英和・和英
海外取引で使える
会計・税務
用語辞典

公認会計士・税理士
佐和 周
著

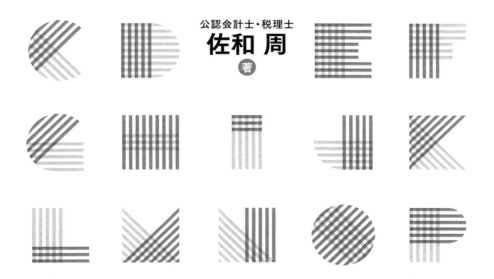

中央経済社

はじめに

　本書の前身である『英和・和英 海外進出の会計・税務用語辞典』が発行されてから６年以上が経過しました。著者自身も「この６年間，自らの辞典を常に開いて，仕事をしながら辞典にない単語を日々メモし，新しいIFRS基準書やOECDガイドラインが出たら用語をチェックしつつ，他にも思いついた単語はどんどん追加していく」，そんなふうにしておけばよかったなあと深く後悔しながら，半べそで本書の執筆作業を行いました。

　本書のコンセプトは，前身である『英和・和英 海外進出の会計・税務用語辞典』のときと変わらず，「使える辞典」という一点です。海外取引のある企業の管理部門や内部監査部門の方々，そのような日本企業をサポートする公認会計士・税理士等の専門家の方々にとって，実際のビジネスで『使える』辞典を目指しました。

　本書の最大の特徴として，以下のような具体的な状況をイメージし，それに合わせてピンポイントで用語を抽出しているという点があります（付録として，英和対照財務諸表様式やメール文例を加えたのも，同様の趣旨です）。

　　会計について
- 海外関係会社から連結パッケージなどで情報を収集する
- 海外関係会社に日本の制度やその趣旨を説明する
- 最終結果としての（連結）財務諸表を英訳する

　　税務について
- 日本の税制上必要な情報を海外関係会社から集める
- 海外関係会社に日本の税制を説明する
- 海外関係会社で発生した現地の税務上の問題を把握する

　また，会計・税務に限定せず，デュー・デリジェンスなど，海外事業に関連する他の分野の用語も幅広くピックアップしている点も本書の特徴です。

　その他の特徴として，税務用語のピックアップや解説にも力を入れている点があります。IFRSという共通言語がある会計に比べて，税務は国ごとに制度も異なり，海外とのコミュニケーションはより難しいというのが実情です。本書では，海外の税制に関連する用語のうち，よく目にするものは（国を問わず）英和編に含めるとともに，日本の税制に関連する用語については，日本語を直訳するよりも，「伝わる英語」という視点から和英編に英訳を入れています。

　本書の前身である『英和・和英 海外進出の会計・税務用語辞典』をベースに，今回は，英和・和英とも，ただひたすら新しい用語を追加していき，英和は6,713語→9,866語，和英は4,079語→6,931語と，収録語数は大幅に増えました。新たに使われるようになった用語はもちろんですが，それ以外でも，「これがないとストレスになる」という用語もしっかり追加できたと思います。

　本書が，「連結パッケージ提出期限を守らず，しかも悪びれない」現地担当者に苦労されている日本企業の実務担当者や，現地専門家に「If you have any questions, please feel free to **"call"** me.」とメールに書かれてひるんでしまう会計・税務の専門家の方々の一助になることを心から願っています。

　最後になりましたが，いつもながらの的確なアドバイスに加えて，最近はやさしく見守ってくだ

さる中央経済社の末永芳奈氏に改めて厚く御礼申し上げます。また，自分たちのほうが忙しくなり，全然チェックを手伝ってくれなくなった娘たちに代わって，スペリングや整合性の確認を手伝ってくれた妻にも，ここに感謝の意を表します。

2018年10月

佐和　周

本書の内容と構成

　本書は，海外での事業や海外関係会社とのコミュニケーションの際に必要になる会計・税務用語を中心に収録した英和・和英用語辞典であり，以下のような方々にお使い頂くことを念頭に，収録用語を選択しています。
- 海外取引のある日本企業の実務担当者
- 上記のような日本企業をサポートする公認会計士・税理士等の専門家

　このような目的に照らし，会計については，世界的な共通言語となりつつある国際財務報告基準（IFRS）を中心に用語を抽出し，日本基準特有の用語や実際の財務諸表上の勘定科目も収録しています。税務については，国際税務の実務から用語を抽出し，日本の税法に根拠を置く独自の用語については，定訳はないものの，意味の通じやすい用語あるいは表現を選択しています。

本書の構成は以下の通りです。
Ⅰ　英和編
Ⅱ　和英編
Ⅲ　付　録
　1．英和対照　財務諸表様式（IFRS ベース）
　2．IFRS 基準書別　会計用語
　3．国際税務の分野別　税務用語
　4．知っていると便利！　e-mail 表現

本書の使い方

Ⅰ　英和編
- 見出し語はアルファベット順に配列しています。
- 会計・税務で使用される用語を中心に収録していますが，海外関係会社とのやりとりで使われるであろう用語（例えば，deadline（期限，締切））も取り上げています。
- 基本的に，会計・税務の文脈でよく使われる意味のみを記載しています。
- 複数の英訳語があるものについては，品詞が同じで意味が類似するものは読点（，）で区切り，品詞や意味が異なるものは①，②…の番号で区切っています。
- 品詞については，名詞のみならず，動詞や形容詞も収録しており，日本語訳から品詞がわかりづらいものには次のように品詞を示しています。
（【動】動詞，【形】形容詞，【副】副詞，【前】前置詞）
- 見出し語のうち，名詞については，基本的に冠詞を省略して単数形で示していますが，複数形で使われることが多いものは複数形で示しています（例えば，accounts payable（買掛金，仕入債務，債務））。
- 見出し語のうち，動詞に関しては，目的語が入る場所がわかりづらいものについて，「〜」で目的語の位置を示しています（例えば，contribute 〜 in kind（to）（（〜に）〜を現物出資する））
- 適切な日本語訳がないものや，用語だけでは意味がわかりづらいものには，解として解説を付しています。
- 用例を示したほうが使い方がわかりやすいと思われる見出し語には，用として【用例】を追加しています。例えば，operating activity（営業活動）の項には，net cash generated by operating activities（営業活動によるキャッシュ・フロー）等の用例が記載されています。
- 使い方に注意を要する用語については，使い方注意！として，その用語の使い方の留意点を示し

- 頭文字語（acronym）については，その省略前の用語のみを記載しています。例えば，CPA の項には，certified public accountant とだけ記載し，certified public accountant の項で「公認会計士」という訳を付しています。
- スペリングは IFRS で使われている英国式を主に使用し，米国式のスペリングには 米 を付しています。
- 見出し語について，（ ）および ［ ］の使い方は以下のとおりです。
  common share ［stock］ ⇒ common share または commom stock
  current and deferred (income) tax ⇒ current and deferred tax または current and deferred income tax

II 和英編

- 用語は，「英和編」の訳語のなかから名詞を中心に選択して収録しています。
- 見出し語は五十音順に配列しています。
- 複数の英語訳がある場合には，基本的に使用頻度が高いものを選択し，複数の英語訳を付している用語もあります。
- 実際の英訳にご活用頂けるよう，いくつかの名詞には，【頻出フレーズ：頻】として，セットで使いやすい動詞や前置詞（および名詞）も示しています。例えば，「子会社」：subsidiary については，「子会社を設立する」：to establish a subsidiary 等のセット表現を示しています。
- また，いくつかの名詞には，【関連フレーズ：関】として，「その名詞自体は使わないが関連するフレーズ」を追加しています。例えば，「清算」：liquidation については，「子会社を清算する」：to liquidate a subsidiary という表現を付しています（liquidate は liquidation の動詞形）。
- なお，頻 や 関 において，目的語を入れる場所がわかりづらいものについては，「~」で目的語の位置を示しています。
- 使い方に注意を要する用語については， 使い方注意！ として，その用語の使い方の留意点を示しています。
- 英国式スペリングの使用や，（ ）および ［ ］の使い方については，「英和編」と同様です。

III 付　録

1．英和対照　財務諸表様式（IFRS ベース）

IFRS ベースの以下の連結財務諸表について，英和対照で様式を示しています。
- 連結財政状態計算書
- 連結包括利益計算書
- 連結持分変動計算書
- 連結キャッシュ・フロー計算書

2．IFRS 基準書別　会計用語

　実務的に使用頻度の低い基準書を除く大半の基準書について，超重要用語に絞って解説しています。ピックアップする用語は，例えば net realisable value など，その一語でかなりの意味を伝えることができ，かつそれを知らないと英文の文書の意味が理解できないようなものを厳選しています。

３．国際税務の分野別　税務用語
　海外進出企業が関わることが多いと思われる国際税務の分野（移転価格税制やタックス・ヘイブン対策税制）について，「２．IFRS 基準書別　会計用語」と同様の基準で抽出した用語を解説しています。

４．知っていると便利！　e-mail 表現
　海外関係会社の担当者とのメールでのコミュニケーションを念頭に，メールの大まかな構成や英文メールでよく使われる表現を収録しています。

英和編

English ⇨ Japanese

- 米 米国式のスペリング
- 解 解説
- 使い方注意! 用語を使う際の留意点
- 用 用例

A

AA ▶annual allowance
abandon 廃棄する，処分する
abandoned and unclaimed property (AUP) 未請求及び請求者不明の預り資産（米国） [解]米国の各州の規制で，例えば一定期間を経過した未取付の小切手など，未請求の預り資産については，本来の権利者に返還できない場合，それを州が収用し，保管するというもの
abandoned asset 廃棄した資産
abandonment 廃棄
abatement 減殺（税金の）
ABC ▶① activity-based costing, ② anti bribery & corruption programme
abolish 廃止する
abolishment 廃止
ABS ▶asset backed securities
absence 欠如
absence fee アブセンス・フィー，派遣社員の不在補償料
absolute amount 絶対値
absolute power 絶対的な力（パワー）
absorption costing 全部原価計算
abuse ①濫用，悪用，②悪用する
abuse of law 法の濫用
accelerated 加速した
accelerated depreciation ①加速度償却，②割増償却，③特別償却
accept ①受け入れる，②検収する
acceptance 受入，検収
acceptance basis 検収基準
acceptance report 受入報告書，検収報告書
accepted 許容された
access アクセス
accomplice 共犯者（不正などの）
accord 一致する，調和する
accordance 一致，調和
account ①勘定，②口座
accountability 説明責任

accountable 説明責任のある
account analysis 勘定分析
accountancy 会計職
accountant 会計士
account balance 勘定残高
account code 勘定コード
account for 会計処理する [用] account for A as B （A を B として会計処理する）
account form 勘定形式（表示方法としての） [解]貸借対照表でいえば，左に資産，右に負債と純資産を配列した様式
accounting 会計
accounting book 会計帳簿
accounting book value 会計簿価
accounting change 会計上の変更
accounting cycle 会計サイクル [解]取引の認識から財務諸表作成までの一連の手続
accounting data 会計データ
accounting department [division] 経理部門，会計部門
accounting depreciation 会計上の減価償却費 [使い方注意!] 会計上の減価償却費は税務上の減価償却費（tax depreciation）と金額が異なることが多いので，会計・税務のいずれを指すのかを明確にする必要がある
accounting election 会計上の選択
accounting equation 会計等式 [解] 資産＝負債＋資本
accounting estimate 会計上の見積り
accounting firm 会計事務所
accounting judgement 会計上の判断 [米] accounting judgment
accounting judgements and estimates 会計上の判断及び見積り [米] accounting judgments and estimates
accounting manual 経理マニュアル，経理規程
accounting method 会計処理方法
accounting mismatch 会計上のミスマッチ [解]資産または負債の測定や，関連する利得または損失の認識を異なる基準に基づいて行うことにより生じる，測定または認識の不整合
accounting model 会計モデル
accounting period 会計期間

accounting perspective	会計の観点 用
from an accounting perspective（会計の観点からは）	
accounting policy	会計方針 解 企業が財務諸表を作成・表示するにあたって適用する特定の原則，基準，慣行，ルール及び実務
accounting practice	会計慣行
accounting principles	会計原則
accounting principles generally accepted in Japan	日本基準（会計基準について）
accounting principles generally accepted in the United State (of America)	米国基準（会計基準について）
accounting procedures	会計手続
accounting process	会計上のプロセス
accounting profit	会計上の利益 解 税務上の利益（taxable profit）と区別するための表現
accounting records	会計記録
accounting software	会計ソフトウェア
Accounting Standard Codification (ASC)	FASB 会計基準（編纂書）（米国）
accounting standards	会計基準
Accounting Standards Board of Japan (ASBJ)	企業会計基準委員会（日本）
accounting system	会計システム，経理システム
accounting treatment	会計上の取扱い，会計処理
accounting unit	会計単位
accounting viewpoint	会計の観点 用
from an accounting viewpoint（会計の観点からは）	
account name	①勘定科目名，②口座名義
account number	口座番号
account reconciliation	勘定の照合・調整
accounts payable (A/P)	買掛金，仕入債務，債務
accounts payable details	買掛金明細
accounts payable ledger	買掛金元帳
accounts payable-other	未払金
accounts payable subsidiary ledger	仕入先元帳
accounts payable-trade	買掛金
accounts payable turnover (A/P turnover)	仕入債務回転率，買掛金回転率
accounts payable turnover period	仕入債務回転期間，買掛金回転期間
accounts receivable (A/R)	売掛金，売掛債権，債権
accounts receivable details	売掛金明細
accounts receivable ledger	売掛金元帳
accounts receivable-other	未収入金
accounts receivable subsidiary ledger	得意先元帳
accounts receivable-trade	売掛金
accounts receivable turnover (A/R turnover)	売掛債権回転率，売掛金回転率
accounts receivable turnover period	売掛債権回転期間，売掛金回転期間
account title	勘定科目
accrete	増大させる
accreted interest	発生利息（債券などの）
accretion	①増加，②増値，増価
accrual	発生（収益や費用の）
accrual accounting	発生主義会計
accrual basis [method]	発生主義，発生基準
accrual method of accounting	発生主義会計
accruals	未収・未払勘定
accrue	未収・未払計上する
accrued	未収・未払計上された
accrued bonus	未払賞与
accrued dividend	未収・未払配当金
accrued dividend income	未収配当金
accrued expense	未払費用
accrued income	未収収益
accrued income taxes	未払法人税等，未払法人所得税
accrued interest	未収・未払利息
accrued interest expense	未払利息
accrued interest income	未収利息
accrued pension cost	年金負債
accrued revenue	未収収益
accrued salaries and wages	未払給料・賃金，未払人件費
accrued vacation (pay)	未払有給休暇，有給休暇引当金
accumulate	①蓄積させる，②蓄積する
accumulated amortisation	償却累計額（無形資産などの） 米 accumulated amor-

tization
accumulated benefit obligation　累積給付債務　[解] 将来の昇給を加味しない給付債務
accumulated deficit　欠損金, 累積損失
accumulated depreciation (account)　減価償却累計額, 償却累計額
accumulated depreciation and amortisation　減価償却及び償却の累計額　[米] accumulated depreciation and amortization
accumulated depreciation, amortisation and impairment　減価償却, 償却及び減損の累計額　[米] accumulated depreciation, amortization and impairment
accumulated impairment (losses)　減損損失累計額
accumulated losses　欠損金, 累積損失, 累損
accumulated other comprehensive income (AOCI)　その他の包括利益累計額
accumulating compensated absences　累積型の有給休暇
accumulation　①累積, ②アキュムレーション（債券などの）
accuracy　正確性
accurate　正確な
acid-test ratio　当座比率　[解] 企業の短期的な支払能力を判断するための安全性指標であり, 次の算式で計算される
当座比率＝当座資産（現金・売上債権・短期保有の有価証券等）/ 流動負債
acknowledge　認める（事実を）
acknowledgement　①認めること, 承認, ②受取の通知, 受取確認
a complete set of financial statements　完全な1組の財務諸表　[解] 構成要素は, 財政状態計算書, 包括利益計算書, 持分変動計算書, キャッシュ・フロー計算書, 注記,（一定の場合には）比較対象期間のうち最も早い年度の期首時点の財政状態計算書
acquire　取得する, 買収する
acquired goodwill　取得のれん
acquiree　被取得企業　[解] IFRS3の文脈では, 企業結合において, 取得企業により支配を獲得された企業
acquirer　①取得企業, ②買手, 買主　[解] ①IFRS3の文脈では, 企業結合において, 被取得企業の支配を獲得した企業
acquirer's previously-held equity interest in the acquiree　取得企業の被取得企業に対する既存の持分
acquiring company　取得企業
acquisition　①取得, ②買収（企業の）, ③譲受け
acquisition cost　取得原価, 取得価額
acquisition date　取得日　[解] IFRS3の文脈では, 取得企業が被取得企業に対する支配を獲得した日を指す。多くの場合, 契約上の企業結合実施日と一致する
acquisition-date fair value　取得日の公正価値　[解] 取得法（acquisition method）においては, 取得資産及び引受負債の測定に取得日の公正価値が使用される
acquisition finance　買収に伴う資金調達
acquisition funding　買収に伴う資金調達
acquisition method　取得法　[解] 企業結合の会計処理方法で, 取得企業（acquirer）により取得される被取得企業（acquiree）の資産及び負債を, 原則として取得日の公正価値で測定する方法
acquisition of interest　持分の取得
acquisition of replacement property　代替資産の取得
acquisition of shares　株式取得, 株式買収
acquisition of treasury shares　自己株式の取得
acquisition-related cost　取得関連コスト, 買収関連コスト　[解] 取得企業側で取得に関連して発生する種々の費用（外部アドバイザーへの報酬等）
acquisitions through business combinations　企業結合による取得（固定資産などの）
acquisition vehicle　買収ビークル, 投資ビークル　[解] 日本企業が海外で買収を行う場合, 税務その他の目的で, 現地あるいは第三国に設立した買収ビークルを経由して, ターゲットを買収することがある
act　①法令, ②行為, ③行動する
action list　アクション・リスト, 実行リスト
action plan　行動計画
active　能動的な, 積極的な
active detection　積極的な摘発（不正など

の)
active detection method　積極的な摘発手段（不正などの）
active income　能動的所得
active market　活発な市場　[解]IFRS13の文脈では、継続的な価格付けの情報を提供するのに十分な頻度及び取引量をもって、資産または負債が取引される市場を指す
activity-based costing（ABC）　活動基準原価計算
Act on Special Measures Concerning Taxation　租税特別措置法
actual　実際の
actual capacity　実際生産能力
actual cost　実際原価
actual costing　実際原価計算
actual return on plan assets　実際運用収益（制度資産，年金資産の）　[解]退職給付会計の文脈では，制度資産からの実際の運用収益で，期待運用収益（expected return on plan assets）に対する用語
actual tax rate　実際（負担）税率
actuarial assumption　数理計算上の仮定　[解]IAS19の文脈では，確定給付債務等の金額を数理計算するにあたって用いられる仮定を指し，従業員の離職率や死亡率といった人口統計上の（demographic）変数や将来の給与上昇等の財務上の（financial）変数を含む　[用]actuarial assumption of discount rates（割引率に関する数理計算上の仮定），actuarial assumption of expected rates of salary increases（予想昇給率に関する数理計算上の仮定），actuarial assumption of mortality rates（死亡率に関する数理計算上の仮定）
actuarial basis　数理計算ベース
actuarial gains and losses　数理計算上の差異　[解]IAS19の文脈では，数理計算上の仮定の変更や実績値との差異により生じる確定給付債務の現在価値の変動を指し，発生時にその全額をその他の包括利益として認識する
actuarial gains [losses] on defined benefit plans　確定給付制度の数理計算上の差異（益［損］）
actuarial present value　数理計算上の現在価値
actuarial risk　数理計算上のリスク
actuarial valuation　数理計算上の評価
actuarial valuation method　数理計算上の評価方法，年金数理評価方式
actuary　アクチュアリー，年金数理人
add　①加える，②税務加算する
add back　①足し戻す，②税務加算する　[用] add □ back to income [profit]（□を税務加算する）
added value component (of enterprise [business] tax)　付加価値割（事業税の外形標準部分の構成要素）
added value levy　付加価値割（事業税の外形標準部分の構成要素）
addendum　補遺，付録
addition　①追加，②（税務）加算
additional　追加的
additional disclosure　追加的な開示
additional information　追加的な情報
additional minimum liability　追加最小負債
additional paid in capital　（株式）払込剰余金
additional retirement benefit　割増退職金
additional tax　①追徴税額，②加算税
additional tax assessed　追徴税額
additional tax on underpayment　過少申告加算税
additions from acquisitions　取得による増加
address　①対処する，②住所
adequacy　十分性
adequate　十分な
adjust　修正する，調整する
adjusted book value　調整後簿価
adjusted earnings　調整後利益
adjusted EBITDA　調整後EBITDA
adjusted income　調整後所得
adjusted market assessment approach　調整後市場評価アプローチ　[解]IFRS15の文脈では，独立販売価格の見積りに際して，財またはサービスを販売する市場を評価し，顧客が支払ってもよいと考える価格を見積もるという方法を指す
adjusted trial balance　決算整理後残高試算

表
adjusted working capital　調整後運転資本
adjusting entry　修正仕訳
adjusting event　修正を要する事象
adjusting event after reporting period　修正後発事象, 修正を要する後発事象　[解]報告期間の末日に存在した状況についての証拠を提供する事象で, 財務諸表の金額等の修正が必要になるもの
adjusting journal entry　修正仕訳
adjustment　①修正, ②精算
adjustments to provisional values　暫定的な評価の修正
administer　管理する
administration　①管理, ②行政, ③執行
administration and control test　管理支配基準　[解]タックス・ヘイブン対策税制における経済活動基準の1つで, 外国関係会社がその本店所在地国において事業の管理, 支配及び運営を自ら行っていることを確認する基準
administration cost　管理コスト
administration expense　管理費
administrative　①管理の, ②行政上の
administrative action　行政処分
administrative appeal　不服申立て
administrative cost [expense]　管理費
administrative department　管理部門
administrative direction　行政指導
Administrative Litigation Law　行政事件訴訟法
administrative monetary penalty　行政上の罰金
administrative penalty　行政罰
administrative ruling　行政通達
admissible　許容される【形】
admission　①入場, 入会, ②入場料, 入会金, ③許可
adopt　採用する
adoption　①採用, ②アドプション　[解]②アドプションは, 一般にIFRSの採用を意味し, コンバージェンスに対する用語
ADR　▶① alternative dispute resolution, ② American Depositary Receipt
ad valorem tax　従価税　[解]課税物件の価格を基準に税率が定められている租税

advance　①事前の, ②前金の, 前渡しの, ③前金, 前渡し
advance approval　事前承認
advance approval of tax authorities　税務当局の事前承認
advance consideration　①前払対価, ②前受対価
advance notice　事前通知
advance payment　前渡金
advance payments to suppliers　前渡金（仕入先への）
advance pricing agreement (APA)　事前確認（制度）　[解] advance pricing arrangement の項を参照
advance pricing arrangement (APA)　事前確認（制度）　[解]移転価格税制の関係では, 独立企業間価格（arm's length price）の算定方法の合理性等につき税務当局が事前に確認する制度を指す
advance receipt　前受金
advance receipts from customers　前受金（得意先からの）
advance ruling　事前照会制度, 事前確認　[解]日本では一般に「国税照会」と呼ばれるもの
advances　①前渡金, ②前受金
advances from customers　前受金（得意先からの）
advances from employees　前受金（従業員からの）
advances paid　前払金, 前渡金
advances received　前受金
advances received for contracts in progress　未成工事に係る前受金
advances to employees　前渡金（従業員への）
advances to suppliers　前渡金（仕入先への）
advantage　利点
advantageous　有利な
adverse　①不利な, ②逆の, ③不適正の（監査意見について）
adverse opinion　不適正意見（監査報告書における）
adverse publicity　悪評
adverse tax consequence　不利な税務上の影響

advertise	広告する，宣伝する
advertisement	広告，宣伝
advertising cost [expense]	広告宣伝費
advice	助言
advisable	望ましい
advise	助言する
adviser	アドバイザー
advisor	アドバイザー
advisory	アドバイザリー，助言の
advisory fee	アドバイザリー・フィー
advisory service	アドバイザリー・サービス
AEOI	▶Automatic Exchange of Information
affect	影響する
affiliate	関連会社
affiliated company	関連会社
affirmative	断定的な
aforementioned	前述の
AFS	▶available-for-sale financial assets
after	〜（日付）より後　使い方注意！ after を使うと，基本的にその日を含まないことになる。その日を含める場合には，on or after といういい方をする
after-tax	税引後の
after-tax operating income	税引後営業利益
after-tax profit	税引後利益
age analysis	年齢調べ　解 売掛金等の債権科目の滞留状況の分析
agency	代理店・代理人
agenda	アジェンダ，議題
agent	代理人，エージェント　解 一般には何らかの行為を依頼人（principal）の利益のために代わって行う者をいい，法人も含む。PE（恒久的施設）との関係では，代理人は，大きく従属代理人（dependent agent）と独立代理人（independent agent）に区分される
agent fee	エージェント・フィー，代理人報酬
agent of an independent status	独立代理人
agent PE	代理人 PE
aggregate	①合算する，②集計，総計
aggregated	合算された
aggregate income	合算所得
aggregation	①合算（特に所得の合算），②集約
aggregation criteria	集約基準　解 IFRS8 の文脈では，報告セグメント（reportable segment）を決定する際に考慮される基準で，いくつかの事業セグメントが類似の経済的特徴を有している場合等に，複数のセグメントを単一のセグメントとして集約すること
aggregation of income	所得の合算，合算課税　解 例えば，タックス・ヘイブン対策税制による合算課税を指す
aggregation of income on an entity basis	会社単位の合算課税（タックス・ヘイブン対策税制による）
aggregation of passive income	受動的所得の合算課税（タックス・ヘイブン対策税制による）
aggregation of profit and loss	損益通算
aggressive tax planning	濫用的租税回避
aging list	年齢調べ表（売掛金などの）
aging schedule	年齢調べ表（売掛金などの）
agio	打歩，プレミアム
agreed-upon procedures (AUP)	合意手続
agreed-upon procedures report	合意手続報告書
agreement	①契約（書），合意，②一致（数値などの）
agriculture	農業
AICPA	▶American Institute of Certified Public Accountants
aid	①援助，②援助する
aircraft	航空機
airframe	航空機の機体
air waybill (AWB)	エア・ウェイビル，航空運送状　解 航空会社などが発行する航空貨物の受取証。海上輸送の場合の船荷証券（B/L）に相当するが，船荷証券とは異なり，有価証券ではない
a.k.a.	通称（also known as）
alien	外国人，在留外国人
alienation	譲渡
alienator	譲渡人
align	①合わせる，②提携させる
alignment	①整列，②提携
allegation	主張，申立て
alleviate	緩和する，軽減する
alleviation	緩和，軽減

alliance	提携，連合
allocate	配賦する，配分する
allocation	配賦，配分
allocation basis	配賦基準
allocation method	配賦方法（費用等の）
allocation of consideration	対価の配分
allocation of head office expenses	本社費の配賦
allocation of purchase price	取得原価の配分
allot	割り当てる
allotment	割当て
allow	許容する
allowable	①許容された【形】，②損金算入可能な
allowable expense [charge]	損金算入可能な費用
allowable limit	損金算入限度額
allowance	①控除（課税所得からの），損金算入（税務上の），②引当金，③手当 [解] allowanceには様々な意味があるので，和訳する場合には注意が必要
allowance account for credit losses	信用損失引当金，貸倒引当金 [用] allowance account for credit losses of financial assets（金融資産の信用損失引当金）
allowance for	～に対する引当金
allowance for bad debt	貸倒引当金
allowance for credit losses	信用損失引当金，貸倒引当金
allowance for depreciation	減価償却累計額
allowance for doubtful accounts	貸倒引当金
along with	～とともに
ALP	▶arm's length price
alternative	①代替的な，②代替案
alternative dispute resolution (ADR)	裁判外紛争処理
alternative minimum tax (AMT)	代替ミニマム課税 [解] 優遇税制の適用等による過度な節税を防止することを目的として，通常の税金計算とは異なる方法で計算された税額の支払いを要求するもの
alternative procedure	代替（的）手続
alternative treatment	代替処理，代替的な取扱い
amalgamate	合併する
amalgamation	合併
ambit	範囲
amend	修正する
amended standard	改訂された基準書
amended tax return	修正申告書
amendment	修正
American Depositary Receipt (ADR)	米国預託証書 [解] 日本企業の普通株式を米国の銀行に預託し，それを対象として米国で発行される預託証書で，投資家は預託証書を購入すれば株式所有と同じ権利を保有することができる
American Institute of Certified Public Accountants (AICPA)	米国公認会計士協会
amortisable	償却可能な（無形資産について）[米] amortizable
amortisable goodwill	償却可能な「のれん」[米] amortizable goodwill [解] 税務上の「のれん」は国によっては償却可能である
amortisable intangible asset	無形減価償却資産 [米] amortizable intangible asset
amortisation	①償却（無形資産などの），②アモチゼーション（債券などの）[米] amortization [使い方注意!] 有形固定資産の減価償却については，amortisationではなく，depreciationを使う
amortisation charge [expense]	償却費（無形資産などの）[米] amortization charge [expense]
amortisation method	償却方法（無形資産などの）
amortisation of goodwill	のれん償却費 [米] amortization of goodwill
amortisation period	償却期間（無形資産などの）[米] amortization period
amortisation rate	償却率（無形資産などの）
amortise	償却する（無形資産などを）[米] amortize
amortised cost	償却原価 [米] amortized cost [解] 当初認識額をもとに額面金額との差額を実効金利法（effective interest method）に基づいて調整した結果をもって金融商品を測定する方法
amount	金額
amounts payable	債務金額

amounts receivable	債権金額
AMT	▶alternative minimum tax
analyse	分析する　㊍analyze
analysis	分析
analyst	アナリスト
analytic(al)	分析的な
analytical procedures	分析的手続
ancillary	付随的な
ancillary agreement	付随契約
ancillary cost	付随費用
annex	付録, 付属品
announce	発表する, 公表する
announced tax rate	公表された税率
announcement	発表, 公表
annual	年次の, 年間の　[解]期中報告期間を表す interim に対する用語
annual accounts	年次財務諸表, 年次決算書
annual allowance (AA)	年次償却　[解]英国等の税制で, 税務上の減価償却費(capital allowance)のうち, 毎年一定の率で, 損金の額に算入されるもの
annual budget	年間予算, 年度予算
annual control	年次統制
annual filing	年次申告
annual financial statements	年次財務諸表, 年次決算書
annual general meeting	年次(定時)株主総会
annualise	年ベースの数値にする(利率などを)　㊍annualize
annual leave	年次休暇, 年次有給休暇
annually	毎年, 年1回
annual rate of tax write-off	①税務上の減価償却率, ②キャピタル・アローワンスの年率
annual report	アニュアル・レポート, 年次報告書
annual securities report	有価証券報告書
annual target	年間目標(値)
annuity	年金
anomalous	例外的な
anomaly	例外
anti-abuse provision	濫用防止規定
anti-avoidance rules	租税回避防止規定
anti bribery & corruption programme (ABC)	贈収賄防止プログラム　㊍anti bribery & corruption program (ABC)
anticipate	予測する
anticipated	予測された
anticipation	予測
anti-conduit provision	導管防止規定　[解]導管取引に対して租税条約の適用を認めない(条約相手国の居住者を受益者として取り扱わない)とする規定。主に, 租税条約の配当・利子・使用料等に関する条項に盛り込まれている
anti-dilution	逆希薄化　[解]希薄化(dilution)の逆で, 転換型金融商品(convertible instrument)の転換等を仮定した場合の1株当たり利益の増加
anti-dilutive	逆希薄化を有する【形】
anti-fraud control	不正対策手段
anti-fraud policy	不正対策方針
anti-sandbagging clause	アンチ・サンドバギング条項　[解]買収契約などにおいて, 買手が売手による表明・保証違反を知っていた場合には, 当該違反に基づく補償請求を認めないとする条項
anti-tax haven rules	タックス・ヘイブン対策税制　[解]CFC rulesの項を参照
anti-treaty shopping provision	トリーティー・ショッピング防止規定　[解]トリーティー・ショッピングに対応するために租税条約に定められる濫用防止規定
anti-trust	反トラストの, 独占禁止の
anti-trust act [law]	独占禁止法
AOA	▶Authorised OECD Approach
AOCI	▶accumulated other comprehensive income
A/P	▶accounts payable
APA	▶① advance pricing arrangement [agreement], ② asset purchase agreement
APAC	▶Asia-Pacific
APA rollback	ロールバック(遡及適用)　[解]移転価格税制の関係では, 事前確認(APA)の結果を, (将来年度のみならず)過年度にも適用することを指す
APA status	事前確認の有無(移転価格税制に係る)
appeal	控訴, 上告, 不服申立て
appendices	appendixの複数形

appendix 別紙，付録
appliances 器具，備品
applicability ①適用可能性，②適用範囲
applicable (to) （〜に）適用できる，適用される【形】
applicable tax rate 適用税率
application ①適用，②申請，申込み
application control 業務処理統制
application form 申請用紙
application form for income tax convention 租税条約に関する届出書 [解] 租税条約による源泉税等の減免を受ける場合には，通常何らかの届出書等の提出が必要であり，日本ではこの「租税条約に関する届出書」がそれに該当する
application guidance 適用指針
applied ①適用されて，②応用の
applied research 応用研究
apply 適用する [用] new standards or interpretations not applied（未適用の新しい基準または解釈指針）
appoint 指名する，任命する
appointment ①約束，予約，②指名，任命
apportion 配賦する，配分する，割り当てる [用] lease payments are apportioned between interest expense and reduction in liability（リース料支払いは，利息費用と負債の減額として割り振られる）
apportionment 配賦，割当
apportionment method 配賦方法（費用等の）
appraisal 評価，鑑定
appraisal approach 評価アプローチ
appraisal date 評価日
appraisal method 評価方法
appraisal practice 評価実務
appraisal procedure 評価手続
appraisal report 鑑定評価書，評価書
appraise 評価する，鑑定する
appraised value 評価額
appreciate ①値上がりする（通貨などの），②感謝する
appreciation 増価 [解] depreciation の反意語
approach アプローチ，方法
appropriate 適切な

appropriate tax office 所轄税務署
appropriation 利益処分
appropriation account 利益処分勘定
appropriation of retained earnings 剰余金処分
approval 承認
approve 承認する
approximate おおよその，近似の
approximately 約，おおよそ
approximation 近似，概算
A/P turnover ▶accounts payable turnover
A/R ▶accounts receivable
arbitrage 裁定（取引）
arbitrarily 恣意的に
arbitrary 恣意的な
arbitrary basis 恣意的な方法 [用] on an arbitrary basis（恣意的な方法で）
arbitration 仲裁 [解] 租税条約の関係では，相互協議（mutual agreement procedure）が不調に終わった場合の救済手段として，第三者により行われる仲裁を指す
area of responsibility 責任の領域
arise 発生する，起こる
arm's length 独立企業間の，第三者間の
arm's length price (ALP) 独立企業間価格 [解] 移転価格税制の関係では，独立の第三者間で取引される際に成立するであろう価格水準を指す
arm's length principle 独立企業間原則
arm's length range 独立企業間価格レンジ
arm's length transaction 独立企業間取引
ARO ▶asset retirement obligation
arrange 準備する，手配する
arrangement ①準備，手配，②協定，取り決め
arrangement fee アレンジメント・フィー [解] loan arrangement fee の項を参照
arranger アレンジャー [解] 社債発行やシンジケート・ローン組成に際して，主幹事となる金融機関
arrears ①延滞金，②支払残金 [解] 通常複数形
article 条，条項
articles of incorporation 定款
artistic-related intangible asset 芸術関連無

形資産
A/R turnover ▶accounts receivable turnover
ASBJ ▶Accounting Standards Board of Japan
ASC ▶(FASB) Accounting Standard Codification
ascending ①昇順の，②上がっていく
ascertain 確かめる，確認する
a set of condensed financial statements 1組の要約財務諸表 [解] IAS34の文脈では，構成要素は，要約財政状態計算書，要約包括利益計算書，要約持分変動計算書，要約キャッシュ・フロー計算書，一定の説明的注記等
Asia-Pacific (APAC) アジア太平洋地域
ask ①質問する，②依頼する
ask price アスク価格（売呼値）
as per ～によると，～のとおり [使い方注意!] the amount as per the invoice（インボイス上の金額）のように，後ろに文書や資料の名称を付けることが多い
assembled workforce 集合的な人的資源，集合的な労働力 [解] IFRSにおいて，無形資産として計上できないこととされている
assembly ①組み立て，②組立品
assert 主張する
assertion 主張（経営者の）
assess 評価する，査定する
assessable income 総所得，課税所得
assessed 評価された
assessed value 評価額（主に税務上の）
assessment ①賦課決定（税金の），②評価
assessment of hedge effectiveness ヘッジ有効性の評価
asset 資産
asset acquisition 資産買収 [解] asset purchaseの項を参照
asset and liability approach 資産負債アプローチ
asset approach アセット・アプローチ（評価手法としての）
asset backed securities (ABS) 資産担保証券
asset-backed financing 資産担保金融

asset-based approach アセット・アプローチ（評価手法としての）
asset ceiling 資産上限額，アセット・シーリング [解] IAS19の文脈では，制度からの返還（または将来の掛金の減額）の形で利用可能な経済的便益の現在価値であり，確定給付制度が積立超過である場合の資産計上の上限額を意味する
asset deal 資産買収，資産取引
asset dismantlement, removal and restoration costs 資産の解体，撤去及び原状回復のコスト
asset finance アセット・ファイナンス [解]（企業ではなく）資産の信用力により行う資金調達
asset for recovery 回収資産
asset held under a finance lease ファイナンスリースにより保有する資産
asset in its entirety 資産全体
asset manager アセット・マネジャー
asset misappropriation 資産の流用
asset purchase 資産買収 [解] 買収形態の1つで，海外に新会社を設立し（または既存の海外子会社を利用して），その海外子会社が買収対象会社の資産等を買収する方法。株式買収（share purchase）に対する用語
asset purchase agreement (APA) 資産買収契約
asset-related grant 資産に関する補助金
asset retirement obligation (ARO) 資産除去債務
asset revaluation 資産再評価
assets acquired 取得した資産 [解] IFRS3の文脈では，取得企業が取得する被取得企業の資産
asset sale 資産売却
assets classified as held for sale 売却目的で保有する資産
assets held for sale 売却目的で保有する資産
assets held by a long-term employee benefit fund 長期の従業員給付基金が保有している資産
assets held for disposal 処分目的で保有する資産

assets held for rental to others　（他者への）賃貸目的で保有する資産
asset turnover　資産回転率
asset utilisation　資産の有効活用　[米] asset utilization
assign　①割り当てる（仕事を），②譲渡する
assignee　譲受人
assignment　①割当，②譲渡
assignment of receivables　債権譲渡
assignor　譲渡人
assistance　支援
associate　関連会社　[解] 投資企業が重要な影響力（significant influence）を有している企業
associate accounted for by the equity-method　持分法適用関連会社
associated cost [expense]　関連費用
associated enterprise　①関連会社，②関連者（移転価格税制における）
assume　①仮定する，②引き受ける（負債などを）
assumption　①仮定，②引受け（負債などの）
assurance　保証（監査証明などの）
assurance engagement　保証業務（監査などの）
at cost　原価で
at fair value　公正価値で
ATM　▶at the money
at market value　市場価格で
ATO　▶Australian Taxation Office
at par　額面で
at sight　一覧払い（の）
at source　源泉地で（所得の）
attachment　①添付（ファイル），②差押え
attest　証明する
attestation　証明
at the money (ATM)　アット・ザ・マネー　[解] オプション取引の買方が権利行使したときに，損益が生じない状態
attorney　弁護士
attorney's letter　弁護士のレター
attributable (to)　（〜に）帰属する【形】
attributable income principle　帰属主義　[解] 企業がある国にPE（恒久的施設）を有し，そのPEを通じて事業を行う場合，その国の税務当局は当該PEに帰属する所得に対してのみ課税できるという考え方。総合主義（entire income principle）に対する用語
attributable to non-controlling interest　非支配持分に帰属する　[解] 純損益やその他包括利益のうち非支配持分に帰属する部分
attributable to owners of the parent　親会社の所有者に帰属する　[解] 純損益やその他包括利益のうち親会社の所有者の持分に帰属する部分
attribute　①帰属させる，②属性
attribution　帰属
attribution of losses　損失の帰属
auction　オークション，競売
auction process　オークション手続（企業・事業売却などの）
auction sale　オークションによる売却（企業や事業などの）
audit　監査
audit adjustment　監査（による）修正
audit & supervisory board　監査役会
audit & supervisory board member　監査役
audit committee　監査委員会（委員会設置会社の）
audit documentation　監査調書
audited　監査済みの
audited financial statements　監査済財務諸表
audit engagement　監査業務
audit evidence　監査証拠
audit fee　監査報酬
audit findings　監査上の発見事項
audit firm　監査法人
auditing standards　監査基準
audit instructions　監査指示書
audit materiality　監査上の重要性
audit objective　監査目的
auditor　監査人
auditor's remuneration　監査人の報酬　[用] auditor's remuneration for audit services（監査業務に係る監査人の報酬），auditor's remuneration for other services（その他の業務に係る監査人の報酬）
auditor's report　監査報告書
audit planning　監査計画

audit procedures　監査手続
audit programme　監査プログラム，監査手続書　㋳audit program
audit report　監査報告書
audit risk　監査リスク
audit sampling　監査サンプリング
audit scope　監査範囲
audit trail　監査証跡
AUP　▶①agreed-upon procedures，②abandoned and unclaimed property
Australian Taxation Office (ATO)　オーストラリア税務局
authenticate　認証する
authentication　認証
authorisation　承認　㋳authorization
authorisation for　〜の承認　㋳authorization for
authorisation limit　承認の限度額　㋳authorization limit
authorisation matrix　職務権限マトリックス　㋳authorization matrix
authorisation of financial statements　財務諸表の承認　㋳authorization of financial statements
authorise　承認する　㋳authorize
authorised number of shares　授権株式数　㋳authorized number of shares
Authorised OECD Approach (AOA)　OECD承認アプローチ　㋳Authorized OECD Approach　㋕OECDモデル租税条約第7条（事業所得）におけるPE（恒久的施設）帰属所得の算定方法。端的には，PEの果たす機能及び事実関係に基づいて外部取引，資産，リスク及び資本をPEに帰属させるとともに，独立企業間価格の算定方法を適用して，PEと本店等との内部取引を認識する
authorised share　授権［発行可能］株式　㋳authorized share
authority　①当局，②権限
Automatic Exchange of Information (AEOI)　自動的情報交換
automobile　車両
auxiliary　①補助的な，②予備の
auxiliary activity　補助的活動
auxiliary company　補助的機能を有する会社
auxiliary function　補助的機能
auxiliary material　補助材料，副資材
availability　入手可能性，利用可能性
availability for immediate sale　即時売却可能性
available　入手可能な，利用可能な
available-for-sale financial assets (AFS)　売却可能金融資産（旧）
available-for-sale securities　その他有価証券
average　平均
average collection period　売掛債権回転期間，売掛金回転期間，平均回収期間
average cost method　平均原価法
average days' inventory on-hand　棚卸資産回転期間，在庫回転期間
average days' sales uncollected　売掛債権回転期間，売掛金回転期間
average inventory period　棚卸資産回転期間，在庫回転期間
average method　平均法（棚卸資産の評価方法など）
average number of employees　平均従業員数
average payment period　仕入債務回転期間，買掛金回転期間
average remaining service period　平均残存勤務期間
average remaining working lives　平均残存勤務期間
avoidance　①回避，②租税回避
avoidance of double taxation　二重課税の排除
award　賞，授与
AWB　▶air waybill

B

background 背景
background check 身元調査
background information 背景情報
backlog 受注残高
backstop 補完するもの
back-to-back certificate of origin 連続する原産地証明書 [解]貿易の中継地国において発行される証明書で，当初輸出国の原産性が維持されていることを証明するもの
back-to-back loan バック・ツー・バック・ローン [解]国外親会社等の保証等により，子会社が第三者からの借入を行うことなど
backup バックアップ
bad debt 不良債権
bad debt allowance 貸倒引当金
bad debt loss [expense] 貸倒損失
bad debt provision 貸倒引当金
bad debt recovered 償却債権取立（益）
bad debts account 不良債権勘定
bad debt written off 貸倒償却
bad leaver バッド・リーバー [解]契約期間を満了せずに（特に，契約に定める一定の事由に該当して）退職する者
bad publicity 悪評
balance 残高
balance confirmation 残高確認
balance confirmation letter 残高確認書，残高確認状
balance confirmation request 残高確認依頼（書）
balance sheet 貸借対照表
balance sheet account 貸借対照表勘定
balance sheet date 貸借対照表日
balance sheet item 貸借対照表項目
balancing allowance バランシング・アローワンス，差額償却 [解]英国等の税制で，キャピタル・アローワンス（capital allowance）を控除した資産を売却する場合の税務調整のうち，売却価額が税務簿価よりも小さい場合に，差額を所得から控除するもの
balancing charge バランシング・チャージ，差額賦課 [解]バランシング・アローワンスの逆で，所得に加算されるもの
balancing item 調整項目
balancing payment バランシング・ペイメント [解]費用分担契約（CCA/CSA）などにおいて，持分額を調整するために行う支払い
balloon payment バルーン・ペイメント [解]借入金などについて，期限満了時に一括弁済するという返済方法
bank 銀行
bank account ①銀行口座，②銀行勘定
bank balance 銀行残高
bank borrowings 銀行借入
bank certificate 銀行残高証明書
bank certification 銀行残高証明書
bank charge 銀行手数料
bank confirmation 銀行残高確認状
bank loan 銀行借入
bank notes payable 銀行借入
bank overdraft ①当座借越，②当座貸越
bank reconciliation 銀行勘定調整表
bank reference 銀行信用照会
bankrupt 倒産した
bankruptcy 倒産，破産
Bankruptcy Act 破産法
bankruptcy remote 倒産隔離
bank statement 銀行取引残高報告書
bank usance バンク・ユーザンス [解]貿易取引の決済に関連して，銀行が支払いを一定期間猶予する形で，輸入者に対して信用を供与すること
BAPA ▶bilateral advance pricing arrangement
bargain ①安売り，バーゲン，②取引，③交渉する
bargaining power 交渉力
bargain purchase バーゲン・パーチェス，割安購入（益） [解]IFRS3の文脈では，計算された「のれん」がマイナスになる場合，つまり割安で購入できた場合をいい，日

本基準でいう「負ののれん」に相当する。取得日における純損益として処理される

bargain purchase option 割安購入選択権［オプション］（リース契約などの）

bargain renewal option 割安更新選択権［オプション］（リース契約などの）

barrier 障害

barrister 法廷弁護士（英国等の）

barter transaction バーター取引

base company ベース・カンパニー [解]通常，タックス・ヘイブンに所在し，高税率国に所在する親会社やグループ会社への役務提供等を行う。グループ会社の所得をその会社に移転し，グループ全体の租税負担を引き下げる目的で設立される

base cost 取得原価 [解]主として，キャピタル・ゲイン課税（capital gain tax）の際の譲渡原価のベースとなる取得原価を指す

Base Erosion and Profit Shifting (BEPS) 税源浸食と利益移転

base period 基準期間

base salary 基本給

base stock 基準棚卸残高

base year 基準年度

basic 基礎的な

basic and diluted earnings [loss] per share 基本的及び希薄化後1株当たり利益［損失］

basic earnings per share 基本的1株当たり利益 [解]親会社の普通株主に帰属する損益を，当期中の発行済普通株式数の加重平均で除したもの

basic loss per share 基本的1株当たり損失

basic research 基礎研究

basis ①基礎，②基準，③取得価額

basis adjustment ベーシス・アジャストメント [解]IFRS9の文脈では，キャッシュ・フロー・ヘッジ剰余金に関する事後的な会計処理として，（資本に累積された）その金額をヘッジ対象である資産または負債の帳簿価額に加減することを意味する

basis for conclusions 結論の根拠

basis for consolidation 連結の基礎

basis of accounting 会計処理の基礎

basis of allocation 配賦基準

basis of consolidation 連結の基礎

basis of measurement 測定の基礎

basis of preparation 作成の基礎 [解]財務諸表の作成の基礎を指すことが多い

basis point (bp) ベーシスポイント [解]0.01％のこと

basis step-up 簿価のステップアップ（増額）

basis step-up in assets acquired 取得資産簿価のステップアップ [解]企業買収の際に資産買収（asset purchase）の形態をとれば，（時価が簿価よりも高い前提で）取得価額が増額（step up）され，例えば将来の減価償却費が大きくなる等の税務メリットがある

BCM ▶business continuity management

BCP ▶business continuity plan(ning)

B/E ▶bill of exchange

bear 負担する（費用などを） [使い方注意!] cost is borne by（負担者）の形で用いられることが多い。borne は bear の過去分詞形

bearer ①持参人（小切手などの），②無記名の

bearer bond 無記名債券

bearer securities 無記名証券

before 〜（日付）より前 [使い方注意!] before を使うと，基本的にその日を含まないことになる。その日を含める場合には，on or before といういい方をする

beforehand 事前に，あらかじめ

beginning balance 期首残高

beginning of (accounting) period 期首

bellow-market rate of interest 市場金利よりも低利の金利

benchmark ベンチマーク，基準となるもの

benchmark analysis ベンチマーク分析

benchmarking ベンチマーク分析

benchmark study ベンチマーク分析

beneficial 有益な

beneficial interest 受益権

beneficial interest in trust 信託受益権

beneficial owner 受益者

beneficial ownership declaration 受益所有者申告書

beneficial tax consequence 有利な税務上の

影響
beneficiary 受益者
benefit ①便益，給付，②福利厚生
benefit and cost 便益とコスト
benefit entitlement 給付を受ける権利
benefits in kind 現物給付，現物給与
benefits paid 支払済給付，支払われた給付（退職給付制度などについて）
benefits paid or payable 支払済給付または未払給付
benefits payable 未払給付
BEP ▶break-even point
BEPS ▶Base Erosion and Profit Shifting
bequest 遺産
berry ratio ベリー・レシオ，営業費用売上総利益率 [解]移転価格税制の関係では，取引単位営業利益法（TNMM）等で用いられる利益水準指標の1つを指し，以下の算式で計算される
ベリー・レシオ＝売上総利益／販売費及び一般管理費
best efforts 最善の努力，ベスト・エフォート
best estimate 最善の見積り
best method rule ベスト・メソッド・ルール [解]移転価格税制の関係では，独立企業間価格の算定方法について，事案に応じた最適な手法を選択すべき，という原則を指す
best practice 最善の実務，ベスト・プラクティス
beta ベータ
beta coefficient ベータ係数 [解]市場全体の動きに対する個別証券（株式）の動きを示す係数で，個別証券（株式）の市場感応度の指標となる
betterment （固定資産の）改良
b/f ▶brought forward
BIA ▶business impact analysis
bid 入札，ビッド
bidding process 入札手続
bid letter ビッド・レター
bid price ビッド価格（買呼値）
bid rigging 不正入札
bifurcate （2つに）区分処理する
big picture 全体像

bilateral advance pricing arrangement (BAPA) 二国間APA，バイラテラルAPA [解]移転価格税制の関係では，事前確認（APA）のうち，関係する2か国の税務当局から確認を受けるものを指す
bilateral CVA 双方向CVA [解]デリバティブについて，取引相手の信用リスクのみならず，自社の信用リスクも考慮して計算されるCVA
bill ①請求書，②手形
bill-and-hold arrangement 請求済未出荷契約
bill-and-hold sales 未出荷売上（請求済み）
billing 請求
billing scheme 請求書不正スキーム
billion 10億
bill of exchange (B/E) 為替手形
bill of lading (B/L) 船荷証券，貨物引換証
bind ①法的に拘束する，②締結する（契約などを）
binding 法的拘束力のある
binding agreement 法的拘束力のある契約
binding bid 法的拘束力のある入札（買収案件などの）
binding offer 法的拘束力のある意向表明（買収案件などの）
binding ruling 法的拘束力のあるルーリング
binding sale agreement 法的拘束力のある販売契約
binomial model 二項モデル [解]オプション評価モデルの1つ
biological asset 生物資産
BJR ▶business judgement rule
B/L ▶bill of lading
black list company ブラックリスト国所在会社 [解]タックス・ヘイブン対策税制における特定外国関係会社の1つで，外国関係会社のうち，「租税に関する情報の交換に関する国際的な取組への協力が著しく不十分な国または地域として財務大臣が指定する国または地域」に本店または主たる事務所を有するもの
Black-Scholes formula ブラック・ショールズ方程式
blank 白紙の

blue chip	優良会社，優良株
blue-form tax return	青色申告書
blue-form tax return filing status	青色申告
board	取締役会
board of auditors	監査役会
board of directors (BOD)	取締役会
Board of Investment (BOI)	投資委員会（タイ）［解］タイにおける優遇税制を所管する委員会
BOD	▶board of directors
body corporate	法人
BOI	▶Board of Investment
bona fide	①真正の，②誠実な
bond	債券
bond discount	債券ディスカウント
bonded area	保税地域　［解］港湾や空港の近くで，海外から輸入した貨物を，税関の輸入許可を得ない状態で関税を留保（保税）したまま置いておける地域
bond futures	債券先物
bondholder	債券保有者
bond issue cost	社債発行費
bond market	債券市場
bond premium	債券プレミアム
bond rating	債券格付け
bond redemption	社債償還，債券償還
bonds issued	発行した社債
bonds payable	社債（勘定）
bond with warrant	新株予約権付社債
bond yield	債券利回り，社債利回り
bonus	賞与
bonus accrual	未払賞与，賞与引当金
bonus payment	賞与の支払い
bonus plan	賞与制度
bonus (share) issue	株式の無償交付
book	帳簿
book closing	決算
bookkeeping	簿記
book-tax difference	会計と税務の差異
book to physical adjustment	実際残高への修正（棚卸後の）
book to tax difference	会計と税務の差異
book value	帳簿価額，簿価
book value per share (BPS)	1株当たり純資産
boot	交換差金
bootstrapping	ブートストラップ，自己資金による起業
borne	bear（負担する）の過去分詞形
borrow	借りる
borrower	借手（資金の）
borrowing costs	借入コスト，借入費用　［解］IAS23の文脈では，企業の資金の借入に関連して発生する利息及びその他の費用
borrowing costs capitalised	資産化した借入コスト　［米］borrowing costs capitalized
borrowing costs eligible for capitalisation	資産化に適格な借入コスト　［米］borrowing costs eligible for capitalization
borrowing costs incurred	発生した借入コスト
borrowing costs recognised as expense	費用として認識した借入コスト
borrowing facility	借入枠，借入限度額
borrowings	借入金
bottom	底，一番下
bottom line	①純損益，②話の要点
bottom of range	範囲の下限
bottom-up approach	ボトムアップ・アプローチ
bought ledger	仕入元帳
bp	▶basis point
BPM	▶business process management
BPO	▶business process outsourcing
BPS	▶book value per share
BPT	▶branch profits tax
bracket	階層，区分（累進課税などの）
branch	支店
branch account	支店勘定
branch accounting	支店会計
branch financial statements	支店財務諸表
branch profits tax (BPT)	支店利益税
brand	ブランド，商標
brand name	ブランド名
brand royalty	ブランド使用料，ブランド・ロイヤルティ
breach	違反（契約違反）
breach of contract	契約違反，契約不履行
breakdown	ブレークダウン，内訳
breakdown information	内訳情報
break-even analysis	損益分岐点分析

break-even point (BEP)	損益分岐点
break-even point analysis	損益分岐点分析
break-even sales	損益分岐点売上高
break-even units	損益分岐点売上数量
break-up	①解体，②離別
break-up fee	ブレイクアップ・フィー，違約金，解約料（特に買収契約に関する）
break-up value	清算価値，解体価値
bribe	①賄賂，②贈賄する
bribery	贈収賄
bribery and corruption	贈収賄（汚職）
bridge finance [financing]	ブリッジ・ファイナンス，つなぎ融資［資金調達］ [解]次のファイナンスを行うまでの「橋」渡しとしての短期の資金調達
bridge loan	ブリッジ・ローン，つなぎ融資
brief	簡潔な
briefing	簡潔な報告
bring forward	繰り越す
broad	幅広い【形】
broad-based	広範囲の，包括的な
broad-based employee share plan	広範囲の従業員株式制度
broker	ブローカー，仲買人，仲立人
brokerage	①仲買，②仲買手数料，口銭
brokerage account	証券口座
brokerage fee	仲介手数料
brokerage fee expense	仲介手数料費用
brokerage fee income	仲介手数料収益
broker quotes	ブローカー相場
brother company	兄弟会社
brought forward (b/f)	前期繰越し
brought-forward tax losses	繰越欠損金（前期以前から繰り越されてきた税務上の欠損金）
budget	予算
budget/actual variance report	予算実績対比表
budgetary	予算の
budgetary accounts	予算勘定
budgetary control	予算統制，予算管理
budget constraint	予算の制約
budgeting	予算編成，予算管理
budgeting system	予算制度
budget to actual	予算対実績，予実
budget vs. actual	予算対実績，予実
buffer	バッファー，クッション，余裕
building	建物
building block	構成要素
building site	建築工事現場，建設現場
build up	①蓄積，積上げ，②積み上げる（在庫などを）[用]② to build up inventory（在庫を積み上げる）
built-in gain	含み益
built-in gains and losses	含み損益
built-in loss	含み損
bullet payment	一括払い，一括返済
burden	負担
burden of proof	立証責任
burden rate	間接費配賦率
bureaucracy	官僚制 [解]比較的規模の大きい社会集団や組織における管理・支配制度
burn rate	バーン・レート [解]会社維持のために，例えば月当たりで必要になる資金の額（特にスタートアップ企業について）
business	事業，ビジネス [解]IFRS3の文脈では，投資家等に対して，配当等の形でのリターンを直接的に提供する目的で実施及び管理される活動及び資産の統合された組合せ。インプット（例えば，原材料），プロセス（例えば，製造プロセス），及びアウトプット（例えば，製品）の3要素で構成される
business assets	事業用資産
business combination	企業結合 [解]取得企業が被取得企業の事業（business）の支配を獲得する取引
business combination achieved in stages	段階的に達成された企業結合 [解]取得企業が被取得企業の支配を段階的に獲得する形態の企業結合
business combination date	企業結合日
business combination under common control	共通支配下の企業結合
business continuity management (BCM)	事業継続マネジメント [解]不測の事態が発生した場合でも，事業の継続を可能とする経営管理手法
business continuity plan(ning) (BCP)	事業継続計画 [解]企業が災害等の緊急事態に備えて，早期復旧や事業の継続に必要な

対応などを計画すること
business day　営業日
business divestiture　事業分離
business divestiture date　事業分離日
business due diligence　ビジネス・デュー・デリジェンス
business enterprise　企業
business impact analysis (BIA)　ビジネス影響度分析　[解]BCP策定の一環として，「不測の事態の発生により業務が中断した場合の影響」を分析すること
business income　事業所得
business interruption　事業の中断
business judgement rule (BJR)　経営判断の原則　[米]business judgment rule (BJR)　[解]経営陣が合理的な経営判断を行ったと考えられる場合には，その結果の如何にかかわらず，株主に対する責任は生じないとする原則
business model test　事業モデルによるテスト　[解]IFRS9の文脈では，それぞれの金融資産がどのような目的で保有・管理されているかを判定するもので，事業モデルには「回収」・「回収及び売却」・「その他」の3つがある
business occupancy tax　事業所税
business office tax　事業所税
business performance　業績
business plan　事業計画
business practice　事業慣行，商慣行，実務
business process description　業務記述書
business process management (BPM)　ビジネス・プロセス・マネジメント　[解]業務フローの最適化など，ビジネス・プロセスを継続的に改善するための管理手法
business process outsourcing (BPO)　ビジネス・プロセス・アウトソーシング　[解]企業内部の業務プロセス（全体）を外部の専門業者に委託すること
business purchase agreement　事業買収契約
business purpose test　①事業基準，②事業目的テスト　[解]①タックス・ヘイブン対策税制における経済活動基準の1つで，外国関係会社の主たる事業が，株式等または債券の保有，工業所有権等または著作権の提供，船舶または航空機の貸付などの事業ではないことを確認する基準（一定の例外あり）
business relationship　事業関係，事業上の関係
business revitalisation　事業再生　[米]business revitalization
business risk　事業リスク，ビジネス・リスク
business segment　事業セグメント
business size　事業規模
business strategy　事業戦略
business tax　事業税
business tax payable　未払事業税
business tax rate　事業税率
business tax return　事業税申告書
business transfer　事業譲渡
business trip　出張
business unit　事業部門
business valuation　事業評価
business workout　事業整理
business year　事業年度
bust-up　離別
bust-up fee　違約金，解約料（特に買収契約に関する）
buyback　買戻し
buyback clause　買戻条項
buyback of ordinary shares　自己株式の取得
buyer　買手，購入者
buyer's value　バイヤーズ・バリュー，買手にとっての（企業）価値
buying agent　買付代理人
buy-in payment　費用分担契約参加のための支払い　[解]費用分担契約（CCA/CSA）に新規に参加する企業が，その参加に際して支払うもの
buyout　バイアウト，買収
buy-out payment　費用分担契約離脱の際の受取り　[解]費用分担契約（CCA/CSA）から離脱する企業が，その離脱に際して受け取るもの
buy-sell agreement　売買契約
buy side　バイサイド，買手側（買収案件などの）
bylaws　付属定款
by-product　副産物

C

CA ▶①confidentiality agreement, ②competent authority, ③chartered accountant, ④capital allowance
CAAT ▶computer assisted audit techniques
cafeteria plan　カフェテリア・プラン
CAGR ▶compound annual growth rate
calculate　計算する
calculation　計算
calendar year　暦年　[解]1月1日から12月31日まで
callable　償還可能な
call deposit　通知預金
call loan　コール・ローン
call option　コール・オプション　[解]基礎商品を将来のある期日までにあらかじめ定められた権利行使価格で買い付ける権利
Canada Revenue Agency (CRA)　カナダ歳入庁（カナダの税務当局）
cancel　取り消す
cancellation　取消し，解除（契約の），キャンセル
cancellation charge　キャンセル料，解約料
cancellation fee　キャンセル料，解約料
cancellation of debt (COD)　①債権放棄，②債務免除
cancellation of treasury shares　自己株式の消却
cancellation penalty　キャンセル料，解約料
C&F ▶cost and freight
CAO ▶chief administrative officer
cap　①キャップ，上限，②金利キャップ取引
capacity　生産能力，キャパシティ
capacity portion of an asset　資産の稼働能力部分
capacity utilisation　操業度，稼働率（工場などの）　[米]capacity utilization
capacity variance　操業度差異（製造間接費に係る）

capex ▶capital expenditure
capital　資本
capital account　資本勘定
capital adequacy　自己資本の十分性
capital allowance (CA)　キャピタル・アローワンス　[解]主として英国系の国で用いられる用語で，一般的には税務上の減価償却費（tax depreciation）とほぼ同義
capital allowances pool　未控除のキャピタル・アローワンス　[解]通常，未控除のキャピタル・アローワンスは将来に繰り越せる
capital and capital surplus (for tax purposes)　資本金等（税務上の）
capital appreciation　値上がり益，資本増価
capital asset　固定資産，資本資産
capital asset pricing model (CAPM)　資本資産評価モデル
capital budget(ing)　資本予算
capital charge　キャピタル・チャージ，資本費用　[解]無形資産の評価の局面では，収益を生み出すために使用される評価対象資産以外の資産（運転資本，有形固定資産，その他の無形固定資産など）に係るコストを指し，一般的に各資産の公正価値にそれぞれの期待収益率を乗じて計算される
capital commitment　資本的支出のコミットメント
capital component (of enterprise [business] tax)　資本割（事業税の外形標準部分の構成要素）
capital contribution　出資
capital decrease　減資
capital deficit　債務超過
capital employed (CE)　使用資本
capital enhancement　資本増強
capital expenditure (capex)　資本的支出　[解]収益的支出（revenue expenditure）に対する用語
capital gain　キャピタル・ゲイン，譲渡利益　[解]不動産や有価証券等の譲渡益　[用]capital gains from the sale of land（土地譲渡益），capital gains from the sale of securities（有価証券譲渡益）
capital gain rollover　譲渡益課税の繰延べ

capital gains tax (CGT)　譲渡益課税
capital gearing　レバレッジ
capital grant　固定資産取得のための補助金
capital increase　増資
capital injection　資本注入
capital investment　設備投資
capitalisation　資産化, 資産計上　㊌ capitalization
capitalisation factor　資本化係数　㊌ capitalization factor
capitalisation of borrowing costs　借入コストの資産化　㊌ capitalization of borrowing costs　㊙ IAS23の文脈では, 借入コストを適格資産の取得原価の一部として処理すること
capitalisation of exchange differences　為替差額の資産化　㊌ capitalization of exchange differences
capitalisation policy　資産計上に係る方針　㊌ capitalization policy　㊙ 例えば, 資本的支出と修繕費の区分
capitalisation rate (cap rate)　①資産化率, ②キャップ・レート, 還元利回り, 収益還元率　㊌ capitalization rate　㊙ ① IAS23の文脈では, 適格資産を取得するために特別に行った借入を除く, 企業の当期中の借入金残高に対する借入コストの割合（加重平均）
capitalisation table　キャップ・テーブル, 資本政策表　㊌ capitalization table
capitalise　資産計上する　㊌ capitalize
capitalise □ into　□を〜（資産）の取得価額に含める　㊌ capitalize □ into
capitalised　資産計上された　㊌ capitalized
capitalised development expenditure　資産化した開発支出　㊌ capitalized development expenditure
capitalised interest　資産計上された利息　㊌ capitalized interest
capital lease　キャピタル・リース（ファイナンス・リース）
capital legal reserve　資本準備金
capital levy　資本割（事業税の外形標準部分の構成要素）
capital loss　キャピタル・ロス, 譲渡損失　㊙ 不動産や有価証券等の譲渡損　㊍ capital losses from the sale of land（土地譲渡損）, capital losses from the sale of securities（有価証券譲渡損）
capital maintenance　資本維持
capital management　資本管理
capital market　資本市場
capital outlay　資本的支出
capital policy　資本政策
capital rationing　資本割当
capital reduction　減資
capital relationship　資本関係
capital requirements　自己資本規制, 必要資本
capital reserve　資本準備金, 資本剰余金
capital spending　設備投資
capital stock　資本金, 株式資本
capital structure　資本構成
capital surplus　資本剰余金
capital tax　資本税
capital transaction　資本取引
capital transaction within 100% group　100%グループ内の資本取引
CAPM　▶capital asset pricing model
cap rate　▶capitalisation rate
captive insurance company　キャプティブ保険会社　㊙ 事業会社の子会社で, 保険会社としての機能を有するもの。主にその事業会社及びグループ会社に保険を提供する
cargo　貨物
carried forward (c/f)　次期繰越し
carried-forward excess credit limit　繰越控除余裕額（外国税額控除の）　㊙ 外国税額控除制度の関係では, 控除対象外国法人税の額が控除限度額を下回るときのその余裕額につき, 将来3年にわたり繰り越すもの
carried-forward tax losses　繰越欠損金　㊙ 過年度に発生した税務上の損失で, 将来の課税所得と相殺できるもの
carried-forward unused foreign tax　繰越控除限度超過額（外国税額控除の）　㊙ 外国税額控除制度の関係では, 控除対象外国法人税の額が控除限度額を上回るときのその超過額につき, 将来3年にわたり

繰り越すもの
carrier　運送業者
carry　帳簿に記載する　[用] to be carried at cost　（取得原価で帳簿に記載される）
carryback　繰戻し（損失などの）
carry back　繰り戻す
carryback period　繰戻期間
carryforward　繰越し（損失などの）
carry forward　繰り越す
carryforward of unused tax credits　繰越税額控除　[解] IAS12の文脈では，税額控除のうち翌期以降に使用されるもの。将来その使用対象となる課税所得（税額）が稼得される可能性が高い場合，繰延税金資産が認識される
carryforward of unused tax losses　税務上の繰越欠損金　[解] IAS12の文脈では，当期以前に発生した欠損金のうち翌期以降に繰り越されるもの。将来その使用対象となる課税所得が稼得される可能性が高い場合，繰延税金資産が認識される
carryforward period　繰越期間
carrying amount　帳簿価額（会計上の）　[解] 資産が財政状態計算書に認識されている金額
carrying charge　保有費用，在庫費用
carry out　実行する
carryover　繰越し（損失などの）
carry over　繰り越す
carryover basis　引継簿価　[解] stepped-up basis（時価移転にあたり増額された簿価）に対して，資産が簿価移転するようなケースを指す
carve-out　カーブアウト　[解] (1)企業の中から事業を切り出し，別組織として独立させること，(2) IFRSが強制適用になった場合に，（国が）その一部の会計基準を採用しないこと
case　①ケース，場合，②判例
case law　判例法
cash　①現金，②資金，キャッシュ　[解] IAS7の文脈では，手許現金及び要求払預金を指す
cash account　現金勘定
cash accounting　現金主義会計
cash and bank balances　現金及び預金

cash and cash equivalents　現金及び現金同等物
cash and cash equivalents at the beginning of the year　現金及び現金同等物の期首残高　[解] キャッシュ・フロー計算書などでよく使われる用語
cash and cash equivalents at the end of the year　現金及び現金同等物の期末残高　[解] キャッシュ・フロー計算書などでよく使われる用語
cash at bank　預金
cash at bank in foreign currencies　外貨預金
cash balance plan　キャッシュ・バランス・プラン，キャッシュ・バランス年金制度　[解] 退職給付制度の1つで，確定給付制度の特徴である一定の給付水準の保障を維持しながら，確定拠出制度の特徴である（仮想）個人別残高も併せ持つ制度
cash balance projection　資金残高予測，資金繰り表
cash basis　現金主義，現金基準
cash basis accounting　現金主義会計
cash book　現金出納帳
cash box　キャッシュ・ボックス　[解] 一般には軽課税国の利用を目的とし，豊富な資本を持ちながら，能動的な事業遂行やリスク管理に必要な機能をほとんど果たしていない事業体。日本税制上は，タックス・ヘイブン対策税制における特定外国関係会社の1つであり，外国関係会社のうち，総資産に対する受動的所得の割合や，総資産に占める金融資産等の割合に関する一定の基準に抵触するものがこれに該当する
cash collateral　現金担保
cash consideration　現金対価　[解] 株式対価（share [stock] consideration）に対する用語
cash conversion cycle (CCC)　キャッシュ・コンバージョン・サイクル　[解] 運転資本の管理などに用いられる指標で，一般的には「売掛金回転期間＋在庫回転期間－買掛金回転期間」という算式で計算される。端的には，仕入に伴う現金支払いから販売に伴う現金回収までの期間（日数または月数）を示す

cash count	現金カウント，現金実査
cash disbursement	出金，現金支払い
cash disbursement slip	出金伝票
cash discount	①現金割引，②売上割引，③仕入割引
cash dividend	現金配当　[解]現物配当（dividend in kind）に対する用語
cash equivalent	現金同等物　[解]IAS7の文脈では，短期の流動性の高い投資のうち，容易に一定金額に換金可能であり，かつ価値の変動について僅少なリスクしか負わないもの
cash flow	キャッシュ・フロー
cash flow analysis	キャッシュ・フロー分析
cash flow characteristics test	（契約上の）キャッシュ・フローの特性によるテスト　[解]IFRS9の文脈では，金融資産の契約条件によって発生するキャッシュ・フローが元本及び利息のみかどうかを判定するもの
cash flow forecast	キャッシュ・フロー予測
cash flow hedge	キャッシュ・フロー・ヘッジ　[解]IFRS9の文脈では，ヘッジ対象のキャッシュ・フローが特定のリスクに起因して変動し，かつ，純資産に影響を与えうる場合における，そのキャッシュ・フローの変動に対するエクスポージャーのヘッジを意味する
cash flow hedge reserve	キャッシュ・フロー・ヘッジ剰余金　[解]その他の資本の構成要素
cash flow management	資金繰り，キャッシュ・フロー管理
cash flow projection	キャッシュ・フロー予測
cash flow return on invested capital (CFROI)	キャッシュ・フロー投下資本利益率
cash flow return on investment (CFROI)	キャッシュ・フロー投下資本利益率
cash flows from [used in] discontinued operation	非継続事業のキャッシュ・フロー
cash flows from financing activities	財務活動によるキャッシュ・フロー
cash flows from investing activities	投資活動によるキャッシュ・フロー
cash flows from operating activities	営業活動によるキャッシュ・フロー
cash flow statement	キャッシュ・フロー計算書
cash flow worksheet	資金繰り表
cash free debt free	キャッシュや有利子負債の影響を受けない【形】
cash free debt free value	キャッシュや有利子負債の影響を受けない（企業の）価値
cash-generating unit (CGU)	資金生成単位　[解]IAS36の文脈では，他の資産または資産グループからのキャッシュ・インフローとはほぼ独立したキャッシュ・インフローを生成するものとして識別される資産グループの最小単位を指す
cashier's cheque	自己宛小切手（銀行の）　[米]cashier's check
cash inflow	資金流入
cash in hand	手許現金
cash instrument	現金性商品
cash larceny	窃盗（資金の）
cash-like item	キャッシュライク・アイテム，資金同等物
cash management	資金管理
cash method	現金主義
cash on delivery	代金引換払い
cash on delivery sales	代金引換払いの売上
cash on hand	手許現金
cash on hand and in banks	現金及び預金
cash-on-hand misappropriation	手許現金の不正流用
cash outflow	資金流出
cash outlay	現金支出
cash-out merger	キャッシュアウト・マージャー　[解]吸収合併により消滅した会社の株主に，合併対価として（存続会社の株式ではなく）金銭を交付する合併形態
cash over and short	現金過不足
cash payments journal	現金出納帳
cash pool(ing)	キャッシュ・プーリング　[解]企業グループ内の資金をマスター口座に集中させること
cash receipt(s)	入金，現金収入
cash receipts journal	現金出納帳
cash receipt slip	入金伝票

cash register disbursement scheme　レジ不正スキーム
cash requirements　資金需要
cash-settled　現金決済される【形】
cash-settled option　現金決済オプション
cash-settled share-based payment　現金決済型の株式に基づく報酬　解 株式に基づく報酬取引の一形態であり，企業が，自社の資本性金融商品の価格を基礎とする金額の「負債」(後に現金決済される) を負うことを対価として，財またはサービスを取得する取引
cash-settled share-based payment liability　現金決済型株式報酬債務
cash settlement　現金決済，差金決済
cash shortage　資金不足
cash shortfall　資金不足
cash surplus　余剰資金
casualty　①災害，②死傷者
casualty loss　災害損失
catastrophe　大災害
catch-all clause　包括条項
catch-up adjustment　処理遅れの修正　解 過年度の処理漏れを当期に修正する場合などを指す
categorisation　分類すること　米 categorization
categorise　分類する　米 categorize
category　分類，区分
causal connection　因果関係
cause　①原因，②引き起こす【動】
cause and effect (relationship)　原因と結果，因果関係
caveat　①警告，②差止め
CbCR　▶Country-by-Country Report
CbC Report　▶Country-by-Country Report
CCA　▶cost contribution arrangements
CCC　▶cash conversion cycle
CCO　▶chief compliance officer
C corporation　Cコーポレーション，C法人　解 米国における法人の一形態で，株式会社を指す
CD　▶certificate of deposit
CDO　▶collateralised debt obligation
CDS　▶credit default swap
CE　▶capital employed

cease　やめる，終了する　用 to cease capitalisation (資産化を終了する)
ceiling　上限，シーリング
central bank　中央銀行
centralise　集中させる　米 centralize
centralised purchasing　集中購買　米 centralized purchasing
central management and control　管理支配地 (主義)　解 実質的な管理支配の中心地をもって法人の居住地国とする考え方
CEO　▶chief executive officer
certificate　証明書，証
certificate of deposit (CD)　譲渡性預金
certificate of incorporation　法人設立許可書
certificate of origin　原産地証明 (書)
certificate of residence [residency]　居住者証明 (書)　解 権限ある当局 (税務当局) が法人や個人について自国の居住者であることを証明するもの。租税条約に基づく租税の減免等を受けるためには，(租税条約に関する届出書に加えて) 居住者証明 (書) が必要になる場合がある
certificate of tax payment　納税証明書
certified　公認の
certified fraud examiner (CFE)　公認不正検査士
certified internal auditor (CIA)　公認内部監査人
certified management accountant (CMA)　公認管理会計士
certified public accountant (CPA)　公認会計士
cessation　中止，停止
cessation of capitalisation　資産化の終了　米 cessation of capitalization
cessation of consolidation of subsidiaries　子会社の連結の停止
cession　譲渡
c/f　▶carried forward
CFC　▶controlled foreign company [corporation]
CFC rules　タックス・ヘイブン対策税制　解 低税率国に所在する海外子会社を利用した租税回避行為を防止することを目的として，低税率国の海外子会社の所得を日本企業の所得と合算して，日本で課税す

る税制
CFE ▶certified fraud examiner
CFO ▶chief financial officer
CFR ▶cost and freight
CFROI ▶① cash flow return on invested capital, ② cash flow return on investment
CGT ▶capital gains tax
CGU ▶cash-generating unit
chain of title 所有権の変遷（を示す文書）
chain reaction 連鎖反応
challenge ①異議を唱える，疑念を持つ，②異議 [使い方注意！]税務当局（tax authorities）が，税務調査（tax audit）の局面で，企業の税務上の処理について異議を唱える，という文脈で使われることが多い
change ①変更する，②変更，③（数値等の）変動
change in accounting estimate 会計上の見積りの変更
change in accounting policy 会計方針の変更
change in business model 事業モデルの変更
change in classification 表示区分の変更
change in financial position 財政状態の変動
change in functional currency 機能通貨の変更
change in measurement 測定の変動
change in non-controlling interests 非支配持分の増減 [解]持分変動計算書などでよく使われる用語
change in ownership interest 所有持分の変動
change in presentation 表示方法の変更
change in tax rates 税率の変更
change in tax laws 税法の変更
change in the level of ownership interest in subsidiary 子会社に対する所有持分の変動 [解]IFRS10の文脈では，子会社に対する親会社の持分変動のうち，支配の喪失とならないものは，持分（資本）の内部で会計処理される
change in value 価値変動
change of control (CoC) 株主変更，チェンジ・オブ・コントロール [解]税務デュー・デリジェンスの関係では，買収による株主変更は，繰越欠損金の失効等を通じて，買収対象会社の税務ポジションに影響を与える可能性がある。change of ownership も同様の意味で使われる
change of control clause チェンジ・オブ・コントロール条項 [解]ライセンス契約（licensing agreement）や取引先との基本契約において，企業買収等で主要株主の交代等があった場合，何らかの制約条件が生じること（例えば，相手方の了承がない限り，ライセンス契約が無効となる等）を規定した条項
change of ownership 株主変更
channel 経路，ルート
channel stuffing 押込販売
Chapter 11 (of Federal Bankruptcy Act) チャプター・イレブン [解]米国の連邦倒産法第11章を指し，日本の民事再生法に相当する
character 特徴，特性
characterise 特徴を決定づける（税務上の） [米]characterize
characteristic ①特徴，②特徴的な
charge ①請求する，②費用
chargeable ①課されるべき，負担すべき，②請求可能な，③課税対象の
chargeable income 課税所得
charitable trust チャリタブル・トラスト，慈善信託
chart チャート，図表，グラフ
charter 定款
chartered accountant (CA) 勅許会計士（英国）
chart of accounts 勘定科目一覧表
cheat ごまかす
check ①チェック，②【米】小切手
checking account 当座預金
checklist チェックリスト
check-the-box classification regulations チェックザボックス規定 [解]米国の税務上，米国内外の一定の事業体（例えばLLC）について，法人課税または構成員課税（パススルー）のどちらと取り扱うかを納税者自らが選択できるという規定

cheque	小切手　㊕check
cheque book	小切手帳　㊕check book
cheque register	小切手台帳　㊕check register
cheque tampering	小切手の改竄　㊕check tampering
cheque tampering scheme	小切手改竄スキーム（不正の一形態）　㊕check tampering scheme
cherry pick	いいとこ取りをする
cherry picking	いいとこ取り　㊟例えば，移転価格調査の局面で，税務当局が自らに有利な形で比較対象取引を選定すること
chief administrative officer (CAO)	最高管理責任者
chief compliance officer (CCO)	最高コンプライアンス責任者，チーフ・コンプライアンス・オフィサー
chief executive officer (CEO)	最高経営責任者
chief financial officer (CFO)	最高財務責任者
chief operating decision maker (CODM)	最高経営意思決定者　㊟IFRSの文脈では，事業セグメントの業績を評価し，資源を配分する機能を意味し，通常最高経営責任者（CEO）や最高執行責任者（COO）がこれに該当するが，経営会議等のグループがこれに該当することも考えられる
chief operating officer (COO)	最高執行責任者
choice	選択
choice of accounting policy	会計方針の選択（肢）
choice of presentation currency	表示通貨の選択（肢）
choice of settlement	決済方法の選択（肢）
choose	選択する
CIA	▶certified internal auditor
CIF	▶cost, insurance, and freight
CIF destination	着荷地渡し
CIF price	CIF価格
CIF value	CIF評価
circular	通達（税務当局の）
circulation	①循環，②回覧，サーキュレーション
circumstance	状況
circumvent	回避する，すり抜ける
CIT	▶corporate income tax
cite	引用する
city planning tax	都市計画税
civil law	民法，シビル・ロー
civil monetary penalty	民事上の罰金
civil penalty	民事罰，制裁金
Civil Rehabilitation Act [Law]	民事再生法
civil suit	民事訴訟
claim	①請求する，②請求，③賠償請求
claim for damages	損害賠償請求
claim for refund	還付請求
clarification	明確化
clarify	明確化する
clarity	明瞭性，透明性
class	種類
class action	集団訴訟
classification	分類　㊟財務諸表における科目の分類を指すことが多い
classification as	～としての分類，～への分類　㊗classification as held for sale（売却目的保有への分類）
classification of expenses by function	費用項目の機能別分類
classification of expenses by nature	費用項目の形態別分類
classify	分類する
class of assets	資産の種類
class of inventory	棚卸資産の種類
class of shares	株式の種類
class shares	種類株式　㊟剰余金の配当その他の権利の内容が異なる2種類以上の株式で，例えば，いわゆる優先株式も種類株式に該当する
clause	条項
clean opinion	無限定適正意見（監査報告書の）
clean-up	浄化
clean-up cost	浄化費用
clear	明らかな
clearance	①許可，クリアランス，②通関
clearance fee	通関手数料
clearance from tax authorities	税務当局からの許可

clearing house	①清算機関，②手形交換所
clearing party	清算機関
clerical	事務の
clerical work	事務，事務作業
client	クライアント
CLO	▶collateralised loan obligation
close	①決算，②閉じた【形】，③親密な
close association	親密な関係
close company	閉鎖的会社，非公開会社
closely held company	閉鎖会社,非公開会社, 同族会社　[解]税務上の同族会社を指す場合，closely held company for tax purposes などのいい方がある
closely related	密接に関連する【形】
close members of the family of a person	個人の近親者　[解] IAS124 の文脈では，その個人に影響を与えるかまたは影響を受けると予測される親族
close of business (COB)	終業時間（までに）
closing	①クロージング,②決算　[解]①企業買収において，対価の決済（株券との交換）を行い，取引を完結させること
closing balance	期末残高
closing conditions	クロージングの前提条件（買収案件などの）
closing date	①クロージング日，②決算日，期末日　[解] ① IFRS3 の文脈では，契約に基づく最終的な取得企業及び被取得企業の義務が履行される日を指し，具体的には取得企業側が対価を決済し，被取得企業側が資産及び負債を引き渡す日
closing entry	決算（整理）仕訳
closing foreign exchange rate	期末の為替レート，決算日レート，期末日レート
closing memorandum	クロージング・メモ　[解]買収案件などで，有効にクロージングが行われていることを当事者間で確認するための文書
closing procedures	決算手続
closing rate	決算日レート，期末日レート
closing rate method	期末日レート法，決算日レート法
closing schedule	決算スケジュール
closing the books	決算
closure	閉鎖
CMA	▶certified management accountant
COB	▶close of business
CoC	▶change of control
COD	▶cancellation of debt
code	①コード，②規約
code of conduct	行動規範
code of ethics	倫理規定
codify	成文化する
COD income	債務免除益
CODM	▶chief operating decision maker
co-founder	共同創業者
COGS	▶cost of goods sold
co-investment	共同投資
collaboration	協力
collaborative	共同の
collaborative arrangement	共同契約
collateral	担保
collateral held	保有している担保
collateralise	担保提供する　[米] collateralize
collateralised debt obligation (CDO)	債務担保証券　[米] collateralized debt obligation (CDO)
collateralised loan obligation (CLO)	ローン担保証券　[米] collateralized loan obligation (CLO)
collateral pledged	差し入れている担保
collateral sold	売却した担保
collect	①回収する，②徴収する（税金などを）
collectibility	回収可能性
collectible	回収可能な
collectible in full	全額回収可能な
collection	①回収，②徴収（税金などの）
collection period	回収期間
collective	集合的な
collective bargaining	団体交渉（労使間の）
collective impairment	集合的減損（営業債権などの）
collective investment vehicle	集団投資ビークル
collectively	集合的に
collude	共謀する
collusion	共謀，通謀
column	列（行・列の）
combination	①結合，②組み合わせ
combination of businesses	事業の結合

combination of contracts	契約の結合
combination of entities	企業の結合
combine	①結合する，②組み合わせる
combined entity	被結合企業　[解] 結合企業（combining entity）に対する用語
combined instrument	結合金融商品
combining entity	結合企業　[解] 被結合企業（combined entity）に対する用語
come into effect	発効する
comfort letter	コンフォート・レター　[解]「監査人から事務幹事証券会社への書簡」を意味し，企業が社債発行等により資金調達を行う際に，監査人が事務幹事証券会社等からの依頼に基づき作成する確認書
co-mingling	混同
commence	開始する
commencement	開始
commencement date	開始日
commencement date for capitalisation	資産化の開始（日）　[米] commencement date for capitalization
commencement of capitalisation	資産化の開始　[米] commencement of capitalization
commencement of lease term	リース期間の開始日
commensurate with income standard	所得相応性基準　[解] 米国等の一定の国の移転価格税制に関連して，無形資産の移転取引等の後に，無形資産に帰属する所得に大幅な変動がある場合には，無形資産の取引価格の修正を求めるという基準
comment	コメント
commentary	①注釈，論評，②コメンタリー（OECDモデル租税条約などの）　[解] ②OECDモデル租税条約には，コメンタリー（解説）があり，その解釈に利用される
commentary by management	経営者による説明
commercial	商業の
commercial bank	商業銀行
commercial database	商業データベース
commercial due diligence	コマーシャル［ビジネス］・デュー・デリジェンス
commercial intangible	コマーシャル・インタンジブル，商業上の無形資産　[解] 一般に，製品の製造あるいは役務の提供のために使用される特許，ノウハウ，デザイン及び形式等を指す
commercial law	商法
commercially	商業的に
commercially justifiable	商業的に正当化可能な
commercial motive	商業的動機　[使い方注意！]「商業的動機がある」＝「租税回避目的ではない」という文脈で用いられることが多い
commercial motive test	商業的動機テスト
commercial paper (CP)	コマーシャル・ペーパー
commercial papers issued	発行したコマーシャル・ペーパー
commercial production	商業生産
commercial property	商業用不動産
commercial substance	商業的実体
commercial value	商業的価値，商品価値
commission	①手数料，委託手数料，②委託
commission agent	問屋
commissionaire	コミッショネア，問屋　[解] 代理人の1つで，日本の商法における定義は，「自己の名をもって他人のために物品の販売または買入れをすることを業とする者」。OECDモデル租税条約では，general commission agentという呼び方をしている
Commissioner (of the National Tax Agency)	国税庁長官
Commissioner's Directive on Interpretation of the Corporation Tax Act	法人税法基本通達
Commissioner's Directive on the Operation of Transfer Pricing	移転価格事務運営要領　[解] 日本の国税庁が発行している，移転価格税制の執行に関する指針
commission expense	手数料，支払手数料
commission income	手数料収入，受取手数料
commission revenue	手数料収入，受取手数料
commitment	コミットメント

Committee on Fiscal Affairs (OECD の)　租税委員会
commodities futures　商品先物
commodity　商品，コモディティ
commodity price risk　コモディティ価格リスク
commodity swap　コモディティ・スワップ
common control　共通支配　[解] 企業結合において，結合当事者が同一企業の支配下にあること
common law　慣習法，コモン・ロー　[解] 特に成文法 (statute law) に対して，判例法 (case law) を指す
common ownership　共同所有
Common Reporting Standard (CRS)　共通報告基準　[解] 自動的情報交換 (AEOI) の対象となる非居住者の口座の特定方法や情報の範囲等を各国で共通化するための国際基準
common sense　常識
common share　普通株式
common stock　①普通株式，②資本金
communication and network equipment　通信及びネットワーク機器
communication cost [expense]　通信費
Companies Act [Law]　会社法
company　会社
company brochure　会社案内，パンフレット
company level control　全社的な内部統制
company's contribution to social security　会社負担の社会保険拠出
company split　会社分割
company with a board of corporate auditors　監査役会設置会社
company with committees　委員会設置会社
comparability　比較可能性　[解] 財務諸表の質的特性の1つ
comparability analysis　比較分析
comparable　比較可能な
comparable company　比較対象会社，類似企業
comparable company analysis　類似企業分析
comparable profits method (CPM)　利益比準法（米国）　[解] 移転価格税制の関係では，米国における独立企業間価格の算定方法の1つを指し，取引単位営業利益法 (TNMM) に類似
comparable transaction　比較対象取引　[解] 移転価格税制の関係では，独立企業間価格の算定の基礎となる比準取引を指す
comparable uncontrolled price method (CUP method)　独立価格比準法，CUP法　[解] 移転価格税制の関係では，独立企業間価格の算定方法の1つで，独立企業間の同種の取引で同様の状況下で行われた取引を比較対象とし，その価格を国外関連取引の価格と比較する方法を指す
comparable uncontrolled transaction method (CUT method)　独立取引比準法，CUT法
comparative　比較対象となる【形】
comparative analysis　比較分析
comparative financial statement　比較財務諸表
comparative information　比較情報　[解] 当期の情報と比較するための前期以前の情報（過年度財務諸表等）
comparative prior-period information　比較対象となる過年度情報
compare　比較する
comparison　比較
compensate　補償する，埋め合わせる
compensated absence　有給休暇
compensating adjustment　補償調整　[解] 移転価格税制の関係では，実際の利益水準等が事前確認 (APA) における合意内容などと異なるときに，それを合意された利益レンジに収めるために行う調整
compensation　①報酬，②賠償（金），補償（金）
compensation committee　報酬委員会（委員会設置会社の）
compensation payment　補償金（の支払い）
compensatory　①報酬としての，②補償としての
compensatory stock option　報酬としてのストック・オプション
competence　①能力，②権限
competency　①能力，②高い業績を上げた社員の行動様式
competent　①法的資格のある，正当な権限

を持つ【形】, ②有能な
competent authority (CA)　権限ある当局　[解]租税条約により, 相互協議 (mutual agreement procedure) を行うべき者として定められている者
competitive bid　競争入札
competitive harm　競争上の障害
competitive quotes　相見積り
compilation　調製・作成 (財務諸表の)
compilation engagement　財務諸表作成業務
compilation of financial statements　財務諸表の作成
compilation report　財務諸表作成に係る報告書
compile　調製する・作成する (財務諸表を)
complain　不満をいう, 不平をいう
complaint　不満, 不平
complement　補足
complementary　補足的な
complete　完成させる
completed contract method　完成基準, 工事完成基準
completeness　完全性, 網羅性
completion　完成, 完了
completion accounts　クロージング日における決算書 (買収対象会社などの)
completion accounts rules　クロージング日における決算書の作成ルール (買収案件などの)
completion adjustment　価格修正方式　[解]買収価格の調整について, クロージング日の貸借対照表等 (completion accounts) に基づき最終的に価格修正を行う方式。固定価格方式 (locked box) に対する用語
completion of sale　売却の完了
compliance　①法令遵守, ② tax compliance の項を参照
compliance audit　コンプライアンス監査
compliance programme　コンプライアンス・プログラム, 法令遵守プログラム　[米] compliance program
compliance with capital requirements　自己資本規制の遵守
comply　遵守する

component　①部品, ②構成要素, 部分
component approach　コンポーネント・アプローチ (減価償却の)
component depreciation　コンポーネント単位の減価償却
componentise　コンポーネント化する　[米] componentize　[解]固定資産の取得原価を重要な構成部分に配分し, その構成部分ごとに耐用年数や減価償却方法を決定すること
component of an entity　企業の構成単位　[解] IFRS5 の文脈では, 事業活動上及び財務報告目的で, 企業の他の部分から明確に区分できる事業活動及びキャッシュ・フローをいう
components of equity　資本の内訳項目
components of tax expense　税金費用の内訳
composite　①複合の, ②複合
composite asset　複合的な資産
composition　構成
composition of a group　グループの構成
compound　複合の, 合成の
compound annual growth rate (CAGR)　年平均成長率
compound financial instrument　複合金融商品　[解]複数の金融商品が組み合わされている金融商品
compound interest　複利　[解]単利 (simple interest) に対する用語
comprehensive　包括的な
comprehensive anti-tax avoidance provisions　包括的租税回避防止規定
comprehensive income　包括利益
comprise　構成する
comptroller　経理責任者
compulsory　強制的な
compulsory liquidation　強制清算
computation　①計算, ② tax computation の項を参照
compute　計算する
computer assisted audit techniques (CAAT)　コンピュータ利用監査技法
computer equipment　コンピュータ機器
computer software　コンピュータ・ソフトウェア　[解]無形資産の例

con | 騙す
conceal | 隠す，隠蔽する，秘密にする
concealed liabilities and expenses | 負債・費用の隠蔽
concealment | 隠蔽
concentration | 集中
concentrations of risk | リスクの集中
concept | 概念
conceptual | 概念の，概念上の
conceptual framework | 概念フレームワーク
Conceptual Framework for Financial Reporting | 財務報告に関する概念フレームワーク
concern | 関心事，懸念事項
concession | ①免許（政府から得る），②利権，③譲歩，④ tax concession の項を参照
conclude | 結論付ける
conclusion | 結論
conclusive | 決定的な
concurrent | 同時の
concurrently | 同時に
condensed | 要約された
condensed (financial) statements | 要約財務諸表
condition | ①条件，②状況
conditional | 条件付きの
conditioned | 条件付きの
condition precedent (CP) | ①先行条件，②停止条件，③クロージングの前提条件（買収案件などの）
conditions for exception | 適用除外要件，適用除外基準（特に旧タックス・ヘイブン対策税制における）[解]タックス・ヘイブン対策税制の関係では，平成29年度税制改正前の制度において，新制度の「経済活動基準」に相当するもの
conditions for qualified reorganisation | 適格要件（組織再編の）[米]conditions for qualified reorganization [解]日本の組織再編税制において，組織再編が適格組織再編となるために充足すべき要件。適格要件は，大きくグループ内再編とその他の再編（共同事業を行うための再編）に分かれている
conditions for tax-qualified reorganisation | 適格要件（組織再編の）[米]conditions for tax qualified reorganization
conduit | 導管
conduit company | 導管事業体
conduit transaction | 導管取引 [解]租税条約の関係では，租税条約の特典を享受するために，あえて条約相手国を経由させて第三国と取引を行うこと
conference | 会議
conference call | 電話会議
confession | 自白（不正などの）
confidence | ①秘密，②信用
confidential | 秘密の
confidentiality | ①守秘義務，②秘密性
confidentiality agreement (CA) | 秘密保持契約
configuration | コンフィギュレーション，設定（システムの），機器構成，配置
confirm | 確認する
confirmation | 確認
confirmation letter | 確認書，確認状
confirmation request | 確認依頼（書）
confirmatory | 確認の
confirmatory due diligence | コンファーマトリー・デュー・デリジェンス [解]買収案件などで，（契約直前などに）確認目的で行われるデュー・デリジェンス
confirmatory value | 確認価値，検証可能価値
conflict | 対立
conflict of interest | 利害対立，利益相反
conform | 従う
conformity | 適合，整合，一致
conglomerate | コングロマリット
conglomerate discount | コングロマリット・ディスカウント [解]多角化した企業において，企業全体の価値が各事業（単体）の価値合計を下回っている状態
consecutive | 連続した
consensual | 合意の上の
consensus | 合意事項
consensus pricing | 合意価格
consent | ①同意する，②同意
consent letter | 同意書
consequence | 結果
conservatism | 保守主義
conservative | 保守的な
consideration | 対価

consideration in the form of cash　現金対価
consideration in the form of shares　株式対価　[解]現金対価に対する用語
consideration paid　支払対価
consideration received　受取対価
consideration transferred　対価，移転された対価　[解]IFRS3の文脈では，取得企業が企業結合の対価として引き渡す現金や株式等を指す
consign　委託する
consigned goods　委託品，販売委託品
consignee　受託者（委託販売の）
consigner　委託者（委託販売の）
consignment　委託（販売）
consignment agreement　委託（販売）契約
consignment arrangement　委託(販売)契約
consignment sales　委託販売
consist (of)　（〜により）構成される
consistency　一貫性，首尾一貫性，整合性
consistent　一貫した【形】
consistent basis　一貫した方法　[用] on a consistent basis（継続的に，一貫した方法で）
consolidate　連結する
consolidated accounts　連結財務諸表
consolidated and separate financial statements　連結及び個別財務諸表
consolidated balance sheet　連結貸借対照表
consolidated filing　連結納税
consolidated financial accounts　連結財務諸表，連結決算書
consolidated financial statements　連結財務諸表　[解]親会社及びその子会社の資産，負債，資本，収益，費用及びキャッシュ・フローを，単一の経済的実体のものとして表示する企業集団の財務諸表
consolidated income　連結所得
consolidated income statement　連結損益計算書
consolidated statement of cash flows　連結キャッシュ・フロー計算書
consolidated statement of changes in equity　連結持分変動計算書
consolidated statement of changes in net assets　連結株主資本等変動計算書
consolidated statement of comprehensive income　①連結包括利益計算書（２計算書方式の場合），②連結損益及び包括利益計算書（１計算書方式の場合）
consolidated statement of financial position　連結財政状態計算書
consolidated statement of income　連結損益計算書
consolidated structured entity　連結対象の組成された企業［ストラクチャード・エンティティ］
consolidated subsidiary　連結子会社
consolidated supplemental schedule　連結附属明細表
consolidated taxable income　連結所得
consolidated taxation system　連結納税制度
consolidated tax loss　連結欠損金
consolidated tax return　連結申告書
consolidated tax return filing (system)　連結納税（制度）
consolidation　連結
consolidation accounting system　連結会計システム
consolidation adjustment　連結修正
consolidation adjustment entry　連結修正仕訳
consolidation closing　連結決算
consolidation entry　連結（修正）仕訳
consolidation group　連結グループ
consolidation period　連結期間
consolidation procedure　連結手続
consortium　コンソーシアム，共同事業体
conspirator　共謀者
conspire　共謀する
constant　①不変の，一定の，②普段の　[用] ① to remain constant（（数値などが）変動しない）
constituent　①構成要素たる【形】，②構成要素，③構成員
constituent unit　構成単位（企業の）
constitute　構成する
constitution　①定款，②憲法
constraint　制限，制約条件
construct　建設する
construction　建設，工事
construction contract　工事契約

construction contract cost　工事原価，工事契約原価
construction contract revenue　工事収益，工事契約収益
construction in progress　①建設仮勘定，②未成工事支出金
construction or installation project　建設または据付プロジェクト
construction sales　工事売上，完成工事高
construction work　工事
constructive　①建設的な，②擬制の，みなし
constructive dividend　みなし配当
constructive obligation　推定的債務，みなし債務　[解]IAS37の文脈では，確立された過去の実務慣行等により，企業が外部の第三者に何らかの責務を受諾することを表明しており，その結果，企業がその責務を果たすであろうという期待が外部の第三者に生じている場合のその債務
constructive ownership　みなし所有
consultancy agreement　コンサルタント契約
consultant　コンサルタント
consultation　コンサルテーション，（専門家への）相談
consulting　コンサルティング
consulting agreement　コンサルティング契約
consulting expense [fee]　コンサルティング費用
consulting service　コンサルティング・サービス
consumables　消耗品　[解]通常複数形
consumer goods　消費財
consumer price index (CPI)　消費者物価指数
consumption　消費
consumption tax　消費税
Consumption Tax Act　消費税法
consumption tax payable　未払消費税
consumption tax receivable [refundable]　未収消費税
consumption tax return　消費税申告書
contaminated　汚染された【形】
contamination　汚染
contemporaneous　同時期の，同時発生の
contemporaneous documentation　同時文書（化）　[解]移転価格税制の関係では，移転価格の文書化を確定申告期限までに行うことを指す
contemporaneous transfer pricing documentation　同時文書（化）
context　文脈
contingency　偶発
contingent　①条件付きの，②偶発の
contingent asset　偶発資産　[解]IAS37の文脈では，過去の事象から発生し得る（潜在的な）資産のうち，将来の不確実な事象の発生または不発生によってのみその存在が確認されるもの（例えば，還付される可能性のある税金）
contingent consideration　条件付対価　[解]IFRS3の文脈では，企業結合後の特定の事象または取引の結果に依存して，企業結合日後に被取得企業の旧所有者に対して追加的に引き渡される取得対価
contingent fee　成功報酬
contingent liability　偶発負債，偶発債務　[解]IAS37の文脈では，(1)過去の事象から発生し得る（潜在的な）債務のうち，将来の不確実な事象の発生または不発生によってのみその存在が確認される債務，あるいは(2)過去の事象から発生した現在の債務であるが，債務決済のために経済的便益が流出する可能性が高くないか，また債務の金額が十分な信頼性をもって測定できないという理由で認識されていない債務　[用]contingent liability for guarantees（保証に係る偶発負債）
contingently issuable ordinary share　条件付発行可能普通株式　[解]条件付株式発行契約（contingent share agreement）に定める一定の条件を満たす場合に（対価をほとんど必要とせずに）発行可能となる普通株式
contingently issuable share　条件付発行可能株式
contingent payment　条件付支払い
contingent purchase price　条件付対価
contingent rent　変動賃借［賃貸］料，条件付賃借［賃貸］料
contingent settlement provision　条件付決済条項

contingent share agreement　条件付株式発行契約　[解] 一定の条件を満たす場合に株式を発行するという契約
continuation　継続
continuing　継続的な
continuing and discontinued operations　継続事業及び非継続事業
continuing auditor　継続監査人
continuing involvement　継続的関与　[用] continuing involvement in derecognised financial assets（認識の中止をした金融資産に対する継続的関与）
continuing managerial involvement　継続的な管理上の関与
continuing operation　継続事業　[解] IFRS5 の文脈では、非継続事業（discontinued operation）以外の事業を指す
continuing use　継続的な使用
continuity　継続性
continuity of beneficial ownership test　株主変動テスト　[解] シンガポールにおける規制で、過年度の欠損金について、主要株主に変動がないことを条件として、繰越しを認めるというもの
continuous　連続的な、継続的な
continuous assessment　継続的な判定
contra account　相殺勘定、反対勘定　[解] 例えば売上勘定に対する売上値引勘定など
contract　①契約、②契約書
contract asset　契約資産　[解] IFRS15 の文脈では、企業が顧客に移転した財またはサービスと交換に受け取る対価に対する企業の権利で、当該権利が時の経過以外の何か（例えば、企業の将来の履行）を条件としているものを指す。条件の観点で、債権（receivable）とは区別される
contract-based intangible asset　契約に基づく無形資産
contract cost　①契約コスト、②契約原価、工事契約原価
contract duration　契約の存続期間
contract for work　請負
contracting state　締約国
contract liability　契約負債　[解] IFRS15 の文脈では、顧客に財またはサービスを移転する企業の義務のうち、企業が顧客から対価を受け取っている（またはその期限が到来している）ものを指す
contract manufacturer　契約製造業者　[解] 他の企業（親会社を含む）から製品製造を請け負う企業
contract modification　契約変更
contractor　請負者、施工者
contract revenue　工事契約収益
contract termination costs　契約終了に係る費用
contract to buy or sell a non-financial item　非金融商品項目を売買する契約
contractual　契約上の
contractual arrangement　契約上の取決め
contractual cash flows　契約上のキャッシュ・フロー
contractual commitment　契約上のコミットメント
contractual legal criterion　契約・法的要件　[解] 無形資産認識の要件の1つ
contractual life　有効期間、契約期間
contractual life of options　オプション契約の有効期間
contractually　契約により
contractually agreed sharing of control　契約により合意された支配の共有
contractual maturity　契約上の満期
contractual obligation　契約上の義務
contractual payment　契約上の支払い　[用] contractual payments are more than 30 days past due（契約上の支払いが期限から30日超遅れている）
contractual right　契約上の権利
contractual term　契約条件
contract with a customer　顧客との契約
contradict　①否定する、②矛盾する
contradiction　①否定、②矛盾
contrast　対比、対照
contribute　①出資する、②寄附する、③貢献する
contributed capital　拠出資本
contribute □ in kind (to)　（〜に）□を現物出資する
contribution　①出資、②拠出（年金基金などへの）、③貢献
contribution analysis　貢献度分析

contribution in kind	現物出資
contribution margin	貢献利益　[解] (1) 各部門の売上高から，その部門が管理可能な費用を差し引いて算出した利益。または，(2) 限界利益（marginal profit）と同義
contribution margin ratio	貢献利益率
contributions by an employer	事業主による拠出（退職給付制度などへの）
contributions by a plan participant	制度加入者による拠出（退職給付制度などへの）
contributions from [by] owners	（企業の）所有者からの出資
contributions to defined contribution plans	確定拠出制度への拠出
contribution to social security	社会保険拠出，社会保険料
contributory	拠出を伴う（退職給付制度が）【形】
contributory asset	拠出資産
control	①支配，②統制，③支配する　[解] ①IFRS10の文脈では，投資企業（investor）が被投資企業（investee）への関与から生じる変動リターン（variable return）にさらされ，または変動リターンに対する権利を有しており，かつ，被投資企業に対する力（パワー）を通じてそれらのリターンに影響を及ぼすことができる場合には，被投資企業を支配していることになる
control account	総勘定元帳（科目）
control activity	統制活動
control deficiency	内部統制の不備
control environment	統制環境
controllability	管理可能性
controllable	管理可能な
controllable cost	管理可能費用
controlled company	①被支配企業，②被連結会社（税務上の）　[解] ①支配企業（controlling company）に対する用語
controlled foreign company [corporation] (CFC)	被支配外国法人　[解] 一般にタックス・ヘイブン対策税制の適用対象となる法人を指し，日本の税制では「外国関係会社」がこれに該当する
controlled transaction	①関連者取引，②国外関連取引　[解] ②移転価格税制の関係では，国外関連者との取引を指す
controller	コントローラー，経理責任者
controlling company	支配企業　[解] 被支配企業（controlled company）に対する用語
controlling interest	支配持分，経営支配権
controlling shareholder	支配株主
control number	管理番号，判定用数値
control of an asset	資産に対する支配
control of an investee	投資先に対する支配
control over the reporting entity	報告企業に対する支配
control premium	コントロール・プレミアム，企業支配対価　[解] 企業買収の局面で，買収対象会社の支配権の獲得に対して支払う対価の上乗せ分
control risk	統制リスク
control self assessment (CSA)	コントロール・セルフ・アセスメント　[解] 統制活動の担当者による，自らの活動の検証・評価
control test	内部統制テスト
convenience translation	便宜的な換算
convention	慣行，慣習
conventional	慣行上の，慣習的な
Convention on Mutual Administrative Assistance in Tax Matters	税務行政執行共助条約
converge	収斂する
convergence	①コンバージェンス，②収斂，収束　[解] ①会計基準間の相違を埋めることで，具体的には自国の会計基準をIFRSに近づけること
conversion	①転換，②改造，③会計基準の変更（例えば，日本基準からIFRS）
conversion cost	加工費
conversion option	転換オプション
convertible (to)	（〜に）転換可能な
convertible bond	転換社債
convertible debt	転換社債
convertible instrument	転換可能な金融商品，転換型金融商品
convertible note	転換社債
convertible preferred share [stock]	（普通株式）転換型優先株式
convertible securities	転換可能証券
COO	▶chief operating officer

cook the books	粉飾する
cooperation	協力，提携
co-operative	協同組合
copyright	コピーライト，著作権，版権
core principle	主要な原則，基本となる原則
corporate	法人の，組織の
corporate assets	全社資産 [解] IAS36の文脈では，検討対象の資金生成単位（CGU）と他の資金生成単位の両方の将来キャッシュ・フローの獲得に寄与する資産
corporate auditor	監査役
corporate body	法人
corporate bond	社債
corporate debt instrument	社債
corporate debt securities	社債，負債性証券
corporate division	会社分割
corporate expense	全社費用
corporate finance	コーポレート・ファイナンス，企業金融
corporate governance	コーポレート・ガバナンス，企業統治
corporate governance code	コーポレート・ガバナンス・コード
corporate guarantee	企業保証
corporate headquarters	本店，本社，本部
corporate income tax (CIT)	法人税，法人所得税
corporate income tax rate	法人税率
corporate inversion	コーポレート・インバージョン [解] 海外に法人を設立し，その法人を企業グループの最終親会社とするための組織再編。海外親会社の設立
corporate officer	執行役員，執行役
corporate planning	経営企画
corporate planning department [division]	経営企画部門
corporate real estate (CRE)	企業不動産 [解] 文字どおり，企業が所有する不動産
corporate reorganisation	組織再編 [米] corporate reorganization
Corporate Reorganisation Act [Law]	会社更生法 [米] Corporate Reorganization Act [Law]
corporate reorganisation without consideration	無対価組織再編 [米] corporate reorganization without consideration	[解] 組織再編の対価として交付されるべき株式または金銭等の交付なしに行われる合併や分割等の組織再編
corporate revitalisation	企業再生 [米] corporate revitalization
corporate social responsibility (CSR)	企業の社会的責任
corporate spin-off	会社分割
corporate tax	法人税
corporate tax return	法人税申告書
corporate valuation	企業評価
corporate value	企業価値
corporation	会社，法人，株式会社
corporation tax	法人税
Corporation Tax Act [Law]	法人税法
corporation tax return	法人税申告書
correct	①修正する，②正しい [用] ① to correct an error（誤りを修正する）
correction	①修正，訂正，②更正
correction notice	更正通知（書）
correction of error	誤謬の訂正
correction of income	更正（税務当局による）
correction of tax return	更正（税務当局による）
corrective	是正の，訂正の
corrective action plan	対応策（監査における指摘事項などに対する）
correlation	相関関係
correlative	相関の，相関関係にある【形】
correlative adjustment	対応的調整 [解] corresponding adjustmentの項を参照
correspondence	文書によるやり取り
corresponding	対応する
corresponding adjustment	対応的調整 [解] 移転価格税制の関係では，関連者の一方が移転価格課税（増額更正）された場合に，相互協議（mutual agreement procedure）における合意に従い，他方の国外関連者に対して還付（減額更正）を行って二重課税を排除することを指す
corresponding figure	対応する数値
corridor	コリドー，回廊
corridor approach	コリドー（回廊）アプローチ（旧）

corroborate　補強する（証拠などで）
corroboration　補強（証拠などによる）
corroborative　補強するような
corrupt　腐った，腐敗した
corruption　汚職，腐敗
corruption case　汚職
COS　▶cost of sales
co-sale　共同売却
co-sale right　共同売却権
cost　取得原価，原価，費用，経費
cost accounting　原価計算
cost allocation　原価配賦，原価配分，費用配分
cost analysis　コスト分析
cost and benefit　費用・便益，コスト・ベネフィット
cost and freight (C&F/CFR)　運賃込み条件（価格）　[解]貿易条件の1つで，売主（輸出者）が荷揚げ地の港で荷揚げするまでの運賃を負担し，保険料は買主（輸入者）が負担する（危険負担は，積み地の港で貨物が本船に積み込まれた時点で移転）
cost approach　コスト・アプローチ（評価手法［技法］としての）　[解]一般的な資産の評価において，資産の取得原価や再調達原価を基準とするアプローチ。企業評価の局面では，対象会社の純資産価値をベースとする。また，IFRS13の文脈では，公正価値測定に際して，資産の用役能力を再調達するために現在必要とされる金額（いわゆる現在再調達原価）を用いるアプローチを指す
cost-based pricing　原価に基づく価格設定
cost basis　原価基準
cost-benefit relationship　費用対効果
cost centre　コスト・センター，原価責任単位　[米]cost center　[解]責任会計（responsibility accounting）において，原価に責任を持つ部門
cost centre code　コスト・センター・コード　[米]cost center code
cost constraint　コストの制約
cost containment　コスト削減，費用削減
cost contribution arrangement (CCA)　費用分担契約　[解]移転価格税制の関係では，研究開発活動等の一定の活動に係る費用を，複数の企業が共同で負担することを取り決める契約を指す。CSA (cost sharing arrangement) とも呼ばれる
cost control　原価管理
cost coverage　コスト・カバレッジ，費用補償
cost driver　コスト・ドライバー　[解]活動基準原価計算（ABC）等において，間接費の配賦計算を行う際の基準となる指標
cost formula　原価算定方式　[解]先入先出法（FIFO）や加重平均法（weighted average cost formula）など，棚卸資産の原価を売上原価や期末残高に配分する方法
cost incurred to fulfil a contract　契約を履行するためのコスト　[米]cost incurred to fulfill a contract
costing　原価計算
costing system　原価計算システム
cost, insurance, and freight (CIF)　運賃・保険料込み条件（価格）　[解]貿易条件の1つで，売主（輸出者）が荷揚げ地の港で荷揚げするまでの運賃や保険料を負担する（危険負担は，積み地の港で貨物が本船に積み込まれた時点で移転）
cost management system　原価管理システム
cost method　原価法　[解]投資を取得原価で評価する方法
cost model　原価モデル，取得原価モデル　[解]IAS16の文脈では，当初認識後の測定として，有形固定資産項目を「取得原価から減価償却累計額及び減損損失累計額を控除した価額」で計上する方法であり，再評価モデル（revaluation model）に対する用語
cost object　コスト・オブジェクト，原価集計対象
cost of acquisition　取得原価
cost of bond issue　社債発行費
cost of capital　資本コスト
cost of debt　負債コスト
cost of disposal　処分コスト，処分費用
cost of equity　株主資本コスト
cost of finished goods　完成品原価
cost of goods manufactured　製品製造原価
cost of goods sold (COGS)　売上原価
cost of hedging　ヘッジ・コスト

cost of issuing an equity instrument	資本性金融商品の発行コスト
cost of purchase	購入原価
cost of reacquiring an equity instrument	資本性金融商品の再取得コスト
cost of revenue	営業原価, 売上原価
cost of sales (COS)	売上原価
cost of share issue	株式交付費
cost planning	原価企画
cost-plus contract	コスト・プラス契約　[解] 原価に一定率または固定の報酬額を加算した対価で請け負う役務提供などの契約
cost-plus mark-up	原価基準法によるマークアップ
cost plus method (CPM)	原価基準法, CP法　[解] 移転価格税制の関係では, 独立企業間価格の算定方法の1つで,「国外関連取引に係る棚卸資産の売手 (製造会社など) の製造原価等の額に通常の利潤の額を加算して計算した金額」をもって独立企業間価格とする方法を指す
cost pool	原価集計額, コスト・プール
cost principle	原価基準
cost records	原価記録
cost recovery method	原価回収基準　[解] 回収が不確実な販売について, 回収が原価を上回った時点で初めて収益を計上する方法
cost reduction	原価低減, コスト削減
cost report	原価報告書
cost saving	コスト削減, 費用削減
cost sharing agreement (CSA)	費用分担契約
cost sharing arrangement (CSA)	費用分担契約　[解] 移転価格税制の関係では, 研究開発活動等の一定の活動に係る費用を, 複数の企業が共同で負担することを取り決める契約を指す。CCA (cost contribution arrangement) とも呼ばれる
cost technique	取得原価法
cost to fulfil a contract	契約を履行するためのコスト　[米] cost to fulfill a contract
cost to sell	売却コスト
cost variance	原価差異, 原価差額
cost variance analysis	原価差異分析
cost-volume-profit (CVP) analysis	CVP分析　[解] コスト (Cost)・販売量 (Volume)・利益 (Profit) の関係から導かれる損益分岐点に係る分析
coterminous	(時間・空間などが) 重なる【形】
coterminous year-ends	一致した (事業) 年度末 (連結子会社などの)
count	①カウントする, 数える, ②カウント
counter	①反対の, 逆の, ②カウント実施者 (棚卸の際の)
counterbalance	相殺する, バランスさせる
counterbalancing error	(翌期に) 自動的に訂正される誤謬 (期ズレなど)
countermeasure	対応策
counter offer	カウンター・オファー
counterpart	取引相手, 対の一方, 対応するもの
counterparty	カウンターパーティー, 取引相手, 相手方
counterparty risk	カウンターパーティー・リスク　[解] デリバティブ契約の相手方が契約通りに履行しないおそれ
count error	数え間違い, カウント・エラー　[解] 実地棚卸の際のカウント・エラー (inventory count error) を指すことが多い
country	国
Country-by-Country Report (CbC Report/CbCR)	国別報告書, 国別報告事項　[解] 移転価格税制の関係では, 移転価格文書の1つで, 多国籍企業グループが事業を行う国ごとの情報をサマリーしたものをいう。事業を行う国ごとの収入金額, 税引前当期利益の額, 納付税額などの情報を記載する
country of domicile	居住地国, 所在地国
country of incorporation	設立国
country of location test	所在地国基準　[解] タックス・ヘイブン対策税制における経済活動基準の1つで, 外国関係会社が事業を主としてその本店所在地国において行っていることを確認する基準
country risk	カントリー・リスク　[解] 海外への投資について, 投資先国における政治・経済・社会環境等の変化によりもたらされるリスク
country risk premium	カントリー・リスク・プレミアム　[解] カントリー・リスクに対

して，追加的に要求されるプレミアム
coupon ①利札（公社債の），②表面利率，③クーポン
coupon bond 利付債
coupon rate クーポン・レート
court 裁判所，法廷
court case 訴訟事件，裁判事例
court decision 判決
covenant コベナンツ，誓約条項
covenant not to compete 競業避止義務
coverage ①カバレッジ，対象範囲，②補償範囲（保険の）
coverage ratio カバレッジ・レシオ [解]債務や金利などの負担能力を示す指標全般
CP ▶① commercial paper, ② condition precedent
CPA ▶certified public accountant
CPI ▶consumer price index
CPM ▶① comparable profits method, ② cost plus method
Cr. ▶creditor
CRA ▶Canada Revenue Agency
crash 暴落，恐慌
CRE ▶corporate real estate
creative accounting クリエイティブ・アカウンティング [解]都合のよい会計数値を「創出」すること。粉飾決算とほぼ同義
credible 信用できる【形】
credit ①貸方，②信用，与信，掛（売り），③貸方記入する【動】，④税額控除の対象とする【動】
creditable 税額控除の対象となる【形】
creditable foreign tax 控除対象外国法人税 [解]外国法人税のうち，外国税額控除の対象となるもの
credit-adjusted effective interest rate 信用調整後の実効金利［利子率］ [解]将来の現金支払いまたは受取りの見積額を，購入または組成した信用減損金融資産（credit-impaired financial asset）の償却原価に割り引くための率
credit agency 信用調査機関
credit agency information 信用調査機関の情報
credit agreement 融資契約
credit analysis 与信分析
credit authorisation 信用照会 [米] credit authorization
credit balance 貸方残高
credit card クレジット・カード
credit check 信用調査
credit control 与信管理
credit default swap (CDS) クレジット・デフォルト・スワップ [解]デリバティブの1つで，CDSの買手はプレミアムを支払う代わりに，対象債権が契約期間中に債務不履行（デフォルト）になった場合，（CDSの売手から）それによる損失相当額を受け取ることができる
credit derivative クレジット・デリバティブ
credit enhancement 信用増強，信用補完
credit entry 貸方記入
credit event 信用事象
credit exposure 信用エクスポージャー
credit facility [facilities] 融資枠，信用枠，与信（主として金融機関からの）
credit grade 信用格付け
credit-impaired 信用減損のある【形】
credit-impaired financial asset 信用減損金融資産，信用減損のある金融資産 [解]見積将来キャッシュ・フローに不利な影響を与える事象（例えば，債務者の重大な財政的困難）が発生している金融資産
credit impairment 信用減損 [用] credit impairment of financial instruments（金融商品の信用減損）
credit information 信用情報
credit limit ①控除限度額（外国税額控除などの），②与信限度額
credit limitation 控除限度額（外国税額控除などの）
credit line 融資枠，与信限度額
credit loss 信用損失，貸倒損失
credit memo ①貸方伝票，取消伝票，②クレジット・メモ［ノート］
credit method 外国税額控除方式（国際課税における）
credit note クレジット・ノート [解]売上金額の減額通知で，値引や返品などに対して発行される
creditor ①債権者，②貸方（Cr.）

creditor protection　債権者保護
creditors　買掛金，債務　[使い方注意！] creditor 自体は「債権者」という意味もあるが，勘定科目としての creditors は「買掛金」という意味になる（主として英国系の国）
creditors(') meeting　債権者集会
credit period　与信期間
credit policy　信用方針，与信方針
credit rating　信用格付け
credit risk　信用リスク
credit risk rating grade　信用リスク格付け
credit sales　掛売り
credit spread　信用スプレッド
credit terms　与信条件，掛売条件
credit value adjustment (CVA)　信用評価調整，CVA　[解] デリバティブについて，取引相手の信用リスクを時価に反映させるための調整
creditworthiness　信用力（があること）
creditworthy　信用力のある【形】
crime　犯罪
criminal　犯罪の，刑事上の
criminal action　刑事裁判
criminal prosecution　刑事訴追
crisis　危機
criteria　criterion の複数形
criteria for　〜の基準，要件　[用] criteria for exemption（免除の要件）
criterion　基準
critical　決定的な，重大な
critical feature　重要な特徴
cross-border　クロスボーダーの，国境を越えた
cross-border acquisition　クロスボーダーの買収
cross-border transaction　クロスボーダー取引
cross entry　振替仕訳
cross shareholding　株式の相互保有，株式の持合い
CRS　▶Common Reporting Standard
crucial　重要な，重大な
crude oil　原油
crystallisation　①（含み損益の）実現，②具体化　[米] crystallization

crystallisation of built-in gains and losses　含み損益の実現　[米] crystallization of built-in gains and losses
crystallise　①（含み損益を）実現させる，②（含み損益が）実現する，③具体化する　[米] crystallize
CSA　▶① cost sharing arrangement [agreement], ② control self assessment
CSR　▶corporate social responsibility
C-Suite　CEO, CFO, COO など C がつく役員の総称
cumbersome　面倒な，厄介な
cumulative　累積の
cumulative change　累積的変動
cumulative dividend　累積型配当（優先株式などの）
cumulative effect　累積的影響　[解] IAS8 の文脈では，会計方針の変更を遡及適用することによる当期残高への影響
cumulative losses　欠損金，累積損失，累損
cumulative preference dividend　累積型優先配当
cumulative preference share　累積型優先株式　[解] 配当を受け取る優先権が累積する優先株式
cumulative tax losses　税務上の欠損金（累計額）　[解] to incur a tax loss of 100, increasing cumulative tax losses to 1,000（税務上の欠損が 100 発生し，その累計額が 1,000 になる）
cumulative translation differences　換算差額累計額
CUP method　▶comparable uncontrolled price method
currency　通貨
currency fluctuation　為替変動
currency forward market　為替先物市場
currency futures　通貨先物
currency market　外為市場
currency option　通貨オプション
currency rate　為替相場
currency risk　為替リスク，通貨リスク　[解] 為替レートの変動により，金融商品の公正価値または将来キャッシュ・フローが変動するリスク

currency spot market　為替直物市場
currency swap　通貨スワップ
currency translation differences　①為替換算差額，②在外営業活動体の換算差額
current　①流動（区分）の，②現在の
current and deferred (income) tax　税金及び税効果
current asset　流動資産
current bonds issued　発行した短期社債
current borrowings　短期借入金
current cost　現在原価　[解]資産であれば，現時点で取得するとしたときに支払う金額を指す
current cost accounting　現在原価会計
current deposit　当座預金
current investments　短期投資
current item　流動項目
current liability　流動負債
currently　現在【副】
current / non-current classification　流動・固定［非流動］分類
current / non-current distinction　流動・固定［非流動］区分
current period　当期
current portion　流動部分　[解]固定資産・負債のうちの流動部分（例えば，1年内に決済される部分）　[用]current portion of non-current borrowings（長期借入金の1年以内返済分）
current portion of long-term debt　固定負債の流動部分（1年内返済予定分など）
current prepaid expenses　前払費用（流動資産）
current ratio　流動比率　[解]企業の短期的な支払能力から安全性を判断するための指標であり，以下の算式で計算される　流動比率＝流動資産／流動負債
current replacement cost　現在再調達原価，現在の再調達コスト
current service cost　当期勤務費用，勤務費用　[解]勤務費用のうち，当期の従業員の勤務による給付見積額の増加額（確定給付債務の現在価値の変動額）
current tax　当期税金　[解]実際に納付すべき（または還付を受ける）税金で，繰延税金（deferred tax）に対する用語
current tax assets　未収還付法人税等，未払法人所得税，当期税金資産
current tax expense　当期税金費用，法人税，住民税及び事業税　[解]当期の税金計算の結果，実際に納付すべき（あるいは納付した）税額であり，繰延税金費用（deferred tax expense）に対する用語
current tax income　当期税金収益
current tax liabilities　未払法人税等，未払法人所得税，当期税金負債
current tax payable　未払法人税等，未払法人所得税
current tax receivable　未収還付法人税等，未収法人所得税
current version　現行版
current year　当年度
curtail　削減する，縮小する
curtailment　削減，縮小
cushion　クッション，余裕
custodian　カストディアン　[解]証券の受渡しや保管の代理人
custody　保管，管理
custom　①慣習，慣例，②（複数形で）税関，関税
customary　慣習の
customer　顧客
customer acceptance　顧客による検収（棚卸資産などの）
customer advances　顧客からの前受金
customer list　顧客リスト　[解]無形資産の例
customer loyalty programme　カスタマー・ロイヤルティ・プログラム　[米]customer loyalty program
customer-related intangible asset　顧客関連無形資産
customer relationship　顧客との関係　[解]無形資産の例
customer's acceptance basis　検収基準
customer's acceptance report　顧客による検収報告書
customer's option　顧客のオプション
customer's unexercised rights　顧客の権利不行使（未使用商品券など）
customs　①税関，②関税　[解]通常複数形
customs broker　通関業者

customs clearance　通関（許可）
customs duties　関税
customs valuation　関税評価
customs value　関税評価額
CUT method　▶comparable uncontrolled transaction method
cut-off　カットオフ，締切（会計の）
cut-off date　カットオフ日，締切日
cut-off error　カットオフ・エラー，期ズレ
cut-off point　カットオフ・ポイント，締切時点
cut-off test　カットオフ・テスト
CVA　▶credit value adjustment
CVP analysis　▶cost-volume-profit analysis
cycle　循環，周期，サイクル
cycle stocktaking　循環棚卸
cyclical　循環の，周期性の
cyclical inventory count　循環棚卸
cyclicality of operations　事業活動の循環性　[解]IAS34の文脈では，事業活動の季節性及び循環性については，注記により説明する必要がある

D

DA　▶definitive agreement
D/A　▶documents against acceptance
daily　日次の
daily average　日次平均
daily control　日次統制
daily proration　日数に基づく按分計算
damage　損害，損傷
damaged inventory　損傷在庫
damages　損害賠償，損害賠償金　[解]通常複数形
D&O　▶directors and officers
DAP　▶delivered at place
DAT　▶delivered at terminal
data　データ
database　データベース　[解]無形資産の例
data flow chart　データ・フロー・チャート
data gap　データ・ギャップ，データ不足
data processing　データ処理
data room　データ・ルーム（デュー・デリジェンスなどの）
date　日付
dated　①日付の（ある），期限のある【形】，②旧式の
dated subordinated liabilities　期限付劣後負債
date of acquisition　取得日
date of audit report　監査報告書日
date of authorisation for issue of financial statements　財務諸表の発行承認日
date of dissolution　解散日
date of end of reporting period　報告期間の期末日
date of transition to IFRS　IFRS移行日　[解]最初のIFRS財務諸表において，IFRSによる完全な比較情報を表示する最初の期間の期首。IFRS開始財政状態計算書の作成基準日
date when financial statements are authorised for issue　財務諸表の発行承認日　[米]

date when financial statements are authorized for issue
dawn raid　事前通知のない実地調査
day 1　初日
days in inventory　棚卸資産回転期間，在庫回転期間
days inventory outstanding (DIO)　棚卸資産回転期間，在庫回転期間
days payable outstanding (DPO)　仕入債務回転期間，買掛金回転期間
days sales outstanding (DSO)　売掛債権回転期間，売掛金回転期間
day-to-day servicing　日々の保守作業
day-to-day transactions　日常の取引
DB　▶defined benefit
d.b.a.　屋号（doing business as）
DC　▶defined contribution
DCF　▶discounted cash flow
DCR　▶debt coverage ratio
DD　▶due diligence
DDP　▶delivered duty paid
DDS　▶debt-debt swap
deadline　期限，締切
deadlock　行き詰まり（交渉などの）
dead stock　滞留在庫
deal　取引
deal breaker　ディール・ブレイカー　[解]買収案件などで，取引成立の妨げになる事項
dealer　ディーラー，販売業者
dealer lessor　販売業者である貸手（リースの）
deal flow　ディール・フロー　[解]案件（特に買収案件）の流れ
dealing　商取引，売買
deal killer　ディール・キラー　[解] deal breakerの項を参照
deal maker　ディール・メーカー　[解]買収案件の主要なプレイヤー
deal structure　ディール・ストラクチャー　[解]買収の方法や対価
death　死亡
death-in-service benefit　勤務期間中の死亡給付
debenture　（無担保）社債
debit　借方

debit balance　借方残高
debit card　デビット・カード
debit entry　借方記入
debit memo　①借方伝票，②デビット・メモ［ノート］
debit note　デビット・ノート　[解]売掛金等の債権金額の増額通知で，売上単価の増額修正や通常の売上以外の債権増額に対して発行される
debt　負債
debt assumption　債務引受，デット・アサンプション　[解]企業が自社発行社債を満期日より前に償還したい場合で，買入消却等による実現が難しい場合などに，社債の元利金の支払いなどに必要な資金を第三者に引き渡し，その債務の履行も引き受けてもらう取引形態
debt capital　他人資本，負債資本
debt component　負債部分（金融商品などの）
debt covenants　財務制限条項
debt coverage ratio (DCR)　デット・カバレッジ・レシオ　[解] debt service coverage ratioの項を参照
debt-debt swap (DDS)　デット・デット・スワップ　[解]デット・エクイティ・スワップ（DES）と同様の金融支援策であり，銀行等の債権者が債務者（融資先）に対する債権を劣後化することで，債務者の財務内容を改善するスキーム。例えば通常の融資から劣後ローンへの切替えなど
debt dumping　不良債権の移転
debt/equity ratio (D/E ratio)　負債・資本比率，負債比率
debt-equity swap (DES)　デット・エクイティ・スワップ　[解]債務の株式化とも言われ，債権者が債務者に債権（融資など）を現物出資することにより，債権者の株式を取得するというスキーム。主に経営不振企業の再生を図る目的で実行される
debt financing　デット・ファイナンス
debt for equity swap (DES)　デット・エクイティ・スワップ
debt holder　債権者
debt instrument　負債性金融商品，負債商品
debt leveraging　債務レバレッジ

debt-like item　デットライク・アイテム，有利子負債同等物
debtor　①債務者，②借方（Dr.）
debtors　売掛金，債権　使い方注意！ debtor自体は「債務者」という意味もあるが，勘定科目としてのdebtorsは「売掛金」という意味になる（主として英国系の国）
debt push-down　デット・プッシュダウン　解 グループ内の資金貸借により，親会社から子会社方向へ借入金等の負債を移転させること。利息負担が実質的に子会社側で発生することになり，買収対象会社が利益体質の場合や，子会社所在地国の税率が高い場合には，税務メリットがある
debt ratio　負債比率（総資本に対する）
debt restructuring　負債の再構成，債務整理
debt retirement　債務弁済，負債の返済
debt securities　債券
debt service　負債の返済
debt service coverage ratio (DSCR)　デット・サービス・カバレッジ・レシオ　解 債務返済余力を示す指標で，計算方法は1つではないが，例えば「元利金返済前キャッシュ・フロー÷元利金返済所要額」で計算される
debt to equity ratio (D/E ratio)　負債・資本比率，負債比率
debt value adjustment (DVA)　DVA　解 双方向CVA（bilateral CVA）において，自社の信用リスクに応じて計算されるCVA
debt waiver　①債権放棄，②債務免除
deception　詐欺
decision　①意思決定，②判決，裁決　用 ② decision taken [made] by the National Tax Tribunal （国税不服審判所の裁決）
decision maker　意思決定者
decision making　意思決定
decision point　意思決定時点
declaration　①宣言，②申告
declare　①宣言する，②申告する
decline　①下落する，②下落
decline in value　価値の低下
declining balance method　定率法
decommission　閉鎖する，廃棄する

decommissioning cost　閉鎖コスト，廃棄コスト
decommissioning, restoration or similar liabilities　廃棄，原状回復または類似の負債
decomposition　分解
decrease　①減少する，②減少
decrease in　～の減少（額）　用 decrease in inventories（棚卸資産の減少額）
decrease in capital　減資
decrement　減少，減額
decremental　減分の
dedicated asset　専用資産
deduct　控除する（所得から），損金算入する
deductibility　損金性，損金算入可能性
deductible　損金算入可能な，損金の額に算入できる【形】
deductible charge [expense]　損金算入可能な費用，損金算入費用
deductible dividend　損金算入配当　解 支払側で損金算入される配当
deductible limit　損金算入限度額
deductible temporary difference　将来減算一時差異　解 一時差異のうち，解消の際に課税所得を減額させるもので，繰延税金資産の計上対象となる（回収可能と判断された場合）　用 deductible temporary differences for which no deferred tax asset is recognised（繰延税金資産を認識していない将来減算一時差異）
deduction　①損金算入，（税務）減算，②控除
deduction at source　源泉課税
deed　①証書，権利証書，②行為
deem　みなす
deemed　みなし～　解 例えば，みなし配当（deemed dividend）のように，擬制されるものを指す
deemed acquisition date　みなし取得日
deemed cost　みなし原価　解 IFRSの初度適用の際に，有形固定資産等の原価の代用として使用することが許容される金額で，その有形固定資産の公正価値など
deemed dividend　みなし配当　解 会社法上の剰余金の配当には該当しないものの，経済的実質がそれと同様ということ

で，税務上は剰余金の配当として取り扱われるもの
deemed interest　みなし利息
deemed joint business operations requirements　みなし共同事業要件
deemed profit　みなし利益
deep discount　大幅な割引（証券発行の際などの）
deep market　十分な資本市場
de facto　事実上の
de facto control　①事実上の支配，②実質支配（関係）　[解]②タックス・ヘイブン対策税制における外国関係会社には，居住者または内国法人との間に実質支配関係がある外国法人も含まれる
de facto power　事実上の力（パワー）
de facto standard　事実上の標準
defalcate　横領する
defalcation　横領，使い込み
default　①債務不履行，デフォルト，②既定，既定値
default depreciation method　法定減価償却方法
default rate　デフォルト率
defaults and breaches　債務不履行及び契約違反
default translation method　法定換算方法
defeasance　①ディフィーザンス，②消滅，失効　[解]①債務の現在価値分を銀行等に預託し，預託を受けた銀行等が国債等の運用を通じて債務の肩代わりに合意することによって，債務者が貸借対照表からその債務を抹消すること
defect　①欠点，問題点，②欠陥（製品などの）
defective　欠陥のある
defendant　被告
defer　繰り延べる
deferment　繰延べ
deferment of tax　税金の繰延べ
deferral　繰延べ
deferral hedge accounting　繰延ヘッジ（会計）
deferral of capital gains and losses　譲渡損益の繰延べ
deferral of tax　税金の繰延べ
deferred　繰り延べられた

deferred and accrued accounts　経過勘定
deferred charge　①繰延費用，②（税務上の）繰延資産
deferred compensation　繰延報酬，後払報酬
deferred consideration　対価支払いの繰延べ　[解]買収において，買収後の買収対象会社の業績等に応じて，事後的に支払われる対価
deferred cost　繰延費用
deferred expense [expenditure]　①繰延費用，②（税務上の）繰延資産
deferred gains and losses　繰延損益
deferred gains and losses on hedges　繰延ヘッジ損益
deferred income　繰延収益
deferred income tax asset　繰延税金資産
deferred income tax liability　繰延税金負債
deferred purchase price　後払い（延払い）の買収対価
deferred recognition　繰延べ，遅延認識
deferred revenue　繰延収益
deferred tax　繰延税金　[解]繰延税金資産・負債の認識に伴い発生するもので，当期税金（current tax）に対する用語
deferred tax assets (DTA)　繰延税金資産
deferred tax assets and liabilities　繰延税金資産及び繰延税金負債
deferred tax expense　繰延税金費用，法人税等調整額　[解]当期の税効果計算の結果，税金費用として認識される額であり，当期税金費用（current tax expense）に対する用語
deferred tax income　繰延税金利益［収益］，法人税等調整額
deferred tax liabilities (DTL)　繰延税金負債
deficiency　①不足，②欠陥，不備（内部統制などの）
deficiency in design　整備に関する不備（内部統制の）
deficiency in operation　運用に関する不備（内部統制の）
deficient　欠陥のある，不備のある
deficit　①赤字，欠損，未処理損失，②積立不足（退職給付制度などの）
deficit balance　赤字残高
deficit in plan　制度の積立不足（退職給付制

度などの）
define ①定義する，②確定させる，限定する
defined benefit (DB) 確定給付（退職給付制度について）
Defined Benefit Corporate Pension Act 確定給付企業年金法
defined benefit cost 確定給付費用 [解]確定給付制度について発生する費用
defined benefit liability 確定給付負債 [解]確定給付制度に係る年金負債
defined benefit obligation 確定給付債務，確定給付制度債務 [解]確定給付制度における債務で，数理計算上の仮定に基づく現在価値計算により算定される
defined benefit plan 確定給付制度 [解]退職後給付制度のうち，確定拠出制度以外のもの。企業が従業員（退職者を含む）に対して合意した給付を支給するという債務を負うもの
defined contribution (DC) 確定拠出（退職給付制度について）
defined contribution plan 確定拠出制度 [解]退職後給付制度のうち，企業が一定の掛金を基金等に支払い，仮に基金に十分な資産がない場合でも，企業はそれ以上の債務を負わないもの
definite 明確な，確定的な
definite useful life 確定した耐用年数
definition 定義
definitive 決定的な，最終的な
definitive agreement (DA) 正式契約，最終契約
deflation デフレーション
defraud 欺く
degree 程度
delay ①遅らせる，②遅延
delayed payment ①遅延支払い，②延納
delayed recognition 遅延認識
delegate ①委任する，権限を委譲する，②派遣する
delegation 委任
delegation of authority 権限委譲
delinquency ①滞納（税金等の），②不履行，③犯罪
delinquency tax 延滞税
delinquent ①滞納の（税金等），②債務不履行の
delisted 上場を廃止した
delisting 上場廃止
deliver ①配達する，②引き渡す
deliverables 成果物
delivered at place (DAP) 仕向地持込み渡し条件（価格） [解]貿易条件の1つで，DATと同じD型。引渡しは貨物ターミナルよりさらに先の場所
delivered at terminal (DAT) ターミナル持込み渡し条件（価格） [解]貿易条件の1つで，売主（輸出者）が輸入地までの費用とリスクを負担する（D型）。引渡しは港湾・空港・鉄道などの貨物ターミナル
delivered duty paid (DDP) 関税込み持込み渡し条件（価格） [解]貿易条件の1つで，DATと同じD型。売主（輸出者）が輸入通関費用まで負担し，所定の場所で引渡しを行う
delivery ①配達，配送，②引渡し，受渡し
delivery basis 引渡基準
delivery conditions 受渡条件
delivery cost 輸送費
delivery date ①配送日，納品日，②受渡日（証券などの）
delivery slip 納品書
demand ①要求する，②需要
demandable 要求払いの
demand deposit 要求払預金
demand feature 要求払いの特徴，性質
demand loan 要求払貸付
de minimis 無視できるほど小さい
de minimis rule デミニマス基準（少額所得除外基準） [解]タックス・ヘイブン対策税制において，受動的所得の金額が少額である場合には，受動的所得の合算課税を適用しないという基準
demographic assumption 人口統計上の仮定
demography 人口統計学
demolition 取壊し
demonstrate 論証する，示す
demonstration 論証，証明
denial 否定，否認
denominate (in) （～(通貨)）で表示する【動】[用] to be denominated in US dol-

lars（米ドル表示される）
denominated in foreign currency　外貨建ての
denominator　分母　[解]分子（numerator）に対する用語
denote　示す，意味する
deny　否定する
department　部門
departmental　部門の
departmental budget　部門予算
departmental cost　部門費
department head　部門長
Department of Revenue　インド税務局（インドの税務当局）
departure　①逸脱（基準や規定されている内部統制からの），②出発，出国
departure tax　出国税
dependent agent　従属代理人　[解]法律的・経済的に本人（企業）に従属している代理人で，独立代理人に対する用語。基本的に当該企業のPE（恒久的施設）に該当する
deplete　①減耗させる，②枯渇させる（資源などを）
depletion　①減耗，②枯渇（資源などの）
deposit　①預金，②敷金，③預り金
depositary　寄託者
deposit at notice　通知預金
deposit for share [stock] subscription　新株式申込証拠金
deposit received　預り（保証）金
deposits from customers　顧客からの預り金
deposits in transit　未達預金　[解]銀行に持ち込んでいない小切手など
depreciable　償却可能な（有形固定資産について）
depreciable amount　償却可能額　[解]資産の取得原価から残存価額を控除した額
depreciable asset　償却可能資産，減価償却資産
depreciable assets tax　償却資産税
depreciable basis　償却可能な取得原価
depreciable capital asset　減価償却資産
depreciable tangible asset　有形減価償却資産
depreciate　①減価償却する，②値下がりする（通貨などが）
depreciated book value　減価償却後の帳簿価額
depreciated replacement cost　減価償却後の再調達コスト
depreciated replacement value　減価償却後の再調達価額
depreciated value　減価償却後の価額
depreciation　①減価償却（費），償却（費），②減価　[使い方注意!]無形資産の減価償却については，depreciationではなく，amortisationを使う
depreciation and amortisation expense　減価償却費及び（無形資産）償却費　[米]depreciation and amortization expense
depreciation charge [expense]　減価償却費
depreciation method　減価償却方法
depreciation on a pool basis　総合償却
depreciation period　減価償却期間，償却期間（有形固定資産の）
depreciation rate　減価償却率
D/E ratio　▶debt to equity [debt/equity] ratio
derecognise　認識を中止する　[米]derecognize
derecognition　認識の中止　[解]過去に認識した金融資産または金融負債などを財政状態計算書から取り除くこと
deregulation　規制緩和
derivative　デリバティブ　[解]（1）その価値が金利や為替等の基礎数値の変動に応じて変動し，（2）当初の純投資が必要ないか相対的に小さく，（3）将来のある日において決済されるような金融商品。一般にデリバティブと呼ばれる金融商品以外でも，これらの要素を持つものはデリバティブとして会計処理する必要がある
derivative feature　デリバティブの特徴・性質
derivative financial assets　デリバティブ（金融）資産
derivative financial assets held for hedging　ヘッジ目的で保有しているデリバティブ（金融）資産
derivative financial instrument　①派生金融商品，デリバティブ金融商品，②デリバ

ティブ資産・負債
derivative financial liabilities　デリバティブ（金融）負債
DES　▶debt for equity [debt-equity] swap
descending　①降順の，②下がっていく【形】
describe　記述する
description　記述
descriptive　記述的な
descriptive information　記述的情報　[解]財務情報（financial information）に対する用語
design　①設計，デザイン，②整備（内部統制の）
designate　指定する
designated　所定の，指定された
designated bank　指定銀行
designated bank account　指定（銀行）口座
designation　指定
designation of hedging relationship　ヘッジ指定，ヘッジ関係の指定
design of control　内部統制のデザイン・整備
design right　意匠権
desk audit　書面調査（税務調査のうち）
destruction　破壊，取壊し
detachable　分離可能な
detachment　分離
detail　詳細，明細
details of accounts　勘定明細
detect　発見する
detected　発見された
detection　発見，検出
detection method　摘発手段（不正などの）
detective control　発見的コントロール（内部統制のうち）
deter　抑止する
deteriorate　悪化する，劣化する
deterioration　悪化，劣化
determinable　決定できる，確定できる
determinant　決定要因
determination　決定
determination of tax liability　決定（税務当局による税額の）
determine　決定する
deterrence　抑止力
deterrent　抑止力

devaluation　価値の低下，価値の切下げ
develop　開発する
development　開発　[解]研究成果または他の知識を新製品等の計画や設計へ適用すること
development cost [expense]　開発費
development expenditure　開発支出
development phase　開発局面
deviation　逸脱（基準や所定の内部統制からの）
DGT　▶Directorate General of Taxation
diagram　ダイアグラム，図表
dialogue　会話，対話　[米]dialog
difference　差異，差額
difference between accounting and tax book value　会計簿価と税務簿価の差
different　異なる
differentiate　差別化する
differentiation　差別化
differing year-ends　異なる決算期
digital services　電気通信利用役務（の提供）
diluted earnings per share　希薄化後1株当たり利益　[解]希薄化性潜在的普通株式（dilutive potential ordinary share）による影響を調整した後の1株当たり利益
diluted loss per share　希薄化後1株当たり損失
dilution　希薄化　[解]転換型金融商品の転換，オプションやワラントの行使，または特定の条件の充足による普通株式の発行等を仮定した場合の1株当たり利益の減少または1株当たり損失の増加
dilution protection　希薄化防止
dilutive　希薄化効果のある
dilutive effect　希薄化効果　[用]dilutive effect of share options on number of ordinary shares（ストック・オプションが普通株式数に与える希薄化効果）
dilutive instrument　希薄化性金融商品
dilutive potential ordinary share　希薄化性潜在的普通株式　[解]普通株式への転換等により1株当たり利益が減少する場合または1株当たり損失が増加する場合の潜在的普通株式
diminish　減少する，減少させる
diminishing balance method　定率法　[解]

減価償却方法の1つで,定率法によると,減価償却費が毎期逓減していく

diminution 減少
DIO ▶days inventory outstanding
direct ①直接の,②向ける【動】
direct charge method 直接賦課方式
direct cost 直接費,直接原価
direct costing 直接原価計算 [解] 変動費のみを製造原価とし,固定費は期間費用として扱う原価計算方法
direct credit 直接貸方入力 [解] 評価勘定(valuation account)を用いず,直接勘定残高に影響させること
direct debit 直接借方入力 [解] 評価勘定(valuation account)を用いず,直接勘定残高に影響させること
direct expense 直接費
direct finance lease 直接金融リース
direct financing 直接金融
direct foreign tax credit 直接外国税額控除 [解] 一般には,外国税額控除のうち,自らが外国で納付した外国税額(利子・配当等に課された源泉所得税も含まれる)を控除対象とするもの
direct insurance contract 元受保険契約
direct investment 直接投資
direction 方向
directive 指令
direct labour cost 直接労務費 [米] direct labor cost
direct labour efficiency variance 時間差異(直接労務費に係る),作業時間差異,直接労務時間差異 [米] direct labor efficiency variance
direct labour hours 直接労務時間
direct labour rate variance 賃率差異(直接労務費に係る) [米] direct labor rate variance
directly 直接,直接的に
direct manufacturing cost 製造直接費
direct material 直接原材料
direct material cost 直接材料費
direct material price variance 価格差異(直接材料費に係る)
direct material usage variance 数量差異(直接材料費に係る)
direct material variance 直接材料費差異
direct method 直接法 [解] IAS7の文脈では,営業活動によるキャッシュ・フローについて,主要な区分ごとに収入総額と支出総額を分けて表示する方法
director 取締役
Directorate General of Taxation (DGT) インドネシア国税総局(インドネシアの税務当局)
directors and officers (D&O) 役員
director's bonus 役員賞与
director's compensation 役員報酬
director's remuneration 役員報酬
director's retirement benefit 役員退職給付,役員退職慰労金
direct selling cost 販売直接費
direct shareholding 直接保有(株式の)
direct tax 直接税
direct transport rule 積送基準 [解] 関税について,原産品が輸入国に到着するまでの間,原産品としての資格を維持しているかどうかを判断するための基準
direct write-off 直接減額(貸倒損失などの)
disability ①障がい,②無能力,無資格
disability benefit 障がい者給付
disadvantage 不利な点
disaggregate 分解する
disaggregation 分解,内訳
disaggregation of revenue 収益の分解
disagree ①一致しない【動】,②合意しない【動】
disagreement ①不一致,②意見の相違
disallow 損金不算入とする
disallowable 損金不算入の
disallowable expense 損金不算入の費用
disallowance 損金不算入
disappearing company 消滅会社(合併による)
disaster 災害
disburse 支出する,支払う
disbursement 支払い,支出,出金
discharge ①解放する(義務などから),②履行する(債務などを),③解放,免除,④履行,遂行 [使い方注意!] ①と②(③と④)は正反対の意味になる場合があるので注意が必要

discharge of indebtedness 債務免除
discipline ①規律，②懲罰
disclaimer ディスクレイマー，免責条項
disclose 開示する
disclose separately 別個に開示する
disclosure 開示
disclosure letter ディスクロージャー・レター，開示確認書 [解]買収案件などで，売手から買手に交付されるレターであり，開示される情報のリストなどが含まれている
disclosure of interests in other entities 他の企業への関与の開示
Disclosure of Tax Avoidance Schemes (DOTAS) 租税回避スキームの開示義務（英国）
disclosure requirement 開示要求
discontinuance 廃止，中止，非継続
discontinue 廃止する，中止する，継続しない【動】
discontinued operations 非継続事業，廃止事業 [解]IFRS5の文脈では，非継続事業とは，すでに処分されたかまたは売却目的保有に分類されている企業の構成単位で，(1)独立の主要な事業分野等，(2)独立の主要な事業分野等を処分する計画の一部，(3)転売のために取得した子会社，のいずれかに該当するものを指す
discount ①割引，②値引
discount bond 割引債
discounted cash flow (DCF) 割引キャッシュ・フロー
discounted cash flow (DCF) method DCF法，割引キャッシュ・フロー法
discounted future cash flows 割引（後）将来キャッシュ・フロー
discount for lack of control マイノリティ・ディスカウント（株式評価などの）
discount for lack of marketability 非流動性ディスカウント（株式評価などの） [解]illiquidity discountの項を参照
discount on notes payable 手形割引料，手形売却損
discount rate 割引率 [解]IAS19の文脈では，確定給付債務の現在価値を算定する際の割引計算等に用いられる率で，期末時点の優良社債の市場利回りを基礎とし

て決定される
discrepancy 不一致
discrepant 不一致の，矛盾した
discrete 個別の，別々の
discrete event 個別の事象
discretion 裁量
discretionary 裁量権のある
discretionary dividend 裁量権のある配当
discretionary participation feature 裁量権のある有配当性
discrimination 差別
discuss 議論する
discussion paper (DP) ディスカッション・ペーパー
disguise or hide 仮装または隠蔽する
dishonour 不渡り ㊍dishonor
dishonoured cheque 不渡小切手 ㊍dishonored check
dishonoured draft [note] 不渡手形 ㊍dishonored draft [note]
dismantle 分解する，解体する，取り壊す
dismantlement 分解，解体，取壊し
dismiss 解雇する，解任する
dismissal 解雇，解任
disparate 異なる，異種の
disparity 不均衡
disposable income 可処分所得
disposal 処分，売却，除却，廃却
disposal gain 処分益
disposal group 処分グループ [解]IFRS5の文脈では，処分や売却等の方法により，単一の取引として処分される資産のグループ，及びそれに直接関連して移転される負債を指す
disposal group held for sale 売却目的で保有する処分グループ
disposal loss 処分損，除却損，廃却損
disposal of interest in ～（子会社など）の持分の処分 [用]additional non-controlling interests arising on the disposal of interest in (…（子会社など）の持分の処分による非支配持分の追加)
disposal of investment property 投資不動産の処分［売却］
disposal of subsidiary 子会社の処分［売却］
disposal of treasury shares 自己株式の処分

disposal proceeds　処分に伴う収入
disposal value　処分価額
dispose (of)　（〜を）処分する，廃棄する
disproportion　不釣り合い，不均衡
disproportionate　不釣り合いな，不均衡の
disproportionate class of shares　不均一分配株式
disproportionately　不釣り合いに
dispute　係争，議論
dispute resolution　紛争解決
disqualify　資格を失わせる
disregard　無視する
disregarded entity　（それ自体は）課税対象とならない事業体
dissent　①反対する，異議を唱える，②不同意，異議
dissenting opinion　反対意見
dissenting shareholder　反対株主
dissolution　解散
dissolution of corporation　会社の解散
dissolve　解散させる（会社を）
distinct　別個の
distinction　区別
distinctive　特有の
distinguish　区別する
distinguishable　区別できる
distort　歪める　使い方注意!「数値などを歪める」という文脈で用いられることが多い
distortion　歪み
distressed　困窮した【形】
distressed debt　ディストレスト債　解 経営破綻（不振）企業が発行する債券など
distributable　分配可能な
distributable amount　分配可能額
distributable profit　分配可能利益
distributable reserve　分配可能積立金
distribute　分配する
distribution　①分配，②配分，③流通
distribution and administrative expense　販売費及び管理費
distribution channel　流通経路，販売経路
distribution cost [expense]　流通費，販売費
distribution network　流通網
distribution of profit　利益分配
distribution of residual assets　残余財産の分配
distribution received from investee　被投資企業から受け取った分配　解 持分法では，被投資企業から受け取った分配は，投資の帳簿価額の減額として処理される
distributions to owners　（企業の）所有者への分配
distributor　販売業者，流通業者
district　地区，地域
diverse　多様な
diversification　多角化
diversify　多角化する
diversity　多様性
divestiture　投資の処分
divestment　投資の処分，引き揚げ
divide　分割する
divided by　÷（割る）　使い方注意! A divided by Bで，「A÷B」の意味になる
dividend　配当（金）
dividend calculation period　配当計算期間
dividend declaration　配当宣言，配当決議
dividend declared　宣言済みの配当
dividend distribution　配当金の支払い
dividend from capital surplus　資本剰余金の配当
dividend income　①受取配当金，配当収益，②配当所得
dividend in kind　現物分配，現物配当　解 剰余金の配当または（税務上の）みなし配当により株主に対して金銭以外の資産を交付すること
dividend in kind within 100% group　100%グループ内の現物分配
dividend on a preference share　優先株式に係る配当
dividend paid　支払配当金
dividend payment　配当金の支払い
dividend payout ratio　配当性向　解 利益のうち配当として株主に分配する金額の割合
dividend per share (DPS)　1株当たり配当金
dividend policy　配当政策，配当方針
dividend received　受取配当金
dividend received from a foreign subsidiary　外国子会社配当
dividend restriction　配当制限

dividends paid　配当金の支払額　[解]キャッシュ・フロー計算書などでよく使われる用語　[用] dividends paid to owners of the parent（親会社の所有者に対する配当金の支払額）, dividends paid to non-controlling interests（非支配持分に対する配当金の支払額）

dividends payable　未払配当金

dividends proposed　提案済みの配当

dividends received　配当金の受取額　[解]キャッシュ・フロー計算書などでよく使われる表現

dividends received deduction (DRD)　受取配当金益金不算入，配当控除（米国）

dividend yield　配当利回り　[解]株価に対する配当の割合を示す指標であり，以下の算式で計算される
配当利回り＝1株当たりの年間配当金／株価

division　①部門，事業部，②分割

division code　部門コード

division of roles　役割分担

divisor　除数

document　①文書，書類，資料，②文書化する

documentation　①文書化，②証拠書類　[解]①移転価格税制の関係では，移転価格文書を作成することを意味する

documentation completion date　文書化完了日

documentation of hedging relationship　ヘッジ関係の文書化

document request list　依頼資料リスト（デュー・デリジェンスなどの）

documents against acceptance (D/A)　手形引受書類渡し　[解]銀行信用状（L/C）なしの荷為替手形で，輸入者が銀行に対して期限付き荷為替手形の支払いを引き受けることを条件に，船積書類が銀行から輸入者に引き渡され，貨物を受け取ることができるようになるという貿易決済形態

documents against payment (D/P)　手形支払書類渡し　[解]銀行信用状（L/C）なしの荷為替手形で，輸入者が銀行に代金を支払うことを条件に，船積書類が銀行から輸入者に引き渡され，貨物を受け取ることができるようになるという貿易決済形態

domain　ドメイン

domain name　ドメイン名

domestic　国内の

domestic cargo　内国貨物

domestic company [corporation]　内国法人

domestic dividend　国内配当

domestic double taxation　国内における二重課税

domestic sales　国内売上

domestic source income　国内源泉所得　[解]国外源泉所得（foreign source income）に対する用語

domestic subsidiary　国内子会社

domestic tax law　国内（税）法

domicile　居住地，所在地

dominant　支配的な

dominate　支配する

donate　寄附する，贈与する

donation　寄附金

donation granted　贈与

donation in kind　現物寄附

donation received　受贈

donation to foreign related person　国外関連者に対する寄附金　[解]移転価格税制の関係では，国外関連者に対する「資産や経済的利益の贈与または無償の供与」を指し，日本の税制上，全額損金不算入となる

donation within 100% group　100%グループ内の寄附金

donee　寄附金の受入側，受贈者

donor　寄附金の支出側，贈与者，寄贈者

dormant　休眠の

dormant company　休眠会社

DOTAS　▶ Disclosure of Tax Avoidance Schemes

double count　ダブルカウント，二重計算

double dipping　ダブル・ディッピング　[解]国際税務の用語で，1つの費用や損失について，2つの国で税務上損金の額に算入すること

double entry　複式記帳

double-entry bookkeeping　複式簿記

double tax agreement (DTA) 租税条約 [解] tax treaty の項を参照
double taxation 二重課税
double taxation relief 二重課税防止規定 [解]租税条約には，国際的な二重課税を防止するための規定が盛り込まれている
double taxation treaty (DTT) 租税条約 [解] tax treaty の項を参照
double tax convention 租税条約 [解] tax treaty の項を参照
doubt ①疑う，②疑い
doubtful 疑わしい，不確実な
doubtful account [debt] 不良債権，貸倒懸念債権
Dow Jones Industrial Average ダウ・ジョーンズ工業株価平均
downgrade 格下げする
down payment 頭金，手付金
downplay 少なめに見積もる
downside ①下側，②マイナス面
downside risk ダウンサイド・リスク，値下がりリスク
downsize 規模を縮小する
downsizing ダウンサイジング
downstream loan ダウンストリーム・ローン [解]親会社から子会社への貸付け
downstream merger ダウンストリーム・マージャー [解]合併の形態のうち，子会社が親会社を吸収合併するもの
downstream sales ダウンストリーム売上 [解]親会社から子会社方向への売上
downstream transaction ダウンストリーム取引 [解]連結グループ内の取引のうち，親会社から子会社へ資産等を売却する方向の取引
downturn 下降，下落
downward ①下に，②下方の
downward adjustment 下方修正，減額修正
DP ▶discussion paper
D/P ▶documents against payment
DPO ▶days payable outstanding
DPS ▶dividend per share
Dr. ▶debtor
draft ドラフト
drag along clause ドラッグ・アロング条項
drag along right ドラッグ・アロング・ライト，強制売却権 [解]（一定の条件の下）株式の売却を他者に強制する権利
drastic 徹底的な
draw 引き出す（預金などを）
drawback 欠点
draw-down ドローダウン，融資の実行（融資枠からの資金の引出し）
draw-down period 融資の実行可能期間
drawing 引出し（預金などの）
DRD ▶dividend received deduction
drop 下落する
drop ship ①直送，②直送する
DSCR ▶debt service coverage ratio
DSO ▶days sales outstanding
DTA ▶① deferred tax asset，② double tax agreement
DTL ▶deferred tax liability
DTT ▶double taxation treaty
dual 二重の，2つの
dual effect 二重の効果
dual GAAP accounting 2つの会計基準に基づく会計 [解] IFRSへの移行期等において，自国の会計基準とIFRSの二本立てで会計処理を行うこと
dual purpose test 二重目的テスト
dual residence 二重居住（地）
dual resident 二重居住者 [解] 各国の法令の相違により，2か国の居住者になる者
due ①賦課金，会費，②期限の到来した【形】，③正当な
due care 正当な注意
due care of prudent manager 善管注意義務
due date 期限
due diligence (DD) デュー・デリジェンス [解]企業買収の意思決定を行うに際して，買収対象会社の実態を把握し，問題点を洗い出すとともに，買収後の事業計画のベースとするために実施する調査
due diligence report デュー・デリジェンス報告書
due from 〜に対する債権（貸し）
due process 適法な手続，正当な手続
due professional care 職業的専門家としての正当な注意
dues and subscriptions 会費及び購読料
due to ①〜に対する債務（借り），②〜に

によって
duly　正しく
dummy stock　名義株
duplicate　①複製する，②二重計上する，③複製，④二重の
duration　期間
Dutch auction　ダッチ・オークション　[解] 応札により，売買が成立するまで徐々に価格を下げていく競売方式
dutiable　関税が課される【形】
dutiable goods　課税品，関税の対象品
duty　①義務，②関税（通常複数形）
duty of confidentiality　守秘義務，秘密保持義務
duty of due care　善管注意義務
duty of loyalty　忠実義務
DVA　▶debt value adjustment

E

E&O　▶errors and omissions
E&P　▶earnings & profits
earlier adoption　早期適用（会計基準などの）
earlier application　早期適用（会計基準などの）
early adoption　早期適用（会計基準などの）
early application　早期適用（会計基準などの）
early recognition　早期認識
early repayment　早期返済（債務の）
early retirement　早期退職
early retirement programme [plan]　早期退職制度　[米] early retirement program [plan]
earmark　取っておく（資金などを特定の用途のために）
earn　稼得する
earned income　①給与所得，②稼得所得
earned legal reserve　利益準備金
earned surplus　利益剰余金
earned surplus brought / carried forward　繰越利益剰余金
earnings　利益
earnings & profits (E&P)　税務上の利益（米国）
earnings before interest and tax (EBIT)　支払利息控除前税引前利益
earnings before interest, tax, depreciation and amortisation (EBITDA)　減価償却費及び支払利息控除前税引前利益　[米] earnings before interest, tax, depreciation and amortization
earnings before interest, taxes and amortisation (EBITA)　無形資産償却前営業利益（税引前）　[米] earnings before interest, taxes and amortization
earnings before taxes (EBT)　税引前利益
earnings per share (EPS)　1株当たり利益

[解] 端的には利益を発行済株式総数で除したもので、基本的1株当たり利益（basic earnings per share）と希薄化後1株当たり利益（diluted earnings per share）がある

earnings per share from continuing operations　継続事業からの1株当たり利益

earnings per share from discontinued operations　非継続事業からの1株当たり利益

earnings stripping rules　①アーニングス・ストリッピング・ルール、②過大支払利子税制（日本）　[解]①米国などの税制で、関連者からの借入に係る支払利息に一定の損金算入制限（所得の一定割合など）を課すもの。②日本にも、過大支払利子税制という同様の税制がある

earn-out clause　アーンアウト条項　[解] 買収対価の一部について、クロージング日後に、一定の条件（買収対象事業の業績要件など）を充足することを条件に支払いを行うという条項

earn-out payment　アーンアウト条項に基づく分割払い

earthquake　地震

earthquake-related expenses　地震関連費用

EBIT　▶earnings before interest and tax

EBITA　▶earnings before interest, taxes and amortisation

EBITDA　▶earnings before interest, tax, depreciation and amortisation

EBITDA margin　EBITDAマージン

EBO　▶employee buy-out

EBT　▶earnings before taxes

ECJ　▶European Court of Justice

ECL　▶expected credit loss

ECL model　予想信用損失モデル

e-commerce　電子商取引

economic activity test　経済活動基準（タックス・ヘイブン対策税制における）　[解] タックス・ヘイブン対策税制において、外国関係会社がその国に所在することに経済合理性があるか否かを判定するための基準。特定外国関係会社以外の外国関係会社については、（租税負担割合が20％未満でも）経済活動基準を充足できれば会社単位の合算課税は行われない。平成29年度税制改正前の「適用除外基準」に相当するもの

economic allegiance　経済的帰属

economic benefit　経済的便益

economic characteristic　経済的特徴

economic consequence　経済的帰結

economic double taxation　経済的二重課税　[解] 1つの所得に対して、異なる納税者に2つの国が課税することをいい、移転価格税制がその代表である

economic entity assumption　企業実体の公準

economic environment　経済環境

economic extortion　利益供与の強要

economic feasibility　採算可能性

economic growth rate　経済成長率

economic hedge　経済的ヘッジ

economic life　経済的耐用年数

economic partnership agreement (EPA)　経済連携協定

economic resource　経済的資源

economic resources and claims　経済的資源及び請求権

economic substance　経済的実質　[解] 法的形式（legal form）に対する用語

economic value added (EVA)　経済的付加価値

economic viability　経済的実行可能性

economy　経済

eco tax　環境税

ED　▶exposure draft

E/D　▶export declaration

EDI　▶electronic data interchange

edition　版

EDP　▶electronic data processing

effect　①効果、②影響

effective　有効な

effective date　発効日

effective income tax rate　実効税率

effective interest method　①実効金利法、②利息法　[解] ① IFRS9の文脈では、金融資産または負債の当初認識額と額面金額の差額につき、実効利回りを考慮した複利計算で各期の配分額（金利収益または費用）を決定し、償却原価を計算する方

法。日本基準でいう利息法に相当する
effective interest rate　実効金利, 実効利子率
effective internal control　有効な内部統制
effectiveness　有効性
effective portion　有効部分（ヘッジなどの）
effective tax rate　実効税率
effective tax rate for CFC purposes　租税負担割合（タックス・ヘイブン対策税制における）　[解] タックス・ヘイブン対策税制（CFC rules）における租税負担割合は、各国の法定税率（statutory tax rate）ではなく、その外国関係会社固有のものである
effect of movement in exchange rates　為替レートの変動による影響
effect of tax rates in foreign jurisdictions　在外管轄地域における税率の影響　[解] 税率差異の内訳
effects of exchange rate changes　為替変動による影響額
effects of exchange rate changes on the balance of cash and cash equivalents in foreign currencies　現金及び現金同等物の為替変動による影響
efficiency　効率性, 能率
efficiency variance　能率差異（製造間接費に係る）
efficient　効率的な
EFT　▶electronic funds transfer
EIN　▶employer identification number
elect　選択する　[用] elect (not) to apply IFRS XX（IFRS XX を適用する（しない）ことを選択する）
election　選択
electronic banking　エレクトロニック・バンキング
electronic data interchange (EDI)　電子データ交換
electronic data processing (EDP)　電子データ処理
electronic funds transfer (EFT)　電子資金振替
electronic tax (return) filing　電子申告
element　要素
element of financial statements　財務諸表の構成要素

eligibility　適格性
eligibility criteria　適格性に関する基準（ヘッジなどの）
eligibility for capitalisation　資産化への適格性　[米] eligibility for capitalization
eligible　適格な
eliminate　消去する　[用] to eliminate the carrying amount of the parent's investment in each subsidiary and the parent's portion of equity of each subsidiary（親会社の各子会社に対する投資の帳簿価額と、各子会社の資本のうち親会社の持分相当額を相殺消去する）
eliminate on consolidation　連結上消去する
elimination　①消去, ②相殺消去（連結財務諸表作成のための）
elimination entry　相殺消去仕訳（連結財務諸表作成のための）
elimination of inter-segment profit　セグメント間利益の消去
elimination of inter-segment revenue　セグメント間収益の消去
elimination of unrealised profit　未実現利益の消去　[米] elimination of unrealized profit　[用] elimination of unrealised profit on downstream sales（ダウンストリーム売上に係る未実現利益の消去）
eLTAX　エルタックス　[解] 地方税の電子申告システム（日本）
embed　組み込む
embedded derivative　組込デリバティブ　[解] デリバティブ以外の金融商品にデリバティブの要素が組み込まれたもの
embezzle　横領する, 着服する
embezzlement　横領
embody　具体化する
EMEA　▶Europe, the Middle East and Africa
emergency　緊急
emerging economies　新興経済圏
emission　排出
emission rights　排出権
emphasis　強調
emphasise　強調する　[米] emphasize
empirical　経験上の
employ　①雇用する, ②採用する（戦略など

を）
employee　従業員
employee benefit　従業員給付　[解] 従業員が提供した勤務などと交換に，企業が従業員に与える対価。従業員給付には様々な形態があるが，IAS19 では，短期従業員給付・退職後給付・その他の長期従業員給付・解雇給付の４つに分類して会計処理を規定している
employee benefit assets　従業員給付資産
employee benefit expense　従業員給付費用
employee benefit liabilities　従業員給付債務，従業員給付負債
employee benefit obligations　従業員給付債務
employee benefit plan　従業員給付制度
employee benefits expense　従業員給付費用
employee buy-out (EBO)　エンプロイー・バイアウト，従業員による企業買収
employee compensation　従業員報酬
employee contributions　従業員掛金
employee dismissal　従業員の解雇
employee profit sharing　従業員に対する利益分配
employees and others providing similar services　従業員及び他の類似サービス提供者
employees' contribution to social security　従業員負担の社会保険拠出
employee share option　従業員ストック・オプション
employee share plan　従業員株式制度
employee share purchase plan　従業員株式購入制度
employees' pension insurance　厚生年金保険
employees' pension fund (EPF)　厚生年金基金
employee stock option　従業員に対するストック・オプション
employee stock ownership plan (ESOP)　従業員持株制度
employee stock ownership programme　従業員持株制度　[米] employee stock ownership program
employee stock purchase plan (ESPP)　従業員株式購入制度
employee support programme　従業員支援プログラム　[米] employee support program
employee turnover　退職率（従業員の）
employer　雇用者
employer contributions　事業主掛金
employer identification number (EIN)　納税者番号（米国）
employer's contribution to social security　雇用主負担の社会保険拠出
employment　雇用
employment contract　雇用契約（書）
employment income　給与所得
employment insurance　雇用保険
empowerment　権限委譲
emptor　買手，買主
E/N　▶exchange of notes
enable　可能にする
enact　制定する（法律を）
enacted or announced　制定または発表された【形】
enacted tax rate　施行されている税率
enactment　制定（法律の）
encompass　包含する
encryption　暗号化
encumbrance　資産に対する制限，財産上の負担　[解] 例えば，抵当権は encumbrance に該当する
end　①最後，②目的
ending balance　期末残高
ending inventory　棚卸資産期末残高
end of accounting period　期末日
end of business day (EOB)　終業時間（までに）
end of day (EOD)　一日の終わり（までに）
end of period　期末日
end of reporting period　報告期間の末日　[解] いわゆる期末日を指し，この日以降に発生した事象が後発事象となる
endorse　①支持する，②裏書きする
endorsee　被裏書人
endorsement　①支持，②裏書き，③承認　[解] ③IFRS を自国の基準として承認すること
endorser　裏書人

enforce 施行する（法令を）
enforceable ①実施できる，②強制できる
enforceable agreement 強制力のある契約
enforceable right ①執行可能な権利，②強制力のある権利
enforcement ①施行（法令の），②執行
engage 従事する
engagement ①業務，②契約
engagement letter 契約書（監査契約等の）
engineer エンジニア
engineering エンジニアリング
enhance 高める，強化する
enhanced 高められた（価値などが）
enhanced retirement entitlement 割増退職金の受給権
enhancement 強化，増強
enquiry ①質問，②引合い
entail 伴う
enter into 締結する（契約を） 用 to enter into a forward contract（先渡契約を締結する）
enterprise 企業，事業
enterprise resource planning (ERP) 企業資源計画，統合基幹業務システム 解 経営資源を企業全体で最適配分し，有効活用するという経営概念。または，その実現のため，生産・販売・物流・財務などの企業活動全般にわたる業務を統合した企業情報システム
enterprise risk management (ERM) 全社的リスクマネジント 解 起こり得るあらゆるリスクを組織全体で管理しようとする体制
enterprise tax 事業税
enterprise tax payable 未払事業税
enterprise tax rate 事業税率
enterprise tax return 事業税申告書
enterprise value (EV) 企業価値 解 一般に事業価値に事業外資産の価値を加えたもので，この企業価値からネット・デットを差し引くことで株主価値が計算される
entertainment cost [expense] 交際費
entire すべての
entire income principle 総合主義 解 PE（恒久的施設）の所在地国のすべての国内源泉所得を総合して課税するという考え方。帰属主義（attributable income principle）に対する用語
entirely 完全に
entirety 全体，全額
entitle 権利を付与する
entitlement ①権利，②権利付与，③受給権
entity 事業体
entity approach 団体課税（アプローチ） 解 構成員課税（pass-through taxation）に対する用語で，通常の企業等（の団体）に対する課税を指す
entity level control 全社統制
entity's own equity instrument 企業自身の資本性金融商品
entity-specific 企業固有の
entity-specific measurement 企業固有の測定（値） 用 market-based, rather than entity-specific, measurement（企業固有の測定値というよりは，市場ベースの測定値）
entity-specific value 企業固有の価値
entity under common control 共通支配下の企業
entity-wide 全社の
entity-wide disclosure 全社情報の開示，企業全体の開示 解 IFRS8の文脈では，企業が単一の報告セグメントしか有しない場合でも，製品及びサービスに関する情報など，一定の全社情報の開示は必要となる
entrepreneur 企業家，起業家
entrepreneurial 企業家的な，起業家的な
entrust 委託する
entry ①入力，記入，②仕訳 用 ② entries are made in a journal（仕訳帳に記入される）
entry price 入口価格 解 資産を取得するために支払った価格（または負債を引き受けるために受け取った価格）で，出口価格（exit price）に対する用語
environment 環境
environmental 環境の
environmental damage 環境被害［損害］
environmental due diligence 環境デュー・デリジェンス
environmental obligations 環境（改善）債務

environmental provision　環境引当金，環境対策引当金
environmental regulations　環境規制
environmental rehabilitation　環境の再生
environmental standards　環境基準
environmental tax　環境税
environment related expense　環境関連費用
envisage　想定する
EOB　▶end of business day
EOD　▶end of day
EPA　▶economic partnership agreement
EPF　▶employees' pension fund
EPS　▶earnings per share
equal　等しい
equal footing　対等な立場
equalisation　均等化，平等化　㊤equalization
equalisation levy　平衡税　㊤equalization levy　[解]特定の電子商取引に対する源泉課税
equal prominence　同等に目立つ場所
equate　等しくする
equation　等式，方程式
equilibrium　均衡
equipment　備品，機器
equity　持分，資本　[解]企業の資産から負債を控除した残余に対する請求権
equity account　資本勘定
equity-accounted investee　持分法適用会社
equity accounting　持分法会計
equity and liabilities　負債及び資本
equity attributable to (the) owners of the parent　親会社の所有者に帰属する持分　[解]資本合計のうち，非支配持分（non-controlling interest）を除く部分
equity capital　（自己）資本
equity component　資本部分（金融商品などの）
equity conversion option　資本への転換オプション
equity distribution　資本の分配
equity financing　エクイティ・ファイナンス
equity holder　持分投資者，出資者，株主
equity instrument　資本性金融商品，持分金融商品　[解]企業の資産から負債を控除した残余に対する持分を証する契約で，例えば株式がこれに該当する
equity instrument granted　付与された資本性金融商品　[解]IFRS2の文脈では，株式に基づく報酬として，企業により他の当事者に付与された（当該企業の）資本性金融商品
equity interest　持分，株式，資本持分
equity investment　資本性金融商品，持分投資，株式投資
equity method　持分法　[解]関連会社や共同支配企業に対する投資につき，当初は取得原価で認識するが，その後の被投資企業の純資産に対する投資企業の持分の変動に応じて，投資額を修正する会計処理の方法
equity of (the) owners of the parent　親会社の所有者に帰属する持分
equity price risk　株価リスク
equity ratio　自己資本比率
equity reclassified into financial liabilities　金融負債に分類変更された資本
equity risk premium　エクイティ・リスク・プレミアム
equity securities　資本性証券，持分証券
equity-settled　持分決済型の
equity-settled share-based payment　持分決済型の株式に基づく報酬　[解]株式に基づく報酬取引の1形態であり，企業が，自社の資本性金融商品（株式やストック・オプション等）を対価として，財またはサービスを受け取る取引など
equity transaction　資本取引
equity value　株主価値
equivalent　①同等の，②同等物
erection　組立て，建設
ERM　▶enterprise risk management
ERP　▶enterprise resource planning
erroneous　誤った
erroneously　誤って
error　誤謬
errors and omissions (E&O)　誤差脱漏
escalation clause　エスカレーション条項　[解]物価や為替レートの変動に応じて，取引価格や工事請負金額等を変更することをあらかじめ決めておくこと
escrow　エスクロー　[解]企業買収等におい

て，取引の安全性を保証するための資産の第三者寄託をいい，取引の決済は金融機関等に設けたエスクロー口座を通じて行われる
escrow account　エスクロー口座
ESOP　▶employee stock ownership plan
especially　特に
ESPP　▶employee stock purchase plan
essence　本質，要点
essential　本質的な，非常に重要な
establish　設立する
establishment　設立
estate　財産
estate tax [duty]　相続税，遺産税
estimable　見積可能な
estimate　①見積もる，②見積り
estimated cost　見積原価
estimated effective tax rate　見積実効税率
estimated forfeiture rate　予想失効率（ストック・オプションなどの）
estimated payment　見込納付（税金などの）
estimated tax　見積税額
estimated tax rate　見積税率
estimated time of arrival (ETA)　入港予定日，到着予定日
estimated useful life　見積耐用年数
estimate of financial effect　財務的影響の見積り　[解]重要な「修正を要しない後発事象」(non-adjusting event after reporting period)については，その財務的影響の見積りを開示する必要がある
estimate of future cash flows　将来キャッシュ・フローの見積り
estimation　見積り，見積もること
estimation technique　見積技法
estimation uncertainty　見積りの不確実性
estoppel　禁反言　[解]自己の行為または捺印証書に反する主張をすることを法律上禁止すること
ETA　▶estimated time of arrival
e-Tax　イータックス　[解]国税の電子申告システム（日本）
EU　▶European Union
EU directive　EU指令　[解]EU委員会が，加盟各国に対し，各国の関連法の見直しを求めるために出す指令。採択された指令の内容は一定の期間内に加盟国の国内法として立法化されなくてはならないこととされている
euro　ユーロ
Eurobond　ユーロ債　[解]欧州以外の企業が欧州金融市場で発行する債券
European Commission　欧州委員会　[解]EUの執行機関の１つ
European Court of Justice (ECJ)　欧州裁判所
European Union (EU)　欧州連合
Europe, the Middle East and Africa (EMEA)　ヨーロッパ，中東及びアフリカ地域
EV　▶enterprise value
EVA　▶economic value added
evaluate　評価する
evaluation　評価
EV/EBITDA ratio　EV/EBITDA倍率　[解]企業価値（EV）がEBITDAの何倍になっているかを示す指標
EV/EBIT ratio　EV/EBIT倍率　[解]企業価値（EV）がEBITの何倍になっているかを示す指標
even　平らな，一様な
evenly　均等に
event　事象
event after reporting period　後発事象　[解]IAS10の文脈では，報告期間の末日と財務諸表の発行承認日との間に発生する事象を指す
eventual　結果としての
eventually　結果的に
evergreen contract　自動更新契約
eviction　立退き
evidence　証拠，証拠資料，監査証拠
evident　（証拠があって）明らかな
evidential　証拠の，証拠となる【形】
evidential matter　証拠資料，監査証拠
exact　正確な
exactly　正確に
examination　①調査，検査，②税務調査
examine　調査する，検査する
example　例
example financial statements　財務諸表の例
ex ante　事前の
exceed　超過する，上回る
except (for)　〜を除いて

exception 例外
exceptional 例外的な
exceptional item 例外項目，異常項目
exception conditions 適用除外要件，適用除外基準（特に旧タックス・ヘイブン対策税制における）
excerpt 抜粋
excess ①過剰，②超過（額） 用in excess of（〜を超えて）
excess cash 余剰資金
excess credit limit 控除余裕額 解外国税額控除の関係では，控除対象外国法人税の額が控除限度額を下回るときのその余裕額をいい，将来3年にわたり繰越可能
excess depreciation 減価償却超過額
excess earnings 超過収益，超過利益
excess earnings method 超過収益法（資産評価などの）
excess foreign taxes 控除限度超過額（外国税額控除の）
excess inventory 過剰在庫
excessive 過度の
excessive director's remuneration 過大役員報酬
excess profit tax 超過利潤税 解一定の所得金額（適正利潤）を超える所得に対して課される税
excess supply 供給過多，過剰供給
excess tax 高率部分の税額
exchange ①交換する，②交換，③取引所
exchange control 為替管理
exchange difference 為替差額 解IAS21の文脈では，ある通貨を他の通貨に換算することにより生じる差額で，純損益で認識される場合とその他包括利益で認識される場合がある
exchange differences on translating foreign operations 在外営業活動体の換算差額，為替換算調整勘定
exchange differences on translation 為替換算差額
exchange gain 為替差益
exchange gains and losses 為替差損益
exchange loss 為替差損
exchange of assets 資産の交換
exchange of information 情報交換 解租税条約には，国際的な租税回避取引の防止のために，情報交換の規定が設けられている
exchange of notes (E/N) 交換公文 解国家間で書簡を往復させて権利義務を設定するもので，広義の条約に含まれる。議定書と同様，租税条約の解釈が記載されていることがある
exchange of properties 資産の交換
exchange rate 為替レート
exchange rate at the date of the transaction 取引日レート
exchange-traded 上場の
exchange-traded derivatives 上場デリバティブ
exchange transaction 交換取引
excise (tax) 物品税，消費税，間接税
exclude 除外する
excluded income 非課税所得,益金不算入収益
exclusion ①課税対象外，②除外
exclusion from operating segments 事業セグメントからの除外
exclusive 排他的な，独占的な
exclusive agreement 独占契約，排他的契約
exclusive licence 専用実施権，独占的実施権，排他的ライセンス 米exclusive license
exclusive negotiating rights 独占交渉権
exclusive right 独占権
exclusivity ①独占権，②競合品の取扱制限
exclusivity agreement 独占交渉権に係る合意・契約（買収案件などの）
exclusivity period 独占交渉期間（買収案件などの）
ex-dividend 配当落ちの
execute ①実行する（取引などを），②執行する
execution ①実行（取引などの），②執行
executive 役員
executive officer 執行役員，執行役
executive summary エグゼクティブ・サマリー 解報告書等のうち，特に重要な部分の要約
executory 未履行の，未済の
executory contract 未履行契約

executory cost　維持管理費（リースなどの）
exempt　①免除する【動】，②免除された【形】
exempt income　非課税所得，免税所得，益金不算入収益
exemption　①免除規定，②免責，③免税　[解] ①IFRSの初度適用にあたっては，従前の資産及び負債の認識，測定及び分類等の見直しが必要になるが，いくつかの項目については免除規定がある
exemption certificate　免税証明書
exemption for foreign dividend　国外配当免税
exemption from consolidation　連結の免除
exemption from tax　免税
exemption method　国外所得免税方式（国際課税における）
exempt organisation　非課税組織　[米] exempt organization
exempt sales　免税売上
exercisability　行使可能性
exercisable　行使可能な
exercise　①行使する，②(権利) 行使
exercise date　権利行使日　[解]（ストック・）オプションを行使する日
exercise period　権利行使可能期間　[解]（ストック・）オプションを行使できる期間
exercise price　権利行使価格　[解]（ストック・）オプションを行使する際の価格
ex factory　工場渡し条件（価格）
exhaustive　網羅的な
exhibit　①示す，②付属書類，③証拠資料
existence　①実在性，②存在
existing　既存の　[解]「新規の」(new) に対する用語
existing interest　既存の持分　[用] existing 25% interest（既存の25%の持分）
existing right　既存の権利
exit　①イグジット, 出口, 投資の売却, 撤退, ②出口
exit activities　撤退活動
exit plan　イグジット・プラン，出口戦略
exit price　出口価格　[解] 資産を売却する際に受け取るであろう（または負債を移転する際に支払うであろう）価格であり，入口価格（entry price）に対する用語。IFRS13 においては，公正価値は出口価格

として定義されている
exit strategy　出口戦略
exit tax　出国税, 国外転出時課税（制度）
ex nunc　現在時点から，将来効の
expand　拡大する
expansion　拡大
expat　▶expatriate
expatriate (expat)　①国外居住者，②海外駐在員
expatriate staff　海外駐在員
expats　expatriate(s)
expectation　①期待，②期待値
expected capacity　予定生産能力
expected cash flow　期待キャッシュ・フロー
expected cost　予想コスト
expected cost plus a margin approach　予想コストにマージンを加算するアプローチ　[解] IFRS15 の文脈では，独立販売価格の見積もりに際して，履行義務を充足するためのコストを予想し，それに適切なマージンを加算するという方法を指す
expected credit loss (ECL)　予想信用損失　[解] 信用損失を債務不履行発生確率でウェイト付けした期待値
expected credit losses collectively assessed　集合的に評価した予想信用損失
expected credit losses individually assessed　個別的に評価した予想信用損失
expected credit loss rate　予想信用損失率
expected impact　予想される影響　[用] expected impact of initial application of new standards or interpretations（新しい基準または解釈指針の適用開始により予想される影響）
expected loss　予想損失
expected loss on construction contract　予測される工事契約損失
expected rate of return　期待収益率
expected return on plan assets　期待運用収益（制度資産，年金資産の）　[解] 退職給付会計の文脈では，期首時点で予測される制度資産からの運用収益をいい，実際運用収益（actual return on plan assets）に対する用語
expected value　期待値
expected value approach　期待値アプロー

チ
expected volatility　予想ボラティリティ
expedient　手段，便法
expenditure　費用，支出
expenditure on qualifying asset　適格資産に係る支出　[解]IAS23の文脈では，資産化される借入費用の額を算定する際，資産化率を乗じる対象
expense　①費用，②経費，③費用処理する【動】　[解]①会計期間における資産の減少または負債の増加という形での経済的便益の減少で，持分参加者への分配以外のもの
expense as incurred　即時費用処理する
expense reimbursement　経費精算
expense reimbursement scheme　経費精算スキーム（不正の一形態）
expenses related to　～関連費用
expenses related to post-employment defined benefit plans　退職後確定給付制度関連費用
experience　経験
experience adjustment　実績による修正（数理計算上の仮定などの）
experienced　経験のある
expert　専門家
expertise　専門知識
expiration　満了（期間の），満期
expiration date　①満期日，②失効日（税務上の繰越欠損金などの）
expire　有効期限が切れる
expiry　①満了（期間の），満期，②失効
expiry date　①満期日，②失効日
explain　説明する
explanation　説明
explanatory　説明的な
explanatory information　説明情報
explanatory material　説明資料
explanatory note　説明的注記　[解]IAS34の文脈では，直近の年次財務報告期間の末日からの財政状態や経営成績の変化を理解する上で重要な事象や取引について説明するもの
explicit　明示的な
explicitly　明示的に
exploit　利用する

exploitation　①開発，②搾取
exploration　探鉱，探査
export　①輸出する，②輸出
export charges　輸出諸掛
export control　輸出規制，安全保障貿易管理
export declaration (E/D)　①輸出申告書，②輸出許可通知書　[解]製品の輸出にあたっては，品目・数量・価格等を記載した「輸出申告書」を税関に提出する。税関がその輸出を許可し，許可印を押すと，それが「輸出許可通知書」となる
export duty　輸出税　[解]一定の輸出品に課される税金
exporter　輸出企業
export sales　輸出売上
expose　さらす（リスクに）
ex post　事後の
exposure　エクスポージャー　[解]（リスクに）さらされていること
exposure draft (ED)　公開草案
express　表明する，表現する
expression　表明，表現
expropriate　収用する（国などが土地等を）
expropriated property　収用資産
expropriation　収用（国などによる土地等の）　[用]expropriation of major assets by government（主要な資産の政府による収用）
extend　延長する
eXtensible Business Reporting Language (XBRL)　XBRL，拡張可能な事業報告言語　[解]財務報告目的に特化したコンピュータ言語
extension　延長
extension for the filing of tax returns　申告期限の延長
extension for the payment of taxes　納付期限の延長
extension of useful life　耐用年数の延長
extension option　延長選択権［オプション］（リース期間などの）
extent　①範囲，②程度　[用]to the extent that hedge is effective（ヘッジが有効である範囲において）
extent of tests of control　コントロール・テストの範囲
external　外部の

external comparable 外部比較対象（取引）
external credit grade 外部信用格付け
external credit grading system 外部の信用格付けシステム
external customer 外部顧客 [解] 連結グループ外の顧客
external financing 外部金融，外部資金調達
external funds 外部資金
external investigation 外部調査
external rating 外部格付け
external reporting 外部報告
external revenue 外部（顧客からの）収益
external sales 外部売上
external transaction 外部取引
extinguish 消滅させる
extinguishment 消滅
extinguishment of debt 負債の消滅
extinguishment of pre-consolidation losses 連結納税開始前の繰越欠損金の消滅
extra 余分な
extract 抽出する
extraction 抽出
extra depreciation 増加償却
extraordinary 異常な
extraordinary gain [income] 特別利益
extraordinary gain and loss 特別損益
extraordinary item ①特別項目，②異常項目，③臨時項目
extraordinary loss 特別損失
extraordinary profit 特別利益
extraordinary report 臨時報告書
extrapolate 外挿する，推測する [解] ある変数について，観察した範囲から，その範囲外の値を推定すること
extrapolation 外挿，推測
extraterritorial 域外の，治外法権の
extraterritorial application 域外適用
extreme 極端な
extremely 極端に
ex tunc その時点から，遡及効の
EXW ▶ex works
ex works (EXW) 工場渡し条件（価格） [解] 貿易条件の1つで，売主は自らの敷地（工場）で買主に商品を移転し，それ以降の運賃，保険料，リスクの一切は買主が負担する

F

FA ▶financial adviser [advisor]
face value 額面金額，券面額
facilitate ①促進する，②容易にする
facilitation ①促進，②容易にすること
facilities attached to buildings 建物附属設備
facility ①設備，②融資枠
fact 事実
fact book ファクト・ブック
factor ①要素，②要因，③ファクタリング会社，④ファクタリングをする
factor-based enterprise [business] tax 外形標準課税（事業税）
factoring ファクタリング [解] 売掛債権を（ファクタリング会社などに）売却して早期に資金化すること
factoring of receivables 債権のファクタリング
factory 工場
factory cost 工場原価，製造原価
factory overhead 製造間接費
factory premises 工場敷地
facts and circumstances 事実及び状況
factual 事実の
factual analysis 事実分析
fail 失敗する
failure 失敗
failure to withhold 源泉徴収漏れ
fair 公正な，公平な
fair disclosure フェア・ディスクロージャー，公平な情報開示
fairly 適正に，公正に
fair market value 時価，公正市場価値
fairness 適正性
fairness opinion フェアネス・オピニオン [解] 公平な第三者が，企業買収における買収価格の適正性に関して表明する意見
fair presentation 公正な表示，適正な表示
fair value 公正価値 [解] IFRS13の文脈で

は，測定日時点の市場参加者（market participant）間の秩序ある取引（orderly transaction）において，資産の売却により受け取る，または負債の移転により支払うであろう価格を指す

fair value changes　公正価値の変動

fair value hedge　公正価値ヘッジ
[解] IFRS9の文脈では，ヘッジ対象の公正価値の変動のうち，特定のリスクに起因して変動し，かつ，純資産に影響を与えうる場合における，その公正価値の変動に対するエクスポージャーのヘッジ

fair value hierarchy　公正価値ヒエラルキー
[解] IFRS11の文脈では，公正価値を測定する際のインプットについて，観察可能性に応じて3つのレベルに区分し，優先順位付けしたもの　[用] all levels of fair value hierarchy（公正価値ヒエラルキーのすべてのレベル）

fair value less costs of disposal　処分コスト控除後の公正価値　[解] 資産等の公正価値から処分に直接要する増分コストを控除した額

fair value less costs to sell　売却コスト控除後の公正価値　[解] 資産または資金生成単位を独立第三者間価格で売却した場合の売却価額から処分費用を控除した額

fair value measurement　公正価値による測定

fair value model　公正価値モデル
[解] IAS40の文脈では，当初認識の後，投資不動産を公正価値で測定する方法で，公正価値の変動は損益として認識される

fair value option　公正価値オプション　[解] IFRS9の文脈では，本来は償却原価またはFVTOCIの負債性金融商品（例えば，債券）を（一定の要件の下で）FVTPLに指定できるという選択肢を指す　[用] an asset is designated at FVTPL [FVPL] under the fair value option（公正価値オプションにより，資産がFVTPLに指定される）

fair value principle　公正価値基準

fair value reserve　フェア・バリュー・リザーブ，公正価値変動による評価差額　[解] その他の資本の構成要素

fair values measured on a provisional basis　暫定的に測定された公正価値

fair value through other comprehensive income (FVOCI / FVTOCI)　その他の包括利益を通じて公正価値（で測定する区分）　[解] IFRS9の文脈では，金融資産の区分の1つで，公正価値で測定され，変動はその他の包括利益として計上されるもの

fair value through profit or loss (FVPL / FVTPL)　純損益を通じて公正価値（で測定する区分）　[解] IFRS9の文脈では，金融資産（または負債）の区分の1つで，公正価値で測定され，変動は純損益として計上されるもの

faithful　忠実な

faithfulness　忠実性

faithful representation　忠実な表現

fall　下落する

fallacious　誤った

fall due　期限が到来する

fallout　副産物，副次的影響

fall under　〜に分類される，属する

false　誤った，偽りの

false refund　不正な還付

falsification　偽造，改竄

falsified　偽造された，改竄された

falsified financial statements　改竄された財務諸表

falsify　偽造する，改竄する

family company [corporation]　同族会社

FAS　▶① Financial Accounting Standards, ② free alongside ship

FASB　▶Financial Accounting Standards Board

FASB Accounting Standard Codification (ASC)　FASB会計基準（編纂書）（米国）

FASB Interpretation (FIN)　FASB解釈指針（旧）

FASF　▶Financial Accounting Standards Foundation

fast close　決算早期化

FATCA　▶Foreign Account Tax Compliance Act

fat payment　高額の支払い

favourable　有利な，好ましい　[米] favorable

favourable issuance　有利発行　[米] favor-

able issuance
favourable tax consequence　有利な税務上の影響　㋖favorable tax consequence
favourable variance　有利差異　㋖favorable variance
FCA　▶free carrier
FCF　▶free cash flow
FCFE　▶free cash flow to equity
FCFF　▶free cash flow to the firm
FCPA　▶Foreign Corrupt Practices Act
FCT　▶foreign contractor tax
FDD　▶financial due diligence
feasibility　実行可能性
feasibility analysis　実行可能性分析
feasibility study　フィージビリティ・スタディ，実行可能性調査
feasible　実行可能な
feature　特徴，特性
federal　連邦の
federal income tax　連邦所得税
federal tax　連邦税
fee　報酬，フィー
fee and commission expense　報酬及び手数料費用
fee and commission income　報酬及び手数料収益
fee estimate [quote]　報酬見積り
fee expense　手数料費用
fee income　手数料収益
fee letter　フィー・レター　㋔買収案件などで，アドバイザーに対するフィーの支払いを約定するもの
fellow subsidiary　兄弟会社
fictitious　架空の
fictitious expense　架空費用
fictitious profit　架空利益
fictitious revenue　架空収益
fictitious transaction　架空取引
fiduciary　①信託の，②受託者（信託の）
fiduciary duty　受託者義務
fiduciary out (clause)　フィデュシャリー・アウト（条項）　㋔買収契約締結後に他社からより好条件の買収提案を受けた場合，その新しい買収提案への乗換えを可能にするような条項
field audit　実地調査［監査］，実地税務調査

field tax audit　実地税務調査
field work　実地作業，現場作業（監査人などの）
FIFO　▶first in, first out
figure　①数値，②図形
file　提出する
filing　提出（公的機関などへの）
filing due date　申告期限
filing extension　申告期限の延長　㋕one-month filing extension（1か月の申告期限の延長）
filing requirement　申告義務
filter　選別する
FIN　▶FASB Interpretation
FIN 48　FASB解釈指針第48号「法人税等における不確実性に関する会計処理」（旧）（米国）
final　最終の，確定の
final customer　最終顧客
finalise　最終化する　㋖finalize
finally　最終的に，最後に
final payment　最終支払い，確定納付（税金などの）
final tax　確定税額，最終税額
final tax return　確定申告書
finance　ファイナンス
finance charge　金融費用，財務費用
finance company　金融会社
finance cost (s)　金融費用，財務費用
finance department [division]　財務部門
finance income　金融収益，財務収益
finance lease　ファイナンス・リース
finance lease without transfer of ownership　所有権移転外ファイナンス・リース
finance lease with transfer of ownership　所有権移転ファイナンス・リース
finance subsidiary　金融子会社
financial　財務の
Financial Accounting Standards (FAS)　財務会計基準（旧）（米国）
Financial Accounting Standards Board (FASB)　財務会計基準審議会（米国）　㋕米国の会計基準設定主体
Financial Accounting Standards Foundation (FASF)　財務会計基準機構（日本）
financial adviser [advisor] (FA)　フィナン

シャル・アドバイザー [解]企業に対して財務面での助言を行う投資銀行等を指す。企業買収の局面では、買収対象会社の選定に始まり、最終のクロージングまで継続的にアドバイスを行う

financial analysis　財務分析

financial and operating policies　財務及び営業の方針

financial asset　金融資産　[解]IAS32の文脈では、(1)現金、(2)他の企業が発行する資本性金融商品、(3)他の企業から金融資産を受け取る契約上の権利、または金融資産等を有利な条件で他の企業と交換する契約上の権利、(4)その企業の資本性金融商品で決済される契約のうち一定のもの

financial asset pledged as collateral　担保として差し入れた金融資産　[用]financial assets pledged as collateral for liabilities or contingent liabilities（負債または偶発負債の担保として差し入れた金融資産）

financial assets mandatorily measured at FVTOCI [FVOCI]　強制的にその他の包括利益を通じて公正価値で測定される金融資産

financial assets measured at amortised cost　償却原価で測定される金融資産　[米]financial assets measured at amortized cost

financial assets measured at fair value　公正価値で測定される金融資産

financial assets measured at FVTOCI [FVOCI]　その他の包括利益を通じて公正価値で測定される金融資産

financial assets measured at FVTPL [FVPL]　純損益を通じて公正価値で測定される金融資産

financial assistance　財務支援

financial assumption　財務上の仮定

financial buyer　フィナンシャル・バイヤー　[解]単に買収対象会社の解散価値や割安度合いに着目して投資を行う買収者で、対象者の事業の取得を目的とするストラテジック・バイヤー（strategic buyer）に対する用語

financial closing　決算

financial component approach　財務構成要素アプローチ　[解]認識の中止に関して、金融商品等をその構成要素に分解した上で、それぞれの支配の有無を判定する方法

financial controller　財務コントローラー

financial cost　金融費用、財務費用

financial covenants　財務制限条項

financial damage　金銭的損害（不正などによる）

financial data　財務データ

financial deterioration　財政状態の悪化

financial difficulties　財務上の困難、財政状態の悪化

financial distress　財務上の困難

financial due diligence (FDD)　財務デュー・デリジェンス　[解]買収対象会社の財務内容の調査。財務諸表の分析等により、資産の実在性や含み損益の実態、また租税債務を含む簿外負債の把握などを行う

financial effect　財務的影響

financial forecast　財務予測

financial guarantee　金融保証、債務保証　[用]to provide financial guarantee for subsidiaries' liabilities（子会社の負債に対して債務保証を行う）

financial guarantee contract　金融保証契約、債務保証契約

financial implication　財務上の意味合い・影響

financial information　財務情報

financial institution　金融機関

financial institution confirmation request　金融機関への確認依頼

financial instrument　金融商品　[解]一方の企業にとっての金融資産と他方の企業にとっての金融負債または資本性金融商品の双方を生じさせる契約

Financial Instruments and Exchange Act　金融商品取引法

financial investor　フィナンシャル・インベスター

financial leverage　財務レバレッジ

financial liabilities reclassified into equity　資本に分類変更された金融負債

financial liability 金融負債 [解] IAS32の文脈では，(1)他の企業に金融資産を支払う契約上の義務，または金融資産等を不利な条件で他の企業と交換する契約上の義務，(2)その企業の資本性金融商品で決済される契約のうち一定のもの

financial liability at amortised cost 償却原価で測定される金融負債 [米] financial liability at amortized cost

financial liability at fair value 公正価値で測定される金融負債

financial liability at FVTPL [FVPL] 純損益を通じて公正価値で測定される金融負債

financial liability held for trading 売買目的［トレーディング目的］保有の金融負債

financial market 金融市場

financial metric 財務指標

financial performance 業績，財務業績

financial position 財政状態

financial projection 財務予測

financial ratio 財務比率

financial reporting 財務報告

financial review 財務概要，財務概況

financial risk 財務リスク

financial risk management 金融リスク管理，財務リスク管理

financial services 金融サービス

Financial Services Agency (FSA) 金融庁

financial services firm 金融機関

financial situation 財務状況

financial statement audit 財務諸表監査

financial statement close process (FSCP) 決算財務報告プロセス，決算プロセス

financial statement fraud 財務諸表不正

financial statements 財務諸表

financial structure 財務構成，資本構成，財務構造

financial support 財務支援 [用] to provide financial support to a subsidiary（子会社に財務支援を行う）

financial transaction 金融取引

financial year (FY) 事業年度

financing 資金調達

financing activity 財務活動 [解] キャッシュ・フロー計算書上の活動区分で，拠出資本や借入金の規模や構成に変動をもたらす活動をいう [用] net cash generated by financing activities（財務活動によるキャッシュ・フロー（プラスの場合）），net cash used in financing activities（財務活動によるキャッシュ・フロー（マイナスの場合））

financing arrangement 資金調達

financing cash flows 財務活動によるキャッシュ・フロー

financing cost 資金調達費用

financing out (clause) ファイナンシング・アウト（条項）[解] 買収案件などで，買手が資金調達に成功しない限り，買手は買収を完了させる義務を負わないとする条項

finder's fee 斡旋手数料，仲介手数料（M&Aに関する）

finding 発見事項

fine 罰金

finished goods 製品，完成品

finished goods inventory 製品在庫

finite 有限の，確定できる（耐用年数が）[解] 耐用年数を確定できる無形資産の償却可能価額は，その耐用年数にわたり規則的に配分される

finite useful life 有限の耐用年数

firm ①企業，②確定した【形】

firm commitment 確定約定［コミットメント］[解] 将来の特定の日に所定の数量の資源を所定の価格で交換することを約する拘束力のある契約

firm purchase commitment 確定購入契約［コミットメント］

1st half 上半期，上期

first IFRS financial statements 最初のIFRS財務諸表 [解] 明示的かつ無限定にIFRSに準拠している旨を示して，IFRSを採用する最初の財務諸表

first IFRS reporting period 最初のIFRS報告期間 [解] 比較情報を含む最初のIFRS財務諸表が対象とする期間のうち，直近の期間

first-in, first-out (FIFO) 先入先出法 [解] 原価算定方式の1つで，先に入庫したものから順に出庫されるという仮定に基づく方式

1st quarter　第1四半期
first sale　ファースト・セール　[解]関税に関するプランニングの手法の1つ。一定の要件のもと，販社を経由する米国やEUへの輸出につき，販社からの販売価格ではなく，販社への販売価格（first sale）をもって関税評価額とし，関税を低減する手法
first-tier subsidiary　第1階層（子会社層）の子会社　[解]第2階層（孫会社層）の子会社（second-tier subsidiary）に対する用語
first-time adopter　初度適用企業　[解]IFRSに基づく財務諸表を初めて作成する企業
first-time adoption　初度適用　[解]IFRSに基づく財務諸表を初めて作成すること
first-time adoption of International Financial Reporting Standards　国際財務報告基準の初度適用
first-time offender　初犯者（不正などの）
fiscal　会計の，財政上の
fiscal domicile　居住地，所在地
fiscally transparent entity　課税対象とならない事業体
fiscal period　会計期間
fiscal policy　財政政策
fiscal residence　居住（地）
fiscal year (FY)　事業年度
fittings　備品　[解]通常複数形
five-step model (framework)　5ステップの収益認識モデル　[解]IFRS15が採用する収益認識モデル
five-year business plan　5年間の事業計画
fixed asset　固定資産
fixed asset ledger　固定資産台帳
fixed asset register　固定資産台帳
fixed assets tax　固定資産税
fixed assets to net worth ratio　固定比率　[解]企業の長期的な安全性を判断するための指標であり，以下の算式で計算される
　　固定比率＝固定資産／自己資本
fixed cost　固定費
fixed fee　固定報酬
fixed income　①固定収入，②金利収入
fixed income investment　債券投資，確定利付投資
fixed interest rate　固定金利
fixed manufacturing cost　固定製造費用
fixed maturity　固定満期
fixed overhead　固定（製造）間接費
fixed overhead variance　固定間接費差異
fixed payment　固定支払い　[解]IFRS16の文脈では，固定リース料を指す
fixed place of business　事業を行う一定の場所　[解]OECDモデル租税条約におけるPE（恒久的施設）は，「事業を行う一定の場所」であって，企業がその場所を通じてその事業の全部または一部を行っている場所とされている
fixed price　固定価格
fixed price contract　固定価格契約
fixed rate　固定金利
fixed-rate debt　固定金利債券
fixed-rate instrument　固定利付金融商品
fixed-rate loan　固定金利ローン
fixture　備品
fixtures and fittings　備品
fixtures, fittings, tools and equipment　工具，器具及び備品
f.k.a　旧（formerly known as）
flash earnings report　速報ベースの業績開示
flash report　速報
flat　平坦な
flat fee　定額報酬，定額料金
flat tax　フラット・タックス，均一課税（税率）　[解]累進課税（graduated taxation）に対して，均一の税率による課税を指す
flaw　欠点，問題点
flexibility　柔軟性
flexible　柔軟な，融通のきく
floating　変動する【形】
floating interest rate　変動金利
floating-rate loan　変動金利ローン
floor　①下限，②金利フロア取引　[解]②金利オプション取引の一種で，金利フロアの買手が売手に対してオプション料を支払うことにより，契約期間中に基準金利が下限金利を下回った場合，その差額を受け取ることができるというもの
flotation　証券発行

flotation cost　証券発行費用
flow　流れ
flowchart　フローチャート
flow of funds　資金の流れ
flow of inventories　在庫品の動き
flow-through entity　フロースルー事業体，導管事業体　[解]その事業体自体は課税対象とならず，出資者（構成員）が課税されるような事業体
fluctuate　変動する
fluctuation　変動，増減
fluctuation analysis　増減分析
fluidity　流動性
FMV　▶fair market value
FOB　▶free on board
FOB destination　到着港本船渡し（価格）
FOB price　FOB 価格
FOB shipping point　積出港本船渡し（価格）
FOB value　FOB 評価
foci　focus の複数形
focus　フォーカス，焦点
following　以下の，それに続く
following year　翌年
foot　合計する
footing　計算突合
footnote　脚注
for accounting purposes　会計上の　[使い方注意!]例えば，会計と税務で金額が異なる減価償却費等については，depreciation for accounting purposes（会計上の減価償却費）のような形で，それが会計上の金額であることを明確にするのが望ましい
forced liquidation value　強制処分価値
force of attraction principle　総合主義　[解]entire income principle の項を参照
forecast　①予測，②予測する
forecast annual amounts　年度の予測数値
forecast balance sheet　予測貸借対照表
forecast income statement　予測損益計算書
forecast intra-group transaction　グループ内の予定取引
forecast non-financial asset purchase　非金融資産の購入予定取引
forecast of cash flow　キャッシュ・フロー予測

forecast transaction　予定取引　[解]IFRS9 の文脈では，確定ではないが，予想される将来の取引
foreclose　抵当流れにする
foreclosure　質流れ，抵当流れ
forego　失う，〜の権利を失う
foreign　海外の
Foreign Account Tax Compliance Act (FATCA)　外国口座税務コンプライアンス法（米国）
foreign activity　海外活動
foreign cargo　外国貨物
foreign company　外国法人　[解]内国法人以外の法人
foreign contractor tax (FCT)　外国契約者税（ベトナム）　[解]外国の個人及び組織が，ベトナムの個人及び組織に対して役務を提供し，その対価を得る際に，その所得や付加価値に対して課される税金
foreign controlling shareholder　国外支配株主等　[解]日本の過少資本税制（thin capitalisation）の適用対象となる外国法人等で，例えば，内国法人の発行済株式総数の 50％以上を保有する外国法人等がこれに該当する
foreign corporation　外国法人
foreign corporation (income) tax　外国法人税
Foreign Corrupt Practices Act (FCPA)　海外腐敗行為防止法（米国）
foreign country　外国
foreign currency　外国通貨　[解]企業の機能通貨（functional currency）以外の通貨
foreign currency basis spread　外貨ベーシス・スプレッド
foreign currency borrowings　外貨建借入金
foreign currency derivative　外貨デリバティブ
foreign currency forward　為替予約
foreign currency futures　通貨先物
foreign currency loan　①外貨建貸付金，②外貨建借入金
foreign currency option　通貨オプション
foreign currency payables　外貨建債務
foreign currency receivables　外貨建債権
foreign currency receivables and payables　外貨建金銭債権債務

foreign currency risk　為替リスク
foreign currency swap　通貨スワップ
foreign currency transaction　外貨建取引　[解]外国通貨による取引
foreign currency translation　外貨換算
foreign currency translation adjustments　為替換算調整勘定
foreign dividend　国外配当，外国配当
foreign dividend exclusion　外国子会社配当益金不算入制度（日本）　[解]外国子会社配当益金不算入制度とは，外国子会社からの配当を原則として95％益金不算入とする制度をいう。本制度により，海外子会社で稼得した利益は，大きな追加の税負担なしに日本へ還流させることが可能となっている（ただし，配当源泉税は純粋な税務コストとなる）
foreign exchange (forex/FX)　外国為替
foreign exchange control　為替管理
foreign exchange gain　為替差益
foreign exchange loss　為替差損
foreign exchange market　外国為替市場
foreign exchange rate　外国為替レート
foreign exchange risk　為替リスク
foreign jurisdiction　在外管轄地域
foreign local tax　外国地方税
foreign operation　在外営業活動体　[解]IAS21の文脈では，報告企業と異なる国または通貨に基盤を置いて活動している子会社，関連会社，共同支配企業，または支店
foreign parent company　外国親会社
foreign related company　外国関係会社　[解]タックス・ヘイブン対策税制の関係では，外国法人のうち，日本資本（内国法人等）により50％超保有されている，または実質支配されている外国法人。この外国関係会社が日本の税制上のCFCに該当する
foreign related party [person]　国外関連者　[解]移転価格税制の関係では，発行済株式総数の50％以上の株式を直接または間接に保有する関係にある外国法人（形式基準），あるいは50％以上の出資関係がない場合でも役員関係，取引依存関係，資金依存関係等で実質的な支配関係にある外国法人（実質基準）を指す
foreign related transaction　国外関連取引　[解]controlled transactionの項を参照
foreign source income　国外源泉所得　[解]居住地国（日本）以外の国で得た所得。国内源泉所得（domestic source income）に対する用語
foreign subsidiary　①外国子会社，②海外子会社，(海外)現地法人　[解]①外国子会社配当益金不算入制度でいう外国子会社とは，日本企業がその発行済株式等の25％以上（ただし，租税条約による軽減あり）を配当等の支払義務が確定する日以前6か月以上引き続き保有している外国法人をいう　[用]foreign subsidiary for the purpose of foreign dividend exclusion（外国子会社配当益金不算入制度における外国子会社）
foreign tax　外国法人税　[解]日本の外国税額控除制度にいう外国法人税とは，日本の法人税に相当する税で，外国の法令に基づき外国またはその地方公共団体により，法人の所得を課税標準として課される税をいう
foreign tax credit (FTC)　外国税額控除（制度）　[解]日本における外国税額控除制度とは，国際的な二重課税を排除するために，外国法人税を一定の条件のもと日本の法人税等から差し引く制度をいう
foreign tax deduction　外国法人税の損金算入
foreign tax eligible for a credit　控除対象外国法人税
foreign taxes paid　外国法人税
foreign tax in excess of credit limit　控除限度超過額（外国税額控除の）
foreign tax relief　国際的二重課税の排除
foreign withholding tax　外国源泉税
foreign withholding tax on dividends　外国配当源泉税　[解]外国子会社配当益金不算入制度の適用を受ける配当については，その配当源泉税に外国税額控除は適用できず，原則として損金の額に算入することもできない
foreseeable　予見できる【形】
foreseeable future　予見しうる将来

foreseeable loss　予見しうる損失
forex　▶foreign exchange
forfeit　失効する，失う（財産・権利などを）　使い方注意！ストック・オプションや繰越欠損金の失効について使う
forfeiture　失効
forfeiture of carried-forward tax losses　繰越欠損金の切捨て　解 税務デュー・デリジェンスの関係では，買収対象会社が繰越欠損金の残高を保有している場合，買収による株主の変更により，繰越欠損金が自動的に切捨てになるケースがある
forfeiture rate　失効率
for financial reporting purposes　財務報告目的の，会計上の　解 for accounting purposes の項を参照
forge　偽造する（文書などを）
forged endorsement　偽造裏書き
forged maker　署名の偽造（小切手などの）
forgery　偽造
forgivable loan　返済免除条件付融資　解 一定の条件を満たせば，返済が免除される融資
forgive　免除する
forgiveness of debt　債務免除
form　①形成する，②形式，③様式
form 8-K　様式 8-K　解 米国で，財務状況や株価に影響を与える可能性のある重要事項が発生した場合に，証券取引委員会への提出が義務付けられている報告書
form 10-K　様式 10-K　解 米国で，証券取引委員会への提出が義務付けられている年次報告書
form 10-Q　様式 10-Q　解 米国で，証券取引委員会への提出が義務付けられている四半期報告書
formal　公式の
formal agreement　公式の契約
formal / informal agreement　公式・非公式の契約
formally　公式に
formal plan　公式の計画
format　フォーマット，形式
formation　形成，組成
formation of a joint arrangement　共同支配の取決めの形成

former　①以前の，②前者（the former で）
formerly　以前は【副】
former subsidiary　前子会社
formula　算式，公式
for-profit corporation　営利企業
for-profit organisation　営利団体　米 for-profit organization
for taxation purposes　課税上の，税務上の　解 for tax purposes の項を参照
for tax purposes　税務上の　使い方注意！例えば，会計と税務で金額が異なる減価償却費等については，depreciation for tax purposes（税務上の減価償却費）のような形で，それが税務上の金額であることを明確にするのが望ましい
forthcoming　来たる，今度の
forward(s)　先渡取引
forward contract　先渡契約，フォワード・コントラクト　解 将来のある時点にあらかじめ定めた価格である商品を売買することを約する契約
forward contract to buy shares　株式を購入する先渡契約
forward contract to sell shares　株式を売却する先渡契約
forwarder　フォワーダー，貨物利用運送事業者　解 自らは輸送手段を持たず，他の業者の輸送手段（船舶・航空機など）を利用し，荷主と直接契約して輸送を行う事業者
forward exchange contract　為替予約（契約）
forward exchange rate　予約レート（為替予約の），先物（為替）レート
forward foreign currency contract　為替予約（契約）
forward-looking　将来を考慮した，前向きな【形】
forward-looking information　将来予測的情報
forward point　フォワード・ポイント　解 為替予約の先渡要素。通貨間の金利差から生じるもので，これを直物レートに加減算することで先渡レートが計算される
forward rate　①金利先渡，②予約レート，先物（為替）レート

forward rate agreement (FRA)　金利先渡取引
found　設立する
foundation　①基礎，②財団
founder　創業者，設立者
401(k) plan　確定拠出型企業年金制度（米国）
4th quarter　第４四半期
FRA　▶forward rate agreement
fraction　①一部，断片，②分数
fractional　一部の，断片的な
fractional elimination　部分的な相殺消去
fractional share　端株
framework　フレームワーク，枠組み
framework agreement　包括協定，枠組み合意
franchise　フランチャイズ
franchise agreement　フランチャイズ契約
franchisee　フランチャイジー
franchise fee　フランチャイズ手数料
franchiser　フランチャイザー
franchise tax　フランチャイズ・タックス　[解]米国の州税の１つ
franchisor　フランチャイザー
franchisor's right　フランチャイザー［フランチャイズ本部］の権利
franking credit　フランキング・クレジット　[解]インピュテーション・システムにおける，個人が受け取った配当金に対応する法人税額相当額であり，配当を受領した個人の所得税額から控除できる
fraud　不正　[用]to commit fraud（不正を行う），to prevent and detect fraud（不正を防止及び摘発する）
fraud detection　不正検出
fraud investigation　不正調査
fraud investigation team　不正調査チーム
fraud prevention　不正防止
fraud reporting mechanism　不正の通報システム
fraud risk　不正リスク
fraud risk assessment　不正リスク評価
fraud scheme　不正スキーム
fraudster　不正実行者
fraudulent　不正の
fraudulent activity　不正行為
fraudulent conduct　不正行為
fraudulent document　書類の改竄
free alongside ship (FAS)　船側渡し条件（価格）　[解]貿易条件の１つ
free carrier (FCA)　運送人渡し条件（価格）　[解]貿易条件の１つで，FOBと同じF型。輸出地の指定場所で買主（輸入者）指定の運送人に貨物を引き渡した時点で，危険負担と費用負担が買主に移転する
free cash flow (FCF)　フリー・キャッシュ・フロー
free cash flow to equity (FCFE)　株主に帰属するフリー・キャッシュ・フロー
free cash flow to the firm (FCFF)　株主及び債権者に帰属するフリー・キャッシュ・フロー
freehold　自由保有権の
freehold land　自己所有の土地
free on board (FOB)　本船渡し条件（価格）　[解]貿易条件の１つで，売主（輸出者）が貨物を積み地の港で本船に積み込むまでの費用とリスクを負担し，それ以降の費用（運賃や保険料を含む）とリスクは買主（輸入者）が負担する
free trade agreement (FTA)　自由貿易協定
free trade zone (FTZ)　自由貿易地域　[解]貿易の振興目的で政府が指定する，関税が賦課されない地域
freight　①運賃，②貨物運送
freight in　仕入運賃，引取運賃
freight out　販売運賃，発送運賃
frequency　頻度
frequent　頻繁な
frequently　頻繁に
fresh start　フレッシュ・スタート
fresh start method　フレッシュ・スタート法　[解]一般に，企業結合にあたって，すべての結合当事企業の資産および負債を（企業結合時の）時価に評価替えする会計処理の方法
friendly takeover　友好的買収
fringe benefit　フリンジ・ベネフィット　[解]給与以外の経済的利益で，例えば社宅の供与や家賃補助などがこれに該当する
FSA　▶Financial Services Agency
FSCP　▶financial statement close process

FTA	▶free trade agreement
FTC	▶foreign tax credit
FTSE 100	FTSE 100 種総合株価指数（英国）
FTZ	▶free trade zone
fuel cost [expense]	燃料費
fulfil	遂行する（職務などを），履行する，実行する　㊇fulfill　㊒to fulfil a contract with a customer（顧客との契約を履行する）
fulfilment	遂行，実行　㊇fulfillment
full consolidation	全部連結
full cost	全部原価
full disclosure	フル・ディスクロージャー
full elimination	全部消去
full extinguishment	完全な消滅（負債などの）
full goodwill method	全部のれん方式
full lifetime ECLs	▶full lifetime expected credit losses
full lifetime expected credit losses (full lifetime ECLs)	全期間の予想信用損失　㊐金融商品について，予想存続期間内のすべての債務不履行事象から生じる予想信用損失
full-time	常勤の
full-time corporate auditor	常勤監査役
fully	完全に
fully amortised intangible asset	償却済みの無形資産　㊇fully amortized intangible asset
fully depreciated asset	減価償却済資産
fully diluted basis	完全希薄化ベース
function	機能　㊒expenses are classified either by nature or by function（費用は性質別または機能別に分類される）
functional analysis	機能分析　㊐移転価格税制の関係では，移転価格の適正性を判断するうえで，法人とその国外関連者の果たす機能を分析すること
functional and economic obsolescence	機能的または経済的な陳腐化
functional and factual analysis	機能及び事実分析
functional currency	機能通貨　㊐企業が営業活動を行う主たる経済環境における通貨。機能通貨以外の通貨で表示されている取引が外貨建取引となる
functional department	機能部門
function and risk	機能とリスク
function of expense method	費用機能法　㊐費用の機能に基づいて費用を分類する方法
fund	①資金，②基金
fundamental	基礎的な
fundamental analysis	ファンダメンタル分析
fundamental characteristic	基本的な特性
fundamental research	基礎研究
funded pension plan	外部積立（基金）を有する年金制度
funding	資金拠出，積立て
funding arrangement	積立ての取決め
funding policy	積立方針
funding requirement	積立要件
fungibility	代用性，代替可能性
furnish	①供給する，②備え付ける
furnishings and equipment	備品
furniture	備品
furniture and fixtures	備品
furniture, fixtures and equipment (FF&E)	家具，什器及び備品（ホテルなどの）
future(s)	先物
future cash flow	将来キャッシュ・フロー
future economic benefit	将来の経済的便益
future event	将来の事象　㊒a future event that is outside the control of the entity（企業がコントロールできない将来の事象）
future loss	将来損失
future mortality	予想死亡率
future operating losses	将来の営業損失
future pension growth	予想年金増加率
future profit	将来利益
future result	将来の業績
future salary growth	予想昇給率
futures contract	先物取引契約
futures exchange	先物取引所
futures market	先物市場
future taxable income [profit]	将来課税所得
future tax deduction	将来の損金算入　㊐資産の税務上の取得価額は，譲渡原価や

減価償却費の形で将来損金算入される
future value　将来価値
FVOCI　▶fair value through other comprehensive income
FVPL　▶fair value through profit or loss
FVTOCI　▶fair value through other comprehensive income
FVTPL　▶fair value through profit or loss
FX　▶foreign exchange
FY　▶① fiscal year, ② financial year

G

GAAP　▶Generally Accepted Accounting Principles
GAAS　▶Generally Accepted Auditing Standards
gain　利得　[解] 広義の収益（income）のうち，狭義の収益（revenue）以外のもの。主として企業の通常の事業過程以外から稼得したものを指すが，IFRS 上は狭義の収益と特段区別はされていない
gain contingencies　偶発利益
gain on [from] a bargain purchase　割安購入益，バーゲン・パーチェスによる利益
gain on disposal　処分益　[用] gain on disposal of subsidiary（子会社処分益）
gain on debt waiver　債務免除益
gain on forgiveness of debt　債務免除益
gain on recovery of loans previously written off　過去に直接償却した貸付金の回収に係る利得
gain on sale of fixed assets　固定資産売却益
gain on sale of investment securities　投資有価証券売却益
gain on sale of property, plant and equipment　（有形）固定資産売却益
gain on sale of securities　有価証券売却益
gain recognised in bargain purchase transaction　割安購入取引で認識した利益
gains and losses　利得及び損失
G&A　▶general and administrative expense
Gantt chart　ガント・チャート，日程計画表
gazette　官報
GDT　▶General Department of Taxation
gearing　レバレッジ
general affairs department [division]　総務部門
general and administrative expense (G&A)　一般管理費
general commission agent　問屋，コミッ

ショネア
General Department of Taxation (GDT)　ベトナム税務総局（ベトナムの税務当局）
generalised system of preferences (GSP)　一般特恵関税制度　㊍ generalized system of preferences (GSP)　㊙新興国から輸入される一定の物品に対して、一般の関税率よりも低い特恵税率を適用する制度
general journal　仕訳帳
general ledger (G/L)　総勘定元帳
general ledger trial balance　総勘定元帳残高試算表
generally　一般的に
Generally Accepted Accounting Principles (GAAP)　一般に公正妥当と認められる会計基準
Generally Accepted Auditing Standards (GAAS)　一般に公正妥当と認められる監査の基準
general meeting　総会
general meeting of shareholders　株主総会
general partner (GP)　ジェネラル・パートナー、無限責任組合員　㊙パートナーシップの運営や管理を行う無限責任のパートナー
general partnership　ジェネラル・パートナーシップ、無限責任組合　㊙パートナーシップの一形態で、各パートナーがパートナーシップの負債を全額返済する責任を負うもの
general price index　一般物価指数
general principles　一般原則
general provision for bad debt　一般評価金銭債権に対する貸倒引当金
general purpose financial statements　一般目的財務諸表
general reserve　別途積立金
generate　発生させる
geographic(al)　地理的な
geographic(al) area　地域
geographic(al) area of operations　営業地域
geographic(al) information　地域別情報
geographic(al) segment　地域別セグメント
ghost employee　幽霊社員
gift　贈与
gift income　受贈益

gift received　受贈
gift tax　贈与税
GK　▶Godo Kaisha
G/L　▶general ledger
global　世界的な
globalisation　グローバリゼーション　㊍ globalization
global trading　グローバル・トレーディング
glossary　用語集
GM　▶gross margin
goal　目的、目標
Godo Kaisha (GK)　合同会社
going concern　継続企業
going concern assumption　継続企業の前提　㊙予見しうる将来にわたって、企業が事業活動を継続するという前提
going concern value　継続企業価値
going private　非上場化
going public　上場、株式公開
golden handshake　退職金（特に、解雇や早期退職に伴い支払われる多額の）
golf club membership　ゴルフ会員権
good faith　①善意、②誠実
good leaver　グッド・リーバー　㊙自らに責任のない事由（例えば、死亡）で退職する者
goods　商品、財
Goods and Services Tax (GST)　物品サービス税　㊙オーストラリア等の一定の国の付加価値税
goods available for sale　販売可能商品
goods in transit　未着品
goods or services　財またはサービス
goods or services transferred at a point in time　一時点で移転される財またはサービス
goods or services transferred over time　一定の期間にわたり移転される財またはサービス
goods sold directly to consumers　消費者に直接販売される財
goods sold through intermediaries　仲介業者を通じて販売される財
good standing　グッド・スタンディング　㊙会社が法的に正常に存在していること
goodwill　のれん　㊙IFRS3の文脈では、企

業結合において，取得企業が支払った対価の公正価値が，取得した資産の公正価値（から引き受けた負債の公正価値を控除したもの）を上回る場合のその差額をいい，個別には識別されない将来の経済的便益を意味する

go-shop clause　ゴーショップ条項　[解] 買収案件などで，最終契約締結後の一定期間，売手が他の買手候補を探して交渉することを認める条項

go under　失敗する，破産する
govern　統治する
governance　ガバナンス，統治
governing body　運営組織
governing law　準拠法
government　政府
governmental　政府の
governmental agency　政府機関
government assistance　政府援助　[解] 一定の条件を満たす企業または企業群に対して，経済的便益を提供することを目的とする政府の活動
government bond　国債
government grant　①政府補助金，②国庫補助金　[解] ① IAS20 の文脈では，企業が一定の条件を過去に満たしたこと，またはそれを将来満たすことの見返りとして，政府が企業へ資源を移転するという形の援助　[用] nature and extent of government grant（政府補助金の性質と範囲）
government levy　政府の賦課金
government official　役人，政府職員
government-related entity　政府関連企業
government subsidy　①政府補助金，②国庫補助金
GP　▶general partner
grace period　①猶予期間，②支払猶予期間
gradual　段階的な
gradually　段階的に，徐々に
graduated rates　累進税率
graduated taxation　累進課税
graduated tax rates　累進税率
grand　①重大な，②全体の
grandfather clause　グランドファーザー条項　[解] 新しい法律により事業活動に制約を受ける場合，法律の導入時点ですでに規制の対象となる活動に従事している企業は規則の適用外となることを規定する条項

grand total　総合計
grant　①付与する，②付与，③補助金
grant date　付与日　[解] IFRS2 の文脈では，企業と他の当事者（従業員等）が株式に基づく報酬契約に合意した日（当該株式に基づく報酬契約に基づき，権利が付与される日）
grantee　補助金受領者
grantor　①補助金譲与者，②付与者
grant related to assets　資産に関する補助金　[解] 補助を受ける企業が固定資産を取得することを主要な条件とする政府補助金
grant related to income　収益に関する補助金　[解] 資産に関する補助金以外の政府補助金
graph　グラフ
graphic　図表による
gratuity　チップ，謝礼
greater use of estimation methods　より多くの見積りの方法の使用　[解] IAS34 の文脈では，期中財務報告書作成にあたっては，例えば税金費用や年金費用等の処理に代表されるように，年次財務報告書に比べ，より多くの見積りの方法が用いられる
gross　①全体的な，総額の，②ひどい，甚だしい
gross average method　総平均法
gross capital employed　総使用資本　[解] 総資産の金額を指す
gross carrying amount　総額での帳簿価額（減価償却累計額や損失評価引当金などの控除前の）
gross cash payments　総支出
gross cash receipts　総収入
gross income　総所得，総収入
gross investment in lease　（総）リース投資未回収額
gross loss　売上総損失
gross margin (GM)　①売上総利益，粗利，②売上総利益率，粗利率
gross margin percentage　売上総利益率

gross margin ratio　売上総利益率
gross negligence　重過失
gross profit　売上総利益，粗利
gross profit margin [ratio]　売上総利益率
gross profit method　売価還元法
gross profit percentage　売上総利益率
gross profits tax　売上総利益に対する課税
gross purchases　総仕入高
gross receipts　総収入
gross receipts tax　総収入に対する課税，総収入税
gross sales [turnover]　総売上高
gross up　グロス・アップ　[解]純額から総額を逆算すること
gross-up calculation　グロスアップ計算　[解]海外駐在員（expatriate）などについて，現地で発生する個人所得税や社会保険料などを企業が負担する場合の総支給額の計算
gross-up clause　グロスアップ条項　[解]源泉税などが課される場合に，（支払側が必要なグロスアップを行って）受取側の手取額を保証する条項
grounds　理由，根拠　[解]通常複数形
group　企業集団，グループ　[解]IFRS10の文脈では，親会社及びそのすべての子会社を指す
group accounting manual　グループ会計マニュアル
group accounting policy　グループ会計ポリシー
group company　グループ会社
group controller　グループ・コントローラー　[解]一般にグループ全体の経理を統括する役職
group formation　グループ化，企業集団の形成
grouping　グルーピング
group management　グループ経営
group of assets　資産グループ
group organisation chart　資本関係図，出資関係図　[米]group organization chart
group relief　グループ・リリーフ制度　[解]一定の保有比率を満たすグループ企業内で，税務上の損益を振替・相殺するという英国等の制度で，日本の連結納税制度に類似する
group reporting package　連結パッケージ
group service centre　グループ会社に対する役務提供部門　[米]group service center
group's share　グループの持分
group taxation (regime)　グループ（法人）税制
group transaction　グループ取引
group treatment　グループ税制　[解]連結納税制度，グループ法人税制，グループ・リリーフ等の複数の企業を課税上一体とみなす税制の総称
growth　成長
growth opportunity　成長機会
growth rate　成長率
GSP　▶generalised system of preferences　[米]generalized system of preferences
GST　▶Goods and Services Tax
guarantee　①保証する，②保証　[用]to issue a guarantee to a bank（銀行に対して保証を付ける）
guaranteed benefit　保証給付
guaranteed element　保証要素
guarantee deposits　（差入）保証金
guarantee deposits received　預り保証金
guaranteed residual value　保証残存価値
guarantee fee　保証料
guarantor　保証人
guaranty　①保証，②保証書
guidance　ガイダンス，手引
guideline　ガイドライン，指針

H

habitually　常習的に
half year　半期
half year budget　半期予算
half-yearly　半期の
handle　処理する，対応する
handling　①取扱い，②荷扱い，出荷
handling cost [expense]　出荷関連費用，荷役費用
hard close　ハード・クローズ　[解] 決算の1〜数か月前に決算手続（及びその監査）を行い，決算早期化の際の本決算時の負担を軽減する方法
hard copy　ハード・コピー
hard numbers　具体的な数値
hard-to-value intangibles (HTVI)　評価困難な無形資産
hardware　ハードウェア
harmonisation　調和　[米] harmonization
harmonise　調和させる　[米] harmonize
haulage　運送，運搬
headcount　人数，員数
heading　表題，見出し
heading and subtotal　見出し及び小計　[解] 期中財務報告書（interim financial report）に含まれる要約財務諸表（condensed financial statements）においては，少なくとも直近の年次財務諸表中に掲記された各見出し及び小計を含んでいる必要がある
head lease　ヘッド・リース　[解] サブリース（sub-lease）に対する用語で，当初の貸手と借手との間のリース
head office　本店，本社
head office account　本店勘定，本社勘定
head office expense　本社費
head office expense allocation　本社費の配賦
head office overhead　本社費
headquarters (HQ)　本店，本社，本部
heads of agreement (HOA)　基本合意書
heads of terms　基本合意書
health care　ヘルスケア
health insurance　健康保険
hearing　聴聞会
heating and lighting cost [expense]　光熱費
heavy additional tax　重加算税
heavy penalty tax　重加算税
hedge　ヘッジ
hedge accounting　ヘッジ会計
hedge counterparty　ヘッジ取引の相手方
hedge fund investment　ヘッジファンド投資
hedged item　ヘッジ対象　[解] 公正価値またはキャッシュ・フローの変動リスクがあり，ヘッジ手段によりヘッジされる対象
hedge effectiveness　ヘッジの有効性　[解] ヘッジ対象の公正価値またはキャッシュ・フローの変動がヘッジ手段により相殺されている割合
hedge effectiveness requirements　ヘッジの有効性に関する要件
hedge ineffectiveness　ヘッジの非有効性
hedge of a net investment in a foreign operation　在外営業活動体に対する純投資のヘッジ
hedge of forecast transactions　予定取引のヘッジ
hedge ratio　ヘッジ比率
hedging instrument　ヘッジ手段　[解] ヘッジ対象の公正価値またはキャッシュ・フローの変動リスクをヘッジするものとして指定されたデリバティブ等の金融商品など　[用] financial instruments designated as hedging instruments（ヘッジ手段に指定された金融商品）
hedging relationship　ヘッジ関係　[解] IFRS9の文脈では，ヘッジ関係は一定の要件を満たす場合ヘッジ会計の対象となるが，ヘッジ関係には大きく分けて，(1) 公正価値ヘッジ，(2) キャッシュ・フロー・ヘッジ，(3) 在外営業活動体に対する純投資のヘッジの3種類がある
hedging reserve　ヘッジ・リザーブ，ヘッジ損益　[解] その他の資本の構成要素
hedging strategy　ヘッジ戦略

hedging transaction	ヘッジ取引
held for disposal	処分目的保有の
held for distribution	分配目的保有の
held for distribution to owners	所有者への分配目的保有の 用 a non-current asset that is classified as held for distribution to owners（所有者への分配目的保有の非流動資産）
held for rental to others	賃貸目的保有の
held for sale	売却目的保有の 解 非流動資産（または処分グループ）の帳簿価額が，継続的使用よりも主として売却取引により回収される場合には，売却保有目的に分類される
held for trading	売買目的保有の，トレーディング目的保有の 解 IFRS9の文脈では，主として短期間に売却（または買戻し）を行う目的で取得（または発生した）金融資産（または金融負債）を指す
held-to-maturity	満期保有目的の
held-to-maturity bond	満期保有目的の債券
held-to-maturity investments (HTM)	満期保有目的投資（旧）
held-to-maturity securities	満期保有目的証券
hereafter	今後
hidden	隠れた
hidden reserves	含み益
hierarchical	階層的な
hierarchy	ヒエラルキー，階層
highest and best use	最有効使用，最有効利用 解 IFRS13の文脈では，市場参加者による資産（非金融資産）の使用のうち，その価値を最大化するものを指す
high-level	概括的な，大局的な，ハイレベルの
high-level analysis	大局的視点からの分析
highlight	強調する
highly probable	可能性が非常に高い
highly probable forecast transaction	実行可能性が非常に高い予定取引
high yield debt	ハイ・イールド債
historical	過去の
historical cost	取得原価 解 資産であれば，取得したときに支払った金額を指す
historical cost accounting	取得原価主義会計
historical cost basis	取得原価ベース
historical cost principle	取得原価基準
historical exchange rate	取得時レート，発生時レート
historical summary	過去の推移の要約
historical tax liabilities	過去の租税債務
historical volatility	ヒストリカル・ボラティリティ，実績ボラティリティ
history	履歴，過去の事象
history of tax audits	税務調査履歴 解 税務デュー・デリジェンスの関係では，買収対象会社が過去に受けた税務調査についての情報を指す。調査終了年度については，指摘事項とその顛末を把握し，現状の税務リスクの判断の参考とする
HMRC	▶HM Revenue and Customs
HM Revenue and Customs (HMRC)	英国歳入税関庁（英国の税務当局）
HOA	▶heads of agreement
hold	保有する
holdback clause	ホールドバック条項 解 買収案件などで，（税務を含む）補償条項（indeminity）が適用される場合に備えて，購入代金の一部を一定期間買主が留保（または中立な第三者が保管）するという条項
HoldCo	holding company（持株会社）の略
holder	保有者
holder of a vested option	確定したオプションの保有者
hold harmless	免責
hold harmless letter	ホールドハームレス・レター，同意書 解 デュー・デリジェンス業務等にあたって，公認会計士等が自らの報告書を第三者に開示する場合に，その第三者から入手する確認書で，報告書や業務の内容及び性質，また公認会計士等の責任を明確化するもの
holding	保有（株式などの）
holding company	持株会社
holding cost	①保有費用，②在庫保有費用
holding period	保有期間（株式などの）
holding ratio	保有比率（株式などの）
holistic	全体的な
home company	出向元法人 解 出向先法

人（host company）に対する用語
home leave　ホーム・リーブ　[解]海外駐在員が，休暇のために帰国すること
honour　（債務を）引き受けて支払う　[米] honor
horizontal integration　水平統合　[解]バリューチェーン上の特定の工程を担う複数の企業がM&A等を通じて一体化すること
horizontal-type corporate division　分割型分割
host company　出向先法人　[解]出向元法人（home company）に対する用語
host contract　本体契約，主契約　[解]例えば，組込デリバティブの本体契約を指す
host financial instrument　本体部分の金融商品（組込デリバティブについて）
hostile　敵対的な
hostile takeover　敵対的買収
hotline　内部通報（制度）
hourly　1時間単位の
hourly rate　時間単価（報酬，賃金等の）
household　家計，世帯
housing　①住宅，②住宅供給
housing allowance　住宅手当
HQ　▶headquarters
HR　▶human resources
HS code　HSコード　[解]関税について，物品（輸入貨物）の帰属を示すコード
HTM　▶held-to-maturity investments
HTVI　▶hard-to-value intangibles
human resources department [division]　人事部門
hurdle　障害
hurdle rate　ハードル・レート
hybrid contract　混合契約
hybrid derivative　ハイブリッド・デリバティブ　[解]デリバティブのうち，例えばスワプション（スワップ＋オプション）など，複数のデリバティブの要素をもつもの
hybrid entity　ハイブリッド事業体　[解]一方の国と他方の国で課税上の取扱いが異なる事業体
hybrid financing　ハイブリッド・ファイナンス
hybrid instrument　ハイブリッド金融商品

hybrid mismatch arrangement　ハイブリッド・ミスマッチ方式　[解]ハイブリッド事業体（hybrid entity）を利用して税負担の軽減を図る仕組み
hybrid securities　ハイブリッド証券　[解]株式（資本）と債券（負債）の両方の性質を持つ証券
hyperinflation　ハイパーインフレーション，超インフレ
hyperinflationary　ハイパーインフレーションの
hypothesis　仮説，仮定
hypothetical　仮定上の
hypothetical derivative　仮想デリバティブ
hypothetical tax　みなし税金，ハイポ・タックス　[解]タックス・イコライゼーション（tax equalisation）の関係では，海外駐在員が仮に派遣元の国に残ったとすれば支払ったであろう税額を指す

I

IA ▶initial allowance
IAS ▶International Accounting Standard
IASB ▶International Accounting Standards Board
IASC ▶International Accounting Standards Committee
IBAN (International Bank Account Number) code　IBANコード
IC ▶invested capital
ICOFR ▶internal control over financial reporting
I/D ▶import declaration
identical　同一の
identically　同様に
identifiability　識別可能性
identifiability criteria　識別可能性要件（無形資産についての）
identifiable　識別可能な　[解]無形資産が識別可能とは，その無形資産が(1)企業から分離可能（個別に売却等可能）な場合，(2)契約またはその他の法的な権利から生じている場合，をいう
identifiable asset　識別可能資産
identifiable intangible asset　識別可能な無形資産　[解]IFRS3の文脈では，企業結合の結果取得される無形資産のうち，資産として認識できるものを指し，「のれん」とは区別される
identifiable liability　識別可能負債
identifiable net assets　識別可能な純資産
identification　①識別，②特定
identification of the acquirer　取得企業の識別
identify　①識別する，②特定する
idiosyncratic　特異な
idle　遊休の
idle asset　遊休資産
IFRIC ▶International Financial Reporting Interpretations Committee

IFRS ▶International Financial Reporting Standard
IFRS Advisory Council　IFRS諮問会議
IFRS Foundation　IFRS財団
IFRS Interpretations Committee　IFRS解釈指針委員会
IFRSs ▶International Financial Reporting Standards　[解]IFRSsという略語は，国際財務報告基準（IFRS）に，国際会計基準（IAS）やその他の解釈指針も合わせた関連基準の総称として使われる場合もある
IGS ▶intra-group service
IHQ ▶international headquarters
illegal　違法な
illegal act　違法行為
illegal activity　違法行為
illegal gratuity　違法な謝礼
illiquid　流動性の低い，非流動的な
illiquid asset　流動性の低い資産
illiquidity　非流動性
illiquidity discount　非流動性ディスカウント（株式評価などの）　[解]企業買収の局面で，買収対象会社が非上場会社である場合に行われる割引であり，一般的にはDCF法等の評価結果に一定率を乗じることで計算される
illustrate　説明する
illustration　説明
illustrative　説明に役立つ
illustrative example　設例
IM ▶information memorandum
IMF ▶International Monetary Fund
immaterial　重要性のない
immateriality　重要性がないこと
immeasurable　測定不可能な
immediate　即時の
immediately　すぐに，即時に
immediate parent company　直接の親会社　[解]究極の親会社（ultimate parent company）に対する用語
immediate recognition　即時認識
immediate sale　即時売却
immediate tax consequence　即時の税務上の影響
immovable property　不動産

immovable property company　不動産保有法人
impact　影響
impair　減損させる
impairment　減損
impairment gain　減損利得
impairment gain or loss　減損利得または減損損失　[解]IFRS9の文脈では、予想信用損失の金額の修正に伴って純資産に認識されるもの
impairment loss　減損損失　[用] to recognise an impairment loss（減損損失を認識する）
impairment loss on contract assets arising from contracts with customers　顧客との契約から生じた契約資産に係る減損損失
impairment loss on financial assets　金融資産に係る減損損失
impairment loss on remeasurement of disposal group　処分グループの再測定による減損損失
impairment loss on trade receivables　営業債権に係る減損損失
impairment of assets　資産の減損
impairment test (ing)　減損テスト
implement　実行する
implementation　実行
implementation guidance　適用ガイダンス
implication　意味合い、含意
implicit　暗黙の
implicitly　暗示的に
implied value　推定価値
implied volatility　インプライド・ボラティリティ
imply　暗示する
import　①輸入する、②輸入
importance　重要性
important　重要な
import cargo　輸入貨物
import charges　輸入諸掛
import declaration (I/D)　①輸入申告書、②輸入許可通知書　[解]製品の輸入にあたっては、品目・数量・価格・関税・消費税等を記載した「輸入申告書」を税関に提出する。税関がその輸入を許可し、許可印を押すと、それが「輸入許可通知書」となる
import duty　輸入関税
importer　輸入企業
import quota (IQ)　輸入割当て　[解]輸入数量等が制限される貨物について、輸入者等に割り当てられた数量等
impose　課す（税金などを）
imposition　賦課（税金などの）
imposition of tax　課税
imposition of withholding tax　源泉税の課税　[用]imposition of withholding tax at the rate of X%（X%での源泉税の課税）
impost　①税、②（特に）関税、輸入税
impracticability　実行不可能性
impracticable　①実行不可能な、②実務上不可能な　[解]②IAS1の文脈では、ある要求事項について、あらゆる合理的な努力を行ったとしても、それを適用することができないという状況を指す
impractical　①実行不可能な、②実務的でない
imprecise　不正確な
imprest system　定額資金前渡制度
improbable　ありそうもない【形】
improper　不適切な
improper asset valuation　不適切な資産評価
improper disclosure　不適切な開示
improve　改善する
improvement　改善、改良
imputation　①帰属（税金などの）、②転嫁
imputation credit　インピュテーション・クレジット　[解]インピュテーション・システムにおける、個人が受け取った配当金に対応する法人税額相当額で、配当を受領した個人の所得税額から控除できる
imputation system　インピュテーション・システム　[解]法人から株主への配当に係る二重課税を調整する方法で、個人が受け取った配当金に対応する（法人の）法人税額を差し引いて個人の所得税額を計算する方式
impute　帰属させる（税金などを）
imputed income　帰属所得、帰属収入
imputed interest　帰属利子　[解]無利息または低利融資等について、実際には支払われていないが、実質的に支払われている

とみなされる利子
in accordance with 　〜に従って
inactive 　①不活発な，②休眠の
inadequacy 　不十分，不足
inadequate 　不十分な
in advance 　事前に
inappropriate 　不適切な
in arrears 　滞納して
inbound 　国内に向けての
inbound transaction 　インバウンド取引　[解] 海外企業が日本に進出する形態の取引で，アウトバウンド取引（outbound transaction）に対する用語
incentive 　①報奨金，②誘因
incentive compensation 　インセンティブ型報酬
incentive payment 　インセンティブ支払い，奨励給支給
incentive stock option (ISO) 　税制適格ストック・オプション（米国）　[解] 米国において，課税の繰延べ等の取扱いを受けられるストック・オプション
inception 　開始
inception date 　開始日　[解] IFRS16の文脈では，リースの契約日を指す
inception of lease 　リースの開始
incidence 　発生
incident 　事件，出来事
incidental (to) 　付随的な，（〜に）付随する【形】
incidental cost [expense] 　付随費用
include 　含む
inclusion 　含めること
inclusive 　含んだ
income 　①（広義の）収益，②所得　[解] ①会計期間における資産の増加または負債の減少という形での経済的便益の増加で，持分参加者からの出資以外のもの
income approach 　インカム・アプローチ（評価手法［技法］としての），収益還元法　[解] 一般的な資産の評価において，資産（買収対象会社）が将来生み出すであろう収益の価値を基準とするアプローチで，例えばDCF法がこれに該当する。また，IFRS13の文脈では，公正価値測定に際して，将来発生するキャッシュ・フロー（または収益及び費用）を割り引くことで，現在価値を算出するアプローチを指す
income-based approach 　インカム・アプローチ
income-based enterprise [business] tax 　事業税所得割
income from a structured entity 　組成された企業からの収益
income from operations 　営業利益
income from performance of services 　役務提供対価，役務提供による所得
income inclusion 　①課税所得に含まれること，②合算課税
income or loss for the year 　単年度損益　[解] 事業税付加価値割の構成要素
income property 　収益性資産
income-related grant 　収益に関する補助金
income shifting 　所得移転
income smoothing 　利益の平準化
income splitting 　所得分割，所得移転
income statement 　損益計算書
income statement item 　損益計算書項目
income subject to tax 　課税所得
income tax 　法人所得税　[解] IAS12の文脈では，所得を課税標準として課される国内外のすべての税金。課税標準が所得ではない税金（例えば，日本の住民税均等割等）はIFRSにおける法人所得税には該当しない
Income Tax Act 　所得税法
income tax allocation 　税金の期間配分
income tax basis 　課税標準，課税所得
income tax credit 　所得税額控除
income taxes paid 　法人税等の支払額　[解] キャッシュ・フロー計算書などでよく使われる表現
income taxes payable 　未払法人税等，未払法人所得税
income taxes receivable [refundable] 　未収還付法人税等，未収法人所得税
income taxes refund 　法人税等の還付額
income tax expense 　税金費用，法人所得税（費用）
income tax withheld 　預り源泉所得税
incompatible 　両立しない，矛盾した
incompatible duties 　両立しない職務，兼務

できない職務
incomplete　不完全な
in compliance with　～に従って
in conformity with　～に従って
inconsequential　重要性のない【形】
inconsistency　不整合
inconsistent　整合しない【形】
incorporate　①組み入れる（レポートなどに），②株式会社化する，設立する
incorporation　会社設立，法人格付与
incorrect　不正確な
incorrectly　不正確に，誤って
Incoterms　インコタームズ　[解]貿易取引に係る標準的な取引条件
increase　①増加する，②増加
increase in　～の増加（額）　[用]increase in inventories（棚卸資産の増加額）
increase in capital　増資
increasingly　ますます
increasing rate preference share　配当逓増優先株式
increment　増分
incremental　増分の
incremental analysis　増分分析
incremental borrowing rate　追加借入利率
incremental cash flow　増分キャッシュ・フロー
incremental cost　増分コスト
incremental costs of obtaining a contract　契約獲得の増分コスト
incremental direct costs　追加直接費用（リースなどの）
incur　①発生させる，②負担させる（費用などを）
incurred　発生した（費用などが）
incurred but not reported　既発生未報告の
incurred loss model　発生損失モデル　[解]IFRS9の予想信用損失（ECL）に対する（IAS39の）用語
incurrence　①発生，②負担（費用や負債の）
indebted　負債があって【形】
indebtedness　負債
indefinite　確定できない（耐用年数などの）【形】　[解]IAS38の文脈では,耐用年数が確定できない無形資産は償却されないが，減損テストを行う必要がある。ちなみにinfinite（無限の）とは区別する必要がある
indefinite useful life　不確定の耐用年数
indemnification　賠償，補償
indemnification asset　補償資産　[解]IFRS3の文脈では，企業結合において，被取得企業が取得企業に対して行う契約上の補償（例えば，資産や負債の偶発性に係る補償）について，取得企業側が資産として認識したものを指す
indemnified party　賠償を受ける側の当事者
indemnify　賠償する
indemnifying party　賠償を行う側の当事者
indemnity　①賠償，補償，②賠償金，補償金
indemnity clause　補償条項
indenture　契約書，証書
independence　独立性
independent　独立した
independent agent　独立代理人　[解]本人（企業）から独立して業務を行う一定の代理人で，従属代理人（dependent agent）に対する用語。基本的に当該企業のPE（恒久的施設）には該当しない。OECDモデル租税条約では，agent of an independent statusという呼び方をしている
independent auditor　独立監査人
independent auditor's report　独立監査人の監査報告書
independent check　独立の立場からのチェック
independent committee　第三者委員会
independent contractor　独立の請負業者
independent enterprise　独立企業
independent officer　独立役員
indeterminable　確定できない【形】
indeterminate　不確定の
index　指数，指標
indexation　指数化
index-linked　指数にリンクした
index-linked adjustment　指数連動の調整
indicate　示す
indication　兆候（減損などの）
indication of impairment　減損の兆候
indicative　兆候がある，示して（～ということを）【形】

indicative bid	法的拘束力のない入札（買収案件などの）
indicative offer	法的拘束力のない意向表明（買収案件などの）
indicator	示すもの，指標
indices	index の複数形
indirect	間接的な
indirect charge	間接費
indirect-charge method	間接配賦方式
indirect cost	間接費
indirect fallout	間接的な副産物
indirect financing	間接金融
indirect foreign tax credit	間接外国税額控除 [解]一般には，外国税額控除の一形態で，一定の要件を満たす外国子会社等の所得に課された外国税額のうち，受け取った配当等に対応する部分の金額につき，その法人が納付したものとみなして控除対象とするもの
indirect labour cost	間接労務費 [米] indirect labor cost
indirectly	間接的に
indirect manufacturing cost	製造間接費，間接製造費用
indirect material cost	間接材料費
indirect materials	間接原材料
indirect method	間接法 [解]IAS7 の文脈では，営業活動によるキャッシュ・フローについて，収入総額と支出総額を分けず，純損益からスタートし，非資金項目等の種々の調整を行う形で表示する方法
indirect selling cost	販売間接費
indirect shareholding	間接保有（株式の）
indirect tax	間接税
individual	①個人，②個人の，③個別の
individual asset	個別資産
individual impairment	個別の減損（営業債権などの）
individual income tax	個人所得税，所得税
individual income tax rate	個人所得税率，所得税率
individual income tax return	所得税申告書
individually	個々に，個別（的）に
individually immaterial	個別にみて重要性のない，個々には重要性のない【形】
industrial	産業の
industrial property right	工業所有権 [解]特許権・実用新案権・意匠権・商標権などの総称
industry	産業，業界
industry information	業界情報
industry practice	業界慣行
industry sector	業種
ineffective	有効でない【形】
ineffectiveness	非有効性
ineffective portion	非有効部分
inefficiency	非効率性
inefficient	非効率な
inevitable	不可避の
inevitably	不可避的に
inexpensive	安価な
inference	①推論，②推定
inferior	より下位の
infinite	無限の
inflate	①インフレーションが起こる，②水増しする
inflation	インフレーション
inflationary	インフレーションの
inflation level	インフレーションの水準
inflation rate	インフレーション率
inflow	流入
influence	影響力
influence criteria	影響力基準
in force	施行されて，効力のある
inform	通知する
informal	非公式の
informal agreement	非公式の契約
informal practices	非公式の実務
information	情報
information gathering	情報収集
information memorandum (IM)	インフォメーション・メモランダム [解]買収案件などで，売却対象企業・事業に関する情報が記載された資料
information needs	情報ニーズ
information processing	情報処理
information request	資料依頼，情報提供依頼
information return	情報申告 [解]税金計算ではなく，情報の提供を目的とする申告書
information security	情報セキュリティ

information system　情報システム
information system audit　システム監査
information technology (IT)　情報技術
informative　情報価値のある
infrastructure　インフラストラクチャー，産業基盤
infringe　侵害する（権利などを）
infringement　違反，侵害
in full　全部，全額，すべて
inhabitant　住民
inhabitant tax　住民税
inhabitant tax rate　住民税率
inhabitant tax return　住民税申告書
inherent　固有の
inherently　本質的に
inherent risk　固有リスク
inheritance　相続
inheritance tax　相続税
in-house　社内の
in-house investigation　社内調査（不正などの）
in-house lawyer　企業内弁護士
in-house specialist　社内専門家
initial　当初の，最初の
initial adoption　最初の適用
initial allowance (IA)　取得時償却　[解] 英国等の税制で，税務上の減価償却費（capital allowance）のうち，取得時に取得価額の一定割合につき，損金の額に算入されるもの
initial application　最初の適用，適用開始　[用] initial application of standards or interpretations（基準または解釈指針の適用開始）
initial cost　初期費用
initial direct cost　当初直接コスト（リースなどの）　[解] IFRS16の文脈では，リースによる増分コストのうち，リースがなければ発生しなかったであろうコストを指す
initial investment　初期投資
initial loss　当初損失　[解] 会社等の設立直後の損失を指すことが多い
initially　最初に
initial measurement　当初測定　[解] 認識時点での測定，つまり計上金額の決定を意味する

initial public offering (IPO)　新規上場
initial recognition　当初認識　[解] 財務諸表への最初の計上
initial royalty　イニシャル・ロイヤルティ
initiate　開始する
initiation　開始
initiative　イニシアティブ，主導権
in kind　現物の（金銭以外の）
in-kind contribution　現物出資
inland　①国内の，内国の，②内陸の
Inland Revenue Authority of Singapore (IRAS)　シンガポール内国歳入庁（シンガポールの税務当局）
Inland Revenue Board (IRB)　マレーシア内国歳入庁（マレーシアの税務当局）
Inland Revenue Department (IRD)　香港税務局（香港の税務当局）
in line with　～に即して，～に沿って
in non-compliance with　～を遵守せず
innovation　イノベーション，技術革新
innovation box　イノベーション・ボックス
in part　部分的に
in principle　原則として
in-process research　仕掛中の研究
in-process research and development project　仕掛中の研究開発プロジェクト　[解] 仕掛中の研究開発プロジェクトが企業結合により取得された場合で，それが無形資産の定義を満たす場合には，取得企業はそのプロジェクトを「のれん」とは区別して資産として認識する
in proportion to　～に比例して
input　①インプット，入力，②投入　[解] ①IFRS13の文脈では，公正価値測定のための入力値を指す。評価手法の適用にあたっては，適切なインプットを選択する必要があるが，関連性のある観察可能なインプット（observable inputs）の使用を最大限にし，観察不能なインプット（unobservable inputs）の使用を最小限にする必要がある
input consumption tax　仮払消費税等
input tax　インプット・タックス　[解] input VATの項を参照
input VAT　インプットVAT　[解] 仕入・費用に対する付加価値税であり，日本の仮払

消費税等に相当
inquire　質問する
inquiry　①質問，②引合い
inseparable　分離できない【形】
insert　挿入する
inside　内部，内側
inside director　社内取締役
inside information　内部情報
insider information　インサイダー情報
insider trading　インサイダー取引，内部者取引
insight　見識，洞察
insignificant　重要でない【形】
insolvency　①支払不能，②債務超過
insolvent　①支払不能の，②債務超過の
inspect　検査する
inspection　①検査，②検収（作業）
inspection cost　検査費用
inspection report　検査報告書
in stages　段階的に
install　据え付ける，設置する
installation　据付け，設置
installation fee　据付費用，設置費用
instalment　分割払い 〖米〗installment
instalment method　割賦基準 〖米〗installment method
instalment receivables　割賦売掛金，割賦債権 〖米〗installment receivables
instalment sale　割賦販売 〖米〗installment sale
instance　①例，②場合
instant　①時点，②即時の
institute　協会
Institute of internal Auditors (IIA)　内部監査人協会
institution　①協会，②機関投資家
institutional investor　機関投資家
instruct　指示する
instruction　指示，指示書
instrument　①金融商品,②器具,③法律文書
insufficient　不十分な
in support of　〜の根拠となる
insurable　保険に適した
insurance　保険
insurance asset　保険資産
insurance company　保険会社

insurance contract　保険契約
insurance expense　保険費用
insurance liability　保険負債
insurance policy　保険契約書，保険証券
insurance premium　保険料
insurance premium withheld　預り金ー保険料，預り保険料
insurance risk　保険リスク
insured benefit　保険が付された給付
insured event　保険対象事象
insurer　保険業者
intact　無傷の
intangible　無形の
intangible asset　無形資産，無形固定資産 〖解〗物理的実体のない識別可能な非貨幣性資産
intangible asset under development　開発中の無形資産
intangible asset with indefinite useful life　耐用年数を確定できない無形資産
intangible property　無形資産 〖解〗移転価格税制の関係では，無形資産は,「重要な価値を有し所得の源泉となるもの」として，例えば，(1)技術革新を要因として形成される特許権，営業秘密等，(2)従業員等が経営，営業，生産，研究開発，販売促進等の企業活動における経験等を通じて形成したノウハウ等，(3)生産工程，交渉手順及び開発，販売，資金調達等に係る取引網等，を含む
intangibles　無形資産
integral　必要不可欠な
integral part　必要不可欠な部分
integrate　統合する
integrated reporting　統合報告 〖解〗財務・非財務に係る情報が統合された，包括的な事業報告
integration　統合
integrity　誠実性，インテグリティ
integrity programme　インテグリティ・プログラム，倫理プログラム 〖米〗integrity program
intellectual property (IP)　知的財産権
intended use　意図した使用 〖用〗all costs necessary to get an asset ready for its intended use（資産を意図した使用目的

で稼動可能な状態にするために必要なすべての費用）
intent　意思，意図
intention　意図
interact　相互に作用する【動】
interaction　相互作用
interactive　相互作用する【形】
inter alia　特に
interbank market　インターバンク市場
interchange　交換する，入れ替える
interchangeable　交換可能な，入替え可能な
interchangeably　交換可能で，交互に
intercompany　①会社間の，②連結会社間の，グループ会社間の
intercompany account　グループ会社間勘定
intercompany balance　グループ内［関係会社間］債権債務
intercompany balance confirmation　グループ内［関係会社間］債権債務の確認
intercompany cost allocation　グループ内の費用付替え
intercompany dividend　グループ内［関係会社間］配当
intercompany elimination　グループ会社間勘定の相殺消去
intercompany payables　グループ内［関係会社間］債務
intercompany pricing　グループ会社間振替価格の決定
intercompany profit　グループ会社間取引による利益
intercompany receivables　グループ内［関係会社間］債権
intercompany receivables and payables　グループ内［関係会社間］債権債務
intercompany receivables and payables schedule　グループ内［関係会社間］債権債務管理表
intercompany tax allocation　グループ会社間の税金配分（連結納税制度に基づく）
intercompany transaction　グループ内［関係会社間］取引
interdepartmental　部門間の
interdependence　相互依存
interdependency　相互依存性

interdependent　相互依存する【形】
interest　①利息，金利，②持分，③利子税
interest-bearing　有利子の
interest-bearing debt [liability]　有利子負債
interest cost　利息費用，金利コスト　解 退職給付会計の文脈では，確定給付債務の現在価値の増加のうち金利部分
interest cost capitalised　資産化した金利コスト　米 interest cost capitalized
interest cost incurred　発生した金利コスト
interest coverage ratio　インタレスト・カバレッジ・レシオ　解 企業の利息支払能力を示す指標であり，以下の算式で計算される

インタレスト・カバレッジ・レシオ
$$= \frac{営業利益＋受取利息・配当金}{支払利息}$$

interest deductibility　利息の損金性
interest expense　支払利息，金利費用
interest-free loan　無利息融資
interest in　〜に対する持分
interest in a joint venture　共同支配企業に対する持分，ジョイント・ベンチャーに対する持分
interest in an associate　関連会社に対する持分
interest in an equity-accounted investee　持分法適用会社に対する持分
interest in another entity　①他の企業に対する持分，②他の企業への関与　解 ② IFRS12の文脈では，企業を他の企業の業績からのリターンの変動性にさらすような関与（契約上及び非契約上）を意味する
interest in a subsidiary　子会社に対する持分
interest income　①受取利息，金利収益，②利子所得
interest margin　利鞘（金利の）
interest on bonds　社債利息
interest on delinquent tax　利子税
interest on deposits　預金利子
interest on loans　①借入金利息，②貸付金利息
interest paid　利息の支払額　解 キャッシュ・フロー計算書などでよく使われる用語

interest payable	未払利息
interest payment	利息支払い
interest rate	利率
interest rate cap	金利キャップ取引 [解] 金利オプション取引の１つで，金利キャップの買手が売手に対してオプション料を支払うことにより，契約期間中に基準金利が上限金利（cap）を上回った場合，その差額を受け取ることができるというもの
interest rate collar	金利カラー取引 [解] 金利カラーの買いは，金利キャップの買いと金利フロアの売りの組み合わせであり，基準金利の金利低下メリットを放棄する代わりに，通常の金利キャップの買いに比べてオプション料を低く抑えることができる。金利カラーの売りはその逆
interest rate implicit in the lease	リース計算上の利子率 [解] IFRS16の文脈では，「リース料総額と無保証残存価値（unguaranteed residual value）の現在価値の合計」を「原資産の公正価値と貸手の初期直接コストの合計」と等しくするような（計算上の）利子率を指す
interest rate option	金利オプション
interest rate risk	金利リスク [解] 市場金利の変動により，金融商品の公正価値または将来キャッシュ・フローが変動するリスク
interest rate swap	金利スワップ [解] 同一の通貨で種類の異なる金利を交換する取引で，元本交換は行われず，金利のみを交換する。固定金利と変動金利との交換が一般的 [用] pay-floating (receive-fixed) interest rate swap（変動払い（固定受け）の金利スワップ）
interest receivable	未収利息
interest received	利息の受取額 [解] キャッシュ・フロー計算書などでよく使われる用語
interest tax	利子税，延滞税
interfirm	①会社間の，②会計事務所間の
interim audit	期中監査
interim audit procedures	中間（四半期）監査手続
interim billing	中間請求
interim dividend	中間配当
interim financial information	期中財務情報，中間（四半期）財務情報
interim financial report	期中財務報告書，中間（四半期）財務報告書 [解] IAS34の文脈では，期中財務報告書とは，期中報告期間に係る完全な１組の財務諸表（a complete set of financial statements）または１組の要約財務諸表（a set of condensed financial statements）のいずれかを含む財務報告書
interim financial reporting	期中財務報告，中間（四半期）財務報告
interim financial statements	期中財務諸表，中間（四半期）財務諸表
interim payment	中間納付（税金などの）
interim period	期中報告期間，中間期間 [解] IAS34の文脈では，期中報告期間とは，１事業年度全体よりも短い財務報告の期間で，半期のみならず四半期も含む
interim (tax) return	中間申告書
intermediary	①中間の，②仲介者，仲介人
intermediary company	中間会社
intermediate	中間の
intermediate holding company	中間持株会社
intermediate lessor	中間の貸手（転貸などの） [用] an intermediate lessor in a sub-lease（サブリースにおける中間の貸手）
intermediate parent	中間親会社 [解] 最終親会社（ultimate parent）に対する用語
intermediation	仲介
internal	内部の
internal audit	内部監査
internal audit department [division]	内部監査部門
internal auditor	内部監査人
internal comparable	内部比較対象（取引）
internal control	内部統制
internal control over financial reporting (ICOFR)	財務報告に係る内部統制
internal control questionnaire	内部統制質問書
internal control weakness	内部統制の不備，内部統制の脆弱性

internal credit grade	内部信用格付け
internal credit grading system	内部の信用格付けシステム
internal direct cost	社内直接費用（リースなどの）
internal discipline	内部処分
internal financing	内部金融，内部資金調達
internal funds	内部資金
internal investigation	内部調査，社内調査（不正などの）
internally	内部的に
internally developed	内部開発の
internally developed intangibles	内部生成無形資産
internally generated	自己創設の
internally generated goodwill	自己創設のれん
internally generated intangible assets	自己創設の無形資産　解 IAS38の文脈では，自己創設の無形資産については，一般的な無形資産の認識要件に加えて，追加の認識要件がある。例えば，自己創設のブランドなどは無形資産としては認識されない
internal management	内部管理　用 for internal management purposes（内部管理目的の［で］）
internal management report	内部管理報告
internal market	内部市場
internal profit	内部利益
internal rate of return (IRR)	内部収益率　解 投資の可否の判断に用いられる概念で，プロジェクトの正味現在価値（NPV）をゼロにする割引率をいう。IRRが資本コストより大きければ，基本的には投資を行うべきという判断になる
Internal Revenue Code (IRC)	内国歳入法（典）（米国の税法）
Internal Revenue Service (IRS)	内国歳入庁（米国の税務当局）
internal transaction	内部取引
internal use	内部使用，社内使用
internal-use software	内部使用のソフトウェア，自社利用のソフトウェア
international	国際的な
International Accounting Standard (IAS)	国際会計基準（書）
International Accounting Standards Board (IASB)	国際会計基準審議会
International Accounting Standards Committee (IASC)	国際会計基準委員会
international double taxation	国際的二重課税
International Financial Reporting Interpretations Committee (IFRIC)	国際財務報告解釈指針委員会
International Financial Reporting Standard (IFRS)	国際財務報告基準
International Financial Reporting Standards (IFRSs)	国際財務報告基準
international headquarters (IHQ)	国際統括本部　解 シンガポールなどで，優遇税制の対象となるステイタスの1つ
internationally	国際的に
International Monetary Fund (IMF)	国際通貨基金
International Organization of Securities Commissions (IOSCO)	証券監督者国際機構
international securities identification number (ISIN)	国際証券識別番号
international shipment	輸出
International Swaps and Derivatives Association (ISDA)	国際スワップ・デリバティブ協会
international taxation	国際課税
international tax planning	国際タックス・プランニング
internet	インターネット
internet domain (name)	インターネットのドメイン（名）　解 無形資産の例
interperiod allocation	期間配分（費用などの）
interperiod tax allocation	税金の期間配分
interpose	～を間に置く　使い方注意! 中間持株会社などについての表現
interposition	介在
interpret	解釈する
interpretation	解釈，解釈書　解 IFRSについていえば，IFRICとSICが解釈書に該当する
interpretative	解釈の，解釈上の

inter-quartile range	四分位レンジ，四分位範囲 [解]データ（例えば，移転価格税制の関係では，比較対象取引の利益率など）を小さい順に並べたときの25%目から75%目の値のレンジ（範囲）
interrelate	相互に関連する
interrelationship	相互関連性
inter-segment	セグメント間の [使い方注意!]inter-segment sales（セグメント間売上）のような使い方をする
inter-segment profit	セグメント間利益
inter-segment purchase	セグメント間購入
inter-segment revenue	セグメント間収益
inter-segment sales	セグメント間売上
in the money (ITM)	イン・ザ・マネー [解]オプション取引について，権利行使価格と基礎商品の価格との関係で見て，買方が権利行使した時に，利益が生じる状態
intra-group	グループ内[関係会社間]の
intra-group assets and liabilities	グループ内の資産及び負債
intra-group balances	グループ内[関係会社間]債権債務
intra-group elimination	連結会社間の消去
intra-group reorganisation	グループ内組織再編 [米]intra-group reorganization [解]日本の組織再編税制における適格組織再編の一形態で，100%の資本関係がある場合と50%超100%未満の資本関係がある場合のそれぞれについて，異なる適格要件が定められている
intra-group service (IGS)	企業グループ内の役務提供 [解]移転価格税制の関係では，企業グループ内の役務提供をいい，多くの場合，日本企業が海外子会社等に対して行う経営・財務・業務・事務管理等の面でのサポートを指す
intra-group transaction	グループ内[関係会社間]取引
intrinsic value	本源的価値 [解]オプションの価値のうち，時間的価値以外の部分で，現時点での権利行使価格と基礎商品価格の差額をいう
intrinsic value basis	本源的価値ベース
intrinsic value measurement	本源的価値による測定（ストック・オプションなどの）
introduce	導入する
introduction	導入
inventory	棚卸資産 [解]通常の事業過程において販売目的で保有されている製品，製造過程にある仕掛品，製造過程で消費する原材料等
inventory book	在庫管理表
inventory count	実地棚卸
inventory in transit	未着品
inventory level	在庫水準
inventory list	棚卸表
inventory management	在庫管理
inventory management system	在庫管理システム
inventory observation	棚卸立会
inventory records	在庫記録
inventory risk	在庫リスク
inventory shortage	在庫不足，品切れ
inventory shrinkage	棚卸減耗（損）
inventory tag	タグ（棚卸用）
inventory turnover	棚卸資産回転率，在庫回転率
inventory turnover period	棚卸資産回転期間，在庫回転期間
inventory valuation	在庫評価
inventory variance	棚卸差異
inventory write-down	棚卸資産の評価減
inverse	逆の
inversely	逆に
invest	投資する
invested capital (IC)	投下資本，総資本
investee	被投資企業，投資先
investigate	調査する
investigation	①調査，②税務調査
investing activity	投資活動 [解]キャッシュ・フロー計算書上の活動区分で，有形固定資産などの長期性資産への投資やその処分等の活動をいう [用]net cash generated by investing activities（投資活動によるキャッシュ・フロー（プラスの場合）），net cash used in investing activities（投資活動によるキャッシュ・フロー（マイナスの場合））
investing cash flows	投資活動によるキャッシュ・フロー
investment	投資

investment allowance　投資控除
investment bank　投資銀行
investment centre　インベストメント・センター　[米]investment center　[解]責任会計（responsibility accounting）において，利益に加えて投資額にも責任を持つ部門
investment certificate　投資証書
investment company　投資会社
investment contract　投資契約
investment credit　投資税額控除
investment deduction　投資控除
investment entity　投資企業
investment fund　投資ファンド
investment grade　投資適格
investment grade bond　投資適格債
investment grade debt securities　投資適格債
investment grade rating　投資適格の格付け
investment in a joint venture　共同支配企業に対する投資　[解]IAS28の文脈では，共同支配企業に対する投資は，原則として持分法により会計処理される
investment in an associate　関連会社に対する投資　[解]IAS28の文脈では，関連会社に対する投資は，原則として持分法により会計処理される　[用]investments in associates accounted for using equity method（持分法で会計処理している関連会社に対する投資）
investment in a subsidiary　子会社に対する投資
investment incentives　投資インセンティブ
investment income　投資収益，投資所得
investment income received　投資収益の受取額　[解]キャッシュ・フロー計算書などでよく使われる用語
investment in the lease　リース投資（未回収額）
investment loss　投資損失
investment management　投資管理
investment management fee　投資管理手数料
investment property　投資不動産　[解]IAS40の文脈では，賃貸収益や価値増加の目的で保有する不動産（土地や建物の全部または一部）を指し，自己使用目的の不動産（IAS16の対象）や販売目的の不動産（IAS2の対象）は除かれる
investment property rental income　投資不動産の賃貸収入
investment risk　投資に係るリスク
investments accounted for using the equity method　持分法で会計処理されている投資
investments and other assets　投資その他の資産
investment securities　投資有価証券
investments in subsidiaries, jointly controlled entities, and associates　子会社，共同支配企業及び関連会社に対する投資
investments other than investments accounted for using equity method　持分法で会計処理されている投資以外の投資
investment tax credit　投資税額控除
investment trust　投資信託
investment vehicle　投資ビークル　[解]acquisition vehicle の項を参照
investor　①投資企業，②投資家
investor relations (IR)　インベスター・リレーションズ，投資家向け広報活動　[解]投資家に対し，投資判断に必要な情報を提供する活動全般
investor's proportionate interest in an investee　投資企業の被投資企業に対する比例持分
investor's share of the other comprehensive income of an investee　被投資企業のその他の包括利益のうち投資企業の持分額
investor's share of the profit or loss of investee　被投資企業の純損益のうち投資企業の持分額
invoice　請求書，インボイス
invoicing company　インボイシング・カンパニー　[解]一般に，関係会社から購入した製品等を（価値を付加せずに）転売することで所得を稼得する法人を指す
involve　①関係させる，巻き込む，②伴う
involvement　関与
IOSCO　▶International Organization of Securities Commissions
IP　▶intellectual property
IPO　▶initial public offering
IQ　▶import quota

IR	▶investor relations
IRAS	▶Inland Revenue Authority of Singapore
IRB	▶Inland Revenue Board
IRC	▶Internal Revenue Code
IRD	▶Inland Revenue Department
IRR	▶internal rate of return

irregular　①不規則な，②不法な
irregularity　①不規則性，②不正
irregularly　不規則に
irrelevant　見当外れの，関連性のない
irrevocable　取り消せない【形】
irrevocable contract　取消不能契約
irrevocable election　取消不能の選択
IRS　▶Internal Revenue Service
ISDA　▶International Swaps and Derivatives Association
ISDA master agreement　ISDAマスター契約
ISIN　▶international securities identification number
ISO　▶incentive stock option
issuable　発行可能な
issuance　発行（証券などの）
issuance cost　発行費用（証券などの）
issue　①論点，問題（点），②発行（証券などの），③発行する（証券などを）
issue cost　発行費用（証券などの）
issued and outstanding　発行済
issue date　発行日（証券などの）
issued capital　資本金
issued share capital　資本金（発行済株式に対応する）
issued shares　発行済株式
issue of equity　株式の発行
issue of ordinary shares　普通株式の発行
issuer　発行者，発行会社（証券などの）
issuer's option　発行者［発行会社］の選択　用 convertible bonds settled in shares or cash at the issuer's option（発行会社の選択により株式または現金で決済される転換社債）
IT　▶information technology
IT application control　IT業務処理統制
item　項目
item by item basis　個別の項目ごと　用 on an item by item basis（個別の項目ごとに）
itemised deduction　項目別控除　米 itemized deduction
IT general control　IT全般統制
ITM　▶in the money

J

Japanese Consumption Tax (JCT)　消費税
Japanese Institute of Certified Public Accountants (JICPA)　日本公認会計士協会
Japanese withholding tax　源泉所得税（日本の）
Japan GAAP　日本基準
Japan-US tax treaty　日米租税条約
jeopardy　危険
jig　治具
JITSIC　▶Joint International Tax Shelter Information Centre
job　仕事，作業
job costing　個別原価計算
job description　職務記述書
job order　作業指示書
job order costing　個別原価計算
job rotation　人事異動，配置転換，ローテーション
joint　共同の
joint arrangement　共同支配の取決め　[解] IFRS11の文脈では，複数の当事者が共同支配を有する取決め。共同支配の取決めは，共同支配企業または共同支配事業のいずれかに分類される
joint business　共同事業
joint business reorganisation　共同事業を行うための組織再編　[米] joint business reorganization　[解] 日本の組織再編税制における適格組織再編の一形態で，50％以下の資本関係の場合の適格要件を充足するもの
joint business requirements　共同事業要件（共同事業を行うための組織再編の）
joint control　共同支配　[解] 契約上合意された支配の共有。IFRS11の文脈では，共同支配は，関連性のある活動の意思決定に際して，支配を共有する当事者の一致した合意（unanimous consent）を必要とする場合にのみ存在する

joint control over the reporting entity　報告企業に対する共同支配
Joint International Tax Shelter Information Centre (JITSIC)　国際タックスシェルター情報センター
jointly controlled　共同支配の
jointly controlled asset　共同支配の資産（旧）
jointly controlled entity　共同支配事業体（旧）
jointly controlled operation　共同支配の事業（旧）
joint operation　共同支配事業，ジョイント・オペレーション　[解] IFRS11の文脈では，共同支配の取決め（joint arrangement）のうち，共同支配の当事者が，その取決めに関する「資産に対する権利及び負債に対する義務」を有しているものを指す
joint operator　共同支配事業者　[解] IFRS11の文脈では，共同支配事業（joint operation）に対して共同支配を有する当事者を指す
joint products　連産品
joint project　共同プロジェクト
joint-stock company　株式会社（主として英国の）
joint venture　①ジョイント・ベンチャー，合弁事業，合弁会社，②共同支配企業　[解] ② IFRS11の文脈では，共同支配の取決め（joint arrangement）のうち，共同支配の当事者が，その取決めに関する「純資産に対する権利」を有しているもの
joint venturer　共同支配投資者，共同支配投資企業　[解] IFRS11の文脈では，共同支配企業（joint venture）に対して共同支配を有する当事者を指す　[用] joint venture where the entity is a joint venturer（企業が共同支配投資者となっている共同支配企業）
journal　仕訳帳
journal entry　仕訳，仕訳入力　[用] journal entries are posted to the ledger（仕訳が元帳に転記される）
journal slip　仕訳伝票
judge　判断する
judgement　①判断，②判決　[米] judgment

judgemental 判断の，判断の要素が含まれる ㊨judgmental
judicial 司法の，裁判の
judicial double taxation 法的二重課税 [解] 1つの所得に対して，1社の納税者に2か国（例えば，源泉地国と居住地国）が課税すること。外国税額控除により解消が図られる
judicially 司法上，裁判により
judicial precedent 判例
junior ①下位の，劣後する【形】，②年少の
junior debt 劣後債務
junk 屑，がらくた
junk bond ジャンク債
jurisdiction 管轄，管轄区
justifiable 正当化可能な
justification 正当化
justify 正当化する
just-in-time ジャスト・イン・タイム
JV ▶joint venture

K

Kabushiki Kaisha (KK) 株式会社
keepwell agreement キープウェル契約 [解]保証類似行為の1つ。子会社等の外部借入等に関連して，親会社等がその子会社等を適切に指導，監督し，存続させる旨を約すること
keepwell letter キープウェル・レター，経営指導念書 [解]keepwell agreement の項を参照
key 主要な，重要な
key assumption 主要な仮定
key competency キー・コンピテンシー，主要能力
key employee 主要な従業員
key factor for success (KFS) 主要な成功要因
key industry 主要な産業
key management personnel 経営幹部，主要なマネジメント（経営者）
key management personnel compensation 経営幹部の報酬
key money 権利金
key performance indicator (KPI) 主要な業績指標 [解]業績管理のための指標のうち，特に重要なもの
key success factor (KSF) 主要な成功要因
KFS ▶key factor for success
kickback キックバック
kind 種類
kiting 空手形の振出し
KK ▶Kabushiki Kaisha
know-how ノウハウ
knowledge 知識
knowledgeable 知識のある
KPI ▶key performance indicator
KSF ▶key success factor

L

labour　労働，労働力　[米] labor
labour cost　①労務費，②報酬給与額　[米] labor cost　[解]②事業税付加価値割の構成要素
labour hour　作業時間，労務時間　[米] labor hour
labour insurance　労働保険　[米] labor insurance
lack of evidence　証拠不十分
land　①土地，②陸揚げする
land and buildings　土地及び建物
landed cost　①陸揚費込み原価，②陸揚費
land improvements　土地改良（費）
landing　荷揚げ
landing charge　荷揚費用
L&R　▶loans and receivables
lapping　ラッピング　[解]売掛金の入金等の横領を隠蔽する不正
lapping scheme　ラッピング・スキーム（不正の一形態）
lapse　①失効（契約などの），②経過（時の）
larceny　窃盗
large corporation　大法人，大企業
last-in, first-out (LIFO)　後入先出法　[解]原価算定方式の１つで，後に入庫したものから順に出庫されるという仮定に基づく方式。IFRS では後入先出法の使用は認められていない
last purchase price method　最終仕入原価法
late　遅れた【形】
late charge　延滞料金
late filing　期限後申告
late filing charge [penalty]　期限後申告に対するペナルティ（加算税，延滞税）
late payment　期限後納付
late payment charge [penalty]　期限後納付に対するペナルティ（加算税，延滞税）
latest　最新の，最近の
latest information　最新情報
latitude　①自由度，裁量，②緯度
latter　①（時間的に）後の，後半の，②後者（the latter で）
law　法，法律
laws and ordinances　法令
lawsuit　訴訟
lawyer　弁護士
lawyer's letter　弁護士のレター
layer　層
layer of management　管理階層
layoff　レイオフ，一時解雇
LBO　▶leveraged buyout
L/C　▶letter of credit
LDD　▶legal due diligence
leakage　①漏れ，②キャッシュ・フローの流出
learning curve　学習曲線
lease　①リース，②賃貸借　[解]① IFRS16 の文脈では，資産（原資産）を使用する権利を，対価との交換により，一定期間にわたって移転する契約（またはそのような契約の一部）
lease agreement [contract]　①リース契約，②賃貸借契約
lease asset　リース資産
leaseback　リースバック
lease classification　リースの分類
lease commencement　リースの開始
lease component　リース構成要素　[解] IFRS16 の文脈では，リース契約に含まれるリースとしての構成要素であり，非リース構成要素（non-lease component）に対する用語
leased asset　リース資産
lease deposit　敷金
leased plant and equipment　リースしている工場及び設備
leased property　リース物件
lease expense　リース費用
leasehold　①借地（権），②賃借の
leasehold improvements　リース物件改良費，賃貸物件改良設備
lease incentive　リース・インセンティブ　[解] 一般にリースの借手に与えられるインセンティブで，例えば，初期リース料の免除や移転費用の負担など

lease incentive cost	リース・インセンティブ・コスト
lease liability	リース負債 [解] リース料の支払義務
lease modification	リース契約の変更，リースの条件変更
lease obligation	リース債務
lease of a low value item	少額資産のリース
lease payables	リース債務［未払金］，未払リース料
lease payment (s)	リース料（支払い）
lease receivables	リース債権［未収入金］，未収リース料
lease renewal option	リース更新選択権［オプション］
lease term	リース期間 [解] IFRS16の文脈では，「リース開始日から起算した解約不能期間＋延長オプション期間（借手が延長オプションを行使することが合理的に確実な場合）＋解約オプション期間（借手が解約オプションを行使しないことが合理的に確実な場合）」
lease [leasing] transaction	リース取引
leave	①休暇，②去る，③残す
leaver	退職者
ledger	元帳
ledger account	元帳科目
legal	①法的な，②合法な，適法な
legal acquiree	法的な被取得企業
legal acquirer	法的な取得企業
legal action	訴訟
legal adviser [advisor]	法務アドバイザー，顧問弁護士
Legal Affairs Bureau	法務局
legal affairs department [division]	法務部門
legal capital reserve	資本準備金
legal cost	法務費用
legal counsel	法律顧問，顧問弁護士
legal department [division]	法務部門
legal due diligence (LDD)	法務デュー・デリジェンス [解] 買収対象会社に対する法的な観点からの調査であり，予定されている取引の障害となりうる法律上の問題点を検出するほか，買収価格のベースとなる企業評価や今後の事業計画に影響のある項目をピックアップするもの
legal entity	法的事業体，法的実体
legal fee	法務費用
legal form	法的形式，法的形態 [解] 経済的実質（economic substance）に対する用語 [用] legal form of a transaction（取引の法的形式）
legal form of a lease	リースとしての法的形式 [用] an arrangement that is not in the legal form of a lease（リースとしての法的形式をとらない契約）
legal form of an entity	企業の法的形態
legal jurisdiction	法的な管轄
legal life	法的有効期限
legally	法的に
legally enforceable right	法律上強制力のある権利
legal matter	法的事項
legal obligation	法的債務 [解] 契約や法律に基づく債務
legal opinion	法律意見（書）
legal proceedings	法的手続，訴訟手続
legal proceedings contingent liability	訴訟に係る偶発負債
legal proceedings provision	訴訟引当金
legal requirement	法的要件
legal reserve	法定準備金
legal restrictions	法律上の制限
legal retained earnings	利益準備金
legal title	法的所有権
legal welfare cost	法定福利費
legislation	法律，立法
legislative	法律の，立法上の
legislative requirement	法的要件
lend	貸す
lender	貸手（資金の）
lending	貸出，融資
length of service	勤務期間，勤続期間
leniency	①寛容，②懲罰の減免
leniency programme	リーニエンシー・プログラム，課徴金減免制度 [米] leniency program
less	①より小さい【形】，②〜をマイナスした【前】 [使い方注意] ② A less B で，「AからBをマイナスしたもの」という意味になる
lessee	リースの借手

lessee's incremental borrowing rate　借手の追加借入利率　[解] リースの借手が追加的に借入を行う際に適用されるべき利率

lessor　リースの貸手

less than　〜未満　[解] less than はその値を含まない。例えば、less than 50%は「50%未満」で、50%を含まない。「50%以下」なら、50% or less といういい方をする

letter-box company　ペーパー・カンパニー

letter of appointment　任命書

letter of awareness　覚書、レター・オブ・アウェアネス　[解] 保証類似行為の1つで、親会社等が（対象となる）子会社等の借入を認識していること等を示すもの

letter of comfort　念書、レター・オブ・コンフォート　[解] 保証類似行為の1つで、親会社等が（対象となる）子会社等を適切に指導、監督し、存続させる旨を約すること

letter of confirmation　確認書、確認状

letter of consent　同意書

letter of credit (L/C)　（銀行）信用状　[解] 銀行が指定期間及び金額まで、顧客の手形支払を保証する証書。貿易で使用される

letter of engagement　業務委託契約書、委任契約書

letter of intent (LOI)　基本合意書　[解] 企業買収などの特定の案件に関連して、買収条件等の基本的な内容につき、売手と買手が合意した段階で取り交わされる書面。法的拘束力は持たないことが多い

letter ruling　レター・ルーリング、文書回答（税務当局による）

level 1 inputs　レベル1のインプット　[解] IFRS13の文脈では、測定日において企業がアクセス可能な、同一の資産または負債に関する活発な市場における（調整なしの）相場価格

level 2 inputs　レベル2のインプット　[解] IFRS13の文脈では、レベル1に含まれる相場価格以外の、直接または間接的に観察可能な、資産または負債に関するインプット（例えば、活発な市場における類似の資産の相場価格）

level 3 inputs　レベル3のインプット　[解] IFRS13の文脈では、資産または負債に関する観察不能なインプット（例えば、企業自身のデータを用いた見積り）

level payment　均等払い

leverage　レバレッジ　[解] 資本構成の決定にあたり、負債（他人資本）を使用することで、自己資本の利益率を相対的に高めること

leveraged buyout (LBO)　レバレッジド・バイアウト　[解] 企業買収の一形態で、買収対象会社の資産を資金調達の際の担保とし、買収後に被買収会社の資産により借入等を返済するもの

leveraged lease　レバレッジド・リース　[解] リースの一形式で、リース会社が多額の借入金を行ってリース物件を購入し、その物件をリースするというもの

leverage effect　レバレッジ効果

leverage ratio　レバレッジ比率　[解] 総資本に対する負債の比率など、負債と自己資本のバランスを示す指標全般を指す用語

leveraging　レバレッジ

levered beta　レバード・ベータ　[解] 負債がある場合のβ（ベータ）で、アンレバード・ベータ (unlevered beta) に対する用語

levy　①徴収する、課す（税金などを）、②徴収、徴税、賦課金

liabilities and equity　負債及び資本

liabilities assumed　引き受けた負債　[解] IFRS3の文脈では、取得企業が引き受ける被取得企業の負債

liabilities held for sale　売却目的で保有する負債

liability　負債

liability cap　補償上限額、責任限度額

liability component　負債部分（金融商品などの）

liability for long-service leave　長期勤続休暇に係る債務

liability for social security contributions　社会保険拠出に係る債務

liable (for)　（〜に対して）責任のある

LIBOR　▶London Inter-Bank Offered Rate

licence　ライセンス　[米] license

licence fee　ライセンス・フィー、ライセンス

報酬　⦅米⦆license fee
licence fee income　ライセンス報酬収益　⦅米⦆license fee income
licence-in　他社から受けるライセンス供与　⦅米⦆license-in
licence-out　他社へのライセンス供与　⦅米⦆license-out
license　ライセンスする
licensee　ライセンシー　⦅解⦆ライセンス契約において，ライセンスを付与される側
licensing　ライセンス（すること），ライセンス供与
licensing agreement　ライセンス契約
licensor　ライセンサー　⦅解⦆ライセンス契約において，ライセンスを付与する側
lien　先取特権　⦅解⦆債務者の財産について，他の債権者に先立って，優先的に自己の債権の弁済を受ける権利
lifecycle　ライフサイクル
life insurance　生命保険
lifetime ECLs　▶lifetime expected credit losses
lifetime expected credit losses (lifetime ECLs)　全期間の予想信用損失
LIFO　▶last-in, first-out
like　同様の，類似の
like items　同様の項目，類似の項目　⦅用⦆to combine like items of assets of the parent with those of its subsidiaries（親会社と子会社の資産について，同様の項目を統合する）
like-kind exchange　同種交換，同種資産の交換
like-kind property　同種資産
likelihood　可能性，発生可能性
likely　ありそうな【形】
like transactions　同様の取引，類似の取引
limit　制限，限度，限界
limitation　制約，制限，限界
limitation of liability　責任限定
limitation on benefits　特典の制限（租税条約などの）
limitation on benefits (LOB) provision　特典制限条項（LOB 条項）　⦅解⦆一定の条件を満たした者にしか租税条約の適用を認めないという形で，租税条約の特典を制限する条項
limitation on deductibility　損金算入制限
limited deductibility　損金算入制限
limited liability　有限責任
limited liability company (LLC)　有限責任会社
limited liability company membership interest　LLC に対する持分
limited liability entity　有限責任事業体
limited liability partnership (LLP)　有限責任組合
limited partner (LP)　リミテッド・パートナー，有限責任組合員　⦅解⦆パートナーシップへの出資を行うが，その管理・運営には関与しない有限責任のパートナー
limited partnership (LPS)　リミテッド・パートナーシップ，有限責任組合　⦅解⦆管理責任を負うジェネラル・パートナーと，出資金額までしか責任を負わないリミテッド・パートナーにより構成されるパートナーシップ
limited risk distributor　リスク限定型卸売会社
limit of loss deduction　欠損金控除限度額
limit tax rate　制限税率
line　①線，②行，列
line by line　1 行ごとに
line item　開示科目，項目　⦅用⦆line item titled（～という開示科目）
line of authority　権限系統
line of business　事業部門，事業分野
line of credit　信用枠，融資限度額
liner　定期船
link　①関連させる，②リンク
linkage　つながり
link between power and returns　パワーとリターンの関係
linked　関連した
linking rule　リンキング・ルール　⦅解⦆国際課税に関して，他国の税務上の取扱いに依拠して，整合する自国の税務上の取扱いを決定するというルール
liquid　流動性のある
liquid asset　流動性のある資産
liquidate　清算する
liquidating company　清算中の法人

liquidating distribution [dividend]　清算配当，清算分配金
liquidation　清算
liquidation basis　清算価値ベース
liquidation basis accounting　清算基準会計
liquidation distribution [dividend]　清算配当，清算分配金
liquidation income　清算所得
liquidation period　清算期間
liquidation procedures　清算手続
liquidation sale　清算に伴う資産売却
liquidation value　清算価値
liquidator　清算人
liquidity　流動性
liquidity discount　（非）流動性ディスカウント（株式評価などの）　[解]illiquidity discountの項を参照
liquidity ratio　流動性に関する財務比率全般
liquidity risk　流動性リスク　[解]企業の金融負債に関連する債務の履行が困難になるリスク
list　①一覧表にする，②上場する，③一覧表，リスト
listed　上場の
listed company　上場会社
listed securities　上場有価証券
listing　上場
listing rules　上場規則
list of accounts　勘定科目一覧表
list price　表示価格
literature　文献
litigation　訴訟
litigation settlement　訴訟の解決
litigation support　訴訟支援
LLC　▶limited liability company
LLP　▶limited liability partnership
loading　荷積み，船積み
loan　①貸付金，②借入金
loan agreement　融資契約
loan arrangement fee　アレンジメント・フィー　[解]主としてシンジケート・ローンのアレンジャーに対して支払うフィーを意味する
loan capital　借入資本
loan collateral　借入金担保
loan commitment　ローン・コミットメント，貸出コミットメント
loan covenant　財務制限条項（借入金に係る）
loan covenant waiver　財務制限条項の免除（借入金に係る）
loan guarantee　借入保証，債務保証
loan participation　ローン・パーティシペーション　[解]（金融機関等の）貸出債権に係る債権者・債務者間の権利・義務関係を変更することなく，貸出債権についての経済的利益とリスク（の一部）を参加者に移転させる契約
loans and receivables (L&R)　貸付金及び債権（旧）
loan(s) payable　借入金（勘定）
loan(s) receivable　貸付金（勘定）
loan syndication fee　シンジケーション・フィー
LOB　▶limitation on benefits
local　①地方の，②現地の
local consumption tax　地方消費税
local corporate income tax　地方法人税
local corporation tax　地方法人税
local currency　現地通貨
local enterprise [business] tax　事業税
local file　ローカル・ファイル（独立企業間価格を算定するために必要と認められる書類）　[解]移転価格税制の関係では，移転価格文書の1つで，国外関連取引の内容を記載し，その取引に係る独立企業間価格を算定するものをいう。日本においては，一定金額以上の国外関連取引について，ローカル・ファイルの同時文書化義務が定められている
local GAAP　現地会計基準
local government　地方自治体
local inhabitant tax　住民税
local regulator　現地規制当局
local tax　地方税
local tax jurisdiction　地方自治体（地方税を管轄する）
local tax office　所轄税務署
local tax returns　地方税申告書
locate　置く
location　位置，所在地
location of assets　資産の所在地

location savings　ロケーション・セービング　[解]移転価格税制の関係では、活動拠点を高コスト国（地域）から低コスト国（地域）に移すことにより、コストが削減されることを指す

locked box　固定価格方式　[解]買収価格の調整について、買収価格は価値算定の基準日におけるバランス・シートをもとに算定し、その後の価値変動については価格調整を行わないという方式。価格修正方式（completion adjustment）に対する用語

lock-up　ロックアップ　[解]株式公開前の株主が、株式公開後の一定期間、市場で保有株式を売却できないという制限

lock-up agreement　ロックアップ契約
lock-up period　ロックアップ期間
logic　論理
logical　論理的な
logically　論理的に
logistic (al)　物流の
logistics　物流
logistics cost [expense]　物流費
logo　ロゴ
LOI　▶letter of intent
London Inter-Bank Offered Rate (LIBOR)　ロンドン銀行間取引金利　[解]変動金利の指標
long bond　長期債
longevity risk　長寿リスク
long list　ロング・リスト　[解]買収案件において、買収対象の候補などをリストアップしたもの。これが絞り込まれてショート・リスト（short list）になる
long-lived　長期性の
long-lived asset　長期性資産
long position　ロング・ポジション　[解]金融資産の買い持ちの状態
long-service leave　長期勤続休暇
long-stop date　クロージングの最終期日（買収案件などの）
long-term　長期の、固定の
long-term asset　長期性資産、固定資産
long-term average growth rate　長期の平均成長率
long-term borrowings　長期借入金

long-term capital gain　長期譲渡所得
long-term contract　長期契約
long-term debt　長期性負債、固定負債
long-term deposit　長期性預金
long-term employee benefit fund　長期の従業員給付基金
long-term investment　長期投資
long-term lease obligation　長期リース債務
long-term liability　長期性負債、固定負債
long-term loan　①長期貸付金、②長期借入金
long-term loans payable　長期借入金（勘定）
long-term loans receivable　長期貸付金（勘定）
long-term management plan　長期経営計画
long-term other accounts payable　長期未払金
long-term other accounts receivable　長期未収入金
long-term prepaid expense　長期前払費用
long-term unearned revenue　長期前受収益
loophole　抜け穴（法の）
lose　失う、喪失する　[用]a parent loses control of a subsidiary（親会社が子会社に対する支配を喪失する）
loss　損失　[解]広義の費用（expense）のうち、主として企業の通常の事業過程以外から発生したものを指すが、IFRS上はその他の費用と特段区別はされていない
loss allowance　損失評価引当金　[解]IFRS9の文脈では、金融資産、リース債権、契約資産などに係る予想信用損失に対する引当金を指す
loss before extraordinary items　経常損失
loss contingencies　偶発損失
loss contract　損失が見込まれる契約
loss for the year　当期損失
loss for the year from continuing operations　継続事業からの当期損失
loss for the year from discontinued operations　非継続事業からの当期損失
loss from continuing operations　継続事業からの純損失
loss from discontinued operations　非継続事業からの純損失
loss from operating activities　営業活動から

の純損失
loss from operations　営業損失
loss-making　損失が発生する【形】
loss-making contract　損失が発生する契約（工事契約など）
loss of control　支配の喪失
loss of control of subsidiary　子会社に対する支配の喪失
loss on debt waiver　債権放棄損
loss on disaster　災害損失
loss on disposal　処分損　[用] loss on disposal of subsidiary（子会社処分損）
loss on disposal of fixed assets　固定資産処分損，固定資産除却損
loss on disposal of property, plant and equipment　（有形）固定資産処分損,（有形）固定資産除却損
loss on revaluation of investment securities　投資有価証券評価損
loss on revaluation of securities　有価証券評価損
loss on sale of fixed assets　固定資産売却損
loss on sale of investment securities　投資有価証券売却損
loss on sale of property, plant and equipment　（有形）固定資産売却損
loss on sale of securities　有価証券売却損
loss per share　1株当たり損失
loss relief　損失控除　[解] 損失の繰戻しや繰越しなど，損失が発生した場合の税務上の措置の総称
lower limit　下限
lower of cost and net realisable value　低価法　[米] lower of cost and net realisable value　[解] 取得原価と正味実現可能価額のいずれか低いほうで財政状態計算書上の価額とする方法
lower of cost or market (basis)　低価基準，低価法
low tax jurisdiction　低税率国［地域］，軽課税国［地域］
low value asset　少額資産
loyalty　忠実，忠誠心
loyalty programme　ロイヤルティ・プログラム　[米] loyalty program
LP　▶limited partner
LPS　▶limited partnership
lucrative　儲かる，有利な
lump-sum　一括の，一時払いの
lump-sum deduction　一括控除
lump-sum exempt amount　定額控除限度額
lump-sum payment　一括支払い
lump-sum payment for know-how　ノウハウの頭金
lump-sum purchase　一括購入
lump-sum retirement benefit　一時払いの退職給付
lump-sum taxation　一括課税
luxury　贅沢，高級品
luxury taxes　奢侈税

M

MAC ▶material adverse change
MAC clause　MAC 条項　[解] 買収案件において，買収対象会社の事業等に重大な悪影響を及ぼす事由（MAC）が発生した場合には，買手は取引から離脱できるという権利を定めたもの
machine　機械　[使い方注意!] 個々の機械を指す可算名詞
machine hours　機械稼働時間
machinery　機械　[使い方注意!] 総称としての機械を指す不可算名詞
machinery and equipment　機械及び装置
macro hedge　マクロ・ヘッジ
magnitude　重要性，規模
mail order catalogue　メール・オーダー・カタログ
main　主要な
main assets and liabilities　主要な資産及び負債
main business　主たる事業
main office　本社
maintain　維持する
maintenance　維持，メンテナンス
maintenance cost [expense]　保守費，維持管理費
major　①過半の，②主要な
major components　主要な内訳　[用] major components of tax expense（税金費用の主要な内訳）
major customer　主要な顧客　[解] IFRS8 の文脈では，主要な顧客との取引に係る情報は開示対象となる
majority　過半数，大部分
majority interest　過半数の持分
majority of interests　持分の過半
majority stake　マジョリティ出資・持分
majority vote　多数決
major production plant　主要な生産設備
major products and services　主要な製品及びサービス
malfunction　機能不全，故障
malpractice　①背任行為，②業務上の過誤
manage　管理する
management　マネジメント，経営者
management accounting　管理会計
management accounts　管理会計数値，管理会計ベースの決算書
management approach　マネジメント・アプローチ（セグメント情報に関する）
management assessment　経営者による評価
management buy-in (MBI)　マネジメント・バイイン　[解] 外部の次期経営陣による対象会社の買収
management buy-out (MBO)　マネジメント・バイアウト　[解] 現経営陣による対象会社（自社）の買収
management by objectives (MBO)　目標管理制度　[解] 年度ごとに目標を設定し，年度末にその達成度を評価する制度
management certification of financial statements　経営陣による財務諸表への宣誓
management commentary　経営者による説明
management fee [expense]　マネジメント・フィー，経営指導料　[解] 親会社等が子会社等に経理・財務・人事等の管理業務サービスを提供し，その対価として回収するもの
management interview　マネジメント・インタビュー
management letter　マネジメント・レター　[解] 監査人が監査上の問題点を経営者に報告するもの
management of capital　資本管理
management override of controls　経営者による内部統制の無効化
management plan　経営計画
management presentation　マネジメント・プレゼンテーション
management relationship　役員関係
management representation　経営者による確認，経営者確認書
management representation letter　経営者

確認書
management review　マネジメント・レビュー
management's discussion and analysis (MD&A)　経営者による討議と分析　[解] 経営者が，有価証券報告書等において，自社の財政状態や経営成績に対する分析及び検討内容を，具体的に記載するもの
management service　マネジメント・サービス，経営指導
management service fee　マネジメント・フィー，経営指導料
management's report　経営者の報告書
management's view　経営者の見解
management vision　経営ビジョン
managerial accounting　管理会計
managerial involvement　経営上の関与，管理上の関与
managing director　代表取締役
M&A　▶mergers & acquisitions
mandate　権限，命令
mandatorily　強制的に
mandatorily effective　強制的に適用されて（会計基準などが）【形】
mandatory　強制的な
mandatory redemption　強制償還
mandatory vacation　休暇取得の義務付け
manifestation　表明
manipulate　操作する（数字などを）
manipulated financial statements　操作された財務諸表
manipulation　操作
manner　方法
manual　①手動の，手作業の，②マニュアル
manual controls　マニュアル・コントロール
manual entry　手入力による仕訳
manufacture　①製造する，②製造
manufactured goods　製品
manufacturer　メーカー，製造会社
manufacturing account　製造勘定
manufacturing and distribution　製造及び販売
manufacturing company　製造会社
manufacturing cost　製造原価，製造費用
manufacturing department [division]　製造部門

manufacturing facility　製造設備
manufacturing overhead　製造間接費
manufacturing overhead allocation　製造間接費の配賦
manufacturing process　工程，製造工程
MAP　▶mutual agreement procedure
MAP APA　相互協議を伴う事前確認（二国間APA）
mapping chart　対応表
margin　①マージン，利鞘，②証拠金
margin account　証拠金勘定，委託証拠金
marginal　①わずかな，②限界の
marginal cost　限界費用
marginal profit [income]　限界利益　[解] 売上高から，変動費のみを差し引いて計算した利益。固定費の回収に貢献するため，貢献利益（contribution margin）とも呼ばれる
marginal rate of tax　限界税率
marginal tax rate　限界税率
margin of profit　利鞘
mark　①マークをつける，②マーク
mark-down　値下げ，マークダウン
market　市場
marketability　市場性
marketability discount　（非）流動性ディスカウント（株式評価などの）　[解] illiquidity discount の項を参照
marketable　市場性のある
marketable securities　市場性のある有価証券
market analysis　市場分析
market approach　マーケット・アプローチ（評価手法 [技法] としての）　[解] 一般的な資産の評価において，資産の市場価格をベースとするアプローチ。また，IFRS13 の文脈では，公正価値測定に際して，同一または類似の資産または負債の市場から得られる価格及び関連する情報を利用するアプローチを指す
market-based approach　マーケット・アプローチ（評価手法としての）
market-based measurement　市場ベースの測定（値）　[用] market-based, rather than entity-specific, measurement（企業固有の測定値というよりは，市場ベース

の測定値）
market-based performance condition　市場条件，株式市場条件　[解]株式に基づく報酬契約における業績条件の１つ
market cap　時価総額
market capitalisation　時価総額　[米]market capitalization
market comparable company　市場における類似会社
market comparable price　類似会社の市場価格
market comparison technique　市場比較法
market condition　市場条件，株式市場条件　[解]IFRS2の文脈では，株式に基づく報酬契約における業績条件のうち，企業の資本性金融商品の市場価格に関連するもの
market-corroborated input　市場の裏付けのあるインプット
market expectations　市場の予想
market index　市場指標
marketing　マーケティング
marketing department [division]　マーケティング部門
marketing expense　マーケティング費
marketing intangible　マーケティング・インタンジブル，マーケティング上の無形資産　[解]一般に，製品あるいはサービスの宣伝に役立つ商標及び商号，顧客リスト，販売網等を指す
marketing-related intangible asset　マーケティング関連無形資産
marketing right　販売権
market interest rate　市場利子率
market multiple　マーケット・マルチプル，市場倍率
market participant　市場参加者
market penetration　市場浸透
marketplace　市場
market price　市場価格
market price risk　市場価格リスク
market rentals　市場の賃貸料
market research　市場調査，マーケット・リサーチ
market risk　市場リスク
market share　マーケット・シェア
market trend　市場の趨勢
market value (MV)　市場価値
market yield　市場利回り
mark to market (MTM)　時価評価
mark-to-market taxation　時価評価課税
mark-to-market valuation　時価法
mark-up　①マークアップ，利潤の上乗せ，②契約書の修正　[解]①仕入原価に利潤を上乗せして販売価格を決めること，またその上乗せされる部分
master agreement　マスター契約，基本契約
master file　マスター・ファイル，事業概況報告事項　[解]移転価格税制の関係では，移転価格文書の１つで，多国籍企業グループの組織構造，事業の概要，財務状況等に関する情報を記載するものをいう。移転価格税制に係るグループのポリシーや全体像を示す文書という位置付け
master netting agreement　マスター・ネッティング契約，基本相殺契約
master plan　基本計画
masthead　マストヘッド（新聞・雑誌等の発行人欄）　[解]無形資産の例
matching (of cost with revenue)　費用収益の対応
matching principle　費用収益対応の原則
material　①重要な，重要性のある，②材料，③資料
material adverse change (MAC)　重大な悪影響（特に買収対象会社の事業等について生じた）
material cost　材料費
materiality　重要性
materiality level　重要性の水準
materiality threshold　重要性の判断基準，重要性の基準値
materials consumed　材料消費高
materials inventory　材料在庫
materials ledger　材料元帳
material weakness　重要な不備
material weakness in internal control　内部統制の重要な不備
material yield　材料歩留
material yield variance　歩留差異（直接材料費に係る）
maternity leave　産休
mathematical　数学の

matrix	①マトリックス，②行列
matrix form of an organisation	マトリックス組織（構成）　㈱matrix form of an organization
matter	問題
maturity	満期
maturity date	満期日
maturity value	満期日における価額，満期償還額
maximisation	最大化　㈱maximization
maximise	最大化する　㈱maximize
maximum	最大
maximum capacity	最大生産能力
maximum creditable amount	控除限度額（税額控除の）
maximum exposure	最大のエクスポージャー　用 maximum exposure to credit risk（信用リスクに対する最大のエクスポージャー）
maximum tax rate	制限税率
MBI	▶management buy-in
MBO	▶① management buy-out, ② management by objectives
MBS	▶mortgage backed securities
MD&A	▶management's discussion and analysis
mean	①意味する，②平均
meaning	意味
meaningless	意味のない【形】
measurability	測定可能性
measurable	測定可能な
measure	①測定する，②手段　用① when fair value cannot be measured reliably（公正価値が信頼性をもって測定できない場合）
measurement	測定　解 財務諸表への計上を決定（認識）した後，その計上金額を決定するプロセス
measurement after recognition	認識後の測定
measurement at recognition	認識時の測定
measurement base	測定の基礎　解 取得原価，現在原価，実現可能価額，現在価値の4つ
measurement date	測定日　解 IFRS2の文脈では，付与された資本性金融商品の公正価値を測定する日。従業員等との取引については，基本的に付与日が測定日となる
measurement inconsistency	測定に関する不一致・不整合
measurement period	測定期間
measurement principle	測定の原則
measure on a provisional basis	暫定的に測定する
mechanism	メカニズム，仕組み
median	中央値
mediation	調停
medical cost	医療費
medium	中間，中位
medium-term	中期の
medium-term management plan	中期経営計画
medium term note (MTN)	ミディアム・ターム・ノート　解 中期債のうち，発行企業があらかじめ設定した社債発行総額の範囲内で，（年限や金利等の）条件を変えて何回でも債券を発行できるもの
medium- to long-term management plan	中長期経営計画
meet	充足する（条件・要件を）
meeting	会議
meeting cost [expense]	会議費
meeting minutes	議事録（会議などの）
member	メンバー，構成員
member firm	メンバー・ファーム　解 大手監査法人と提携関係にある海外の監査法人
member of board of directors	取締役
member of key management personnel	経営幹部の一員
membership	会員権
membership fee	会費
memo	伝票
memorandum	メモ，覚書
memorandum of association	定款，基本定款
memorandum of understanding (MoU)	合意書，覚書
mention	言及する
merchandise	商品
merchandise inventory	商品在庫

merge	合併する
merged company	消滅会社（被合併法人）
merger	合併
merger control	企業結合［合併］規制
merger control clearance	企業結合［合併］規制のクリアランス
merger ratio	合併比率
mergers & acquisitions (M&A)	（企業の）合併・買収
merit	利点
message	メッセージ
method	方法
methodology	方法，方法論
metric	測定基準，指標
metropolitan	首都の，都会の
metropolitan inhabitant tax	都民税（住民税）
mezzanine	メザニン ［解］もともとは中二階という意味で，デット（借入金など）とエクイティ（株式）の中間に位置するファイナンス。例えば，メザニン・デットは弁済順位が通常の借入金（シニア・デット）より劣後する借入金を指す
mezzanine financing	メザニン・ファイナンス
middle-man	仲買人，中間商人
mid-point	中間点
mid-year	期中
migration	移転
milestone	マイルストン，主要管理点
million	100万
mineral	鉱物
mineral resource	鉱物資源
minimal	最小の，ごくわずかの
minimisation	最小化 ［米］minimization
minimise	最小化する ［米］minimize
minimum	最小
minimum disclosure	最低限の開示
minimum disclosure requirements	最低限の開示要求
minimum funding requirement	最低積立要件
minimum lease payment	最低リース料支払額，最低支払リース料
minimum rental payment	最低レンタル料支払額，最低支払レンタル料
minimum standard	ミニマム・スタンダード，最低基準
minimum tax	ミニマム・タックス ［解］利益の有無にかかわらず支払いが必要とされる最低税負担額
mining right	鉱業権
Ministry of Finance (MOF)	財務省
Ministry of Finance Ordinance	財務省令
minor	より小さい，重要でない
minority discount	マイノリティ・ディスカウント ［解］企業買収の局面で，支配権を取得できない場合に行われる割引。コントロール・プレミアム（control premium）の逆
minority interest	少数株主持分
minority owner	少数株主
minority shareholder	少数株主
minority stake	マイノリティ出資・持分
minority veto right	少数株主拒否権
minor variance	軽微な差異
minus	マイナス
minutes	議事録
minutes of board of directors' meeting	取締役会議事録
minutes of shareholders' meeting	株主総会議事録
misapplication	①誤用，②不正使用
misappropriate	横領する
misappropriation	横領
miscellaneous	種々雑多な
miscellaneous assets	諸資産
miscellaneous expense(s)	雑費
miscellaneous equity	資本の諸項目
miscellaneous income	①雑益，雑収入，②雑所得
miscellaneous income and loss	雑損益
miscellaneous liabilities	諸負債
miscellaneous loss	雑損，雑損失
misc expense	雑費
misclassify	分類を誤る
misconduct	①不法行為，②誤った行為
misinterpret	解釈を誤る
misinterpretation	解釈誤り
mislead	誤解させる【動】
misleading	誤解を与えるような
misrepresentation	虚偽表示，虚偽記載，不

当表示
mission 任務，業務
misstatement 虚偽表示，記載誤り
mistake 誤り
misunderstanding 誤解
misuse 誤用，不正使用
mitigate 緩和する，軽減する
mitigation 緩和（リスクなどの）
mix 混合する
mixed-use property 複数用途の不動産 [解] 不動産の一部を自己使用し，残りの部分を賃貸するなど，複数の用途で使用される不動産
mixture 混合
MLTN ▶more likely than not
MNC ▶multinational corporation
MNE ▶multinational enterprise
model モデル
modelling ①モデリング，②モデル製作 [米]modeling
model tax conventions [treaties] モデル租税条約 [解] OECDモデル租税条約及び国連モデル租税条約
moderate 中程度の
modification 修正，変更
modification gain or loss 条件変更による利得または損失 [解] IFRS9の文脈では，条件変更による契約上のキャッシュ・フローの変更を金融資産の帳簿価額に反映させることにより生じる利得または損失を指す
modified retrospective approach 修正遡及アプローチ
modify 修正する，変更する
MOF ▶Ministry of Finance
monetary 金銭の，貨幣の
monetary asset ①貨幣性資産，②金銭債権 [解] ①保有している貨幣，及び固定額の貨幣を受け取ることとなる資産
monetary assumption 貨幣測定の公準
monetary item 貨幣性項目 [解] IAS21の文脈では，保有している通貨単位で受け取るかまたは支払うこととなる資産または負債
monetary liability 金銭債務
monetary penalty 課徴金，制裁金

monetary policy 金融政策
money 金銭
money box company ペーパー・カンパニー
money laundering マネー・ロンダリング
money market 短期金融市場
money market investment 短期金融投資
monitor モニターする，監視する
monitoring モニタリング
monopoly 独占
Monte Carlo simulation モンテカルロ・シミュレーション
monthly 月次の
monthly average 月次平均
monthly close [closing] 月次決算
monthly closing procedures 月次決算手続
monthly control 月次統制
monthly filing 月次申告
monthly proration 月数に基づく按分計算
monthly report 月次報告書
monthly reporting 月次報告
monthly trial balance 月次試算表
more likely than not (MLTN) 50%超の確率で発生する，ありそうな
more than 〜超 [解] more thanはその値を含まない。例えば，more than 50%は「50%超」で50%を含まない。「50%以上」なら，50% or moreといういい方をする
more than half 過半数
mortality 死亡率
mortality table 死亡率表
mortgage ①モーゲージ，②抵当権，③住宅ローン
mortgage backed securities (MBS) モーゲージ担保証券，抵当証券
most advantageous market 最も有利な市場 [解] IFRS13の文脈では，取引コスト及び輸送コストを考慮したうえで，資産の売却により受け取る金額が最大となる（または負債の移転により支払う金額が最小となる）市場を指す
most favoured nation clause 最恵国待遇条項 [米]most favored nation clause [解] もともとは条約などにおいて，相手国の国民・企業を，他国の国民・企業よりも不利に取り扱わないとする条項であり，

同様の考え方が，（国家間ではなく）私人間の取引に取り入れられたもの
most likely amount　最も発生可能性の高い金額
most likely outcome　最も起こりそうな結果　[解]IAS37の文脈では，引当金の測定方法の1つとして，最も起こりそうな結果（金額）で見積もる方法がある
most recent　直近の
most recent purchase method　最終仕入原価法
motive test　動機テスト　[解]租税回避への対応策の基本的な考え方として，ある取引に商業的な動機があり，税務コストの低減だけを目的としていないかを判定すること
motor vehicle　車両
MoU　▶Memorandum of Understanding
mould　金型　[米]mold
movement　①動き，②移動，③変動　[用]movement in deferred tax balances（繰延税金残高の増減）
moving average　移動平均
moving average method　移動平均法
moving target　ムービング・ターゲット
MTM　▶mark-to-market
MTN　▶medium term note
multi-employer (benefit) plan　複数事業主（給付）制度　[解]共通支配下にない複数の企業が拠出資産をプールし，それを当該複数の企業の従業員に給付するために使用する等の一定の基準に該当する退職給付制度
multi-employer defined benefit plan　複数事業主の確定給付制度
multilateral advance pricing arrangement　多国間APA，マルチラテラルAPA　[解]移転価格税制の関係では，事前確認（APA）のうち，3か国以上の税務当局から確認を受けるものを指す
multinational　多国籍の
multinational corporation (MNC)　多国籍企業
multinational enterprise (MNE)　多国籍企業
multiple　①多数の，②倍数，③乗数，倍率，マルチプル　[解]③企業価値評価の局面では，企業価値が収益指標（EBITDA等）の何倍あるかを示すもの
multiple components　複数の要素（取引などに含まれる）
multiple ledgers　複数元帳
multiple-step　多段階の
multiple-step income statement　多段階形式の損益計算書　[解]段階損益を表示する損益計算書の形式
multiplied by　×（掛ける）　[使い方注意！]A×Bは，A multiplied by B
municipal　市町村の
municipal bond　地方債
municipality　市町村，地方自治体
municipal tax　市町村民税（住民税）　[解]住民税（inhabitant tax）は，基本的に道府県民税（prefectural tax）と市町村民税により構成される
municipal tax office　市町村税事務所
mutual　①相互の，②共通の
mutual agreement procedure (MAP)　相互協議　[解]租税条約締結国の税務当局間の協議。主として移転価格課税に係る二重課税の排除のために行われる
mutual entity　相互会社　[解]投資家所有企業以外の企業で，配当等を所有者等に直接的に提供するもの。例えば，相互保険会社，信用組合及び協同組合などがこれに該当する
mutual fund　ミューチュアル・ファンド　[解]米国におけるオープンエンド型の投資信託
mutual shareholding　株式相互保有
MV　▶market value

N

narration　説明部分（仕訳の）
narrative　①説明部分（仕訳の），②業務記述書，記述（内部統制に関する）
narrative description　説明的な記述
NASDAQ　▶National Association of Securities Dealers Automated Quotations
national　国の
National Association of Securities Dealers Automated Quotations (NASDAQ)　ナスダック（米国）
nationalisation　国有化　㊎nationalization
national tax　国税　[解]地方税（local tax）に対する用語
National Tax Agency (NTA)　国税庁（日本の）
national tax office　税務署
National Tax Service (NTS)　韓国国税庁（韓国の税務当局）
National Tax Tribunal　国税不服審判所
natural disaster　自然災害
natural resources　天然資源
nature　性質　[用] expenses are classified either by nature or by function（費用は性質別または機能別に分類される）
nature and extent of government grant　政府補助金の性質と範囲
nature of expense method　費用性格法　[解]費用の性格に基づいて費用を分類する方法
nature of the event　事象の性質　[解]重要な「修正を要しない後発事象」（non-adjusting event after reporting period）については，その性質を開示する必要がある
NAV　▶net asset value
NCI　▶non-controlling interest
NDA　▶non-disclosure agreement
necessarily　必ず
necessary　必要な
necessity　必要性

negate　①否定する，②無効にする
negation　否定，否認
negative　①負の，マイナスの，②消極的な
negative assurance　消極的保証
negative balance　マイナス残高
negative confirmation　消極的確認
negative confirmation request　消極的確認（依頼）
negative equity　債務超過
negative goodwill　負ののれん
negligence　過失
negotiable　①交渉可能な，②譲渡可能な
negotiate　交渉する
negotiated sale　相対取引による売却（特に買収案件における）
negotiated transaction　相対取引
negotiation　交渉
net　純額の
net assets　純資産
net assets adjustment　純資産調整（買収対価などについての）
net asset value (NAV)　純資産価額
net basis　純額ベース　[用] on a net basis（純額で）
net capital employed　純使用資本　[解]固定資産＋（流動資産－流動負債）を指す
net cash　ネット・キャッシュ　[解]キャッシュが有利子負債を上回る場合のその差額
net cash inflow on disposal of subsidiaries　子会社の売却による収入（売却時の現金保有額控除後）　[解]キャッシュ・フロー計算書などでよく使われる用語
net cash outflow on acquisition of subsidiaries　子会社の取得による支出（取得時の現金受入額控除後）　[解]キャッシュ・フロー計算書などでよく使われる用語
net cash used　使用した資金
net change　純変動（額）
net change in fair value　公正価値の純変動額
net cost plus (margin/ratio)　対総費用営業利益率　[解]移転価格税制の関係では，利益水準指標（PLI）の1つで，事業活動に費やされたコストがどの程度営業利益を生み出しているかを示すもの。以下の算

式で計算される
対総費用営業利益率＝
　　　　　　営業利益
　　売上原価＋販売費及び一般管理費

net current assets　純流動資産

net current liabilities　純流動負債

net debt　ネット・デット，純（有利子）負債，正味負債　[解]（有利子）負債から現金及び現金同等物を差し引いたもの

net decrease in cash and cash equivalents　現金及び現金同等物の減少額　[解] キャッシュ・フロー計算書などでよく使われる用語

net deferred tax assets and liabilities　繰延税金資産及び負債の純額

net defined benefit asset　確定給付資産の純額，退職給付に係る資産　[解] 報告期間の末日において，制度資産が確定給付債務を上回っている部分。ただし，計上額にアセット・シーリング（asset ceiling）と呼ばれる一定の制限がある

net defined benefit liability　確定給付負債の純額，退職給付に係る負債　[解] 報告期間の末日において，確定給付債務が制度資産を上回っている部分

net finance costs　金融費用（純額）

net gain　純利益　[用] net gain (arising) on（～により発生した利益）

net gain on available-for-sale securities　その他有価証券評価差額金（益）

net income　当期純利益

net increase in cash and cash equivalents　現金及び現金同等物の増加額　[解] キャッシュ・フロー計算書などでよく使われる表現

net interest　純利息（費用）

net interest on the net defined benefit liability [asset]　確定給付負債[資産]の純額に対する利息純額，純利息費用[収益]　[解] 確定給付費用の1つで，確定給付債務から制度資産を控除したネットの金額に（確定給付債務を求める際に用いた）割引率を乗じて計算される

net interest payment　純支払利子　[解] 事業税付加価値割の構成要素

net investment　純投資

net investment hedge　純投資ヘッジ

net investment in a foreign operation　在外営業活動体に対する純投資額　[解] 在外営業活動体の純資産のうち報告企業の持分の額

net investment in lease　正味リース投資未回収額

net liabilities　純負債

net loss　①純損失，②欠損金額　[用] net loss (arising) on（～により発生した損失）

net loss on available-for-sale securities　その他有価証券評価差額金（損）

net off　相殺

net of income tax　税引後（の）

net of tax　税抜き，税引後（の）

net operating income (NOI)　営業純利益

net operating loss (NOL)　①欠損金（税務上の），②営業（純）損失

net operating loss carryback　欠損金の繰戻（還付）

net operating loss carryforward　欠損金の繰越，繰越欠損金

net operating profit after tax (NOPAT)　税引後営業利益

net operating profit less adjusted taxes (NOPLAT)　みなし税引後営業利益

net present value (NPV)　正味現在価値　[解] 投資の可否の判断に用いられる概念で，プロジェクトの投資回収期間のキャッシュ・フローの割引現在価値から初期投資額を差し引いた金額をいう。NPVがプラスであれば，基本的には投資を行うべきという判断になる

net present value (NPV) method　正味現在価値法，NPV法

net proceeds　純収入

net profit　純利益

net profit margin　純利益率

net profit or loss　純損益

net purchases　純仕入高

net realisable value (NRV)　正味実現可能価額　[米] net realizable value　[解] 通常の事業過程における見積売価から，完成までに要する見積原価及び販売に要する見積費用を控除した額

net rent payment　純支払賃料　[解] 事業税

付加価値割の構成要素
net sales　純売上高
net selling price　正味売却価格，正味売却価額（売却費用控除後）
net selling value　正味売却価額
net settlement　純額決済
net settlement feature　純額決済の要素
netting　ネッティング，相殺
netting agreement　ネッティング契約
net unrealised gain on land revaluation　土地再評価差額金（益）　[米] net unrealized gain on land revaluation
net unrealised loss on land revaluation　土地再評価差額金（損）　[米] net unrealized loss on land revaluation
network　ネットワーク
network infrastructure　ネットワーク基盤
net working capital　純（正味）運転資本　[解] 一般に運転資金といわれるもので，以下の算式で計算される
純（正味）運転資本＝流動資産－流動負債
net worth　正味財産，自己資本
neutral　中立の
neutralise　無効化する　[米] neutralize
neutrality　中立性
NewCo　new company（新会社）の略
new cost basis　新取得価額
newly acquired asset　新規取得資産
newly formed subsidiary　新設子会社
newly listed entity　新規上場企業
newspaper masthead　新聞のマストヘッド　[解] 無形資産の例
New York Stock Exchange (NYSE)　ニューヨーク証券取引所
next business day　翌営業日
next period　翌期，来期，次期
nexus　ネクサス　[解] 端的には「課税ポイントとなるつながり」を意味し，例えば，米国の州税は，基本的に企業がネクサスを有する州においてのみ課される
nexus link　ネクサス，つながり
niche　ニッチ，隙間
nil　ゼロ
Nini Kumiai (NK)　任意組合
NK　▶Nini Kumiai

NOI　▶net operating income
NOL　▶net operating loss
NOL deduction　欠損金控除
nominal　①名目の，②額面の，③記名式の
nominal accounts　総勘定元帳科目
nominal amount　①額面金額，②名目金額
nominal capital　名目資本
nominal interest rate　名目金利，名目利子率
nominal ledger　総勘定元帳
nominal tax rate　表面税率
nominal value　①額面金額，②名目価値
nominate　指名する
nomination　指名
nomination committee　指名委員会（委員会設置会社の）
nominee　名義人
non-accomplice vendor (scheme)　共犯でない仕入先（を利用したスキーム）（不正の一形態）　[解] 仕入先との共謀ではなく，例えば，仕入先に敢えて過払いし，その返還を横領するような不正のスキームを指す
non-accumulating compensated absence　非累積型の有給休暇
non-adjusting event　修正を要しない事象
non-adjusting event after reporting period　非修正後発事象，修正を要しない後発事象　[解] 報告期間の末日後に新たに発生した状況を示す事象で，日本基準でいう開示後発事象に相当する
non-amortisable intangible asset　非償却の無形資産　[米] non-amortizable intangible asset
non-arbitrary basis　恣意的でない方法　[用] on a non-arbitrary basis（恣意的でない方法で）
non-binding　（法的）拘束力のない
non-binding bid　法的拘束力のない入札（買収案件などの）
non-binding offer　法的拘束力のない意向表明（買収案件などの）
non-building structure　構築物
non-cancellable　解約不能の
non-cancellable lease　解約不能リース
non-cancellable period　解約不能期間（リース契約などの）

non-cash asset	非現金資産，非資金資産
non-cash expense	非資金支出費用
non-cash item	非資金項目
non-cash misappropriation	現金以外の資産（棚卸資産など）の流用
non-cash transaction	非資金取引　[解] IAS7の文脈では，現金及び現金同等物の増減を伴わない取引（例えば，リース資産の取得）を指す
non-compete clause	競業避止義務，競合禁止条項
non-competition obligation	競業避止義務
non-compliance	法令不遵守
non-consolidated financial statements	個別財務諸表
non-contributory	拠出を伴わない（退職給付制度が）[形]
non-controllable	管理不能の
non-controllable cost	管理不能費用
non-controlling interest (NCI)	非支配持分，非支配株主持分　[解] 子会社に対する持分のうち，親会社に帰属しないもので，従来の少数株主持分（minority interest）[用] non-controlling interests arising on the acquisition of（～（子会社）の取得による非支配持分の追加）
non-coterminous year-ends	異なる（事業）年度末（連結子会社などの）
non-counterbalancing error	（翌期に）自動的に訂正されない誤謬
non-credit-impaired financial asset	信用減損のない金融資産
non-cumulative	非累積型の
non-cumulative dividend	非累積型配当（優先株式などの）
non-cumulative preference share	非累積型優先株式　[解] 配当を受け取る優先権が累積せず，単年度で失効する優先株式
non-current	非流動（区分）の
non-current asset	非流動資産，固定資産　[解] 流動資産以外の資産
non-current assets held for sale	売却目的で保有する非流動資産
non-current asset (that is) to be abandoned	廃棄予定の非流動資産
non-current bonds issued	発行した長期社債
non-current borrowings	長期借入金
non-current item	非流動項目，固定項目
non-current liability	非流動負債，固定負債
non-deductibility	損金不算入
non-deductible	損金不算入の
non-deductible expense	損金不算入の費用
non-default depreciation method	法定減価償却方法以外の減価償却方法　[解] 法定減価償却方法（default depreciation method）に対する用語
non-default translation method	法定換算方法以外の換算方法　[解] 法定換算方法（default translation method）に対する用語
non-depreciable asset	非償却資産，非減価償却資産（有形固定資産）
non-derivative	非デリバティブ
non-derivative financial asset	非デリバティブ金融資産
non-derivative financial instrument	非デリバティブ金融商品
non-derivative financial liability	非デリバティブ金融負債
non-derivative host	デリバティブでない本体部分（組込デリバティブなどの）
non-disclosure	非開示
non-disclosure agreement (NDA)	秘密保持契約　[解] 企業買収等の局面で，企業が自社の情報を開示する場合に，相手方に自社の秘密情報を第三者に開示しないことを約させるもの
non-discretionary dividend	裁量権のない配当
non-discrimination	無差別
non-discrimination provisions	無差別条項　[解] 租税条約の一般原則の1つで，国籍無差別，PE無差別，資本無差別等がある
non-employees	非従業員
non-exclusive	非独占的な，非排他的な
non-exclusive agreement	非独占契約，非排他的契約
non-exclusive licence	通常実施権，非独占的実施権，非排他的ライセンス　[米] non-exclusive license
non-existence	不存在

non-financial asset　非金融資産
non-financial information　非財務情報
non-financial instrument　非金融商品
non-financial liability　非金融負債
non-financial obligation　非金融債務
non-interference　不干渉
non-investment grade　投資不適格
non-lease component　非リース構成要素　[解] IFRS16の文脈では，リース契約に含まれる，リース以外の財またはサービス（例えば，維持管理）の取引に係る合意であり，リース構成要素（lease component）に対する用語
non-marketability of equity securities　資本性証券が市場で取引されていないこと
non-marketable securities　市場性のない有価証券
non-market-based performance condition　株式市場条件以外の業績条件　[解] 株式に基づく報酬契約における業績条件の1つ
non-monetary asset　非貨幣性資産
non-monetary benefits　非貨幣性給付
non-monetary grant　非貨幣性の補助金　[解] IAS20の文脈では，例えば，企業が使用するための土地の移転であり，非貨幣性の補助金は公正価値により測定される
non-monetary item　非貨幣性項目
non-monetary liability　非貨幣性負債
non-monetary transaction　非貨幣性取引，非金銭取引
non-occurrence　発生しないこと
non-operating asset　非事業用資産，事業外資産
non-operating expense　営業外費用
non-operating income　営業外収益
non-operating loss　営業外費用
non-operating revenue　営業外収益
non-ownership-transfer finance lease　所有権移転外ファイナンス・リース
non-performance risk　不履行リスク　[解] 企業が債務を履行しないリスク
non-performing loans　不良債権
non-permanent resident　非永住者
non-profit organisation (NPO)　非営利組織　[米] non-profit organization

non-public　公開されていない【形】
non-public enterprise　非上場企業，非公開企業
non-qualified　非適格の
non-qualified reorganisation　非適格組織再編　[米] non-qualified reorganization　[解] 日本の組織再編税制において，組織再編のうち，適格要件を充足しないもの。譲渡益課税やみなし配当課税が行われる可能性がある
non-qualified stock option (NQSO)　税制非適格ストック・オプション　[解] 税制適格ストック・オプション以外のストック・オプション
non-recourse　ノンリコース
non-recourse debt　ノンリコースの債務
non-recourse loan　ノンリコース・ローン，責任財産限定特約付融資　[解] 返済原資の範囲に限定を加えたローンで，通常は責任財産となる原資からのキャッシュ・フローを返済原資とし，その範囲以上の返済義務を負わないというもの
non-recurring　非経常の，非継続の，再度発生しない
non-recurring basis　非経常ベース　[用] on a recurring or non-recurring basis（経常的または非経常的な［に］）
non-recurring cost　非経常原価
non-recurring fair value measurement　非経常的な［単発の］公正価値評価
non-recurring item　非経常項目
non-redeemable　非償還の，弁済されない【形】
non-redeemable preference share　非償還優先株式
non-refundable　還付されない【形】
non-refundable fee　返金不能の報酬
non-refundable purchase taxes　還付されない取得税（有形固定資産などの）
non-refundable upfront fee　返金不能の前払報酬
non-resident　非居住者
non-resident alien　非居住外国人
non-resident individual　非居住者（個人）
non-routine transaction　非経常的取引
non-share consideration　株式以外の対価

non-solicitation clause　勧誘禁止条項
non-sufficient funds cheque (NSF cheque)　不渡小切手　［米］non-sufficient funds check (NSF check)
non-taxable　非課税の，益金不算入の
non-taxable corporate reorganisation　非課税組織再編　［米］non-taxable corporate reorganization
non-taxable income　非課税所得，益金不算入収益
non-taxable sales　非課税売上
non-taxable transaction　非課税取引
non tax-qualified　非適格の，税制非適格の
non tax-qualified contribution in kind　非適格現物出資
non tax-qualified corporate division　非適格分割
non tax-qualified corporate reorganisation　非適格組織再編　［米］non tax-qualified reorganization
non tax-qualified dividend in kind　非適格現物分配
non tax-qualified horizontal-type corporate division　非適格分割型分割
non tax-qualified merger　非適格合併
non tax-qualified reorganisation　非適格組織再編　［米］non tax-qualified reorganization
non tax-qualified share for share exchange　非適格株式交換
non tax-qualified share transfer　非適格株式移転
non tax-qualified vertical-type corporate division　非適格分社型分割
non-vessel-operating common carrier (NVOCC)　非船舶運航業者　［解］自らは海上運送を行う船舶を運航しない運送業者
non-vesting condition　権利確定条件以外の条件
no-par stock　無額面株式
no-par value　無額面
no-par value stock [share]　無額面株式
NOPAT　▶net operating profit after tax
NOPLAT　▶net operating profit less adjusted taxes
norm　標準

normal　通常の，標準の
normal capacity　正常生産能力，通常の操業度
normal course of business　通常の事業過程
normalisation　標準化　［米］normalization
normalise　標準化する，正常化する　［米］normalize
normalised working capital　正常化された運転資本　［米］normalized working capital
normal operating capacity　正常操業度
normal operating cycle　通常の営業循環
normal operating cycle basis [rule]　正常営業循環基準
normal working capital　正常運転資本
Norwalk agreement　ノーウォーク合意
no-shop clause　ノーショップ条項　［解］買収案件などで，売手が他の買手候補と交渉することを原則として禁止する条項
notable　顕著な
notably　特に
no-talk clause　ノートーク条項　［解］買収案件などで，売手が他の買手候補と交渉し，情報を提供することを禁止する条項
not applicable　該当なし
notary public　公証人
note　①注記，②手形，③注，注釈，④紙幣
notes　注記　［解］財務諸表の本体に追加する形で，財務諸表作成の基礎や採用している具体的な会計方針，またその他の情報（財務諸表に表示している項目の説明や個別の項目の分解など）を開示するもの
notes discounted　割引手形
notes payable　①支払手形，②手形借入
notes payable to banks　銀行借入
notes payable-trade　支払手形
notes receivable　受取手形
notes receivable discounted　割引手形
notes receivable endorsed　裏書手形
notes receivable-trade　受取手形
notes to financial statements　注記，財務諸表注記　［解］notesの項を参照
not-for-profit　非営利の
not-for-profit organisation (NPO)　非営利組織　［米］not-for-profit organization
notice　①通知，②気付く

notice of assessment	賦課決定通知書（税金の）
notice of correction	更正通知（書）
notice of deficiency	延滞通知（納税の），不足税額通知書
notification	①通知，届出，②通知書
notify	通知する
notion	概念
notional	概念的な
notional (principal) amount	想定元本
novation	更新，更改（契約などの）
NPO	▶non-profit [not-for-profit] organisation 米 non-profit [not-for-profit] organization
NPV	▶net present value
NRV	▶net realisable value 米 net realizable value
NSF cheque	▶non-sufficient funds cheque
NTA	▶National Tax Agency
NTS	▶National Tax Service
nullify	取り消す
number	数字
number of employees	従業員数
number of shares	株式数
number of shares authorised	授権株式数 米 number of shares authorized
number of shares issued	発行済株式総数
number of shares issued and fully paid	全額払込済みの発行済株式数
number of shares issued but not fully paid	未払込額のある発行済株式数
number of shares outstanding	発行済株式総数
numerator	分子 解 分母(denominator)に対する用語
numerical	数字の
numerous	多数の
NVOCC	▶non-vessel-operating common carrier
NYSE	▶New York Stock Exchange

O

object	①対象，②反対する
objective	①目的，②客観的な
objective evidence	客観的な証拠
objectivity	客観性
obligate	義務を負わせる
obligating event	偶発発生事象 解（その決済以外に企業に現実的な選択肢がない）法的債務または推定的債務を生じさせる事象
obligation	義務，債務
obligation to withhold tax	源泉徴収義務
obligator	債務者
obligee	債権者
obligor	債務者
obliterate	痕跡が残らないように消す
obscure	①不明瞭な，②不明瞭にする，隠蔽する
observable	観察可能
observable input	観察可能なインプット
observable market	観察可能な市場
observable market data	観察可能な市場のデータ
observable market price	観察可能な市場価格
observation	①観察，②立会（棚卸などの）
observe	①観察する，②遵守する
observer	観察者，第三者
obsolescence	陳腐化
obsolete	陳腐化した
obsolete inventory	陳腐化在庫
obtain	入手する
obtainable	入手可能な
occasional	①時折の，②偶発的な
occasional income	①臨時の収益，②一時所得
occasional revenue	臨時の収益
occupancy	占有
occupancy rate	稼働率（投資不動産などの）
occupation	①占有，②職業

occupational fraud	職業上の不正
occupy	占有する
occur	発生する
occurrence	発生
OCI	▶other comprehensive income
OCI option	▶other comprehensive income option
odd share	端株
OECD	▶Organisation for Economic Co-operation and Development
OECD Model Tax Convention on Income and on Capital	OECDモデル租税条約 [解] OECD（経済協力開発機構）が公表している租税条約のひな型。法的拘束力は有しないが，特に先進国の間での国際的なコンセンサスとして機能している
OECD Model Tax Treaty	OECDモデル租税条約
OECD Transfer Pricing Guidelines for Multinational Enterprises and Tax Administrations	OECD移転価格ガイドライン [解] OECD（経済協力開発機構）が，移転価格に関連する税務上の問題について，多国籍企業及び各国の税務当局のための解決の方策を示したもの。法的拘束力は有しないが，実務上は国際的なコンセンサスとして機能している
OEM	▶original equipment manufacturing [manufacturer]
off-balance (sheet)	オフバランスの，簿外の
off-balance sheet asset	簿外資産
off-balance sheet liability	簿外負債
offer	①提供する，②提案する，③オファー，意向表明
offering	売出し，提供物
offering memorandum	募集要項
offer letter	①雇用契約書，②オファー・レター
office	事務所，事業所
office audit	書面調査（税務調査のうち）
office equipment	事務用（備）品，オフィス機器
office expense	事務所費
office furniture	オフィス用家具
officer	①役員，幹部，オフィサー，②役人
office relocation	事務所移転
office supplies	事務用消耗品
office supplies expense	事務用消耗品費
official	①公的な，②役人，公務員
official document	公文書，事務文書
official gazette	官報
offset	相殺する
offsetting	相殺
offsetting of financial assets and liabilities	金融資産・負債の相殺
offsetting of financial instruments	金融商品の相殺
offshore	海外の，国外の
offshore bank	オフショア・バンク（海外に所在する銀行）
offshore company	オフショア・カンパニー（海外に所在する会社）
offshore subsidiary	海外子会社
OID	▶original issue discount
OIP	▶original issue premium
oligopoly	寡占
ombudsman	オンブズマン
omission	①漏れ，②省略
omit	①忘れる，②省略する
on account	掛で
on behalf of	～の代理で
on call services	オンコール・サービス [解] 要求に応じて，いつでも提供されるサービス
on credit	掛で [用] sell □ on credit（□を掛で売る）
on demand	要求払いの
183-day rule	183日ルール [解] 租税条約に定める，給与所得に関する短期滞在者免税を指す
100% control relationship	完全支配関係
100% reduction of capital	100%減資
one-off	単発の
onerous contract	不利な契約 [解] IAS37の文脈では，企業にとって不利な契約であり，正確には，契約上の義務の履行に不可避なコストが，契約から得られる経済的便益を上回る契約を指す
onerous contract charge	不利な契約による負担
onerous contracts contingent liability	不利な契約に係る偶発負債

onerous contracts provision　不利な契約に係る引当金
onerous performance obligation　不利な履行義務
one-sided risk　片側リスク
one-year rule　1年基準
ongoing　継続中の，進行中の　[用] on an ongoing basis（継続的に）
online　オンライン
on or after　〜以後　[使い方注意!] on or after は，その日を含めて，「その日以後」という意味
on or before　〜以前　[使い方注意!] on or before は，その日を含めて，「その日以前」という意味
onshore company　オンショア・カンパニー（国内に所在する会社）
on the books　帳簿上の
onus　責任，義務
onus of proof　立証責任
opaque　不透明な
OPEB　▶other post-retirement employee benefit
open-door policy　開放的な政策
open-ended mutual fund　オープンエンド型ミューチュアル・ファンド
opening balance　期首残高，開始残高
opening entry　開始記入
opening IFRS statement of financial position　IFRS開始財政状態計算書　[解] IFRS移行日現在の財政状態計算書
opening inventory　棚卸資産期首残高
open invoice　未払いの請求書
open issue　未解決の課題
open order　未出荷の注文書
open (tax) years　税務調査未了年度，税務申告書修正可能年度　[解] 税務デュー・デリジェンスの関係では，税務調査未了年度は税務調査終了年度よりも税務リスクが高い
operate　事業を行う
operating activity　営業活動　[解] キャッシュ・フロー計算書上の活動区分で，企業の主たる収益稼得活動をいうが，投資活動や財務活動に含まれないその他の活動も含む　[用] net cash generated by operating activities（営業活動によるキャッシュ・フロー（プラスの場合）），net cash used in operating activities（営業活動によるキャッシュ・フロー（マイナスの場合））
operating asset　事業資産，営業資産
operating capacity　事業規模
operating cash flows　営業活動によるキャッシュ・フロー
operating cycle　営業循環，営業サイクル
operating cycle rule　営業循環基準
operating expense　営業費用
operating income　営業利益
operating lease　オペレーティング・リース　[解] IFRS16の文脈では，原資産の所有に伴うリスクと経済価値の実質的移転を伴わないリース（貸手にとっての分類）
operating leverage　営業レバレッジ　[解] 変動費に対して固定費の割合が大きく，売上の変動に対して利益の変動が増幅される状況
operating loss　営業損失
operating margin　①営業利益率，売上高営業利益率，②営業利益
operating margin ratio　営業利益率
operating payables　営業債務
operating profit　営業利益
operating profit and loss　営業損益
operating receivables　営業債権
operating result　営業成績，業績
operating revenue　営業収益
operating segment　事業セグメント　[解] IFRS8の文脈では，企業の構成単位であって，(1)その単位で事業活動を行って収益を稼得，費用を負担しており，(2)その単位で最高経営意思決定者が業績評価を行って資源の配分方法の決定しており，(3)その単位で区分された財務情報が入手可能なもの
operation　①業務，オペレーション，②事業，③運用（内部統制の）
operational　業務上の，運用上の
operational audit　業務監査
operational efficiency　業務効率
operational efficiency review　業務効率の調査

operational risk　オペレーショナル・リスク，業務運営上のリスク，事業リスク　[解]事務ミス等により損失を被るリスク
operation of control　内部統制の運用
operation service　運営サービス
operator　営業者
opinion　意見
opportunity　機会
opportunity cost　機会費用
opposite　逆の
optimal　最適な
optimal capital structure　最適資本構成
optimistic　楽観的な
option　①オプション，②選択肢
optional　任意の，自由選択の
optional exemption　任意の免除規定
optional lease payment　オプション・リース料　[解]リースの延長または解約オプションの対象期間のうち，リース期間に含まれていない期間に係るリース料
option exercise price　オプション行使価格
option granted (to)　(～に)付与されたオプション
option holder　オプション保有者
option premium　オプション料
option pricing model　オプション価格算定モデル
options, warrants and their equivalents　オプション，ワラント及びその同等物　[解]所有者に対して普通株式の購入の権利を付与する金融商品
option to be taxed　課税の選択　[解]例えば，消費税における課税事業者の選択など
order　①順序，②注文，③命令
order acceptance　受注
order backlog　受注残高
Order for Enforcement of the Act on Special Measures Concerning Taxation　租税特別措置法施行令
Order for Enforcement of the Consumption Tax Act　消費税法施行令
Order for Enforcement of the Corporation Tax Act　法人税法施行令
Order for Enforcement of the Income Tax Act　所得税法施行令
orderly　整然とした，秩序ある【形】

orderly liquidation value　通常処分価額
orderly transaction　秩序ある取引
order quantity　注文数量，発注量
ordinance　法令，政令
Ordinance for Enforcement of the Act on Special Measures Concerning Taxation　租税特別措置法施行規則
Ordinance for Enforcement of the Consumption Tax Act　消費税法施行規則
Ordinance for Enforcement of the Corporation Tax Act　法人税法施行規則
Ordinance for Enforcement of the Income Tax Act　所得税法施行規則
ordinary　普通の，通常の
ordinary activities　経常的活動，通常の活動
ordinary course of business　通常の事業過程
ordinary deposit　普通預金
ordinary depreciation　普通償却
ordinary dividend　普通配当
ordinary donation　一般寄付金
ordinary income　経常利益
ordinary loss　経常損失
ordinary operations　通常の活動
ordinary profit　経常利益
ordinary profit and loss　経常損益
ordinary share [stock]　普通株式　[解]他のすべての資本性金融商品に劣後する資本性金融商品
ordinary shareholder　普通株主　[解]普通株式の保有者
organic　有機的な
organic growth　有機的成長　[解]M&A等によらない事業拡大
organisation　組織　[米]organization
organisational　組織の　[米]organizational
organisational structure　組織構造　[米]organizational structure
organisation chart　組織図　[米]organization chart
organisation cost [expense]　創立費　[米]organization cost [expense]
Organisation for Economic Co-operation and Development (OECD)　経済協力開発機構
organise　組織する　[米]organize

origin　①源泉（所得などの），②原産地
original　当初の，元の
original contract　原契約
original copy　原本
original cost　原始取得原価
original equipment manufacturing [manufacturer] (OEM)　発注元企業ブランドによる製品の受託製造（者）
original issue discount (OID)　割引発行（債券の）
original issue premium (OIP)　打歩発行（債券の）
originally　もともとは
original state　原状
originate　①発生させる，②発生する，③組成する（金融商品などを）
originated credit-impaired financial asset　信用減損組成金融資産
originating goods　原産品
origination　①発生，②組成
origination of temporary differences　一時差異の発生
or less　以下
or more　以上
Osaka Regional Tax(ation) Bureau　大阪国税局
OTC　▶over-the-counter
other accounts payable　未払金
other accounts receivable　未収入金
other capital surplus [reserve]　その他資本剰余金
other components of equity　その他の資本の構成要素　[用] transfer from other components of equity to retained earnings（その他の資本の構成要素から利益剰余金への振替）
other comprehensive income (OCI)　その他の包括利益
other comprehensive income for the year　当期その他の包括利益
other comprehensive income option (OCI option)　OCIオプション　[解] IFRS9の文脈では，本来はFVTPLの資本性金融商品（例えば，株式）をFVTOCIに指定できるという選択肢（一定の要件あり）を指す
other comprehensive income section　その他の包括利益の部（包括利益計算書などの）
other comprehensive income that will be reclassified to profit or loss　純損益に振り替えられるその他の包括利益
other comprehensive income that will not be reclassified to profit or loss　純損益に振り替えられることのないその他の包括利益
other current assets　その他の流動資産
other current liabilities　その他の流動負債
other earned surplus　その他利益剰余金
other income　①その他の収益，②その他の所得
other long-term benefits　その他の長期給付
other long-term employee benefits　その他の長期従業員給付　[解] 従業員給付の一形態であり，短期従業員給付，退職後給付，解雇給付以外のすべて従業員給付。例えば，長期勤務休暇がこれに該当する
other non-current assets　その他の非流動資産
other non-current liabilities　その他の非流動負債
other operating expense　その他の営業費用
other operating income　その他の営業収益
other payables　未払金，その他の債務　[解] 仕入債務（trade payables）に対する用語
other post-employment benefit　その他の退職後従業員給付
other post-retirement employee benefit (OPEB)　その他の退職後従業員給付
other price risk　その他の価格リスク　[解] IFRS7の文脈では，金利リスクまたは為替リスク以外で，市場価格の変動により，金融商品の公正価値または将来キャッシュ・フローが変動するリスク
other receivables　未収入金，その他の債権　[解] 売上債権（trade receivables）に対する用語
other retained earnings　その他利益剰余金
OTM　▶out of the money
outbound　海外に向けての
outbound transaction　アウトバウンド取引　[解] 日本企業が海外に進出する形態の取

引で，インバウンド取引（inbound transaction）に対する用語
outcome　結果
outlay　支出
outline　概要
outlook　①見解，②見通し
out-of-court settlement　裁判外の解決，示談
out-of-pocket expense　立替費用
out of the money (OTM)　アウト・オブ・ザ・マネー　[解]権利行使価格と基礎商品の価格との関係で，オプション取引の買方が権利行使したときに，損失が発生する状態
out of the scope　対象外（業務範囲などの）　[使い方注意!]「業務内容に含まれていない」という意味で，専門家がよく用いる表現
output　①生産，②出力，③アウトプット
output consumption tax　仮受消費税等
output tax　アウトプット・タックス　[解]output VAT の項を参照
output VAT　アウトプット VAT　[解]売上・収益に対する付加価値税であり，日本の仮受消費税等に相当
outright　完全な
outright sale　売切り
outside　外側
outside corporate auditor　社外監査役
outside director　社外取締役
outside the scope　対象外（業務範囲などの）　[解]out of the scope の項を参照
outsource　外部から調達する，外部委託する
outsourcing　アウトソーシング，外部委託
outstanding　①未決済の，②発行済の
outstanding balance　未決済残高　[解]IAS24 の文脈では，関連当事者（related party）との取引に係る未決済残高及びそれに関連する貸倒引当金の残高は開示対象となる　[用]outstanding balances for related party transactions（関連当事者との取引に係る未決済残高）
outstanding borrowings　借入金残高
outstanding cheques　未決済小切手　[米]outstanding checks　[解]銀行に持ち込まれているが，残高に未反映の小切手

outstanding shares　発行済（残存）株式
outstanding shares basis　発行済株式ベース
outstanding share options　未行使のストック・オプション
overall　全体的な
overallotment　追加割当て（有価証券の公募・売出しにおける）
over a period (of time)　一定の期間にわたって
overarching　包括的な
overcapitalisation　過大資本　[米]overcapitalization
overdraft　①当座借越，②当座貸越
overdraft facility　当座借越枠
overdue　期限を経過した，延滞の
overdue accounts receivable　滞留売掛金
overdue receivables　滞留債権，延滞債権
overestimate　①過大評価する，②過大に見積もる
overfunded　積立超過の
overhaul　①修理する，オーバーホールする，②修理，オーバーホール
overhead　①間接費，②間接経費
overhead allocation rate　間接費配賦率
overhead cost [expense]　間接費
overhedged　オーバーヘッジの
overinvestment　過大投資
overlap　①重複する，重なる，②重複
overlay　①上書きする，②上書き
overleveraging　過大なレバレッジ，過大借入れ
overlook　見落とす
overpaid　過払いの
overpayment　過払い，過大支払い，過大納付
overreport　過大申告する
override　①優先する，②無効にする，③無効化
override of internal controls　内部統制の無効化
overseas　①海外の，②海外に
overseas investment　海外投資
overseas subsidiary　海外子会社
oversee　監視する，監督する，管理する
oversight　①監視，監督，審査，②見落とし　[使い方注意!]①「監視」という意味と，②「見落とし」という（ほぼ逆の）意味があ

るので，文脈に注意が必要
overstate 過大計上する
overstated liabilities and expenses 過大計上された負債・費用
overstatement 過大計上
over-the-counter (OTC) 店頭
over-the-counter (OTC) derivative 店頭デリバティブ
over-the-counter market 店頭市場
over time 一定の期間にわたって [用]revenue is recognised either over time or at a point in time（収益は一定期間にわたって，または一時点で認識される）
overtime 時間外労働
overtime allowance 残業手当
overvaluation 過大評価
overvalue 過大評価する
overview 概要，概観
owe 借りている
owner 所有者 [解]IAS1の文脈では，資本に分類される金融商品の保有者
owner-occupied property 自己使用不動産 [解]IAS40の文脈では，財またはサービスの供給等，または管理の目的で保有している不動産であり，投資不動産（investment property）に対する用語
owner's equity 自己資本，株主資本
ownership 所有
ownership change 株主変更
ownership structure 株主構成，所有者の構成
ownership-transfer finance lease 所有権移転ファイナンス・リース
owners of the parent 親会社の所有者（株主）
own share 自己株式

P

p.a. ▶per annum
package ①連結パッケージ，②パッケージ
packaging 梱包，包装
packaging material 梱包（資）材，包装（資）材
packing 荷造り，梱包，包装
packing cost 荷造費
packing list 梱包明細，パッキング・リスト
packing slip 納品書
paid absence 有給休暇
paid in capital 払込資本，資本金
paid invoice 支払済みの請求書
paid leave 有給休暇
paid time-off (PTO) 有給休暇
paid-up share capital 払込資本金
PAN permanent account number
P&L ▶profit and loss
paper company ペーパー・カンパニー [解]タックス・ヘイブン対策税制の関係では，特定外国関係会社の1つで，外国関係会社のうち，主たる事業を行うに必要と認められる固定施設を有しておらず，本店所在地国においてその事業の管理，支配及び運営を自ら行っていないもの
par 額面
paragraph 段落，パラグラフ
parameter パラメータ，媒介変数
parent (company) 親会社 [解]他の企業（子会社）を支配している企業
parentheses parenthesisの複数形
parenthesis 括弧
parent-only accounts （親会社の）個別財務諸表，単体財務諸表
parent-only financial statements （親会社の）個別財務諸表，単体財務諸表
parent's separate 親会社単体の
parent's separate earnings per share 親会社単体の1株当たり利益
partial 部分的な

partial completion method	部分完成基準
partial deduction	部分的な損金算入，部分的な控除
partial disposal	部分除却
partial exemption	一部免税　[解] 優遇税制等で，所得の一定割合が免税となること
partial extinguishment	部分的な消滅（負債などの）
partial goodwill method	購入のれん方式
partially	部分的に
partially-owned subsidiary	一部所有子会社，部分所有子会社　[解] 100％子会社（wholly-owned subsidiary）に対する用語
partially-taxable	部分的に課税される
partially-tax deductible	部分的に損金算入可能な
participant	参加者
participate	参加する
participating equity instrument	参加型資本性金融商品
participating preferred stock	参加型優先株式
participation	参加
participation exemption	資本参加免税　[解] オランダの税制で，オランダの持株会社が他社に資本参加（出資）する場合，一定の要件を満たせば，その出資先からの配当やキャピタル・ゲインが免税になるというもの
particular	特有の，特別な
particularly	特に
particulars	詳細
partly	部分的に
partly finished goods	半製品
partly-owned subsidiary	一部所有子会社，部分所有子会社　[解] 100％子会社（wholly-owned subsidiary）に対する用語
partly paid share	部分払込株式
partner	パートナー，組合員
partnership	パートナーシップ，組合
partnership interest	パートナーシップの持分
parts	部品
part-time	パートタイムの，非常勤の
part-time corporate auditor	非常勤監査役
part-way	部分的に
party	当事者
party to a joint arrangement	共同支配の取決めの当事者　[解] IFRS11の文脈では，共同支配の取決めに「参加」している企業であり，当該取決めに対する共同支配を有しているものに限らない
par value	額面金額
par value stock [share]	額面株式
passage	通過，経過
passage of time	時の経過
passive	受動的な，消極的な
passive detection	消極的な摘発（不正などの）
passive income	①パッシブ・インカム，②受動的所得，資産性所得（旧タックス・ヘイブン対策税制における）　[解] ②タックス・ヘイブン対策税制の関係では，受動的所得とは，企業の能動的な活動を必要としない所得であり，持分比率25％未満の株式等に係る配当など一定のものを指す。平成29年度税制改正前は「資産性所得」と呼ばれていた
pass-through	パススルーの
pass-through arrangement	パススルーの取決め
pass-through entity	パススルー事業体　[解] その事業体自体は課税対象とならず，出資者（構成員）が課税されるような事業体
pass-through taxation	構成員課税，パススルー課税　[解] 事業体の所得に課税せず，その出資者（構成員）に対して課税する方式
password	パスワード
past	①過去の，②過ぎ去った【形】，③過去
past customary business practices	過去の商慣習
past due	期限を経過して，期日経過の，延滞の　[用] financial assets past due but not impaired（期日は経過しているが減損はしていない金融資産）
past due receivables	回収期限を経過した債権，延滞債権，滞溜債権
past due status	期日経過の状況

past event	過去の事象
past experience	過去の経験
past service cost	過去勤務費用　[解] 勤務費用のうち，制度改訂（確定給付制度の導入や変更）または縮小により発生する，過去の期間の従業員の勤務に対応する確定給付債務の現在価値の変動額
past service credit	過去勤務費用（貸方）
past service liability	過去勤務債務
patent	特許（権）　[解] 無形資産の例
patent box	パテント・ボックス　[解] 一定の知的財産（特許権等）から生じた所得に対する租税優遇措置
patented technology	特許技術　[解] 無形資産の例
patent infringement	特許権侵害
pattern	パターン，型
pattern of benefit consumption	便益の消費パターン
payable	未払の，支払うべき
payables	①債務，②支払勘定　[用] payables to related parties（関連当事者に対する債務）
payable within one year	1年以内に支払義務のある【形】
pay as you earn (PAYE)	源泉課税
pay-as-you-go	現金払いの
payback	回収，リターン（投資の）
payback period	回収期間（投資の）
payback period method	回収期間法　[解] 投資の可否を判断する手法の1つで，プロジェクトの初期投資額が何年で回収されるかを算定し，その期間に基づいて投資を評価すること
PAYE	▶pay as you earn
payee	受取人
payer	支払人
payment	①支払い，出金，②納付（税金などの）
payment due date	納付期限，納期限
payment extension	納付期限の延長
payment in kind (PIK)	現物による支払い，物納，現物給付
payment on behalf of	〜のための立替金　[用] parent's payment on behalf of a subsidiary（親会社が支払う子会社のための立替金）
payment process	支払（処理）プロセス
payment record	支払調書
payments for	〜のための支出　[解] キャッシュ・フロー計算書などでよく使われる用語　[用] payments for purchase of property, plant and equipment（有形固定資産の取得による支出），payments for purchase of investment securities（投資有価証券の取得による支出），payments for buyback of shares（自己株式の取得による支出）
payment slip	①支払伝票，出金伝票，②納付書
payment system	支払システム
payment terms	支払条件
pay on delivery	引渡時払い
payout	①支払い，②配当金
payout ratio	配当性向　[解] 利益のうち，配当として株主に還元する金額の割合
payroll	①賃金台帳，②給与計算
payroll cost [expense]	人件費
payroll table	給与テーブル
payroll tax	賃金税，給与税
pay-through taxation	ペイスルー課税
pay to play clause	Pay-to-Play条項　[解] 一定のファイナンスに対して，既存の投資家が（持分割合ベースで）参加しない場合，その投資家に与えられている何らかの優遇措置（権利）が喪失するという条項
PBO	▶projected benefit obligation
PBR	▶price book-value ratio, price-to-book ratio
P/B ratio	▶price book-value ratio, price-to-book ratio
PCAOB	▶Public Company Accounting Oversight Board
PE	▶①permanent establishment, ②private equity
peer group	ピア・グループ，同業他社（集団）
penalty	ペナルティ（加算税），罰金
penalty charge	罰金，違約金
penalty clause	違約条項
penalty tax	加算税
pending	未決定の

pending lawsuit	係争中の訴訟
pending tax audit	継続中の税務調査
pension	年金
pensioner	年金受給者
pension fund	年金基金
pension plan	年金制度
PER	▶price earnings ratio
per annum (p.a.)	1年当たり，1年につき
P/E ratio	▶price earnings ratio
per capita	1人当たりの
per capita inhabitant tax	住民税均等割
per capita levy	均等割（住民税の）
per capita metropolitan tax	都民税均等割
per capita municipal tax	市町村民税均等割
per capita prefectural tax	道府県民税均等割
per capita tax	均等割（住民税の） [解]住民税のうち，法人税額に連動しない部分
percentage	割合，パーセンテージ
percentage of completion method	進行基準，工事進行基準 [解]役務提供などの進捗度に合わせて収益及び原価を計上する方法
percentage of ownership	保有［持株］割合（株式などの）
percentage (of) ownership interest	所有持分割合，保有［持株］割合（株式などの）
per diem	日当
perform	実施する
performance	①実績，業績，②履行
performance assessment	業績評価
performance audit	業績監査
performance-based compensation	業績連動給与
performance-based fee	成果報酬
performance bonus	業績賞与
performance condition	業績条件 [解]IFRS2の文脈では，権利確定条件のうち，勤務条件に加えて，一定の業績目標を達成することを求めるもの。株式市場条件（market-based performance condition）とそれ以外のもの（例えば，利益目標など）がある
performance evaluation	業績評価
performance obligation	履行義務 [解]IFRS15の文脈では，財またはサービスを移転するという顧客との契約上の約束
performance obligation satisfied at a point in time	一時点で充足される履行義務
performance obligation satisfied over time	一定の期間にわたり充足される履行義務
performance target	業績目標
period	期間
period cost	期間費用
period covered by financial statements	財務諸表の対象期間
period-end adjustment	決算修正，期末修正
periodic	定期的な
periodically	定期的に
periodic inventory	定期棚卸法
periodicity	定期性
periodicity assumption	会計期間の公準
period of use	使用期間
period presented	表示される期間（財務諸表に）
period-specific	特定期間の
period-specific effect	特定期間への影響
period-specific effects for retrospective application	遡及適用による特定期間への影響
permanent	恒久的な，永久の
permanent account number (PAN)	納税者番号（インド）
permanent audit documentation	継続監査調書
permanent difference	①一時差異以外の差異，永久差異，②社外流出項目（税務調整のうち） [解]①一時差異（temporary difference）や，②留保項目（timing difference）に対する用語で，例えば，交際費等のように会計と税務の差が将来的にも解消しないもの
permanent establishment (PE)	恒久的施設 [解]恒久的施設（PE）とは，事業を行う一定の場所であって，企業がその場所を通じてその事業の全部または一部を行っている場所をいう。例えば，日本企業が海外で事業を行うために設けた（海外）支店などがこれに該当する
permanent resident	永住者
permissible	許容される
permission	許可

permit　許可する
permitted leakage　許容されたキャッシュ・フローの流出　[解]買収価格の調整の際の固定価格（locked box）方式において，契約上で許容されているキャッシュ・フローの流出項目
perpetrate　実行する（不正などを）
perpetrator　犯行者，実行者（不正などの）
perpetual　永続する【形】
perpetual inventory　継続記録法，常時棚卸法
per se　それ自体は，それ自体で
per share　1株当たり
personal　個人の，個人に属する【形】
personal holding company　個人持株会社
personal income tax　個人所得税
personal income tax rate　個人所得税率，所得税率
personal income tax return　所得税申告書
personal property　動産
personal property tax　動産税
personal purchase　個人的購入（会社経費などによる）
personal service　人的役務（の提供）
person in charge　①担当者，②責任者
personnel　従業員，人員
perspective　観点，見方
persuade　説得する
persuasive　説得力のある
pertinent　適切な
pertinent condition　適切な状況
pertinent factor　適切な要素
pervasive　浸透している，普及している
pessimistic　悲観的な
petition　①嘆願（書），②訴状
petty cash　小口現金
petty cash book　小口現金出納帳
petty cash slip　小口現金伝票
phantom stock plan　ファントム・ストック・プラン　[解]仮想の株価と株数を設定し，通常のストック・オプションと同じ方法で，一定期間内に個人が権利行使した時点の株式の評価差益を現金等で支給するもの
phase　フェーズ，段階
physical　物理的な

physical capital maintenance　実体資本維持
physical count (of cash)　（現金）実査
physical damage　物理的損害
physical data room　フィジカル・データ・ルーム（デュー・デリジェンスなどの）　[解]ヴァーチャル・データ・ルーム（virtual data room）に対する用語
physical deterioration　物理的な劣化
physical inspection　実査，現物確認，現物検査
physical inventory (count)　実地棚卸（在庫の）
physical inventory instructions　棚卸実施要領
physical possession　物理的な所有
physical safeguard　物理的保護（不正などに対する）
picture　状況，描写
piercing the corporate veil　法人格否認の法理　[解]法人格が形骸的なものである場合や法人格が濫用されている場合に，紛争解決に必要な範囲で，法人とその株主等との分離を否定する法理
PIK　▶payment in kind
pioneer certificate　パイオニア・ステイタス証明書
pioneer status　パイオニア・ステイタス　[解]優遇税制の一形態で，パイオニア・ステイタスの認定を受けた企業には，一定期間の法人税の減免等が認められる
place　①配置する，②（注文など）を出す，③場所
placement　①配置，②起債，発行証券の消化
place of business　事業を行う場所
place of central management and control　管理支配地（基準）　[解]法人の居住地国を決定する際の概念で，法人がどこで設立されているかにかかわらず，実際に事業の管理・支配が行われている国をもって，その法人の居住地国とする考え方
place of incorporation　本店所在地（基準）　[解]法人の居住地国を決定する際の概念で，法人の本店所在地国をもって，その法人の居住地国とする考え方
place of management　事業の管理の場所　[解]事業を管理している場所は，OECDモ

デル租税条約において PE(恒久的施設)として例示されている
plan 計画
plan amendment 制度の変更（退職給付制度などの）
plan assets 制度資産，年金資産 [解]退職後給付（post-employment benefit）のために保有する資産
plan curtailment 制度の縮小（退職給付制度などの）
plan participant 制度加入者（退職給付制度などの）
plan settlement 制度の清算（退職給付制度などの）
plant 工場
plausible ありそうな，もっともらしい
pledge ①担保提供する，②担保 [用]① inventories pledged as security for liabilities（負債の担保に供されている棚卸資産）
pledged asset 担保提供資産
PLI ▶profit level indicator
plow back 再投資する
PLTA ▶profit and loss transfer agreement
PMI ▶post-merger integration
PMO ▶project management office
P/N ▶promissory note
PO ▶purchase order
PoA ▶power of attorney
point ①ポイント，②時点，③小数点
pointer 指針
point in time 時点 [用] at a point in time（一時点の［で］），revenue is recognised either over time or at a point in time（収益は一定期間にわたって，または一時点で認識される）
point of production (POP) 生産時点
point of sales (POS) 販売時点
point of time 時点
policy ①方針，②保険契約，保険証券
policyholder 保険契約者
policy loan 保険契約者貸付［借入］
policy making 方針策定
pollute 汚染する
pollution 汚染
pooling method プーリング法

pooling of interests 持分プーリング
pooling-of-interests method 持分プーリング法
POP ▶point of production
portfolio ポートフォリオ
portfolio company 投資対象企業（投資会社などが投資の対象にしている企業）
portfolio hedge ポートフォリオ・ヘッジ
portfolio investment ポートフォリオ投資
portion 部分
position ①状態，②位置，③立場
position paper ポジション・ペーパー [解]移転価格税制の関係では，相互協議において，相手国に対して自国の立場を提示するための書簡
positive ①正の，プラスの，②積極的な，③確信して
positive assurance 積極的保証
positive balance プラス残高
positive confirmation 積極的確認
positive confirmation request 積極的確認（依頼）
possess 所有する
possession 所有
possibility 可能性
possible 可能性がある【形】
possible obligation 発生しうる債務
possible outcome 発生しうる結果
post 元帳に転記する（仕訳帳から）
post- 事後の
post-acquisition 取得後の，買収後の
post-acquisition due diligence 買収後のデュー・デリジェンス
post-acquisition performance 買収後の業績
post-acquisition retained earnings 取得後利益剰余金
post audit 事後監査
post-closing ①決算整理後の，②クロージング後の
post-closing due diligence 買収後［クロージング後］のデュー・デリジェンス
post-closing trial balance 決算整理後残高試算表
post-combination 企業結合後の
post-dated 先日付の，将来日付が記入され

た【形】
post-dated cheque　先日付小切手　[米] postdated check
post-employment　退職後の
post-employment benefit　退職後給付　[解] 従業員給付の一形態で，雇用関係の終了後に支払われるもの（解雇給付及び短期従業員給付を除く）
post-employment benefit expense　退職後給付費用
post-employment benefit plan　退職後給付制度　[解] 企業が従業員に対して退職後給付を支給する公式または非公式の取り決め。退職後給付制度は，確定拠出制度か確定給付制度のいずれかに分類される
post-employment life insurance　退職後生命保険
post-employment medical benefits　退職後医療給付
post-formation acquisition (of assets)　事後設立
posting　転記（仕訳帳から元帳への）
post-M&A　M&A後の
post-merger integration (PMI)　ポストマージャー・インテグレーション，買収後の統合　[解] M&A実行後の統合プロセス
postpone　延期する
post-retirement　退職後の
post-tax　税引後の　[解]「税引前の」(pre-tax)に対する用語
post-tax profit or loss　税引後損益
potential　潜在的な
potential buyer　潜在的買手
potential investor　潜在的投資家
potential loss　潜在的損失
potentially　潜在的に
potential ordinary share　潜在的普通株式　[解] その所有者に普通株式を付与する可能性がある金融商品またはその他の契約
potential risk　潜在的リスク
potential share　潜在株式
potential tax exposure　潜在的税務エクスポージャー，潜在的税務リスク
potential tax liability　潜在的租税債務　[解] 税務デュー・デリジェンスの関係では，いまだ顕在化していないものの，買収対象会社に潜在的に存在する租税債務で，買収後の税務調査により顕在化する可能性があるもの
potential value　潜在的価値
potential voting right　潜在的議決権
power　力（パワー）　[解] IFRS10の文脈では，被投資企業の関連する活動を左右する現在の能力
power of attorney (PoA)　委任状
power over an investee　被投資企業［投資先］に対する力（パワー）
power to govern　支配する力
PPA　▶purchase price allocation
PP&E　▶property, plant and equipment
PPM　▶private placement memorandum
PPT　▶principal purpose test
practicability　実行可能性
practicable　実行可能な
practical　実行可能な，実務的な
practical expedient　実務上の便法，現実的手段
practicality　実用性
practice　実務
practitioner　実務家
pre-　事前の
pre-acquisition　取得前の，買収前の
pre-acquisition contingency　買収前の偶発事象
pre-acquisition retained earnings　取得時利益剰余金
pre-acquisition tax losses　買収前の繰越欠損金
preamble　前文，序文
pre-approval　事前承認
precede　先行する【動】
precedence　①先行，②優先
precedent　①慣例，②先例，③判例
preceding　先立つ【形】
preceding year　前年
precise　正確な
precision　正確性
pre-closing　①決算整理前の，②クロージング前の
pre-closing trial balance　決算整理前残高試算表
preclude　排除する

preclusion	除外，排除
pre-consolidation	①連結前の，②連結納税開始前の
pre-consolidation losses	連結納税開始前の繰越欠損金
pre-contract	契約前の
pre-contract cost	契約前のコスト
pre-deal	取引実行前の
predecessor	前任者
predecessor auditor	前任の監査人
predecessor company	①被合併法人，②消滅会社
pre-determined	事前に決定された
pre-determined cost	予定原価
pre-determined costing	予定原価計算
pre-determined overhead rate	予定間接費配賦率
predict	予測する
predictable	予測可能な
prediction	予測
predictive	予測の
predictive value	予測価値
predominant	顕著な，優勢な
pre-emptive	①先取りの，②先買権のある【形】
pre-emptive [pre-emption] right	①優先的（新株）引受権，②先買権 【解】①既存株主が，持分比率維持のため，新株発行の際に優先的に新株を引き受ける権利など
pre-established goal	事前に設定された目標
pre-existing	既存の
pre-existing interest	既存の持分
pre-existing interest in an acquiree	被取得企業に対する既存持分
pre-existing relationship	既存の関係，以前からの関係（被取得企業などとの）
preface	序文
prefectural	都道府県の
prefectural tax	道府県民税（住民税） 【解】住民税（inhabitant tax）は，基本的に道府県民税と市町村民税（municipal tax）により構成される
prefectural tax office	道府県税事務所
prefer	より好む
preferable	より望ましい【形】
preference	選好，好み
preference dividend	優先配当 【解】優先株式（preference share）からの配当
preference right	優先権
preference share [stock]	優先株式 【解】その株主に優先権（通常は配当に関する優先権）が付与されている株式
preference share dividend	優先株式配当
preferential tax treatment	優遇税制，税制優遇措置
preferred share [stock]	優先株式
pre-filing consultation [conference]	事前相談 【解】移転価格税制の関係では，事前確認（APA）を受けようとする法人が，事前確認の申出前に，独立企業間価格の算定方法等について国税局の担当課等と行う相談
preliminary	予備の，準備の
preliminary assessment	予備評価，初期評価
preliminary comments	初期のコメント
pre-merger	合併前の
pre-merger losses	合併前の繰越欠損金
premise	前提，仮定
premises	建物，家屋 【解】通常複数形
premium	プレミアム
premium at the issue of shares	株式発行プレミアム
premium bond	プレミアム債 【解】額面を上回る価格で発行または取引される債券
pre-notified director's compensation	事前確定届出給与
pre-numbered	連番の付された【形】
pre-numbered invoices	予め連番の付された請求書
pre-opening [pre-operating] cost	開業費
prepaid	前払いの
prepaid expense	前払費用
prepaid insurance premium [expense]	前払保険料
prepaid pension cost	前払年金費用
prepaid rent	前払賃借料，前払家賃
prepaid service contract	前払式のサービス契約
preparation	作成，準備 【解】財務諸表や税務申告書などの作成という意味で使われることが多い

preparation of financial statements　財務諸表の作成
preparatory activity　準備的活動
preparatory or auxiliary activity　準備的または補助的な活動　[解]例えば，情報の提供など，企業の生産性に貢献するものではあるが，実際の利得の実現とは関係が薄い活動。準備的または補助的な性格の活動を行うことのみを目的として，事業を行う一定の場所を保有する場合，一般にその場所はPEには該当しない
prepare　作成する，準備する
preparer　作成者（財務諸表や税務申告書などの）
prepay　前払いする
prepayment　①前払い，前払金，②前払費用，③期限前返済
prepayment asset　前払費用　[用] prepayment asset for advertising expenditure（広告宣伝費に係る前払費用）
prepayment of contributions　前払いの拠出（年金基金などへの）
pre-production　生産開始前の
pre-reorganisation　組織再編前の　[米] pre-reorganization
pre-reorganisation losses　組織再編前の繰越欠損金　[米] pre-reorganization losses
prerequisite　要件，必要条件
pre-sale dividend　売却前の配当　[解]子会社等を売却する際に，売却前に配当させること。売却益（capital gain）と配当の課税に差があれば，税務メリットが取れることがある
prescribe　規定する
prescribed period　所定の期間
prescription　規定
present　現在の
presentation　表示
presentation and disclosure　表示及び開示
presentation based on liquidity　流動性に基づく表示
presentation currency　表示通貨　[解]財務諸表を表示する通貨で，表示通貨が機能通貨（functional currency）と異なる場合には，表示通貨への換算が必要になる
presentation currency other than the functional currency　機能通貨以外の表示通貨
presentation of financial statements　財務諸表の表示
present obligation　現在の債務　[解]現在の債務には，法的債務（legal obligation）のほか推定的債務（constructive obligation）も含まれる
present separately　（〜を）区分掲記する
present value　現在価値　[解]資産であれば，将来キャッシュ・フロー（流入）の現在価値を指す
preservation clause　プリザベーションの原則　[解]国内法上の減免措置や納税者にとって有利な取扱いが租税条約の締結によって損なわれることはない，という原則
preserve　保存する
pressing　差し迫った
press release　プレス・リリース
presumably　おそらく
presumption　①前提，仮定，②推定
presumptive　①仮定の，②推定に基づく
presumptive assessment [taxation]　推計課税，推定課税
pre-tax　税引前の
pre-tax cash flow　税引前キャッシュ・フロー
pre-tax income　税引前利益，税引前所得
pre-tax loss　税引前損失
pre-tax profit　税引前利益
pre-tax rate　税引前の利率
pre-transaction　取引前の
prevail　優勢である，流行している【動】
prevailing rate　広く使用されている利率
prevent　妨げる
prevention　防止，予防
preventive　予防的な
preventive control　予防的コントロール（内部統制のうち）
previous　以前の
previous accounting period　前期
previous GAAP　従前のGAAP［会計原則］　[解] IFRS採用の直前に採用していた会計基準
previously　以前

previous period	前期
previous year	前年（度）
price	価格
price book-value ratio (P/B ratio, PBR)	株価純資産倍率，PBR
price concession	値引
price earnings ratio (P/E ratio, PER)	株価収益率，PER [解]株価が利益の何倍かを算出して，株価が割安か割高かを判断する指標
price index	価格指数
price range	価格レンジ
price risk	価格リスク
price setting	価格設定
price-to-book ratio (P/B ratio, PBR)	株価純資産倍率，PBR
price variance	価格差異
pricing	価格設定，価格算定
pricing model	価格算定モデル
pricing policy	価格政策
pricing service	プライシング・サービス
prima facie	一見したところでは
primarily	主に
primary	①主要な，②最初の
primary adjustment	第一次調整（移転価格課税に係る） [解]第二次調整（secondary adjustment）に対する用語で，当初の移転価格課税を指す
primary assets	主要資産
primary market	発行市場（証券などの）
primary perpetrator	主犯者（不正などの）
primary user	主要な利用者
prime	①主要な，②最良の
prime rate	プライムレート
principal	①本人（代理人に対して），②元本（借入金などの），③主要な，主たる
principal/agent status	本人・代理人の立場
principal amount	元本
principal auditor	主たる監査人
principal business	主たる事業
principally	主に
principal market	主要な市場 [解]IFRS13の文脈では，資産または負債について，活動の量や水準（取引量や取引額）が最も大きい市場を指す
principal place of business	主たる事業の場所
principal purpose test（PPT）	主要目的テスト [解]取引の主たる目的が租税条約の特典の享受である場合には，その取引に租税条約の適用を認めないとする考え方（租税条約上の規定）
principal repayment	元本返済
principal vs. agent considerations	本人か代理人かの検討
principle	原則
principles-based	原則主義
printing cost [expense]	印刷費用
prior	①過去の，②事前の
prior approval	事前承認 [用]prior approval of tax authorities（税務当局の事前承認）
prior consent	事前の同意 [用]prior consent of tax authorities（税務当局の事前の同意）
priority	優先，優先権
prior notice	事前通知
prior period	前期，過年度
prior period adjustment	過年度修正
prior period error	過年度の誤謬 [解]信頼性の高い情報の不使用または誤用により生じた，過去の財務諸表における脱漏または誤表示
prior period information	過年度の情報
prior service cost	過去勤務費用（債務）
prior service liability	過去勤務債務
prior year	過年度
prior year tax expense	過年度税金費用，過年度法人税等
private	①非公開の，②私有の，個人の
private company	非公開会社
private equity (PE)	プライベート・エクイティ
private equity fund	プライベート・エクイティ・ファンド，PEファンド
private letter ruling	プライベート・レター・ルーリング [解]private rulingの項を参照
privately	①非公開で，②個人として
private monopoly	私的独占
private placement	私募（証券の） [解]特定の少数の投資者に対する証券発行

private placement memorandum (PPM)　目論見書

private ruling　プライベート・ルーリング　[解] 特定の納税者からの個別の照会に対する税務当局の回答で，その納税者に限って有効とされる

privatisation　民営化　[米] privatization
privatise　民営化する　[米] privatize
privilege　特権，特典
privity　当事者関係
probability　確率，可能性
probability of default　債務不履行の確率
probability-weighted basis　発生確率による加重平均ベース
probability-weighted expected value　発生確率で加重平均した期待値　[解] IAS37の文脈では，引当金の測定方法の1つとして，発生可能性のあるすべての結果を，その発生確率で加重平均した期待値として見積もる方法がある
probable　発生の可能性が高い　[解] IAS37の文脈では，more likely than not（発生の可能性が50%より高い）と同義
probably　おそらく
problem　問題
problematic　問題のある【形】
procedure　手続
proceedings　①法的手続, 訴訟手続, ②審理, ③議事録
proceeds　収入，収益　[解] 通常複数形
proceeds from　〜による収入　[解] キャッシュ・フロー計算書などでよく使われる表現　[用] proceeds from disposal of property, plant and equipment（有形固定資産の売却による収入），proceeds from disposal of investment securities（投資有価証券の売却による収入），proceeds from issue of ordinary shares（普通株式の発行による収入），proceeds from long-term borrowings（長期借入れによる収入）
process　プロセス，過程
process costing　総合原価計算
process letter　プロセス・レター　[解] 買収案件などで，売手から買手候補に対して提示される，今後のプロセス（例えば，入札プロセスなど）を記載した書面
process level control　業務プロセスに係る内部統制
process narrative　業務記述書
process owner　プロセス・オーナー
process ownership　プロセス・オーナーシップ　[解] 業務プロセスごとにプロセス・オーナーを定め，プロセス・オーナーにそれぞれの業務プロセスの適切な構築・運用に係る責任（権限）を割り当てる制度
processing　加工
processing cost　加工費
procure　調達する
procurement　調達，購買
procurement department [division]　購買部門, 調達部門
produce　生産する
product　製品
production　生産，製造
production capacity　生産能力
production control　生産管理
production cost　製造原価
production cycle　製造サイクル
production facilities　生産設備，製造設備
production line　生産ライン，製造ライン
production order　製造指図書
production overhead　製造間接費
production plan　生産計画
production process　工程，製造工程
production supplies　製造用貯蔵品
production volume　生産量
productive　生産的な，生産性の高い
productivity　生産性
product line　製品ライン
products and services　製品及びサービス　[解] IFRS8の文脈では，製品及びサービスは，全社情報の開示の一環として開示対象となる
product warranty　製品保証
professional　専門家の
professional fee　専門家報酬
professional fees expense　専門家報酬費用
professional qualification　専門的資格
professional service　専門家による役務（の提供），人的役務（の提供）

professional services fee 人的役務の提供に係る報酬
proficiency 熟練
profit 利益
profitability 収益性
profitable 収益性の高い
profit and loss (P&L) 損益
profit and loss account 損益勘定
profit and loss statement 損益計算書
profit and loss transaction 損益取引 [解]資本取引（equity transaction）に対する用語
profit and loss transfer agreement (PLTA) 損益移転契約
profit attributable to 〜に帰属する当期利益 [用] profit attributable to non-controlling interests（非支配持分に帰属する当期利益）, profit attributable to owners of the parent（親会社の所有者に帰属する当期利益）
profit attributable to PE PEに帰属する利益
profit-based compensation 利益連動給与
profit before extraordinary items 経常利益
profit before tax 税引前（当期）利益
profit centre プロフィット・センター, 利益責任単位 [米] profit center [解]責任会計（responsibility accounting）において、利益に責任を持つ部門
profit for the year 当期利益
profit for the year from continuing operations 継続事業からの当期利益
profit for the year from discontinued operations 非継続事業からの当期利益
profit from continuing operations 継続事業からの純利益
profit from discontinued operations 非継続事業からの純利益
profit from operating activities 営業活動からの純利益
profit from operations 営業利益
profit level indicator (PLI) 利益水準指標 [解]移転価格税制の関係では、移転価格分析で用いられる利益水準の指標を指す
profit margin 利益率（特に売上高総利益率）
profit mark-up 利益の上乗せ、マークアップ

profit method 利益法
profit or loss 損益, 純損益
profit or loss for the period 当期の純損益
profit or loss for the year 当期の純損益, 当期損益
profit or loss section 純損益の部（包括利益計算書などの）
profit plan 利益計画
profit ratio 利益率
profits available for distribution 分配可能利益
profit sharing プロフィット・シェアリング, 利益分配
profit sharing plan 利益分配制度
profit shifting 利益移転
profit smoothing 利益の平準化
profit split method (PSM) 利益分割法 [解]移転価格税制の関係では、独立企業間価格の算定方法の1つで、対象となる国外関連者取引について、日本企業と国外関連者の利益の合計額を計算し（切り出し計算）、それを両者の寄与度を表す一定のアロケーション・ファクターで配分し、それをもとに独立企業間価格を算定する方法を指す
profits tax 利益に対する課税
profit-taking 利食い [解]利益を確定させる取引
pro forma ①プロ・フォーマ（の）, ②形式上の [解]①企業が過年度との比較等の目的で独自に算定する実質ベースの利益指標等
pro-forma financial statements プロフォーマ財務諸表 [解]仮定の数字（例えば、予測値など）に基づく財務諸表
pro-forma invoice プロフォーマ・インボイス [解]製品の発送前に送付するインボイス
pro-forma taxation 外形標準課税
programme プログラム [米] program
progress ①進歩, 進捗, ②経過
progress billing 分割請求, 中間請求 [解]役務提供などの進捗等に応じて分割して対価を請求すること
progression 累進（課税）
progressive 累進的な

progressive rates　累進税率
progressive tax rates　累進税率
progress payment　出来高払い，中間払い
prohibit　禁止する
prohibition　禁止
project　①プロジェクト，②予測する
projected benefit obligation (PBO)　予測給付債務　[解] 一般に退職給付債務と呼ばれるもの
projected unit credit method　予測単位積増方式
project finance　プロジェクト・ファイナンス　[解] 特定のプロジェクトから予想される収益のみを基礎としたファイナンスであり，通常ノンリコース・ローン（non-recourse loan）の形態をとる
projection　予測，計画
project management office (PMO)　プロジェクト・マネジメント・オフィス　[解] 組織内の複数のプロジェクトの管理を支援するため設置されるスタッフ部門
prolonged　長引く，長期化した【形】
prolonged decline　継続的な下落
promise　①契約，②保証，③約束
promissory note (P/N)　①約束手形，②借用証書
promote　促進する
promoted　奨励対象となる【形】　[解] 優遇税制の文脈では，その対象となる地域，事業，活動，製品等を指す
promoted activity　奨励対象活動
promoted area　奨励対象地域
promoted business　奨励対象事業
promoted product　奨励対象製品
promoter　発起人
promotion　①昇進，②促進
prompt　迅速な
pronouncement　①見解，②判決
proof　証明
proper　適切な
property　①財産，資産，②所有地，不動産
property and equipment　有形固定資産（工場が含まれない場合）
property development　不動産開発
property income　資産所得
property interest　不動産持分

property management　不動産管理
property, plant and equipment (PP&E)　有形固定資産　[解] 製品の製造や役務の提供に使用する目的等で企業が保有し，1会計期間を超えて使用されると予想される有形の資産
property tax　財産税，固定資産税
property valuer　（不動産）鑑定人
proportion　①割合，②比例
proportional　比例した【形】
proportional allocation　比例配分
proportionally　比例して
proportional taxation　比例課税
proportionate　比例した【形】
proportionate consolidation　比例連結
proportionate interest　比例持分
proportionately　比例して
proportionate share　比例割合，比例持分
proportion of ownership interest (in)　所有持分割合　[用] proportion of ownership interest in a subsidiary（子会社に対する所有持分割合）
proportion of ownership interests held by non-controlling interests　非支配持分の所有持分割合
proportion of voting rights held (in)　議決権の保有割合　[用] proportion of voting rights held in a subsidiary（子会社に対して保有している議決権の割合）
proportion of voting rights held by non-controlling interests　非支配持分の議決権の保有割合
proposal　提案，提案書
propose　提案する
proprietary　①所有（主）の，②独占的な
proprietor　①所有者（土地などの），②経営者，事業主
proprietorship　①個人事業，②個人事業者
pro rata　①プロラタ，②比例的な【形】，③比例的に【副】
pro rata allocation　比例配分
pro rata rule　プロラタ・ルール
pro rata share　比例割合，比例持分
proration　比例配分，按分計算
pro-sandbagging clause　プロ・サンドバギング条項　[解] 買収契約などにおいて，売

手による表明・保証違反を買手が知っていたかどうかを問わず，当該違反に基づく補償請求を認めるという条項

prospective ①将来の，②見込みのある

prospective application 将来に向かっての適用 [解] 会計方針の変更についていうと，変更時点から新しい会計方針を適用すること。遡及適用(retroactive application)に対する用語

prospective financial information 将来に関する財務情報

prospectively 将来にわたり

prospectus 目論見書 [解] 証券発行時の届出書の一部で，会社内容やその証券の内容を説明する資料

protect 保護する

protection 保護

protective 保護的な

protective rights 防御的な権利，保護的な権利 [解] IFRS10の文脈では，権利を有する当事者の利益を保護するように設計された権利（例えば，一定の拒否権）で，当該権利が関係する企業に対する力（パワー）を与えないもの

protocol 議定書 [解] 租税条約に付随して国会の承認を得るもので，議定書には租税条約の解釈が記載されていることがある

prototype プロトタイプ，模型

protracted 長引く，長引いた【形】

prove 証明する

prove-out 適用除外基準

provide ①提供する，供給する，②引当金を設定する，③規定する

provide for 〜に対して引当金を設定する

provider 供給者

provision ①引当金，②規定，条項，③提供，供給 [解] ①時期または金額が不確実な負債 [用] ① to make additional provisions（引当金を積み増す）

provisional 暫定的な，仮の

provisional amount 暫定的な金額，仮の金額

provisional assessment ①暫定賦課課税，②暫定的な評価査定

provisionally 仮に

provisional tax payment 予定納税

provisional value 暫定的な評価 [用] a business combination is accounted for using provisional values（企業結合は暫定的な評価を用いて会計処理される），adjustments to provisional values（暫定的な評価に対する修正）

provision for 〜に対する引当金

provision for bad debt 貸倒引当金

provision for bonuses 賞与引当金

provision for decommissioning costs 除去費用引当金，解体費用引当金

provision for directors' bonuses 役員賞与引当金

provision for directors' retirement benefits 役員退職慰労引当金

provision for employee benefits 従業員給付に係る引当金

provision for environmental rehabilitation costs 環境引当金，環境対策引当金

provision for investment losses 投資損失引当金

provision for litigation 訴訟引当金，訴訟損失引当金

provision for loss on construction contracts 工事損失引当金

provision for loss on disaster 災害損失引当金

provision for loss on guarantees 債務保証損失引当金

provision for onerous contracts 不利な契約に対する引当金

provision for product warranties 製品保証引当金

provision for repairs 修繕引当金

provision for restructuring costs リストラクチャリング引当金，構造改革費用引当金

provision for retirement benefits 退職給付引当金

provision for sales rebates 売上割戻引当金

provision for sales returns 返品調整引当金

provision for site restoration 土地原状回復引当金

provision for warranties 製品保証引当金

provision of services 役務提供

proximity 近似
proxy 委任状（議決権行使の）
prudence 慎重性
prudent 慎重な
prudential 慎重な
prudent man rule 善管注意義務
PSM ▶profit split method
PTO ▶paid time-off
PTP ▶publicly traded partnership
public ①公開の，②政府による，③公衆
public company 公開会社
Public Company Accounting Oversight Board (PCAOB) 公開会社会計監督委員会（米国） [解] 米国において，公開会社を監査する会計事務所の監査業務の品質を監視する機関
public letter ruling パブリック・レター・ルーリング [解] public ruling の項を参照
publicly 公に
publicly held company [corporation] 上場会社
publicly traded company [corporation] 上場会社
publicly traded partnership (PTP) 上場パートナーシップ
public market 公開市場
public notice 公告
public offering 公募，公開（証券の）
public official 役人，公務員
public placement 公募（証券の）
public relations 広報
public relations cost [expense] 広報費
public ruling パブリック・ルーリング [解] 特定の状況における税法の適用関係についての税務当局の見解のうち，一般に公表されるもの
public-to-private service arrangement 公から民へのサービス契約
public works 公共事業
publish ①公表する，②発行する
published price quotation 公表された価格相場
published statistics 公表された統計値
publishing title 出版の題名
punishment 刑罰，罰則，懲罰

punitive 懲罰的な
punitive damages 懲罰的損害賠償金
purchase ①購入する，②購入，購買，仕入
purchase allowance 仕入値引
purchase budget 購買予算
purchase cost 購入原価
purchase cut-off 仕入のカットオフ（締切）
purchased call option 買建コール・オプション
purchased call option on shares 株式に係る買建コール・オプション
purchased credit-impaired financial asset 購入した信用減損金融資産
purchased goods 購入品，商品
purchased goodwill 購入のれん
purchase discount 仕入割引
purchased option 買建オプション
purchased or originated credit-impaired financial assets 購入または組成した信用減損金融資産
purchased put option 買建プット・オプション
purchased put option on shares 株式に係る買建プット・オプション
purchase ledger 仕入元帳
purchase method パーチェス法
purchase of treasury shares 自己株式の取得
purchase option 購入選択権［オプション］（リースなどの）
purchase order (PO) 注文書
purchase price ①購入価格，買収価格，②取得原価
purchase price adjustment 買収価格の調整
purchase price adjustment mechanism 買収価格の調整メカニズム [解] 企業買収にあたって，デュー・デリジェンス等における発見事項を買収価格の調整として織り込むこと
purchase price allocation (PPA) 取得原価の配分 [解] 買収の対価を取得した各資産に配分する作業
purchase price variance 仕入価格差異，購入価格差異
purchase process 購買プロセス
purchaser 購入者，買手

purchaser due diligence　買手によるデュー・デリジェンス
purchase rebate　仕入割戻し
purchase requisition　購入申請書
purchase return　仕入戻し高，仕入返品
purchase taxes　取得税（有形固定資産などの）
purchasing budget　購買予算
purchasing department [division]　購買部門
pure research　基礎研究
purport　趣旨
purpose　目的
pursuant to　〜に従って
push-down accounting　プッシュダウン会計　[解]米国基準において，子会社を取得した場合に，子会社の個別財務諸表上の資産・負債の金額を，親会社にとっての取得価額ベースに修正すること
push □ down to　□（負債・費用など）を〜（子会社方向など）へ移転させる　[解]親会社で発生した費用を子会社に負担させる場合など
put option　プット・オプション　[解]基礎商品を将来のある期日までにあらかじめ定められた権利行使価格で売る権利
puttable　買取請求権付きの
puttable instrument　プッタブル金融商品　[解]現金または他の金融資産と交換に，当該金融商品を発行者に売り戻す権利が保有者に与えられている金融商品など

Q

Q&A process　Q&Aプロセス　[解]デュー・デリジェンスなどにおいて，買手が買収対象会社に質問を行い回答を入手するという一連のプロセス
QC　▶quality control
qualification　資格
qualified　①適格の，②限定付きの
qualified corporate reorganisation　適格組織再編　[米]qualified corporate reorganization　[解]日本の組織再編税制において，組織再編のうち適格要件を充足するもので，基本的に課税が繰り延べられる
qualified opinion　限定意見（監査報告書における）
qualified resident　適格居住者
qualified stock option　適格ストック・オプション　[解]ストック・オプションのうち，税務上の適格要件を満たすもの。権利行使時の課税は繰り延べられ，株式売却時に初めて課税が行われる
qualify　①資格を与える，適格とする，②資格がある，適格である【動】
qualify for　〜の資格がある
qualifying asset　適格資産　[解]IAS23の文脈では，企業の意図した使用または販売が可能となるまでに相当の期間を要する資産。建設期間中の有形固定資産や投資不動産，開発期間中の無形資産などが適格資産になりうる
qualifying insurance policy　適格な保険証券　[解]報告企業の関連当事者でない保険会社の発行した保険証券のうち一定の要件を満たすもので，（従業員給付制度の）制度資産を構成する
qualifying project　適格プロジェクト　[解]一般に，優遇税制の対象となるプロジェクト
qualitative　定性的な，質的な　[解]「定量的な」（quantitative）に対する用語

qualitative analysis　定性的分析
qualitative and quantitative information　定性的及び定量的情報
qualitative characteristics　定性的な特性，質的特性
qualitative disclosure　定性的開示，定性的情報の開示　[解]数値化された「定量的開示（quantitative disclosure）」に対する用語。IFRS7の文脈では，金融商品から生じるリスクの管理に関する経営者の目的，方針，及び手続などを説明するもの
qualitative factor　質的要素
qualitative information　定性的情報
qualitatively　定性的に，質的に
quality　品質
quality assurance　品質保証
quality control (QC)　品質管理
quality inspection　品質検査
quality of earnings　利益の質　[解]利益の質は，会計制度自体の歪みや企業の会計処理の保守性等により左右される
quantifiable　数値化可能な，定量化可能な
quantification　数値化，定量化
quantified　数値化された，定量化された
quantify　数値化する，定量化する
quantitative　定量的　[解]「定性的な」（qualitative）に対する用語
quantitative analysis　定量的分析
quantitative disclosure　定量的開示，定量的情報の開示　[解]数値化されていない「定性的開示（qualitative disclosure）」に対する用語。IFRS7の文脈では，金融商品から生じるリスクなどを数値として示すもの
quantitative factor　量的要素
quantitative information　定量的情報
quantitatively　定量的に
quantitative threshold　量的基準，定量的な基準値　[解]IFRS8の文脈では，定量的な基準値とは，報告セグメントを決定する際に考慮される基準で，収益，純損失，資産等が全セグメント合計の10%以上など，一定の基準を満たす事業セグメントを報告対象とするものを指す
quantity　量
quantity of earnings　利益の量　[解]利益の質（quality of earnings）に対する用語
quantity variance　数量差異
quarter　四半期
quarterly　①四半期の，②四半期に1度
quarterly budget　四半期予算
quarterly control　四半期統制
quarterly filing　四半期ごとの申告
quarterly financial statements　四半期財務諸表
quarterly period　四半期
quarterly report　四半期報告書
quarterly reporting　四半期報告
quarterly review　四半期レビュー
quarterly securities report　四半期報告書
quartile　四分位値［数］　[解]第1四分位値（first quartile）・第3四分位値（third quartile）は，データ（例えば，比較対象取引の利益率など）を小さい順に並べたときの，それぞれ25%目・75%目の値を意味する。なお，第2四分位値は中央値（median）である
quasi-　①準-，②疑似-
quasi-debt equity swap　疑似デット・エクイティ・スワップ，疑似DES　[解]デット・エクイティ・スワップ（DES）と同様の金融支援策であり，債権者が債務者（融資先）の増資を引き受け，その資金をもって債権を回収するスキーム。経済的実質としてはDESと同様であるが，税務上の取扱いが異なるケースがある
quasi-fixed cost　準固定費
quasi-reorganisation　準組織再編　[米]quasi-reorganization
quasi-variable cost　準変動費
query　質問
question　質問
questionable　疑わしい
questionnaire　質問書
quick　迅速な
quick assets　当座資産　[解]現金・売上債権・短期保有の有価証券等を指す
quickly　迅速に
quick ratio　当座比率　[解]企業の短期的な支払能力を判断するための安全性指標であり，以下の算式で計算される
当座比率＝当座資産（現金・売上債権・

短期保有の有価証券等）/流動負債
quota　数量割当　[解] 製造や輸出入の数量割当を意味する
quotation　①相場，②引用
quote　①値付けする，②引用する
quoted market price　公表された市場価格
quoted price　公表価格
quoted prices in active markets　活発な市場における公表価格
quoted securities　時価のある有価証券

R

raise　①高める，②掲げる，③調達する（資金を）　[用] ③ to raise funds（資金を調達する）
ramification　分岐
R&D　▶research and development
R&M　▶repair and maintenance
random　ランダムな
range　①幅，範囲，レンジ，②変動する
rate　率
rate of return　収益率，利益率
ratification　批准，承認
ratify　批准する，承認する
rating　格付け，評価
rating agency　格付機関
ratio　比率
ratio analysis　比率分析
rational　合理的な
rationale　合理的な根拠
rationing　割当て，配給
raw material　原材料
RCM　▶risk control matrix
reacquire　再取得する
reacquired right　再取得した権利　[解] IFRS3の文脈では，取得企業が企業結合前に被取得企業に使用を認めていた権利（例えば，技術ライセンス契約）を，企業結合の結果，取得企業が取得した場合のその権利を指す
reacquisition　再取得
react　①反応する，②反対する
readily　容易に
readily convertible to cash　容易に換金できる【形】
real estate　不動産
real estate acquisition tax　不動産取得税
real estate agent　不動産業者
real estate appraisal　不動産鑑定評価
real estate appraisal report　不動産鑑定評価書

real estate held for resale	販売用不動産
real estate holding company	不動産保有法人，不動産関連法人
real estate income	不動産所得
real estate inventories	販売用不動産
real estate investment trust (REIT)	不動産投資信託，リート
real estate transfer tax (RETT)	不動産譲渡税
real income	実質所得
real interest rate	実質利子率
realisability	実現可能性　㋎realizability
realisable	実現可能な　㋎realizable
realisable value	実現可能価額　㋎realizable value　[解]資産であれば，通常の事業過程で処分することにより得られる金額を指す
realisation	実現　㋎realization
realisation principle	実現主義　㋎realization principle
realise	実現する　㋎realize
realised gains and losses	実現損益　㋎realized gains and losses　[解]未実現損益（unrealised gains and losses）に対する用語
realised profit	実現利益　㋎realized profit
realistic	現実的な
realistically	現実的に
reallocate	再配賦する
reallocation	再配賦
real property	不動産
real property acquisition tax	不動産取得税
real property holding corporation	不動産保有会社
real property interest	不動産持分
real rate of return	実質収益率
rearrange	①再調整する，②再編成する
rearrangement	①再調整，②再編成
reason	理由，根拠
reasonable	合理的な
reasonable assurance	合理的な保証
reasonable estimate	合理的な見積り
reasonableness	合理性
reasonably	合理的に
reassess	再評価する，再査定する
reassessment	①再評価，再査定，②更正（税務当局による）
reassessment notice	更正通知（書）
reaudit	再監査
rebalance	再調整する，バランスを調整する
rebalancing	再調整，バランス調整
rebalancing of hedge relationships	ヘッジ関係のバランス調整
rebate	リベート，割戻し
rebut	反論する
rebuttable	反論可能な
rebuttable presumption	反論可能な前提
recalculate	再計算する
recalculation	再計算
recapitalisation	資本再構成，資本構成の変更　㋎recapitalization
recapture	取り返す
recast	修正する，再表示する（過年度の財務諸表などを）
recast book value	修正後簿価，調整後簿価
recast earnings	修正後利益，調整後利益
recasting	修正，再表示（過年度の財務諸表などの）
receipt	①受領，②領収書
receipt of goods	入荷
receipt of money	入金
receipt slip	入金伝票
receivable	①未収の，②債権　[解]② IFRS15の文脈では，企業が顧客に移転した財またはサービスと交換に受け取る対価に対する企業の権利で，無条件のもの（時の経過のみが要求されているもの）。条件の観点で，契約資産（contract asset）は区別される
receivables	①債権，②受取勘定　[用]① receivables due from related parties（関連当事者に対する債権）
receivables and payables	債権債務
receivables and payables schedule	債権債務管理表
receivables turnover	債権回転率
receive	受け取る
receiver	管財人，破産管財人
receiving report	入荷報告書
recent	最近の
recently	最近
recession	景気後退
recharacterise	みなす　㋎recharacterize

recipient 受取人

[解] 取引の経済的実質が法的形式と異なる場合などに，税務当局などが課税関係を検討するうえで，(法的形式ではなく) 経済的実質に注目すること

recipient company 受領した会社（寄附金などを）

reciprocity 相互主義　[解] 外国人に権利を認める場合，その外国人の本国が自国民に対して，同様の権利を認めていることを条件とするもの

recitals 前文（契約書などの）

reclassifiable 組替可能な　[用] items of other comprehensive income are grouped based on whether or not they are potentially reclassifiable to profit or loss at a later date（その他の包括利益の項目は，純損益への組替可能性の有無によりグループ分けされる）

reclassification ①分類変更, 再分類, ②組替

reclassification adjustment 組替調整（額）　[解] 当期または過去の期間に「その他包括利益」として認識されていたもので，当期において「純損益」に組み替えられた金額　[用] reclassification adjustments on cash flow hedges（キャッシュ・フロー・ヘッジに係る組替調整額）

reclassification adjustment to profit or loss for the year 当期利益（損失）への組替調整額

reclassification date 分類変更日

reclassification entry 組替仕訳

reclassify ①再分類する, ②組み替える　[用] to be reclassified from OCI（その他の包括利益から組み替えられる）

recognisable 認識可能な　[米] recognizable

recognise 認識する　[米] recognize

recognise in profit or loss 純損益として認識する　[米] recognize in profit or loss　[用] to be recognised as a bargain purchase in profit or loss（割安購入益として純損益に認識される）

recognise outside profit or loss 純損益の外で認識する　[米] recognize outside profit or loss

recognition 認識　[解] 財務諸表への計上を決定するプロセス

recognition and measurement 認識及び測定

recognition criteria 認識基準

recognition inconsistency 認識に関する不一致・不整合

recognition of previously unrecognised deductible temporary differences 過去に認識されていなかった将来減算一時差異の認識　[米] recognition of previously unrecognized deductible temporary differences

recognition of previously unrecognised tax losses 過去に認識されていなかった税務上の欠損金の認識　[米] recognition of previously unrecognized tax losses

recognition principle 認識の原則

recommend 推奨する

recommendation 推奨

recomputation 再計算

reconcile 調整する

reconciliation ①調整, 差異調整, ②調整表　[解] ①期首残高と期末残高の「調整」という意味で，増減内訳という意味で用いられることもある, ② IFRS の初度適用にあたっては，従前の GAAP による純資産や包括利益（または当期純損益）等について，IFRS に基づく包括利益への調整表の開示が必要となる

reconciliation from A to B A から B への調整（表）　[用] reconciliation from the opening balances to the closing balances（期首から期末残高への調整（表））

reconciliation item 調整項目

reconciliation of changes in deferred tax assets [liabilities] 繰延税金資産［負債］の増減の調整表

reconciliation of effective tax rate 実効税率の調整（表），税率差異の調整（表）

reconfirm 再確認する

reconsider 再検討する

reconsideration 再検討

reconstruct 再構築する

record ①記録する, ②記帳する, 認識する, ③記録

record date 基準日（配当などの）

recordkeeping	記録保管（業務），文書保存
recordkeeping requirement	文書保存義務
record master	レコード原盤 [解] 無形資産の例
record retention	記録の保存
record retention period	記録の保存期間
recoup	取り戻す
recourse	遡及，遡及権 [用] with recourse（遡及権のある），without recourse（遡及権のない）
recover	①回復する，②取り戻す（損失などを），③回収する（投資などを）
recoverability	回収可能性
recoverable	回収可能な，回復可能な
recoverable amount	回収可能価額 [解] 文字通り，資産等から回収可能な金額であり，IAS36の文脈では，処分コスト控除後の公正価値と使用価値のいずれか高い金額を指す
recovery	①回復，②回収
recovery of bad debt	償却債権取立益
recovery of losses	損失の回復
recovery of tax	①還付（納税者から見て），②延滞額の回収（税務当局から見て）
recovery period	回収期間
recruit	①募集する，採用する，②新入社員
recruiting cost [expense]	採用費用
recruitment	採用
rectification	修正
rectify	修正する
recur	①繰り返される，②循環する
recurring	経常の，継続する【形】
recurring basis	経常ベース，継続ベース [用] on a recurring or non-recurring basis（経常的または非経常的な）
recurring fair value measurement	経常的な公正価値評価
recycle	リサイクルする
recycling	リサイクリング
redeem	償還する
redeemable	償還可能な
redeemable preference share [stock]	償還優先株式
redemption	買戻し，償還
redemption amount [value]	償還金額
redesignate	再指定する
redesignation	再指定
redevelop	再開発する
redevelopment	再開発
red flag	レッド・フラッグ，危険信号
red flag due diligence	レッド・フラッグ・デュー・デリジェンス [解] 買収にあたって重要な事項（例えば，ディール・ブレイカー（deal breaker）となりうるもの）のみを調査の対象とするデュー・デリジェンス
red flag report	レッド・フラッグ・レポート
redistribute	再分配する
redistribution	再分配
reduce	減少させる
reduced (tax) rate	軽減税率
reducing balance method	定率法
reduction	減少，削減
reduction in capital	減資
reduction in future contributions	将来掛金の減額
reduction in tax rate	税率引下げ
reduction of capital	減資
reduction or exemption	減免 [解] 租税条約の規定により，源泉税などは減免の対象となることが多い。なお，(tax) relief の1語で減免を表すこともできる
redundancy	①余分，②余剰従業員
redundancy payment	解雇手当
redundancy plan	人員整理計画
redundant	余分な，余剰とされた
redundant asset	余剰資産
reestimate	①再見積り，②再見積りする
refer (to)	①（～を）参照する，②（～に）言及する
reference	参照 [用] to be measured by reference to the fair value of the equity instruments granted（付与した資本性金融商品の公正価値を参照する形で測定される）
refinancing	リファイナンス，借換え
refinancing agreement	リファイナンス契約，借換契約
refinancing fee	借換手数料
refine	洗練する [解] 例えば，報告書などの内容を精緻化すること
reflect	反映する

reform	①改正する，②改正
refund	払戻し，返金，還付
refundable	返金可能な，還付可能な
refunding	借換え
refund liability	返金負債
refund of tax	税金の還付
refund policy	返金方針，返済方針
refusal	拒否
refuse	拒否する
regime	制度，体制
region	地域
regional	地域の
regional headquarters (RHQ)	地域統括本部 [解]シンガポールなどで，優遇税制の対象となるステイタスの1つ
regional headquarters (company)	①地域統括会社，②統括会社 [解]②タックス・ヘイブン対策税制の関係では，統括会社とは，外国関係会社のうち，内国法人の100％子会社で，複数の被統括会社に対して統括業務を行っている等の一定の要件を充足するものを指す
Regional Tax(ation) Bureau	国税局
register	①登録する，②登記する，③小口現金出納帳，④金銭登録器
register disbursements scheme	レジ不正スキーム
registered bond	記名債券
registered capital	授権資本
registered office	登記上の本社，登録事業所
registered securities	記名証券
registered trademark	登録商標
registrar	①登録機関，②登記官
registration	①登録，②登記
registration and license tax	登録免許税
registration duty	登録免許税
registration fee	登録（手数）料
registration statement	①登録書類，②有価証券届出書
registration tax	登録免許税
regression analysis	回帰分析
regressive	逆進的な
regressive rate	逆進税率
regular	規則的な，定期的な [用]on a regular basis（規則的に，定期的に）
regular hybrid	レギュラー・ハイブリッド [解]源泉地国においてパス・スルー課税を受け，構成員の居住地国で団体課税を受けること。リバース・ハイブリッド（reverse hybrid）に対する用語
regular inspection	定期点検
regularly	規則的に，定期的に，通常
regular way	通常の方法
regular way contract	通常の契約，通常の方法による契約
regular way purchase or sale	通常の方法による売買
regular way trade	通常の取引
regulate	規制する
regulation	規制
regulator	規制当局，規制機関
regulatory	規制の
regulatory agency	規制官庁
regulatory authority	規制当局
regulatory body	規制機関
regulatory deferral account	規制繰延勘定
regulatory organisation	規制機関，規制団体 [米]regulatory organization
reimburse	①払い戻す，②弁済する
reimbursement	①払戻し（立替費用などの），②弁済
reimbursement right	補填の権利
reinforce	補強する
reinsurance	再保険
reinsurance asset	再保険資産
reinsurance company	再保険会社
reinsurance contract	再保険契約
reinsurer	再保険者
reinvest	再投資する
reinvestigate	再調査する
reinvestigation	再調査
reinvestment	再投資
reinvestment rate	再投資比率
REIT	▶real estate investment trust
related company	関係会社
related cost [expense]	関連費用
related party	①関連当事者（会計），②関連者（税務） [解]①報告企業と一定の関連のある個人または企業，②国外関連者より広く，国内の関連者も含む概念
related party transaction	①関連当事者取引（会計），②関連者取引（税務） [解]①報

告企業と関連当事者との間の資源，役務または債務の移転をいい，対価のやり取りの有無を問わない，②国外関連取引より広く，国内の関連者との取引も含む概念

relationship　関係
relative　①相対的な，②関係のある【形】
relatively　相対的に，比較的
relax　緩和する（法規制や条件などを）
release　①公表する，②解放する，③公表，④解放
release letter　リリース・レター，確認書　[解]　デュー・デリジェンス業務等にあたり，公認会計士等が「自らの報告書を第三者が利用することによる不利益につき，何らの責任も負わないこと」を明確にするために，業務の委託者から入手するレター
release of provisions　引当金の目的外使用（取崩し）
relevance　目的適合性　[解]　財務諸表の質的特性の１つ
relevant　適切な，関連性のある
relevant activities　関連性のある活動　[解]　IFRS10の文脈では，被投資企業のリターンに重要な影響を及ぼす被投資企業の活動を指す
relevant tax office　所轄税務署
relevant (to)　（〜と）関連性がある
reliability　信頼性
reliability of measurement　測定の信頼性
reliable　信頼性のある
reliably　信頼性をもって　[用]　the fair value of employee services received can be estimated reliably（従業員から受け取るサービスの公正価値が信頼性をもって測定できる）
reliance　信頼，依存
relief　軽減，免除
relinquish　①放棄する，②譲渡する
relist　再上場する
relisting　再上場
reload feature　リロード特性　[解]　オプション保有者が，オプション行使に伴って（現金ではなく）株式を払込みに使用する場合，追加的にストック・オプションを自動付与するという規定
reload option　リロード・オプション
relocate　①移転させる，②移転する
relocation　移転
relocation cost [expense]　移転費用
remain　①残存する，②〜のままである　[用]　② remain the same（変わらない），remain unchanged（変わらない）
remainder　残余
remaining　残存する【形】
remaining amortisation period　残存償却期間（無形資産などの）　[米]　remaining amortization period
remaining amount　残額，残りの金額
remaining performance obligation　残存履行義務
remaining service period　残存勤務期間
remaining useful life　残存耐用年数
remaining working lives　残存勤務期間
remark　①備考，②所見
remarks column　備考欄
remeasure　再測定する
remeasurement　再測定　[解]　IAS19の文脈では，確定給付負債（資産）の再測定結果（例えば，数理計算上の差異）は，発生時にその全額をその他の包括利益として認識し，事後的な純損益へのリサイクリングも行わない
remedial action　是正措置
remediation　改善，是正
remedy　①救済する，②救済，③改善（方法）
remit　送金する
remittance　送金
remittance advice　送金通知（書）
remote　①起こりそうにない【形】，②遠隔の
removal　①除去，撤去，②排除，③解任
removal cost　除去費用
removal rights　解任権　[解]　IFRS10の文脈では，意思決定者から意思決定権限を剥奪する権利を指す
remove　取り除く
remunerate　報酬を与える
remuneration　報酬
remuneration derived from rendering professional [personal] services　人的役務提供事業の対価

render	提供する
rendering of services	役務提供
renegotiate	再交渉する
renew	更新する（契約などを）
renewable	①更新可能な，②再生可能な
renewal	更新（契約などの）
renewal option	更新選択権［オプション］（リースなどの）
rent	①賃借料，②賃貸料
rental	①賃貸借，②賃貸借の
rent(al) expense	支払賃借料，支払家賃
rent(al) income	賃貸収入
rental of investment property	投資不動産の賃貸
rental of property	不動産賃貸
rent(al) payment	賃借料・レンタル料（の支払い）
rent(al) period	賃貸期間
rent(al) revenue	受取賃貸料，受取家賃
rental value	賃貸価値，賃貸価格（不動産などの）
rent-free (arrangement)	フリーレント（の取決め）
rent-free period	フリーレント期間
rent payment	賃借料（の支払い）
reorganisation	①組織再編，②更生（会社更生）［米］reorganization
reorganisation without consideration	無対価組織再編　［米］reorganization without consideration
reorganise	再編する　［米］reorganize
repair	①修繕する，②修繕
repair and maintenance (R&M)	修繕及び保守
repair cost [expense]	修繕費
repairs and maintenance expense	維持修繕費
repatriate	本国に送り返す（利益・資産などを）
repatriation	利益還流，資金還流
repay	返済する
repayable	返済すべき
repayment	返済　［用］repayment of long-term borrowings（長期借入金の返済による支出）
repayment of grant	補助金の返還
repeal	廃止する
repeat	繰り返す
repercussion	影響
reperformance	再実施（監査人による）
repetition	繰り返し
repetitive	繰り返しの，反復的な
replace	取り替える
replacement	取替え，差替え
replacement award	代替報酬
replacement cost	再調達原価
replacement method	取替法
replacement of property	資産の買換え
replacement property	代替資産
replacement value	再調達価額
repledge	再担保
replicate	複製する
repo	レポ
report	①報告書，②報告
reportability	報告可能性
reportable segment	報告セグメント　［解］IFRS8の文脈では，報告の対象となる事業セグメント（または特定の条件に合致して集計された事業セグメントの合計数値）を指す
report date	報告日
reported earnings	報告利益
report form	報告様式
reporting	報告
reporting date	報告日
reporting deadline	報告期限
reporting entity	報告企業　［解］財務諸表を作成する企業
reporting hotline	内部通報制度
reporting mechanism	報告の枠組み
reporting method	報告方法
reporting package	連結パッケージ
reporting period	報告期間
reporting unit	報告単位
report of payment	支払調書
repossession	①担保の差押え，②再取得
repo transaction	レポ取引
represent	①表す，②表明する，③代表する
representation	①表示，②表明，③経営者確認書
representation and warranty	表明・保証　［解］買収契約書（株式譲渡契約書など）に

おいて，その取引に関連する各種の事実について各当事者がそれが真実であることを表明・保証すること。その事実が真実でない場合には金銭による補償の請求などを可能とする補償条項が通常セットで規定される
representation and warranty clause　表明・保証条項
representation letter　経営者確認書
representations (reps)　表明
representations and warranties (reps & warranties)　表明・保証
representative　①代表する【形】，②代表者
representative director　代表取締役
representative office　駐在員事務所
reproduction cost　再生産原価
reps　▶representations
reps & warranties　▶representations and warranties
repurchase　買戻し，再購入
repurchase agreement　買戻契約，再購入契約
repurchase arrangement　買戻契約，買戻しの取決め
repurchase cost　再調達原価
request　①依頼する，②依頼
request for information (RFI)　情報提供依頼（書），資料依頼（書）
request form　申請書
request for proposal (RFP)　提案依頼書
request for reconsideration (to National Tax Tribunal)　審査請求（国税不服審判所に対する）
request for refund　還付請求
request for reinvestigation　再調査の請求（税務当局に対する）
request for remittance　送金依頼
require　要求する
required rate of return　要求収益率
requirement　①要件，②要求
requisite　必要な
requisition　要求，購買要求
rerate　再評価する
rerating　再評価，評価見直し
resale　再販売，転売
resale price　再販売価格

resale price margin　再販売による粗利
resale price method (RPM)　再販売価格基準法, PR法　[解]移転価格税制の関係では，独立企業間価格の算定方法の１つで,「国外関連取引に係る棚卸資産の買手（販売会社など）が独立第三者に対して当該棚卸資産を販売した対価の額から通常の利潤の額を控除して計算した金額」をもって独立企業間価格とする方法を指す
reschedule　①計画を変更する，②返済スケジュールを変更する
rescind　①無効にする，取り消す，②廃止する（法律などを）
rescission　取消し（契約などの）
research　研究　[解]新規の科学的知識等を得る目的で実施される基礎的な調査
research and development (R&D)　研究開発
research and development (R&D) cost [expense/expenditure]　研究開発費，試験研究費　[使い方注意]会計上は「研究開発費」と呼ぶことが多く，税務上は「試験研究費」と呼ぶことが多い
research and development (R&D) department [division]　研究開発部門
research and development (R&D) tax credit　試験研究費の税額控除
research expense　研究費
research phase　研究局面
resell　再販売する，転売する
reservation　①留保，②予約
reservation of title　所有権の留保
reserve　①剰余金，②積立金，準備金
reserve for　〜積立金
residence　居住（地）
residence certificate　居住者証明（書）
resident　居住者
resident alien　居住外国人
residual　残余の
residual analysis　残余利益分析　[解]residual profit split method (RPSM) の項を参照
residual approach　残余アプローチ　[解]IFRS15の文脈では，独立販売価格の見積りに際して,「取引価格の総額」から「他の財またはサービスの独立販売価格の合計」を控除するという方法を指す。財ま

たはサービスの独立販売価格の変動性が高い，または不確実な場合に限って使用が認められる

residual assets 残余財産
residual claim 残余財産請求権
residual income (RI) 残余利益
residual interest ①残余持分，②残余財産請求権
residual profit 残余利益
residual profit split method (RPSM) 残余利益分割法 [解]移転価格税制の関係では，独立企業間価格の算定方法の1つで，まず重要な無形資産を有しない非関連者間取引において通常得られる基本的利益の金額を日本企業及び国外関連者に配分し，配分後の残額である超過利益または残余利益を，それぞれが有する重要な無形資産の価値に応じて（例えば，重要な無形資産の開発のために支出した費用等の額に応じて）合理的に配分することにより，各関連者が稼得すべき利益を決定し，これをもとに独立企業間価格を算定する方法を指す
residual value 残存価額，残存価値 [解]資産の耐用年数終了時点における処分可能価額（見積処分コスト控除後）の現時点での予測額
residual value guarantee 残価保証 [解]IFRS16の文脈では，リース終了時の原資産の価値が（最低でも）所定の金額になるという保証で，貸手と関連のない者が貸手に対して行うもの
residual value method 残余アプローチ（独立販売価格の見積りの際の） [解]residual approachの項を参照
resign 辞職する
resignation 退職，辞任
resolution ①決議，②解決
resolution date 決議日（配当などの）
resolution of a court case 訴訟事件の解決
resolution of uncertainty 不確実性の解消
resolution on dividend payment 配当決議
resource 資源
respective それぞれの
respectively それぞれ（に）
respond 返答する

respondent 返答者
response 返答
responsibility 責任
responsibility accounting 責任会計
responsibility centre 責任センター [米]responsibility center
responsible 責任のある
rest 残り
restart ①再開する，②再起動する
restate 修正再表示する，遡及修正する [用] to restate the opening balances of assets, liabilities, and equity（資産，負債及び資本の期首残高を修正再表示する）
restatement 修正再表示
restatement of previously reported information 過去に報告した情報の修正再表示
restoration 原状回復
restoration cost 原状回復費用
restoration obligation 原状回復義務
restore 元に戻す，修復する
restraint 制限
restrict 制限する
restricted cash and cash equivalents 制限付きの現金及び現金同等物
restricted fund 拘束資金，使途制限のある資金
restricted share [stock] 制限株式，売却制限株式
restricted stock plan リストリクテッド・ストック・プラン [解]端的には，ストック・オプションに代えて現物株式（自社株）を付与するインセンティブ・プラン。株式には，通常譲渡制限がかかっており，雇用期間の経過とパフォーマンス等によって，その制限が解消されていく
restriction (on) （〜に対する）制限
restriction on deductibility 損金算入制限
restriction on foreign investment 外資規制
restriction on interest deductibility 利息の損金算入制限 [解]過少資本税制に代表されるように，税務上，利息の損金算入が制限されることがある
restriction on share transferability 株式の譲渡制限
restriction on the disposal of shares 株式の処分制限 [米]restriction on the dispos-

al of shares ［解］例えば，日本の適格再編における株式継続保有要件のようなものを指す ［用］restriction on the disposal of shares received in a tax-free reorganisation（非課税組織再編における取得株式の処分制限）
restriction on the transfer of funds　送金に対する制限
restriction on the use of carried-forward tax losses　繰越欠損金の使用制限
restriction on the use of tax attributes　繰越項目（繰越欠損金や繰越税額控除）の使用制限
restrictive　制限のある
restrictive covenant　制限条項，規制条項 ［解］契約の当事者に一定の制約（例えば，一定の行為の禁止）を課す条項
restructure　再構築する，構造改革を行う
restructuring　①リストラクチャリング，②事業再編，③再構築 ［解］① IAS37 の文脈では，企業が従事する事業の範囲または運営方法を大きく変更する経営者の計画（例えば，工場閉鎖や再編等）
restructuring charge　リストラクチャリング費用，事業再編費用
restructuring contingent liability　リストラクチャリングに係る偶発負債
restructuring provision　リストラクチャリング引当金，構造改革費用引当金
result　結果，成果 ［用］results of discontinued operation（非継続事業の業績）
result from　～から結果として生じる
result in　結果として～になる
resulting　結果としての【形】
resume　①再開する，②履歴書
retail　小売
retailer　小売業者
retail method　売価還元法
retail price index (RPI)　小売物価指数
retain　①留保する，②引き留める
retainage　留保金（工事などで完了まで支払いを留保する部分）
retainage withheld　預り留保金
retained earnings　①利益剰余金，②留保利益，内部留保
retained earnings reserve　利益準備金

retainer fee　リテイナー・フィー（弁護士などの顧問報酬）
retention　維持，保留
retention account　留保口座
retention for contracts in progress　未成工事に係る保留金
retention of title　所有権の留保
retention period　保存期間（帳簿などの）
retention ratio　内部留保率
retire　①退職する，②退職させる
retired employee　退職従業員
retiree　退職者
retirement　①退職，②除却（資産の），③消却（株式などの），④償還（負債の）
retirement age　退職年齢
retirement allowance　退職金
retirement benefit　退職給付，退職金
retirement benefit cost　退職給付費用 ［解］退職後給付制度に関連する費用
retirement benefit obligation　①退職給付債務，②退職給付引当金（勘定）
retirement benefit plan　退職給付制度
retirement entitlement　退職金の受給権
retirement income　退職所得
retirement of debt　債務弁済
retirement of shares　株式の消却
retirement of treasury shares　自己株式の消却
retranslate　換算替えする
retroactive　遡及的な
retroactive application　遡及適用
retroactive effect　遡及効
retroactively　遡及的に，遡及して
retroactive restatement　遡及的修正再表示
retrospective　遡及的な
retrospective adjustment　遡及的調整
retrospective application　遡及適用 ［解］IAS8 の文脈では，新しい会計方針について，あたかも過去からその会計方針が適用されていたかのように適用すること
retrospective application of IFRS　IFRS の遡及適用 ［解］IFRS の初度適用にあたっては，基本的には IFRS を遡及的に適用する必要があるが，企業結合等の一定の項目については免除規定がある
retrospective approach　遡及アプローチ

retrospectively 遡及的に
retrospective restatement 遡及的修正再表示 [解]あたかも過年度の誤謬がなかったかのように，財務諸表項目の金額及び表示を修正すること
RETT ▶real estate transfer tax
return ①リターン，②運用収益，③申告書，④返品，返却 [解]① IFRS10 の文脈では，被投資企業への関与から生じるリターンには，利益のみならず，損失も含まれる。リターンの典型例は配当であり，その他被投資企業に対する投資の価値変動などもリターンの１つである
returned goods 返品（された商品）
return for routine contribution 基本的利益 [解]residual profit split method の項を参照
return of capital 資本の払戻し
return of goods 返品
return on assets (ROA) 総資産利益率
return on equity (ROE) 自己資本利益率
return on invested capital (ROIC) 投下資本利益率 [解]NOPLAT（みなし税引後営業利益）を投下資産で除したもの
return on investment (ROI) 投資利益率
return on new invested capital (RONIC) 新規投下資本に対する利益率
return on plan assets 制度資産に係る利益（従業員給付制度の）
return on sales 売上高利益率
return on total costs 総費用営業利益率
revaluation 再評価
revaluation difference on land 土地再評価差額金
revaluation gain 評価益
revaluation loss 評価損
revaluation model 再評価モデル [解]IAS16の文脈では，当初認識後の測定として，公正価値が信頼性をもって測定できる有形固定資産等の資産につき，再評価実施日の公正価値からその後の減価償却累計額及び減損損失累計額を控除した価額で計上する方法を指す。原価モデル（cost model）に対する用語
revaluation reserve 再評価剰余金 [解]その他の資本の構成要素
revaluation surplus 再評価剰余金
revalue 再評価する
revalued amount 再評価額
revalued assets 再評価された資産，再評価資産
revamp 改訂
revenue （狭義の）収益 [解]広義の収益（income）のうち，企業の通常の事業活動により生じる経済的便益の総流入であり，持分参加者（株主）からの拠出等以外で，持分の増加をもたらすもの
revenue centre レベニュー・センター [米] revenue center [解]責任会計（responsibility accounting）において，収益に責任を持つ部門
revenue cycle 収益サイクル
Revenue Department タイ歳入局（タイの税務当局）
revenue expenditure 収益的支出 [解]資本的支出（capital expenditure）に対する用語
revenue from construction contracts 工事契約による収益
revenue from contracts with customers 顧客との契約から生じた収益
revenue from rendering of services サービスの提供による収益
revenue recognition 収益認識
revenue recognition criteria 収益認識基準
revenue ruling 内国歳入庁通達（米国） [解]租税法規や租税条約に関する米国内国歳入庁の公的解釈を示すもの
revenue stamp 収入印紙
reversal ①戻入，②取崩し，③（過年度の加算に対する）認容減算，④（過年度の減算に対する）認容加算
reversal entry 逆仕訳，反対仕訳
reversal of impairment losses 減損損失の戻入 [解]reversal of prior years' impairment losses（過年度の減損損失の戻入）のようないい方もある
reversal of inventory write-down 棚卸資産の評価減の戻入
reversal of temporary differences 一時差異の解消
reversal of write-down 評価減の戻入

reverse	①逆，②逆の，③取り崩す，④（過年度の加算を）認容減算する，⑤（過年度の減算を）認容加算する
reverse acquisition	逆取得　[解] IFRS3 の文脈では，取得企業の決定において，法律上の被取得企業が会計上は取得企業とされるような企業結合を指す
reverse break-up fee	リバース・ブレイクアップ・フィー　[解] 特に買収契約に関して，買手が支払うブレイクアップ・フィー（break-up fee）
reverse charge mechanism	リバース・チャージ方式（消費税等の）　[解] 消費税等（付加価値税等）の納税義務者を，供給元から供給先に転換する課税方式
reverse hybrid	リバース・ハイブリッド　[解] 源泉地国において団体課税を受け，構成員の居住地国でパス・スルー課税を受けること。レギュラー・ハイブリッド（regular hybrid）に対する用語
reverse repurchase agreement	売戻契約
reverse share [stock] split	株式併合
reverse triangular merger	逆三角合併
reversing entry	逆仕訳，反対仕訳
revert	戻る
review	①レビューする，見直す，②再吟味する，③レビュー
review control	レビュー統制
review engagement	レビュー業務
review report	レビュー報告書
revise	改訂する，改定する
revised budget	修正予算
revised tax return	修正申告書
revision	改訂，改定
revision to an estimate	見積りの見直し
revitalisation	再生　[米] revitalization
revocation	取消し
revocation of previous designations	従来の指定の取消し（ヘッジなどの）
revoke	取り消す，撤回する，無効にする，廃止する
reward	報酬
RFI	▶request for information
RFP	▶request for proposal
RHQ	▶regional headquarters
RI	▶residual income
rider	特約，追加条項
right	権利
right and obligation	権利義務
right of first refusal	ファースト・リフューザル・ライト，優先交渉権，先買権　[解] 意味合いとしては，「最初に拒否する権利」。例えば，株主間契約において，ある株主が他の株主にファースト・リフューザル・ライトを与えた場合，その株主が保有する株式を第三者に譲渡する場合，その譲渡と同一の条件で，まずは当該他の株主に対して同株式の買取りをオファーしなければならない
right of return	返品権，返品する権利
right of set-off	相殺権
right of substitution	差替えの権利，資産を取り替える権利
right of use	使用権
right-of-use asset	使用権資産　[解] IFRS16 の文脈では，借手が原資産を（リース期間にわたり）使用する権利を表す資産
rights issue	ライツ・イシュー，新株予約権無償割当て，株主割当増資　[解] 既存の株主に新株予約権を無償で割り当てることで，（その新株予約権の行使に伴って）新株を発行する増資の方法
rights offering	ライツ・オファリング，新株予約権無償割当て，株主割当増資　[解] rights issue の項を参照
rights of minority shareholders	少数株主権
right to control the use of an identified asset for a period of time	一定期間にわたり識別された資産の使用を支配する権利
right to set off	相殺権
right to use	使用権
ring fence	リング・フェンス　[解] 英国の税制上の概念で，課税上一定の事業（リング・フェンス内の事業）の損益をリング・フェンス外の事業と通算できない等の制約を意味する
risk	リスク
risk-adjusted discount rate	リスク調整後の割引率
risk analysis	リスク分析
risk assessment	リスク評価
risk assessment procedures	リスク評価手

続
risk associated with　〜に関連するリスク
risk averse　リスク回避型の
risk bearing　リスク負担
risk component　リスク要素
risk control matrix (RCM)　リスク・コントロール・マトリックス　[解]「財務諸表に虚偽記載が発生するリスク」と「リスクを低減する内部統制」との対応表。通常それぞれの項目が「適切な財務情報を作成するための要件」とどのように関連するかが示されている
risk diversification　リスク分散
risk diversification effect　リスク分散効果
risk-free interest rate　リスクフリー・レート　[解]理論的には無リスク資産から得ることのできる利回りのことをいうが、実務的には国債の利回りやLIBOR等のインターバンク・レートなどを指す
risk limit　リスクの上限
risk management　リスク・マネジメント、リスク管理
risk management policy　リスク管理方針
risk premium　リスク・プレミアム、リスク調整　[解]一般に、株式等の金融商品において、そのリスクに対して投資家が要求する対価。IFRS13の文脈では、資産または負債のキャッシュ・フローに固有の不確実性に対して、リスク回避型の市場参加者が要求する報酬を指す
risks and rewards　リスクと経済価値
risks and rewards incidental to ownership　所有に伴うリスクと経済価値
risks and rewards of ownership　所有に伴うリスクと経済価値
risks and uncertainties　リスクと不確実性
risk sharing　リスク分担
ROA　▶return on assets
ROE　▶return on equity
ROI　▶return on investment
ROIC　▶return on invested capital
role　役割
rollback　巻き戻し、ロールバック　[解]移転価格税制の関係では、APA rollbackの項を参照
roll forward　ロール・フォワード

roll forward procedure　ロール・フォワード手続　[解]内部統制の評価などにおいて、評価時点からの変更点を確認することで、期末日における最終評価を行う手続
rolling budget　継続予算　[解]月次や四半期等の一定の期間で定期的に更新される予算
roll over　①繰り越す、②繰り延べる（課税を）、③延期する（支払いを）、④再投資する
rollover　①繰越し、②繰延べ
rollover relief　譲渡益課税の繰延べ
RONIC　▶return on new invested capital
roster　名簿
roster of workers　労働者名簿
round down　切り捨てる（端数を）
rounding　全額表示単位、数値の丸め　[用] level of rounding used in financial statements（財務諸表に使用している金額表示単位）
round off　四捨五入する
round trip transaction　循環取引
round up　切り上げる（端数を）
routine　定型的な、ルーティンの
routine transaction　経常的取引、通例取引
row　行（行・列の）
royalty (fee)　ロイヤルティ、使用料
royalty expense　支払ロイヤルティ、ロイヤルティ費用
royalty from intellectual property　知的財産権の使用料
royalty income　受取ロイヤルティ、ロイヤルティ収益
royalty revenue　ロイヤルティ収益、受取ロイヤルティ　[用] sales or usage-based royalty revenue（売上または使用連動のロイヤルティ収益）
RPI　▶retail price index
RPM　▶resale price method
RPSM　▶residual profit split method
rule　規則、規定、規程
rule off　線を引いて区切る
rule of thumb　経験則
rules-based　規則主義
rules of employment　就業規則
ruling　①裁定、判示、②通達（税務当局の）

running 連続する，繰り返しの
running cost 運営経費，維持管理費
running royalty ランニング・ロイヤルティ
run rate ラン・レート [解]直近の実績値がそのまま継続すると仮定した場合の将来予測値

S

safe box 金庫
safeguard ①保護する，②セーフガード（条項） [解]②海外からの特定品目の輸入が増加しすぎた場合に政府が行う緊急輸入制限
safe harbour セーフ・ハーバー [米] safe harbor [用] safe harbour of debt-equity ratio（負債資本比率についてのセーフ・ハーバー）
safe harbour rule セーフ・ハーバー・ルール [米]safe harbor rule [解]税務当局が簡易な一定のルールや範囲をあらかじめ設定し，納税者がそのルールや範囲内で取引を行っている限り，税務当局はその結果を税務上妥当なものとして自動的に受け入れるという規定
salaries and wages 人件費
salary 給料，給与
salary level 給与水準
sale ①売上（高），②売却，販売
saleability 販売可能性 [米]salability
saleable 販売可能な [米]salable
sale and leaseback (transaction) セール・アンド・リースバック（取引） [解]所有物件をいったん売却し，その購入者（リースの貸手）から当該物件のリースを受ける取引
sale and purchase agreement 売買契約
sale-leaseback transaction セール・アンド・リースバック取引
sale limit 販売限度額
sales 売上（高）
sales allowance 売上値引
sales and marketing expense 販売及びマーケティング費用
sales-based royalty 売上連動のロイヤルティ
sales budget 販売予算，売上予算
sales by operating segment セグメント別

売上
sales by product　製品別売上
sales channel　販売経路
sales commission　販売手数料
sales cut-off　売上のカットオフ（締切）
sales cut-off error　売上のカットオフ・エラー（期ズレ）
sales cut-off test　売上のカットオフ・テスト
sales department [division]　販売部門, 営業部門
sales discount　売上割引
sales forecast　売上予測
sales incentive　販売インセンティブ
sales ledger　売上元帳
sales management　販売管理
sales mix　売上構成, セールス・ミックス
sales mix variance　売上構成（セールス・ミックス）差異
sales network　販売網
sales of goods　物品の販売
sales order　注文書
sales performance　販売実績
sales price　販売価格
sales price variance　販売価格差異
sales proceeds　売上収入
sales promotion　販売促進
sales promotion cost [expense]　販売促進費
sales rebate　売上割戻し
sales representative　営業担当者
sales return　売上返品
sales slip　売上伝票
sales system　販売システム
sales tax　売上税
sales territory　販売地域
sales transaction　販売取引, 売却取引
sales-type lease　販売型リース
sales volume　販売数量
sales volume variance　販売数量差異
sale transaction　売却取引
sale with a right of repurchase　買戻権付販売［売却］
sale with a right of return　返品権付販売［売却］
salvage　残存価値, 廃物利用
salvage value　残存価額, 処分価額
sample　サンプル, 見本
sampling　サンプリング
sanction　制裁
sandbagging　サンドバギング　[解]買収案件などで, 買手が売手の表明・保証違反を知りながら取引を実行し, 事後的に表明・保証違反に基づく補償を請求すること
SAR　▶share [stock] appreciation right
Sarbanes-Oxley Act (SOX)　企業改革法, サーベインス・オクスリー法, SOX法（米国）　[解]財務報告の透明性や正確性を高めることを目的として, コーポレート・ガバナンスの在り方及び監査制度を抜本的に改革するとともに, 投資家に対する企業経営者の責任や罰則を定めた米国の法律
SAS　▶Statements on Auditing Standards
SAT　▶State Administration of Taxation
satisfaction　①満足, ②充足（条件・要件の）
satisfaction of performance obligation　履行義務の充足
satisfy　充足する（条件・要件を）
saving　貯蓄
saving clause　セービングの原則　[解]自国の居住者に対する自国での課税関係は租税条約の影響を受けない, という原則
savings account　普通預金
SBU　▶strategic business unit
scale　規模
scam　詐欺
scenario　シナリオ
scenario analysis　シナリオ分析
scepticism　懐疑心　[米]skepticism
schedule　①明細, ②別表（法人税申告書などの）, ③スケジュール, 予定, ④スケジュールを立てる
Schedule 4　別表四
Schedule 5(1)　別表五（一）
scheduling　スケジューリング
scheme　スキーム, 計画
scheme of arrangement　スキーム・オブ・アレンジメント, 債務整理計画
SCM　▶supply chain management
scope　スコープ, 範囲, 対象範囲
scope limitation　範囲の制限
scope of consolidation　連結の範囲

scope of work　業務範囲
S corporation　Sコーポレーション，S法人　[解]米国における法人の一形態であり，税務上の一定の要件を充足することで，株式会社ではあるが構成員課税の適用を受けるもの（一般に小規模）
scrap　①くず，スクラップ，②スクラップにする
scrap value　処分価格
screen　選別する
screening　選別，選考，審査
seal　印鑑，判
seasonal　季節の
seasonal fluctuation　季節変動
seasonality　季節性
seasonality of operations　事業活動の季節性　[解]IAS34の文脈では，事業活動の季節性及び循環性は，注記により説明する必要がある
SEC　▶Securities and Exchange Commission
SEC filing　SECへの提出書類，ファイリング
second　出向させる【動】
secondary adjustment　第二次調整　[解]移転価格税制の関係では，みなし配当やみなし出資といった第二次取引（secondary transaction）に対する源泉税や資本税の課税を指す。第二次調整は基本的に国内法をその根拠とするため，制度の有無や内容は国によって異なる
secondary lease　再リース
secondary lease payment　再リース料（支払い）
secondary lease period　再リース期間
secondary market　流通市場（証券の）
secondary period　第二次期間，再リース期間
secondary transaction　第二次取引　[解]移転価格税制の関係では，国外関連取引に関して，関連者の一方が移転価格課税による増額更正を受けた場合，相互協議の結果，他方の関連者の所得を減額する対応的調整（corresponding [correlative] adjustment）により還付が行われることがある。この場合，（所得が減額になった）他方の関連者から（所得が増額になった）一方の関連者に見合いの金額の送金が行われない場合には，本来一方の関連者が保有すべき資産を，他方の関連者が保有していることになる。第二次取引は，これを一方の関連者から他方の関連者に対する資産の流出と考え，配当や出資とみなすものである
seconded employee　出向者
secondee　出向者
2nd half　下半期，下期
second-hand　中古の
second-hand property　中古資産
secondment　出向
secondment arrangement　出向契約
secondment period　出向期間
2nd quarter　第2四半期
second-tier subsidiary　第2階層（孫会社層）の子会社　[解]第1階層（子会社層）の子会社（first-tier subsidiary）に対する用語
secret comparable　シークレット・コンパラブル　[解]移転価格税制の関係では，移転価格税制に基づく調査や更正処分にあたり，独立企業間価格を算定するために必要な帳簿書類等の提示・提出がなされない場合等に，課税当局が（調査対象会社の）同業者に対する質問検査を通じて収集する比較対象取引を指す。シークレット・コンパラブルは調査対象会社が入手不可能な非公開情報である
section　①部分，②部門，③条（法令の）
Section 482 (of the Internal Revenue Code)　内国歳入法典（IRC）第482条（米国）　[解]米国の移転価格税制に関する規定
secured bank loan　担保付銀行借入金
secured bond　担保付債券
secured debt　担保付負債
secured loan　①担保付貸付金，②担保付借入金
secured transaction　担保付取引
securities　有価証券　[解]通常複数形
Securities and Exchange Commission (SEC)　証券取引委員会（米国）
securities borrowed　借入有価証券
securities commission　証券委員会
securities firm　証券会社
securities held for other than trading purposes

売買目的外有価証券
securities held for trading purposes　売買目的有価証券
securities holder　証券の保有者
securities lending　有価証券貸借
securities lent　貸付有価証券
securities registration statement　有価証券届出書
securitisation　証券化，流動化　[米]securitization
securitisation vehicle　証券化ビークル
security　①（通常複数形で）有価証券，②担保，保証
security deposit　敷金，保証金
security interest　担保権
segment　①セグメント，②セグメントを決定する【動】
segmental　セグメントの
segmental cash flow　セグメント別キャッシュ・フロー
segmental information　セグメント情報
segmental reporting　セグメント別報告
segment assets　セグメント資産
segmentation　セグメントの分割
segmented financial statements　セグメント別財務諸表
segment expense　セグメント費用
segment information　セグメント情報
segmenting　セグメントの決定
segment liabilities　セグメント負債
segment profit [loss]　セグメント利益［損失］
segment profit [loss] before tax　セグメント別の税引前利益［損失］
segment reporting　セグメント報告
segment result　セグメント業績
segment revenue　セグメント収益
segregate　区分する
segregation　区分
segregation of duties　職務分掌
select　選択する
selection　選択
selective　選択的な
self assessment　①申告納税，②自己評価，自己査定
self-constructed assets　自己建設資産

self-created　自己創設の
self-employed　自営業の
self-generated goodwill　自己創設のれん
sell　売却する
seller　売手，譲渡人，販売者
seller's note　セラーズ・ノート　[解]vendor loanの項を参照
seller's value　セラーズ・バリュー，売手にとっての（企業）価値
selling cost [expense]　販売費
selling, general and administrative expenses (SG&A)　販売費及び一般管理費
sell side　セルサイド，売手側（買収案件などの）
semi-annual　半期の
semi-annual closing　半期決算
semi-annual control　半期統制
semi-annually　半期に一度
semi-finished goods　半製品
semi-fixed cost　準固定費
semi-variable cost　準変動費
senior　①上位の，②年上の
senior debt　優先的に弁済される債務
senior employee　上級従業員
senior executives　上級経営者，役員
seniority　①返済の優先順位（金融商品の），②年功
senior management　上級経営者
sensitivity　感応度
sensitivity analysis　感応度分析　[解]ある変数が変動したとき，結果にどの程度の影響を与えるかを分析する手法で，例えば，為替レートの変動が事業計画にどの程度の影響を与えるかをあらかじめ分析することなどが該当する
separability　分離可能性
separability criterion　分離可能性要件
separable　分離可能な
separate　別個の
separate account　区分経理　[解]例えば，優遇税制を適用している場合などに，その対象となる事業の所得計算を区分計算すること
separate assessment　分離課税
separate entity　別個の（独立した）事業体
separate financial statements　個別財務諸

表，単体財務諸表　[解]（特に親会社等が）単体として作成する財務諸表で，連結財務諸表（consolidated financial statements）に対する用語。IAS27の文脈では，企業が表示する財務諸表のうち，子会社，共同支配企業及び関連会社に対する投資の会計処理を，(1)取得原価による会計処理，(2)IFRS9に従った会計処理，(3)IAS28に従った会計処理（持分法）のいずれの方法で行うかを企業が選択できるもの

separate legal entity　法的に独立した事業体　[解]例えば，子会社はseparate legal entityに該当するが，支店は該当しない

separate line item　別掲項目

separately　別個に

separately identifiable　別個に（区別して）識別可能な

separate taxation　分離課税

separate vehicle　別個のビークル　[解]別個に識別可能な財務構造（financial structure）であり，例えば，株式会社などがこれに該当する。IFRS11の文脈では，共同支配の取決めが別個のビークルを通じて組成されていない場合は，その取決めは共同支配事業に該当する

separation　分離

separation of duties　職務分掌・分離

sequence　①連続，②結果

sequential　①連続する【形】，②結果として起こる【形】

serial　連続する【形】

serial bond　連続償還債券　[解]一定の間隔で，順次（元本を）償還していく債券

service　サービス，役務

service agreement　役務提供契約，業務委託契約

service company　役務提供会社（グループ内の）

service concession arrangement　サービス委譲契約　[解]政府等が公共サービスの提供を民間業者に委託するもの

service condition　勤務条件，サービス条件　[解]IFRS2の文脈では，権利確定条件のうち，従業員などに所定の期間の勤務を完了することを求めるもの

service cost　①勤務費用，②役務費用　[解]①IAS19の文脈では，確定給付費用の1つで，当期勤務費用・過去勤務費用・確定給付制度の清算損益により構成される

service fee　サービス・フィー

service level agreement (SLA)　サービス水準に係る合意　[解]サービスを提供する側と受ける側との間のサービスの水準（内容や品質）に関する合意

service PE　サービスPE　[解]企業がある国に従業員等を派遣して役務提供（例えば，コンサルティング・サービス）を行う場合，その従業員等をその国における派遣元企業のPE（恒久的施設）として取り扱うという考え方

service provider　サービス提供者，役務提供者

servicer　サービサー，債権回収会社　[解]債権回収を専門に行う会社

service received　受領したサービス

service rendered　提供された役務

service revenue　役務収益

services in progress　仕掛役務，未成業務支出金

servicing contract　回収業務契約

set forth　明らかにする【動】

set of accounts　勘定組織，勘定体系

set-off　相殺

setter　設定者

settle　決済する

settlement　①決済，②解決，和解

settlement agreement　和解契約書

settlement date　決済日，受渡日

settlement date accounting　決済日会計

settlement of employee benefit obligations　従業員給付債務の清算　[解]確定給付制度に係る給付について，すべての追加的な債務（法的債務または推定的債務）を解消する取引

settlement of pre-existing relationship　既存の関係の清算

settlement option　決済方法の選択肢

settlor　委託者，設定者（信託の）

severance　解雇

severance payment　解雇手当

SFAS　▶Statement of Financial Accounting

Standards
SG&A ▶selling, general and administrative expenses
S/H ▶shareholder
SHA ▶shareholders(') agreement
shady 胡散臭い
sham 偽物
sham transaction 仮装取引
shape 形
share ①株式，②シェア
share acquisition 株式買収，株式取得 [解] share purchase の項を参照
share appreciation right (SAR) 株式増価受益権 [解] 現金決済型の株式に基づく報酬契約（cash-settled share-based payment）の１つ
share-based payment 株式に基づく報酬，株式報酬
share-based payment arrangement 株式に基づく報酬契約
share-based payment award 株式に基づく報酬（の授与）
share-based payment plan 株式に基づく報酬制度，株式報酬制度
share-based payment transaction 株式に基づく報酬取引 [解] 財またはサービス（例えば，従業員の勤務）の対価として，企業の資本性金融商品やそれを基礎とする現金等を取引相手（例えば，従業員）に与える取引。株式に基づく報酬取引には，(1)持分決済型，(2)現金決済型，(3)持分決済と現金決済の選択ができるもの，がある
share buyback 自己株式の取得
share buyback cost 自己株式取得費用
share capital 資本金
share capital and share premium 資本金及び資本剰余金
share certificate 株券
share consideration 株式対価 [解] 現金対価（cash consideration）に対する用語
share consolidation 株式併合
share deal 株式取引，株式買収
share dividend 株式配当
shared service シェアード・サービス [解] 経営効率化の一手段で，間接部門の機能など，グループ内の複数の企業で共通する業務を，個々の組織から切り出して１つの会社に集中させること
shared service agreement シェアード・サービス契約
share for share exchange (kabushiki kokan) 株式交換
shareholder (S/H) 株主
shareholder activity 株主活動 [解] 移転価格税制の関係では，親会社が，専ら自らのために行う株主としての法令上の権利の行使または義務の履行に係る活動をいい，企業グループ内の役務提供（IGS）とは区別される
shareholder ownership structure 株主構成
shareholder registry 株主名簿
shareholders(') agreement (SHA) 株主間契約，株主間合意
shareholders' derivative action 株主代表訴訟
shareholders' equity 株主資本，株主持分
shareholders' meeting 株主総会
shareholder structure 株主構成
shareholder value 株主価値
share issue 株式発行
share issue cost 株式交付費
share issue related cost 株式発行関連コスト，株式交付費
share of loss of investments accounted for using the equity method 持分法による投資損失
share of other comprehensive income of investments accounted for using the equity method 持分法適用会社におけるその他の包括利益に対する持分
share of profit of investments accounted for using the equity method 持分法による投資利益
share option ①ストック・オプション，②株式オプション，③新株予約権 [解] 一定の期間，所定の価格で企業の株式を取得する権利を付与する契約
share option programme ストック・オプション・プログラム ㊍ share option program
share premium 株式プレミアム，資本剰余

金
share price 株価
share purchase 株式買収，株式購入 [解] 買収対象会社の株式を取得する方法
share purchase agreement (SPA) 株式購入契約（書）
share purchase plan 株式購入制度
share purchase programme 株式購入制度 [米] share purchase program
share redemption 株式償還，減資
share sale 株式売却，株式譲渡
share sale agreement (SSA) 株式譲渡契約（書）
shares issued 発行済株式
shares outstanding 発行済株式
share split 株式分割
share subscription 株式の引受け
share transfer 株式譲渡
share transfer (kabushiki iten) 株式移転
share warrant 新株予約権
sharing control 支配の共有
shelf company シェルフ・カンパニー [解] 設立済みではあるものの，まだ事業活動を行っていない（売却目的の）会社
shell company 休眠会社，ペーパー・カンパニー
shift ①移す，移転する，②移行する
shifting of profits 利益移転
shift to 〜に移行する
ship 船舶
shipment 出荷
shipment basis 出荷基準
shipment request 出荷依頼
shipper ①荷主，②運送業者
shipper's usance シッパーズ・ユーザンス [解] 貿易取引の決済に関連して，輸出者が支払いを一定期間猶予する形で，輸入者に対して信用を供与すること
shipping 船積み，運送，輸送
shipping advice 出荷通知
shipping basis 出荷基準
shipping cost [expense] 出荷費用，輸送費
shipping document 出荷関連書類，船積書類
shipping instruction (S/I) 船積依頼書，船積指示書

shipping report 出荷報告書
shipping request 出荷依頼
ships and vessels 船舶
shopping centre ショッピング・センター [米] shopping center
short ①不足して【形】，②短い
shortage 不足
short bond 短期債券
short-cut method 簡便法
short depreciation 減価償却不足額
shorten 短縮する（耐用年数などを）
shortening of useful life 耐用年数の短縮
shortfall 不足
short-form report 短文式の報告書（デュー・デリジェンスなどの）
short list ショート・リスト [解] ロング・リスト (long list) の候補を絞り込んだもの
shortly まもなく
short position ショート・ポジション [解] 金融資産の売り持ちの状態
short sale 空売り
short-term 短期の
short-term benefit 短期給付
short-term borrowings 短期借入金
short-term capital gain 短期譲渡所得
short-term contract 短期契約
short-term debt 短期負債，流動負債
short-term deposit 短期の預金
short-term employee benefit 短期従業員給付 [解] 従業員給付の一形態で，従業員が関連する役務を提供した期間の末日後12か月以内に決済されると予想されるもの（解雇給付を除く）。例えば，給料や年次有給休暇
short-term employee benefits accruals 短期従業員給付費用発生額
short-term employee benefits expense 短期従業員給付費用
short-term investment 短期投資
short-term item 短期項目
short-term lease 短期リース [解] リース開始日において，リース期間が12か月以内であるリース
short-term lease obligation 短期リース債務
short-term liability 短期負債，流動負債

short-term loan　①短期貸付金，②短期借入金
short-term loans payable　短期借入金（勘定）
short-term loans receivable　短期貸付金（勘定）
short-term management plan　短期経営計画
short-term paid absence　短期有給休暇
shrinkage　減耗（棚卸資産などの）
S/I　▶shipping instruction
SIC　▶Standard Interpretations Committee
SIC Code　▶Standard Industrial Classification Code
sick leave　傷病休暇
side effect　副作用
side letter　サイド・レター　[解]本契約の内容を補足する文書
sidestep　回避する
signature　署名
significance　重要性
significant　重要な
significant account　重要な勘定
significant accounting policies　重要な会計方針
significant business unit　重要な事業拠点
significant deficiency　重要な不備
significant doubt　重要な疑義　[用]significant doubt upon the entity's ability to continue as a going concern（継続企業の前提に関する重要な疑義）
significant financing arrangement　重大な金融要素，重要な金融要素
significant financing component　重大な金融要素，重要な金融要素　[解]IFRS15の文脈では，対価の前払いや後払いなどの場合に契約に含まれる金利部分のうち重要なものを指す
significant finding　重要な発見事項
significant influence　重要な影響力　[解]被投資企業の財務及び営業の方針の決定に関与する力（パワー）ではあるが，支配または共同支配には該当しないもの
significant influence over the reporting entity　報告企業に対する重要な影響力
significant issue　重要な論点
significant location　重要な（事業）拠点
significant restriction　重大な制限
significant risk　重要なリスク
sign-off　①承認（最終化された文書などの），②（監査）証明　[用]to require a sign-off by a local auditor（現地監査法人の監査証明を求める）
sign off on　（署名して）〜を承認する
silent partnership　匿名組合（主に米国などの）　[解]日本の匿名組合は，そのままTokumei Kumiai（TK）と呼ばれることが多い
silo　サイロ　[解]IFRS10の文脈では，被投資企業の一部を別個の事業体とみなしたもの
similar　類似の
similarity　類似性
similarly　同様に
similar transaction　類似の取引
simple interest　単利　[解]複利（compound interest）に対する用語
simplified approach　簡素化したアプローチ
simulation　シミュレーション
simultaneous　同時の
simultaneously　同時に
single lessee accounting model　リースの借手に関する単一の会計モデル
single point of contact　単一の窓口
single-statement presentation　1計算書方式の表示（包括利益計算書などの）
single-step　単一段階の
single-step acquisition　一括取得　[解]段階取得（step acquisition）に対する用語
single-step approach　1ステップ・アプローチ　[解]減損テストに際し，第1段階としての割引前将来キャッシュ・フローを用いたテストを行わない方法
single-step income statement　単一区分の損益計算書　[解]段階損益を表示しない損益計算書の形式
single year　単年度
sinking fund　減債基金　[解]社債等の長期債務を返済するために積み立てる基金
sister company [corporation]　姉妹会社，兄弟会社
site　①現場，②用地，敷地

site restoration　（用地の）原状回復
site restoration provision　土地原状回復引当金
site visit　現場［現地］訪問，現場［現地］視察
situation analysis　状況分析
situs rule　所在地ルール
six months' rule　183日ルール　[解]183-day rule の項を参照
size-based enterprise [business] tax　外形標準課税（事業税）
skilled workforce　熟練した労働力
skimming　スキミング
SKU　▶stock keeping unit
skyrocket　急上昇する
S/L　▶① subsidiary ledger, ② sub-ledger
slack　余裕，余裕分
slide　①スライドする，②下落する，低下する
slight　僅かな
slightly　僅かに
slip　伝票
slow-moving inventory　滞留在庫
small and medium enterprise (SME)　中小法人
small and medium-sized company　中小法人
small and medium-sized enterprise (SME)　中小企業，中小法人
SME　▶small and medium (-sized) enterprise
smooth　①滑らかな，②平らにする，ならす
smoothing　平準化
so-called　いわゆる
social insurance　社会保険
social insurance premium　社会保険料
socially responsible investment (SRI)　社会的責任投資　[解]CSRの観点で一定の基準を満たす企業に投資するというスタイル
social security　社会保障
social security agreement　社会保障協定　[解]社会保険料の二重払いや掛捨てといった問題を回避するために結ばれる協定
social security contribution　社会保険拠出
social security payable　未払社会保険料

software　ソフトウェア
software development　ソフトウェア開発
soil　土壌
soil contamination　土壌汚染
sole proprietor　個人事業者
sole proprietorship　個人事業
sole trader　個人事業者
solicitor　事務弁護士（英国等の）
solution　解決策
solve　解決する
solvency　支払余力
solvent　支払余力のある
sound　健全な（財務的に）
soundness　健全性（財務的な）
source　①出典，②源泉
source document　根拠資料（仕訳等の）
source of estimation uncertainty　見積りの不確実性の発生要因
source of funds　資金調達源
source of income　①所得の源泉，②収入源
source of risk　リスクの源泉
source rule　ソース・ルール　[解]所得の源泉地（国内源泉所得か国外源泉所得か）の決定基準。ソース・ルールが国内法と租税条約で異なっている場合，租税条約が優先される
sovereign　主権国，ソブリン
sovereign bond　国債
SOX　▶Sarbanes-Oxley Act
SPA　▶① share purchase agreement, ② stock purchase agreement
space　スペース
spare　①予備の，②予備
spare parts　予備品，予備部品，交換用部品
SPC　▶special purpose company
SPE　▶special purpose entity
special　特別な
special concession　特別措置（税務上の）
special deduction　特別控除
special depreciation　特別償却
special income tax for reconstruction　復興特別所得税
specialise　特化する，専門化する　[米]specialize
specialist　専門家
special liquidation　特別清算

special local corporation tax　地方法人特別税
special purpose company (SPC)　特別目的会社
special purpose entity (SPE)　特別目的会社
special purpose vehicle (SPV)　特別目的会社
special tariffs　特殊関税（制度）　[解]不公正な貿易取引等に対して，通常の関税に加え，割増関税を賦課する制度
Special Taxation Measures Law　租税特別措置法
special tax due by specified family company　特定同族会社の留保金課税
special tax for reconstruction　復興特別税
specific　特定の
specification　仕様，仕様書
specific cost　個別費
specific identification method　個別法
specific identification of costs　個別法　[解]代替性のない棚卸資産の原価算定方式
specific provision for bad debt　個別評価金銭債権に対する貸倒引当金
specified asset　特定の資産
specified family company　特定同族会社
specified foreign related company　特定外国関係会社（タックス・ヘイブン対策税制における）　[解]タックス・ヘイブン対策税制における外国関係会社のうち，(1)ペーパー・カンパニー，(2)事実上のキャッシュ・ボックス，(3)ブラックリスト国所在会社に該当するもの。基本的に会社単位の合算課税の対象となる（ただし，租税負担割合が30％以上の場合を除く）
specified foreign subsidiary　特定外国子会社等（旧タックス・ヘイブン対策税制における）　[解]平成29年度税制改正前のタックス・ヘイブン対策税制において，外国関係会社のうち，租税負担割合が20％未満のもの
specify　特定する
spectrum　範囲
speculation　投機
speculative　投機的な
spend　支出する
spending　支出

spillover effect　波及効果
spin-off　スピン・オフ　[解]一般に，企業が事業部などの一部門を独立させ，別会社（例えば，子会社）化すること
split　①分割する，②分割
split-off　スプリット・オフ　[解]主として米国における会社分割の一形態。まず，企業（親会社）が事業部門の分離により設立した子会社の株式を取得する。次に，それを自らの株主に交付し，自己株式を受け取る形で減資を行うというもの
split-up　スプリット・アップ　[解]主として米国における会社分割の一形態。まず，企業（親会社）が2つ以上の子会社を新設し，その子会社に事業用資産のすべてを移転する。そのうえで，親会社が清算し，株主に子会社株式を分配するというもの
spoilage　仕損
sponsor　①スポンサー，②保証人
spot　①現物，直物，②点
spot element of a forward contract　先渡契約に含まれる直物の要素
spot exchange rate　直物為替レート　[解]為替を即時受渡しする際の為替レートで，一般にいう為替レートは直物為替レートを指す。為替予約に係る予約レート（forward exchange rate）に対する用語
spot market　現物市場，直物市場
spouse　配偶者
spread　①利鞘，スプレッド，②配分する　[用]② the cost of a fixed asset is spread over the useful life（固定資産の原価は，その耐用年数にわたって配分される）
spread proportionately over the period　均等に期間配分する
spreadsheet　スプレッドシート，表計算　[解]表計算ソフトの表
SPV　▶special purpose vehicle
squeeze out　スクイーズ・アウト　[解]組織再編の局面において，少数株主を排除し，対象会社を完全子会社とすること
SRI　▶socially responsible investment
SSA　▶share sale agreement
stability　安定性

stable　安定した
staff　スタッフ
staffing　人員配置，スタッフィング
staff skills　スタッフの技能
staff training cost [expense]　教育訓練費
stage　段階，ステージ
stage of completion　進捗度
stage of completion of contract activity　工事進捗度
stake　利害関係
stakeholder　利害関係者
stamp duty [tax]　印紙税
stance　スタンス，姿勢，態度
stand-alone　①単体の，個別の，②単独の　[解]①「連結の」(consolidated) に対する用語
stand-alone issue　スタンドアロン・イシュー，スタンドアロン問題　[解]買収案件などで，買収対象会社がもともとのグループから離脱した結果，グループ内で受けていたベネフィットが得られなくなるという問題
stand-alone selling price　独立販売価格　[解]IFRS15の文脈では，企業が財またはサービスを独立して顧客に提供する場合の価格を指す
standard　標準，基準
standard cost　標準原価
standard costing　標準原価計算
standard cost method　標準原価法　[解]原価算定方式ではなく，原価の直接的な測定方法であり，IFRSでは実際原価に近似する場合のみ簡便法として使用が認められる
standard cost sheet　標準原価表
standard cost variance　標準原価差異
standard deduction　定額控除，標準控除
standard deviation　標準偏差
Standard Industrial Classification Code (SIC Code)　標準産業分類コード（米国の）
Standard Interpretations Committee (SIC)　解釈指針委員会
standardisation　標準化　㊆standardization
standardise　標準化する　㊆standardize
standard procedure　標準的手続

Standards Advisory Council　基準諮問会議（日本）
standard setter　（会計）基準設定者
standard setting body　会計基準の設定主体
standard tax rate　標準税率
standby credit　スタンドバイ・クレジット
standby letter of credit　スタンドバイ信用状　[解]取引限度額と有効期間があり，商品代金に関する支払いではなく，債務不履行に対して支払いの確約を行う信用状であり，銀行保証と同様の効果がある。日本企業の海外子会社などが現地の銀行から融資を受ける場合に，債務保証の位置付けで，日本の取引銀行が発行する場合もある
standing cost　固定費
standpoint　観点，見地
standstill　停止
standstill agreement　スタンドスティル契約
standstill clause　スタンドスティル条項，再買収停止条項　[解]買収案件などで，買収対象会社の株主が，株式を一定期間買い戻せないことを定める条項
stapled financing　ステイプル・ファイナンス　[解]買収案件などで，売手のFAが買手候補に買収資金を融資する形態
start-up　①開業間もない会社，②開始
start-up cost　開業費
state　①述べる，②国，③州
State Administration of Taxation (SAT)　中国国家税務総局（中国の税務当局）
state defined benefit plan　公的確定給付制度
stated value　①額面金額，②表示金額
statement　①計算書，②述べること，記載
statement of cash flows　キャッシュ・フロー計算書　[解]1会計期間のキャッシュ・フローの内訳を示す計算書
statement of changes in equity　持分変動計算書　[解]1会計期間の資本の変動内訳を示す計算書
statement of changes in net assets　株主資本等変動計算書
statement of comprehensive income　包括利益計算書　[解]1会計期間の企業の所

有者（株主）以外との取引による資本の変動（単純にいうと経営成績）を示す計算書で，従来の損益計算書にその他の包括利益の要素を加えたもの
statement of cost of goods manufactured　製造原価報告書
statement of earnings　損益計算書
Statement of Financial Accounting Standards (SFAS)　財務会計基準書（旧）（米国）
statement of financial condition　貸借対照表
statement of financial position　財政状態計算書　[解]　企業の期末時点の財政状態を表現したもので，従来の貸借対照表と同様
statement of income　損益計算書
statement of operations　損益計算書
statement of profit or loss　損益計算書
statement of profit or loss and other comprehensive income　純損益及びその他の包括利益計算書
statement of shareholders' equity　株主資本等変動計算書
Statements on Auditing Standards (SAS)　監査基準書（米国）
state plan　①国の制度，②公的制度（退職給付制度について）
state tax　①州税，②国税
statistical　統計上の
statistics　統計
status　状況
status quo　現状
statute　法令，成文法
statute law　成文法
statute of limitations　時効，出訴期間　[解]　税務デュー・デリジェンスの関係では，買収対象会社の税務リスクを判断するうえで，租税債権の時効は重要な情報となり，税務調査未了年度のうち，消滅時効にかかっていない年度が税務リスクの観点から特に重要とされる
statutory　法定の
statutory audit　法定監査
statutory auditor　監査役
statutory income　法定総所得
statutory rate　法定税率

statutory requirement　法的要請
statutory reserve　法定準備金
statutory tax rate　法定税率，法定実効税率
statutory useful life　法定耐用年数
steering committee　運営委員会　[解]　プロジェクトの運営責任を持つ委員会
step　①段階，②手段
step acquisition　段階取得，段階的取得
step-by-step acquisition method　段階法
step-down in basis　簿価のステップダウン（減額）
stepped down basis　ステップダウン（減額）された簿価
stepped up basis　ステップアップ（増額）された簿価
step-up in basis　簿価のステップアップ（増額）
stewardship　管理，財務管理
stipulate　規定する（法律や契約書などが）
stipulation　規定（法律や契約書などの）
stock　①株式，②在庫
stock acquisition　株式買収，株式取得
stock appreciation right (SAR)　株式増価受益権
stock award plan　株式報奨制度
stock certificate　株券
stock compensation plan　株式に基づく報酬制度，株式報酬制度
stock consideration　株式対価　[解]　share consideration の項を参照
stock consolidation　株式併合
stock deal　株式買収，株式取引
stock dividend　株式配当
stock exchange　証券取引所
stockholder　株主
stockholders' equity　株主資本，株主持分
stock index　株価指数
stock issue cost　株式交付費
stock keeping unit (SKU)　在庫管理単位　[解]　企業が在庫を管理する上での最小単位で，例えば，商品の品目や型番ごとなど
stock lending　株式等賃借取引，ストック・レンディング
stock level　在庫水準
stock market　株式市場
stock option　ストック・オプション　[解]

share option の項を参照
stock premium　株式プレミアム
stock price　株価
stock purchase　株式買収
stock purchase agreement (SPA)　株式買収契約書
stock redemption　株式償還，減資
stock right　株式引受権
stock sale　株式売却，株式譲渡
stock sale agreement　株式譲渡契約書
stock split　株式分割
stock subscription　株式の引受け
stock taking　棚卸
stock valuation　在庫評価
stock warrant　新株予約権
storage　保管
storage cost [expense]　保管費用
straight　①直線の，②普通の
straight bond　普通社債
straightforward　単純な
straight-line depreciation　定額法による減価償却
straight-line method　定額法　[解] 減価償却方法の１つで，定額法によると，減価償却費が毎期一定になる
strata　stratum の複数形
strategic　戦略的な
strategic business unit (SBU)　戦略的事業単位　[解] 戦略の策定と実行を独立して行える事業単位をいい，業績管理もこの単位で行われる
strategic buyer　ストラテジック・バイヤー　[解] 買収対象会社の事業を継続的に営むことを前提に投資を行う買収者。単に買収対象会社の解散価値や割安度合いに着目して投資を行うファイナンシャル・バイヤー（financial buyer）に対する用語
strategic decision　戦略的意思決定
strategic investor　ストラテジック・インベスター
strategy　戦略
stratification　層別化，階層化
stratify　層別に分ける
stratum　層
stream　流れ
streamline　合理化する

stress testing　ストレス・テスト　[解] リスク管理手法の１つで，システムに通常以上の負荷をかけて正常に動作するかを確認すること。具体的には，マーケットで不測の事態が生じた場合，自社のポートフォリオについて，どれだけの潜在的リスクがあるかを計測しておくこと
strike price　権利行使価格（オプションの）
structure　①構築物，②構造，構成，③ストラクチャー（買収などの），④ストラクチャーを決定する（買収などの）　[解] ③④ structuring の項を参照
structured entity　ストラクチャード・エンティティ，組成された企業　[解] IFRS12 の文脈では，その企業を支配している主体の決定にあたって，議決権または類似の権利が決定的な要因とならないように設計された企業（例えば，証券化の際のビークルなど）を指す
structure diagram　資本関係図
structuring　ストラクチャリング　[解] 企業買収や組織再編時の手法及び構成の決定
structuring analysis　ストラクチャリング分析
study　調査
sub-account　小科目
sub-category　サブカテゴリー
sub-classification　小分類
sub-consolidation　サブ連結　[解] 下位グループにおける連結を指し，親会社にとっては，例えば子会社が孫会社を連結することなど
subcontract　下請契約
subcontracting cost　外注費
subcontractor　外注先，下請業者
sub-group　下位グループ
subjective　主観的な
subjectivity　主観性
subject to　①〜に従う必要がある，②〜が課される
subject to withholding tax　源泉徴収の対象となる
sub-lease　サブリース，転貸　[解] 貸手から借手にリースされた原資産を，借手がさらに（第三者に）リースすること　[用] rental income from property sub-

leases（転貸不動産からの賃貸収入）
sub-lease arrangement　転貸契約
sub-lease income　転貸収入
sub-lease payment　サブリース料
sub-ledger (S/L)　補助元帳，補助簿
sub-let　転貸する
submission　提出
submit　提出する
sub-national regime　地方自治体
subordinate(d)　劣後した【形】
subordinated debt　劣後債，劣後債務
subordinated liabilities　劣後負債
Subpart F　サブパートF　[解] 米国株主に保有されている被支配外国法人（CFC）の特定の所得を，その持分割合に応じて米国株主の総所得に合算して課税する米国の制度
Subpart F income inclusion　Subpart Fによる合算課税
subpoena　召喚令状
sub-process　サブプロセス
subscribe　①引き受ける（証券などを），②購読する
subscription　①引受け（証券などの），②購読
subscription right　引受権
subsequent　その次の，その後の
subsequent accounting period　翌期，来期
subsequent cost　事後のコスト，取得後のコスト
subsequent event　後発事象
subsequent expenditure　事後の支出，取得後の支出（無形資産などの）
subsequently　その後
subsequent measurement　当初以後の測定，事後の測定
subsequent period　①その後の期間，事後の期間，②翌期，来期
subsequent year　翌年（度），来年（度）
subsidiary　子会社　[解] 他の企業（親会社）に支配されている企業
subsidiary account　補助科目
subsidiary acquired with a view to resale　転売目的で取得した子会社
subsidiary company　子会社
subsidiary ledger (S/L)　補助元帳
subsidise　補助金を支給する　[米] subsidize

subsidy　補助金
substance　実質，実体
substance of transaction　取引の実体
substance over form　実質主義　[解] 形式よりも実質を優先するという会計・税務における一般的な原則であり，IFRSにおける原則の1つでもある
substance over form doctrine　実質主義
substance test　実体基準　[解] タックス・ヘイブン対策税制における経済活動基準の1つで，外国関係会社がその本店所在地国において主たる事業を行うために必要と認められる事務所等の固定施設を有していることを確認する基準
substantial　①実体のある，②重要な，③多数の
substantial doubt　重要な疑義　[用] substantial doubt about entity's ability to continue as a going concern（継続企業の前提に関する重要な疑義）
substantially　①実質的に，②十分に
substantially enacted tax rate　実質的に施行されている税率
substantiate　①根拠づける，実証する，②実体化する，具体化する
substantiation　①実証，立証，②実体化，具体化
substantive　①実証的な，②実体の（ある），実質的な，③相当量（数）の
substantive audit procedures　実証的な監査手続
substantive rights　実質的な権利
substitute　代替する
substitution　代替，代用
subtotal　小計
subtract　引く
subtraction　減算
succeed　①成功する，②承継する
success fee　成功報酬
succession　承継，引継ぎ
succession plan　後継者育成計画
successive　連続した
successor　①承継者，承継法人，②後任
successor auditor　後任の監査人
successor company　承継法人　[解] 分割承継や債務承継に関して

successor liability 引継（者）債務
sue 告訴する
suffice 十分である【動】
sufficiency 十分性
sufficient 十分な
sufficiently 十分に
suggest 提案する
suggestion 提案
suit 訴訟
suitable 適した
sum 合計，金額，総額
summarise 要約する ㊋summarize
summarised financial information 要約財務情報 ㊋summarized financial information
summary 要約
summary of significant accounting policies 重要な会計方針の要約
sundries ①諸口，②雑多な項目
sundry 雑多な，種々の
sundry account 雑勘定
sundry creditors 雑勘定（貸方）
sundry debtors 雑勘定（借方）
sundry expense(s) 雑費
sunk cost 埋没原価，サンク・コスト
superior 上位の
super royalty provision スーパー・ロイヤルティ条項 [解] commensurate with income standard の項を参照
supersede 取って代わる
supervise 管理する，監督する
supervision 管理，監督
supervisor 管理者，監督者
supervisory 管理の，管理上の
supplement 補足，補遺
supplemental 補足的な，追加の
supplemental schedule(s) 附属明細表，補足的な明細
supplementary 補足的な，追加の
supplementary disclosure 補足開示
supplementary information 補足情報，補足説明
supplementary schedule(s) 附属明細表，補足的な明細
supplier 仕入先，供給者
supplies 貯蔵品，消耗品

supplies expense 消耗品費
supply ①貯蔵品（通常複数形で），②供給，③供給する
supply chain サプライ・チェーン
supply chain management (SCM) サプライ・チェーン・マネジメント
support ①支援する，支持する，②支援，支持，③根拠（資料）
supportable 支持可能な
supportable assumption 支持可能な仮定
supportable information 支持可能な情報 [用] supportable information about past events（過去の事象に関する支持可能な情報）
supporting document 根拠資料
supporting evidence 裏付け，根拠資料
Supreme Court 最高裁判所
surcharge ①追加料金，②付加税，③課徴金
surplus ①剰余，余剰，②剰余金，③積立超過（退職給付制度などの）
surplus in plan 積立超過（退職給付制度などの）
surplus or deficit 積立超過または積立不足（退職給付制度などの）
surprise audit 抜き打ち監査
surrogate ①代用の，②代用物
surtax 付加税
surveillance 監視
survey ①調査する，②調査
survival 存続
surviving company 存続会社（合併に際しての）
suspend ①中止する，中断する，②一時停止する，③猶予する，延期する
suspense account 仮勘定 [解] いわゆる「仮払金」や「仮受金」を意味する場合もあるが，残高試算表などがバランスしないケースで，「差異を埋めるために暫定的に用いる勘定」を意味する場合もある
suspense payment 仮払金
suspense receipt 仮受金
suspension ①中止，②中断，一時停止，③未決
suspension of capitalisation 資産化の中止 ㊋suspension of capitalization
suspicious 疑わしい，不審な

sustain 維持する
sustaining capital reinvestment 更新(再)投資
swap スワップ
swap contract スワップ契約
swaption スワプション [解]スワップ取引を行う権利を対象とするオプション取引
SWIFT code SWIFTコード [解]SWIFT(Society for Worldwide Interbank Financial Telecommunication)が提供する,国際的な送金システム上で相手方の銀行を特定するためのコード
syndicate シンジケート
syndicated loan シンジケート・ローン
syndication シンジケーション
synergistic シナジー[相乗]効果を生むような【形】
synergistic buyer シナジー効果を生むような買手(買収案件などの)
synergistic value シナジー効果の価値
synergy シナジー(効果),相乗効果
synergy with other assets 他の資産とのシナジー
synonymous 同義の
synthetic 合成の,統合的な
synthetic instrument 合成金融商品
system システム
systematic ①規則的な,②組織的な
systematically 規則的に
systematic basis 規則的方法 [用]on a systematic basis(規則的に)
system audit システム監査

T

table 表
tabulation 作表,集計
T account T勘定
tag タグ,札,棚札(棚卸用の)
tag along clause タグ・アロング条項 [解]複数の株主が共同で投資する場合に締結される株主間契約の条項で,株式売却の局面において,ある株主が株式を売却する場合には,他の株主も同条件で買手に売却する権利を有する旨を定めるもの
tag along right タグ・アロング・ライト,売却参加権,共同売却権 [解]ある株主が株式を売却する場合,他の株主(特に少数株主)も同条件で買手に株式を売却できるという(他の株主の)権利
tag control タグ・コントロール,棚札の管理(棚卸の際の)
tailor うまく調整する(条件に適合するように)
tainted 汚れた,腐敗した
tainted income 不浄所得(規制対象となる所得)
takeover ①企業買収,②乗っ取り
takeover bid (TOB) 株式の公開買付け [解]主として支配権獲得目的で不特定多数の株主から株を買い取ること
takeover defence 買収防衛策 [米]takeover defense
take place 発生する,起こる
tangible 有形の
tangible asset 有形資産
tangible fixed asset 有形固定資産
tangible property 有形資産
target ①買収対象会社,②目標
target company 買収対象会社
target cost 目標原価
target group 買収対象会社グループ
target's shareholder 買収対象会社の株主
tariff ①関税,②関税率,③関税率表

tariff classification	関税分類
tariff code	タリフ・コード，関税番号
tax	税金，税金費用
taxable	課税対象となる，課税の
taxable amount	課税対象金額
taxable base	課税標準，課税ベース
taxable earnings	税務上の利益（課税所得）
taxable event	課税事象
taxable income	課税所得，所得
taxable period	課税期間
taxable person	納税（義務）者
taxable profit	税務上の利益（課税所得） [解]会計上の利益（accounting profit）と区別するための表現
taxable retained earnings	課税対象留保利益
taxable sales	課税売上（消費税などの）
taxable temporary difference	将来加算一時差異 [解]一時差異のうち，解消の際に課税所得を増額させるもので，繰延税金負債の計上対象となる
taxable transaction	課税取引（消費税などの）
taxable year	課税年度
tax accounting	税務会計
tax accrual	税金引当 [解]会計上の税金費用及び未払法人税等の計上
tax adviser [advisor]	税務アドバイザー
tax affairs	税務関連事項
tax agent	税務代理人，納税管理人
tax allowable	損金算入可能な
tax allowance	損金算入（税務上の）
tax amount	税額
tax appeal	不服申立て（税務に関する）
tax arbitrage	租税裁定取引 [解]各国の税制の相違などを利用して，節税（あるいは租税回避）を行うための取引
tax assessment	賦課課税
tax assessment notice	賦課決定通知書（税金の）
taxation	課税
taxation at source	源泉課税
tax attributes	①税務上の繰越項目，②租税属性 [解]①繰越欠損金や繰越税額控除等を指す
tax audit	税務調査
tax audit adjustment	税務調査による修正（更正）
tax auditor	税務調査官
tax audit status	税務調査の状況
tax authorities	税務当局
tax avoidance	租税回避
tax avoidance scheme	租税回避スキーム
tax base	①税務基準額，税務上の金額，税務簿価，②課税標準，課税ベース [解]①一時差異を計算する際に会計上の金額（carrying amount）と比較される金額
tax basis	①税務簿価，②課税標準
tax benefit	税務上の恩典，税務上の便益
tax bill	税法に関する法案
tax book value	税務簿価
tax burden	租税負担
Tax Bureau	（財務省）主税局（日本）
tax calculation	税金計算
tax calculation worksheet	税金計算シート
tax case	税務訴訟
tax characterisation	税務上の特徴 [米] tax characterization [解]取引の法的形式（legal form）に対して，「税務的な観点からの取引の実質」という文脈で用いられることが多い
tax clearance certificate	納税証明書
tax compliance	タックス・コンプライアンス [解]税務申告・納付に係る規制の遵守
tax computation	①税金計算，②納付税額計算書
tax concession	税制優遇措置，優遇税制
tax consequence	税務上の影響
tax consideration	税務上の考慮事項
tax consolidated group	連結納税グループ
tax consolidation	連結納税
tax contingent liability	税金に係る偶発負債
tax convention	租税条約
tax court	租税裁判所
tax credit	税額控除
tax credit for job creation	雇用促進税制（日本）
tax credit for research and development (R&D) expenditure	試験研究費の税額控除
tax credit for salary growth	所得拡大促進税制（日本）
tax crime	租税犯罪

tax declaration	税務申告
tax deductibility	損金性, 損金算入可能性
tax deductible	損金算入可能な
tax deduction	損金算入（税務上の）
tax deferral	課税の繰延べ
tax deferral treatment	課税の繰延措置
tax delinquency	税金の滞納
tax department [division]	税務部門
tax depreciation	税務上の減価償却費 [使い方注意!]税務上の減価償却費は会計上の減価償却費（accounting depreciation）と金額が異なることが多いので, 会計・税務のいずれを指すのかは明確にする必要がある
tax dispute	税務上の争い
tax due diligence (TDD)	税務デュー・デリジェンス [解]潜在的な租税債務を含む簿外負債などの把握を行うための調査
tax effect (of)	（～の）税効果 [用]tax effect of non-deductible expenses （損金不算入費用の税効果）, tax effect of tax-exempt income （非課税所得の税効果）, tax effect of tax incentives （税制優遇措置の税効果）, tax effect of current-year losses for which no deferred tax asset is recognised （繰延税金資産が認識されない当事業年度の損失による税効果）
tax effect accounting	税効果会計
tax-effective	税務上有効な
tax-efficient	税務上効率的な
tax equalisation (TEQ)	タックス・イコライゼーション [米]tax equalization [解]海外駐在員について, 企業（雇用者）が従業員の派遣元・派遣先両国の税額を支払う一方, 従業員がみなし税金（派遣元の国にとどまったと仮定した場合の税額）を企業に支払うという取決め
taxes deemed paid	みなし支払税金
taxes other than income tax	法人所得税以外の税金
taxes paid	支払税金
taxes payable	未払税金
taxes receivable	未収税金
tax evader	脱税者
tax evasion	租税回避, 脱税
tax examination	税務調査
tax examiner	税務調査官
tax-exempt	非課税の, 免税の
tax-exempt income	非課税所得, 益金不算入収益
tax-exempt organisation	非課税組織 [米]tax-exempt organization
tax expense	税金費用 [解]当期税金費用（current tax expense）と繰延税金費用（deferred tax expense）の合計額
tax expense at applicable tax rate	適用税率による税金費用
tax expense other than income tax expense	法人所得税費用以外の税金費用
tax exposure	税務エクスポージャー [解]税務リスクにさらされていることをいい, 税務リスクとほぼ同義
tax filing	税務申告
tax foreclosure	税金滞納による差押え
tax form	税務申告書（用紙）
tax fraud	税務上の不正
tax-free	非課税の, 免税の
tax-free reorganisation	非課税組織再編 [米]tax-free reorganization
tax haven	タックス・ヘイブン
tax haven rules	タックス・ヘイブン対策税制
tax holiday	タックス・ホリデイ [解]一定期間の租税の減免
tax impact	税務上の影響
tax implication	税務上の意味合い
tax incentive	優遇税制 [解]税務デュー・デリジェンスの関係では, 買収対象会社が優遇税制（特定事業についての免税や軽減税率等）の適用を受けている場合, 買収による株主変更により, 優遇税制の適用が自動的に終了するケースがある
tax income	税金収益 [解]マイナスの税金費用
tax indemnification [indemnity]	税金に関する補償
tax information exchange agreement (TIEA)	税務に関する情報交換協定
taxing right	課税権
tax investigation	税務調査 [解]tax investigationという用語は, 通常のtax auditと区別され, 租税回避等が疑われる場合

tax

の調査を指すこともある
tax investigator　税務調査官
tax invoice　タックス・インボイス，税額票，請求書
tax jurisdiction　課税管轄区域
tax law　税法
tax liability　納税義務，未払税金
tax lien　租税先取特権
tax loss　欠損金（税務上の），マイナスの課税所得
tax loss carryback　欠損金の繰戻し
tax loss carryforward(s)　繰越欠損金，欠損金の繰越し
tax losses carried forward　繰越欠損金
tax offence　税法違反
tax office　税務署
tax on gross income　総収入に対する課税
taxonomy　タクソノミ，分類（法）　[解]財務報告の電子的なひな型
tax on undistributed profits　留保金課税
tax opinion　税務意見書
tax package　タックス・パッケージ
taxpayer　納税（義務）者
taxpayer identification number (TIN)　納税者番号
taxpayer-specific ruling　特定の納税者に対する確認（税務当局による）
tax payment　納税，税金の納付
tax payment certificate　納税証明書
tax payment slip　納付書
tax perspective　税務の観点
　　　[用] from a tax perspective（税務の観点からは）
tax planning　タックス・プランニング　[解]将来の税務コストの削減や税務リスクの低減を達成するための計画をいい，繰延税金資産の回収可能性を判断するにあたって考慮される
tax position　税務ポジション　[解]過去の所得または欠損の発生状況や税金の納付状況，また繰越欠損金の残高等の全般的な状況
tax profile　税務に関する概略（会社の）
tax provision　税金引当　[解]会計上の税金費用及び未払法人税等の計上
tax-qualified　（税制）適格の

tax-qualified contribution in kind　適格現物出資
tax-qualified corporate division　適格分割
tax-qualified corporate reorganisation　適格組織再編　[米] tax qualified reorganization
tax-qualified dividend in kind　適格現物分配
tax-qualified horizontal-type corporate division　適格分割型分割
tax-qualified merger　適格合併
tax-qualified reorganisation　適格組織再編　[米] tax qualified reorganization
tax-qualified share for share exchange　適格株式交換
tax-qualified share transfer　適格株式移転
tax-qualified stock option　（税制）適格ストック・オプション
tax-qualified vertical-type corporate division　適格分社型分割
tax rate　税率
tax rates that have been enacted or substantively enacted　施行されているまたは実質的に施行されている税率
tax reassessment　更正（税務当局による）
tax reassessment notice　更正通知書
tax rebate　税金の還付
tax reform　税制改正
tax reform bill　税制改正法案
tax reform plan　税制改正案
tax refund　税金の還付
tax regime　税制，租税体系
tax registration　税務登録
tax relief　税金の軽減
tax representative　納税管理人
tax reserve　税金引当
tax residency certificate　居住者証明書（税務上の）
tax return　税務申告書
tax return filing　税務申告，税務申告書の提出
tax return filing obligation　税務申告書の提出義務
tax return preparation　税務申告書の作成
tax return preparer　税務申告書の作成者
tax revenue　税収
tax risk　税務リスク

tax shelter	タックス・シェルター
tax shield	タックス・シールド [解]費用（減価償却費等）の損金算入により，税金が軽減されること
tax sparing credit	みなし外国税額控除 [解]開発途上国等への投資促進を目的とする制度であり，端的には，実際には海外で支払っていない税金をあたかも海外で支払ったかのように日本の税金から控除するもの。一般に租税条約に規定される
tax status	課税上の地位，税務上のステイタス
tax structuring	税務上のストラクチャリング [解]税務の観点からの，企業買収や組織再編時の手法及び構成の決定
tax structuring analysis	税務上のストラクチャリング分析
tax treatment	税務上の取扱い
tax treaty	租税条約 [解]二重課税の排除や脱税の防止などを目的として主権国家の間で締結される成文による合意
tax treaty withholding tax rate	租税条約上の源泉税率
tax viewpoint	税務の観点 [用] from a tax viewpoint（税務の観点からは）
tax withheld (at source)	源泉税
tax write-off	税務上の減価償却費，キャピタル・アローワンス
tax written-down value	減価償却資産の税務簿価
tax year	課税年度，税務目的の事業年度
T/B	▶trial balance
TDD	▶tax due diligence
teaser	ティーザー，ノンネーム・シート [解]買収案件などにおける売却対象企業の（匿名の）企業概要書
technical	技術的な
technical feasibility	技術的実行可能性
technical service	技術役務，技術上の役務
technique	技術
technological	テクノロジーの
technology	テクノロジー
technology-based intangible asset	技術に基づく無形資産
teleconference	電話会議，テレビ会議
telegraphic transfer (T/T)	電信為替（送金）
telegraphic transfer buying rate (TTB)	電信買相場 [解]銀行が顧客から外貨を買う際のレートで，顧客から見ると，外貨を円に交換するときのレート
telegraphic transfer middle rate (TTM)	仲値（TTBとTTSの）
telegraphic transfer selling rate (TTS)	電信売相場 [解]銀行が顧客に外貨を売る際のレートで，顧客から見ると，円を外貨に交換するときのレート
telephone hotline	電話による通報制度（不正などの）
template	テンプレート，ひな型 [用] template for（〜のひな型）
temporarily	一時的に
temporarily idle	一時的に遊休の
temporary	一時的な
temporary control	一時的な支配
temporary difference	一時差異 [解]資産及び負債の会計上の金額と税務上の金額の差異であり，将来減算一時差異（deductible temporary difference）と将来加算一時差異（taxable temporary difference）に分類される [用] origination and reversal of temporary differences（一時差異の発生及び解消）
temporary difference, unused tax losses and unused tax credits	一時差異，税務上の繰越欠損金及び繰越税額控除
temporary joint control	一時的な共同支配
temporary measure	経過措置
temporary significant influence	一時的な重要な影響力
temporary staff	派遣社員
tenancy	借用
tenancy agreement	賃貸借契約
tenant	借家人，借地人，テナント
tendency	傾向
tender offer	テンダー・オファー [解]企業買収等のための株式公開買付け
tentative	仮の
10-year government bond	10年物国債
TEQ	▶tax equalisation
term	①条件，②期間，③用語
term deposit	定期預金
terminal	最終の

terminal value (TV)　ターミナル・バリュー
terminate　終了させる
termination　解除，終了（契約などの）
termination benefit　解雇給付　[解] 従業員給付の一形態で，企業が従業員を解雇する場合などに，雇用の終了と交換に支給されるもの
termination benefits expense　解雇給付費用
termination of employment　雇用の終了，解雇
termination option　解約選択権［オプション］（リース契約などの）
terminology　（専門）用語
term loan　ターム・ローン，証書貸付
terms　条件
terms and conditions　条件（契約などの），取引条件
term sheet　ターム・シート，条件概要書　[解] 契約の概要や骨子となる条件を記載した文書
terms of payment　支払条件
territorial　管轄区域の，領土の
territoriality　属地
territoriality principle　属地主義　[解] territorial system の項を参照
territorial system　国外所得免税方式，属地主義　[解] 国際課税における課税方式の1つで，全世界所得課税方式（worldwide system）に対して，自国の国内源泉所得のみに課税し，国外源泉所得には課税しないという方式
territory　管轄区域，領土
test　テスト
test count　テスト・カウント（棚卸立会における）
tested company　検証対象会社（移転価格税制などの）
testing　テスト
testing procedure　検証手続
test of controls　統制テスト
test of design　整備テスト（内部統制の）
test of detail　詳細テスト
test of operating effectiveness　運用テスト（内部統制の）
theft　盗難
theft of cash on hand　手許現金の窃盗

theft of cash receipts　領収現金の窃盗
theoretical　理論的な，理論上の
theoretically　理論的には，理論上
theory　理論
thin capitalisation　過少資本　[米] thin capitalization
thin capitalisation rules　過少資本税制　[米] thin capitalization rules　[解] 多くの国で利息が損金算入されることを利用して，国外に所在する親会社等から資金提供を受ける際に，出資の比率を下げて，逆に借入を増やすことにより，子会社の租税負担の軽減を行うことを防止する制度
thin corporation　過少資本会社
third party　第三者
third-party appraisal　第三者による評価
third-party document　第三者の書類
third-party hotline　第三者による通報制度（不正などの）
third-party transaction　（対）第三者取引，第三者間取引
3rd quarter　第3四半期
threshold　基準値，閾値，限界値
TIBOR　▶Tokyo Interbank Offered Rate
tick　チェック（照合時に付ける）
tick mark　チェック・マーク
TIEA　▶Tax Information Exchange Agreement
tiebreaker rule　タイブレーカー・ルール　[解] 1つの法人（または個人）が双方の国の居住者とされる場合に，いずれか一方に振り分ける租税条約上の規定
tie-in shares　抱合せ株式
tier　層，階層
time-and-materials contract　実費精算契約（開発業務などの）
time-consuming　時間を要する【形】
time deposit　定期預金
time frame　タイム・フレーム，時間枠
timeline　タイムライン
timeliness　適時性
timely　適時の
timely disclosure　適時開示，タイムリー・ディスクロージャー
time report　作業時間報告書
times　×（掛ける）　[使い方注意!] A×Bは，

A times B
time schedule (of work)　工程表
timetable　予定表
time value　時間的価値　[解]オプションの価値のうち，本源的価値（intrinsic value）以外の部分で，満期日までに原資産価格が変動して，本源的価値が大きくなることを期待した価値
time value of money　貨幣の時間的価値
timing　タイミング，時点
timing benefit　タイミング・ベネフィット　[解]課税タイミングが遅れることで，税務上有利になることを意味し，課税繰延べの効果を指す
timing difference　留保項目（税務調整のうち），[解]社外流出項目（permanent difference）に対する用語
timing of transfer of goods or services　財またはサービスの移転の時期
TIN　▶taxpayer identification number
tip　①通報，②チップ
title　①題名，②（法的）所有権　[用] title passes（所有権が移転する）
title transfer　所有権の移転
TK　▶Tokumei Kumiai
TMK　特定目的会社　[解]資産流動化法に基づいて設立され，資産の流動化業務を行う，日本の特別目的会社
TNMM　▶transactional net margin method
TOB　▶takeover bid
Tokumei Kumiai (TK)　匿名組合（日本の）　[解]匿名組合員が出資を行い，営業者がそれを運用して利益をあげ，匿名組合員に対して分配を行うという契約形態。匿名組合員は営業者の行為に関して，第三者に対する権利義務を有しない
Tokyo Inter-Bank Offered Rate (TIBOR)　東京銀行間取引金利
Tokyo Regional Tax(ation) Bureau　東京国税局
Tokyo Stock Exchange (TSE)　東京証券取引所
tolerable　許容可能な
toll　①通行料金（道路などの），②犠牲
toll manufacturer　委託製造業者
tool　工具

tooling cost　工具費
tools, furniture and fixtures　工具，器具及び備品
top-down approach　トップダウン・アプローチ
top line　①売上高（損益計算書の冒頭），②重要事項
top of range　範囲の上限
tort　不法行為
total　合計
total assets　資産合計，総資産
total assets turnover　総資産回転率
total comprehensive income　包括利益（合計）　[解]当期利益とその他の包括利益の合計
total comprehensive income attributable to ～に帰属する当期包括利益　[用] total comprehensive income attributable to non-controlling interests（非支配持分に帰属する当期包括利益），total comprehensive income attributable to owners of the parent（親会社の所有者に帰属する当期包括利益）
total comprehensive income for the year　当期包括利益　[解]当期利益とその他の包括利益の合計
total contract cost　工事契約総原価
total contract revenue　工事契約総収益
total cost　総原価
total current assets　流動資産合計
total current liabilities　流動負債合計
total equity　資本合計
total equity and liabilities　資本及び負債合計
total liabilities　負債合計
totalling　①合算，集計，②合計で～（金額）の　[米] totaling
total non-current assets　非流動資産合計
total non-current liabilities　非流動負債合計
total posting　合計転記
total quality management (TQM)　全社的品質管理
TP　▶transfer pricing
TPM　▶transfer pricing methodology
TPP　▶Trans-Pacific (Strategic Economic) Partnership (Agreement)

TQM ▶total quality management
trace 証跡
tracking stock トラッキング・ストック，事業部門株式 [解]企業内の特定の事業部門の業績を基礎として，投資家に配当を行う種類株式
track record 実績
trade ①取引，②商業，③業界
trade accounts payable 買掛金，仕入債務，営業債務
trade accounts receivable 売掛金，売掛債権，営業債権
trade and other payables 営業[仕入]債務及びその他の債務
trade and other receivables 営業[売上]債権及びその他の債権
trade credit 企業間与信（信用）
trade date 取引日，約定日
trade date accounting 取引日会計，約定日会計
trade discount 値引き，業者間値引き
trade dress トレード・ドレス [解]商品のデザインや全体的なイメージで，知的財産権の１つとして保護されるもの
trade intangible トレード・インタンジブル [解]一般的には，コマーシャル・インタンジブル（commercial intangible）のうち，マーケティング・インタンジブル（marketing intangible）以外を指す
trade loading 押込販売
trademark 商標，トレードマーク [解]無形資産の例
trademark right 商標権
trade name 商号
trade notes payable 支払手形
trade notes receivable 受取手形
trade payables 仕入債務，営業債務
trader トレーダー
trade receivables 売掛債権，営業債権
trade secret 営業秘密，トレード・シークレット [解]無形資産の例
trading ①取引，②トレーディング
trading account トレーディング勘定
trading expense トレーディング費用
trading history 取引履歴
trading income トレーディング収益

trading income and expense トレーディングの収益及び費用
trading securities トレーディング有価証券
traditional transaction methods 基本三法（旧） [解]平成23年度税制改正前の日本における移転価格税制の関係では，CUP法，RP法，CP法の３法を指す
training トレーニング
training cost [expense] 研修費用
training materials 研修資料
tramper 不定期船
tranche トランシェ
transaction 取引
transactional net margin method (TNMM) 取引単位営業利益法 [解]移転価格税制の関係では，独立企業間価格の算定方法の１つで，取引単位ごとに，検証の対象とする会社（通常は海外子会社）と類似の事業活動を行う会社の営業利益率とを比較することにより，独立企業間価格を算定する方法を指す。主として当事者の一方に（例えば，単純な製造機能等の）基本的な機能しかなく，当該当事者が独自の機能を果たしていない場合に適した算定方法
transaction between entities of a group グループ内取引 [用] to eliminate in full cash flows relating to transactions between entities of the group（グループ内取引に関係するキャッシュ・フローを完全に相殺消去する）
transaction-by-transaction basis 取引ごとのベース [用] on a transaction-by-transaction basis（取引ごとの[に]）
transaction cost 取引コスト
transaction date 取引日
transaction-date exchange rate 取引日（の為替）レート
transaction eliminated on consolidation 連結上消去される取引
transaction flow 取引の流れ
transaction price 取引価格 [解] IFRS15の文脈では，約束した財またはサービスの顧客への移転と引換えに，企業が権利を得ると見込んでいる対価の金額を指す
transactions with employees 従業員との取

引
transactions with non-controlling interests　非支配持分との取引
transactions with owners　（企業の）所有者との取引
transactions with parties other than employees　従業員以外の当事者との取引
transaction tax　取引税
transaction under common control　共通支配下の取引
transaction value　現実支払価格　[解] 関税の関係では，輸入貨物について，輸入者が輸出者に対して，現実に支払う（支払うべき）金額の総額を指す。関税の課税価格の決定の基礎となる
transaction within 100% group　100％グループ内の取引
transfer　①移転，譲渡，②譲受け，③振替え（勘定科目の）
transferability　移転可能性，譲渡可能性
transferable　移転可能な，譲渡可能な
transfer agent　名義書換代理人
transferee　①譲受人，②承継法人，③分割承継法人
transfer entry　振替仕訳
transfer from　①～からの振替，②～からの譲受　[用] ① transfer from construction in progress（建設仮勘定からの振替），transfer from investment property classification（投資不動産からの振替）
transfer of assets within 100% group　100％グループ内の資産譲渡
transfer of business　事業譲渡
transfer of financial assets　金融資産の譲渡
transfer of funds　資金移動
transfer of receivables　債権譲渡
transferor　①譲渡人，②分割法人
transfer price　移転価格
transfer pricing (TP)　移転価格
transfer pricing adjustment　移転価格課税，移転価格調整
transfer pricing document　移転価格文書
transfer pricing documentation　移転価格文書（化），移転価格ドキュメンテーション
transfer pricing methodology (TPM)　独立企業間価格の算定方法
transfer pricing settlement　移転価格に係る決済
transfer pricing study　移転価格スタディ
transfer pricing taxation　移転価格税制，移転価格課税　[解] 日本企業とその国外関連者との取引について，取引価格を独立企業間価格で計算し直して課税所得を計算するもの。国外関連者との取引を通じた恣意的な所得の移転を防止することを目的とした税制
transferred business　移転事業
transfer tax　（財産）譲渡税，移転税　[解] 資産の譲渡に伴い発生する税金全般
transfer to　①～への振替，②～への譲渡　[用] ① transfer to investment property classification（投資不動産への振替），transfer to a disposal group（処分グループへの振替）
transfer to other accounts　他勘定振替高
transition　経過，移行
transition adjustment　移行時の調整
transitional　経過的な，移行的な
transitional liability　移行時負債
transitional measure　経過措置
transitional provision　経過規定，経過措置
transitional services agreement (TSA)　トランジショナル・サービス・アグリーメント，移行期間における役務提供契約　[解] 事業のカーブアウト（carve-out）などに際して，事業のスムーズな買手への移管のために，売却後の移行期間中に売手が行う役務提供（サポート）の内容を取り決めるもの
transition economies　移行経済圏
transition from previous GAAP to IFRS　従前の GAAP［会計原則］から IFRS への移行　[用] financial effect of transition from previous GAAP to IFRS（従前の会計原則から IFRS への移行の財務上の影響）
transition method　移行措置
transitory　一時的な
translate　①換算する，②翻訳する
translation　①換算，②翻訳
translation adjustments　為替換算調整勘定
translation difference　換算差額
translation of foreign operation　在外営業

活動体の換算
translation rate 換算レート
translation reserve 為替換算調整勘定 [解] その他の資本の構成要素
translation to the presentation currency 表示通貨への換算
Trans-Pacific Partnership (TPP) 環太平洋戦略的経済連携協定
Trans-Pacific Strategic Economic Partnership Agreement (TPP) 環太平洋戦略的経済連携協定
transparency 透明性
transparent 透明性の高い
transparent entity 課税対象とならない事業体
transport ①輸送する，②輸送，運送
transportation 輸送，運送
transportation cost [expense] ①輸送費，運搬費，②交通費
transport cost [expense] 輸送コスト，運送費用
travel ①旅行する，②旅行
travel and expense report 出張旅費精算書
travel cost [expense] 旅費，交通費
treasurer ①財務責任者，②財務担当者
treasury 財務部
treasury bill 財務省短期証券（米国）
treasury bond 財務省長期証券（米国）
treasury department [division] 財務部門
Treasury Department Regulations 財務省規則（米国）
treasury note 財務省中期証券（米国）
treasury share [stock] 自己株式
treatment 取扱い
treaty 条約
treaty override トリーティー・オーバーライド [解] 米国等において，租税条約締結後に，租税条約と内容の異なる国内法が制定された場合，その国内法が租税条約に優先される状況をいう
treaty shopping トリーティー・ショッピング，条約漁り [解] 本来であれば租税条約の特典を享受することのできない者が，租税条約の一方の締約国に中間会社を置くなどして，租税条約の特典を受けること

trend 傾向
trend analysis 傾向分析
trial ①裁判，②試行
trial balance (T/B) 残高試算表，試算表
triangular merger 三角合併
tribunal 裁判所，裁決機関
trigger ①起こす，契機となる【動】，②引き金，トリガー [用] ① activity that triggers the payment of the levy（徴税の契機となる活動）
trigger event トリガー・イベント，引き金となる事象 [解] 例えば，繰り延べていた譲渡損益を実現させる契機となる事象
trillion 1兆
trivial 僅少な，ささいな
troublesome 厄介な
true and fair view 真実かつ公正な概観
true sale 真正譲渡
true-up 調整（実績値などへの） [用] true-up for differences between expected and actual outcomes（予測と実績の差異に係る調整）
trust 信託，信託財産
trustee 受託者（信託の）
TSA ▶transitional services agreement
TSE ▶Tokyo Stock Exchange
T/T ▶telegraphic transfer
TTB ▶telegraphic transfer buying rate
TTM ▶telegraphic transfer middle rate
T/T remittance 電信送金
TTS ▶telegraphic transfer selling rate
tumble 下落する，暴落する
turnaround ターンアラウンド，事業再生
turnkey contract ターンキー契約 [解] 元請けとなる業者が施設の建設から試運転等まですべて完了し，あとは「鍵を回す」のみという状態で引き渡すことを約する工事契約
turnover ①売上，②回転率
turnover period 回転期間
turnover tax 売上税（の総称）
TV ▶terminal value
12-month ECLs ▶12-month expected credit losses
12-month expected credit losses (12-month ECLs) 12か月の予想信用損失 [解] 金

融商品について，報告日後 12 か月以内に生じる債務不履行事象から生じる予想信用損失

two-statement presentation　２計算書方式の表示（包括利益計算書などの）
two-step approach　２ステップ・アプローチ　[解]減損テストに際し，第１段階として割引前将来キャッシュ・フローを用いたテストを行う方法
type　種類，類型　[用]types of financial assets（金融資産の種類），types of hedges（ヘッジの種類），types of risks（リスクの種類）
typical　典型的な
typically　典型的には

U

UKBA　▶UK Bribery Act (2010)
UK Bribery Act (2010) (UKBA)　（2010 年）贈収賄法（英国）
ultimate　究極の
ultimate controlling party　最終的な支配当事者
ultimately　究極的に
ultimate parent　最終親会社　[解] 中間親会社（intermediate parent）に対する用語
UN　▶United Nations
unabsorbed　未消化の
unabsorbed business losses (brought forward)　未使用の繰越欠損金
unabsorbed capital allowance (brought forward)　未控除のキャピタル・アローワンス　[解] 過年度において所得から控除できなかったキャピタル・アローワンス（税務上の減価償却費）の繰越額
unacceptable　許容できない【形】
unadjusted　未修正の，未調整の
unadjusted quoted price　（調整なしの）公表価格
unadjusted trial balance　決算整理前残高試算表
unaffiliated　関係会社でない【形】
unallocated　未配賦の，未配分の
unallocated amount　未配分金額，配分しなかった金額
unallocated goodwill　配分されていないのれん
unallotted　未割当の
unamortised　未償却の（無形資産などについて）　[米]unamortized
unamortised balance　未償却残高（無形資産などの）　[米]unamortized balance
unanimous　合意して，満場一致の
unanimous consent　すべての当事者の一致した合意
unanticipated　予期していない【形】

unappropriated	未処分の，未充当の
unappropriated retained earnings	未処分利益
unaudited	未監査の
unaudited financial statements	未監査財務諸表
unauthorised use	不正使用　㊍ unauthorized use
unavailable	入手できない，利用できない【形】
unavoidable	避けられない【形】
unbiased	偏りのない【形】
unbilled receivables	未請求の債権
unbundling	アンバンドリング　[解] 関税に関するプランニング手法の1つで，関税評価額（customs value）について，その価格の構成要素（金利やサービス・チャージ）を分解し，関税の課税対象とならない非課税要素を取り除くことで，関税を低減する手法
uncertain	不確実な
uncertain tax position (UTP)	不確実な税務ポジション　[解] 端的には，税務当局と見解が相違する（つまり，税務上の処理の一部または全部を否認される）可能性のある項目。不確実な税務ポジションも考慮に入れて税金費用を見積もる必要がある
uncertainty	不確実性
uncertainty over income tax treatments	法人所得税の取扱いに関する不確実性
unclear	不明確な
uncollectibility	回収不能
uncollectible	回収不能な
uncollectibles	回収不能債権
uncommitted	コミットしていない【形】
unconditional	無条件の
unconditional requirements	無条件の義務
unconditional right	無条件の権利
unconsolidated	個別の，非連結の
unconsolidated structured entity	非連結の組成された企業［ストラクチャード・エンティティ］
unconsolidated subsidiary	非連結子会社
uncontrolled transaction	第三者間取引
uncorrected	未修正の
uncorrected misstatement	未修正の虚偽記載
uncover	摘発する（不正などを）
undated	日付のない，期限のない【形】
undated subordinated liabilities	期限のない劣後負債
undelivered goods	未着品
undepreciated	未償却の（有形固定資産について）
undepreciated balance	未償却残高（有形固定資産の）
undercapitalisation	過少資本　㊍ undercapitalization
under common control	共通支配下の
under construction	建設中の
under development	開発中の　[用] investment property under construction or development（建設中または開発中の投資不動産）
underestimate	①過小評価する，②過少に見積もる
underestimation	①過小評価，②過少見積り
underfunded	積立不足の
undergo	経験する
underhedged	アンダーヘッジの
underlying	基礎となる【形】
underlying asset	原資産　[解] IFRS16の文脈では，リースの対象となる資産
underlying assumption	基礎となる前提
underlying tax	間接納付税額　[解] 外国税額控除制度の関係では，配当のもととなった利益に課された税金を指し，一般に間接税額控除の対象となるもの
underlying tax credit	間接外国税額控除　[解] indirect foreign tax credit の項を参照
underpaid	十分に支払い（給与）を受けていない
underpayment	過少払い，過少納付
underpinning	土台
underprovision	過少引当
underreport	過少申告する
understand	理解する
understandability	理解可能性
understandable	理解可能な
understanding	理解
understate	過少計上する

understated revenue	過少計上された収益
understatement	過少計上
undertake	引き受ける（仕事などを）
undertaking	①企業，事業，②引受，約束
undervaluation	過小評価
undervalue	過小評価する
underwrite	引き受ける（株式や社債などの証券を）
underwriter	引受人・引受会社（証券などの）
underwriting	証券引受業務
undetected	発見されていない【形】
undisclosed	非開示の
undiscounted	割引前の
undiscounted future cash flows	割引前将来キャッシュ・フロー
undisposed	未処理の
undisposed loss	未処理損失
undistributed	未配分の
undistributed profit	未配分利益，留保利益 [解]IAS12の文脈では，子会社等が親会社に配当せずに保有している利益。将来加算一時差異を構成するが，親会社がその解消時期をコントロールでき，予見しうる将来（foreseeable future）にそれが解消しない可能性が高い場合（例えば，配当させない方針の場合）には，繰延税金負債を認識しない
undistributed profits tax	未配分利益［留保利益］に対する課税
undrawn	未引出しの（融資・融資枠など）
undrawn borrowing facility	未使用の借入枠
undrawn loan commitment	未使用の貸出コミットメント
unduly	過度に，不当に
unearned	①未稼得の，前受の，②不労の
unearned discount	未経過割引料
unearned finance income	未稼得金融収益
unearned income	①前受収益，②不労所得，給与所得等以外の所得 [解]②配当，利子，ロイヤルティ等
unearned interest	未経過利息
unearned revenue	前受収益
unearned service fee	前受サービス・フィー
unemployment	失業
uneven	不均等な
unevenly	不均等に
unexercised	未行使の
unexpired	期限内の
unfair	不公正な
unfair issuance	不公正発行（株式などの）
unfavourable	不利な，好ましくない [米]unfavorable
unfavourable variance	不利差異 [米]unfavorable variance
unforeseen	予期できない【形】
unfulfilled	果たされていない【形】
unfulfilled condition	①未履行の条件，②充足していない条件
unfunded	非積立（制度）の，資金拠出のない【形】
unguaranteed	保証されていない【形】
unguaranteed residual value	無保証残存価値
unidentifiable	確認不可能な
unidentified	未確認の
uniform	①同一の，統一的な，②制服
uniform accounting policies	統一的な会計方針，統一された会計方針 [解]企業集団は，類似の状況における同様の取引等の報告にあたって，統一的な会計方針を用いる必要がある
uniform format	統一フォーム
uniformity	統一性
unilateral	一方的な
unilateral advance pricing arrangement	一国内APA，ユニラテラルAPA [解]移転価格税制の関係では，事前確認（APA）のうち，1か国の税務当局からのみ確認を受けるものを指す
unilaterally	一方的に
unilateral relief	国内法による国際的二重課税の排除
unincorporated	法人化されていない【形】
union	組合，労働組合
union agreement	労働協約
unique	独自の
unissued share [stock]	未発行株式
unit	単位
unitary	①単一の，②単位の
unitary tax system	ユニタリー・タックス・システム，合算課税制度 [解]米国の州税

において，一法人だけでなくその関係会社も含めた企業グループ全体を一体とみなして課税する制度
unit cost　単位当たり原価
United Nations (UN)　国際連合（国連）
unit of account　会計単位　[解] IFRS13 の文脈では，認識目的で集計または分解する，資産・負債の単位
unit of production　生産単位
unit of production method　生産高比例法　[解] 減価償却方法の１つで，毎期の生産高に基づいて減価償却費を決定するもの
unit price　単価
unit trust　ユニット型投資信託
unknown　未知の
unlawful　違法な
unlawful act　違法行為
unlevered beta　アンレバード・ベータ　[解] 負債がないと仮定した場合のβ（ベータ）で，レバード・ベータ（levered beta）に対する用語
unlimited　無限の，無制限の
unlimited liability　無限責任
unlisted　非上場の，未上場の
unlisted entity　非上場企業
unlisted securities　非上場有価証券
unlisted share [stock]　非上場株式，未上場株
unloading　荷揚げ
unmatched　不一致の
unmatched item　不一致項目
UN Model Double Taxation Convention between Developed and Developing Countries　国連モデル租税条約
UN Model Tax Treaty　国連モデル租税条約
unobservable　観察不能な
unobservable input　観察不能なインプット
unpaid　未払の，未納の
unpaid invoice　未払いの請求書
unpaid taxes　未払税金
unqualified　①無条件の，②無資格の
unqualified opinion　無限定適正意見（監査報告書の）
unquoted　非上場の，価格が付されていない【形】
unquoted securities　時価のない有価証券
unrated　評価されていない，未評価の

unrated credit exposures　格付けのない信用エクスポージャー
unrealised　未実現の　[米] unrealized
unrealised gain　未実現利益，含み益　[米] unrealized gain
unrealised gains and losses　未実現損益　[米] unrealized gains and losses　[解] 実現損益（realised gains and losses）に対する用語
unrealised intercompany loss　未実現損失（グループ内の）　[米] unrealized intercompany loss
unrealised intercompany profit　未実現利益（グループ内の）　[米] unrealized intercompany profit
unrealised loss　未実現損失，含み損　[米] unrealized loss
unrealised profit　未実現利益　[米] unrealized profit
unrecognised　未認識の　[米] unrecognized
unrecognised actuarial gains and losses　未認識数理計算上の差異　[米] unrecognized actuarial gains and losses　[用] amortisation of unrecognised actuarial gains and losses（未認識数理計算上の差異の償却）
unrecognised deferred tax assets　未認識の繰延税金資産　[米] unrecognized deferred tax assets
unrecognised deferred tax liabilities　未認識の繰延税金負債　[米] unrecognized deferred tax liabilities
unrecognised firm commitment　未認識の確定コミットメント　[米] unrecognized firm commitment
unrecognised prior service cost　未認識過去勤務費用（債務）　[米] unrecognized prior service cost　[用] amortisation of unrecognised prior service cost（未認識過去勤務費用（債務）の償却）
unrecorded　記録されない（帳簿などに）【形】
unrecorded asset　簿外資産
unrecorded liability　簿外負債
unrelated company　非関連者
unrelated party test　非関連者基準　[解]

タックス・ヘイブン対策税制における経済活動基準の１つで，外国関係会社がその事業を主として関連者以外の者との間で行っていることを確認する基準（一定の例外あり）
unrelated person　非関連者　[解]移転価格税制の関係では，日本企業と特殊の関係にない者を指す
unreserved　無限定の
unrestricted fund　非拘束性資金
unsecured bank loan　無担保借入金
unsecured bond　無担保債券
unsecured debt　無担保債務，無担保負債
unsecured loan　無担保融資
untaxed　課税対象とならない【形】
unused　使用していない【形】
unused asset　遊休資産，未使用資産
unused credit limit　繰越控除余裕額
unused foreign tax (credit)　繰越控除限度超過額（外国税額控除の）
unused provision　未使用の引当金
unused tax credits　繰越税額控除（未使用の）
unused tax losses　繰越欠損金（未使用の）
unusual item　通常でない項目
unutilised　活用されていない【形】　[米]unutilized
unutilised tax losses　繰越欠損金　[米]unutilized tax losses
unwanted assets　不要資産
unweighted average　単純平均
unwind(ing) of discount　割引額の振戻し［巻戻し］（時の経過に伴う）　[用]expense due to unwinding of discount on provisions（引当金に係る割引の振戻しによる費用），unwind of discount on site restoration provision（土地原状回復引当金の時間の経過に伴う増加額）
upcoming period　翌期，来期
update　更新する
updated　最新の
update testing　アップデート・テスト
up-front　前払いの，前金の
up-front fee　アップフロント・フィー　[解]主としてシンジケート・ローンの貸手金融団に支払われる手数料で，融資総額の一定比率で一括して支払われる
up-front payment　前払い
upgrade　アップグレードする，等級を上げる
upgrade service　改修サービス
upload　アップロードする
upper limit　上限
upside　上側
upside potential　アップサイド（・ポテンシャル），値上がり期待
upstream dividend　（子会社から）親会社への配当
upstream loan　アップストリーム・ローン　[解]親会社から子会社への貸付け
upstream merger　アップストリーム・マージャー　[解]合併の形態のうち，親会社が子会社を吸収合併するもの
upstream sales　アップストリーム売上　[解]子会社から親会社方向への売上
upstream transaction　アップストリーム取引　[解]連結グループ内の取引のうち，子会社から親会社へ資産等を売却する方向の取引
up to　～まで
upward　①上に，②上方の
upward adjustment　上方修正，増額修正
urgent　緊急の
usage　使用
usage-based royalty　使用（量・回数）連動のロイヤルティ
usage variance　数量［消費量］差異
usance　ユーザンス　[解]貿易取引の決済に関連して，一定期間代金の支払猶予を行う形で，信用の供与を行うこと
use　①使用する，②使用
useful life　耐用年数　[解]企業がその資産を使用すると予測される期間など
usefulness　有用性
use of judgements and estimates　判断及び見積りの使用　[米]use of judgments and estimates
user　利用者
user of financial statements　財務諸表の利用者
use tax　使用税
use value　使用価値

US GAAP 米国基準
utilisation 利用，活用 ㊤utilization
utilisation of provisions 引当金の目的使用
　　　㊤utilization of provisions
utilisation of tax losses 繰越欠損金の使用
　　　㊤utilization of tax losses
utilise ①利用する，活用する，②使用する
　　（繰越欠損金を）　㊤utilize
utilities cost [expense] 水道光熱費
utility 有用性
utility model right 実用新案権
UTP ▶uncertain tax position

V

vacancy 空き
vacant 空の
vacation 休暇
vague 曖昧な
valid 妥当な
validate ①有効にする（法的に），②検証する
validity 妥当性
valid period 有効期間
valuable 価値のある
valuation （企業）評価，バリュエーション
valuation account 評価勘定
valuation adjustment 評価調整
valuation allowance 評価性引当額　㊥繰延税金資産のうち回収不能と判断された部分
valuation and translation adjustments 評価・換算差額等
valuation approach 評価アプローチ
valuation basis 評価基準
valuation date 評価日
valuation-date exchange rate 評価日（の為替）レート
valuation difference on available-for-sale securities その他有価証券評価差額金
valuation method 評価方法
valuation method of securities 有価証券の評価方法
valuation model 評価モデル
valuation multiple 評価倍率（企業評価に用いるマルチプル）
valuation practice 評価実務
valuation premise 評価前提
valuation principles 評価原則
valuation procedure 評価手続
valuation report バリュエーション・レポート，評価書
valuation technique 評価技法，評価手法　㊥IFRS13の文脈では，公正価値の評価

にあたって用いる技法を指し，マーケット・アプローチ，インカム・アプローチ，及びコスト・アプローチがある
value 価値
value added 付加価値
value added activity 付加価値活動
value added tax (VAT) 付加価値税
value at risk (VaR) バリュー・アット・リスク [解] ポートフォリオの市場リスクを統計的手法を用いて測定した数値であり，そのポートフォリオを将来のある一定期間保有すると仮定した場合に，ある一定の確率の範囲内で，マーケットの変動によりどの程度損失を被り得るかを計測したもの
value driver バリュー・ドライバー [解] 企業価値に影響を与える項目（勘定科目など）
value in use 使用価値 [解] 資産等から生じると見込まれる将来キャッシュ・フローの現在価値
value of business acquired 取得した事業の価値
valuer 評価者
VaR ▶value at risk
variability 変動性
variability in cash flows キャッシュ・フローの変動性
variability of returns リターンの変動性
variable ①変動する【形】, ②変数
variable consideration 変動対価
variable cost 変動費
variable costing 直接原価計算
variable interest rate 変動金利
variable lease payment 変動リース料 [解] リース料のうち，リース開始後に発生する事実や状況の変化により変動する部分
variable manufacturing cost 変動製造費用
variable overhead 変動（製造）間接費
variable overhead variance 変動間接費差異
variable-rate instrument 変動利付金融商品
variable-rate loan 変動金利ローン
variable return 変動リターン [用] variable returns from the investor's involvement with the investee（投資企業による被投資企業への関与から生じる変動リターン）

variance ①差異，②分散（統計学の）
variance analysis 差異分析
variation 変動，変化
variety 種類，多様性
various 種々の
vary ①変化する，②様々である
VAT ▶value added tax
VAT payable 未払付加価値税
VAT receivable 未収付加価値税
VC ▶venture capital
VDD ▶vendor due diligence
VDR ▶virtual data room
vehicle ①車両，運搬具，②ビークル
vehicle tonnage tax 車両重量税
vendor ①売手，売主，②仕入先
vendor due diligence (VDD) ベンダー・デューデリジェンス [解] 売手が実施するデュー・デリジェンス
vendor loan ベンダー・ローン [解] 取引の売手（vendor）が買手に対して行う融資
venture ベンチャー
venture capital (VC) ベンチャーキャピタル
venture capital organisation ベンチャー・キャピタル企業 [米] venture capital organization
venturer 投資企業
verifiability 検証可能性
verifiable 検証可能な
verification 認証，検証，正確性の確認
verify 検証する，正確性を確認する
version バージョン，版
versus 対
vertical 垂直の
vertical integration 垂直統合 [解] バリューチェーンに沿う形で，仕入先あるいは販売先とのM&A等により，事業領域の拡張を行うこと
vertically 垂直に
vertically integrated enterprises 垂直的に統合した企業
vertical-type corporate division 分社型分割
vessel 船舶
vest ①権利を与える，②権利が確定する
vested employee benefit 確定従業員給付
vesting 受給権（の付与）
vesting condition 権利確定条件 [解] IFRS2

の文脈では，株式に基づく報酬契約において，資本性金融商品や現金等を受け取る権利を得るために充足すべき条件。権利確定条件には，①一定期間の勤務を条件とする勤務条件や②業績目標の達成を条件とする業績条件がある
vesting date　権利確定日
vesting period　権利確定期間，権利確定までの期間　[解]IFRS2の文脈では，株式に基づく報酬契約に係る権利確定条件が（その間に）充足されるべき期間
veto　①拒否権，②拒否する
veto right　拒否権
viability　実行可能性
viable　実行可能な
vice versa　逆もまた同様
Vienna Conventions　ウィーン条約
view　観点，意見
viewpoint　観点，見地
violate　違反する
violation　違反（法律などの）
virtual data room (VDR)　ヴァーチャル・データ・ルーム（デュー・デリジェンスなどの）
virtually　実質的には
virtually certain　ほぼ確実な，実質的に確実な
virtual PE　仮想恒久的施設
vis a vis　相対して
visit　①訪問する，②訪問
void　無効の
voidable　無効にできる，取り消せる
void period　空室期間（投資不動産などの）
volatile　不安定な，変動の大きい
volatility　ボラティリティ（変動率）
volume　量，数量
volume variance　数量差異
voluntarily　自発的に
voluntary　自発的な，任意の
voluntary change　自発的変更，任意の変更
voluntary change in accounting policy　自発的な会計方針の変更，会計方針の任意の変更　[解]会計方針の変更のうち，新しいIFRSの基準書等で要求されるもの以外の変更
voluntary discontinuation　任意の中止　[用]
voluntary discontinuation of hedge accounting（ヘッジ会計の任意の中止）
voluntary dissolution　任意解散
voluntary liquidation　任意清算
voluntary reserve　任意積立金
vote　①投票する，②投票
voting power [right]　議決権
voting right basis　議決権ベース
voting stock　議決権付株式
vouch　証憑突合する
voucher　証憑書類

W

w/　with
WACC　▶weighted average cost of capital
wage　賃金
wages and salaries　賃金及び給料
wage tax　賃金税（源泉徴収）
waive　放棄する
waiver　放棄（権利などの）
waiver of liability　免責
walkthrough　ウォークスルー　[解] 内部統制の整備状況をテストするための手法の1つであり，「取引が発生してから，会社の業務システムや会計システムを通じて，財務諸表に反映されるまでの一連の流れ」を帳票上で追跡することにより，文書化内容を実証的に検証すること
warehouse　倉庫
warehouse cost [expense]　倉庫費用, 保管費用
warehousing cost [expense]　倉庫費用, 保管費用
warrant　新株予約権, ワラント
warrant bond　新株予約権付社債
warranty　保証
warranty & indemnity [w&i] insurance　表明・保証保険　[解] 表明・保証違反より生じる（買手の）損失または（売手の）補償をカバーするための保険
warranty against defects　瑕疵担保責任
warranty expense　製品保証費用
warranty provision　製品保証引当金
wastage　①損耗, ②廃棄物
waste　①無駄にする, ②無駄, ③廃棄物
waterfall　ウォーターフォール　[解] プロジェクト・ファイナンスなどに関して，対象プロジェクトが生み出したキャッシュ・フローの（投資家等への）支払いの優先順位を付けたもの
weakness　欠陥, 不備（内部統制などの）
wear and tear　使用による価値低下

weather derivative　天候デリバティブ
website　ウェブサイト
website cost　ウェブサイト費用　[解] IFRSにおいては，ウェブを介したマーケティングや情報システム開発に関連する支出は，無形資産になるものと費用になるものがある
website development cost　ウェブサイト開発費用
weight　ウェイト（加重平均の）
weighted average　加重平均
weighted average borrowing rate　加重平均借入利率
weighted average cost　加重平均原価
weighted average cost formula [method]　加重平均法　[解] 原価算定方式の1つで，期首の原価と期中に購入・製造したものの原価との加重平均により，個々の原価を算定する方式
weighted average cost of capital (WACC)　加重平均資本コスト　[解] IAS36の文脈では，使用価値を算定する際の割引率（discount rate）は，対象となる資産に固有の割引率を用いるのが原則だが，それがない場合には企業の加重平均資本コスト（WACC）が用いられることがある
weighted average number　加重平均数
weighted average number of ordinary shares outstanding (during the period)　（期中の）発行済普通株式の加重平均株式数
weighting　ウェイト（加重平均の）
welfare expense　福利厚生費
whistle-blower　内部告発者
whistle-blowing　内部告発
white paper　白書
wholesale　卸売
wholesaler　卸売業者
wholly-owned subsidiary　100％子会社, 完全子会社
WHT　▶withholding tax
wilful　故意の　[米] willful
wilful misconduct　故意の不法行為　[米] willful misconduct
windfall profit　偶発利益
windfall profit tax　超過利潤税　[解] excess profit taxの項を参照

winding up	清算
window dressing	粉飾
wind up	終わりにする，解散する（会社などを）
wind-up of a plan	制度の解散（退職給付制度などの）
WIP	▶work in process [progress]
wire transfer	振込み，電信送金
withdraw	引き出す
withdrawal	払戻し，引出し（預金などの）
withdrawal from a plan	制度からの脱退（退職給付制度などの）
withhold	①源泉徴収する，②保留する，差し控える
withholding	源泉徴収（すること）
withholding agent	源泉徴収義務者
withholding exemption	源泉徴収の免除
withholding income tax	源泉所得税
withholding income tax credit	所得税額控除
withholding obligation	源泉徴収義務
withholding requirement	源泉徴収義務
withholding tax (WHT)	源泉税
withholding tax credit	源泉税の税額控除
withholding tax exemption certificate	源泉徴収免除証明書
withholding tax obligation	源泉徴収義務
withholding tax on dividends	配当源泉税
withholding tax on interest	利子源泉税
withholding tax on royalties	使用料源泉税
withholding tax payable	未払源泉税
withholding tax slip	源泉徴収票
withholding tax statement	源泉徴収票
without recourse	ノンリコースの，遡及権のない
with recourse	リコース付きの，遡及権のある
w/o	without
W/O	▶work order
wording	文言，表現
work	仕事，労働，作業
workable	実行可能な
workforce	労働力
working capital	運転資本
working capital adjustment	運転資本調整（買収対価などについての）
working capital management	運転資本管理
working condition	労働条件
working papers	調書，監査調書
work in process [progress] (WIP)	仕掛品
workload	仕事量
work of art	美術品
work order (W/O)	作業指示書
work paper (W/P)	調書
workplace misconduct	職場での不適切な行為
worksheet	①精算表，②ワークシート
World Trade Organization (WTO)	世界貿易機関
worldwide	世界的な
worldwide income	全世界所得 [解]国内源泉所得と国外源泉所得の合計
worldwide system	全世界所得課税方式 [解]国外所得免税方式（territorial system）に対して，全世界所得に課税する方式
worst case scenario	（予想できる）最悪のシナリオ
W/P	▶work paper
wrap-up	要約，総括
write back	評価減などを戻入する
write-back	評価減の戻入
write down	①評価減する（簿価の一部），②評価減（簿価の一部）
write-down	評価減（簿価の一部）
write-down and reversal	評価減及びその戻入
write off	①評価減する（簿価全額），②評価減（簿価全額）
write-off	評価減（簿価全額），直接償却
write-up	評価増
written call option	売建コール・オプション
written call option on shares	株式に係る売建コール・オプション
written-down value	①（減価償却資産の）税務簿価，②評価減後簿価
written option	売建オプション
written put option	売建プット・オプション
written put option on shares	株式に係る売建プット・オプション
WTO	▶World Trade Organization
WTO customs value agreement	WTO関税

評価協定　[解]関税評価制度の国際的な統一を目的とする協定
XBRL　▶eXtensible Business Reporting Language

Y

YE　▶year-end
year-end (YE)　年度末，（決算）期末
year-end adjustment　①年度末修正，決算整理，②年末調整
year-end closing　年度（末）決算，年次決算
yearly　年度の
year of assessment　賦課年度（税金の）　[解]税金が賦課される対象の年度
years of service　勤続年数，勤務年数
year-to-date　年初からの累計
year-to-date basis　年初からの累計ベース　[解]期中財務報告目的の測定は，年初からの累計を基準として行われる　[用]on a year-to-date basis（年初からの累計で）
year-to-date calculation　年初からの累計計算
year-to-date period　年初からの累計期間
yield　①利回り，②歩留
yield curve　イールド・カーブ
yield rate　歩留率
yield to maturity　満期利回り
YK　▶Yugen Kaisha
Yugen Kaisha (YK)　有限会社

Z

ZBB ▶zero based budget
zero based budget (ZBB) ゼロベース予算
　[解]予算立案時に，過去の実績を考慮に入れず，ゼロからの積み上げで予算を策定すること
zero coupon bond ゼロ・クーポン債

和英編

Japanese English

- 米 米国式のスペリング
- 使い方注意! 用語を使う際の留意点
- 頻 頻出フレーズ
- 関 関連フレーズ

あ

アーニングス・ストリッピング・ルール　earnings stripping rules
IFRS 移行日　date of transition to IFRS
IFRS 開始財政状態計算書　opening IFRS statement of financial position
IFRS の遡及適用　retrospective application of IFRS
相対取引　negotiated transaction
相対取引による売却（特に買収案件における）　negotiated sale
IT 業務処理統制　IT application control
IT 全般統制　IT general control
相手方　counterparty
相見積り　competitive quotes
アウト・オブ・ザ・マネー　out of the money
アウトソーシング　outsourcing
アウトバウンド取引　outbound transaction
青色申告　blue-form tax return filing status
青色申告書　blue-form tax return
赤字　deficit
赤字残高　deficit balance
空き　vacancy
アキュムレーション（債券などの）　accumulation
アクチュアリー　actuary
悪評　adverse [bad] publicity
悪用　abuse
アジェンダ　agenda
預り金　deposit (received)
預り源泉所得税　income tax withheld
預り保険料　insurance premium withheld
預り保証金　(guarantee) deposit received
預り留保金　retainage withheld
アスク価格　ask price
アセット・アプローチ（評価手法としての）　asset [asset-based] approach
アセット・シーリング　asset ceiling
アセット・ファイナンス　asset finance
アセット・マネジャー　asset manager
頭金　down payment
悪化　deterioration
斡旋手数料（M&Aに関する）　finder's fee
アット・ザ・マネー　at the money
アップサイド（・ポテンシャル）　upside potential
アップストリーム取引　upstream transaction
アップストリーム・ローン　upstream loan
アップデート・テスト　update testing
アップフロント・フィー　up-front fee
後入先出法　last-in, first-out (LIFO)
アドバイザー　adviser [advisor]
アドバイザリー・サービス　advisory services
アドバイザリー・フィー　advisory fee
後払いの買収対価　deferred purchase price
アドプション　adoption
アナリスト　analyst
アニュアル・レポート　annual report
アブセンス・フィー　absence fee
アプローチ　approach
アモチゼーション（債券などの）　amortisation 米amortization
アレンジメント・フィー　(loan) arrangement fee
安定性　stability
按分計算　proration
アンレバード・ベータ　unlevered beta

い

イータックス　e-Tax
委員会設置会社　company with committees
異議　challenge, dissent 頻tax authorities' challenge（税務当局からの異議（指摘））
関tax authorities challenge transfer pricing policies（税務当局が移転価格設定方針に異議を唱える）
域外適用　extraterritorial application
行き詰まり（交渉などの）　deadlock
異議申立て（税務などに関する）　(tax) appeal
頻to file [make] an appeal（異議を申し立てる）

イグジット　exit
イグジット・プラン　exit plan
意見　opinion
移行　transition
移行期間における役務提供契約　transitional services agreement (TSA)
移行経済圏　transition economies
移行時の調整　transition adjustment
移行時負債　transitional liability
移行措置　transition method
意向表明　offer
維持　retention
維持管理費　running cost, maintenance cost
維持管理費（リースなどの）　executory cost
意思決定　decision making
意思決定時点　decision point
意思決定者　decision maker
維持修繕費　repairs and maintenance expense
意匠権　design right
異常項目　exceptional [extraordinary] item
委託　commission
委託（販売の）　consignment
委託（販売）契約　consignment agreement [arrangement]
委託者（委託販売の）　consigner
委託者（信託の）　settlor
委託証拠金　margin account
委託製造業者　toll manufacturer
委託手数料　commission
委託販売　consignment sales
委託品　consigned goods
位置　position
1計算書方式の表示（包括利益計算書などの）　single-statement presentation
一時差異　temporary difference　頻 temporary differences reverse（一時差異が解消する）
一時差異の解消　reversal of temporary differences
一時差異の発生　origination of temporary differences
一時所得　occasional income
一時的な共同支配　temporary joint control
一時的な支配　temporary control
一時的な重要な影響力　temporary significant influence

1日の終わり（までに）　end of day (EOD)
1年基準　one-year rule
一部　fraction
一部所有子会社　partially-owned [partly-owned] subsidiary
一覧表　list
一括課税　lump-sum taxation
一括控除　lump-sum deductions
一括購入　lump-sum purchase
一括取得（段階取得に対して）　single-step acquisition
一括払い　lump-sum payment, bullet payment
一括評価金銭債権に対する貸倒引当金　general provision for bad debt
一括返済　bullet payment
一貫性　consistency　関 consistent across group companies（グループ会社間で一貫して）
一国内APA　unilateral advance pricing arrangement
逸脱（基準や規定されている内部統制からの）　deviation, departure　頻 deviation from prescribed internal control（所定の内部統制からの逸脱）, departure from GAAP（GAAPからの逸脱）
一致　accordance
一致した（事業）年度末　coterminous year-ends
一定期間にわたり識別された資産の使用を支配する権利　right to control the use of an identified asset for a period of time
一般管理費　general and administrative expense (G&A)
一般寄付金　ordinary donation
一般原則　general principles
一般特恵関税制度　generalised system of preferences (GSP)　米 generalized system of preferences (GSP)
一般に公正妥当と認められる会計基準　Generally Accepted Accounting Principles (GAAP)　頻 in accordance with GAAP（GAAPに従って）, departure from GAAP（GAAPからの逸脱）
一般に公正妥当と認められる監査の基準　Generally Accepted Auditing Standards

(GAAS)
一般目的財務諸表　general purpose financial statements
移転（資産などの）　transfer
移転（場所の）　relocation
移転価格（価格自体）　transfer price
移転価格（価格設定）　transfer pricing (TP)
移転価格課税　transfer pricing taxation [adjustment]
移転価格事務運営要領　Commissioner's Directive on the Operation of Transfer Pricing
移転価格スタディ　transfer pricing study
移転価格税制　transfer pricing taxation 〔頻〕 transfer pricing taxation applies（移転価格税制が適用される）
移転価格調整　transfer pricing adjustment
移転価格ドキュメンテーション　transfer pricing documentation
移転価格文書　transfer pricing document
移転価格文書(化)　transfer pricing documentation 〔頻〕 documentation to formalise transfer pricing（移転価格を正式化する文書（化））
移転可能性　transferability
移転された対価　consideration transferred
移転費用　relocation cost [expense]
意図　intent, intention
移動平均　moving average
移動平均法　moving average method
意図した使用　intended use
イニシアティブ　initiative
イニシャル・ロイヤリティ　initial royalty
委任　delegation
委任契約書　letter of engagement
委任状　power of attorney (PoA)
委任状（議決権行使の）　proxy
イノベーション　innovation
イノベーション・ボックス　innovation box
違反（契約や法令に対する）　breach, violation 〔頻〕 breach of contract（契約違反）, violation of laws and regulations（法令違反）
違法行為　illegal act [activity]
違法な謝礼　illegal gratuity
意味　meaning
意味合い　implication

違約金　penalty charge
違約金（特に買収契約に関する）　break-up [bust-up] fee
違約条項　penalty clause
依頼資料リスト（デュー・デリジェンスなどの）　document request list
入口価格　entry price
因果関係　cause and effect (relationship), causal connection
インカム・アプローチ（評価手法としての）　income [income-based] approach
印鑑　seal
インコタームズ　Incoterms
インサイダー情報　insider information
インサイダー取引　insider trading
印刷費用　printing cost [expense]
イン・ザ・マネー　in the money (ITM)
印紙税　stamp duty [tax]
インセンティブ型報酬　incentive compensation
インセンティブ支払い　incentive payment
インターネットのドメイン(名)　internet domain name
インターバンク市場　interbank market
インタレスト・カバレッジ・レシオ　interest coverage ratio
インテグリティ・プログラム　integrity programme 米 integrity program
インバウンド取引　inbound transaction
インピュテーション・クレジット　imputation credit
インフォメーション・メモランダム　information memorandum (IM)
インプット　input
インプライド・ボラティリティ　implied volatility
インフラストラクチャー　infrastructure
インフレーション　inflation
インフレーション率　inflation rate
隠蔽　concealment
インベスター・リレーションズ　investor relations (IR)
インベストメント・センター　investment centre 米 investment center
インボイシング・カンパニー　invoicing company

う

ヴァーチャル・データ・ルーム（デュー・デリジェンスなどの）　virtual data room (VDR)
ウェイト（加重平均の）　weight(ing)
上側　upside
ウェブサイト開発費用　website development cost
ウェブサイト費用　website cost
ウォークスルー　walkthrough
ウォーターフォール　waterfall
受入れ（棚卸資産などの）　acceptance
受入報告書（棚卸資産などの）　acceptance report
請負　contract for work
請負者　contractor
受取確認　acknowledgement
受取対価　consideration received
受取賃貸料　rent(al) revenue
受取手形　(trade) notes receivable
受取手数料　commission revenue [income]
受取人　recipient
受取人（送金や手形などの）　payee
受取配当金　dividend income [received]
受取家賃　rent(al) revenue
受取利息　interest income
受取ロイヤルティ　royalty income [revenue]
受渡し　delivery
受渡条件　delivery conditions
受渡日（証券などの）　delivery date
動き　movement
疑い　doubt
打歩発行（債券の）　original issue premium (OIP)
内訳　breakdown, disaggregation
内訳情報　breakdown information
裏書き　endorsement
裏書手形　notes receivable endorsed
裏書人　endorser
裏付け　supporting evidence

売上　sales, turnover　頻 to recognise sales（売上を認識する）　関 to sell products to related parties（関連当事者に製品を販売する）
売上原価　cost of goods sold (COGS), cost of sales (COS)
売上構成　sales mix
売上構成差異　sales mix variance
売上債権　「売掛債権」の項を参照
売上収入　sales proceeds
売上総損失　gross loss
売上総利益　gross margin [profit]
売上総利益率　gross margin (percentage), gross profit percentage
売上高　sales, turnover
売上高（損益計算書の冒頭）　top line
売上高営業利益率　operating margin
売上高利益率　return on sales
売上伝票　sales slip
売上値引　sales allowance
売上のカットオフ（締切）　sales cut-off
売上返品　sales return
売上元帳　sales ledger
売上予算　sales budget
売上予測　sales forecast
売上連動のロイヤルティ　sales-based royalty
売上割引　sales discount
売上割戻し　sales rebate
売上割戻引当金　provision for sales rebates
売掛金　(trade) accounts receivable　頻 to record accounts receivable（売掛金を計上する）, to collect accounts receivable（売掛金を回収する）
売掛金回転期間　「売掛債権回転期間」の項を参照
売掛金回転率　accounts receivable turnover (A/R turnover)
売掛金明細　accounts receivable details
売掛金元帳　accounts receivable (subsidiary) ledger
売掛債権　(trade) accounts receivable, trade receivables
売掛債権及びその他の債権　trade and other receivables
売掛債権回転期間　accounts receivable turnover period, days sales outstanding (DSO),

average collection period
売掛債権回転率　accounts receivable turnover (A/R turnover)
売建オプション　written option
売建コール・オプション　written call option
売建プット・オプション　written put option
売手　seller, vendor
売手側（買収案件などの）　sell side
売手にとっての（企業）価値　seller's value
売主　seller, vendor
売戻契約　reverse repurchase agreement
売呼値　ask price
上書き　overlay
運営サービス　operation service
運送　transport(ation), shipping
運送業者　carrier, shipper
運送人渡し条件（価格）　free carrier (FCA)
運送費用　transport cost [expense]
運賃　freight
運賃込み条件（価格）　cost and freight (C&F/CFR)
運賃・保険料込み条件（価格）　cost, insurance, and freight (CIF)
運転資本　working capital
運転資本管理　working capital management
運転資本調整（買収対価などについての）　working capital adjustment
運搬　haulage
運搬具　vehicle
運用（内部統制の）　operation
運用収益　return
運用テスト（内部統制の）　test of operating effectiveness
運用に関する不備（内部統制の）　deficiency in operation

え

エア・ウェイビル　air waybill (AWB)
永久差異　permanent difference
影響　impact, effect　使い方注意！impact of A なら、「A が与える影響」で、impact on B なら、「B に与える影響」を意味し、impact of A on B のような使い方もする。effect も同様で、effect of A on B で、「A が B に与える影響」。具体例としては、effects of exchange rate changes on the balance of cash and cash equivalents（現金及び現金同等物に係る為替変動による影響額）[頻] to make an impact on（〜に影響を与える）, to quantify the impact of（〜の影響を数値化する）, there is no net impact on（純額でみれば、〜への影響はない）
営業外収益　non-operating income
営業外費用　non-operating expense
営業活動　operating activity
営業活動からの純損失　loss from operating activities
営業活動からの純利益　profit from operating activities
営業活動によるキャッシュ・フロー　cash flows from operating activities, operating cash flows
営業原価　cost of revenue
営業サイクル　operating cycle
営業債権　trade accounts receivable, trade receivables, operating receivables
営業債権及びその他の債権　trade and other receivables
営業債権に係る減損損失　impairment loss on trade receivables
営業債務　trade accounts payable, trade payables, operating payables
営業債務及びその他の債務　trade and other payables
営業資産　operating asset
営業者　operator
営業収益　operating revenue
営業循環　operating cycle
営業循環基準　operating cycle rule
営業純利益　net operating income (NOI)
営業成績　operating result
営業損益　operating profit and loss
営業損失　operating loss, loss from operations
[頻] recurring operating losses（継続的な営業損失）
営業担当者　sales representative
営業地域　geographic(al) area of operations

えいぎよう

営業日　business day
営業費用　operating expense
営業費用売上総利益率　berry ratio
営業部門　sales department
営業利益　operating profit [income], income from operations
営業利益率　operating margin (ratio)
影響力　influence　頻 to determine the degree of influence（影響力の度合いを決定する）
影響力基準　influence criteria
営業レバレッジ　operating leverage
永住者　permanent resident
営利企業　for-profit corporation
営利団体　for-profit organisation　米 for-profit organization
エージェント　agent
エージェント・フィー　agent fee
益金不算入収益　non-taxable income, (tax-)exempt income, excluded income
役務　service　頻 to render services（役務を提供する）
役務収益　service revenue
役務提供　rendering [provision] of services
役務提供契約　service agreement
役務提供者　service provider
役務提供対価　income from performance of services
役務提供による所得　income from performance of services
役務費用　service cost
エクイティ・ファイナンス　equity financing
エクイティ・リスク・プレミアム　equity risk premium
エクスポージャー　exposure　頻 exposure to risk（リスクへのエクスポージャー）
エグゼクティブ・サマリー　executive summary
エスカレーション条項　escalation clause
エスクロー　escrow
エスクロー口座　escrow account
エルタックス　eLTAX
エレクトロニック・バンキング　electronic banking
エンジニアリング　engineering
援助　aid

延滞金　arrears
延滞金（地方税などの）　late payment charge [penalty]
延滞債権　overdue receivables, past due receivables
延滞税　late payment charge [penalty], delinquency tax
延滞通知（納税の）　notice of deficiency
延長　extension
延長選択権［オプション］（リース期間などの）　extension option
延納　delayed payment
エンプロイー・バイアウト（従業員による企業買収）　employee buy-out (EBO)

お

応用研究　applied research
横領　embezzlement, defalcation
OECD 移転価格ガイドライン　OECD Transfer Pricing Guidelines for Multinational Enterprises and Tax Administrations
OECD モデル租税条約　OECD Model Tax Convention on Income and on Capital
オークション　auction
オークション手続（企業・事業売却などの）　auction process
オークションによる売却（企業や事業などの）　auction sale
大阪国税局　Osaka Regional Tax(ation) Bureau
OCI オプション　other comprehensive income option (OCI option)
大幅な割引（証券発行の際などの）　deep discount
押込販売　channel stuffing, trade loading
汚職　corruption (case)
汚染　contamination, pollution
オファー　offer
オフィス用家具　office furniture
オフィス機器　office equipment
オフショア・カンパニー　offshore company

オプション　option
オプション価格算定モデル　option pricing model
オプション契約の有効期間　contractual life of options
オプション行使価格　option exercise price
オプション保有者　option holder
オプション・リース料　optional lease payment
オプション料　option premium
オプション，ワラント及びその同等物　options, warrants and their equivalents
オペレーショナル・リスク　operational risk
オペレーティング・リース　operating lease
覚書　memorandum (of understanding)
親会社　parent (company)
親会社単体の１株当たり利益　parent's separate earnings per share
親会社の所有者　owners of the parent
親会社の所有者に帰属する当期包括利益　total comprehensive income attributable to (the) owners of the parent
親会社の所有者に帰属する当期利益　profit attributable to (the) owners of the parent
親会社の所有者に帰属する持分　equity of (the) owners of the parent, equity attributable to (the) owners of the parent
卸売　wholesale
卸売業者　wholesaler
オンコール・サービス　on call services
オンショア・カンパニー　onshore company
オンブズマン　ombudsman

か

カーブアウト　carve-out
会員権　membership
海外活動　foreign activity
海外現地法人　foreign subsidiary
海外子会社　foreign [overseas] subsidiary
海外駐在員　expatriate (staff)
海外投資　overseas investment
外貨換算　foreign currency translation
買掛金　(trade) accounts payable　頻 to record accounts payable（買掛金を計上する），to settle accounts payable（買掛金を支払う）
買掛金回転期間　「仕入債務回転期間」の項を参照
買掛金回転率　accounts payable turnover (A/P turnover)
買掛金明細　accounts payable details
買掛金元帳　accounts payable (subsidiary) ledger
外貨建貸付金　foreign currency loan
外貨建借入金　foreign currency borrowings [loan]
外貨建金銭債権債務　foreign currency receivables and payables
外貨建債権　foreign currency receivables
外貨建債権債務　foreign currency receivables and payables
外貨建債務　foreign currency payables
外貨建取引　foreign currency transaction
外貨デリバティブ　foreign currency derivative
外貨ベーシス・スプレッド　foreign currency basis spread
外貨預金　cash at bank in foreign currencies
会議　meeting, conference　頻 to hold a meeting（会議を開催する）
懐疑心　scepticism　米 skepticism
会議費　meeting cost [expense]
回帰分析　regression analysis

開業費　pre-opening [pre-operating] cost, start-up cost
下位グループ　sub-group
会計　accounting
会計慣行　accounting practice
会計期間　accounting [fiscal] period
会計期間の公準　periodicity assumption
会計基準　accounting standards
会計基準の設定主体　standard setting body
会計基準の変更（採用する会計基準の変更）conversion　[頻] conversion from Japan GAAP to IFRS（日本基準からIFRSへの変更）
会計記録　accounting records
会計原則　accounting principles
会計士　accountant
会計システム　accounting system
会計事務所　accounting firm
会計上の　for accounting purposes　[使い方注意!] depreciation for accounting purposes（会計上の減価償却費）のように，会計目的であることを明記したい場合に使う
会計上の減価償却費　accounting depreciation
会計上の選択　accounting election
会計上の取扱い　accounting treatment
会計上の判断　accounting judgement　[米] accounting judgment
会計上の判断及び見積り　accounting judgements and estimates　[米] accounting judgments and estimates
会計上のプロセス　accounting process
会計上の変更　accounting change
会計上のミスマッチ　accounting mismatch
会計上の見積り　accounting estimate
会計上の見積りの変更　change in accounting estimate
会計上の利益　accounting profit
会計処理　accounting treatment　[関] to account for A as B（AをBとして会計処理する）, to account for □ in accordance with IFRS（□をIFRSに従って会計処理する）
会計処理の基礎　basis of accounting
会計処理方法　accounting method

会計ソフトウェア　accounting software
会計単位　accounting unit, unit of account
会計帳簿　accounting book
会計データ　accounting data
会計手続　accounting procedures
会計と税務の差異　book-tax difference
会計の観点　accounting perspective [viewpoint]　[頻] from an accounting perspective [viewpoint]（会計の観点からは）
外形標準課税（事業税）　pro-forma enterprise [business] tax, size-based enterprise [business] tax, factor-based enterprise [business] tax
会計部門　accounting department [division]
会計方針　accounting policy　[頻] to determine accounting policies（会計方針を決定する）
会計方針の選択（肢）　choice of accounting policy
会計方針の任意の変更　voluntary change in accounting policy
会計方針の変更　change in accounting policy　[関] to change accounting policies（会計方針を変更する）
会計簿価　accounting book value, carrying amount　[頻] difference between accounting and tax book value（会計簿価と税務簿価の差）
会計モデル　accounting model
解決　resolution
解決策　solution
解雇　dismissal, severance, termination of employment　[関] to dismiss an employee（従業員を解雇する）
解雇給付　termination benefit
解雇給付費用　termination benefits expense
外国　foreign country
外国親会社　foreign parent company
外国貨物　foreign cargo
外国為替　foreign exchange (forex/FX)
外国為替市場　foreign exchange market
外国為替レート　foreign exchange rate
外国関係会社　foreign related company
外国源泉税　foreign withholding tax
外国公務員　foreign public official
外国子会社　foreign subsidiary

外国子会社配当	dividend received from foreign subsidiary
外国子会社配当益金不算入制度（日本）	foreign dividend exclusion
外国税額控除（制度）	foreign tax credit (FTC) 頻 to claim foreign tax credits（外国税額控除をとる）
外国地方税	foreign local tax
外国通貨	foreign currency
外国配当	foreign dividend
外国配当源泉税	foreign withholding tax on dividends
外国法人	foreign company [corporation]
外国法人税	foreign (corporation) tax, foreign taxes paid 頻 to claim credits for foreign corporation tax（外国税額控除をとる）
解雇手当	severance [redundancy] payment
介在	interposition
解散	dissolution
改竄	falsification
概算	approximation
改竄された財務諸表	falsified financial statements
解散日	date of dissolution
開始	commencement, inception, initiation
開示	disclosure 関 to be disclosed separately（別途開示される）
開示確認書	disclosure letter
開示科目	line item 頻 line item titled（～という開示科目）
外資規制	restriction on foreign investment
開始記入	opening entry
開始日	commencement date, inception date
会社	company, corporation
会社案内（パンフレット）	company brochure
解釈（書）	interpretation
会社更生法	Corporate Reorganisation Act [Law] 米 Corporate Reorganization Act [Law]
会社単位の合算課税（タックス・ヘイブン対策税制による）	aggregation of income on an entity basis
会社の解散	dissolution of corporation
会社の設立	incorporation 関 to be incorporated（設立される，法人化される）
会社負担の社会保険拠出	company's contribution to social security
会社分割	corporate division
会社法	Companies Act [Law]
回収	collection, recovery 関 to recover deferred tax assets（繰延税金資産を回収する）
回収（投資の）	payback
回収可能価額	recoverable amount 頻 a recoverable amount is the higher of fair value less costs of disposal and value in use（回収可能価額は，処分コスト控除後の公正価値と使用価値のいずれか大きいほうである），the carrying amount of an asset is reduced to its recoverable amount（資産の帳簿価額が回収可能価額まで減額される）
回収可能性	collectibility, recoverability 頻 collectibility of accounts receivable（売掛債権の回収可能性），recoverability of deferred tax assets（繰延税金資産の回収可能性）関 accounts receivable are collectible（売掛債権は回収可能である），deferred tax assets are recoverable（繰延税金資産は回収可能である）
回収期間	collection period
回収期間（投資の）	payback period
回収期間法	payback period method
回収期限を経過した債権	past due receivables
回収業務契約	servicing contract
改修サービス	upgrade service
回収資産	asset for recovery
回収不能	uncollectibility
回収不能債権	uncollectibles
解除（契約などの）	termination
開示要求	disclosure requirement
改正	reform
改善	improvement, remediation
改善（方法）	remedy
階層	hierarchy, tier
階層（累進課税などの）	bracket
階層化	stratification
解体	break-up, dismantlement
解体費用引当金	provision for decommissioning costs
買建オプション	purchased option

買建コール・オプション	purchased call option
買建プット・オプション	purchased put option
外為市場	currency market
ガイダンス	guidance
外注先	subcontractor
外注費	subcontracting cost
買付代理人	buying agent
買手	buyer, acquirer
改訂	revision
改訂された基準書	amended standard
買手側（買収案件などの）	buy side
買手にとっての価値	buyer's value
買手によるデュー・デリジェンス	purchaser due diligence
回転期間	turnover period
回転率	turnover
ガイドライン	guideline 頻 guideline for (～に対するガイドライン)
解任	removal, dismissal
解任権	removal rights
概念	concept, notion
概念フレームワーク	conceptual framework
開発	development, exploitation
開発局面	development phase
開発支出	development expenditure
開発中の無形資産	intangible asset under development
開発費	development cost [expense]
会費	membership fee
会費及び購読料	dues and subscriptions
外部委託	outsourcing
外部売上	external sales
外部格付け	external rating
外部金融	external financing
回復	recovery
外部顧客	external customer
外部資金	external funds
外部資金調達	external financing
外部収益（外部顧客からの収益）	external revenue
外部信用格付け	external credit grade
外部調査	external investigation
外部積立（基金）を有する年金制度	funded pension plan
外部取引	external transaction
外部比較対象（取引）	external comparable
外部報告	external reporting
買戻し	buyback, repurchase 関 to buy back shares（自社株買いを行う）
買戻契約	repurchase agreement [arrangement]
買戻権付販売［売却］	sale with a right of repurchase
買戻条項	buyback clause
買戻しの取決め	repurchase arrangement
解約	cancellation
解約選択権［オプション］	termination option
解約不能期間（リース契約などの）	non-cancellable period
解約不能リース	non-cancellable lease
解約料	cancellation fee [penalty]
解約料（特に買収契約に関する）	break-up [bust-up] fee
概要	outline, overview
買呼値	bid price
改良（固定資産の）	betterment
カウンター・オファー	counter offer
カウンターパーティー	counterparty
カウンターパーティー・リスク	counterparty risk
カウント実施者（棚卸の際の）	counter
価格	price 関 to be priced at cost（原価をもって販売価格とする）, to be priced at market value（市場価格をもって販売価格とする）
価格差異	price variance
価格差異（直接材料費に係る）	direct material price variance
価格算定モデル	pricing model
価格指数	price index
価格修正方式（買収価格の調整における）	completion adjustment
価格政策	pricing policy
価格設定	pricing, price setting
価格リスク	price risk
価格レンジ	price range
架空収益	fictitious revenue
架空取引	fictitious transaction
架空費用	fictitious expense
架空利益	fictitious profit

家具，什器及び備品（ホテルなどの）　furniture, fixtures and equipment (FF&E)
学習曲線　learning curve
拡大　expansion
格付け　rating
格付機関　rating agency
確定給付（退職給付制度について）　defined benefit (DB)
確定給付企業年金法　Defined Benefit Corporate Pension Act
確定給付債務　defined benefit obligation
確定給付資産（の純額）　net defined benefit asset
確定給付資産の純額に対する利息純額　net interest on the net defined benefit liability [asset]
確定給付制度　defined benefit plan
確定給付制度債務　defined benefit obligation
確定給付制度の数理計算上の差異（益［損］）　actuarial gains [losses] on defined benefit plans
確定給付費用　defined benefit cost
確定給付負債　defined benefit liability
確定給付負債（の純額）　net defined benefit liability
確定給付負債の純額に対する利息純額　net interest on the net defined benefit liability
確定拠出（退職給付制度について）　defined contribution (DC)
確定拠出制度　defined contribution plan
確定拠出制度への拠出　contributions to defined contribution plans
確定購入契約［コミットメント］　firm purchase commitment
確定したオプションの保有者　holder of a vested option
確定した耐用年数　definite useful life
確定従業員給付　vested employee benefit
確定申告書　final tax return
確定納付（税金などの）　final (tax) payment
確定約定［コミットメント］　firm commitment
確認　confirmation
確認依頼（書）　confirmation request
確認価値　confirmatory value
確認書　confirmation letter, letter of confirmation
確認状　confirmation letter, letter of confirmation
額面　par
額面株式　par value stock [share]
額面金額　face value, par value
確率　probability
掛（売り）　credit
下限　floor, lower limit
過去　past
下降　downturn
加工　processing
加工費　processing [conversion] cost
過去勤務費用（貸方）　past service credit
過去勤務費用（債務）　past service cost　［頻］　unrecognised past service cost（未認識過去勤務費用（債務））
過去の事象　past event
過去の商慣習　past customary business practices
過去の推移の要約　historical summary
過去の租税債務　historical tax liabilities　［頻］　to inherit all historical tax liabilities（過去の租税債務をすべて引き継ぐ）
加算　addition　［関］　to add □ back (to income)（□を税務加算する）
加算税　penalty (tax)　［頻］　a penalty is imposed on additional tax assessed（追徴税額に対して加算税が課される）
貸方　credit
貸方記入　credit entry
貸方残高　credit balance
貸方伝票　credit memo
貸倒懸念債権　doubtful debt
貸倒償却　bad debt written off　［関］　to write off bad debt（不良債権を償却する）
貸倒損失　bad debt loss [expense], credit loss
貸倒引当金　provision [allowance] for bad debt, allowance (account) for credit losses
貸出コミットメント　loan commitment
瑕疵担保責任　warranty against defects
過失　negligence
貸付金　loan, loan (s) receivable
貸付金及び債権（旧）　loans and receivables (L&R)
貸付金利息　interest on loans

かしつけゆ　204

貸付有価証券　securities lent
貸手（資金の）　lender
加重平均　weighted average
加重平均借入利率　weighted average borrowing rate
加重平均資本コスト　weighted average cost of capital (WACC)
加重平均普通株式数　weighted average number of outstanding ordinary shares
加重平均法　weighted average cost formula
過剰　excess
過剰供給　excess supply
過少計上　understatement　[頻] understatement of a profit（利益の過少計上）　[関] to understate a profit（利益を過少計上する）
過少計上された収益　understated revenue
過剰在庫　excess inventory
過少資本　thin capitalisation　[米] thin capitalization　[関] to be thinly capitalised（資本が過少である）
過少資本税制　thin capitalisation rules　[米] thin capitalization rules　[頻] thin capitalisation rules apply（過少資本税制が適用される）
過少申告（課税所得の）　underreporting (of taxable income)
過少申告加算税　additional tax on underpayment
過少納付　underpayment
過少払い　underpayment
過少引当　underprovision
過小評価　undervaluation, underestimation
過少見積り　underestimation
可処分所得　disposable income
カスタマー・ロイヤルティ・プログラム　customer loyalty programme　[米] customer loyalty program
課税　taxation, imposition of tax　[関] to impose tax（課税する）
課税売上（消費税などの）　taxable sales
課税管轄区域　tax jurisdiction
課税期間　taxable period
課税権　taxing right
課税事象　taxable event
課税上の地位　tax status

課税所得　taxable income (profit), income subject to tax　[頻] to constitute taxable income（課税所得を構成する）　[関] income inclusion（課税所得に含まれること）
課税対象外　exclusion
課税対象金額　taxable amount
課税対象とならない事業体　(fiscally) transparent entity, disregarded entity
課税対象留保利益　taxable retained earnings
課税取引（消費税などの）　taxable transaction
課税年度　tax(able) year
課税の繰延べ　tax deferral (treatment)
課税標準　tax(able) base, tax basis
課税ベース　tax base
仮説　hypothesis
寡占　oligopoly
仮想恒久的施設　virtual PE
仮想デリバティブ　hypothetical derivative
仮装取引　sham transaction
加速度償却（減価償却のうち）　accelerated depreciation
過大借入れ　overleveraging
過大計上　overstatement　[頻] overstatement of a profit（利益の過大計上）　[関] to overstate a profit（利益を過大計上する）
過大計上された負債・費用　overstated liabilities and expenses
過大支払い　overpayment
過大支払利子税制（日本）　earnings stripping rules
過大資本　overcapitalisation　[米] overcapitalization
過大投資　overinvestment
過大なレバレッジ　overleveraging
過大納付　overpayment
過大評価　overvaluation
過大役員報酬　excessive director's remuneration
片側リスク　one-sided risk
形　shape
価値　value
価値の切下げ　devaluation
価値の低下　decline in value
価値変動　change in value
課徴金　monetary penalty
課徴金減免制度　leniency programme　[米]

	leniency program	過年度税金費用	prior year tax expense
括弧	parenthesis	過年度の誤謬	prior period error 〔頻〕 correction of a prior period error（過年度の誤謬の訂正）
合算	aggregation		
合算課税	aggregation of income, income inclusion 〔関〕 a company includes in its income the proportionate share of the income of a CFC（CFC（被支配外国法人）の所得を持分割合に応じて合算する）	過年度の情報	prior period information
		過年度法人税等	prior year tax expense
		可能性	likelihood, possibility
		ガバナンス	governance
		過払い	overpayment
活動基準原価計算	activity-based costing (ABC)	カバレッジ	coverage
		カバレッジ・レシオ	coverage ratio
カットオフ	cut-off 〔頻〕 sales cut-off test（売上のカットオフ・テスト）, sales cut-off error（売上のカットオフ・エラー（期ズレ））	過半数	majority
		過半数の持分	majority interest
		株価	share [stock] price
		株価指数	stock index
カットオフ・エラー	cut-off error	株価収益率	price earnings ratio (P/E ratio, PER)
カットオフ・テスト	cut-off test		
カットオフ日	cut-off date	株価純資産倍率	price book-value ratio, price-to-book ratio (P/B ratio, PBR)
カットオフ・ポイント	cut-off point		
活発な市場	active market		
活発な市場における公表価格	quoted prices in active markets	株価リスク	equity price risk
		株券	share [stock] certificate
割賦売掛金	instalment receivables 〔米〕 installment receivables	株式	share, stock 〔頻〕 to issue shares（株式を発行する）, to subscribe shares（株式を引き受ける）
割賦基準	instalment method 〔米〕 installment method		
		株式以外の対価	non-share consideration
割賦債権	instalment receivables 〔米〕 installment receivables	株式移転	share transfer (kabushiki iten) 〔使い方注意！〕 単純に share transfer というと，通常の株式譲渡と誤解される可能性があるので，補足説明が必要
割賦販売	instalment sales 〔米〕 installment sales		
合併	merger, amalgamation 〔頻〕 to implement a merger（合併を実行する） 〔関〕 Company A and Company B merge（A 社と B 社が合併する）, Company A merges with Company B（A 社が B 社と合併する）	株式会社	corporation, Kabushiki Kaisha (KK)
		株式公開	going public
		株式交換	share for share exchange (kabushiki kokan)
		株式購入	share purchase
合併・買収	mergers & acquisitions (M&A)	株式購入契約書	share [stock] purchase agreement (SPA)
合併比率	merger ratio		
合併前の繰越欠損金	pre-merger losses	株式購入制度	share purchase plan [programme] 〔米〕 share purchase program
仮定	assumption 〔頻〕 on the assumption that（〜という仮定のもとで）		
		株式交付費	share [stock] issue cost, share issue related cost
稼働率（工場などの）	capacity utilisation 〔米〕 capacity utilization		
		株式市場	stock market
稼働率（投資不動産などの）	occupancy rate	株式市場条件	market condition, market-based performance condition
金型	mould 〔米〕 mold		
過年度	prior year(s), prior period 〔頻〕 in prior year(s)（過年度において）	株式市場条件以外の業績条件	non-market-based performance condition
過年度修正	prior period adjustment	株式取得	share [stock] acquisition

かぶしきし

株式償還	share [stock] redemption
株式消却	retirement of stock
株式譲渡	share transfer, stock sale
株式譲渡契約（書）	share sale agreement (SSA), stock sale agreement
株式数	number of shares
株式増価受益権	share [stock] appreciation right (SAR)
株式対価	consideration in the form of shares, share [stock] consideration
株式等貸借取引	stock lending
株式取引	share [stock] deal
株式に係る売建コール・オプション	written call option on shares
株式に係る売建プット・オプション	written put option on shares
株式に係る買建コール・オプション	purchased call option on shares
株式に係る買建プット・オプション	purchased put option on shares
株式に基づく報酬	share-based payment
株式に基づく報酬（の授与）	share-based payment award
株式に基づく報酬契約	share-based payment arrangement
株式に基づく報酬制度	share-based payment plan, stock compensation plan
株式に基づく報酬取引	share-based payment transaction
株式の公開買付け	takeover bid (TOB)
株式の種類	class of shares
株式の譲渡制限	restriction on share transferability
株式の処分制限	restriction on the disposal of shares　[頻]　restriction on the disposal of shares received in a tax-free reorganisation（非課税組織再編における取得株式の処分制限）
株式の発行	share issue
株式の無償交付	bonus (share) issue
株式売却	share [stock] sale
株式買収	share [stock] acquisition, share [stock] purchase, share [stock] deal　[頻]　to make a share acquisition（株式買収を行う）　[関]　to acquire shares（株式買収を行う）

株式買収契約書	share [stock] purchase agreement (SPA)
株式配当	share [stock] dividend
株式発行関連コスト	share issue related cost
株式払込剰余金	additional paid in capital
株式引受け	share [stock] subscription
株式引受権	stock right
株式プレミアム	share [stock] premium
株式分割	share [stock] split
株式併合	share [stock] consolidation, reverse share [stock] split
株式報酬	share-based payment
株式報酬契約	share-based payment arrangement
株式報酬制度	share-based payment plan
株式報酬取引	share-based payment transaction
株式を購入する先渡契約	forward contract to buy shares
株式を売却する先渡契約	forward contract to sell shares
株主	shareholder (S/H), stockholder
株主及び債権者に帰属するフリー・キャッシュ・フロー	free cash flow to the firm (FCFF)
株主価値	shareholder value, equity value
株主活動	shareholder activity
株主間契約	shareholders(') agreement (SHA)
株主間合意	shareholders(') agreement (SHA)
株主構成	shareholder (ownership) structure, ownership structure
株主資本	shareholders' [stockholders'] equity, owner's equity
株主資本計算書	statement of shareholders' equity
株主資本コスト	cost of equity
株主資本等変動計算書	statement of shareholders' equity, statement of changes in net assets
株主総会	shareholders' meeting, general meeting of shareholders
株主総会議事録	minutes of shareholders' meeting
株主代表訴訟	shareholders' derivative action
株主に帰属するフリー・キャッシュ・フロー	free cash flow to equity (FCFE)

| 株主変更 | change of control (CoC), change of ownership 〔頻〕 a change of control could have adverse tax consequences（株主変更が不利な税務上の影響をもたらす可能性がある）
| 株主名簿 | shareholder registry
| 株主割当増資 | rights issue, rights offering
| 貨幣性項目 | monetary item
| 貨幣性資産 | monetary asset
| 貨幣測定の公準 | monetary assumption
| 貨幣の時間的価値 | time value of money
| 下方修正 | downward adjustment
| 上期 | 1st half
| 上半期 | 1st half
| 貨物 | cargo
| 貨物引換証 | bill of lading (B/L)
| 空売り | short sale
| 借入金 | borrowings, loan, loan(s) payable
| 借入金残高 | outstanding borrowings
| 借入金担保 | loan collateral
| 借入金利息 | interest on loans
| 借入限度額 | borrowing facility
| 借入コスト | borrowing costs 〔頻〕 borrowing costs incurred（発生した借入コスト）, borrowing costs capitalised（資産化した借入コスト）, borrowing costs recognised as expense（費用として認識した借入コスト）
| 借入コストの資産化 | capitalisation of borrowing costs 〔米〕 capitalization of borrowing costs 〔頻〕 to cease capitalisation of borrowing costs（借入コストの資産化を終了する）
| 借入資本 | loan capital
| 借入費用 | borrowing costs
| 借入有価証券 | securities borrowed
| 借入枠 | borrowing facility
| 仮受金 | suspense receipt
| 仮受消費税等 | output consumption tax
| 借換え | refinancing
| 借換契約 | refinancing agreement
| 借換手数料 | refinancing fee
| 借方 | debit
| 借方記入 | debit entry
| 借方残高 | debit balance
| 借方伝票 | debit memo
| 仮勘定 | suspense account
| 借手（資金の） | borrower
| 借手の追加借入利率（リースについて） | lessee's incremental borrowing rate
| 仮払金 | suspense payment
| 仮払消費税等 | input consumption tax
| 為替換算差額 | currency translation differences, exchange differences on translation
| 為替換算調整勘定 | translation adjustments, exchange differences on translating foreign operations, translation reserve
| 為替管理 | foreign exchange control
| 為替差益 | (foreign) exchange gain
| 為替差額 | exchange difference
| 為替差額の資産化 | capitalisation of exchange differences 〔米〕 capitalization of exchange differences
| 為替先物市場 | currency forward market
| 為替差損 | (foreign) exchange loss
| 為替差損益 | exchange gains and losses
| 為替直物市場 | currency spot market
| 為替相場 | currency rate
| 為替手形 | bill of exchange (B/E)
| 為替変動 | currency fluctuation
| 為替変動による影響額 | effects of exchange rate changes
| 為替予約 | foreign currency forward
| 為替予約（契約） | forward exchange contract, forward foreign currency contract
| 為替リスク | (foreign) currency risk, foreign exchange risk
| 為替レート | exchange rate
| 為替レートの変動による影響 | effect of movement in exchange rates
| 管轄区 | jurisdiction
| 管轄区域 | territory
| 環境 | environment
| 環境改善債務 | environmental obligations
| 環境関連費用 | environment related expense
| 環境基準 | environmental standards
| 環境規制 | environmental regulations
| 環境債務 | environmental obligations
| 環境対策引当金 | provision for environmental rehabilitation costs, environmental provision
| 環境デュー・ディリジェンス | environmental

	due diligence	監査人	auditor
環境の再生	environmental rehabilitation	監査人の報酬	auditor's remuneration 〔頻〕 auditor's remuneration for audit services（監査業務に係る監査人の報酬），auditor's remuneration for other services（その他の業務に係る監査人の報酬）
環境被害［損害］	environmental damage		
環境引当金	provision for environmental rehabilitation costs, environmental provision		
関係	relationship	監査範囲	audit scope
関係会社	related company	監査報告書	audit report, auditor's report
関係会社間債権	intercompany receivables	監査報告書日	date of audit report
関係会社間債権債務	intercompany [intra-group] balance, intercompany receivables and payables	監査報酬	audit fee
		監査法人	audit firm
		監査目的	audit objective
関係会社間債権債務管理表	intercompany receivables and payables schedule	監査役	corporate [statutory] auditor, audit & supervisory board member
関係会社間債権債務の確認	intercompany balance confirmation	監査役会	board of auditors, audit & supervisory board
関係会社間債務	intercompany payables	監査役会設置会社	company with a board of corporate auditors
関係会社間取引	intercompany [intra-group] transaction		
		監査リスク	audit risk
関係会社間配当	intercompany dividend	換算	translation 〔関〕 to be translated at the closing rate（期末日レートで換算される）
慣行	convention		
監査	audit 〔頻〕 to conduct an audit（監査を実施する）	換算差額	translation difference
		換算差額累計額	cumulative translation differences
監査委員会（委員会設置会社の）	audit committee	換算レート	translation rate
管財人	receiver	監視	oversight, surveillance
監査基準	auditing standards	慣習	custom
監査業務	audit engagement	勘定	account
監査計画	audit planning	勘定科目	account title
監査サンプリング	audit sampling	勘定科目一覧表	chart [list] of accounts
監査指示書	audit instructions	勘定科目名	account name
監査修正（監査による修正）	audit adjustment	勘定形式（表示方法としての）	account form
監査証拠	audit evidence	勘定コード	account code
監査証跡	audit trail	勘定残高	account balance
監査上の重要性	audit materiality	勘定組織	set of accounts
監査上の発見事項	audit findings	勘定の調整	account reconciliation
監査済財務諸表	audited financial statements	勘定分析	account analysis
監査調書	audit documentation, working papers	勘定明細	details of accounts
		完成	completion
観察可能なインプット	observable input	関税	(customs) duties 〔使い方注意！〕通常複数形（duties）で使われる
観察可能な市場のデータ	observable market data		
		完成基準	completed contract method
観察不能なインプット	unobservable input	完成工事高	construction sales
監査手続	audit procedure	関税込み持込み渡し条件（価格）	delivered duty paid (DDP)
監査手続書	audit programme 〔米〕audit program		
		関税番号	tariff code

関税評価　customs valuation
関税評価額　customs value
完成品（製品）　finished goods
完成品原価　cost of finished goods
関税分類　tariff classification
関税率表　tariff
間接外国税額控除　indirect foreign tax credit
間接金融　indirect financing
間接経費　overhead (cost)
間接材料費　indirect material cost
間接税　indirect tax
間接製造費用　indirect manufacturing cost
間接納付税額　underlying tax
間接配賦方式　indirect-charge method
間接費　indirect cost, overhead
間接費配賦率　burden rate, overhead allocation rate
間接法（キャッシュ・フロー計算書）　indirect method
間接保有（株式の）　indirect shareholding
間接労務費　indirect labour cost 米 indirect labor cost
完全希薄化ベース　fully diluted basis
完全子会社　wholly-owned subsidiary
完全支配関係　100% control relationship
完全性　completeness
完全な１組の財務諸表　a complete set of financial statements
完全な消滅（負債などの）　full extinguishment
簡素化したアプローチ　simplified approach
鑑定（評価）　appraisal
鑑定評価書　appraisal report
観点　perspective, viewpoint
監督　supervision, oversight
監督者　supervisor
カントリー・リスク　country risk
カントリー・リスク・プレミアム　country risk premium
感応度　sensitivity
感応度分析　sensitivity analysis
還付　refund 頻 to claim a refund（還付請求する）, to receive a refund（還付金を受け取る） 関 to be refundable（還付対象となる）
還付されない取得税（有形固定資産などの）　non-refundable purchase taxes
還付請求　request for refund, claim for refund
簡便法　short-cut method
官報　(official) gazette
元本（借入金などの）　principal (amount)
元本返済　principal repayment 関 interest payment（利息支払い）
関与　involvement
管理　administration
管理会計　management [managerial] accounting
管理会計数値［決算書］　management accounts
管理階層　layer of management
管理可能性　controllability
管理可能費用　controllable cost
管理コスト　administration cost
管理支配基準（タックス・ヘイブン対策税制）　administration and control test 頻 to satisfy the administration and control test（管理支配基準を充足する）, to fail the administration and control test（管理支配基準を充足しない）
管理支配地（基準）　place of central management and control
管理番号　control number
管理費　administrative cost [expense]
管理不能費用　non-controllable cost
管理部門　administrative department
官僚制　bureaucracy
慣例　custom
関連会社　associate, affiliate
関連会社に対する投資　investment in an associate
関連会社に対する持分　interest in an associate
関連者　related party
関連者取引　related party transaction, controlled transaction
関連性のある活動　relevant activities
関連当事者　related party
関連当事者取引　related party transaction
関連費用　associated cost [expense], related cost [expense]
緩和（リスクなどの）　mitigation, alleviation

き

キー・コンピテンシー	key competency
キープウェル・レター	keepwell letter
機会	opportunity
機械	machine, machinery 使い方注意! machinery は集合体としての機械を意味する不可算名詞であり、machine は個々の機械を意味する可算名詞
機械及び装置	machinery and equipment
機械稼働時間	machine hours
機会費用	opportunity cost
期間	period, duration
機関投資家	institutional investor
期間配分（費用などの）	interperiod allocation
期間費用	period cost
企業	(business) enterprise, firm
企業家	entrepreneur
起業家	entrepreneur
企業会計基準委員会（日本）	Accounting Standards Board of Japan (ASBJ)
企業価値	corporate value, enterprise value (EV)
企業間与信（信用）	trade credit
企業金融	corporate finance
企業結合	business combination
企業結合規制	merger control
企業結合規制のクリアランス	merger control clearance
企業結合による取得（固定資産などの）	acquisitions through business combinations
企業結合日	business combination date
企業固有の価値	entity-specific value
企業固有の測定値	entity-specific measurement
企業再生	corporate revitalisation 米 corporate revitalization
企業資源計画	enterprise resource planning (ERP)
企業自身の資本性金融商品	entity's own equity instrument
企業実体の公準	economic entity assumption
企業支配対価	control premium
企業集団	group 頻 member of a group（企業集団の構成員）
企業集団の形成	group formation
企業全体の開示	entity-wide disclosure
企業内弁護士	in-house lawyer
企業の結合	combination of entities
企業の構成単位	component of an entity
企業の社会的責任	corporate social responsibility (CSR)
企業の法的形態	legal form of an entity
企業買収	acquisition, takeover
企業評価	(corporate) valuation
企業不動産	corporate real estate (CRE)
企業保証	corporate guarantee
議決権	voting power [right]
議決権付株式	voting stock
議決権の保有割合	proportion of voting rights 頻 proportion of voting rights held in a subsidiary（子会社に対する議決権の保有割合）, proportion of voting rights held by non-controlling interests（非支配持分の議決権の保有割合）
議決権ベース	voting right basis
危険	jeopardy
期限	deadline, due date
期限後申告	late filing
期限後納付	late payment
期限付劣後負債	dated subordinated liabilities
期限のない劣後負債	undated subordinated liabilities
期限前返済	prepayment
起債	placement
疑似–	quasi-
疑似DES（疑似デット・エクイティ・スワップ）	quasi-debt equity swap
期首	beginning of (accounting) period
期首残高	opening [beginning] balance
記述	description
技術	technique
技術役務	technical service
技術革新	innovation
技術上の役務	technical service

技術的実行可能性　technical feasibility
記述的情報　descriptive information
技術に基づく無形資産　technology-based intangible asset
基準　basis, criterion, standard　[使い方注意！] criterion については，複数形の criteria の形で使うことが多い。[頻] criteria for (〜の基準)，to meet specified criteria (特定の基準に適合する)
基準期間　base period
基準設定者　standard setter
基準棚卸残高　base stock
基準値　threshold　[頻] above the threshold (基準値を上回って), below the threshold (基準値を下回って), to reach the threshold (基準値に到達する)
基準年度　base year
基準日（配当などの）　record date
議事録　minutes
議事録（会議などの）　meeting minutes
期ズレ　cut-off error　[頻] sales cut-off errors (売上の期ズレ)
規制　regulation
規制官庁　regulatory agency
規制緩和　deregulation
規制機関　regulatory body [organisation], regulator　[米] regulatory organization
規制繰延勘定　regulatory deferral account
規制条項　restrictive covenant
規制団体　regulatory organisation　[米] regulatory organization
規制当局　regulatory authority, regulator
季節性　seasonality
季節変動　seasonal fluctuation
基礎　basis
偽造　falsification, forgery
偽造裏書き　forged endorsement
寄贈者　donor
規則　rule
帰属　attribution　[関] to be attributable to (〜に帰属する)
帰属（税金などの）　imputation
規則主義　rules-based
帰属主義（PE に関する）　attributable income principle
規則的方法　systematic basis

基礎研究　basic [pure] research
基礎となる前提　underlying assumption
既存の関係（被取得企業などとの）　pre-existing relationship
既存の関係の清算　settlement of pre-existing relationship
既存の権利　existing right
既存の持分　existing [pre-existing] interest
期待　expectation
期待運用収益（制度資産，年金資産の）　expected return on plan assets
期待キャッシュ・フロー　expected cash flow
期待収益率　expected rate of return
期待値　expected value
期待値アプローチ　expected value approach
寄託者　depositary
期中　mid-year
期中監査　interim audit
期中財務情報　interim financial information
期中財務諸表　interim financial statements
期中財務報告　interim financial reporting
期中財務報告書　interim financial report
期中報告期間　interim period
キックバック　kickback
規定　provision　[関] a law provides that (法は〜と規定している)
規定（特に法律や契約書などの）　stipulation
規程　rules
議定書　protocol
既定値　default
機能　function　[頻] to perform a function (機能を果たす)
機能通貨　functional currency
機能通貨以外の表示通貨　presentation currency other than the functional currency
機能通貨の変更　change in functional currency
機能的または経済的な陳腐化　functional and economic obsolescence
機能とリスク　function and risk
機能分析　functional analysis
希薄化　dilution
希薄化効果　dilutive effect　[頻] dilutive effect of share options on number of ordinary shares (ストック・オプションが普通株式数に与える希薄化効果)

希薄化後1株当たり損失　diluted loss per share
希薄化後1株当たり利益　diluted earnings per share
希薄化性金融商品　dilutive instrument
希薄化性潜在的普通株式　dilutive potential ordinary share
希薄化防止　dilution protection
寄附金　donation　[頻] to make a donation to（～に対して寄附金を支出する）
寄附金の受入側　donee
寄附金の支出側　donor
規模　scale, magnitude
技法　technique
基本給　base salary
基本契約　master agreement
基本合意書　letter of intent (LOI), heads of agreement (HOA), heads of terms
基本相殺契約　master netting agreement
基本的及び希薄化後1株当たり利益［損失］　basic and diluted earnings [loss] per share
基本的な特性　fundamental characteristic
基本的1株当たり損失　basic loss per share
基本的1株当たり利益　basic earnings per share
基本的利益　return for routine contribution
基本となる原則　core principle
期末　end of (accounting) period
期末残高　closing [ending] balance
期末修正　period-end adjustment
期末の為替レート　closing foreign exchange rate
期末日　closing date, end of (accounting/reporting) period
期末日レート　closing (foreign exchange) rate　[頻] to be translated at the closing rate（期末日レートで換算される）
期末日レート法　closing rate method　[頻] to adopt [use] the closing rate method（期末日レート法を採用する）
義務　duty, obligation
記名債券　registered bond
記名証券　registered securities
規約　code
逆希薄化　anti-dilution
逆三角合併　reverse triangular merger

逆取得　reverse acquisition
逆仕訳　reversal [reversing] entry
脚注　footnote
客観性　objectivity
客観的な証拠　objective evidence
キャッシュ・コンバージョン・サイクル　cash conversion cycle (CCC)
キャッシュ・バランス・プラン（年金制度）　cash balance plan
キャッシュ・プーリング　cash pool(ing)
キャッシュ・フロー　cash flow
キャッシュ・フロー管理　cash flow management
キャッシュ・フロー計算書　cash flow statement, statement of cash flows
キャッシュ・フロー投下資本利益率　cash flow return on invested capital (CFROI), cash flow return on investment (CFROI)
キャッシュ・フローの変動性　variability in cash flows
キャッシュ・フロー分析　cash flow analysis
キャッシュ・フロー・ヘッジ　cash flow hedge
キャッシュ・フロー・ヘッジ剰余金　cash flow hedge reserve
キャッシュ・フロー予測　cash flow forecast [projection]
キャッシュ・ボックス　cash box
キャッシュや有利子負債の影響を受けない（企業の）価値　cash free debt free value
キャッシュライク・アイテム　cash-like item
キャップ・テーブル　capitalisation table　[米] capitalization table
キャップ・レート　capitalisation rate (cap rate)　[米] capitalization rate
キャピタル・アローワンス　capital allowance (CA)
キャピタル・ゲイン　capital gain
キャピタル・チャージ　capital charge
キャピタル・リース　capital lease
キャピタル・ロス　capital loss
キャンセル　cancellation
キャンセル料　cancellation charge [fee]
休暇　vacation, leave
休暇取得の義務付け　mandatory vacation
救済　remedy
給付　benefit

給付を受ける権利	benefit entitlement
休眠会社	dormant company
給与	salary
給与計算	payroll
給与所得	employment [earned] income
給与水準	salary level
給与テーブル	payroll table
給料	salary
行（行・列の）	row
教育訓練費	staff training cost [expense]
強化	enhancement
協会	institute, institution
業界	industry
業界慣行	industry practice
業界情報	industry information
供給	supply
供給者	provider, supplier
競業避止義務	covenant not to compete, non-compete clause
競合禁止条項	non-compete clause
業種	industry sector
行政	administration
行政事件訴訟法	Administrative Litigation Law
行政指導	administrative direction
強制償還	mandatory redemption
行政上の罰金	administrative monetary penalty
行政処分	administrative action
強制処分価値	forced liquidation value
強制清算	compulsory liquidation
行政通達	administrative ruling
強制的にその他の包括利益を通じて公正価値で測定される金融資産	financial assets mandatorily measured at FVTOCI [FVOCI]
強制売却権	drag along right
行政罰	administrative penalty
強制力のある契約	enforceable agreement
業績	(financial) performance, operating result
業績条件	performance condition
業績賞与	performance bonus
業績評価	performance evaluation [assessment]
業績目標	performance target
業績連動給与	performance-based compensation

競争上の障害	competitive harm
競争入札	competitive bid
兄弟会社	sister company [corporation], fellow subsidiary
強調	emphasis
共通支配	common control 頻 under common control（共通支配下にある） 関 Company A and Company B are commonly controlled（A社とB社は共通支配下にある）
共通支配下の企業	entity under common control
共通支配下の企業結合	business combination under common control
共通支配下の取引	transaction under common control
共通報告基準	Common Reporting Standard (CRS)
協同組合	co-operative
共同契約	collaborative arrangement
共同事業	joint venture [business]
共同事業体	consortium 頻 to form a consortium（共同事業体を形成する）
共同事業要件（共同事業を行うための組織再編の）	joint business requirements
共同事業を行うための組織再編	joint business reorganisation 米 joint business reorganization
共同支配	joint control
共同支配企業	joint venture
共同支配企業に対する投資	investment in a joint venture
共同支配企業に対する持分	interest in a joint venture
共同支配事業	joint operation
共同支配事業者	joint operator
共同支配事業体（旧）	jointly controlled entity
共同支配投資企業	joint venturer
共同支配投資者	joint venturer
共同支配の事業（旧）	jointly controlled operation
共同支配の資産（旧）	jointly controlled asset
共同支配の取決め	joint arrangement
共同支配の取決めの形成	formation of a joint arrangement
共同支配の取決めの当事者	party to a joint

arrangement	
共同創業者	co-founder
共同投資	co-investment
共同売却	co-sale
共同売却権	co-sale right, tag along right
共同プロジェクト	joint project
共犯者（不正などの）	accomplice
共謀	collusion
共謀者	conspirator
業務	operation, engagement 頻 to cease operations（業務を停止する）
業務委託契約	service agreement
業務委託契約書	letter of engagement
業務監査	operational audit
業務記述書	(process) narrative, business process description
業務効率	operational efficiency
業務効率の調査	operational efficiency review
業務処理統制	application control
業務範囲	scope of work
業務プロセスに係る内部統制	process level control
協力	cooperation, collaboration
許可	clearance, permission, admission 頻 to obtain clearance（in advance）from tax authorities（税務当局から（事前に）許可を得る）
虚偽記載	misrepresentation
虚偽表示	misstatement, misrepresentation
居住	(fiscal) residence
居住外国人	resident alien
居住者	resident
居住者証明（書）	certificate of residence [residency], residence [residency] certificate
居住者証明書（税務上の）	tax residency certificate
居住地	domicile
居住地国	country of domicile
拠出	contribution
拠出資産	contributory asset
拠出資本	contributed capital
拒否	refusal
拒否権	veto right
規律	discipline
記録	record
記録の保存	record retention
記録の保存期間	record retention period
金額	amount
金額表示単位	rounding 頻 level of rounding used in financial statements（財務諸表に使用している金額表示単位）
緊急	emergency
金庫	safe box
均衡	equilibrium
銀行	bank
銀行借入	bank loan [borrowings], bank notes payable
銀行勘定調整表	bank reconciliation
銀行口座	bank account
銀行残高	bank balance
銀行残高確認状	bank confirmation
銀行残高証明書	bank certificate [certification]
銀行信用照会	bank reference
銀行手数料	bank charge
銀行取引残高報告書	bank statement
禁止	prohibition
近似	proximity
金銭	money
金銭債権	monetary asset
金銭債務	monetary liability
金銭的損害（不正などによる）	financial damage
勤続期間	length of service
勤続年数	years of service
均等化	equalisation ㊇ equalization
均等払い	level payment
均等割（住民税の）	per capita inhabitant tax, per capita levy
勤務期間	length of service
勤務期間中の死亡給付	death-in-service benefit
勤務条件	service condition
勤務年数	years of service
勤務費用	(current) service cost
金融機関	financial institution, financial services firm
金融子会社	finance subsidiary
金融サービス	financial services
金融資産	financial asset
金融資産の譲渡	transfer of financial assets
金融資産・負債の相殺	offsetting of financial

金融市場　financial market
金融収益　finance income
金融商品　financial instrument
金融政策　monetary policy
金融庁　Financial Services Agency (FSA)
金融取引　financial transaction
金融費用　finance cost
金融費用（純額）　net finance costs
金融負債　financial liability
金融負債に分類変更された資本　equity reclassified into financial liabilities
金融保証　financial guarantee
金融保証契約　financial guarantee contract
金融リスク管理　financial risk management
金利　interest
金利オプション　interest rate option
金利カラー（取引）　interest rate collar
金利キャップ（取引）　interest rate cap
金利コスト　interest cost
金利先渡　forward rate
金利先渡取引　forward rate agreement (FRA)
金利収益　interest income
金利スワップ　interest rate swap
金利費用　interest expense
金利リスク　interest rate risk

く

偶発　contingency
偶発債務　contingent liability
偶発資産　contingent asset
偶発損失　loss contingencies
偶発発生事象　obligating event
偶発負債　contingent liability
偶発利益　gain contingencies, windfall profit
クーポン　coupon
クーポン・レート　coupon rate
屑（くず）　scrap
具体的な数値　hard numbers
クッション　buffer, cushion
グッド・スタンディング　good standing

グッド・リーバー　good leaver
国　country, state
国別報告事項　Country-by-Country Report (CbC Report / CbCR)
国別報告書　Country-by-Country Report (CbC Report / CbCR)
区分　segregation 関 to segregate 〜 into three categories（〜を3つのカテゴリーに区分する）
区分（累進課税などの）　bracket
区別　distinction
組合　partnership
組合員　partner
組替　reclassification
組替仕訳　reclassification entry
組替調整（額）　reclassification adjustment
組込デリバティブ　embedded derivative
組立て　erection
繰返し　repetition
繰越し（損失などの）　carryforward 関 to carry forward tax losses（税務上の欠損金を繰り越す）
繰越期間　carryforward period
繰越欠損金　tax losses carried forward, unused tax losses, net operating loss carryforward 頻 to use [utilise] tax losses carried forward（繰越欠損金を使用する）, unused tax losses expire [are forfeited]（繰越欠損金が失効する）
繰越欠損金の切捨て　forfeiture of carried-forward tax losses
繰越欠損金の使用　use [utilisation] of tax losses 米 utilization [use] of tax losses
繰越欠損金の使用制限　restriction on the use of carried-forward tax losses
繰越控除限度超過額（外国税額控除の）　unused foreign tax (credit)
繰越控除余裕額（外国税額控除の）　unused credit limit
繰越税額控除　carryforward of unused tax credits
繰越税額控除（未使用の）　unused tax credits
繰越利益剰余金　earned surplus brought / carried forward
繰延べ　deferral, deferment
繰延資産　deferred expense [charge, expendi-

ture]　使い方注意！ 繰延資産について, deferred asset(s) という表現が使われているケースもあるが, deferred expense(s) や deferred charge(s) のほうが, 意味は通じやすい	
繰延収益	deferred income [revenue]
繰延税金	deferred tax
繰延税金資産	deferred tax asset (DTA) 頻 to recognise deferred tax assets (繰延税金資産を認識する), to reverse deferred tax assets (繰延税金資産を取り崩す)
繰延税金資産及び負債の純額	net deferred tax assets and liabilities
繰延税金費用	deferred tax expense
繰延税金負債	deferred tax liability (DTL) 頻 to recognise deferred tax liabilities (繰延税金負債を認識する), to reverse deferred tax liabilities (繰延税金負債を取り崩す)
繰延税金利益［収益］	deferred tax income
繰延損益	deferred gains and losses
繰延費用	deferred expense [charge, expenditure]
繰延ヘッジ（会計）	deferral hedge accounting
繰延ヘッジ損益	deferred gains and losses on hedges
繰戻し（損失などの）	carryback 関 to carry back a tax loss to a prior tax year (税務上の欠損を過年度に繰り戻す)
繰戻期間	carryback period
グルーピング	grouping
グループ	group
グループ化	group formation
グループ会計ポリシー	group accounting policy
グループ会計マニュアル	group accounting manual
グループ会社	group company
グループ会社間勘定	intercompany account
グループ会社間勘定の相殺消去	intercompany elimination 関 to eliminate Intercompany transactions upon consolidation (連結にあたって，グループ内取引を消去する)
グループ会社間取引による利益	intercompany profit 関 to eliminate profit in inventory resulting from intercompany transactions (棚卸資産の未実現利益を消去する)
グループ会社間の税金配分（連結納税制度に基づく）	intercompany tax allocation
グループ・コントローラー	group controller
グループ税制	group taxation (regime), group treatment
グループ取引	group transaction
グループ内役務提供	intra-group service (IGS)
グループ内債権	intercompany receivables
グループ内債権債務	intercompany [intra-group] balance, intercompany receivables and payables
グループ内債権債務管理表	intercompany receivables and payables schedule
グループ内債権債務の確認	intercompany balance confirmation
グループ内債務	intercompany payables
グループ内組織再編	intra-group reorganisation 米 intra-group reorganization
グループ内取引	intercompany [intra-group] transaction, transaction between entities of a group 頻 intercompany transactions are eliminated upon consolidation (連結にあたって，グループ内取引は消去される)
グループ内の資産及び負債	intra-group assets and liabilities
グループ内の費用付替え	intercompany cost allocation
グループ内の予定取引	forecast intra-group transaction
グループ内配当	intercompany dividend
グループの構成	composition of a group
グループの持分	group's share
グループ法人税制	group taxation (regime)
グループ・リリーフ制度	group relief
クレジット・カード	credit card
クレジット・デフォルト・スワップ	credit default swap (CDS)
クレジット・デリバティブ	credit derivative
クレジット・ノート	credit note
クロージング	closing 頻 conditions of [for] closing are satisfied (クロージングのための条件が充足される), conditions of [for]

closing are waived（クロージングのための条件が免除される）
クロージングの前提条件（買収案件などの）　condition precedent (CP), closing conditions
クロージング日　closing date
クロージング・メモ　closing memorandum
グロス・アップ　gross up
グロスアップ計算　gross-up calculation
グロスアップ条項　gross-up clause
クロスボーダー取引　cross-border transaction
クロスボーダーの買収　cross-border acquisition

け

経営幹部　key management personnel　[頻]　key management personnel compensation（経営幹部の報酬）
経営企画　corporate planning
経営企画部門　corporate planning department [division]
経営計画　management plan
経営指導　management service
経営指導念書　keepwell letter
経営指導料　management fee　[頻]　to charge a management fee（経営指導料を請求する、負担させる）, to pay a management fee（経営指導料を支払う）
経営者　management
経営者確認書　(management) representation (letter)
経営者による説明　management commentary
経営者による討議と分析　management's discussion and analysis (MD&A)
経営者による内部統制の無効化　management override of controls
経営者による評価　management assessment
経営者の見解　management's view
経営上の関与　managerial involvement
経営判断の原則　business judgement rule (BJR)　[米]　business judgment rule (BJR)
経営ビジョン　management vision
経過　progress
経過（時の）　passage of time
経過勘定　deferred and accrued accounts
経過規定　transitional provision
計画　plan
軽課税国［地域］　low tax jurisdiction
経過措置　transitional provision, transitional (temporary) measure
経験　experience
軽減　alleviation
軽減税率　reduced (tax) rate
経験則　rule of thumb
傾向　tendency, trend
警告　caveat
経済　economy
経済活動基準（タックス・ヘイブン対策税制における）　economic activity test
経済環境　economic environment
経済成長率　economic growth rate
経済的帰結　economic consequence
経済的帰属　economic allegiance
経済的資源　economic resource
経済的資源及び請求権　economic resources and claims
経済的実行可能性　economic viability
経済的実体　economic substance
経済的耐用年数　economic life　[頻]　to estimate the economic life of an asset（資産の経済的耐用年数を見積もる）
経済的特徴　economic characteristic
経済的二重課税　economic double taxation
経済的付加価値　economic value added
経済的ヘッジ　economic hedge
経済的便益　economic benefit
計算　calculation, computation
計算書　statement
計算突合　footing
形式　form, format
刑事裁判　criminal action
刑事訴追　criminal prosecution
芸術関連無形資産　artistic-related intangible asset
経常損益　ordinary profit and loss

経常損失	ordinary loss, loss before extraordinary items
経常的活動	ordinary activities
経常的取引	routine transaction
経常的な公正価値評価	recurring fair value measurement
経常ベース	recurring basis
経常利益	ordinary profit [income], profit before extraordinary items
形成	formation
係争	dispute
係争中の訴訟	pending lawsuit
継続	continuation
継続監査調書	permanent audit documentation
継続監査人	continuing auditor
継続企業	going concern 【頻】 to continue as a going concern（継続企業として存続する）
継続企業価値	going concern value
継続企業の前提	going concern assumption 【関】 substantial doubt about an entity's ability to continue as a going concern（継続企業の前提に関する重要な疑義）
継続事業	continuing operations
継続事業からの純損失	loss from continuing operations
継続事業からの純利益	profit from continuing operations
継続事業からの当期利益[損失]	profit [loss] for the year from continuing operations
継続事業からの1株当たり利益	earnings per share from continuing operations
継続性	continuity
継続中の税務調査	pending tax audit
継続的関与	continuing involvement 【頻】 continuing involvement in derecognised financial assets by type of instrument（認識の中止をした金融資産に対する継続的関与）
継続的な使用	continuing use
継続的な判定	continuous assessment
継続ベース	recurring basis
継続予算	rolling budget
競売	auction
刑罰	punishment
経費	expense
経費精算	expense reimbursement
軽微な差異	minor variance
契約	contract, agreement 【頻】 to enter into a contract with（～と契約を締結する）
契約違反	breach of contract
契約獲得の増分コスト	incremental costs of obtaining a contract
契約原価	contract cost
契約コスト	contract cost
契約資産	contract asset 【頻】 contract assets arising from contracts with customers（顧客との契約から生じた契約資産）
契約終了に係る費用	contract termination costs
契約書	contract, agreement
契約書（監査契約などの）	engagement letter
契約条件	contractual term
契約上の義務	contractual obligation
契約上のキャッシュ・フロー	contractual cash flows
契約上の権利	contractual right
契約上のコミットメント	contractual commitment
契約上の支払い	contractual payment
契約上の取決め	contractual arrangement
契約上の満期	contractual maturity
契約製造業者	contract manufacturer
契約に基づく無形資産	contract-based intangible asset
契約により合意された支配の共有	contractually agreed sharing of control
契約の結合	combination of contracts
契約の存続期間	contract duration
契約負債	contract liability
契約不履行	breach of contract
契約変更	contract modification
契約・法的要件	contractual legal criterion
契約前のコスト	pre-contract cost
契約を履行するためのコスト	cost (incurred) to fulfil a contract 【米】 cost (incurred) to fulfill a contract
経理規程	accounting manual
経理システム	accounting system
経理責任者	controller, comptroller
経理部門	accounting department [division]

経路	channel
ケース	case
結果	consequence, outcome, result
欠陥（製品などの）	defect
欠陥（内部統制などの）	deficiency, weakness
決議	resolution 頻 resolution of board of directors（取締役会決議）
決議日（配当などの）	resolution date
結合	combination
結合企業	combining entity
結合金融商品	combined instrument
決済	settlement
決済日	settlement date
決済日会計	settlement date accounting
決済方法の選択	choice of settlement
決済方法の選択肢	settlement option
決算	close, closing, book closing, financial closing
決算期末	year-end (YE)
決算財務報告プロセス	financial statement close process (FSCP)
決算修正	period-end adjustment
決算仕訳	closing entry
決算スケジュール	closing schedule
決算整理後残高試算表	post-closing trial balance
決算整理仕訳	closing entry
決算整理前残高試算表	pre-closing trial balance
決算早期化	fast close
決算手続	closing procedures
決算日	closing date, end of (accounting/reporting) period
決算日レート	closing (foreign exchange) rate 頻 to be translated at the closing rate（決算日レートで換算される）
決算日レート法	closing rate method
決算プロセス	financial statement close process (FSCP)
月次決算	monthly close [closing]
月次決算手続	monthly closing procedures
月次試算表	monthly trial balance
月次申告	monthly filing
月次統制	monthly control
月次平均	monthly average
月次報告	monthly reporting
月次報告書	monthly report
欠如	absence
欠損	deficit
欠損金（税務上の）	tax loss, net operating loss (NOL) 頻 to carry forward tax losses（欠損金を繰り越す）
欠損金（累積損失）	accumulated [cumulative] losses
欠損金控除	tax loss deduction, NOL deduction
欠損金控除限度額	limit of loss deduction
欠損金の繰越し	tax loss carryforward(s), net operating loss carryforward
欠損金の繰戻し（還付）	tax loss carryback, net operating loss carryback
決定	determination
決定（税務当局による税額の）	determination of tax liability
決定要因	determinant
欠点	drawback
結論	conclusion
結論の根拠	basis for conclusions
懸念（事項）	concern
下落	decline 頻 decline in（〜の下落）, prolonged decline（継続的な下落）
原因	cause
原価	cost
減価	depreciation
見解	outlook
限界	limit
限界税率	marginal rate of tax, marginal tax rate
限界費用	marginal cost
限界利益	marginal profit [income]
原価回収基準	cost recovery method
原価管理	cost control
原価管理システム	cost management system
原価企画	cost planning
原価基準	cost basis, cost principle
原価基準法	cost-plus method 関 to be priced at cost plus 5%（原価に5%マークアップして販売価格とされる）
原価記録	cost records
原価計算	cost accounting, costing
原価計算システム	costing system
原価差異	cost variance

原価差異分析	cost variance analysis
原価算定方式	cost formula
原価集計額	cost pool
原価集計対象	cost object

減価償却（費）　depreciation　頻 to record depreciation（expense）（減価償却費を計上する）　関 to depreciate fixed assets（固定資産を償却する）
減価償却期間　depreciation period
減価償却後の価額　depreciated value
減価償却後の再調達価額　depreciated replacement value
減価償却後の再調達コスト　depreciated replacement cost
減価償却後の帳簿価額　depreciated book value
減価償却資産　depreciable asset
減価償却済資産　fully depreciated asset
減価償却超過額　excess depreciation
減価償却費　depreciation expense [charge]
減価償却費及び支払利息控除前税引前利益　earnings before interest, tax, depreciation and amortisation (EBITDA)　米 earnings before interest, tax, depreciation and amortization
減価償却不足額　short depreciation
減価償却方法　depreciation method　頻 to determine depreciation methods（減価償却方法を決定する），to change depreciation methods（減価償却方法を変更する）
減価償却率　depreciation rate
減価償却累計額　accumulated depreciation, allowance for depreciation
原価責任単位　cost centre　米 cost center
原価で　at cost　頻 to be priced at cost（原価をもって販売価格とされる），to be sold at cost（原価で販売される）
原価低減　cost reduction
原価配分　cost allocation
原価法　cost method
原価報告書　cost report
原価モデル　cost model
研究　research
研究開発　research and development (R&D)
研究開発費　research and development (R&D) cost [expense/expenditure]
研究開発部門　research and development (R&D) department [division]
研究局面　research phase
研究費　research expense
現金　cash
現金以外の資産の流用　non-cash misappropriation
現金及び現金同等物　cash and cash equivalents
現金及び現金同等物に係る為替変動による影響額　effects of exchange rate changes on the balance of cash and cash equivalents in foreign currencies
現金及び現金同等物の期首[期末]残高　cash and cash equivalents at the beginning [end] of the year
現金及び現金同等物の増加[減少]額　net increase [decrease] in cash and cash equivalents
現金及び預金　cash and bank balances, cash on hand and in banks
現金過不足　cash over and short
現金基準　cash basis
現金決済　cash settlement
現金決済オプション　cash-settled option
現金決済型株式報酬債務　cash-settled share-based payment liability
現金決済型の株式に基づく報酬　cash-settled share-based payment
現金支出　cash outlay
現金実査　cash count, physical count (of cash)　頻 to perform a cash count（現金実査を行う）
現金支払い　cash disbursement
現金収入　cash receipt(s)
現金主義　cash basis
現金主義会計　cash (basis) accounting
現金出納帳　cash book
現金性商品　cash instrument
現金対価　cash consideration, consideration in the form of cash
現金担保　cash collateral
現金同等物　cash equivalent
現金配当　cash dividend
現金割引　cash discount
原契約　original contract

権限	authority
権限ある当局	competent authority (CA)
権限委譲	delegation of authority, empowerment
権限系統	line of authority
健康保険	health insurance
検査	inspection, examination
減殺（税金の）	abatement
現在価値	present value 頻 to discount □ to present value using a pre-tax discount rate（税引前の割引率を使って，□を現在価値に割り引く）
減債基金	sinking fund
現在原価	current cost
現在再調達原価	current replacement cost
現在の債務	present obligation
原材料	raw material
検査費用	inspection cost
検査報告書	inspection report
減算	subtraction
減算（税務上の）	deduction
原産地	origin
原産地証明（書）	certificate of origin
原産品	originating goods
減資	capital reduction [decrease], reduction [decrease] in capital, reduction of capital
見識	insight
原資産	underlying asset
原始取得原価	original cost
現実支払価格（輸入貨物についての）	transaction value
現実的手段	practical expedient
検収	acceptance
研修	training
検収（作業）	inspection
検収基準	(customer's) acceptance basis
研修資料	training materials
研修費用	training cost [expense]
検収報告書	acceptance report
検証	verification
減少	decrease, reduction 頻 decrease in（～の減少（額））
原状	original state
現状	status quo
原状回復	restoration
原状回復（用地）	site restoration
原状回復義務	restoration obligation
原状回復費用	restoration cost
検証可能価値	confirmatory value
検証可能性	verifiability
検証対象会社（移転価格税制などの）	tested company
検証手続	testing procedure
建設	construction
建設仮勘定	construction in progress 頻 to transfer construction in progress to（建設仮勘定を～に振り替える）
建設現場	building site
建設または据付プロジェクト	construction or installation project
源泉（所得などの）	source, origin
源泉所得税	withholding (income) tax
源泉所得税（日本の）	Japanese withholding tax
健全性（財務的な）	soundness
源泉税	withholding tax (WHT), tax withheld (at source)
源泉税の課税	imposition of withholding tax, taxation at source 頻 imposition of withholding tax at the rate of X%（X%での源泉税の課税）関 to be taxed at source（源泉課税される）
源泉税の税額控除	withholding tax credit
源泉徴収	withholding 関 to withhold individual [personal] income tax（所得税を源泉徴収する）
源泉徴収義務	withholding requirement [obligation], withholding tax obligation
源泉徴収義務者	withholding agent
源泉徴収の免除	withholding exemption
源泉徴収票	withholding tax statement [slip]
源泉徴収免除証明書	withholding tax exemption certificate
源泉徴収漏れ	failure to withhold
原則	principle
原則主義	principles-based
減損	impairment
減損損失	impairment loss 頻 to recognise an impairment loss（減損損失を認識する），to reverse an impairment loss（減損損失を戻入する）
減損損失の認識	recognition of impairment

losses
減損損失の戻入　reversal of impairment losses　関 an impairment loss is reversed（減損損失が戻入される）
減損損失累計額　accumulated impairment (losses)
減損テスト　impairment test(ing)　頻 to perform an impairment test（減損テストを実施する）
減損の兆候　indication of impairment　頻 there is an indication of impairment（減損の兆候がある）　関 indication that an asset may be impaired（減損の兆候）
減損利得　impairment gain
減損利得または減損損失　impairment gain or loss
現地会計基準　local GAAP
現地規制当局　local regulator
建築工事現場　building site
現地通貨　local currency
現地法人　foreign subsidiary
現地訪問［視察］　site visit
限定意見（監査報告書における）　qualified opinion
限度　limit
現場　site　頻 on site（現場の，現場に）
現場作業（監査人などの）　field work
現場訪問［視察］　site visit
現物　spot
現物確認　physical inspection
現物寄附　donation in kind
現物給付　benefits in kind
現物検査　physical inspection
現物出資　contribution in kind, in-kind contribution　頻 to make a contribution in kind to（〜に現物出資する）　関 contribute □ in kind to（〜に□を現物出資する）
現物による支払い　payment in kind (PIK)
現物分配　dividend in kind　頻 to distribute [pay (out)] a dividend in kind（現物配当を支払う），to receive a dividend in kind（現物配当を受け取る）
原本　original copy
減免　reduction or exemption, relief
券面額　face value
減耗（資源などの）　depletion
減耗（棚卸資産などの）　shrinkage
原油　crude oil
権利　right, entitlement
権利確定期間　vesting period
権利確定条件　vesting condition
権利確定条件以外の条件　non-vesting condition
権利確定日　vesting date
権利確定までの期間　vesting period
権利義務　right and obligation
権利金　key money
権利行使（オプションなどの）　exercise
権利行使価格　exercise [strike] price
権利行使可能期間　exercise period
権利行使日　exercise date

こ

行為　act
合意　agreement　頻 to reach an agreement（合意に達する）
合意価格　consensus pricing
合意事項　consensus
合意書　memorandum of understanding (MoU)
合意手続　agreed-upon procedures (AUP)
合意手続報告書　agreed-upon procedures report
効果　effect
公開会社　public company
公開買付け（株式の）　takeover bid (TOB), tender offer
公開市場　public market
公開草案　exposure draft (ED)
高額の支払い　fat payment
公から民へのサービス契約　public-to-private service arrangement
交換　exchange　頻 exchange of A for B（AとBとの交換）
交換公文　exchange of notes (E/N)
交換差金　boot
交換取引　exchange transaction

交換用部品	spare parts
恒久的施設	permanent establishment (PE) [頻] to constitute a PE (恒久的施設を構成する、PEとなる), profit attributable to a PE (恒久的施設に帰属する利益)
鉱業権	mining right
公共事業	public works
工業所有権	industrial property right
工具	tool
航空機	aircraft
航空機の機体	airframe
工具, 器具及び備品	fixtures, fittings, tools and equipment, tools, furniture and fixtures
工具費	tooling cost
合計	sum, total
合計転記	total posting
貢献	contribution
貢献度分析	contribution analysis
貢献利益	contribution margin
貢献利益率	contribution margin ratio
公告	public notice
広告 (宣伝)	advertisement
広告宣伝費	advertising cost [expense]
口座	account
交際費	entertainment cost [expense]
口座番号	account number
口座名義	account name
行使	exercise
工事	construction (work)
工事売上	construction sales
行使可能性	exercisability
工事完成基準	completed contract method
公式の計画	formal plan
公式の契約	formal agreement
公式・非公式の契約	formal / informal agreement
工事契約	construction contract
工事契約原価	(construction) contract cost
工事契約収益	(construction) contract revenue
工事契約総原価	total contract cost
工事契約総収益	total contract revenue
工事原価	(construction) contract cost
工事収益	(construction) contract revenue
工事進行基準	percentage of completion method
工事進捗度	stage of completion of contract activity
工事損失引当金	provision for loss on construction contracts
後者	latter
控除 (課税所得計算上の)	allowance, deduction [頻] deduction from (〜からの控除)
控除 (税額計算上の)	(tax) credit
交渉	negotiation [頻] to be currently under negotiation (現在交渉中である)
工場	factory, plant
工場原価	factory cost
工場敷地	factory premises
公証人	notary public
交渉力	bargaining power
工場渡し条件	ex factory, ex works (EXW)
控除限度額 (外国税額控除などの)	credit limit [limitation], maximum creditable amount
控除限度超過額 (外国税額控除の)	excess foreign taxes, foreign tax in excess of credit limit
控除対象外国法人税	creditable foreign tax, foreign tax eligible for a credit
控除余裕額 (外国税額控除の)	excess credit limit
更新 (契約などの)	renewal
更新 (再) 投資	sustaining capital reinvestment
更新選択権 [オプション] (リース契約などの)	renewal option
更生 (会社更生)	reorganisation [米] reorganization
更正 (税務当局による)	correction (of income [tax return]), (tax) reassessment
構成	structure, composition
構成員	constituent
構成員課税	pass-through taxation
公正価値	fair value
公正価値オプション	fair value option
公正価値基準	fair value principle
公正価値で測定される金融資産	financial assets measured at fair value
公正価値で測定される金融負債	financial liability at fair value
公正価値による測定	fair value measurement

こうせいか

公正価値の純変動額	net change in fair value
公正価値の変動	fair value changes
公正価値ヒエラルキー	fair value hierarchy
公正価値ヘッジ	fair value hedge
公正価値変動による評価差額	fair value reserve
公正価値モデル	fair value model
合成金融商品	synthetic instrument
公正市場価値	fair market value (FMV)
構成単位（企業などの）	constituent unit
更正通知（書）	correction notice, notice of correction, (tax) reassessment notice 〔頻〕 to receive a correction notice（更正通知書を受領する）
公正な表示	fair presentation 〔関〕 to present fairly（適正に表示する）
厚生年金基金	employees' pension fund (EPF)
厚生年金保険	employees' pension insurance
構成要素	component, constituent, building block
口銭	brokerage
控訴	appeal
構造	structure
構造改革費用引当金	provision for restructuring costs, restructuring provision
拘束力のある契約	binding agreement
拘束力のある販売契約	binding sale agreement
構築物	structure
交通費	travel cost [expense], transportation cost [expense]
工程（製造工程）	production process, manufacturing process
工程表	time schedule (of work)
公的確定給付制度	state defined benefit plan
公的制度（退職給付制度について）	state plan
合同会社	Godo Kaisha (GK)
行動規範	code of conduct
行動計画	action plan
購読	subscription
購入	purchase 〔関〕 to purchase products from related parties（関連当事者から製品を購入する）
購入価格	purchase price 〔頻〕 to be treated as a reduction in the purchase price（購入価格からの減額として取り扱われる），to allocate a purchase price among（〜（取得資産・負債など）に購入価格を配分する）
購入価格差異	purchase price variance
購入原価	cost of purchase, purchase cost
購入した信用現存金融資産	purchased credit-impaired financial asset
購入者	purchaser
購入申請書	purchase requisition
購入選択権［オプション］（リースなどの）	purchase option
購入のれん	purchased goodwill
購入のれん方式	partial goodwill method
購入品	purchased goods
購入または組成した信用減損金融資産	purchased or originated credit-impaired financial assets
後任	successor
公認会計士	certified public accountant (CPA)
後任の監査人	successor auditor
公認不正検査士	certified fraud examiner (CFE)
光熱費	heating and lighting cost [expense]
購買	purchase, procurement 〔関〕 to procure raw materials（原材料を調達する）
購買部門	purchasing department [division], procurement department [division]
購買プロセス	purchase process
購買予算	purchase [purchasing] budget
後発事象	event after reporting period, subsequent event
広範囲の従業員株式制度	broad-based employee share plan
公表	announcement, release
公表価格	quoted price
公表された価格相場	published price quotation
公表された市場価格	quoted market price
公表された税率	announced tax rate
公表された統計値	published statistics
鉱物	mineral
鉱物資源	mineral resource
公文書	official document
公平な情報開示	fair disclosure
合弁会社	joint venture
合弁事業	joint venture

公募（証券の）	public offering, public placement
広報	public relations
広報費	public relations cost [expense]
公務員	government [public] official
項目	item　頻item by item（項目ごとに）
項目（財務諸表における）	line item
項目別控除	itemised deduction　米itemized deduction
小売	retail
小売業者	retailer
合理性	reasonableness
効率性	efficiency
高率部分の税額	excess tax
合理的な根拠	rationale
合理的な保証	reasonable assurance
合理的な見積り	reasonable estimate
小売物価指数	retail price index (RPI)
コード	code
コーポレート・ガバナンス・コード	corporate governance code
コーポレート・ファイナンス	corporate finance
コール・オプション	call option
コール・ローン	call loan
誤解	misunderstanding
子会社	subsidiary (company)　頻to establish a subsidiary（子会社を設立する），to liquidate a subsidiary（子会社を清算する），to sell a subsidiary（子会社を売却する）
子会社，共同支配企業及び関連会社に対する投資	investments in subsidiaries, jointly controlled entities, and associates
子会社層の子会社（第1階層の子会社）	first-tier subsidiary,　使い方注意!子会社Aの下に子会社Bがある場合，子会社Aがfirst-tier（子会社層）で，子会社Bがsecond-tier（孫会社層）ということになる
子会社に対する支配の喪失	loss of control of subsidiary
子会社に対する所有持分の変動	change in the level of ownership interest in subsidiary
子会社に対する投資	investment in a subsidiary
子会社に対する持分	interest in a subsidiary
子会社の取得	acquisition of subsidiary
子会社の取得による支出（取得時の現金受入額控除後）	net cash outflow on acquisition of subsidiaries
子会社の処分［売却］	disposal of subsidiary
子会社の売却による収入（売却時の現金保有額控除後）	net cash inflow on disposal of subsidiaries
小切手	cheque　米check
小切手台帳	cheque register　米check register
小切手帳	cheque book　米check book
小切手の改竄	cheque tampering　米check tampering
顧客	customer
顧客からの預り金	deposits from customers
顧客関連無形資産	customer-related intangible asset
顧客との関係	customer relationship
顧客との契約	contract with a customer
顧客との契約から生じた収益	revenue from contracts with customers
顧客による検収（棚卸資産などの）	customer acceptance
顧客による検収報告書	customer's acceptance report
顧客のオプション	customer's option
顧客の権利不行使（未使用商品券など）	customer's unexercised rights
顧客リスト	customer list
国外関連者	foreign related party [person]
国外関連者に対する寄附金	donation to foreign related party
国外関連取引	foreign related transaction, controlled transaction
国外居住者	expatriate
国外源泉所得	foreign source income
国外支配株主	foreign controlling shareholder
国外転出時課税（制度）	exit tax
国外配当	foreign dividend
国外配当免税	exemption for foreign dividend
国債	government bond, sovereign bond
国際会計基準（書）	International Accounting Standard (IAS)
国際課税	international taxation

国際財務報告基準（書）	International Financial Reporting Standard (IFRS) 【頻】 to adopt IFRS（IFRSを採用する），in accordance with IFRS（IFRSに準拠して）
国際財務報告基準の初度適用	first-time adoption of IFRS
国際的二重課税	international double taxation
国税	national tax
国税局	Regional Tax(ation) Bureau
国税庁	National Tax Agency (NTA)
国税庁長官	Commissioner (of the National Tax Agency)
国税不服審判所	National Tax Tribunal
小口現金	petty cash
小口現金出納帳	petty cash book
小口現金伝票	petty cash slip
国内売上	domestic sales
国内源泉所得	domestic source income
国内子会社	domestic subsidiary
国内における二重課税	domestic double taxation
国内配当	domestic dividend
国内法（国内税法）	domestic tax law
国有化	nationalisation 【米】nationalization
誤差脱漏	errors and omissions (E&O)
個人	individual
個人事業	(sole) proprietorship
個人事業者	sole proprietor [trader]
個人所得税	personal [individual] income tax
個人所得税率	personal [individual] income tax rate
個人的購入（会社経費などによる）	personal purchase
個人持株会社	personal holding company
コスト・アプローチ（評価手法としての）	cost approach
コスト・オブジェクト	cost object
コスト・カバレッジ	cost coverage
コスト・センター	cost centre 【米】cost center
コスト・ドライバー	cost driver
コストの制約	cost constraint
コスト・プラス契約	cost plus contract
コスト分析	cost analysis
国庫補助金	government grant
固定価格	fixed price
固定価格契約	fixed price contract
固定価格方式（買収価格の調整における）	locked box
固定間接費	fixed overhead
固定間接費差異	fixed overhead variance
固定金利	fixed interest rate
固定金利債券	fixed-rate debt
固定金利ローン	fixed-rate loan
固定項目	non-current item
固定資産	fixed asset, non-current asset
固定資産除却損	loss on disposal of fixed assets
固定資産除却損（有形固定資産除却損）	loss on disposal of property, plant and equipment
固定資産処分損	loss on disposal of fixed assets
固定資産処分損（有形固定資産処分損）	loss on disposal of property, plant and equipment
固定資産税	fixed assets tax, property tax
固定資産台帳	fixed asset ledger [register]
固定資産売却益	gain on sale of fixed assets
固定資産売却益（有形固定資産売却益）	gain on sale of property, plant and equipment
固定資産売却損	loss on sale of fixed assets
固定資産売却損（有形固定資産売却損）	loss on sale of property, plant and equipment
固定支払い	fixed payment
固定製造間接費	fixed overhead
固定製造費用	fixed manufacturing cost
固定費	fixed [standing] cost
固定比率	fixed assets to net worth ratio
固定負債	non-current liability
固定報酬	fixed fee
固定満期	fixed maturity
固定利付金融商品	fixed-rate instrument
異なる決算期	differing year-ends
異なる（事業）年度末	non-coterminous year-ends
5年間の事業計画	five-year business plan
誤謬	error 【頻】errors arising from（〜により発生した誤謬）
誤謬の訂正	correction of error
個別原価計算	job (order) costing

個別財務諸表　separate [non-consolidated] financial statements
個別財務諸表（親会社の）　parent-only financial statements, parent-only accounts
個別資産　individual asset
個別の減損（営業債権などの）　individual impairment
個別の事象　discrete event
個別費　specific cost
個別評価金銭債権に対する貸倒引当金　specific provision for bad debt
個別法　specific identification of costs, specific identification method
コマーシャル・インタンジブル　commercial intangible
コマーシャル・デュー・デリジェンス　commercial due diligence
コマーシャル・ペーパー　commercial paper (CP)
コミッショネア（問屋）　commissionaire, general commission agent
コミットメント　commitment
コメンタリー（OECDモデル租税条約などの）　commentary
コモディティ　commodity
コモディティ価格リスク　commodity price risk
コモディティ・スワップ　commodity swap
顧問弁護士　legal counsel, legal adviser [advisor]
固有リスク　inherent risk
雇用　employment
誤用　misuse
雇用契約（書）　employment contract
雇用契約書　offer letter
雇用者　employer
雇用促進税制（日本）　tax credit for job creation
雇用主負担の社会保険拠出　employer's contribution to social security
雇用保険　employment insurance
コリドー（回廊）　corridor
コリドー（回廊）アプローチ（旧）　corridor approach
ゴルフ会員権　golf club membership 頻 write-off of golf club membership（ゴルフ会員権の評価減）, to write off golf club membership（ゴルフ会員権を評価減する）
根拠　grounds
根拠資料　supporting [source] document, supporting evidence 頻 to provide supporting documents for（〜の根拠資料を提供する）
混合　mixture
混合契約　hybrid contract
コンサルタント　consultant
コンサルタント契約　consultancy agreement
コンサルティング　consulting
コンサルティング契約　consulting agreement
コンサルティング・サービス　consulting service
コンサルティング費用　consulting expense [fee]
コンソーシアム　consortium
コントローラー　controller
コントロール・セルフ・アセスメント　control self assessment (CSA)
コントロール・プレミアム　control premium
コンバージェンス　convergence
コンピュータ機器　computer equipment
コンピュータ・ソフトウェア　computer software
コンピュータ利用監査技法　computer assisted audit techniques (CAAT)
コンファーマトリー・デュー・デリジェンス　confirmatory due diligence
コンフォート・レター　comfort letter
コンプライアンス監査　compliance audit
コンプライアンス・プログラム　compliance programme 米compliance program
梱包　packing
梱包（資）材　packaging material
梱包明細　packing list
コンポーネント・アプローチ（減価償却の）　component approach
コンポーネント単位の減価償却　component depreciation

さ

サービス委譲契約　service concession arrangement
サービス条件　service condition
サービス水準に係る合意　service level agreement (SLA)
サービス提供者　service provider
サービスの提供による収益　revenue from rendering of services
サービス PE　service PE
サービス・フィー　service fee
差異　difference, variance
財　goods　[頻]goods sold directly to consumers（消費者に直接販売される財），goods sold through intermediaries（仲介業者を通じて販売される財）
災害　disaster, casualty
在外営業活動体　foreign operation
在外営業活動体に対する純投資　net investment in a foreign operation
在外営業活動体に対する純投資のヘッジ　hedge of a net investment in a foreign operation
在外営業活動体の換算　translation of foreign operation
在外営業活動体の換算差額（為替換算調整勘定）　exchange differences on translating foreign operations, currency translation differences
在外管轄地域　foreign jurisdiction
在外管轄地域における税率の影響　effect of tax rates in foreign jurisdictions
災害損失　loss on disaster, casualty loss
災害損失引当金　provision for loss on disaster
再開発　redevelopment
再監査　reaudit
最恵国待遇条項　most favoured nation clause　[米]most favored nation clause
再計算　recalculation, recomputation
裁決　decision　[頻]decision taken [made] by the National Tax Tribunal（国税不服審判所の裁決）
裁決機関　tribunal
債券　bond, debt securities
債権　receivables　[頻]to collect receivables（債権を回収する），receivables due from related parties（関連当事者に対する債権）
債権回転率　receivables turnover
債券格付け　bond rating
債権金額　amounts receivable
債権債務　receivables and payables
債権債務管理表　receivables and payables schedule
債券先物　bond futures
債券市場　bond market
債権者　creditor, debt holder
債権者集会　creditors (') meeting
債権者保護　creditor protection
債券償還　bond redemption
債権譲渡　transfer [assignment] of receivables
債券ディスカウント　bond discount
再検討　reconsideration
債券投資　fixed income investment
債券プレミアム　bond premium
債権放棄　debt waiver, forgiveness of debt, cancellation of debt (COD)　[頻]to offer debt waiver（債権放棄を申し出る），to implement debt waiver（債権放棄を実行する）　[関]to waive debt（債権放棄する）
債権放棄損　loss on debt waiver
債券保有者　bondholder
債券利回り　bond yield
在庫　stock, inventory
最高管理責任者　chief administrative officer (CAO)
最高経営意思決定者　chief operating decision maker (CODM)
最高経営責任者　chief executive officer (CEO)
最高コンプライアンス責任者　chief compliance officer (CCO)
最高裁判所　Supreme Court
最高財務責任者　chief financial officer (CFO)
最高執行責任者　chief operating officer (COO)
再構築　restructuring　[関]to restructure operations（事業を再構築する）

再購入	repurchase
在庫回転期間	「棚卸資産回転期間」の項を参照
在庫回転率	「棚卸資産回転率」の項を参照
在庫管理	inventory management
在庫管理システム	inventory management system
在庫管理表	inventory book
在庫記録	inventory records
在庫水準	inventory [stock] level
在庫の動き	flow of inventories
在庫評価	inventory [stock] valuation
在庫不足	inventory shortage
在庫リスク	inventory risk
再査定	reassessment
財産	estate
採算可能性	economic feasibility
財産税	property tax
再実施（監査人による）	reperformance
再指定	redesignation
最終親会社	ultimate parent
最終契約	definitive agreement (DA)
最終顧客	final customer
最終仕入原価法	last purchase price method, most recent purchase method
最終支払い	final payment
最終税額	final tax
最終的な支配当事者	ultimate controlling party
再取得	reacquisition
再取得した権利	reacquired right
最小	minimum
最小化	minimisation 米 minimization
再上場	relisting
最初のIFRS財務諸表	first IFRS financial statements
最初のIFRS報告期間	first IFRS reporting period
最初の適用	initial adoption [application]
再生	revitalisation 米 revitalization
再生産原価	reproduction cost
財政状態	financial position
財政状態計算書	statement of financial position
財政状態の悪化	financial deterioration [difficulties]
財政状態の変動	change in financial position
財政政策	fiscal policy
最善の実務	best practice
最善の努力	best efforts
最善の見積り	best estimate
再測定	remeasurement 関 to be remeasured at each balance sheet date（毎期，貸借対照表日で再測定される）
最大	maximum
最大化	maximisation 米 maximization
最大のエクスポージャー	maximum exposure 頻 maximum exposure to credit risk（信用リスクに対する最大のエクスポージャー）
再担保	repledge
再調査	reinvestigation
再調査の請求（税務当局に対する）	request for reinvestigation
差異調整	reconciliation
再調整	rearrangement, rebalancing
再調達価額	replacement value
再調達原価	replacement [repurchase] cost
裁定（裁判所などの）	ruling
裁定（取引）	arbitrage
最低限の開示	minimum disclosure
最低限の開示要求	minimum disclosure requirements
最低支払リース料	minimum lease payment
最低支払レンタル料	minimum rental payment
最低積立要件	minimum funding requirement
最低リース料支払額	minimum lease payment
最低レンタル料支払額	minimum rental payment
最適資本構成	optimal capital structure
再投資	reinvestment
再投資比率	reinvestment rate
サイド・レター	side letter
再配賦	reallocation
裁判	trial
裁判外紛争処理	alternative dispute resolution (ADR)
裁判所	court, tribunal
再販売価格	resale price

さいはんば

再販売価格基準法　resale price method (RPM)
再評価　revaluation, reassessment, rerating
再評価額　revalued amount
再評価資産　revalued assets
再評価剰余金　revaluation surplus, revaluation reserve
再評価モデル　revaluation model
再表示（過年度の財務諸表などの）　recasting
差異分析　variance analysis
再分配　redistribution
再分類　reclassification　関 to be reclassified as [to]（〜として再分類される）
再保険　reinsurance
再保険会社　reinsurance company
再保険契約　reinsurance contract
再保険資産　reinsurance asset
再保険者　reinsurer
財またはサービス　goods or services　頻 goods or services transferred at a point in time（一時点で移転される財またはサービス）, goods or services transferred over time（一定の期間にわたり移転される財またはサービス）
債務　obligation, payables　頻 to settle an obligation（債務を弁済する）, payables to related parties（関連当事者に対する債務）
財務及び営業の方針　financial and operating policies
財務概況　financial review
財務会計基準機構（日本）　Financial Accounting Standards Foundation (FASF)
財務概要　financial review
財務活動　financing activity
財務活動によるキャッシュ・フロー　cash flows from financing activities, financing cash flows
財務業績　financial performance
債務金額　amounts payable
財務構成　financial structure
財務構成要素アプローチ　financial component approach
財務構造　financial structure
財務コントローラー　financial controller
財務支援　financial assistance [support]　頻 to provide financial support for（〜に対する財務支援を行う）, to withdraw financial support for（〜に対する財務支援を中止する）, to provide financial support to a subsidiary（子会社に財務支援を行う）
財務指標　financial metric
債務者　debtor, obligator
財務省　Ministry of Finance (MOF)
財務状況　financial situation
財務上の意味合い　financial implication
財務上の仮定　financial assumption
財務上の困難　financial difficulties [distress]
財務情報　financial information
財務省令　Ministry of Finance Ordinance
財務諸表　financial statements　頻 to prepare financial statements（財務諸表を作成する）, financial statements are authorised for issue（財務諸表の公表が承認される）
財務諸表監査　financial statement audit
財務諸表注記　notes to financial statements
財務諸表の構成要素　element of financial statements
財務諸表の作成　preparation [compilation] of financial statements
財務諸表の作成業務　compilation engagement
財務諸表の承認　authorisation of financial statements　米 authorization of financial statements
財務諸表の対象期間　period covered by financial statements
財務諸表の発行承認日　date of authorisation for issue of financial statements　米 date of authorization for issue of financial statements
財務諸表の表示　presentation of financial statements
財務諸表の利用者　user of financial statements
財務諸表の例　example financial statements
財務諸表不正　financial statement fraud
財務制限条項　financial covenants, debt covenants　頻 to be in compliance with financial covenants（財務制限条項を遵守している）, to be in non-compliance with financial covenants（財務制限条項を遵守していない）

230

財務制限条項（借入金に係る）　loan covenant
財務制限条項の免除（借入金に係る）　loan covenant waiver
財務制限条項への抵触に係る免除　waiver of the breach of covenant
債務整理　debt restructuring
財務責任者　treasurer
財務担当者　treasurer
債務担保証券　collateralised debt obligation (CDO)　［米］collateralized debt obligation (CDO)
債務超過　insolvency, negative equity, capital deficit
財務データ　financial data
財務的影響　financial effect
財務デュー・デリジェンス　financial due diligence (FDD)　［頻］to perform financial due diligence（財務デュー・デリジェンスを実施する）
債務引受　debt assumption
財務費用　finance charge (cost)
財務比率　financial ratio
財務部門　finance department [division], treasury department [division]
債務不履行　default
債務不履行及び契約違反　defaults and breaches
債務不履行の確率　probability of default
財務分析　financial analysis
債務弁済　debt retirement
財務報告　financial reporting
財務報告に係る内部統制　internal control over financial reporting (ICOFR)
財務報告に関する概念フレームワーク　Conceptual Framework for Financial Reporting
財務報告目的の　for financial reporting purposes
債務保証　financial guarantee　［頻］to provide financial guarantee for subsidiaries' liabilities（子会社の負債に対して債務保証を行う）
債務保証契約　financial guarantee contract
債務保証損失引当金　provision for loss on guarantees
債務免除　debt waiver, forgiveness of debt, cancellation of debt (COD)　［頻］to request debt waiver（債務免除を要請する）, to receive debt waiver from（〜から債務免除を受ける）　［関］debt is waived（債務が免除される）
債務免除益　gain on debt waiver, gain on forgiveness of debt, cancellation of debt (COD) income
財務予測　financial forecast [projection]
財務リスク　financial risk
財務リスク管理　financial risk management
債務レバレッジ　debt leveraging
財務レバレッジ　financial leverage
最有効使用［利用］　highest and best use
採用　recruitment
採用費用　recruiting cost [expense]
再リース　secondary lease
再リース期間　secondary (lease) period
再リース料（支払い）　secondary lease payment
裁量　discretion　［頻］at management's discretion（マネジメントの裁量で［により］）
材料　material
裁量権のある配当　discretionary dividend
裁量権のある有配当性　discretionary participation feature
裁量権のない配当　non-discretionary dividend
材料在庫　materials inventory
材料消費高　materials consumed
材料費　material cost
材料歩留　material yield
材料元帳　materials ledger
サイロ　silo
詐欺　deception, scam
先入先出法　first-in, first-out (FIFO)
先取特権　lien
先日付小切手　post-dated cheque　［米］post-dated check
先物　future(s)
先物為替レート　forward exchange rate
先物契約　futures contract
先物市場　futures market
先物取引契約　futures contract
先物取引所　futures exchange
先物レート　forward rate

作業　　job, work
作業時間　　labour hour　㊗labor hour
作業時間差異　　direct labour efficiency variance　㊗direct labor efficiency variance
作業時間報告書　　time report
作業指示書　　job order, work order (W/O)
先渡契約　　forward contract
先渡契約に含まれる直物の要素　　spot element of a forward contract
先渡取引　　forward(s)
差金決済　　cash settlement
削減　　reduction, curtailment
作成（財務諸表などの）　　compilation　㊗to compile financial statements（財務諸表を作成する）
作成（財務諸表や税務申告書などの）　　preparation　㊗to prepare financial statements（財務諸表を作成する）, to prepare tax returns（税務申告書を作成する）
作成者（財務諸表や税務申告書などの）　　preparer
作表　　tabulation
差入保証金　　guarantee [security] deposits
差押え　　attachment
差替え　　replacement
差替えの権利　　right of substitution
雑勘定　　sundry account
雑勘定（貸方）　　sundry creditors
雑勘定（借方）　　sundry debtors
雑益　　miscellaneous income
雑収入　　miscellaneous income
雑損　　miscellaneous loss
雑損益　　miscellaneous income and loss
雑損失　　miscellaneous loss
雑費　　miscellaneous [misc] expense
サブカテゴリー　　sub-category
サブプロセス　　sub-process
サプライ・チェーン　　supply chain
サプライ・チェーン・マネジメント　　supply chain management (SCM)
サブリース　　sub-lease
サブリース料　　sub-lease payment
サブ連結　　sub-consolidation
差別　　discrimination
差別化　　differentiation
参加　　participation

参加型資本性金融商品　　participating equity instrument
参加型優先株式　　participating preferred stock
残額　　remaining amount
三角合併　　triangular merger
参加者　　participant
残価保証　　residual value guarantee
産業　　industry
算式　　formula
参照　　reference　㊙reference to（〜の参照）
残存価額［価値］　　residual [salvage] value
残存勤務期間　　remaining service period
残存償却期間（無形資産などの）　　remaining amortisation period　㊗remaining amortization period
残存耐用年数　　remaining useful life
残存履行義務　　remaining performance obligation
残高　　balance
残高確認　　balance confirmation
残高確認依頼（書）　　balance confirmation request
残高確認書［状］　　balance confirmation letter
残高試算表　　trial balance (T/B)
暫定的な金額　　provisional amount
暫定的な評価　　provisional value
暫定的な評価の修正　　adjustments to provisional values
暫定的に測定された公正価値　　fair values measured on a provisional basis
サンプリング　　sampling
残余　　remainder
残余アプローチ　　residual approach
残余アプローチ（独立販売価格の見積りの際の）　　residual value method
残余財産　　residual assets
残余財産請求権　　residual claim
残余財産の分配　　distribution of residual assets
残余持分　　residual interest
残余利益　　residual income (RI)
残余利益分割法　　residual profit split method (RPSM)
残余利益分析　　residual analysis

し

シークレット・コンパラブル　secret comparable
仕入　purchase
仕入運賃　freight in
仕入価格　purchase price
仕入価格差異　purchase price variance
仕入債務　(trade) accounts payable, trade payables
仕入債務及びその他の債務　trade and other payables
仕入債務回転期間　accounts payable turnover period, days payable outstanding (DPO), average payment period
仕入債務回転率　accounts payable turnover (A/P turnover)
仕入先　supplier, vendor
仕入値引　purchase allowance
仕入のカットオフ（締切）　purchase cut-off
仕入返品（仕入戻し高）　purchase return
仕入元帳　purchase [bought] ledger
仕入割引　purchase discount
仕入割戻し　purchase rebate
シェアード・サービス　shared service
ジェネラル・パートナー　general partner (GP)
ジェネラル・パートナーシップ　general partnership
シェルフ・カンパニー　shelf company
支援　assistance, support　頻 assistance from (〜からの支援)
時価　fair market value (FMV)
仕掛役務　services in progress
仕掛中の研究　in-process research
仕掛中の研究開発プロジェクト　in-process research and development project
仕掛品　work in process [progress] (WIP)
資格　qualification
時価総額　market capitalisation [cap]　米 market capitalization
時価のある有価証券　quoted securities
時価のない有価証券　unquoted securities
時価評価　mark to market, mark-to-market valuation
時価評価課税　mark-to-market taxation
時間外労働　overtime
時間差異（直接労務費に係る）　direct labour efficiency variance　米 direct labor efficiency variance
時間単価（報酬，賃金等の）　hourly rate
時間的価値　time value
次期　「翌期」の項を参照
閾値　threshold
敷金　security [lease] deposit
次期繰越　carried forward (c/f)
敷地　site
識別　identification
識別可能資産　identifiable asset
識別可能性　identifiability
識別可能性要件（無形資産についての）　identifiability criteria
識別可能な純資産　identifiable net assets
識別可能な負債　identifiable liability
識別可能な無形資産　identifiable intangible asset
直物　spot
直物為替レート　spot exchange rate
事業　business, operation　頻 to wind down operations（事業を縮小する），to cease operations（事業を停止する）
事業概況報告事項（マスター・ファイル）　master file
事業外資産　non-operating asset
事業慣行　business practice
事業基準（タックス・ヘイブン対策税制）　business purpose test　頻 to satisfy the business purpose test（事業基準を充足する），to fail the business purpose test（事業基準を充足しない）
事業規模　operating capacity, business size
事業計画　business plan
事業継続計画　business continuity plan(ning) (BCP)
事業継続マネジメント　business continuity management (BCM)
事業再生　turnaround, business revitalisation　米 business revitalization

事業再編　restructuring
事業再編費用　restructuring charge
事業資産　operating asset
事業所　office
事業譲渡　transfer of business, business transfer
事業所税　business office [occupancy] tax
事業税　enterprise [business] tax, local enterprise [business] tax
事業税資本割　capital component of enterprise [business] tax
事業税所得割　income-based enterprise [business] tax
事業税申告書　enterprise [business] tax return
事業税の外形標準課税　size-based enterprise [business] tax
事業税付加価値割　added value component of enterprise [business] tax
事業整理　business workout
事業税率　enterprise [business] tax rate
事業セグメント　operating [business] segment
事業セグメントからの除外　exclusion from operating segments
事業戦略　business strategy
事業体　entity
事業主　proprietor
事業主掛金　employer contributions
事業主による拠出（退職給付制度などへの）　contributions (paid) by an employer
事業年度　financial [fiscal] year (FY)　関 for the year ended 31 March 202X（202X年3月31日に終了した事業年度の）
事業の管理の場所　place of management
事業の結合　combination of businesses
事業の中断　business interruption
事業買収契約　business purchase agreement
事業評価　business valuation
事業部　division
事業部門　business unit, line of business
事業分離　business divestiture
事業分離日　business divestiture date
事業モデルによるテスト　business model test
事業リスク　business risk, operational risk
事業を行う一定の場所　fixed place of business
事業を行う場所　place of business
資金　cash, fund
資金移動　transfer of funds
資金管理　cash management
資金還流　repatriation
資金拠出　funding
資金繰り　cash flow management
資金繰り表　cash flow worksheet
資金繰り表（予測）　cash balance projection
資金残高予測　cash balance projection
資金需要　cash requirements
資金生成単位　cash-generating unit (CGU)　頻 to identity □ as a cash-generating unit（□を資金生成単位として特定する）, goodwill is allocated to each cash-generating unit for the purpose of impairment testing（のれんは減損テスト目的で各資金生成単位に配分される）
資金調達　financing (arrangement)
資金調達源　source of funds
資金調達費用　financing cost
資金同等物　cash-like item
資金不足　cash shortage [shortfall]
資金流出　cash outflow
資金流入　cash inflow
治具　jig
資源　resource
試験研究費　research and development (R&D) cost [expense/expenditure]
試験研究費の税額控除　research and development (R&D) tax credit, tax credit for research and development (R&D) expenditure
自己宛小切手（銀行の）　cashier's cheque　米 cashier's check
施行（法令の）　enforcement
時効　statute of limitations　頻 statute of limitations for the assessment and collection of taxes（税金の賦課及び徴収に関する時効）, closure of a statute of limitations（時効の到来）, a statute of limitations expires（時効が到来する）
自己株式　treasury share [stock], own share
自己株式の取得　purchase [acquisition] of treasury shares, buyback of ordinary

shares, share buyback	
自己株式の取得費用	share buyback cost
自己株式の消却	cancellation [retirement] of treasury shares
自己株式の処分	disposal of treasury shares
事後監査	post audit
自己建設資産	self-constructed assets
自己査定	self assessment
自己資本	equity (capital), owner's equity
自己資本規制	capital requirements
自己資本規制の遵守	compliance with capital requirements
自己資本の十分性	capital adequacy
自己資本比率	equity ratio
自己資本利益率	return on equity (ROE)
自己使用不動産	owner-occupied property
自己所有の土地	freehold land
事後設立	post-formation acquisition (of assets)
自己創設の無形資産	internally generated intangible assets
自己創設のれん	internally generated goodwill, self-generated goodwill
仕事	work, job
仕事量	workload
事後のコスト	subsequent cost
事後の支出	subsequent expenditure
事後の測定	subsequent measurement
資産	asset
資産化	capitalisation ㋞ capitalization ㋕ to be capitalised as an asset（資産計上される）
資産回転率	asset turnover
資産化された利息	capitalised interest ㋞ capitalized interest
資産化した開発支出	capitalised development expenditure ㋞ capitalized development expenditure
資産化した金利コスト	interest cost capitalised ㋞ interest cost capitalized
資産化に適格な借入コスト	borrowing costs eligible for capitalisation ㋞ borrowing costs eligible for capitalization
資産化の開始	commencement of capitalisation ㋞ commencement of capitalization
資産化の開始日	commencement date for capitalisation ㋞ commencement date for capitalization
資産化の終了	cessation of capitalisation ㋞ cessation of capitalization
資産化の中止	suspension of capitalisation ㋞ suspension of capitalization
資産化への適格性	eligibility for capitalisation ㋞ eligibility for capitalization
資産化率	capitalisation rate (cap rate) ㋞ capitalization rate
資産グループ	group of assets
資産計上	capitalisation ㋞ capitalization
資産合計	total assets
資産再評価	asset revaluation
資産取得	asset acquisition
資産上限額	asset ceiling
資産除去債務	asset retirement obligation (ARO)
資産性所得（旧タックス・ヘイブン対策税制における）	passive income
資産全体	asset in its entirety
資産担保金融	asset-backed financing
資産担保証券	asset backed securities (ABS)
資産取引	asset deal
資産に関する補助金	grant related to assets, asset-related grant
資産に対する支配	control of an asset
持参人（小切手などの）	bearer
資産の買換え	replacement of property
資産の解体、撤去及び原状回復のコスト	asset dismantlement, removal and restoration costs
資産の稼働能力部分	capacity portion of an asset
資産の減損	impairment of assets
資産の交換	exchange of assets [properties]
資産の種類	class of assets
資産の所在地	location of assets
資産の有効活用	asset utilisation ㋞ asset utilization
資産の流用	asset misappropriation
資産売却	asset sale
資産買収	asset acquisition [purchase], asset deal ㋡ to make an asset acquisition（資産買収を行う） ㋕ to acquire assets（資産買収を行う）

資産買収契約	asset purchase agreement (APA)
試算表	trial balance (T/B)
資産負債アプローチ	asset and liability approach
資産を取り替える権利	right of substitution
指示	instruction
支持可能な情報	supportable information
事実	fact
事実及び状況	facts and circumstances
事実上の支配	de facto control
事実上の力（パワー）	de facto power
事実上の標準	de facto standard
事実分析	factual analysis
自社利用のソフトウェア	internal-use software
支出	expenditure, spending, disbursement
市場	market
事象	event 頻 an event occurs（事象が発生する）
市場価格	market price [value] 頻 to be priced at market value（市場価格をもって販売価格とされる），to be sold at market value（市場価格で販売される）
市場価格リスク	market price risk
市場価値	market value (MV)
市場金利よりも低利の金利	bellow-market rate of interest
市場参加者	market participant
市場指標	market index
市場条件	market condition, market-based performance condition
市場浸透	market penetration
市場性	marketability
市場性のある証券	marketable securities
市場性のない証券	non-marketable securities
市場調査	market research
市場における類似会社	market comparable company
市場の裏付けのあるインプット	market-corroborated input
市場の趨勢	market trend
事象の性質	nature of the event
市場の賃貸料	market rentals
市場の予想	market expectations
市場倍率	market multiple
市場比較法	market comparison technique
市場分析	market analysis
市場ベースの測定（値）	market-based measurement
市場利子率	market interest rate
市場リスク	market risk
市場利回り	market yield
指針	guideline 頻 guideline for（～に対する指針）
地震	earthquake
地震関連費用	earthquake-related expenses
指数	index
指数化	indexation
システム監査	(information) system audit
姿勢	stance
事前確定届出給与	pre-notified director's compensation
事前確認（移転価格税制に関する）	advance pricing arrangement [agreement] (APA) 頻 to obtain an APA（APAを取得する）
事前確認（税務当局に対する）	advance ruling 頻 to apply for an advance ruling（事前確認を申請する），to obtain an advance ruling（事前確認を得る）
事前確認（文書による）	letter ruling
事前確認の有無（移転価格税制に関する）	APA status
自然災害	natural disaster
事前承認	prior [advance] approval, pre-approval 頻 prior approval of tax authorities（税務当局の事前承認）
事前相談（税務当局への）	pre-filing consultation
事前通知	prior [advance] notice
事前通知のない実地調査	dawn raid
事前の同意	prior consent 頻 prior consent of tax authorities（税務当局の事前の同意）
仕損	spoilage
下請業者	subcontractor
下請契約	subcontract
下側	downside
示談	out-of-court settlement
市町村	municipality
市町村税事務所	municipal tax office
市町村民税（住民税）	municipal tax

市町村民税均等割	per capita municipal tax
失業	unemployment
実現	realisation ㊊ realization
実現（含み損益の）	crystallisation ㊊ crystallization
実現可能価額	realisable value ㊊ realizable value
実現可能性	realisability ㊊ realisability
実現主義	realisation principle ㊊ realization principle
実現損益	realised gains and losses ㊊ realized gains and losses
実現利益	realised profit ㊊ realized profit
失効	expiration, forfeiture ［頻］ forfeiture of tax losses carried forward（繰越欠損金の失効）
執行	execution
実行	implementation
実行（取引などの）	execution
実行可能性	feasibility
実行可能性が非常に高い予定取引	highly probable forecast transaction
実行可能性分析	feasibility analysis
実効金利	effective interest rate
実効金利法	effective interest method
実行者（不正などの）	perpetrator
実効税率	effective (income) tax rate
実効税率の調整（表）	reconciliation of effective tax rate
失効日	expiration date
実行不可能性	impracticability
執行役員	corporate officer, executive officer
実効利子率	effective interest rate
失効率	forfeiture rate
実査	physical count, physical inspection ［頻］「現金実査」の項を参照
実際運用収益（制度資産の）	actual return on plan assets
実際原価	actual cost
実際原価計算	actual costing
実際残高への修正（棚卸後の）	book to physical adjustment
実在性	existence
実際生産能力	actual capacity
実際（負担）税率	actual tax rate
実質	substance
実質支配（関係）	de facto control
実質収益率	real rate of return
実質主義	substance over form
実質所得	real income
実質的な権利	substantive rights
実質的な受益者	beneficial owner
実質的に施行されている税率	substantially enacted tax rate
実質利子率	real interest rate
実証的監査手続	substantive audit procedure
実績	track record
実績による修正（数理計算上の仮定などの）	experience adjustment
実績ボラティリティ	historical volatility
実体	substance
実体基準（タックス・ヘイブン対策税制）	substance test ［頻］ to satisfy the substance test（実体基準を充足する）, to fail the substance test（実体基準を充足しない）
実地監査	field audit
実地作業	field work
実地税務調査	field (tax) audit
実地棚卸（在庫の）	inventory count, physical inventory (count) ［頻］ to perform an inventory count（実地棚卸を行う）
実地調査	field audit
質的特性	qualitative characteristics
質的要素	qualitative factor
失敗	failure
実費精算契約（開発業務などの）	time-and-materials contract
実務	practice
実務家	practitioner
実務上の便法	practical expedient
質問	enquiry, query, question ［頻］ to make an enquiry（質問する）, to ask a question（質問する）
質問書	questionnaire
実用新案権	utility model right
実用性	practicality
指定	designation ［頻］ designation of a hedging relationship（ヘッジ指定）［関］ a derivative instrument is designated as a hedging instrument（デリバティブがヘッ

ジ手段として指定される）
指定銀行　designated bank
指定銀行口座　designated bank account
指定の取消し（ヘッジなどの）　revocation of previous designations
支店　branch　頻 to establish a branch（支店を設置する), to close a branch（支店を閉鎖する）
時点　point of [in] time
支店会計　branch accounting
支店勘定　branch account
支店財務諸表　branch financial statements
自動更新契約　evergreen contract　関 This contract is automatically renewed（この契約は自動更新される）
自動的情報交換　Automatic Exchange of Information (AEOI)
自動的に訂正されない誤謬　non-counterbalancing error
自動的に訂正される誤謬（期ズレなど）　counterbalancing error
品切れ　inventory shortage
シナジー（効果）　synergy
シナジー効果の価値　synergistic value
シナジー効果を生むような買手（買収案件などの）　synergistic buyer
シナリオ　scenario
シナリオ分析　scenario analysis
辞任　resignation
支配　control　頻 to obtain control over（〜の支配を獲得する), to lose control over（〜の支配を喪失する）
支配株主　controlling shareholder
支配企業　controlling company
支配の共有　sharing control
支配の喪失　loss of control
支配持分　controlling interest　頻 to acquire controlling interest in（〜の支配持分を取得する）
自白（不正などの）　confession
自発的な会計方針の変更　voluntary change in accounting policy
自発的な変更　voluntary change
支払い　payment, disbursement　頻 to make a payment（支払う）
支払システム　payment system

支払条件　payment terms, terms of payment
支払済給付（退職給付制度などについて）　benefits paid
支払済給付または未払給付　benefits paid or payable
支払済みの請求書　paid invoice
支払税金　taxes paid
支払対価　consideration paid
支払調書　report of payment, payment record
支払賃借料　rent(al) expense
支払手形　(trade) notes payable
支払手数料　commission expense
支払伝票　payment slip
支払人　payer
支払配当金　dividend paid
支払不能　insolvency
支払（処理）プロセス　payment process
支払家賃　rent(al) expense
支払猶予期間　grace period
支払余力　solvency
支払利息　interest expense
支払利息控除前税引前利益　earnings before interest and tax (EBIT)
支払ロイヤルティ　royalty expense
支払われた給付（退職給付制度などについて）　benefits paid
四半期　quarter, quarterly period
四半期財務諸表　quarterly financial statements
四半期統制　quarterly control
四半期報告　quarterly reporting
四半期報告書　quarterly (securities) report
四半期予算　quarterly budget
四半期レビュー　quarterly review
指標　indicator, index
四分位値　quartile
四分位レンジ　inter-quartile range
私募（証券の）　private placement
死亡　death
死亡率　mortality
死亡率表　mortality table
資本　capital, equity, equity capital
資本維持　capital maintenance
資本及び負債　equity and liabilities
資本及び負債合計　total equity and liabilities
資本化係数　capitalisation factor　米 capital-

資本	
ization factor	
資本関係	capital relationship
資本関係図	group organisation chart 米 group organization chart
資本管理	capital management, management of capital
資本金	share capital, capital stock, issued capital
資本金及び資本剰余金	share capital and share premium
資本金等（税務上の）	capital and capital surplus (for tax purposes)
資本合計	total equity
資本構成	capital [financial] structure
資本コスト	cost of capital
資本参加免税	participation exemption
資本資産	capital asset
資本資産評価モデル	capital asset pricing model (CAPM)
資本市場	capital market
資本準備金	(legal) capital reserve, capital legal reserve
資本剰余金	capital surplus [reserve], share premium
資本剰余金の配当	dividend from capital surplus
資本性金融商品	equity instrument [investment]
資本性金融商品の再取得コスト	cost of re-acquiring an equity instrument
資本性金融商品の発行コスト	cost of issuing an equity instrument
資本政策	capital policy
資本政策表	capitalisation table 米 capitalization table
資本性証券	equity securities
資本増価	capital appreciation
資本増強	capital enhancement
資本注入	capital injection
資本的支出	capital expenditure (capex), capital outlay
資本的支出のコミットメント	capital commitment
資本取引	capital [equity] transaction
資本に分類変更された金融負債	financial liabilities reclassified into equity
資本の内訳項目	components of equity
資本の払戻し	return of capital
資本の分配	equity distribution
資本費用	capital charge
資本部分（金融商品などの）	equity component
資本への転換オプション	equity conversion option
資本持分	equity interest
資本予算	capital budget (ing)
資本割（事業税の外形標準部分の構成要素）	capital component [levy]
資本割当	capital rationing
姉妹会社	sister company [corporation]
シミュレーション	simulation
仕向地持込み渡し条件（価格）	delivered at place (DAP)
事務（作業）	clerical work
事務所	office
事務所移転	office relocation
事務所費	office expense
事務用消耗品	office supplies
事務用消耗品費	office supplies expense
事務用（備）品	office equipment
指名	nomination
指名委員会（委員会設置会社の）	nomination committee
締切	deadline
締切（会計の）	cut-off
締切時点	cut-off point
締切日	cut-off date 頻 the cut-off date for invoices is the 25th of each month（請求書の締め日は毎月 25 日）
下期	2nd half
下半期	2nd half
社外監査役	outside corporate auditor
社会的責任投資	socially responsible investment (SRI)
社外取締役	outside director
社会保険	social insurance
社会保険拠出	social security contribution, contribution to social security
社会保険拠出に係る債務	liability for social security contributions
社会保険料	social insurance premium, contribution to social security

| 社会保障 social security
| 社会保障協定 social security agreement
| 社外流出項目（税務加算のうち） permanent difference
| 借地（権） leasehold
| 借地人 tenant
| 借用証書 promissory note (P/N)
| 社債 corporate bond, bonds payable, corporate debt securities [instrument]
| 社債償還 bond redemption
| 社債発行費 bond issue cost, cost of bond issue
| 社債利息 interest on bonds
| 社債利回り bond yield
| 借家人 tenant
| 社内使用 internal use
| 社内専門家 in-house specialist
| 社内調査（不正などの） internal [in-house] investigation
| 社内直接費用（リースなどの） internal direct cost
| 社内取締役 inside director
| 車両 (motor) vehicle, automobile
| 車両重量税 vehicle tonnage tax
| 州 state
| 収益（狭義の） revenue 使い方注意！広義の収益（income）のうち、主として企業の通常の事業過程で稼得したもの 頻 to recognise revenue（収益を認識する）
| 収益（広義の） income 使い方注意！会計期間における資産の増加または負債の減少という形での経済的便益の増加で、持分参加者からの出資以外のもの。狭義の収益（revenue）を含む
| 収益還元法 income approach
| 収益還元率 capitalisation rate (cap rate) 米 capitalization rate
| 収益サイクル revenue cycle
| 収益性 profitability
| 収益的支出 revenue expenditure
| 収益に関する補助金 grant related to income, income-related grant
| 収益認識 revenue recognition
| 収益認識基準 revenue recognition criteria
| 収益の分解 disaggregation of revenue
| 収益率 rate of return
| 重加算税 heavy penalty [additional] tax
| 重過失 gross negligence
| 従価税 ad valorem tax
| 従業員 employee, personnel
| 従業員以外の当事者との取引 transactions with parties other than employees
| 従業員及び他の類似サービス提供者 employees and others providing similar services
| 従業員掛金 employee contributions
| 従業員株式購入制度 employee share purchase plan, employee stock purchase plan (ESPP)
| 従業員株式制度 employee share plan
| 従業員給付 employee benefit
| 従業員給付債務 employee benefit obligations [liabilities]
| 従業員給付債務の清算 settlement of employee benefit obligations
| 従業員給付資産 employee benefit assets
| 従業員給付制度 employee benefit plan
| 従業員給付に係る引当金 provision for employee benefits
| 従業員給付費用 employee benefit(s) expense
| 従業員給付負債 employee benefit liabilities
| 従業員支援プログラム employee support programme 米 employee support program
| 従業員数 number of employees
| 従業員ストック・オプション employee share option
| 従業員との取引 transactions with employees
| 従業員に対する利益分配 employee profit sharing
| 従業員の解雇 employee dismissal
| 従業員負担の社会保険拠出 employees' contribution to social security
| 従業員報酬 employee compensation
| 従業員持株制度 employee stock ownership plan (ESOP), employee stock ownership programme 米 employee stock ownership program
| 就業規則 rules of employment
| 終業時間（までに） close of business (COB), end of business day (EOB)
| 集計 aggregate

集合的減損（営業債権などの） collective impairment
集合的な人的資源 assembled workforce
集合的な労働力 assembled workforce
住所 address, domicile
修正 adjustment, amendment 頻 to make an adjustment to（～を修正する）
修正（誤りの） correction
修正（過年度の財務諸表などの） recasting
州税 state tax
修正後発事象 adjusting event after reporting period
修正後簿価 recast book value
修正後利益 recast earnings
修正再表示 restatement 頻 restatement of previously reported information（過去に報告した情報の修正再表示）
修正仕訳 adjusting (journal) entry
修正申告書 amended [revised] tax return
修正遡及アプローチ modified retrospective approach
修正予算 revised budget
修正を要しない後発事象 non-adjusting event after reporting period
修正を要しない事象 non-adjusting event
修正を要する後発事象 adjusting event after reporting period
修正を要する事象 adjusting event
修繕 repair
従前のGAAP［会計原則］ previous GAAP 頻 transition from previous GAAP to IFRS（従前のGAAP［会計原則］からIFRSへの移行）
修繕費 repair cost [expense], maintenance cost [expense]
修繕引当金 provision for repairs
充足（要件などの） satisfaction
従属代理人 dependent agent
重大な悪影響（特に買収対象会社の事業等について生じた） material adverse change (MAC)
重大な金融要素 significant financing component
重大な制限 significant restriction
住宅 housing
集団訴訟 class action

集団投資ビークル collective investment vehicle
集中 concentration
集中購買 centralised purchasing 米 centralized purchasing
柔軟性 flexibility
12か月の予想信用損失 12-month expected credit losses (12-month ECLs)
収入 proceeds
収入印紙 revenue stamp
収入源 source of income
10年物国債 10-year government bond
重複 overlap
十分性 adequacy, sufficiency 頻 the adequacy of disclosure of（～についての開示の十分性）
自由貿易地域 free trade zone (FTZ)
住民 inhabitant
住民税 (local) inhabitant tax
住民税均等割 per capita inhabitant tax
住民税申告書 inhabitant tax return
住民税率 inhabitant tax rate
集約 aggregation
集約基準（セグメントの） aggregation criteria
収用（国などによる土地等の） expropriation 頻 expropriation of major assets by government（主要な資産の政府による収用）
重要事項 top line
収用資産 expropriated property
重要性 materiality, significance, magnitude
重要性がないこと immateriality
重要性の基準値 materiality threshold
重要性の水準 materiality level
重要性の判断基準 materiality threshold
重要な影響力 significant influence 頻 an entity over which the group has significant influence（グループが重要な影響力を行使する立場にある事業体）
重要な会計方針 significant accounting policies
重要な会計方針の要約 summary of significant accounting policies
重要な勘定 significant account
重要な疑義 substantial [significant] doubt 頻 substantial doubt about an entity's ability

to continue as a going concern（継続企業の前提に関する重要な疑義）
重要な拠点　significant location
重要な金融要素　significant financing component
重要な事業拠点　significant business unit
重要な特徴　critical feature
重要な発見事項　significant finding
重要な不備　material weakness, significant deficiency
重要なリスク　significant risk
重要な論点　significant issue
終了（契約などの）　termination
受益権　beneficial interest
受益者　beneficiary, beneficial owner
主観性　subjectivity
受給権　entitlement
受給権（の付与）（年金などの）　vesting
縮小　curtailment
主契約　host contract
授権（発行可能）株式　authorised shares 米 authorized shares
授権株式数　authorised number of shares, number of shares authorised 米 authorized number of shares, number of shares authorized
授権資本　registered capital
趣旨　purport
受贈　donation [gift] received
受贈益　gift income
受贈者　donee
受託者（委託販売の）　consignee
受託者（信託の）　trustee, fiduciary
受託者義務　fiduciary duty
主たる監査人　principal auditor
主たる事業　principal [main] business
主たる事業の場所　principal place of business
手段　measure
受注　order acceptance
受注残高　(order) backlog
主張（経営者の）　assertion
出荷　shipment
出荷依頼　shipping [shipment] request
出荷関連書類　shipping document
出荷関連費用　handling cost [expense]
出荷基準　shipment [shipping] basis

出荷通知　shipping advice
出荷費用　shipping cost [expense]
出荷報告書　shipping report
出金　payment, (cash) disbursement
出金伝票　payment slip, cash disbursement slip
出向　secondment 関 to second an employee to（従業員を〜に出向させる）
出向期間　secondment period
出向契約　secondment arrangement
出向先法人　host company
出向者　seconded employee, secondee
出向元法人　home company
出国　exit, departure
出国税　exit [departure] tax
出資　(capital) contribution 頻 to make a capital contribution to（〜に出資する）
出資関係図　group organisation chart 米 group organization chart
出資者　equity holder
出張　business trip
出張旅費精算書　travel and expense report
受動的所得　passive income
受動的所得の合算課税（タックス・ヘイブン対策税制による）　aggregation of passive income
取得　acquisition 頻 to carry out an acquisition of（〜の買収・取得を実行する）, to make an acquisition of（〜の買収・取得を行う）
取得関連コスト　acquisition-related cost
取得企業　acquirer, acquiring company
取得企業の識別　identification of the acquirer
取得企業の被取得企業に対する既存の持分　acquirer's previously-held equity interest in the acquiree
取得原価　acquisition cost, historical cost
取得原価基準　historical cost principle
取得原価主義会計　historical cost accounting
取得原価の配分　purchase price allocation (PPA), allocation of purchase price 関 to allocate a purchase price among（〜（取得資産・負債）に購入価格を配分する）
取得原価ベース　historical cost basis
取得原価法　cost technique
取得原価モデル　cost model

取得後のコスト	subsequent cost
取得後の支出（無形資産などの）	subsequent expenditure
取得後利益剰余金	post-acquisition retained earnings
取得した事業の価値	value of business acquired
取得時利益剰余金	pre-acquisition retained earnings
取得時レート	historical exchange rate
取得税（有形固定資産などの）	purchase taxes
取得による増加	additions from acquisitions
取得のれん	acquired goodwill
取得日	acquisition date, date of acquisition
取得日の公正価値	acquisition-date fair value
取得法	acquisition method
主犯者（不正などの）	primary perpetrator
首尾一貫性	consistency
守秘義務	(duty of) confidentiality
授与	award
需要	demand
主要資産	primary assets
主要な内訳	major components 頻 major components of tax expense（税金費用の主要な内訳）
主要な原則	core principle
主要な市場	principal market
主要な成功要因	key factor for success (KFS), key success factor (KSF)
主要な生産設備	major production plant
主要なマネジメント（経営者）	key management personnel
主要な利用者	primary user
主要目的テスト	principal purpose test (PPT)
受領	receipt
受領した会社（寄附金などを）	recipient company
種類	class, kind, type 頻 types of financial assets（金融資産の種類）, types of hedges（ヘッジの種類）, types of risks（リスクの種類）
種類株式	class shares
純売上高	net sales
純運転資本	net working capital
純額決済	net settlement
純額決済の要素	net settlement feature
純額ベース	net basis 頻 on a net basis（純額で）
循環	cycle, circulation
循環棚卸	cyclical inventory count, cycle stocktaking
循環取引	round trip transaction
準拠法	governing law
準固定費	semi-fixed [quasi-fixed] cost
純仕入高	net purchases
純資産	net assets
純資産価額	net asset value (NAV)
純資産調整（買収対価などについての）	net assets adjustment
純支払賃料	net rent payment
純支払利子	net interest payment
純収入	net proceeds
順序	order
純使用資本	net capital employed
準組織再編	quasi-reorganisation 米 quasi-reorganization
純損益	(net) profit or loss
純損益及びその他の包括利益計算書	statement of profit or loss and other comprehensive income
純損益に振り替えられることのないその他の包括利益	other comprehensive income that will not be reclassified to profit or loss
純損益に振り替えられるその他の包括利益	other comprehensive income that will be reclassified to profit or loss
純損益の部（包括利益計算書などの）	profit or loss section
純損益を通じて公正価値（で測定する区分）	fair value through profit or loss (FVPL / FVTPL)
純損益を通じて公正価値で測定される金融資産	financial assets measured at FVTPL [FVPL]
純損益を通じて公正価値で測定される金融負債	financial liability at FVTPL [FVPL]
純損失	net loss
純投資	net investment
純投資ヘッジ	net investment hedge
準備	preparation
準備金	reserve
準備的活動	preparatory activity

準備的または補助的な活動　preparatory or auxiliary activity
純負債　net liabilities, net debt
純変動（額）　net change
準変動費　semi-variable [quasi-variable] cost
純利益　net profit
純利益率　net profit margin
純利息（費用）　net interest
純流動資産　net current assets
純流動負債　net current liabilities
ジョイント・オペレーション　joint operation
ジョイント・ベンチャー　joint venture　[頻] to form a joint venture（ジョイント・ベンチャーを形成する）, to dissolve [terminate] a joint venture（ジョイント・ベンチャーを解散する）
ジョイント・ベンチャーに対する持分　interest in a joint venture
賞　award
使用　usage
仕様（書）　specification
条（法令，契約書などの）　article, section
浄化　clean-up
障害　barrier, hurdle
障がい（身体などの）　disability
障害者給付　disability benefit
少額資産　low value asset
少額資産のリース　lease of a low value item
少額所得除外基準（デミニマス基準）　de minimis rule
使用価値　value in use, use value
浄化費用　clean-up cost
小科目　sub-account
償還（負債の）　redemption, retirement
償還金額　redemption amount [value]
商慣行　business practice
償還優先株式　redeemable preference share [stock]
使用期間　period of use
消却（株式などの）　retirement
償却（無形資産などの）　amortisation　[米] amortization
償却（有形固定資産の）　depreciation
償却可能額（有形固定資産の）　depreciable amount
償却可能資産（有形固定資産のうち）　depreciable asset
償却期間（無形資産などの）　amortisation period　[米] amortization period
償却期間（有形固定資産の）　depreciation period
償却原価　amortised cost　[米] amortized cost
償却原価で測定される金融資産　financial assets measured at amortised cost　[米] financial assets measured at amortized cost
償却原価で測定される金融負債　financial liability at amortised cost　[米] financial liability at amortized cost
償却債権取立益　recovery of bad debt, bad debt recovered
償却資産税　depreciable assets tax
償却済みの無形資産　fully amortised intangible asset　[米] fully amortized intangible asset
償却費（無形資産などの）　amortisation charge [expense]　[米] amortization charge [expense]
償却費（有形固定資産の）　depreciation charge [expense]
償却方法（無形資産などの）　amortisation method
償却率（無形資産などの）　amortisation rate
償却累計額（無形資産などの）　accumulated amortisation　[米] accumulated amortization
償却累計額（有形固定資産の）　accumulated depreciation
上級経営者　senior management [executives]
上級従業員　senior employee
消去　elimination
状況　circumstance, condition, status
商業銀行　commercial bank
商業上の無形資産　commercial intangible
商業生産　commercial production
商業データベース　commercial database
商業的価値　commercial value
商業的実体　commercial substance
商業的動機　commercial motive
状況分析　situation analysis
商業用不動産　commercial property
消極的確認　negative confirmation
消極的な摘発（不正などの）　passive detec-

しょうにん

tion	
常勤監査役	full-time corporate auditor
小計	subtotal
承継	succession
承継者	successor
承継法人	successor (company)
使用権	right to [of] use
証券	securities
条件	condition 頻 to meet [satisfy] a condition（条件を充足する）, to waive a condition（条件を免除する）
条件（契約などの）	terms and conditions
上限	cap, ceiling, upper limit
証券委員会	securities commission
証券化	securitisation 米 securitization
証券会社	securities firm
条件概要書	term sheet
証券化ビークル	securitisation vehicle
証券口座	brokerage account
使用権資産	right-of-use asset
条件付株式発行契約	contingent share agreement
条件付決済条項	contingent settlement provision
条件付支払い	contingent payment
条件付対価	contingent consideration, contingent purchase price
条件付賃借料	contingent rent
条件付賃貸料	contingent rent
条件付発行可能株式	contingently issuable share
条件付発行可能普通株式	contingently issuable ordinary share
証券取引所	stock exchange
証券の保有者	securities holder
証券発行	flotation
証券発行費用	flotation cost
証券引受（業務）	underwriting
条件変更による利得または損失	modification gain or loss
証拠	evidence
商号	trade name
条項	article, clause, provision
証拠金	margin
証拠金勘定	margin account
上告	appeal
証拠資料	evidence, evidential matter
証拠不十分	lack of evidence
詳細	detail, particulars
詳細テスト	test of detail
常識	common sense
証書	certificate, deed
上場	listing
上場会社	listed company, publicly traded company
上場規則	listing rules
上場デリバティブ	exchange-traded derivatives
上場パートナーシップ	publicly traded partnership (PTP)
上場廃止	delisting
上場有価証券	listed securities
証書貸付	term loan
昇進	promotion
乗数	multiple
少数株主	minority shareholder [owner] 頻 a minority owner in（〜（会社名）の少数株主）
少数株主拒否権	minority veto right
少数株主権	rights of minority shareholders
少数株主持分	minority interest
証跡	trace
譲渡	transfer, assignment
譲渡益	capital gain
譲渡益課税	capital gains tax (CGT)
譲渡益課税の繰延べ	capital gain rollover, rollover relief
譲渡可能性	transferability
譲渡制限（株式の）	restriction on share transferability
譲渡性預金	certificate of deposit (CD)
譲渡損	capital loss
譲渡損益の繰延べ	deferral of capital gains and losses
譲渡損失	capital loss
譲渡人	transferor, assignor
譲渡利益	capital gain
承認	approval, authorisation 米 authorization 頻 to obtain approval from（〜から承認を得る）, authorisation for（〜の承認）
承認（最終化された文書などの）	sign-off

し

しょうにん

承認の限度額	authorisation limit ㊇ authorization limit
消費	consumption
消費財	consumer goods
消費者物価指数	consumer price index (CPI)
消費税	consumption tax, Japanese Consumption Tax (JCT)
消費税申告書	consumption tax return
消費税法	Consumption Tax Act
消費税法施行規則	Ordinance for Enforcement of the Consumption Tax Act
消費税法施行令	Order for Enforcement of the Consumption Tax Act
商標	trademark
商標権	trademark right
証憑書類	voucher
消費量差異	usage variance
商品	goods, merchandise ㊇ merchandize
商品価値	commercial value
商品在庫	merchandise inventory
商品先物	commodities futures
小分類	sub-classification
商法	commercial law
情報	information
情報交換	exchange of information
情報システム	information system
情報収集	information gathering
上方修正	upward adjustment
情報処理	information processing
情報申告	information return
情報セキュリティ	information security
情報提供依頼（書）	request for information (RFI)
情報ニーズ	information needs
正味現在価値	net present value (NPV)
正味現在価値法	net present value (NPV) method
正味財産	net worth
正味実現可能価額	net realisable value (NRV) ㊇ net realizable value
正味売却価格	net selling price
正味売却価額	net selling value
正味負債	net debt
正味リース投資未回収額	net investment in the lease
証明	proof
証明（監査証明など）	attestation, sign-off
証明書	certificate
消滅	extinguishment ㊇ to extinguish financial liabilities（金融負債を消滅させる）
消滅（主に債務の）	defeasance
消滅会社（合併による）	merged company, predecessor company
消耗品	consumables, supplies
消耗品費	supplies expense
条約	treaty
条約漁り	treaty shopping
賞与	bonus
剰余	surplus
剰余金	reserve, surplus
剰余金処分	appropriation of retained earnings
賞与制度	bonus plan
賞与の支払い	bonus payment
賞与引当金	provision for bonuses, bonus accrual
将来掛金の減額	reduction in future contributions
将来加算一時差異	taxable temporary difference ㊇ deferred tax liabilities are recognised for taxable temporary differences（繰延税金負債は将来加算一時差異に対して認識される）
将来課税所得	future taxable income [profit] ㊇ future taxable profit will be available to absorb tax losses（税務上の（繰越）欠損金を吸収できるだけの将来課税所得が予想される）
将来価値	future value
将来キャッシュ・フロー	future cash flow ㊇ the amount, timing, and uncertainty of future cash flows（将来キャッシュ・フローの金額、発生タイミング及び不確実性）
将来キャッシュ・フローの見積り	estimate of future cash flows
将来減算一時差異	deductible temporary difference ㊇ deferred tax assets are recognised for deductible temporary differences（繰延税金資産は将来減算一時差異に対して認識される）, recognition of previously unrecognised deductible temporary

differences（過去に認識されていなかった将来減算一時差異の認識）
将来損失　future loss
将来に関する財務情報　prospective financial information
将来に向かっての適用　prospective application
将来の営業損失　future operating losses
将来の経済的便益　future economic benefit
将来の事象　future event
将来予測的情報　forward-looking information
将来利益　future profit
使用料　royalty (fee) 〔頻〕 to charge royalty fees（使用料を課す），to collect royalty fees（使用料を回収する）
使用料源泉税　withholding tax on royalties
使用連動のロイヤルティ（量・回数など）　usage-based royalty
ショート・ポジション　short position
ショート・リスト　short list
除外　exclusion, preclusion
所轄税務署　relevant [appropriate] tax office
初期投資　initial investment
初期のコメント　preliminary comments
初期費用　initial cost
初期評価　preliminary assessment
除却　disposal, retirement 〔関〕 to dispose of（〜を処分する，除却する）
除却損　disposal loss
除去　removal
除去費用　removal cost
除去費用引当金　provision for decommissioning costs
職業上の不正　occupational fraud
職業的専門家としての正当な注意　due professional care
諸口　sundries
職場での不適切な行為　workplace misconduct
職務記述書　job description
職務権限マトリックス　authorisation matrix 〔米〕 authorization matrix
職務分掌　segregation [separation] of duties
所見　remark
助言　advice

所在地　location, (fiscal) domicile
所在地国　country of domicile
所在地国基準（タックス・ヘイブン対策税制）　country of location test 〔頻〕 to satisfy the country of location test（所在地国基準を充足する），to fail the country of location test（所在地国基準を充足しない）
諸資産　miscellaneous assets
除数　divisor
ショッピング・センター　shopping centre 〔米〕 shopping center
所得　income, taxable income
所得移転　income shifting
所得拡大促進税制（日本）　tax credit for salary growth
所得税　income tax
所得税（個人の）　personal [individual] income tax
所得税額控除　(withholding) income tax credit
所得税申告書　personal [individual] income tax return
所得税法　Income Tax Act
所得税法施行規則　Ordinance for Enforcement of the Income Tax Act
所得税法施行令　Order for Enforcement of the Income Tax Act
所得税率　personal [individual] income tax rate
所得の合算　aggregation of income
所得の源泉　source of income
初度適用　first-time adoption
初度適用企業　first-time adopter
初日　day 1
初犯者（不正などの）　first-time offender
諸負債　miscellaneous liabilities
処分　disposal
処分益　disposal gain, gain on disposal
処分価額　disposal [scrap] value
処分グループ　disposal group
処分グループの再測定による減損損失　impairment loss on remeasurement of disposal group
処分コスト　cost of disposal
処分コスト控除後の公正価値　fair value less costs of disposal

しょぶんそ

処分損　disposal loss, loss on disposal
処分に伴う収入　disposal proceeds
処分費用　cost of disposal
処分目的で保有する資産　assets held for disposal
処分目的保有の　held for disposal
署名　signature
書面調査（税務調査のうち）　office [desk] audit
所有　ownership, possession
所有権　title
所有権移転外ファイナンス・リース　finance lease without transfer of ownership, non-ownership-transfer finance lease
所有権移転ファイナンス・リース　finance lease with transfer of ownership, ownership-transfer finance lease
所有権の移転　title transfer
所有権の変遷（を示す文書）　chain of title
所有権の留保　reservation [retention] of title
所有者　owner
所有者（土地などの）　proprietor
所有者からの出資　contributions from [by] owners
所有者との取引　transactions with owners
所有者の構成　ownership structure
所有者への分配　distributions to owners
所有者への分配目的保有の　held for distribution to owners
所有に伴うリスクと経済価値　risks and rewards incidental to ownership, risks and rewards of ownership
所有持分の変動　change in ownership interest
所有持分割合　proportion [percentage] of ownership interest　[頻]　proportion of ownership interest in a subsidiary（子会社に対する所有持分割合）, proportion of ownership interests held by non-controlling interests（非支配持分の所有持分割合）
書類　document
書類の改竄　fraudulent document
資料　material, document
資料依頼（書）　information request, request for information (RFI)

指令　directive
仕訳　(journal) entry　[頻]　to make a journal entry（仕訳を記帳する）
仕訳帳　(general) journal
仕訳伝票　journal slip
人員　personnel
人員整理計画　redundancy plan
人員配置　staffing
侵害　infringement
新株式申込証拠金　deposit for share [stock] subscription
新株の優先引受権　pre-emptive [pre-emption] right
新株予約権　share [stock] option, share [stock] warrant
新株予約権付社債　bond with warrant, warrant bond
新株予約権無償割当て　rights issue [offering]
新規取得資産　newly acquired asset
新規上場　initial public offering (IPO)
新規上場企業　newly listed entity
新規投下資本に対する利益率　return on new invested capital (RONIC)
人件費　payroll cost [expense], salaries and wages
進行基準　percentage of completion method
新興経済圏　emerging economies
新興国　emerging country
人口統計学　demography
人口統計上の仮定　demographic assumption
申告　declaration, filing
申告期限　filing due date, deadline for (filing) tax returns
申告期限の延長　filing extension, extension for the filing of tax returns　[頻]　1 month extension for the filing of tax returns（申告期限の1か月延長）
申告義務　filing requirement
申告書　(tax) return　[頻]「税務申告書」の項を参照
申告納税　self assessment
審査　screening
審査請求（国税不服審判所に対する）　request for reconsideration (to National Tax Tribunal)
人事異動　job rotation

シンジケーション	syndication
シンジケート・ローン	syndicated loan
人事部門	human resources department [division]
申請	application
申請書	request form
真正譲渡	true sale
申請用紙	application form
新設子会社	newly formed subsidiary
信託	trust
信託受益権	beneficial interest in trust
慎重性	prudence
進捗度	stage of completion
人的役務	personal service
人的役務提供事業の対価	remuneration derived from rendering professional [personal] services
人的役務の提供	professional service
人的役務の提供に係る報酬	professional services fee
新聞のマストヘッド	newspaper masthead
親密な関係	close association
信用	credit
信用エクスポージャー	credit exposure 頻 unrated credit exposures（格付けのない信用エクスポージャー）
信用格付け	credit rating, credit grade
信用減損	credit impairment 頻 credit impairment of financial instruments（金融商品の信用減損）
信用減損金融資産	credit-impaired financial asset
信用減損組成金融資産	originated credit-impaired financial asset
信用減損のある金融資産	credit-impaired financial asset
信用減損のない金融資産	non-credit-impaired financial asset
信用事象	credit event
信用状	letter of credit (L/C)
信用情報	credit information
信用スプレッド	credit spread
信用増強	credit enhancement
信用損失	credit loss
信用損失引当金	allowance (account) for credit losses 頻 allowance account for credit losses of financial assets（金融資産の信用損失引当金）
信用調査	credit check
信用調査機関	credit agency
信用調査機関の情報	credit agency information
信用調整後の実効金利[利子率]	credit-adjusted effective interest rate
信用評価調整（CVA）	credit value adjustment (CVA)
信用方針	credit policy
信用リスク	credit risk
信用リスク格付け	credit risk rating grade
信用力	creditworthiness
信用枠	line of credit
信頼	reliance
信頼性	reliability 頻 can be measured with reliability（信頼性をもって測定できる） 関 can be measured reliably（信頼性をもって測定できる）

す

推計課税	presumptive assessment
遂行	fulfilment 米 fullfillment
推奨	recommendation
垂直的に統合した企業	vertically integrated enterprises
垂直統合	vertical integration
推定	presumption, inference
推定課税	presumptive assessment
推定価値	implied value
推定的債務	constructive obligation
水道光熱費	utilities cost [expense]
水平統合	horizontal integration
推論	inference
数値	figure
数値化	quantification
数値の丸め	rounding
数理計算上の仮定	actuarial assumption
数理計算上の現在価値	actuarial present value

数理計算上の差異　actuarial gains and losses　[頻] unrecognised actuarial gains and losses（未認識数理計算上の差異）
数理計算上の評価　actuarial valuation
数理計算上の評価方法　actuarial valuation method
数理計算上のリスク　actuarial risk
数理計算ベース　actuarial basis
数量差異　volume variance, quantity variance
数量差異（消費量差異）　usage variance
数量差異（直接材料費に係る）　direct material usage variance
据付け　installation
据付費用　installation fee
スキーム　scheme
スキミング　skimming
スクイーズ・アウト　squeeze out
スクラップ　scrap
図形　figure
スケジューリング　scheduling
スタートアップ（開業間もない企業）　start-up
スタンス　stance
スタンドアロン・イシュー［問題］　stand-alone issue
スタンドバイ・クレジット　standby credit
スタンドバイ信用状　standby letter of credit
ステイプル・ファイナンス　stapled financing
ステップアップ（簿価の）　step-up in basis　[関] stepped up basis（ステップアップ（増額）された簿価）
ステップダウン（簿価の）　step-down in basis　[関] stepped down basis（ステップダウン（減額）された簿価）
ストック・オプション　share [stock] option　[頻] to issue a share option（ストック・オプションを発行する）, to grant a share option to（〜にストック・オプションを付与する）, to exercise a share option（ストック・オプションを行使する）
ストック・オプション・プログラム　share option programme　[米] share option program
ストック・レンディング　stock lending
ストラクチャー（買収などの）　structure　[頻] to rearrange a structure（（買収などの）ストラクチャーを変更する）
ストラクチャード・エンティティ　structured entity
ストラクチャリング　structuring
ストラクチャリング分析　structuring analysis
ストラテジック・インベスター　strategic investor
ストレス・テスト　stress testing
図表　diagram
スピン・オフ　spin-off
スプリット・アップ　split-up
スプリット・オフ　split-off
すべての当事者の一致した合意　unanimous consent
スワップ　swap
スワップ契約　swap contract

せ

成果　result
税額　tax amount
税額控除　tax credit　[関] to be credited against Japanese corporation tax（日本の法人税から控除する）
正確性　accuracy, precision　[頻] can be measured with precision（正確に測定できる）
成果物　deliverables
成果報酬　performance-based fee
税関　customs
請求　billing, claim
請求書　invoice, bill　[頻] to issue [raise] an invoice（請求書を発行する）
請求済未出荷売上　bill-and-hold sales
請求済未出荷契約　bill-and-hold arrangement
税金　tax　[頻] a tax is imposed on（〜に税金が課される）　[関] to be taxed（課税される）
税金及び税効果　current and deferred (income) tax
税金計算　tax computation [calculation]

税金計算シート　　tax calculation worksheet
税金収益　　tax income
税金に係る偶発負債　　tax contingent liability
税金に関する補償　　tax indemnity [indemnification]
税金の還付　　refund of tax, tax refund
税金の期間配分　　income tax allocation, interperiod tax allocation
税金の繰延べ　　deferral [deferment] of tax
税金の軽減　　tax relief
税金の滞納　　tax delinquency
税金の滞納による差押え　　tax foreclosure
税金引当　　tax provision, tax accrual, tax reserve
税金費用　　(income) tax expense　頻 difference between tax expense and tax at the applicable tax rate on accounting profit（税率差異）
税金費用の内訳　　components of tax expense 頻 major components of tax expense（主要な税金費用の内訳）
制限　　limitation, restriction　頻 limitation on deductibility（損金算入制限）　関 to be restricted（制限される）
制限株式　　restricted share [stock]
制限条項　　restrictive covenant
税源浸食と利益移転　　Base Erosion and Profit Shifting (BEPS)
制限税率　　limit [maximum] tax rate
税効果（〜の）　　tax effect (of)　頻 tax effect of non-deductible expenses（損金不算入費用の税効果），tax effect of tax exempt income（非課税所得の税効果），tax effect of tax incentives（税制優遇措置の税効果），tax effect of current-year losses for which no deferred tax asset is recognised（繰延税金資産が認識されない当事業年度の損失による税効果）
税効果会計　　tax effect accounting
整合性　　consistency
成功報酬　　success fee, contingent fee
制裁　　sanction
制裁金　　civil penalty
生産　　production
生産（物）　　output
清算（会社の）　　liquidation, winding up　関 to liquidate a subsidiary（子会社を清算する）
精算　　adjustment
清算価値　　liquidation [break-up] value
生産管理　　production control
清算期間　　liquidation period
清算機関　　clearing house [party]
清算基準会計　　liquidation basis accounting
生産計画　　production plan
清算所得　　liquidation income
生産性　　productivity
生産設備　　production facilities
生産高比例法　　unit of production method
生産単位　　unit of production
清算中の法人　　liquidating company
清算手続　　liquidation procedures　頻 under liquidation procedures（清算手続中の），during liquidation procedures（清算期間中に）
清算人　　liquidator
生産能力　　production capacity
清算配当　　liquidating [liquidation] distribution, liquidating [liquidation] dividend
精算表　　worksheet
生産ライン　　production line　頻 to set up a new production lline（新しい生産ラインを立ち上げる）
生産量　　production volume
正式契約　　definitive agreement (DA)
性質　　nature
誠実性　　integrity
税収　　tax revenue
正常運転資本　　normal working capital
正常営業循環基準　　normal operating cycle basis [rule]
正常化された運転資本　　normalised working capital 米 normalized working capital
正常生産能力　　normal capacity
正常操業度　　normal operating capacity
税制　　tax regime
税制改正　　tax reform
税制改正案　　tax reform plan
税制改正法案　　tax reform bill
税制適格―　　適格―の各項を参照
税制優遇措置　　preferential tax treatment, tax incentive [concession]

製造　production, manufacture
製造及び販売　manufacturing and distribution
製造会社　manufacturer, manufacturing company
製造勘定　manufacturing [factory] account
製造間接費　manufacturing [production] overhead, indirect manufacturing cost
製造間接費の配賦　manufacturing overhead allocation
製造原価　manufacturing [production] cost
製造原価報告書　statement of cost of goods manufactured
製造工程　production process, manufacturing process
製造サイクル　production cycle
製造指図書　production order
製造指示書　work order (W/O)
製造設備　manufacturing facility, production facility
製造直接費　direct manufacturing cost
製造費用　manufacturing cost
製造部門　manufacturing department [division]
製造用貯蔵品　production supplies
製造ライン　production line
成長　growth
成長機会　growth opportunity
成長率　growth rate
制定（法律の）　enactment
正当化　justification
正当な注意　due care
制度加入者（退職給付制度などの）　plan participant　[頻] contributions by a plan participant（制度加入者による拠出）
制度からの脱退（退職給付制度などの）　withdrawal from a plan
制度資産（従業員給付制度の）　plan assets
制度資産に係る収益（従業員給付制度の）　return on plan assets
制度の解散（退職給付制度などの）　wind-up of a plan
制度の縮小（退職給付制度などの）　plan curtailment
制度の清算（退職給付制度などの）　plan settlement
制度の積立不足（退職給付制度などの）　deficit in plan
制度の変更（退職給付制度などの）　plan amendment
税抜き　net of tax
整備（内部統制の）　design
税引後　net of tax
税引後営業利益　net operating profit after tax (NOPAT), after-tax operating income
税引後損益　post-tax profit or loss
税引後利益　after-tax profit
税引前キャッシュ・フロー　pre-tax cash flow
税引前所得　pre-tax income
税引前損失　pre-tax loss
税引前の利率　pre-tax rate
税引前利益　earnings before taxes (EBT), pre-tax profit [income], profit before tax
整備テスト（内部統制の）　test of design
整備に関する不備（内部統制の）　deficiency in design
製品　product, manufactured goods
製品（完成品）　finished goods
製品及びサービス　products and services
製品在庫　finished goods inventory
製品製造原価　cost of goods manufactured
製品別売上　sales by product
製品保証　product warranty
製品保証引当金　provision for (product) warranties, warranty provision
製品保証費用　warranty expense
製品ライン　product line
政府　government
政府援助　government assistance
政府関連企業　government-related entity
政府機関　governmental agency
制服　uniform
生物資産　biological asset
政府の賦課金　government levy
政府補助金　government grant
税法　tax law
税法違反　tax offence
税法の変更　change in tax laws
税務アドバイザー　tax adviser [advisor]
税務意見書　tax opinion
税務エクスポージャー　tax exposure　[頻] to assess tax exposure（税務エクスポージャ

ーを評価する），to quantify tax exposure（税務エクスポージャーを定量化する），to reduce tax exposure（税務エクスポージャーを低減する）
税務会計　tax accounting
税務加算　addition　関「加算」の項を参照
税務基準額　tax base
税務行政執行共助条約　Convention on Mutual Administrative Assistance in Tax Matters
税務減算　deduction
税務署　(national) tax office
税務上の　for tax purposes　使い方注意！ depreciation for tax purposes（税務上の減価償却費）のように，税務目的であることを明記したい場合に使う
税務上の意味合い　tax implication
税務上の影響　tax consequence [impact]
税務上の恩典　tax benefit　頻 to claim tax benefit（税務上の恩典を請求する），to enjoy [obtain] tax benefit（税務上の恩典を享受する）
税務上の金額　tax base
税務上の繰越欠損金　carryforward of unused tax losses　頻 繰越欠損金の項を参照
税務上の繰越項目　tax attributes
税務上の欠損金（累計額）　cumulative tax losses
税務上の減価償却費　tax depreciation
税務上のステイタス　tax status
税務上のストラクチャリング　tax structuring
税務上のストラクチャリング分析　tax structuring analysis
税務上の取扱い　tax treatment
税務上の不正　tax fraud
税務上の紛争　tax dispute　頻 to resolve a tax dispute（税務上の紛争を解決する）
税務上の便益　tax benefit
税務上の利益（課税所得）　taxable profit [earnings]
税務申告　tax (return) filing, tax declaration
税務申告書　tax return　頻 to prepare tax returns（税務申告書を作成する），to file [submit] tax returns（税務申告書を提出する）
税務申告書修正可能年度　open (tax) years
税務申告書の作成　tax return preparation
税務申告書の作成者　tax return preparer
税務申告書の提出　tax return filing
税務申告書の提出義務　tax return filing obligation
税務訴訟　tax case
税務代理人　tax agent
税務調査　tax audit, (tax) examination, (tax) investigation　頻 to undergo a tax audit（税務調査を受ける），a tax audit is carried out（税務調査が実施される）
税務調査官　tax auditor, tax examiner, tax investigator
税務調査による修正（更正）　tax audit adjustment
税務調査の状況　tax audit status
税務調査未了年度　open (tax) years
税務調査履歴　history of tax audits
税務デュー・ディリジェンス　tax due diligence (TDD)　頻 to perform tax due diligence（税務デュー・ディリジェンスを実施する）
税務当局　tax authorities
税務当局からの許可　clearance from tax authorities
税務当局の事前承認　advance [prior] approval of tax authorities
税務当局の事前の同意　prior consent of tax authorities
税務登録　tax registration
税務の観点　tax perspective [viewpoint]　頻 from a tax perspective [viewpoint]（税務の観点からは）
税務部門　tax department [division]
税務簿価　tax base [basis], tax book value　頻 differences between the carrying amount in the balance sheet and the tax base of assets and liabilities（会計簿価と税務簿価の差異）
税務ポジション　tax position
税務リスク　tax risk　頻 to assess tax risk（税務リスクを評価する），to quantify tax risk（税務リスクを定量化する），to mitigate tax risk（税務リスクを低減する），to manage tax risk（税務リスクを管理する）
生命保険　life insurance

誓約条項	covenant
税率	tax rate
税率差異（の調整）	reconciliation of effective tax rate 関 reconciliation of tax expense and the accounting profit multiplied by domestic tax rate (「税金費用」と「会計上の利益に国内の税率を乗じた金額」との調整表)
税率の変更	change in tax rates, tax rate change
税率引下げ	reduction in tax rate
セーフガード（条項）	safeguard
セーフ・ハーバー	safe harbour 米 safe harbor
セーフ・ハーバー・ルール	safe harbour rule 米 safe harbor rule
セール・アンド・リースバック取引	sale and leaseback (transaction), sale-leaseback transaction
セールス・ミックス	sales mix
セールス・ミックス差異	sales mix variance
積送基準	direct transport rule
責任	responsibility
責任会計	responsibility accounting
責任限定	limitation of liability
責任限度額	liability cap
責任者	person in charge
責任センター	responsibility centre 米 responsibility center
責任の領域	area of responsibility
セグメント	segment
セグメント間売上	intersegment sales
セグメント間購入	inter-segment purchase
セグメント間収益	inter-segment revenue
セグメント間収益の消去	elimination of inter-segment revenue
セグメント間利益	inter-segment profit
セグメント間利益の消去	elimination of inter-segment profit
セグメント業績	segment result
セグメント資産	segment assets
セグメント収益	segment revenue
セグメント情報	segment information, segmental information
セグメント税引前利益[損失]	segment profit [loss] before tax
セグメント損失	segment loss
セグメントの決定	segmenting
セグメントの分割	segmentation
セグメント費用	segment expense
セグメント負債	segment liabilities
セグメント別売上	sales by operating segment
セグメント別キャッシュ・フロー	segmental cash flow
セグメント別財務諸表	segmented financial statements
セグメント別報告	segmental reporting
セグメント報告	segment reporting
セグメント利益	segment profit
施行（法令の）	enforcement
施行されている税率	enacted tax rate
施行されているまたは実質的に施行されている税率	tax rates that have been enacted or substantively enacted
是正	remediation
是正措置	remedial action
積極的確認	positive confirmation
積極的な摘発（不正などの）	active detection
積極的な摘発手段（不正などの）	active detection method
設計	design
絶対値	absolute amount
絶対的な力（パワー）	absolute power
設置	installation
設置費用	installation fee
設定者（信託の）	settlor
窃盗	larceny
窃盗（資金の）	cash larceny
設備	facility
設備投資	capital investment [spending]
説明	explanation, illustration
説明情報	explanatory information
説明資料	explanatory material
説明責任	accountability
説明的注記	explanatory note
説明部分（仕訳の）	narration, narrative
設立	establishment
設立（会社の）	incorporation
設立国	country of incorporation
設立者	founder
設例	illustrative example

セラーズ・ノート	seller's note
セラーズ・バリュー	seller's value
セルサイド	sell side
善管注意義務	duty of due care
前期	previous (accounting) period, prior (accounting) period
全期間の予想信用損失	full lifetime expected credit losses (full lifetime ECLs), lifetime expected credit losses (lifetime ECLs)
前期繰越	brought forward (b/f)
宣言	declaration
選好	preference
選考	screening
先行条件	condition precedent (CP)
前子会社	former subsidiary
潜在株式	potential share
潜在的買手	potential buyer
潜在的価値	potential value
潜在的議決権	potential voting right
潜在的税務エクスポージャー	potential tax exposure
潜在的租税債務	potential tax liability
潜在的損失	potential loss
潜在的投資家	potential investor
潜在的普通株式	potential ordinary share
潜在的リスク	potential risk
前者	former
全社資産	corporate assets
全社情報の開示	entity-wide disclosure
全社的な内部統制	company [entity] level control
全社費用	corporate expense
全世界所得	worldwide income
全世界所得課税方式	worldwide system
船側渡し条件（価格）	free alongside ship (FAS)
全体	entirety
全体像	big picture
選択	choice, election, selection 頻 a choice of two alternative treatments（2つの取扱いのなかからの選択）, to make a selection of（～を選択する）
選択肢	option
前提	premise, presumption
宣伝	advertisement
前任者	predecessor
前任の監査人	predecessor auditor
前年（度）	preceding year, previous year
船舶	ship, vessel, ships and vessels
全部原価	full cost
全部原価計算	absorption costing
全部消去	full elimination
全部のれん方式	full goodwill method
全部連結	full consolidation
選別	screening
専門家	expert, specialist
専門家による役務提供	professional services
専門家報酬	professional fee
専門家報酬費用	professional fees expense
専門知識	expertise
専門的資格	professional qualification
専門用語	terminology
占有	occupancy
専用資産	dedicated asset
専用実施権	exclusive licence 米 exclusive license
戦略	strategy
戦略的意思決定	strategic decision
戦略的事業単位	strategic business unit (SBU)
先例	precedent

そ

層	layer
総売上高	gross sales [turnover]
増加	increase 頻 increase in（～の増加（額））
増価	accretion, appreciation
総会	general meeting
総額	sum
総額での帳簿価額（減価償却累計額や損失評価引当金などの控除前の）	gross carrying amount
増加償却（減価償却のうち）	extra depreciation
総括	wrap-up
相関関係	correlation
総勘定元帳	general ledger (G/L), nominal

	ledger
総勘定元帳（科目）	control account
早期退職	early retirement
早期退職制度	early retirement programme [plan]　米 early retirement program [plan]
早期適用（会計基準などの）	early application [adoption], earlier application [adoption]
早期認識	early recognition　頻 early recognition of expenses（費用の早期認識）
早期返済（債務の）	early repayment
創業者	founder
操業度	capacity utilisation　米 capacity utilization
操業度差異（製造間接費に係る）	capacity variance
送金	remittance
送金依頼	request for remittance
送金通知	remittance advice
送金に対する制限	restriction on the transfer of funds
総計	aggregate
増減	fluctuation
総原価	total cost
増減分析	fluctuation analysis
倉庫	warehouse
相互依存	interdependence
相互依存性	interdependency
総合計	grand total
総合原価計算	process costing
総合主義（PEに関する）	entire income principle, force of attraction principle
総合償却（減価償却のうち）	depreciation on a pool basis
相互会社	mutual entity
相互関連性	interrelationship
相互協議	mutual agreement procedure (MAP)
相互作用	interaction
相互主義	reciprocity
倉庫費用	warehouse cost [expense], warehousing cost [expense]
相互保有（株式の）	cross [mutual] shareholding
操作（利益などの）	manipulation
相殺	offsetting, set-off, netting　関 to be offset against（〜と相殺される）, to offset financial assets and financial liabilities（金融資産と金融負債を相殺する）, to be set off against future profits（（繰越欠損金などが）将来の利益と相殺される）
相殺権	right of set-off, right to set off
相殺消去（連結財務諸表作成のための）	elimination
相殺消去仕訳（連結財務諸表作成のための）	elimination entry
増資	capital increase, increase in capital
総仕入高	gross purchases
総資産	total assets
総資産回転率	total assets turnover
総資産利益率	return on assets (ROA)
総支出	gross (cash) payments
総資本	invested capital (IC)
総収入	gross (cash) receipts
贈収賄	bribery
贈収賄（汚職）	bribery and corruption
贈収賄防止プログラム	anti bribery & corruption programme (ABC)　米 anti bribery & corruption program (ABC)
相乗効果	synergy
総使用資本	gross capital employed
総所得	gross income
相続	inheritance
相続税	inheritance tax
想定元本	notional (principal) amount
相場	quotation
総費用営業利益率	return on total costs
増分	increment
増分キャッシュ・フロー	incremental cash flow
増分コスト	incremental cost
増分分析	incremental analysis
総平均法	gross average method
双方向CVA	bilateral CVA
総務部門	general affairs department [division]
贈与	gift
贈与者	donor
贈与税	gift tax
総リース投資未回収額	gross investment in lease
創立費	organisation cost [expense]　米 organization cost [expense]

ソース・ルール　　source rule
遡及（権）　　recourse　[頻] with recourse（リコース（遡及権）付きの）
遡及アプローチ　　retrospective approach
遡及効　　retroactive effect
遡及的修正再表示　　retrospective [retroactive] restatement
遡及的調整　　retrospective adjustment
遡及適用　　retrospective [retroactive] application
遡及適用による特定期間への影響　　period-specific effects for retrospective application
即時認識　　immediate recognition
即時売却　　immediate sale
即時売却可能性　　availability for immediate sale
促進　　facilitation, promotion
属性　　attribute
属地　　territoriality
属地主義　　territorial system, territoriality principle
測定　　measurement　[関] to be measured at cost（取得原価で測定される）, to be measured at fair value（公正価値で測定される）
測定可能性　　measurability
測定期間　　measurement period
測定基準　　metric
測定に関する不一致・不整合　　measurement inconsistency
測定の基礎　　measurement base, basis of measurement
測定の原則　　measurement principle
測定の信頼性　　reliability of measurement
測定の変動　　change in measurement
測定日　　measurement date
速報　　flash report
速報ベースの業績開示　　flash earnings report
底　　bottom
組織　　organisation　[米] organization
組織構造　　organisational structure　[米] organizational structure
組織再編　　(corporate) reorganisation　[米] (corporate) reorganization　[頻] to implement corporate reorganisation（組織再編を実行する）
組織再編前の繰越欠損金　　pre-reorganisation losses　[米] pre-reorganization losses
組織図　　organisation chart　[米] organization chart
訴訟　　lawsuit, litigation　[頻] litigation against（～に対する訴訟）
訴訟事件　　court case　[頻] settlement of a court case（訴訟事件の解決）
訴訟事件の解決　　resolution of a court case
訴訟損失引当金　　provision for litigation
訴訟手続　　(legal) proceedings
訴訟に係る偶発負債　　legal proceedings contingent liability
訴訟の解決　　litigation settlement
訴訟引当金　　provision for litigation, legal proceedings provision
組成　　origination
租税回避　　tax avoidance [evasion]
租税回避スキーム　　tax avoidance scheme
租税回避防止規定　　anti-avoidance rules
租税裁定取引　　tax arbitrage
租税裁判所　　tax court
租税先取特権　　tax lien
組成された企業　　structured entity
組成された企業からの収益　　income from a structured entity
租税条約　　tax treaty [convention], double taxation treaty (DTT)　[使い方注意！] 日本とX国の租税条約は、通常 Japan-X tax treaty のようないい方をする
租税条約上の源泉税率　　tax treaty withholding tax rate
租税条約に関する届出書　　application form for income tax convention
租税特別措置法　　Act on Special Measures Concerning Taxation
租税特別措置法施行規則　　Ordinance for Enforcement of the Act on Special Measures Concerning Taxation
租税特別措置法施行令　　Order for Enforcement of the Act on Special Measures Concerning Taxation
租税犯罪　　tax crime
租税負担　　tax burden
租税負担割合（タックス・ヘイブン対策税制に

おける） effective tax rate for CFC purposes
その他資本剰余金 other capital surplus [reserve]
その他の営業収益 other operating income
その他の営業費用 other operating expense
その他の価格リスク other price risk
その他の債権 other receivables
その他の債務 other payables
その他の資本の構成要素 other components of equity
その他の収益 other income
その他の所得 other income
その他の退職後従業員給付 other post-employment benefit, other post-retirement employee benefit (OPEB)
その他の長期給付 other long-term benefits
その他の長期従業員債務 other long-term employee benefits
その他の非流動資産 other non-current assets
その他の非流動負債 other non-current liabilities
その他の包括利益 other comprehensive income (OCI) 頻 to be recognised directly in other comprehensive income（その他の包括利益として認識される）
その他の包括利益の部（包括利益計算書などの） other comprehensive income section
その他の包括利益累計額 accumulated other comprehensive income (AOCI)
その他の包括利益を通じて公正価値（で測定する区分） fair value through other comprehensive income (FVOCI / FVTOCI)
その他の包括利益を通じて公正価値で測定される金融資産 financial assets measured at FVTOCI [FVOCI]
その他の流動資産 other current assets
その他の流動負債 other current liabilities
その他有価証券 available-for-sale securities
その他有価証券評価差額金 valuation difference on available-for-sale securities
その他有価証券評価差額金（益） net gain on available-for-sale securities
その他有価証券評価差額金（損） net loss on available-for-sale securities

その他利益剰余金 other retained earnings, other earned surplus
ソフトウェア software
ソフトウェア開発 software development
損益 profit and loss (P&L), profit or loss 頻 to be recognised in profit or loss（損益として認識される）, to be recycled to profit or loss（損益にリサイクルされる）
損益移転契約 profit and loss transfer agreement (PLTA)
損益勘定 profit and loss (P&L) account
損益計算書 income statement, profit and loss (P&L) statement, statement of operations
損益計算書項目 income statement item
損益通算 aggregation of profit and loss
損益取引 profit and loss transaction
損益分岐点 break-even point (BEP)
損益分岐点売上数量 break-even units
損益分岐点売上高 break-even sales
損益分岐点分析 break-even (point) analysis
損害 damage
損害賠償 indemnity 頻 to obtain indemnity for（〜に対する賠償を受ける）
損害賠償（金） damages
損害賠償請求 claim for damages
損金算入（税務上の） (tax) deduction, (tax) allowance 関 to be deducted directly in tax returns（申告書上で損金算入する）
損金算入可能性 (tax) deductibility
損金算入可能な費用 deductible expense [charge], allowable expense [charge]
損金算入限度額 deductible [allowable] limit
損金算入制限 limitation [restriction] on deductibility, limited deductibility
損金算入配当 deductible dividend
損金算入費用 deductible expense [charge]
損金性 (tax) deductibility
損金不算入 non-deductibility, disallowance 関 be disallowed（損金不算入となる）
損金不算入の費用 non-deductible expense, disallowable expense
損失 loss 頻 to make a loss（損失を計上する）, to report a loss（損失を報告する）
損失が発生する契約（工事契約など） loss-making contract

損失が見込まれる契約　loss contract
損失の回復　recovery of losses
損失の帰属　attribution of losses
損失評価引当金　loss allowance
損傷　damage
損傷在庫　damaged inventory
存続　survival
存続会社（合併に際しての）　surviving company
損耗　wastage

た

ターミナル・バリュー　terminal value
ターミナル持込み渡し条件（価格）　delivered at terminal (DAT)
ターム・シート　term sheet
ターム・ローン　term loan
ターンアラウンド　turnaround
ターンキー契約　turnkey contract
第一次調整（移転価格税制などの）　primary adjustment
第1四半期　1st quarter
対応策　countermeasure
対応策（監査における指摘事項などに対する）　corrective action plan
対応的調整　corresponding [correlative] adjustment
対応表　mapping chart
対価　consideration (transferred)
対価の配分　allocation of consideration
大企業　large corporation
代金引換払い　cash on delivery
大災害　catastrophe
第3四半期　3rd quarter
第三者　third party
第三者委員会　independent committee
第三者（間）取引　third-party transaction, uncontrolled transaction
第三者による通報制度（不正などの）　third-party hotline
第三者による評価　third-party appraisal
第三者の書類　third-party document
貸借対照表　balance sheet　[頻] to be recorded on a balance sheet（貸借対照表上で認識される）
貸借対照表勘定　balance sheet account
貸借対照表項目　balance sheet item
貸借対照表日　balance sheet date　[頻] within 12 months of the balance sheet date（貸借対照表日から12か月以内に）
対照　contrast

対象（範囲） scope, coverage
対象外 out of the scope, outside the scope 頻 to fall out of the scope（（業務範囲の）対象外である）
退職 retirement
退職給付 retirement benefit
退職給付債務 retirement benefit obligation
退職給付制度 retirement benefit plan
退職給付に係る資産 net defined benefit asset
退職給付に係る負債 net defined benefit liability
退職給付引当金 provision for retirement benefits, retirement benefit obligation
退職給付費用 retirement benefit cost
退職金 retirement benefit [allowance]
退職金（特に，解雇や早期退職に伴い支払われる多額の） golden handshake
退職金の受給権 retirement entitlement
退職後医療給付 post-employment medical benefits
退職後確定給付制度 post-employment defined benefit plan
退職後確定給付制度関連費用 expenses related to post-employment defined benefit plans
退職後給付 post-employment benefit
退職後給付制度 post-employment benefit plan
退職後給付費用 post-employment benefit expense
退職後生命保険 post-employment life insurance
退職者 retiree, leaver
退職従業員 retired employee
退職年齢 retirement age
退職率（従業員の） employee turnover
対総費用営業利益率 net cost plus (margin / ratio)
代替案 alternative
代替資産 replacement property
代替資産の取得 acquisition of replacement property
代替処理 alternative treatment
代替的な取扱い alternative treatment
代替（的）手続 alternative procedure

代替報酬 replacement award
第二次期間 secondary period
第二次調整（移転価格税制などの） secondary adjustment
第二次取引 secondary transaction
第２四半期 2nd quarter
滞納（税金などの） delinquency
代表者 representative
代表取締役 representative [managing] director 使い方注意! 代表取締役の英訳に定訳はなく，会社により呼称が異なる
タイブレーカー・ルール tiebreaker rule
大法人 large corporation
タイミング timing
タイムライン timeline
耐用年数 useful life 頻 over a useful life（耐用年数にわたって）
耐用年数の延長 extension of useful life
耐用年数の短縮 shortening of useful life
耐用年数を確定できない無形資産 intangible asset with indefinite useful life
第４四半期 4th quarter
対立 conflict
代理店 agency
代理人 agent
代理人 PE agent PE
滞留売掛金 overdue accounts receivable
滞留債権 overdue receivables
滞留在庫 slow-moving inventory, dead stock
ダウンサイジング downsizing
ダウンサイド・リスク downside risk
ダウンストリーム取引 downstream transaction
ダウンストリーム・ローン downstream loan
多角化 diversification
他勘定振替高 transfer to other accounts
抱合せ株式 tie-in shares
タグ（棚卸用の） (inventory) tag
タグ・アロング条項 tag along clause
タグ・コントロール（棚卸の際の） tag control
多国間 APA multilateral advance pricing arrangement
多国籍企業 multinational enterprise (MNE)
多数決 majority vote
多段階形式の損益計算書 multiple-step in-

come statement
立会（棚卸などの） observation
立退き eviction
立場 position
タックス・イコライゼーション tax equalisation (TEQ) ㊕tax equalization
タックス・インボイス tax invoice
タックス・コンプライアンス tax compliance
タックス・シールド tax shield
タックス・シェルター tax shelter
タックス・パッケージ tax package
タックス・プランニング tax planning
タックス・ヘイブン tax haven
タックス・ヘイブン対策税制 CFC rules, (anti-) tax haven rules 使い方注意！CFC は controlled foreign company/corporation の略 ㊙CFC rules apply（タックス・ヘイブン対策税制が適用される）
タックス・ホリデイ（一定期間の租税の減免） tax holiday ㊙ to enjoy a tax holiday（タックス・ホリデイの適用を受ける）
脱税 tax evasion
脱税者 tax evader
立替金（〜のための） payment on behalf of ㊙parent's payment on behalf of a subsidiary（親会社が支払う子会社のための立替金）
立替費用 out-of-pocket expense
建物 building
建物附属設備 facilities attached to buildings
妥当性 validity
棚卸 inventory count, stock taking
棚卸減耗（損） inventory shrinkage
棚卸差異 inventory variance
棚卸資産 inventory ㊙to purchase inventory（棚卸資産を購入する）, to sell inventory（棚卸資産を販売する）
棚卸資産回転期間 days in inventory, days inventory outstanding (DIO), inventory turnover period, average inventory period
棚卸資産回転率 inventory turnover
棚卸資産期首［期末］残高 opening [ending] inventory
棚卸資産の評価減 inventory write-down
棚卸資産の評価減の戻入 reversal of inventory write-down

棚卸実施要領 physical inventory instructions
棚卸立会 inventory observation
棚卸表 inventory list
棚札（棚卸の際の） tag
棚札の管理（棚卸の際の） tag control
他人資本 debt capital
他の企業に対する持分 interest in another entity
他の企業への関与 interest in another entity
他の企業への関与の開示 disclosure of interests in other entities
他の資産とのシナジー synergy with other assets
多様性 diversity
タリフ・コード tariff code
単位 unit
単位当たり原価 unit cost
単一区分の損益計算書 single-step income statement
単一の窓口 single point of contact
単価 unit price
段階 stage, step
段階（的）取得 step acquisition
段階的に達成された企業結合 business combination achieved in stages
段階法 step-by-step acquisition method
嘆願（書） petition
短期 short term
短期貸付金 short-term loan, short-term loans receivable
短期借入金 short-term borrowings, short-term loan, short-term loans payable, current borrowings
短期給付 short-term benefit
短期経営計画 short-term management plan
短期契約 short-term contract
短期項目 short-term item
短期債券 short bond
短期従業員給付 short-term employee benefit
短期従業員給付費用 short-term employee benefits expense
短期譲渡所得 short-term capital gain
短期投資 short-term investment, current investments
短期の預金 short-term deposit
短期有給休暇 short-term paid absence

短期リース　short-term lease
短期リース債務　short-term lease obligation
探鉱　exploration
単純平均　unweighted average
団体課税（アプローチ）　entity approach
単体財務諸表　separate financial statements
単体財務諸表（親会社の）　parent-only financial statements, parent-only accounts
担当者　person in charge
単年度　single year
単年度損益　income [profit] or loss for current year
短文式の報告書（デュー・デリジェンスなどの）　short-form report
断片　fraction
担保　collateral, pledge　[頻] collateral pledged（差し入れている担保）, collateral held（保有している担保）, collateral sold（売却した担保）
担保権　security interest
担保付貸付金［借入金］　secured loan
担保付銀行借入金　secured bank loan
担保付債券　secured bond
担保付取引　secured transaction
担保付負債　secured debt
担保提供資産　pledged asset
担保として差し入れた金融資産　financial asset pledged as collateral　[頻] financial assets pledged as collateral for liabilities or contingent liabilities（負債または偶発負債の担保として差し入れた金融資産）
担保の差押え　repossession
段落　paragraph
単利　simple interest

ち

地域　region, district, geographic(al) area
地域統括会社　regional headquarters (company)
地域別情報　geographic(al) information
地域別セグメント　geographic(al) segment
チェック（照合時に付ける）　tick
チェック・マーク　tick mark
遅延　delay　[頻] without delay（遅滞なく）
チェンジ・オブ・コントロール　change of control (CoC)
チェンジ・オブ・コントロール条項　change of control clause
遅延支払い　delayed payment
遅延認識　deferred [delayed] recognition
力（パワー）　power
知識　knowledge
秩序ある取引　orderly transaction
チップ　tip
知的財産権　intellectual property (IP)
知的財産権の使用料　royalty from intellectual property
地方債　municipal bond
地方自治体　local government, sub-national regime
地方自治体（地方税を管轄する）　local tax jurisdiction
地方消費税　local consumption tax
地方税　local tax
地方税申告書　local tax returns
地方法人税　local corporation tax, local corporate income tax
地方法人特別税　special local corporation tax
着荷地渡し　CIF destination
中央銀行　central bank
中央値　median
仲介　intermediation
仲介者［人］　intermediary
仲介手数料　brokerage fee
仲介手数料（M&Aに関する）　finder's fee
仲介手数料収益　brokerage fee income
仲介手数料費用　brokerage fee expense
中間親会社　intermediate parent
中間会社　intermediary company
中間期間　interim period
中間（四半期）財務情報　interim financial information
中間（四半期）財務諸表　interim financial statements
中間財務報告　interim financial reporting
中間財務報告書　interim financial report
中間申告書（税務申告書）　interim (tax) return

中間請求　interim [progress] billing
中間点　mid-point
中間納付（税金などの）　interim payment
中間の貸手（転貸などの）　intermediate lessor
中間配当　interim dividend
中間払い　progress payment
中間持株会社　intermediate holding company　[頻] to interpose an intermediate holding company between Company A and Company B（A社とB社の間に中間持株会社を置く）
注記　notes (to financial statements)　[頻] disclosure in the notes to financial statements（（財務諸表）注記による開示）
中期　medium term
中期経営計画　medium-term management plan
中古資産　second-hand property
仲裁　arbitration
駐在員（海外）　expatriate (expat), expatriate staff
駐在員事務所　representative office　[頻] to establish a representative office（駐在員事務所を設置する）, to close a representative office（駐在員事務所を閉鎖する）
中止　suspension, discontinuance, cessation
忠実義務　duty of loyalty
忠実性　faithfulness
忠実な表現　faithful representation
注釈　commentary
抽出　extraction
中小企業　small and medium-sized enterprise (SME)
中小法人　small and medium-sized company, small and medium-sized enterprise (SME)
忠誠心　loyalty
中長期経営計画　medium- to long-term management plan
注文　order　[頻] to place an order（発注する）, to receive an order（受注する）
注文書　purchase order (PO), sales order
注文数量　order quantity
中立性　neutrality
超インフレ　hyperinflation
超過（額）　excess　[頻] in excess of（〜を超えて）

超過収益[利益]　excess earnings
超過収益法（資産評価などの）　excess earnings method
長期　long term
長期貸付金　long-term loan, long-term loans receivable
長期借入金　long-term borrowings, long-term loan, long-term loans payable, non-current borrowings
長期勤続休暇　long-service leave
長期勤続休暇に係る債務　liability for long-service leave
長期経営計画　long-term management plan
長期契約　long-term contract
長期債　long bond
長期譲渡所得　long-term capital gain
長期性資産　long-lived asset
長期性預金　long-term deposit
長期投資　long-term investment
長期の従業員給付基金　long-term employee benefit fund
長期の従業員給付基金が保有している資産　assets held by a long-term employee benefit fund
長期の平均成長率　long-term average growth rate
長期前受収益　long-term unearned revenue
長期前払費用　long-term prepaid expense
長期未収入金　long-term other accounts receivable
長期未払金　long-term other accounts payable
長期リース債務　long-term lease obligation
兆候（減損などの）　indication　[頻] indication of impairment（減損の兆候）
調査　investigation, study
徴収（税金などの）　collection
長寿リスク　longevity risk
調書　work paper (W/P)
調整　reconciliation, adjustment　[頻] reconciliation between A and B（AとBの調整）, reconciliation from A to B（AからBへの調整）
調整（実績値などへの）　true-up
調製（財務諸表の）　compilation
徴税　levy

調整項目　　reconciliation item, balancing item
調整後運転資本　　adjusted working capital
調整後市場評価アプローチ　　adjusted market assessment approach
調整後簿価　　adjusted [recast] book value
調整後利益　　adjusted [recast] earnings
調整なしの公表価格　　unadjusted quoted price
調整表　　reconciliation
調達部門　　procurement department [division]
調停　　mediation
懲罰　　punishment, discipline
懲罰的損害賠償金　　punitive damages
懲罰の減免　　leniency
重複　　overlap
帳簿　　book 〔頻〕 to be recorded in the book（帳簿に記載される），to maintain books（帳簿記録を保持する）
帳簿価額　　book value
帳簿価額（会計上の）　　carrying amount 〔頻〕 carrying amount will be recovered principally through a sale transaction（帳簿価額が，主として売却取引により回収される），carrying amount will be recovered principally through continuing use（帳簿価額が，主として継続的な使用により回収される）
聴聞会　　hearing
調和　　harmonisation 〔米〕harmonization
直接外国税額控除　　direct foreign tax credit 〔頻〕to claim direct foreign tax credits（直接外国税額控除をとる）
直接貸方入力　　direct credit 〔頻〕by a direct credit（評価勘定を用いず，直接貸方入力で）
直接借方入力　　direct debit 〔頻〕by a direct debit（評価勘定を用いず，直接借方入力で）
直接金融　　direct financing
直接金融リース　　direct finance lease
直接原価　　direct cost
直接減額（貸倒損失などの）　　direct write-off
直接原価計算　　direct costing, variable costing
直接原材料　　direct material
直接材料費　　direct material cost
直接材料費差異　　direct material variance

直接償却　　write-off
直接税　　direct tax
直接投資　　direct investment
直接の親会社　　immediate parent company
直接費　　direct cost [expense]
直接賦課方式　　direct charge method
直接法（キャッシュ・フロー計算書）　　direct method
直接保有（株式の）　　direct shareholding
直接労務時間　　direct labour hours 〔米〕direct labor hours
直接労務時間差異　　direct labour efficiency variance 〔米〕direct labor efficiency variance
直接労務費　　direct labour cost 〔米〕direct labor cost
直送　　drop ship
著作権　　copyright
貯蔵品　　supplies
貯蓄　　saving
賃金　　wage
賃金及び給料　　wages and salaries
賃金台帳　　payroll
賃借物件改良設備　　leasehold improvements
賃借料　　rent
賃借料（の支払い）　　rent(al) payment
賃貸価値［価格］（不動産などの）　　rental value
賃貸借期間　　rent(al) period
賃貸借契約　　lease agreement [contract], tenancy agreement
賃貸収入　　rent(al) income
賃貸目的で保有する資産　　assets held for rental to others
賃貸料　　rent
陳腐化　　obsolescence
陳腐化在庫　　obsolete inventory 〔関〕inventories become obsolete（在庫が陳腐化する）
賃率差異（直接労務費に係る）　　direct labour rate variance 〔米〕direct labor rate variance

つ

追加 addition
追加借入利率 incremental borrowing rate
追加最小負債 additional minimum liability
追加直接費用（リースなどの） incremental direct costs
追加的な開示 additional disclosure
追加的な情報 additional information
追加料金 surcharge
追加割当て（有価証券の公募・売出しにおける） overallotment
追徴税額 additional tax (assessed) 頻 a penalty is imposed on additional tax assessed（追徴税額に対して加算税が課される）
対の一方 counterpart
通貨 currency
通貨オプション (foreign) currency option
通貨先物 (foreign) currency futures
通貨スワップ (foreign) currency swap
通貨リスク currency risk
通関 (customs) clearance
通関業者 customs broker
通関手数料 clearance fee
通常実施権 non-exclusive licence 米 non-exclusive license
通常処分価値 orderly liquidation value
通常でない項目 unusual item
通常の営業循環 normal operation cycle
通常の活動 ordinary activities [operations]
通常の契約 regular way contract
通常の事業過程 normal [ordinary] course of business
通常の取引 regular way trade
通常の方法 regular way
通常の方法による契約 regular way contract
通常の方法による売買 regular way purchase or sale
通信及びネットワーク機器 communication and network equipment
通信費 communication cost [expense]
２ステップ・アプローチ two-step approach
通達（税務当局の） circular, ruling
通知 notice, notification
通知預金 deposit at notice, call deposit
通報 tip
月数に基づく按分計算 monthly proration
つなぎ融資［資金調達］ bridge finance [financing]
積上げ（在庫などの） build up
積立金 reserve 頻 reserve for（〜積立金）
積立超過（退職給付制度などの） surplus (in plan)
積立超過または積立不足（退職給付制度などの） surplus or deficit
積立ての取決め funding arrangement
積立不足（退職給付制度などの） deficit
積立方針 funding policy
積立要件 funding requirement

て

手当 allowance
提案 proposal, suggestion
提案依頼書 request for proposal (RFP)
提案済みの配当 dividends proposed
Ｔ勘定 T account
ティーザー teaser
ディール・キラー deal killer
ディール・ストラクチャー deal structure
ディール・ブレイカー deal breaker
ディール・フロー deal flow
ディール・メーカー deal maker
低価基準 lower of cost or market (basis)
定額控除限度額 lump-sum exempt amount
定額資金前渡制度 imprest system
定額法（減価償却） straight-line method
定額報酬 flat fee
低価法 lower of cost and net realisable value, lower of cost or market (basis) 米 lower of cost and net realizable value
定款 articles of incorporation, charter, mem-

	orandum of association	データ・ルーム（デュー・デリジェンスなどの） data room
定義	definition	手形	note
定期性	periodicity	手形借入	notes payable
定期船	liner	手形交換所	clearing house
定期棚卸法	periodic inventory	手形割引料（売却損） discount on notes payable
定期点検	regular inspection		
提供	provision	適格合併	(tax-) qualified merger
定期預金	time deposit 頻 time deposit over 3 months（3ヶ月超の定期預金）	適格株式移転	(tax-) qualified share transfer
		適格株式交換	(tax-) qualified share for share exchange
提携	alliance, cooperation	適格居住者	qualified resident
停止	standstill, cessation	適格現物出資	(tax-) qualified contribution in kind
定時株主総会	annual general meeting		
停止条件	condition precedent (CP)	適格現物分配	(tax-) qualified dividend in kind
提出	submission	適格資産	qualifying asset
提出（公的機関などへの） filing	適格資産に係る支出	expenditure on qualifying asset
ディスクロージャー	disclosure		
ディスクロージャー・レター disclosure letter	適格ストック・オプション qualified stock option
ディストレスト債	distressed debt	適格性	eligibility
訂正	correction	適格性に関する基準（ヘッジなどの） eligibility criteria
定性的及び定量的情報 qualitative and quantitative information		
	適格組織再編	(tax-) qualified corporate reorganisation 米 (tax-) qualified corporate reorganization
定性的開示	qualitative disclosure		
訂正的コントロール corrective control		
定性的情報	qualitative information	適格な保険証券 qualifying insurance policy
定性的情報の開示 qualitative disclosure	適格分割	(tax-) qualified corporate division
定性的な特性	qualitative characteristics		
定性的分析	qualitative analysis	適格分割型分割 (tax-) qualified horizontal-type corporate division
低税率国［地域］ low tax jurisdiction		
程度	degree, extent	適格分社型分割 (tax-) qualified vertical-type corporate division
抵当権	mortgage		
抵当証券	mortgage backed securities (MBS)	適格要件（組織再編の） conditions for (tax-) qualified reorganisation 米 conditions for (tax-) qualified reorganization
ディフィーザンス	defeasance		
締約国	contracting state		
定率法（減価償却） declining balance method, diminishing balance method, reducing balance method	適時開示	timely disclosure
	適時性	timeliness
	適正性	fairness
定量化	quantification	適正な表示	fair presentation
定量的開示	quantitative disclosure	敵対的買収	hostile takeover
定量的情報	quantitative information	出来高払い	progress payment
定量的情報の開示 quantitative disclosure	摘発手段（不正などの） detection method
定量的な基準値	quantitative threshold	適法な手続	due process
定量的分析	quantitative analysis	適用	application
データ・ギャップ	data gap	適用開始	initial application 頻 initial application of standards or interpretations（基
データ不足	data gap		
データ・フロー・チャート data flow chart		

準または解釈指針の適用開始）
適用ガイダンス　implementation guidance
適用可能性　applicability
適用指針　application guidance
適用除外基準　prove-out
適用除外基準［要件］（特に旧タックス・ヘイブン対策税制における）　conditions for exception, exception conditions
適用税率　applicable tax rate
出口　exit
出口価格　exit price
出口戦略　exit strategy [plan]
手数料　commission
手数料収益　fee income
手数料収入　commission income, commission revenue
手数料費用　fee expense
テスト・カウント（棚卸立会における）　test count
撤去　removal
手付金　down payment
撤退　exit
撤退活動　exit activities
手続　procedure
デット・エクイティ・スワップ　debt-equity swap (DES), debt for equity swap (DES)
デット・カバレッジ・レシオ　debt coverage ratio (DCR)
デット・サービス・カバレッジ・レシオ　debt service coverage ratio (DSCR)
デット・デット・スワップ　debt-debt swap (DDS)
デット・ファイナンス　debt financing
デット・プッシュダウン　debt push-down
　関 debt is pushed down to a subsidiary（負債が子会社にプッシュダウンされる）
デットライク・アイテム　debt-like item
テナント　tenant
手入力による仕訳　manual entry
手引　guidance
デビット・カード　debit card
デビット・ノート　debit note
デフォルト　default
デフォルト率　default rate
デフレーション　deflation
デミニマス基準　de minimis rule
手許現金　cash on [in] hand
手許現金の窃盗　theft of cash on hand
手許現金の不正流用　cash-on-hand misappropriation
デュー・デリジェンス　due diligence (DD)
　頻 to perform due diligence（デュー・デリジェンスを実施する）
デュー・デリジェンス報告書　due diligence report
デリバティブ　derivative
デリバティブ金融資産　derivative financial assets
デリバティブ金融商品　derivative financial instrument
デリバティブ金融負債　derivative financial liabilities
デリバティブ資産　derivative financial assets
デリバティブでない本体部分（組込デリバティブなどの）　non-derivative host
デリバティブ負債　derivative financial liabilities
転換　conversion
転換オプション　conversion option
転換型優先株式　convertible preferred share [stock]
転換可能証券　convertible securities
転換可能な金融商品　convertible instrument
転換社債　convertible bond [note]
転記（仕訳帳から元帳への）　posting
電気通信利用役務（の提供）　digital services
天候デリバティブ　weather derivative
電子資金振替　electronic funds transfer (EFT)
電子商取引　e-commerce
電子申告　electronic tax (return) filing
電信売相場　telegraphic transfer selling rate (TTS)
電信買相場　telegraphic transfer buying rate (TTB)
電信送金　T/T remittance
転貸　sub-lease
転貸契約　sub-lease arrangement
転貸収入　sub-lease income
店頭　over-the-counter (OTC)
店頭市場　over-the-counter (OTC) market
店頭デリバティブ　over-the-counter (OTC) derivative

天然資源　natural resources
転売　resale
転売目的で取得した子会社　subsidiary acquired with a view to resale
伝票　memo, slip
添付　attachment
電話会議　conference call
電話による通報制度（不正などの）　telephone hotline

と

問屋　commissionaire, (general) commission agent
同意　consent
同意書　consent letter, letter of consent
統一性　uniformity
統一的な会計方針　uniform accounting policies
統一フォーム　uniform format
投下資本　invested capital (IC)
投下資本利益率　return on invested capital (ROIC)
統括会社（地域統括会社）　regional headquarters (company)
導管　conduit
導管事業体　conduit company, flow-through entity
導管取引　conduit transaction
導管防止規定　anti-conduit provision
当期　current period [year]
投機　speculation
登記　registration
登記官　registrar
当期勤務費用　current service cost
当期純損益　profit or loss for the period
当期純損失　net loss, loss for the year
当期純利益　net income, profit for the year
登記上の本社　registered office
当期税金　current tax
当期税金資産　current tax assets
当期税金収益　current tax income
当期税金費用　current tax expense
当期税金負債　current tax liabilities
当期税金利益　current tax income
当期その他の包括利益　other comprehensive income for the year
当期損益　profit or loss for the year
当期損益への組替調整額　reclassification adjustment to profit or loss for the year
当期損失　loss for the year
当期包括利益合計　total comprehensive income for the year
東京国税局　Tokyo Regional Tax(ation) Bureau
東京証券取引所　Tokyo Stock Exchange (TSE)
同業他社（集団）　peer group
当局　authority
当期利益　profit for the year
統計　statistics
統合　integration
統合基幹業務システム　enterprise resource planning (ERP)
統合報告　integrated reporting
当座貸越［借越］　(bank) overdraft
当座借越枠　overdraft facility
当座資産　quick assets
当座比率　quick [acid-test] ratio
当座預金　checking account, current deposit
倒産　bankruptcy
動産　personal property
倒産隔離　bankruptcy remote
投資　investment
投資インセンティブ　investment incentives
投資家　investor
投資会社　investment company
投資回収期間　payback period
投資活動　investing activity
投資活動によるキャッシュ・フロー　cash flows from investing activities, investing cash flows
投資家向け広報活動　investor relations (IR)
投資管理　investment management
投資管理手数料　investment management fee
等式　equation
投資企業　investor, investment entity
投資企業の被投資企業に対する比例持分　investor's proportionate interest in an in-

vestee	
投資銀行	investment bank
投資契約	investment contract
投資控除	investment allowance
投資先	investee
投資先に対する支配	control of an investee
投資先に対する力（パワー）	power over an investee
当事者	party
当事者関係	privity
投資収益	investment income
投資収益の受取額	investment income received
投資証書	investment certificate
投資信託	investment trust
投資税額控除	investment (tax) credit
投資その他の資産	investments and other assets
投資損失引当金	provision for investment losses
投資対象企業（投資会社などが投資の対象にしている企業）	portfolio company
投資適格	investment grade
投資適格債	investment grade bond, investment grade debt securities
投資適格の格付け	investment grade rating
投資に係るリスク	investment risk
投資の処分	divestiture, divestment
投資ビークル	acquisition [investment] vehicle
投資ファンド	investment fund
投資不適格	non-investment grade
投資不動産	investment property 頻 transfer to [from] investment property (classification)（投資不動産への［からの］振替）
投資不動産の処分［売却］	disposal of investment property
投資不動産の賃貸	rental of investment property
投資不動産の賃貸収入	investment property rental income
同時文書（化）	contemporaneous (transfer pricing) documentation
投資有価証券	investment securities
投資有価証券売却益	gain on sale of investment securities
投資有価証券売却損	loss on sale of investment securities
投資有価証券評価損	loss on revaluation of investment securities
同種資産	like-kind property
同種資産の交換	like-kind exchange
当初以後の測定	subsequent measurement
当初測定	initial measurement
当初損失	initial loss
当初直接コスト（リースなどの）	initial direct cost
当初認識	initial recognition
投資利益率	return on investment (ROI)
統制	control
統制活動	control activity
統制環境	control environment
統制テスト	test of controls
統制リスク	control risk
同族会社	family company [corporation], closely held company
統治	governance
同等物	equivalent
盗難	theft
投入	input
導入	introduction
当年度	current year
道府県税事務所	prefectural tax office
道府県民税（住民税）	prefectural tax
道府県民税均等割	per capita prefectural tax
透明性	transparency, clarity
同様の項目	like items
同様の取引	like transactions
登録	registration
登録機関	registrar
登録事業所	registered office
登録商標	registered trademark
登録書類	registration statement
登録手数料	registration fee
登録免許税	registration (and licence) tax 米 registration (and license) tax
登録料	registration fee
時の経過	passage of time
特殊関税（制度）	special tariffs
特性	feature, character
独占	monopoly
独占禁止法	anti-trust act [law]

独占契約　exclusive agreement
独占権　exclusivity, exclusive right
独占交渉期間（買収案件などの）　exclusivity period
独占交渉権　exclusive negotiating rights
独占交渉権に係る合意（買収案件などの）　exclusivity agreement
独占的実施権　exclusive licence　㊪ exclusive license
特徴　characteristic, character, feature
特定　identification
特定外国関係会社（タックス・ヘイブン対策税制における）　specified foreign related company
特定外国子会社等（旧タックス・ヘイブン対策税制における）　specified foreign subsidiary
特定期間への影響　period-specific effect
特定同族会社　specified family company
特定同族会社の留保金課税　special tax due by specified family company
特定の資産　specified asset
特定目的会社　TMK
特典　privilege
特典制限条項　limitation on benefits (LOB) provision
特典の制限（租税条約などの）　limitation on benefits
特別控除　special deduction
特別項目　extraordinary item
特別償却（減価償却のうち）　special depreciation, accelerated depreciation
特別清算　special liquidation
特別措置（税務上の）　special concession
特別損失　extraordinary loss
特別目的会社　special purpose company (SPC), special purpose vehicle (SPV), special purpose entity (SPE)
特別利益　extraordinary gain, extraordinary income, extraordinary profit
匿名組合（主に米国などの）　silent partnership
匿名組合（日本の）　Tokumei Kumiai (TK)
特約　rider
独立価格比準法　comparable uncontrolled price method (CUP method)
独立監査人　independent auditor
独立監査人の監査報告書　independent auditor's report
独立企業　independent enterprise
独立企業間価格　arm's length price (ALP)
独立企業間価格の算定方法　transfer pricing methodology (TPM)
独立企業間価格レンジ　arm's length range
独立企業間価格を算定するために必要と認められる書類（ローカル・ファイル）　local file
独立企業間原則　arm's length principle
独立企業間取引　arm's length transaction
独立性　independence
独立代理人　independent agent, agent of an independent status
独立取引比準法　comparable uncontrolled transaction (CUT method)
独立の立場からのチェック　independent check
独立販売価格　stand-alone selling price
独立役員　independent officer
都市計画税　city planning tax
土壌　soil
土壌汚染　soil contamination
土地　land
土地及び建物　land and buildings
土地改良（費）　land improvements
土地原状回復引当金　provision for site restoration, site restoration provision
土地再評価差額金　revaluation difference on land
土地再評価差額金（益）　net unrealised gain on land revaluation　㊪ net unrealized gain on land revaluation
土地再評価差額金（損）　net unrealised loss on land revaluation　㊪ net unrealized loss on land revaluation
特許　patent
特許技術　patented technology
特許権　patent
特許権侵害　patent infringement
特権　privilege
トップダウン・アプローチ　top-down approach
届出　notification

都民税（住民税）　metropolitan inhabitant tax
都民税均等割　per capita metropolitan tax
ドメイン名　domain name
トラッキング・ストック　tracking stock
ドラッグ・アロング条項　drag along clause
トランシェ　tranche
トランジショナル・サービス・アグリーメント　transitional services agreement (TSA)
取扱い　treatment, handling　[頻] to determine the treatment of [for]（～の取扱いを決定する）　[関] to treat A as B（A を B として取り扱う）
トリーティー・オーバーライド　treaty override
トリーティー・ショッピング　treaty shopping
トリーティー・ショッピング防止規定　anti-treaty shopping provision
トリガー　trigger
トリガー・イベント（引き金となる事象）　trigger (ing) event
取替え　replacement
取替法　replacement method
取決め　arrangement
取崩し　reversal　[頻] reversal of a provision（引当金の取崩し）　[関] to be reversed（取り崩される）
取消し　cancellation, revocation
取消し（契約などの）　rescission
取消伝票　credit memo
取消不能契約　irrevocable contract
取壊し　demolition, destruction, dismantlement
取締役　director, member of board of directors
取締役会　board, board of directors (BOD)
取締役会議事録　minutes of board of directors' meeting
取引　transaction, trading, deal　[頻] to cease trading（取引を停止する）, to carry out/execute a transaction（取引を実行する）, to structure a transaction（取引（組織再編など）を組成する）
取引相手　counterparty, counterpart
取引価格　transaction price
取引コスト　transaction cost

取引ごとのベース　transaction-by-transaction basis　[頻] on a transaction-by-transaction basis（取引ごとに［の］）
取引所　exchange
取引条件　terms and conditions
取引税　transaction tax
取引単位営業利益法　transactional net margin method (TNMM)
取引の法的形式　legal form of a transaction
取引日　trade date, transaction date
取引日会計　trade date accounting
取引日の為替レート　transaction-date exchange rate
取引日レート　exchange rate at the date of the transaction, transaction-date exchange rate
取引履歴　trading history
トレーダー　trader
トレーディング　trading
トレーディング収益　trading income
トレーディング費用　trading expense
トレーディング目的保有の　held for trading
トレーディング目的保有の金融負債　financial liability held for trading
トレーディング有価証券　trading securities
トレード・ドレス　trade dress
トレーニング　training
ドローダウン（融資枠からの資金の引出し）　draw-down
問屋　commissionaire, (general) commission agent

な

内国貨物　domestic cargo
内国法人　domestic company [corporation]
内部監査　internal audit
内部監査人　internal auditor
内部監査人協会　Institute of internal Auditors (IIA)
内部監査部門　internal audit department [division]
内部管理　internal management
内部管理報告　internal management report
内部金融　internal financing
内部告発　whistle-blowing
内部告発者　whistle-blower
内部資金　internal funds
内部資金調達　internal financing
内部市場　internal market
内部収益率　internal rate of return (IRR)
内部使用　internal use
内部使用のソフトウェア　internal-use software
内部情報　inside information
内部処分　internal discipline
内部信用格付け　internal credit grade
内部生成無形資産　internally developed intangibles
内部調査　internal investigation
内部通報制度　(reporting) hotline
内部統制　internal control
内部統制質問書　internal control questionnaire
内部統制テスト　control test
内部統制の運用　operation of control
内部統制の重要な不備　material weakness in internal control
内部統制の脆弱性　internal control weakness
内部統制の整備　design of control
内部統制の不備　control deficiency, internal control weakness
内部統制の無効化　override of internal controls
内部取引　internal transaction
内部比較対象（取引）　internal comparable
内部利益　internal profit
内部留保　retained earnings
内部留保率　retention ratio
仲買　brokerage
仲買手数料　brokerage
仲買人　broker
仲立人　broker
仲値（TTBとTTSの）　telegraphic transfer middle rate (TTM)
流れ　flow, stream

に

荷揚げ　landing, unloading
荷揚費用　landing charge
荷扱い　handling
荷役費用　handling cost [expense]
2計算書方式の表示（包括利益計算書などの）　two-statement presentation
二項モデル　binomial model
二国間APA　bilateral advance pricing arrangement (BAPA)
二重課税　double taxation　頻 to relieve double taxation（二重課税を排除する）
二重課税の排除　avoidance of double taxation
二重課税防止規定　double taxation relief
二重居住（地）　dual residence
二重居住者　dual resident
二重計算　double count
二重の効果　dual effect
日次統制　daily control
日次平均　daily average
日常の取引　day-to-day transactions
日米租税条約　Japan - U.S. tax treaty
荷造り　packing
荷造費　packing cost
日数に基づく按分計算　daily proration
日当　per diem

荷主　　　shipper
日本基準（会計基準について）　　Japan GAAP, accounting principles generally accepted in Japan
日本公認会計士協会　　Japanese Institute of Certified Public Accountants (JICPA)
入荷　　　receipt of goods
入会（金）　　admission
入荷報告書　　receiving report
入金　　　receipt of money, cash receipt(s)
入金伝票　　(cash) receipt slip
入札　　　bid
入札手続　　bidding process
入手可能性　　availability
入力　　　input
任意解散　　voluntary dissolution
任意組合　　Nini Kumiai (NK)
任意清算　　voluntary liquidation
任意積立金　　voluntary reserve
任意の中止　　voluntary discontinuation
任意の変更　　voluntary change
任意の免除規定　　optional exemption
認識　　　recognition　[頻] recognition of A as B (AのBとしての（財務諸表上の）認識), to defer recognition of (〜の認識を遅らせる)
認識及び測定　　recognition and measurement
認識基準　　recognition criteria　[頻] to meet recognition criteria (認識基準を充足する)
認識後の測定　　measurement after recognition
認識時の測定　　measurement at recognition
認識に関する不一致・不整合　　recognition inconsistency
認識の中止　　derecognition　[関] an asset is derecognised on disposal (資産の認識は処分の時点で中止される)
認証　　　verification, authentication
人数　　　headcount　[頻] to allocate □ based on headcount (□を人数割で配賦する)
任務　　　mission
任命　　　appointment
任命書　　letter of appointment
認容加算（過年度の減算に対する）　　reversal
認容減算（過年度の加算に対する）　　reversal

ぬ

抜き打ち監査　　surprise audit
抜け穴（法の）　　loophole

ね

ネクサス　　nexus　[頻] nexus with a state (州とのつながり), to create nexus (ネクサスを発生させる)
値下がりリスク　　downside risk
値下げ　　markdown
ネッティング　　netting
ネット・キャッシュ　　net cash
ネット・デット　　net debt
ネットワーク基盤　　network infrastructure
値引　　　discount, price concession
年間目標（値）　　annual target
年間予算　　annual budget
年金　　　pension, annuity
年金基金　　pension fund
年金資産　　plan assets
年金受給者　　pensioner
年金数理人　　actuary
年金数理評価方式　　actuarial valuation method
年金制度　　pension plan
年金負債　　accrued pension cost
年功　　　seniority
年次休暇　　annual leave
年次決算　　year-end closing
年次決算書　　annual financial statements, annual accounts
年次財務諸表　　annual financial statements, annual accounts
年次申告　　annual filing
年次統制　　annual control

年次有給休暇　annual leave
年次報告書　annual report
年初からの累計期間　year-to-date period
年初からの累計計算　year-to-date calculation
年初からの累計ベース　year-to-date basis
年初来　year to date
年度決算　year-end closing
年度の予測数値　forecast annual amounts
年度末　year-end
年度末決算　year-end closing
年度末修正　year-end adjustment
年度予算　annual budget
年平均成長率　compound annual growth rate (CAGR)
年末調整　year-end adjustment
燃料費　fuel cost [expense]
年齢調べ　age analysis　関 accounts receivable aged greater than 90 days（90日を超えて未回収の売掛金）
年齢調べ表（売掛金などの）　aging list

能率　efficiency
能率差異（製造間接費に係る）　efficiency variance
能力　competence, competency
残り　rest
延払いの買収対価　deferred purchase price
のれん　goodwill　頻 goodwill arrising from a business combination（企業結合により生じるのれん），goodwill is not amortised but is reviewed [tested] for impairment（のれんは償却されないが減損テストの対象となる）
のれん償却費　amortisation of goodwill　米 amortization of goodwill
ノンネーム・シート　teaser
ノンリコース・ローン　non-recourse loan

の

農業　agriculture
納税　tax payment
納税管理人　tax agent [representative]
納税義務　tax liability
納税（義務）者　taxpayer, taxable person
納税者番号　taxpayer identification number (TIN)
納税証明書　tax payment certificate, certificate of tax payment, tax clearance certificate
能動的所得　active income
ノウハウ　know-how
納品書　delivery [packing] slip
納付（税金などの）　payment
納付期限　payment due date
納付期限の延長　payment extension, extension for tax payments
納付書　tax payment slip
納付税額計算書　tax computation

は

場合　case
バーゲン・パーチェス　bargain purchase
バーゲン・パーチェスによる利益　gain on [from] a bargain purchase
バージョン　version
パーチェス法　purchase method
ハードウェア　hardware
ハード・クローズ　hard close
パートナー　partner
パートナーシップ　partnership
パートナーシップの持分　partnership interest
ハードル・レート　hurdle rate
バーン・レート　burn rate
ハイ・イールド債　high yield debt
売価還元法　retail method, gross profit method
廃棄　abandonment　関 non-current asset (that is) to be abandoned（廃棄予定の非流動資産）
廃棄，原状回復または類似の負債　decommissioning, restoration or similar liabilities
廃棄コスト　decommissioning cost
廃棄した資産　abandoned asset
廃棄物　waste
廃却　disposal
売却　sale
売却可能金融資産（旧）　available-for-sale financial assets (AFS)
売却コスト　cost to sell
売却コスト控除後の公正価値　fair value less costs to sell
売却参加権　tag along right
売却制限株式　restricted share [stock]
廃却損　disposal loss
売却取引　sale transaction
売却の完了　completion of sale
売却目的で保有する資産　assets (classified as) held for sale　頻 transfer to assets held for sale（売却目的で保有する資産への振替え）
売却目的で保有する処分グループ　disposal group held for sale
売却目的で保有する非流動資産　non-current assets held for sale
売却目的で保有する負債　liabilities held for sale
廃棄予定の非流動資産　non-current asset (that is) to be abandoned
配偶者　spouse
背景　background
背景情報　background information
バイサイド　buy side
廃止　discontinuance, abolishment
廃止事業　discontinued operations
買収　buyout, acquisition
買収価格　purchase price　頻「購入価格」の項を参照
買収価格の調整　purchase price adjustment
買収関連コスト　acquisition-related cost
買収後［クロージング後］のデュー・デリジェンス　post-acquisition [post-closing] due diligence
買収後の統合　post-merger integration (PMI)
買収対象会社　target (company)
買収対象会社グループ　target group
買収対象会社の株主　target's shareholder
買収に伴う資金調達　acquisition finance, acquisition funding
買収ビークル　acquisition vehicle
買収防衛策　takeover defence　米 takeover defense
買収前の繰越欠損金　pre-acquisition tax losses
排出　emission
排出権　emission rights
賠償　compensation, indemnification, indemnity
賠償金　indemnity
倍数　multiple
配送　delivery
配送日　delivery date
排他的契約　exclusive agreement
排他的ライセンス　exclusive licence　米 exclusive license

配置　placement
配置転換　job rotation
配当（金）　dividend　［頻］to distribute [pay (out)] a dividend（配当金を支払う）, to receive a dividend（配当金を受け取る）, to declare a dividend（配当を宣言する）
配当金の受取（額）　dividends received
配当金の支払い　dividend distribution [payment]
配当計算期間　dividend calculation period
配当決議　resolution on dividend payment
配当源泉税　withholding tax on dividends
配当収益　dividend income
配当所得　dividend income
配当制限　dividend restriction
配当性向　(dividend) payout ratio
配当政策　dividend policy
配当宣言　dividend declaration
配当逓増優先株式　increasing rate preference share
配当利回り　dividend yield
ハイパーインフレーション　hyperinflation
売買　dealing
売買契約　buy-sell agreement, sale and purchase agreement
売買目的外有価証券　securities held for other than trading purposes
売買目的保有の　held for trading
売買目的保有の金融負債　financial liability held for trading
売買目的有価証券　securities held for trading purposes
配賦　allocation
配賦基準　allocation basis, basis of allocation　［関］to be allocated based on（～を基準に配賦される）
配賦方法（費用等の）　allocation method
ハイブリッド金融商品　hybrid instrument
ハイブリッド事業体　hybrid entity
ハイブリッド証券　hybrid securities
ハイブリッド・デリバティブ　hybrid derivative
ハイブリッド・ファイナンス　hybrid financing
ハイブリッド・ミスマッチ方式　hybrid mismatch arrangement
配分　allocation　［関］unallocated goodwill（配分されていないのれん）, unallocated amount（配分しなかった金額）
ハイポ・タックス　hypothetical tax
バイヤーズ・バリュー　buyer's value
倍率　multiple
端株　fractional [odd] share
波及効果　spillover effect
派遣社員　temporary staff
破産　bankruptcy
破産法　Bankruptcy Act
場所　place
パススルー課税　pass-through taxation
パススルー事業体　pass-through entity
パススルーの取決め　pass-through arrangement
派生金融商品　derivative financial instrument
パターン　pattern
罰金　fine, penalty charge
パッケージ　package
発見　detection
発見事項　finding
発見的コントロール（内部統制のうち）　detective control
発行（証券などの）　issuance, issue　［関］commercial papers issued（発行したコマーシャル・ペーパー）, bonds issued（発行した社債）
発行会社（証券などの）　issuer
発行会社の選択　issuer's option
発行市場（証券などの）　primary market
発行者（証券などの）　issuer
発行者の選択　issuer's option
発行済　issued and outstanding
発行済株式　shares outstanding [issued], outstanding [issued] shares
発行済株式総数　number of shares outstanding [issued]
発行済株式ベース　outstanding shares basis
発行済普通株式の加重平均株式数（期中の）　weighted average number of ordinary shares outstanding (during the period)
発行日（証券などの）　issue date
発効日　effective date
発行費用（証券などの）　issue cost
パッシブ・インカム　passive income

抜粋　excerpt
発生　occurrence, incidence, origination　[頻] the occurrence or non-occurrence of（～の発生または不発生）
発生（収益や費用の）　accrual
発生（費用や負債の）　incurrence　[関] costs incur（費用が発生する）
発生確率で加重平均した期待値　probability-weighted expected value
発生確率による加重平均ベース　probability-weighted basis
発生可能性　likelihood
発生基準　accrual basis
発生しないこと　non-occurrence
発生主義　accrual basis [method]
発生主義会計　accrual (method of) accounting
発生時レート　historical exchange rate
発生損失モデル　incurred loss model
発生利息（債券などの）　accreted interest
罰則　punishment
発注量　order quantity
バッド・リーバー　bad leaver
バッファー　buffer
パテント・ボックス　patent box
パブリック・レター・ルーリング　public letter ruling
払込資本　paid in capital
払込資本金　paid-up share capital
払込剰余金　additional paid in capital
払戻し（立替費用などの）　reimbursement
払戻し（預金などの）　withdrawal
パラメータ　parameter
バランシング・ペイメント　balancing payment
バランス調整　rebalancing
バリュー・アット・リスク　value at risk (VaR)
バリュー・ドライバー　value driver
バリュエーション・レポート　valuation report
バルーン・ペイメント　balloon payment
パワー　power
パワーとリターンの関係　link between power and returns
判　seal
範囲　scope, extent, range　[頻] out of the scope（（業務の対象）範囲外）, top of range（範囲の上限）, bottom of range（範囲の下限）
範囲の制限　scope limitation
半期　half year
半期決算　semi-annual closing
半期統制　semi-annual control
半期予算　half year budget
判決　(court) decision, judgement
犯行者　perpetrator
犯罪　crime
半製品　semi-finished goods
反対意見　dissenting opinion
反対株主　dissenting shareholder
反対仕訳　reversal [reversing] entry
判断　judgement　[米] judgment　[頻] to require judgement（判断を要する）
判断及び見積りの使用　use of judgements and estimates　[米] use of judgments and estimates
判定用数値　control number
販売インセンティブ　sales incentive
販売　sale
販売運賃　freight out
販売及びマーケティング費用　sales and marketing expense
販売価格　sales price
販売価格差異　sales price variance
販売型リース　sales-type lease
販売可能商品　goods available for sale
販売可能性　saleability　[米] salability
販売間接費　indirect selling cost
販売管理　sales management
販売業者　distributor, dealer
販売業者である貸手（リースの）　dealer lessor
販売経路　distribution channel, sales channel
販売権　marketing right
販売限度額　sale limit
販売システム　sales system
販売実績　sales performance
販売数量　sales volume
販売数量差異　sales volume variance
販売促進　sales promotion
販売促進費　sales promotion cost [expense]
販売地域　sales territory

はんばいち

販売直接費　direct selling cost
販売手数料　sales commission
販売取引　sales transaction
販売費　selling cost [expense], distribution cost [expense]
販売費及び一般管理費　selling, general and administrative expenses (SG&A)
販売費及び管理費　distribution and administrative expense
販売部門　sales department
販売網　sales network
販売用不動産　real estate inventory, real estate held for resale
販売予算　sales budget
判例　(judicial) precedent, case

ひ

ピア・グループ　peer group
ビークル　vehicle
被裏書人　endorsee
非永住者　non-permanent resident
非営利組織　non-profit [not-for-profit] organisation (NPO) 米 non-profit [not-for-profit] organization
非開示　non-disclosure
比較　comparison
比較可能性　comparability 頻 to enhance comparability（比較可能性を高める）関 to be comparable with the current period（当期と比較可能である）
比較財務諸表　comparative financial statement
比較情報　comparative information
比較対象会社　comparable company
比較対象となる過年度情報　comparative prior-period information
比較対象取引　comparable transaction
比較分析　comparability [comparative] analysis
非課税　exemption (from tax)
非課税売上　non-taxable sales

非課税所得　non-taxable income, (tax-) exempt income, excluded income 関 be excluded from taxable income（非課税とされる）
非課税組織　(tax-) exempt organisation 米 (tax-) exempt organization
非課税組織再編　non-taxable (corporate) reorganisation, tax-free (corporate) reorganisation 米 non-taxable (corporate) reorganization, tax-free (corporate) reorganization 頻 restriction on the disposal of shares received in a tax-free (corporate) reorganisation（非課税組織再編における取得株式の処分制限）
非課税取引　non-taxable transaction
被合併法人　merged company, predecessor company
非貨幣性給付　non-monetary benefits
非貨幣性項目　non-monetary item
非貨幣性資産　non-monetary asset
非貨幣性取引　non-monetary transaction
非貨幣性の補助金　non-monetary grant
非貨幣性負債　non-monetary liability
非関連者　unrelated company [person]
非関連者基準（タックス・ヘイブン対策税制）　unrelated party test 頻 to satisfy the unrelated party test（非関連者基準を充足する）, to fail the unrelated party test（非関連者基準を充足しない）
引合い　enquiry
引当金　provision, allowance 頻 to record [recognise] a provision for（～に対して引当金を設定する）, to revise a provision（引当金の額を変更する）, to reverse a provision（引当金を取り崩す）
引当金の目的外使用(取崩し)　release of provisions
引当金の目的使用　utilisation of provisions
引受け（証券などの）　subscription
引受け（負債などの）　assumption
引受会社（証券などの）　underwriter
引受権　subscription right
引き受けた負債　liabilities assumed
引受人（証券などの）　underwriter
引出し（預金などの）　withdrawal
引継ぎ　succession

引継（者）債務　successor liability
引継簿価　carryover basis
非居住者　non-resident
引渡し　delivery
引渡基準　delivery basis
非金銭取引　non-monetary transaction
非金融債務　non-financial obligation
非金融資産　non-financial asset
非金融資産の購入予定取引　forecast non-financial asset purchase
非金融商品　non-financial instrument
非金融商品項目を売買する契約　contract to buy or sell a non-financial item
非金融負債　non-financial liability
非経常原価　non-recurring cost
非経常項目　non-recurring item
非経常的取引　non-routine transaction
非経常的な公正価値評価　non-recurring fair value measurement
非経常ベース　non-recurring basis
非継続　discontinuance
非継続事業　discontinued operations
非継続事業からの純損失　loss from discontinued operations
非継続事業からの純利益　profit from discontinued operations
非継続事業からの当期利益［損失］　profit [loss] for the year from discontinued operations
非継続事業からの1株当たり利益　earnings per share from discontinued operations
非継続事業のキャッシュ・フロー　cash flows from (used in) discontinued operation
被結合企業　combined entity
非減価償却資産　non-depreciable asset
非現金資産　non-cash asset
備考　remark
非公開会社　private company
非公開企業　non-public enterprise
非公式の契約　informal agreement
備考欄　remarks column
非効率性　inefficiency
被告　defendant
非財務情報　non-financial information
非事業用資産　non-operating asset
非資金項目　non-cash item

非資金資産　non-cash asset
非資金支出費用　non-cash expense
非資金取引　non-cash transaction
ビジネス影響度分析　business impact analysis (BIA)
ビジネス・デュー・デリジェンス　business due diligence
ビジネス・プロセス・アウトソーシング　business process outsourcing (BPO)
ビジネス・プロセス・マネジメント　business process management (BPM)
被支配外国法人　controlled foreign company (CFC)
非支配株主持分　non-controlling interest (NCI)
被支配企業　controlled company
非支配持分　non-controlling interest (NCI) 頻 a non-controlling interest in a subsidiary（子会社の非支配持分），change in non-controlling interests（非支配持分の増減）
非支配持分との取引　transactions with non-controlling interests
非支配持分に帰属する当期包括利益　total comprehensive income attributable to non-controlling interests
非支配持分に帰属する当期利益　profit attributable to non-controlling interests
非従業員　non-employees
非修正後発事象　non-adjusting event after reporting period
被取得企業　acquiree
被取得企業に対する既存持分　pre-existing interest in an acquiree
非償還優先株式　non-redeemable preference share
非償却資産（有形固定資産）　non-depreciable asset
非償却の無形資産　non-amortisable intangible asset 米 non-amortizable intangible asset
非常勤監査役　part-time corporate auditor
非上場化　going private
非上場株式　unlisted share [stock]
非上場企業　unlisted entity, non-public enterprise

非上場有価証券	unlisted securities
ヒストリカル・ボラティリティ	historical volatility
日付	date
ビッド	bid
ビッド価格	bid price
ビッド・レター	bid letter
必要資本	capital requirements
必要条件	prerequisite
必要性	necessity
否定	denial, negation
非適格合併	non tax-qualified merger
非適格株式移転	non tax-qualified share transfer
非適格株式交換	non tax-qualified share for share exchange
非適格現物出資	non tax-qualified contribution in kind
非適格現物分配	non tax-qualified dividend in kind
非適格ストック・オプション	non (tax-) qualified stock option
非適格組織再編	non tax-qualified (corporate) reorganisation 米 non tax-qualified (corporate) reorganization
非適格分割	non tax-qualified corporate division
非適格分割型分割	non tax-qualified horizontal-type corporate division
非適格分社型分割	non tax-qualified vertical-type corporate division
非デリバティブ	non-derivative
非デリバティブ金融資産	non-derivative financial asset
非デリバティブ金融商品	non-derivative financial instrument
非デリバティブ金融負債	non-derivative financial liability
被統括会社（税務上の）	controlled company
被投資企業	investee
被投資企業から受け取った分配	distribution received from an investee
被投資企業に対する力（パワー）	power over an investee
被投資企業の純損益のうち投資企業の持分額	investor's share of the profit or loss of an investee
被投資企業のその他の包括利益のうち投資企業の持分額	investor's share of the other comprehensive income of an investee
1株当たり純資産	book value per share (BPS)
1株当たり損失	loss per share
1株当たり配当金	dividend per share (DPS)
1株当たり利益	earnings per share (EPS)
非独占契約	non-exclusive agreement
非独占的実施権	non-exclusive licence 米 non-exclusive license
1組の財務諸表（完全な）	a complete set of financial statements
1組の要約財務諸表	a set of condensed financial statements
否認	denial, negation
非排他的契約	non-exclusive agreement
非排他的ライセンス	non-exclusive licence 米 non-exclusive license
備品	equipment, fixtures and fittings, furniture and fixtures
秘密	confidence
秘密保持契約	confidentiality agreement (CA), non-disclosure agreement (NDA)
100％グループ	100% group
100％グループ内の寄附金	donation within 100% group
100％グループ内の現物分配	dividend in kind within 100% group
100％グループ内の資産譲渡	transfer of assets within 100% group
100％グループ内の資本取引	capital transaction within 100% group
100％グループ内の取引	transaction within 100% group
100％減資	100% reduction of capital
100％子会社	wholly-owned subsidiary
非有効性	ineffectiveness
非有効部分（ヘッジなどの）	ineffective portion
表	table
費用	expense, expenditure, charge 頻 to recognise expenses（費用を認識する）, an expense is incurred（費用が発生する）関 to be expensed（費用処理される）, to be expensed as incurred（発生時に費用処

理される）, to be expensed immediately（即時費用処理される）
評価　valuation, appraisal
評価アプローチ　valuation [appraisal] approach
評価益　revaluation gain　関 (net) gain on (the) revaluation of（～についての評価益）
評価額　appraised value
評価額（主に税務上の）　assessed value
評価・換算差額等　valuation and translation adjustments
評価勘定　valuation account
評価基準　valuation basis
評価技法　valuation technique
評価減（簿価全額）　write-off
評価減（簿価の一部）　write-down　頻 a write-down is made item by item（個別項目ごとに評価減される）, a write-down is made by groups of items（グループごとに評価減される）　関 an asset is written down to the recoverable amount（資産が回収可能価額まで評価減される）
評価減及びその戻入　write-down and reversal
評価原則　valuation principles
評価減の戻入　reversal of write-down, write-back
評価困難な無形資産　hard-to-value intangibles (HTVI)
評価実務　valuation [appraisal] practice
評価者　valuer
評価手法　valuation technique
評価書　valuation [appraisal] report
評価性引当額　valuation allowance　頻 to recognise a valuation allowance（評価性引当額を設定する）
評価前提　valuation premise
評価増　write-up
評価損　revaluation loss　関 (net) loss on (the) revaluation of（～についての評価損）
評価調整　valuation adjustment
評価手続　valuation [appraisal] procedure
評価倍率（企業評価に用いるマルチプル）　valuation multiple
評価日　valuation [appraisal] date
評価日（の為替）レート　valuation-date exchange rate
評価方法　valuation [appraisal] method
評価見直し　rerating
評価モデル　valuation model
表現　expression
費用項目の機能別分類　classification of expenses by function
費用項目の形態別分類　classification of expenses by nature
費用削減　cost saving, cost reduction
表示　presentation, representation　頻 presentation of A as B（AのBとしての（財務諸表上の）表示）
表示及び開示　presentation and disclosure
表示価格　list price
表示区分の変更　change in classification
表示される期間（財務諸表に）　period presented
表示通貨　presentation currency
表示通貨の選択（肢）　choice of presentation currency
表示通貨への換算　translation to the presentation currency
表示方法の変更　change in presentation
費用収益対応の原則　matching principle
費用収益の対応　matching (of cost with revenue)
標準　standard, norm
標準化　standardisation, normalisation　米 standardization, normalization
標準原価　standard cost
標準原価計算　standard costing
標準原価差異　standard cost variance
標準原価表　standard cost sheet
標準原価法　standard cost method
標準税率　standard tax rate
標準的手続　standard procedure
標準偏差　standard deviation
表題　heading
費用対効果　cost-benefit relationship
費用分担契約　cost sharing arrangement [agreement] (CSA), cost contribution arrangement [agreement] (CCA)　関 to share costs among（～の間で費用を分担する）
費用補償　cost coverage

表明　representation, representations (reps)
表明・保証　representation and warranty, representations and warranties (reps & warranties) 頻 to seek representation and warranty（表明・保証を求める）
表明・保証条項　representation and warranty clause
表明・保証保険　warranty & indemnity [w&i] insurance
表面税率　nominal tax rate
非リース構成要素　non-lease component
比率　ratio
比率分析　ratio analysis
非流動項目　non-current item
非流動資産　non-current asset
非流動資産合計　total non-current assets
非流動性　illiquidity
非流動性ディスカウント（株式評価などの）　illiquidity discount, discount for lack of marketability
非流動負債　non-current liability
非流動負債合計　total non-current liabilities
非累積型の有給休暇　non-accumulating compensated absence
非累積型配当（優先株式などの）　non-cumulative dividend
非累積型優先株式　non-cumulative preference share
比例　proportion 関 assets are reduced proportionately [pro rata]（資産は比例的に減額される）
比例配分　pro rata allocation, proportional allocation, proration
比例持分　pro rata share, proportionate share [interest]
比例連結　proportionate consolidation
非連結子会社　unconsolidated subsidiary
非連結の組成された企業［ストラクチャード・エンティティ］　unconsolidated structured entity
広く使用されている利率　prevailing rate
品質　quality
品質管理　quality control (QC)
品質検査　quality inspection
品質保証　quality assurance
頻度　frequency

ふ

ファースト・リフューザル・ライト　right of first refusal
ファイナンシング・アウト（条項）　financing out (clause)
ファイナンス・リース　finance lease
ファイナンス・リースにより保有する資産　asset held under a finance lease
5ステップの収益認識モデル　five-step model (framework)
ファクタリング　factoring 頻 factoring of receivables（債権のファクタリング）
ファクタリング会社　factor
ファクト・ブック　fact book
ファンダメンタル分析　fundamental analysis
フィー　fee
フィージビリティ・スタディ　feasibility study 頻 to conduct a feasibility study（フィージビリティ・スタディを行う）
フィー・レター　fee letter
フィジカル・データ・ルーム（デュー・デリジェンスなどの）　physical data room
不一致　discrepancy, disagreement 頻 discrepancy between A and B（AとBの不一致）
不一致項目　unmatched item
フィナンシャル・アドバイザー　financial adviser [advisor] (FA)
フィナンシャル・インベスター　financial investor
ブートストラップ（自己資金による起業）　bootstrapping
プーリング法　pooling method
フェア・ディスクロージャー　fair disclosure
フェア・バリュー・リザーブ　fair value reserve
フェーズ　phase
フォーマット　format
フォワーダー　forwarder
フォワード・ポイント　forward point
賦課（税金などの）　imposition

賦課課税　tax assessment
付加価値　value added
付加価値活動　value added activity
付加価値税　value added tax (VAT)
付加価値割（事業税の外形標準部分の構成要素）　added value component [levy]
賦課金　levy
不確実性　uncertainty
不確実性の解消　resolution of uncertainty
不確実な税務ポジション　uncertain tax position (UTP)
不確定の耐用年数　indefinite useful life
賦課決定（税金の）　assessment
賦課決定通知書（税金の）　notice of assessment, tax assessment notice
付加税　surcharge, surtax
賦課年度（税金の）　year of assessment
不干渉　non-interference
不均一分配株式　disproportionate class of shares
不均衡　disparity
複合金融商品　compound financial instrument
複合的な資産　composite asset
副作用　side effect
副産物　by-product
複式記帳　double entry
複式簿記　double-entry bookkeeping
副資材　auxiliary material
副次的影響　fallout
複数事業主給付制度　multi-employer benefit plan
複数事業主制度　multi-employer plan
複数事業主の確定給付制度　multi-employer defined benefit plan
複数の要素（取引などに含まれる）　multiple components
複数用途の不動産　mixed-use property
複製　duplicate
含み益　unrealised gain, built-in gain
含み損　unrealised loss, built-in loss 〖頻〗 to restrict utilisation of built-in losses（含み損の使用を制限する）
含み損益　unrealised gains and losses, built-in gains and losses
含み損益の実現　crystallisation of built-in gains and losses 〖米〗 crystallization of built-in gains and losses
含めること　inclusion
複利　compound interest
福利厚生　(employee) benefit
福利厚生費　welfare expense
不公正発行（株式などの）　unfair issuance
負債　liability, debt 〖頻〗to accrue a liability for（〜を未払計上する）
負債及び資本　liabilities and equity
負債合計　total liabilities
負債コスト　cost of debt
負債・資本比率　debt/equity ratio, debt to equity ratio (D/E ratio)
負債性金融商品　debt instrument
負債性証券　corporate debt securities
負債の再構成　debt restructuring
負債の消滅　extinguishment of debt
負債の返済　debt retirement [service]
負債・費用の隠蔽　concealed liabilities and expenses
負債比率　debt/equity ratio (D/E ratio), debt to equity ratio (D/E ratio)
負債比率（総資本に対する）　debt ratio
負債部分（金融商品の）　liability [debt] component
不十分　inadequacy
付随契約　ancillary agreement
付随費用　ancillary cost, incidental cost [expense]
不正　fraud
不正還付　false refund
不正検出　fraud detection
不整合　inconsistency
不正行為　fraudulent activity [conduct]
不正実行者　fraudster
不正使用　misuse, unauthorised use 〖米〗unauthorized use
不正スキーム　fraud scheme
不正対策手段　anti-fraud control
不正対策方針　anti-fraud policy
不正調査　fraud investigation
不正調査チーム　fraud investigation team
不正入札　bid rigging
不正の通報システム　fraud reporting mechanism

不正防止	fraud prevention
不正リスク	fraud risk
不正リスク評価	fraud risk assessment
不足	shortage, shortfall
付属書類	exhibit
附属明細表	supplementary [supplemental] schedule(s)
札（棚卸の際の）	tag
負担	burden 使い方注意! 費用などを「負担する」という文脈では，bear を使って，the cost is borne by（～がその費用を負担する）という表現を用いることが多い
普通株式	common share [stock], ordinary share [stock]
普通株式の発行	issue of ordinary shares
普通株主	ordinary shareholder
普通社債	straight bond
普通償却（減価償却のうち）	ordinary depreciation
普通配当	ordinary dividend
普通預金	ordinary deposit, savings account
復興特別所得税	special income tax for reconstruction
復興特別税	special tax for reconstruction
プッシュダウン会計	push-down accounting
プッタブル金融商品	puttable instrument
プット・オプション	put option
物品の販売	sales of goods
不釣り合い	disproportion
物理的な所有	physical possession
物理的な劣化	physical deterioration
物理的保護（不正などに対する）	physical safeguard
物流	logistics
物流費	logistics cost [expense]
不定期船	tramper
不適正意見（監査報告書における）	adverse opinion
不適切な開示	improper disclosure
不適切な資産評価	improper asset valuation
不動産	immovable property, real estate [property]
不動産開発	property development
不動産鑑定人	property valuer
不動産鑑定評価	real estate appraisal
不動産鑑定評価書	real estate appraisal report
不動産管理	property management
不動産関連法人	real estate holding company
不動産業者	real estate agent
不動産取得税	real estate [property] acquisition tax
不動産譲渡税	real estate transfer tax (RETT)
不動産所得	real estate income
不動産賃貸	rental of property
不動産投資信託	real estate investment trust (REIT)
不動産保有会社	real property holding corporation
不動産保有法人	immovable property company, real estate holding company
不動産持分	real property interest
歩留	yield
歩留差異（直接材料費に係る）	material yield variance
歩留率	yield rate
船積み	loading, shipping
船積依頼［指示］書	shipping instruction (S/I)
船荷証券	bill of lading (B/L)
負ののれん	bargain purchase, negative goodwill
不備（内部統制などの）	deficiency, weakness
部品	parts, component
不服申立て	(administrative) appeal
不服申立て（税務に関する）	(tax) appeal 頻 to file [make] an appeal（不服を申し立てる）
部分	portion, component
部分完成基準	partial completion method
部分除却	partial disposal
部分所有子会社	partially-owned [partly-owned] subsidiary
部分的な消滅（負債などの）	partial extinguishment
部分的な相殺消去	fractional elimination
部分的な損金算入	partial deduction
部分払込株式	partly paid share
不法行為	illegal act [activity]
部門	department, division
部門コード	division code
部門長	department head
部門費	departmental cost

部門予算	departmental budget
付与（権利などの）	grant
不要資産	unwanted assets
付与されたオプション（〜に）	option granted (to)
付与された資本性金融商品	equity instrument granted
付与日	grant date
プライシング・サービス	pricing service
プライベート・エクイティ	private equity (PE)
プライベート・エクイティ・ファンド	private equity fund
プラス残高	positive balance
ブラック・ショールズ方程式	Black-Scholes formula
ブラックリスト国所在会社	black list company
フランキング・クレジット	franking credit
フランチャイザー	franchisor [franchiser]
フランチャイザーの権利	franchisor's right
フランチャイズ契約	franchise agreement
フランチャイズ手数料	franchise fee
フランチャイズ本部	franchisor [franchiser]
ブランド	brand
ブランド使用料［ロイヤルティ］	brand royalty
ブランド名	brand name
フリー・キャッシュ・フロー	free cash flow (FCF)
フリーレント（の取決め）	rent-free (arrangement)
フリーレント期間	rent-free period
振替え（勘定科目などの）	transfer 頻 transfer from（〜からの振替）, transfer to（〜への振替）
振替仕訳	transfer [cross] entry
不履行リスク	non-performance risk
振込み	wire transfer
不利差異	unfavourable variance 米 unfavorable variance
ブリッジ・ファイナンス	bridge finance [financing]
不利な影響（税務上の）	adverse (tax) consequence 頻 a change of control could have adverse tax consequences（株主変更が不利な税務上の影響をもたらす可能性がある）
不利な契約	onerous contract
不利な契約に係る偶発負債	onerous contracts contingent liability
不利な契約に対する引当金	provision for onerous contracts, onerous contracts provision
不利な契約による負担	onerous contract charge
不利な点	disadvantage
不利な履行義務	onerous performance obligation
不良債権	bad [doubtful] debt, non-performing loans
フリンジ・ベネフィット	fringe benefits
ブレイクアップ・フィー	break-up fee
フレームワーク	framework
プレス・リリース	press release
フレッシュ・スタート	fresh start
フレッシュ・スタート法	fresh start method
プレミアム	premium
プレミアム債	premium bond
不労所得	unearned income
ブローカー	broker
ブローカー相場	broker quotes
フローチャート	flowchart
付録	appendix, annex, addendum
プロジェクト・マネジメント・オフィス	project management office (PMO)
プロセス	process
プロセス・オーナー	process owner
プロセス・オーナーシップ	process ownership
プロセス・レター	process letter
プロトタイプ	prototype
プロフィット・シェアリング	profit sharing
プロフィット・センター	profit centre 米 profit center
プロ・フォーマ	pro forma
プロフォーマ財務諸表	pro-forma financial statements
プロラタ	pro rata
不渡り	dishonour 米 dishonor
不渡小切手	dishonoured cheque, non-sufficient funds cheque (NSF cheque) 米

	dishonored check, non-sufficient funds check (NSF check)
不渡手形	dishonoured note [draft] 米 dishonored note [draft]
分解	disaggregation 関 to disaggregate accounts receivable by type of debtor（売掛金勘定を債務者の種類により分解する）
分解（機械などの）	dismantlement
分割	division, split 関 to be split between A and B（AとBに分割される）
分割型分割	horizontal-type corporate division
分割承継法人	transferee
分割請求	progress billing
分割払い	instalment 米 installment
分割法人	transferor
分岐	ramification
文献	literature
分散（統計学の）	variance
分子	numerator
分社型分割	vertical-type corporate division
文書	document
文書化	documentation
文書回答（税務当局による）	letter ruling
粉飾	window dressing
文書によるやり取り	correspondence
分数	fraction
分析	analysis 頻 to conduct an analysis（分析を行う）
分析的手続	analytical procedure
分配	distribution
分配可能額	distributable amount
分配可能利益	distributable profit, profits available for distribution
分母	denominator
文脈	context
分離	separation, detachment
分離課税	separate taxation [assessment]
分離可能性	separability
分離可能性要件	separability criterion
分類	classification, category 頻 classification of an asset as（資産の〜への分類）関 to be classified as（〜に分類される）
分類すること	categorisation 米 categorization
分類変更	reclassification
分類変更日	reclassification date

へ

平均	average
平均回収期間	average collection period
平均原価法	average cost method
平均残存勤務期間	average remaining service period, average remaining working lives
平均従業員数	average number of employees
平均法（棚卸資産の評価方法など）	average method
平衡税	equalisation levy 米 equalization levy
米国基準（会計基準について）	US GAAP, accounting principles generally accepted in the United State (of America)
閉鎖	closure
閉鎖コスト	decommissioning cost
閉鎖的会社	closely held company
平準化	smoothing
ペイスルー課税	pay-through taxation
ベーシス・アジャストメント	basis adjustment
ベータ	beta
ペーパー・カンパニー	paper company, shell company
ベスト・エフォート	best efforts
ベスト・プラクティス	best practice
ベスト・メソッド・ルール	best method rule
別掲項目	separate line item
別個に（区別して）識別可能な	separately identifiable
別個のビークル	separate vehicle
ヘッジ	hedge 頻 hedge against currency risk（為替リスクに対するヘッジ）関 to hedge against currency risk（為替リスクをヘッジする）
別紙	appendix
ヘッジ会計	hedge accounting
ヘッジ関係	hedging relationship
ヘッジ関係の指定	designation of hedging

relationship	
ヘッジ関係のバランス調整	rebalancing of hedge relationships
ヘッジ関係の文書化	documentation of hedging relationship
ヘッジ・コスト	cost of hedging
ヘッジ指定	designation of hedging relationship
ヘッジ手段	hedging instrument
ヘッジ戦略	hedging strategy
ヘッジ損益	hedging reserve
ヘッジ対象	hedged item
ヘッジ取引	hedging transaction
ヘッジ取引の相手方	hedge counterparty
ヘッジの非有効性	hedge ineffectiveness
ヘッジの有効性	hedge effectiveness
ヘッジの有効性に関する要件	hedge effectiveness requirements
ヘッジの有効性の評価	assessment of hedge effectiveness
ヘッジ比率	hedge ratio
ヘッジファンド投資	hedge fund investment
ヘッジ目的で保有しているデリバティブ（金融）資産	derivative financial assets held for hedging
ヘッジ・リザーブ	hedging reserve
別途積立金	general reserve
ヘッド・リース	head lease
別表（法人税申告書などの）	schedule [頻] to attach a schedule（別表を添付する）
別表五（一）	Schedule 5 (1)
別表四	Schedule 4
ペナルティ	penalty [頻]「加算税」の項を参照
ベリー・レシオ	berry ratio
ヘルスケア	health care
便益	benefit
便益の消費パターン	pattern of benefit consumption
便宜的な換算	convenience translation
返金	refund
返金負債	refund liability
返金不能の報酬	non-refundable fee
返金不能の前払報酬	non-refundable up-front fee
返金方針	refund policy
変更	change, modification
弁護士	lawyer, attorney
弁護士のレター	lawyer's [attorney's] letter
返済	repayment, reimbursement
返済の優先順位（金融商品の）	seniority
返済免除条件付融資	forgivable loan
変数	variable
ベンダー・デューデリジェンス	vendor due diligence (VDD)
ベンダー・ローン	vendor loan
ベンチマーク	benchmark
ベンチマーク分析	benchmark study [analysis], benchmarking
ベンチャー	venture
ベンチャー・キャピタル	venture capital (VC)
ベンチャー・キャピタル企業	venture capital organisation [米] venture capital organization
変動	fluctuation, variation
変動間接費	variable overhead
変動間接費差異	variable overhead variance
変動金利	variable [floating] interest rate
変動金利ローン	variable-rate loan, variable [floating] rate loan
変動性	variability
変動製造間接費	variable overhead
変動製造費用	variable manufacturing cost
変動対価	variable consideration
変動賃借料	contingent rent
変動賃貸料	contingent rent
変動費	variable cost
変動リース料	variable lease payment, contingent rent
変動リターン	variable return
変動利付金融商品	variable-rate instrument
返品	return (of goods)
返品（された商品）	returned goods
返品権	right of return
返品権付販売［売却］	sale with a right of return
返品調整引当金	provision for sales returns
便法	expedient

ほ

補遺　addendum
法　law
包括協定　framework agreement
包括条項　catch-all clause
包括的租税回避防止規定　comprehensive anti-tax avoidance provision
包括利益　comprehensive income
包括利益計算書　statement of comprehensive income
包括利益合計　total comprehensive income
放棄　waiver
防御的な権利　protective rights
方向　direction
報告　reporting, report
報告可能性　reportability
報告期間　reporting period
報告期間の期末日　date of end of reporting period
報告企業　reporting entity
報告企業に対する共同支配　joint control over the reporting entity
報告企業に対する支配　control over the reporting entity
報告企業に対する重要な影響力　significant influence over the reporting entity
報告期限　reporting deadline
報告書　report
報告セグメント　reportable segment
報告単位　reporting unit
報告の枠組み　reporting mechanism
報告日　reporting [report] date
報告方法　reporting method
報告様式　report form
報告利益　reported earnings
報酬　compensation, remuneration
報酬（専門家などに対する）　fee
報酬委員会（委員会設置会社の）　compensation committee
報酬及び手数料収益　fee and commission income
報酬及び手数料費用　fee and commission expense
報酬給与額　labour cost ㊍ labor cost
報酬見積り　fee quote [estimate]
方針　policy
法人　body corporate, corporation
法人格否認（の法理）　piercing the corporate veil
法人所得税　(corporate) income tax
法人所得税以外の税金　taxes other than income tax
法人所得税の取扱いに関する不確実性　uncertainty over income tax treatments
法人所得税費用以外の税金費用　tax expense other than income tax expense
法人税　corporate [corporation] income tax, corporate [corporation] tax
法人税基本通達　Commissioner's Directive on Interpretation of the Corporation Tax Act
法人税，住民税及び事業税　current tax expense
法人税申告書　corporate [corporation] tax return
法人税等調整額　deferred tax expense [income]
法人税等の還付額　income taxes refund
法人税等の支払額　income taxes paid
法人税法　Corporation Tax Act [Law]
法人税法施行規則　Ordinance for Enforcement of the Corporation Tax Act
法人税法施行令　Order for Enforcement of the Corporation Tax Act
法人税率　corporate income tax rate
法人設立許可書　certificate of incorporation
包装　packaging, packing
包装（資）材　packaging material
法廷　court
法定監査　statutory audit
法定換算方法　default translation method
法定換算方法以外の換算方法　non-default translation method
法定減価償却方法　default depreciation method
法定減価償却方法以外の減価償却方法　non-default depreciation method

法定実効税率	statutory tax rate
法定準備金	legal [statutory] reserve
法定税率	statutory (tax) rate
法定耐用年数	statutory useful life
法定福利費	legal welfare cost
法的形式	legal form
法的形態	legal form
法的拘束力のある意向表明（買収案件などの）	binding offer
法的拘束力のある入札（買収案件などの）	binding bid
法的拘束力のあるルーリング	binding ruling
法的拘束力のない意向表明（買収案件などの）	non-binding [indicative] offer
法的拘束力のない入札（買収案件などの）	non-binding [indicative] bid
法的債務	legal obligation
法的所有権	(legal) title
法的手続	(legal) proceedings
法的な管轄	legal jurisdiction
法的な取得企業	legal acquirer
法的な被取得企業	legal acquiree
法的二重課税	judicial double taxation
法的に独立した事業体	separate legal entity
法的有効期限	legal life
法的要件	legal [legislative] requirement
法的要請	statutory requirement
法の濫用	abuse of law
方法	method, approach 頻 to apply a method to（～に方法を適用する）
法務アドバイザー	legal adviser [advisor]
法務局	Legal Affairs Bureau
法務デュー・デリジェンス	legal due diligence (LDD)
法務費用	legal fee [cost]
法務部門	legal department [division], legal affairs department [division]
訪問	visit
暴落	crash
法律	law, legislation
法律意見（書）	legal opinion
法律顧問	legal counsel
法律上の制限	legal restrictions
法令	statute, laws and ordinances
法令遵守	compliance
法令遵守プログラム	compliance programme 米compliance program
ポートフォリオ	portfolio
ポートフォリオ投資	portfolio investment
ポートフォリオ・ヘッジ	portfolio hedge
ホーム・リーブ	home leave
ホールド・ハームレス・レター（同意書）	hold harmless letter
簿価	book value 頻帳簿価額の項を参照
簿外	off-balance sheet
簿外資産	off-balance sheet asset, unrecorded asset
簿外負債	off-balance sheet liability, unrecorded liability 頻 to obtain indemnity for unrecorded liabilities（簿外負債に対する賠償を受ける）
保管	storage
補完（するもの）	backstop
保管費用	storage cost [expense], warehousing cost [expense]
簿記	bookkeeping
補強（証拠などによる）	corroboration
保険	insurance
保険会社	insurance company
保険が付された給付	insured benefit
保険業者	insurer
保険契約	insurance contract
保険契約者	policyholder
保険契約者貸付［借入］	policy loan
保険契約書	insurance policy
保険資産	insurance asset
保険証券	insurance policy
保険対象事象	insured event
保険費用	insurance expense
保険負債	insurance liability
保険リスク	insurance risk
保険料	insurance premium
保護	protection
保護的な権利	protective rights
ポジション・ペーパー	position paper
募集要項	offering memorandum
保守主義	conservatism
保証	guarantee, warranty 使い方注意! guaranteeは主として「債務保証」でいう保証の意味で使われ，warrantyは主として「製品保証」でいう保証（瑕疵担保責任）の意味で使われる

保証（監査証明などの）	assurance
補償	compensation, indemnification, indemnity
保証業務（監査などの）	assurance engagement
補償金	indemnity, compensation
保証金	guarantee [security] deposit
補償金（の支払い）	compensation payment
保証残存価値	guaranteed residual value
補償資産	indemnification asset
補償上限額	liability cap
補償条項	indemnity clause
補償調整	compensating adjustment
保証人	guarantor
保証料	guarantee fee
補助科目	subsidiary account
補助金	grant, subsidy　[頻] receipt of a grant（補助金の受領）, repayment of a grant（補助金の返還）
補助金受領者	grantee
補助金譲与者	grantor
補助材料	auxiliary material
補助的活動	auxiliary activity
補助的機能	auxiliary function
補助簿	sub-ledger (S/L)
補助元帳	subsidiary ledger (S/L), sub-ledger (S/L)
ポストマージャー・インテグレーション	post-merger integration (PMI)
保税地域	bonded area
補足	complement, supplement
補足開示	supplementary disclosure
補足情報	supplementary information
補足的な明細	supplementary [supplemental] schedule(s)
保存（帳簿などの）	retention
保存期間（帳簿などの）	retention period　[頻]　7 year retention period（7年間の保存期間）　[関] documents are retained for 7 years（書類は7年間保存される）
発起人	promoter
補填の権利	reimbursement right
ボトムアップ・アプローチ	bottom-up approach
保有（株式などの）	holding
保有期間（株式などの）	holding period
保有者	holder
保有費用	carrying charge, holding cost
保有比率（株式などの）	holding ratio
保有割合（株式などの）	percentage of ownership, percentage (of) ownership interest
ボラティリティ（変動率）	volatility
保留	retention
本源的価値	intrinsic value
本源的価値による測定（ストック・オプションなどの）	intrinsic value measurement
本源的価値ベース	intrinsic value basis
本質	essence
本社	headquarters (HQ), corporate headquarters, head [main] office
本社費	head office expense [overhead]
本社費の配賦	allocation of head office expenses, head office expense allocation
本船渡し条件	free on board (FOB)
本体契約	host contract
本体部分の金融商品（組込デリバティブについて）	host financial instrument
本店	headquarters (HQ), corporate headquarters, head [main] office
本店勘定	head office account
本店所在地（基準）	place of incorporation
本人（代理人に対して）	principal
本人か代理人かの検討	principal vs. agent considerations
本人・代理人の立場	principal/agent status

ま

マークアップ　(profit) mark-up
マーケット・アプローチ（評価手法としての）　market [market-based] approach
マーケット・マルチプル　market multiple
マーケティング　marketing
マーケティング・インタンジブル　marketing intangible
マーケティング関連無形資産　marketing-related intangible asset
マーケティング費用　marketing expense
マーケティング部門　marketing department [division]
マージン　margin
マイナス残高　negative balance
マイノリティ出資　minority stake
マイノリティ・ディスカウント（株式評価などの）　discount for lack of control
埋没原価　sunk cost
前受金　advances (received), advance receipt 頻advances from customers（顧客からの前受金）
前受サービス・フィー　unearned service fee
前受収益　unearned revenue [income]
前受対価　advance consideration
前金　advance
前払い　prepayment, up-front payment
前払金　prepayment
前払式のサービス契約　prepaid service contract
前払対価　advance consideration
前払賃借料　prepaid rent
前払年金費用　prepaid pension cost
前払いの拠出（年金基金などへの）　prepayment of contributions
前払費用　prepaid expense, prepayment (asset)
前払保険料　prepaid insurance premium [expense]
前払家賃　prepaid rent
前渡金　advances (paid), advance payment 頻advances to suppliers（仕入先への前渡金）
孫会社層の子会社（第2階層の子会社）　second-tier subsidiary　使い方注意！ 子会社Aの下に子会社Bがある場合，子会社Aがfirst-tier（子会社層）で，子会社Bがsecond-tier（孫会社層）ということになる
マジョリティ出資　majority stake
マスター契約　master agreement
マスター・ネッティング契約　master netting agreement
マスター・ファイル（事業概況報告事項）　master file
マトリックス組織（構成）　matrix form of an organisation　米 matrix form of an organization
マニュアル　manual
マニュアル・コントロール　manual controls
マネジメント　management
マネジメント・アプローチ（セグメント情報に関する）　management approach
マネジメント・インタビュー　management interview
マネジメント・サービス　management service
マネジメント・バイアウト　management buy-out (MBO)
マネジメント・バイイン　management buy-in (MBI)
マネジメント・フィー　management fee　頻「経営指導料」の項を参照
マネジメント・プレゼンテーション　management presentation
マネジメント・レター　management letter
マネジメント・レビュー　management review
マルチプル　multiple
満期　maturity, expiry, expiration
満期償還金額　maturity value
満期日　maturity [expiry] date
満期保有目的証券　held-to-maturity securities
満期保有目的投資（旧）　held-to-maturity investments (HTM)
満期保有目的の債券　held-to-maturity bond

満了（期間の）　expiration, expiry

み

見落とし　oversight
未解決の課題　open issue
未稼得金融収益　unearned finance income
未監査財務諸表　unaudited financial statements
未経過利息　unearned interest
未経過割引料　unearned discount
未決済小切手　outstanding cheques　㊥outstanding checks
未決済残高　outstanding balance
未行使のストック・オプション　outstanding share options
見込納付（税金などの）　estimated payment
未実現損益　unrealised gains and losses　㊥unrealized gains and losses
未実現損失　unrealised loss　㊥unrealized loss
未実現損失（グループ内の）　unrealised intercompany loss　㊥unrealized intercompany loss
未実現利益　unrealised profit [gain]　㊥unrealized profit [gain]
未実現利益（グループ内の）　unrealised intercompany profit　㊥unrealized intercompany profit　㊥unrealised intercompany profit in inventory（棚卸資産に含まれる未実現利益）　㊥to eliminate profit in inventory resulting from intercompany transactions（棚卸資産の未実現利益を消去する）
未実現利益の消去　elimination of unrealised profit　㊥elimination of unrealized profit
未収勘定　accruals　㊥to book accruals for（〜を未収計上する）
未収還付法人税等　current tax assets [receivable], income taxes receivable [refundable]
未収収益　accrued revenue, accrued income
未収消費税　consumption tax receivable [refundable]
未修正の虚偽記載　uncorrected misstatement
未収入金　other receivables, other accounts receivable, accounts receivable-other
未収配当金　accrued dividend (income)
未収付加価値税　VAT receivable
未収法人所得税　current tax assets [receivable]
未収法人税等　「未収還付法人税等」の項を参照
未収・未払勘定　accruals
未収リース料　lease receivables
未収利息　accrued interest (income), interest receivable
未出荷売上（請求済み）　bill-and-hold sales
未償却残高（無形資産などの）　unamortised balance　㊥unamortized balance
未償却残高（有形固定資産の）　undepreciated balance
未使用資産　unused asset
未上場株　unlisted share [stock]
未使用の貸出コミットメント　undrawn loan commitment
未使用の借入枠　undrawn borrowing facility
未使用の引当金　unused provision
未処分利益　unappropriated retained earnings
未処理損失　undisposed loss, deficit
未請求の債権　unbilled receivables
未成業務支出金　services in progress
未成工事支出金　construction in progress
未成工事に係る保留金　retention for contracts in progress
未成工事に係る前受金　advances received for contracts in progress
見出し　heading
見出し及び小計　heading and subtotal
未達預金　deposits in transit
未着品　goods [inventory] in transit, undelivered goods
見積り　estimate, estimation　㊥basis of an estimate（見積りの基礎）, to revise an estimate（見積りを改定する）, greater use of estimation methods（より多くの見積りの方法の使用）

見積技法	estimation technique
見積原価	estimated cost
見積実効税率	estimated effective tax rate
見積税額	estimated tax
見積税率	estimated tax rate
見積耐用年数	estimated useful life
見積りの不確実性	estimation uncertainty
見積りの不確実性の発生要因	source of estimation uncertainty
見積りの見直し	revision to an estimate
見積もること	estimation
ミディアム・ターム・ノート	medium term note (MTN)
見通し	outlook
みなし外国税額控除	tax sparing credit
みなし共同事業要件	deemed joint business requirements
みなし原価	deemed cost
みなし支払税金	taxes deemed paid
みなし取得日	deemed acquisition date
みなし所有	constructive ownership
みなし税金	hypothetical tax
みなし税引後営業利益	net operating profit less adjusted taxes (NOPLAT)
みなし配当	deemed [constructive] dividend
みなし利息	deemed interest
ミニマム・スタンダード	minimum standard
未認識過去勤務費用（債務）	unrecognised prior service cost 米 unrecognized prior service cost 頻 amortisation of unrecognised prior service cost（未認識過去勤務費用（債務）の償却）
未認識数理計算上の差異	unrecognised actuarial gains and losses 米 unrecognized actuarial gains and losses 頻 amortisation of unrecognised actuarial gains and losses（未認識数理計算上の差異の償却）
未認識の確定コミットメント	unrecognised firm commitment 米 unrecognized firm commitment
未認識の繰延税金資産	unrecognised deferred tax assets 米 unrecognized deferred tax assets
未認識の繰延税金負債	unrecognised deferred tax liabilities 米 unrecognized deferred tax liabilities
未配分金額	unallocated amounts
未配分利益	undistributed profit 頻 taxable temporary differences associated with undistributed profits of subsidiaries（子会社の留保利益に係る将来加算一時差異）
未配分利益に対する課税	undistributed profits tax
未発行株式	unissued share [stock]
未払勘定	accruals 頻 to book accruals for（〜を未払計上する） 関 to accrue a liability for（〜を未払計上する）
未払給付	benefits payable
未払金	other payables, other accounts payable, accounts payable-other
未払源泉税	withholding tax payable
未払事業税	business [enterprise] tax payable
未払社会保険料	social security payable
未払消費税	consumption tax payable
未払賞与	accrued bonus, bonus accrual
未払人件費	accrued salaries and wages
未払税金	unpaid taxes, taxes payable, tax liability
未払いの請求書	open [unpaid] invoice
未払配当金	dividends payable, accrued dividend
未払費用	accrued expense 関 to accrue expenses（費用を未払計上する）
未払付加価値税	VAT payable
未払法人所得税	current tax liabilities [payable], income taxes payable, accrued income taxes
未払法人税等	current tax liabilities [payable], income taxes payable, accrued income taxes
未払有給休暇	accrued vacation (pay)
未払リース料	lease payables
未払利息	accrued interest (expense), interest payable
身元調査	background check
未履行契約	executory contract
未履行の条件	unfulfilled condition
民営化	privatisation 米 privatization
民事再生法	Civil Rehabilitation Act [Law]
民事上の罰金	civil monetary penalty
民事訴訟	civil suit
民事罰	civil penalty

む

無額面　no-par value
無額面株式　no-par (value) stock [share]
無記名債券　bearer bond
無形減価償却資産　amortisable intangible asset 米 amortizable intangible asset
無形固定資産　「無形資産」の項を参照
無形資産　intangible asset [property], intangibles
無形資産償却前営業利益（税引前）　earnings before interest, taxes and amortisation (EBITA) 米 earnings before interest, taxes and amortization (EBITA)
無限責任　unlimited liability
無限責任組合　general partnership
無限責任組合員　general partner (GP)
無限定適正意見（監査報告書の）　unqualified [clean] opinion
無効化　override
無差別　non-discrimination
無差別条項　non-discrimination provisions
矛盾　contradiction
無条件の義務　unconditional requirement
無条件の権利　unconditional right
無対価組織再編　(corporate) reorganisation without consideration 米 (corporate) reorganization without consideration
無担保借入金　unsecured bank loan
無担保債券　unsecured bond
無担保債務　unsecured debt
無担保社債　debenture
無担保負債　unsecured debt
無担保融資　unsecured loan
無保証残存価値　unguaranteed residual value
無利息融資　interest-free loan

め

明確化　clarification
名義株　dummy stock
名義人　nominee
明細　schedule, detail(s)
名簿　roster
名目金利　nominal interest rate
名目利子率　nominal interest rate
明瞭性　clarity
命令　mandate, order
メール・オーダー・カタログ　mail order catalogue
メザニン　mezzanine
メザニン・ファイナンス　mezzanine financing
免許　licence 米 license
免除（債務などの）　discharge
免除規定　exemption 頻 an exemption applies to（～は免除の対象となる）
免税　exemption (from tax)
免税売上　exempt sales
免税証明書　exemption certificate
免責　exemption, waiver of liability
メンテナンス　maintenance

も

申込み　application
申立て　allegation
網羅性　completeness 頻 completeness of a list（リストの網羅性）
モーゲージ　mortgage
モーゲージ担保証券　mortgage backed securities (MBS)
目的　purpose, end
目的適合性　relevance

目標　　goal, target
目標管理制度　　management by objectives (MBO)
目標原価　　target cost
目論見書　　prospectus, private placement memorandum (PPM)
持合い（株式の）　　cross [mutual] shareholding
持株会社　　holding company
持株比率　　「保有比率」の項を参照
持株割合　　「保有割合」の項を参照
持分　　equity, interest, equity interest 頻 to own an interest in（～に対する持分を有する）
持分金融商品　　equity instrument
持分決済型の株式に基づく報酬　　equity-settled share-based payment
持分証券　　equity securities
持分投資　　equity investment
持分投資者　　equity holder
持分の過半　　majority of interests
持分の取得　　acquisition of interest
持分の処分　　disposal of interest
持分プーリング法　　pooling-of-interests method
持分変動計算書　　statement of changes in equity
持分法　　equity method
持分法会計　　equity accounting
持分法で会計処理されている投資　　investments accounted for using the equity method
持分法で会計処理されている投資以外の投資　　investments other than investments accounted for using equity method
持分法適用会社　　equity-accounted investee
持分法適用会社におけるその他の包括利益に対する持分　　share of other comprehensive income of investments accounted for using the equity method
持分法適用会社に対する持分　　interest in an equity-accounted investee
持分法適用関連会社　　associate accounted for by the equity method
持分法による投資損失　　share of loss of investments accounted for using the equity method
持分法による投資利益　　share of profit of investments accounted for using the equity method
最も起こりそうな結果　　most likely outcome
最も発生可能性の高い金額　　most likely amount
最も有利な市場　　most advantageous market
モデル租税条約　　model tax conventions [treaties]
元受保険契約　　direct insurance contract
戻入れ　　reversal
元帳　　ledger
元帳科目　　ledger account
モニタリング　　monitoring
漏れ　　omission, leakage
文言　　wording
問題　　issue, problem 使い方注意！ issue のほうが problem よりもソフト
モンテカルロ・シミュレーション　　Monte Carlo simulation

や

役員　director, executive, officer, directors and officers (D&O)
役員賞与　director's bonus
役員賞与引当金　provision for directors' bonuses
役員退職慰労金　director's retirement benefit
役員退職慰労引当金　provision for directors' retirement benefits
役員退職給付　director's retirement benefit
役員報酬　director's remuneration [compensation]
約定日　trade date
約定日会計　trade date accounting
約束手形　promissory note (P/N)
役人　government [public] official, officer
役割　role
役割分担　division of roles

ゆ

有価証券　securities
有価証券貸借　securities lending
有価証券届出書　(securities) registration statement
有価証券の評価方法　valuation method of securities
有価証券売却益　gain on sale of securities
有価証券売却損　loss on sale of securities
有価証券評価損　loss on revaluation of securities
有価証券報告書　annual securities report
有給休暇　compensated absence, paid absence [leave], paid time-off (PTO)
有給休暇引当金　accrued vacation (pay)
遊休資産　idle [unused] asset
優遇税制　tax incentive [concession], preferential tax treatment　[頻] to enjoy tax incentives（優遇税制の適用を受ける）
有形減価償却資産　depreciable tangible asset
有形固定資産　property, plant and equipment (PP&E), tangible fixed asset
有形固定資産（工場が含まれない場合）　property and equipment
有形資産　tangible asset [property]
有限会社　Yugen Kaisha (YK)
有限責任　limited liability
有限責任会社　limited liability company (LLC)
有限責任組合　limited partnership (LPS)
有限責任組合員　limited partner (LP)
有限責任事業体　limited liability entity
有限の耐用年数　finite useful life　[頻] an intangible asset with finite useful life（耐用年数が有限の無形資産）
有効期間　valid period
有効期間（契約の）　contractual life
有効性　effectiveness
有効部分（ヘッジなどの）　effective portion
融資　loan, lending
融資契約　loan [credit] agreement
融資限度額　line of credit
融資の実行可能期間　draw-down period
融資枠　credit facility [facilities], credit line
優先（権）　priority
優先株式　preference share [stock], preferred share [stock]
優先株式に係る配当　dividend on a preference share
優先株式配当　preference share dividend
優先権　preference right
優先交渉権　right of first refusal
優先的（新株）引受権　pre-emptive [pre-emption] right
優先的に弁済される債務　senior debt
優先配当　preference dividend
有用性　usefulness, utility
猶予期間　grace period
有利差異　favourable variance　[米] favorable variance
有利子負債　interest-bearing liability [debt]
有利子負債同等物　debt-like item
有利な影響（税務上の）　beneficial [favour-

able] (tax) consequence 米beneficial [favorable] (tax) consequence
有利発行　　favourable issuance　米favorable issuance
幽霊社員　　ghost employee
歪み　　distortion
輸出　　export, international shipment
輸出売上　　export sales
輸出企業　　exporter
輸出規制　　export control
輸出許可通知書　　export declaration (E/D)
使い方注意!　税関に提出した「輸出申告書」に，税関が許可印を押すと，それが「輸出許可通知書」となる
輸出諸掛　　export charges
輸出申告書　　export declaration (E/D)
譲受け　　acquisition, transfer
譲受人　　transferee, assignee
輸送　　transport, transportation, shipping
輸送コスト　　transport cost [expense]
輸送費　　transportation cost [expense], shipping cost [expense]
輸入　　import
輸入貨物　　import cargo
輸入関税　　import duty
輸入企業　　importer
輸入許可通知書　　import declaration (I/D)
使い方注意!　税関に提出した「輸入申告書」に，税関が許可印を押すと，それが「輸入許可通知書」となる
輸入諸掛　　import charges
輸入申告書　　import declaration (I/D)
輸入割当て　　import quota (IQ)
ユニラテラルAPA　　unilateral advance pricing arrangement

よ

要因　　factor
要求　　requirement
要求（購買要求）　　requisition
要求収益率　　required rate of return
要求払預金　　demand deposit
要件　　prerequisite, requirement　頻to meet specified requirements（特定の要件を充足する）
用語　　term, terminology
用語集　　glossary
様式　　form
要素　　element, factor
用地　　site
要約　　summary, wrap-up
要約財務情報　　summarised financial information　米summarized financial information
要約財務諸表　　condensed (financial) statements
預金　　deposit, cash at bank
預金利子　　interest on deposits
翌営業日　　next business day
翌期　　next period, subsequent period, upcoming period
抑止力　　deterrent
翌年（度）　　following year, subsequent year
予見しうる将来　　foreseeable future
予見しうる損失　　foreseeable loss
予算　　budget
予算管理　　budgetary control, budgeting
予算実績対比表　　budget/actual variance report
予算制度　　budgeting system
予算対実績　　budget to actual [budget vs. actual]
予算統制　　budgetary control
予算の制約　　budget constraint
予算編成　　budgeting
予実　　budget to actual [budget vs. actual]
余剰　　surplus
余剰資金　　excess cash, cash surplus
余剰資産　　redundant assets
余剰従業員　　redundancy
与信　　credit
与信（主として金融機関からの）　　credit facility [facilities]
与信管理　　credit control
与信期間　　credit period
与信限度額　　credit limit　頻to set a credit limit（与信限度額を設定する）

与信条件	credit terms
与信分析	credit analysis
与信方針	credit policy
予想コスト	expected cost
予想コストにマージンを加算するアプローチ	expected cost plus a margin approach
予想される影響	expected impact [頻] expected impact of initial application of new standards or interpretations（新しい基準または解釈指針の適用開始により予想される影響）
予想失効率（ストック・オプションなどの）	estimated forfeiture rate
予想死亡率	future mortality
予想昇給率	future salary growth
予想信用損失	expected credit loss (ECL) [頻] expected credit losses collectively assessed（集合的に評価した予想信用損失），expected credit losses individually assessed（個別的に評価した予想信用損失）
予想信用損失モデル	ECL model
予想信用損失率	expected credit loss rate
予想損失	expected loss
予想年金増加率	future pension growth
予想ボラティリティ	expected volatility
予測	forecast, projection
予測価値	predictive value
予測給付債務	projected benefit obligation (PBO)
予測損益計算書	forecast income statement
予測貸借対照表	forecast balance sheet
予定	schedule
予定間接費配賦率	pre-determined overhead rate
予定原価	pre-determined cost
予定原価計算	pre-determined costing
予定生産能力	expected capacity
予定取引	forecast transaction [頻] forecast transactions qualify as hedged items（予定取引はヘッジ対象となりうる）
予定取引のヘッジ	hedge of forecast transactions
予定納税	provisional tax payment
予定表	timetable
予備評価	preliminary assessment
予備部品	spare parts
予防	prevention
予防的コントロール（内部統制のうち）	preventive control
予約レート（為替予約の）	forward (exchange) rate
余裕	buffer, cushion, slack [頻] financial slack（財務上の余裕）

ら

来期　「翌期」の項を参照
ライセンサー　licensor
ライセンシー　licensee
ライセンス　licence 米license
ライセンス供与　licensing
ライセンス供与（他社から受ける）　licence-in 米license-in
ライセンス供与（他社に対する）　licence-out 米license-out
ライセンス契約　licensing (agreement)
ライセンス・フィー　licence fee 米license fee
ライセンス報酬　licence fee 米license fee
ライセンス報酬収益　licence fee income 米license fee income
ライツ・イシュー　rights issue
ライツ・オファリング　rights offering
来年（度）　「翌年（度）」の項を参照
ラッピング（入金等の横領）　lapping
ランニング・ロイヤルティ　running royalty
濫用　abuse
濫用的租税回避　aggressive tax planning
濫用防止規定　anti-abuse provision
ラン・レート　run rate

り

リース　lease
リース・インセンティブ　lease incentive
リース・インセンティブ・コスト　lease incentive cost
リース期間　lease term
リース期間の開始日　commencement of lease term
リース計算上の利子率　interest rate implicit in the lease
リース契約　lease agreement [contract]
リース契約の変更　lease modification
リース更新選択権［オプション］　lease renewal option
リース構成要素　lease component
リース債権　lease receivables
リース債務　lease obligation [payables]
リース資産　lease [leased] asset
リースしている工場及び設備　leased plant and equipment
リース投資（未回収額）　investment in the lease
リースとしての法的形式　legal form of a lease
リース取引　lease [leasing] transaction
リースの開始　lease commencement, inception of lease
リースの貸手　lessor
リースの借手　lessee
リースの借手に関する単一の会計モデル　single lessee accounting model
リースの条件変更　lease modification
リースバック　leaseback
リース費用　lease expense
リース負債　lease liability
リース物件　leased property
リース未収入金　lease receivables
リース未払金　lease payables
リース料（支払い）　lease payment(s)
リーニエンシー・プログラム　leniency programme 米leniency program
利益　profit, earnings 頻 to earn [make] a profit（利益を計上する）, to report a profit（利益を報告する）
利益移転　profit shifting
利益還流　repatriation
利益供与の強要　economic extortion
利益計画　profit plan
利益準備金　retained earnings reserve, legal retained earnings, earned legal reserve
利益剰余金　retained earnings, earned surplus
利益処分　appropriation
利益水準指標　profit level indicator (PLI)
利益責任単位　profit centre 米profit center
利益相反　conflict of interest

利益の上乗せ	profit mark-up
利益の平準化	profit smoothing
利益比準法	comparable profits method (CPM)
利益分割法	profit split method (PSM)
利益分配（従業員などへの）	profit sharing
利益分配（配当などの）	distribution of profit
利益分配制度	profit sharing plan
利益率	profit margin [ratio], rate of return
利益連動給与	profit-based compensation
理解	understanding
理解可能性	understandability
利害関係	stake
利害関係者	stakeholder
履行	performance, discharge
履行義務	performance obligation 頻 performance obligation satisfied at a point in time（一時点で充足される履行義務）, performance obligation satisfied over time（一定の期間にわたり充足される履行義務）
履行義務の充足	satisfaction of performance obligation
リサイクリング	recycling
利鞘	margin
利鞘（金利の）	interest margin
利子	interest
利子源泉税	withholding tax on interest
利子所得	interest income
利子税	interest (on delinquent tax), interest tax
リスク	risk 頻 risks arising from（〜により発生するリスク）, risk associated with（〜に関連するリスク）
リスク管理	risk management
リスク管理方針	risk management policy
リスク・コントロール・マトリックス	risk control matrix (RCM)
リスク調整	risk premium
リスク調整後の割引率	risk-adjusted discount rate
リスクと不確実性	risks and uncertainties
リスクの集中	concentrations of risk
リスクの上限	risk limit
リスク評価	risk assessment
リスク評価手続	risk assessment procedures
リスク負担	risk bearing
リスクフリー・レート	risk-free interest rate
リスク・プレミアム	risk premium
リスク分散	risk diversification
リスク分散効果	risk diversification effect
リスク分析	risk analysis
リスク分担	risk sharing
リスク・マネジメント	risk management
リスク要素	risk component
リストラクチャリング	restructuring
リストラクチャリングに係る偶発負債	restructuring contingent liability
リストラクチャリング引当金	provision for restructuring costs, restructuring provision
リストラクチャリング費用	restructuring charge
利息	interest
利息支払い	interest payment 関 principal repayment（元本返済）
利息の受取額	interest received
利息の支払額	interest paid
利息の損金算入制限	restriction on interest deductibility
利息の損金性	interest deductibility
利息費用	interest cost
利息法	effective interest method
リターン	return
リターン（投資の）	payback
リターンの変動性	variability of returns
利付債	coupon bond
立証	proof, substantiation
立証責任	burden [onus] of proof 頻 the burden of proof is on tax authorities [taxpayers]（立証責任は税務当局［納税者］側にある）
立法	legislation
リテイナー・フィー（弁護士などの顧問報酬）	retainer fee
利点	advantage, merit
利得	gain
利得及び損失	gains and losses
リバース・チャージ方式（消費税等の）	reverse charge mechanism
リバース・ハイブリッド	reverse hybrid
リバース・ブレイクアップ・フィー	reverse break-up fee

リファイナンス　refinancing
リファイナンス契約　refinancing agreement
利札（公社債の）　coupon
リベート　rebate
利回り　yield
リミテッド・パートナー　limited partner (LP)
リミテッド・パートナーシップ　limited partnership (LPS)
理由　reason, grounds
流通　distribution
流通業者　distributor
流通経路　distribution channel
流通市場（証券の）　secondary market
流通費　distribution cost [expense]
流通網　distribution network
流動化　securitisation　米 securitization
流動項目　current item
流動・固定［非流動］区分　current / non-current distinction
流動・固定［非流動］分類　current / non-current classification
流動資産　current asset
流動資産合計　total current assets
流動性　liquidity　頻 to be presented in order of liquidity（流動性の順に表示される）関 liquid asset（流動性のある資産）, illiquid asset（流動性の低い資産）
流動性ディスカウント（株式評価などの）　liquidity [marketability] discount
流動性に基づく表示　presentation based on liquidity
流動性比率　liquidity ratio
流動性リスク　liquidity risk
流動比率　current ratio
流動負債　current liability
流動負債合計　total current liabilities
流動部分　current portion　頻 current portion of long-term debt（固定負債の流動部分（1年内返済部分））
流入　inflow
留保　reservation, retention
留保金（工事などで完了まで支払いを留保する部分）　retainage
留保金課税　tax on undistributed profits
留保口座　retention account
留保項目（税務加算のうち）　timing difference
留保利益　retained earnings, undistributed profit
留保利益に対する課税　undistributed profits tax
量　quantity, volume
利用　utilisation　米 utilization
利用者（財務諸表などの）　user
領収書　receipt
量的基準　quantitative threshold
量的要素　quantitative factor
領土　territory
旅行　travel
旅費（旅費交通費）　travel expense
リリース・レター（確認書）　release letter
利率　interest rate
履歴　history
リロード・オプション　reload option
リロード特性　reload feature
理論　theory
リンキング・ルール　linking rule
臨時項目　extraordinary item
臨時の収益　occasional revenue [income]
臨時報告書　extraordinary report
倫理規定　code of ethics
倫理プログラム　integrity programme　米 integrity program

る

類似企業　comparable company
類似企業分析　comparable company analysis
類似性　similarity
類似の項目　like items
類似の取引　like [similar] transaction
累進課税　graduated taxation
累進税率　graduated [progressive] (tax) rates
累積　accumulation
累積型の有給休暇　accumulating compensated absences
累積型配当（優先株式などの）　cumulative dividend

るいせきが　　　302

累積型優先株式　　cumulative preference share
累積型優先配当　　cumulative preference dividend
累積給付債務　　accumulated benefit obligation
累積損失　　accumulated [cumulative] losses
累積的影響　　cumulative effect
累積的変動　　cumulative change
累損　　accumulated [cumulative] losses

れ

例外　　exception
例外項目　　exceptional item
戻入　　reversal　[頻] reversal of an impairment loss（減損損失の戻入）
暦年　　calendar year
レギュラー・ハイブリッド　　regular hybrid
レジスター（金銭登録機）　　register
レター・オブ・アウェアネス　　letter of awareness
レター・オブ・コンフォート　　letter of comfort
レター・ルーリング　　letter ruling
列（行・列の）　　column
劣化　　deterioration
劣後債務　　junior [subordinated] debt
劣後負債　　subordinated liabilities
レッド・フラッグ（危険信号）　　red flag
レッド・フラッグ・デュー・デリジェンス　　red flag due diligence
レッド・フラッグ・レポート　　red flag report
レバードベータ　　levered beta
レバレッジ　　leverage, gearing
レバレッジ効果　　leverage effect
レバレッジ比率　　leverage ratio
レビュー統制　　review control
レビュー　　review
レビュー報告書　　review report
レベニュー・センター　　revenue centre　[米] revenue center
レベル1のインプット　　level 1 inputs
レベル2のインプット　　level 2 inputs
レベル3のインプット　　level 3 inputs
連結　　consolidation
連結及び個別財務諸表　　consolidated and separate financial statements
連結会計システム　　consolidation accounting system
連結会社間の消去　　intra-group elimination
連結株主資本等変動計算書　　consolidated statement of changes in net assets
連結期間　　consolidation period
連結キャッシュ・フロー計算書　　consolidated statement of cash flows
連結グループ　　consolidation group
連結決算　　consolidation closing
連結決算書　　consolidated financial accounts
連結欠損金　　consolidated tax loss
連結子会社　　consolidated subsidiary
連結財政状態計算書　　consolidated statement of financial position
連結財務諸表　　consolidated financial statements, consolidated (financial) accounts
連結修正　　consolidation adjustment
連結修正仕訳　　consolidation (adjusting) entry
連結上消去される取引　　transaction eliminated on consolidation
連結所得　　consolidated (taxable) income
連結仕訳　　consolidation entry
連結申告書　　consolidated tax return
連結損益及び包括利益計算書　　consolidated statement of comprehensive income
連結損益計算書　　consolidated income statement, consolidated statement of income
連結貸借対照表　　consolidated balance sheet
連結対象の組成された企業[ストラクチャード・エンティティ]　　consolidated structured entity
連結手続　　consolidation procedure
連結納税　　consolidated (tax return) filing, tax consolidation
連結納税開始前の繰越欠損金　　pre-consolidation losses　[頻] extinguishment of pre-consolidation losses（連結納税開始前の繰越欠損金の消滅）
連結納税グループ　　tax consolidated group
連結納税制度　　consolidated tax return filing system, consolidated taxation system

連結の基礎　basis for [of] consolidation
連結の免除　exemption from consolidation
連結パッケージ　(group) reporting package
連結範囲　scope of consolidation
連結附属明細表　consolidated supplemental schedule
連結包括利益計算書　consolidated statement of comprehensive income
連結持分変動計算書　consolidated statement of changes in equity
連鎖反応　chain reaction
連産品　joint products
レンジ　range　関range from A to B（A から B の値をとる）
連続　sequence
連続する原産地証明書　back-to-back certificate of origin
レンタル料（の支払い）　rent(al) payment
連番の請求書（予め連番を付したもの）　pre-numbered invoices

ローテーション　job rotation
ロールバック　rollback
ロールバック（APA の遡及適用）　APA rollback
ロール・フォワード　roll forward
ロール・フォワード手続　roll forward procedure
ローン・コミットメント　loan commitment
ローン担保証券　collateralised loan obligation (CLO)　米collateralized loan obligation (CLO)
ロケーション・セービング　location savings
ロックアップ　lock-up
ロックアップ期間　lock-up period
ロックアップ契約　lock-up agreement
ロング・ポジション　long position
ロング・リスト　long list
論証　demonstration
論点　issue
論理　logic

ろ

ロイヤルティ（使用料）　royalty, royalty fee
ロイヤルティ（忠誠心）　loyalty
ロイヤルティ収益　royalty revenue, royalty income
ロイヤルティ費用　royalty expense
ロイヤルティ・プログラム　loyalty programme　米loyalty program
労働　labour　米labor
労働協約　union agreement
労働組合　union
労働者名簿　roster of workers
労働条件　working condition
労働保険　labour insurance　米labor insurance
労働力　labour, workforce　米labor
労務費　labour cost　米labor cost
ローカル・ファイル（独立企業間価格を算定するために必要と認められる書類）　local file

わ

ワークシート　worksheet
賄賂　bribe
和解　settlement
和解契約書　settlement agreement
枠組み　framework
枠組み合意　framework agreement
ワラント　warrant
割合　percentage, proportion
割当　assignment, allotment, apportionment　[関] cost is assigned to（コストが〜に割り当てられる）, cost is apportioned between A and B（コストがAとBに割り振られる）
割引　discount
割引額の振戻し（時の経過に伴う）　unwind(ing) of discount　[頻] unwind of discount on site restoration provision（土地原状回復引当金の時間の経過に伴う増加額）, expense due to unwinding of discount on provisions（引当金に係る割引の振戻しによる費用）
割引キャッシュ・フロー　discounted cash flow (DCF)
割引キャッシュ・フロー法　discounted cash flow (DCF) method
割引後将来キャッシュ・フロー　discounted future cash flows
割引債　discount bond
割引将来キャッシュ・フロー　discounted future cash flows
割引手形　notes (receivable) discounted
割引発行（債券の）　original issue discount (OID)
割引前将来キャッシュ・フロー　undiscounted future cash flows
割引率　discount rate
割増退職金　additional retirement benefit
割増退職金の受給権　enhanced retirement entitlement
割戻し　rebate
割安更新選択権［オプション］（リース契約などの）　bargain renewal option
割安購入（益）　bargain purchase
割安購入益　gain on [from] a bargain purchase
割安購入選択権［オプション］（リース契約などの）　bargain purchase option
1ステップ・アプローチ　single-step approach

付　録

1　英和対照　財務諸表様式（IFRSベース）
2　IFRS基準書別　会計用語
3　国際税務の分野別　税務用語
4　知っていると便利！　e-mail表現

1. 英和対照 財務諸表様式（IFRS ベース）

ここでは，IFRS ベースの以下の連結財務諸表について，英和対照で様式を示しています。

(1)	Consolidated Statement of Financial Position	連結財政状態計算書
(2)	Consolidated Statement of Comprehensive Income	連結包括利益計算書
(3)	Consolidated Statement of Changes in Equity	連結持分変動計算書
(4)	Consolidated Statement of Cash Flows	連結キャッシュ・フロー計算書

(1) Consolidated Statement of Financial Position（連結財政状態計算書）

ASSETS	資産
NON-CURRENT ASSETS：	**非流動資産：**
Property, plant and equipment	有形固定資産
Investment property	投資不動産
Goodwill	のれん
Other intangible assets	無形資産
Investments accounted for using the equity method	持分法で会計処理されている投資
Other investments	その他の投資
Trade and other receivables	営業債権及びその他の債権
Other financial assets	その他の金融資産
Deferred tax assets	繰延税金資産
Other non-current assets	その他の非流動資産
Total non-current assets	**非流動資産合計**
CURRENT ASSETS：	**流動資産：**
Inventories	棚卸資産
Trade and other receivables	営業債権及びその他の債権
Other financial assets	その他の金融資産
Current tax assets [receivable]	未収法人所得税
Other current assets	その他の流動資産
Cash and cash equivalents	現金及び現金同等物
Sub total	**小計**
Assets held for sale	売却目的で保有する資産
Total current assets	**流動資産合計**
Total assets	**資産合計**

| LIABILITIES AND EQUITY | 負債及び資本 |

LIABILITIES / 負債

NON-CURRENT LIABILITIES： / 非流動負債：

Borrowings	借入金
Other financial liabilities	その他の金融負債
Net defined benefit liabilities	退職給付に係る負債
Provisions	引当金
Deferred tax liabilities	繰延税金負債
Other non-current liabilities	その他の非流動負債
Total non-current liabilities	**非流動負債合計**

CURRENT LIABILITIES： / 流動負債：

Borrowings	借入金
Trade and other payables	営業債務及びその他の債務
Other financial liabilities	その他の金融負債
Current tax liabilities [payable]	未払法人所得税
Provisions	引当金
Other current liabilities	その他の流動負債
Liabilities directly associated with assets held for sale	売却目的で保有する資産に直接関連する負債
Total current liabilities	**流動負債合計**
Total liabilities	**負債合計**

EQUITY / 資本

Share capital	資本金
Share premium	資本剰余金
Treasury shares	自己株式
Retained earnings	利益剰余金
Other components of equity	その他の資本の構成要素
Equity attributable to owners of the Company	親会社の所有者に帰属する持分
Non-controlling interests	非支配持分
Total equity	**資本合計**
Total liabilities and equity	**負債及び資本合計**

(2) Consolidated Statement of Comprehensive Income（連結包括利益計算書）

CONTINUING OPERATIONS:	**継続事業：**
Revenue	売上収益
Cost of sales	売上原価
Gross profit	売上総利益
Selling, general and administrative expenses	販売費及び一般管理費
Research and development expenses	研究開発費
Other operating income	その他の営業収益
Other operating expenses	その他の営業費用
Operating profit	営業利益
Finance income	金融収益
Finance costs	金融費用
Share of profit (loss) of investments accounted for using the equity method	持分法による投資損益
Profit before tax	税引前当期利益
Income tax expense	法人所得税費用
Profit for the year from continuing operations	**継続事業からの当期利益**
DISCONTINUED OPERATIONS:	**非継続事業：**
Profit for the year from discontinued operations	**非継続事業からの当期利益**
Profit for the year	**当期利益**
OTHER COMPREHENSIVE INCOME:	**その他の包括利益：**
Items that will not be reclassified to profit or loss	**純損益に振り替えられることのない項目**
Financial assets measured at FVTOCI	その他の包括利益を通じて公正価値で測定される金融資産
Remeasurements of defined benefit plans	確定給付制度の再測定
Share of other comprehensive income of investments accounted for using the equity method	持分法適用会社におけるその他の包括利益に対する持分
Items that may be reclassified subsequently to profit or loss	**純損益に振り替えられる可能性のある項目**
Exchange differences on translation of foreign operations	在外営業活動体の換算差額
Cash flow hedges	キャッシュ・フロー・ヘッジ
Share of other comprehensive income of investments accounted for using the equity method	持分法適用会社におけるその他の包括利益に対する持分
Other comprehensive income for the year, net of tax	**その他の包括利益合計**
Total comprehensive income for the year	**当期包括利益合計**
Profit for the year attributable to:	**当期利益の帰属：**
Owners of the Company	親会社の所有者
Non-controlling interests	非支配持分
Total comprehensive income attributable to:	**当期包括利益の帰属：**
Owners of the Company	親会社の所有者
Non-controlling interests	非支配持分
Earnings per share	**1株当たり当期利益**
Basic earnings per share	基本的1株当たり当期利益
Diluted earnings per share	希薄化後1株当たり当期利益

（注）非継続事業に係る1株当たり当期利益の情報は省略します

(3) Consolidated Statement of Changes in Equity (連結持分変動計算書)

Equity attributable to owners of the Company
(親会社の所有者に帰属する持分)

	Share capital 資本金	Share premium 資本剰余金	Treasury shares 自己株式	Retained earnings 利益剰余金	Other components of equity その他の資本の構成要素(注)	Total 合計	Non-controlling interests 非支配持分	Total equity 資本合計

(注)内訳の記載は省略します

Balance at 1 April 20X0	20X0年4月1日残高
Profit for the year	当期利益
Other comprehensive income	その他の包括利益：
Total comprehensive income for the year	当期包括利益合計
Issue of ordinary shares	普通株式の発行
Purchase of treasury shares	自己株式の取得
Disposal of treasury shares	自己株式の処分
Dividends	配当
Share-based payments	株式報酬取引
Changes in the ownership interest in subsidiaries	子会社所有持分の変動
Transfer from other components of equity to retained earnings	その他の資本の構成要素から利益剰余金への振替
Total transactions with owners	所有者との取引額合計
Balance at 31 March 20X1	20X1年3月31日残高

(4) Consolidated Statement of Cash Flows（連結キャッシュ・フロー計算書）

CASH FLOWS FROM OPERATING ACTIVITIES:	営業活動によるキャッシュ・フロー：
Profit for the year	当期利益
Adjustments for:	調整：
Income tax expense recognised in profit or loss	法人所得税費用
Depreciation and amortisation	減価償却費及び無形資産償却費
(Gain)/loss on sale and disposal of property, plant and equipment	有形固定資産除売却損益
(Reversal of) impairment loss	減損損失（戻入れ）
Finance income recognised in profit or loss	金融収益
Finance costs recognised in profit or loss	金融費用
Share of (profit) loss of investments accounted for using the equity method	持分法による投資損益
(Increase)/decrease in trade and other receivables	営業債権及びその他の債権の増減
(Increase)/decrease in inventories	棚卸資産の増減
Increase/(decrease) in trade and other payables	営業債務及びその他の債務の増減
Increase/(decrease) in provisions	引当金の増減
Other	その他
Interest received	利息の受取額
Dividends received	配当金の受取額
Interest paid	利息の支払額
Income taxes paid	法人所得税の支払額
Net cash generated from (used in) operating activities	**営業活動によるキャッシュ・フロー**
CASH FLOWS FROM INVESTING ACTIVITIES:	投資活動によるキャッシュ・フロー：
Payments for property, plant and equipment	有形固定資産の取得による支出
Proceeds from sale of property, plant and equipment	有形固定資産の売却による収入
Payments for investment property	投資不動産の取得による支出
Proceeds from sale of investment property	投資不動産の売却による収入
Payments for intangible assets	無形資産の取得による支出
Proceeds from sale of intangible assets	無形資産の売却による収入
Net cash outflow on acquisition of subsidiaries	子会社の取得による支出（取得時の現金受入額控除後）
Net cash inflow on sale of subsidiaries	子会社の売却による収入（売却時の現金保有額控除後）
Payments for other investments	その他の投資の取得による支出
Proceeds from sale of other investments	その他の投資の売却による収入
Other	その他
Net cash generated from (used in) investing activities	**投資活動によるキャッシュ・フロー**

CASH FLOWS FROM FINANCING ACTIVITIES:	**財務活動によるキャッシュ・フロー：**
Net increase/(decrease) in short-term borrowings	短期借入金の純増減額
Proceeds from long-term borrowings	長期借入れによる収入
Repayment of long-term borrowings	長期借入金の返済による支出
Proceeds from issue of ordinary shares	普通株式の発行による収入
Proceeds from disposal of treasury shares	自己株式の処分による収入
Payments for treasury shares	自己株式の取得による支出
Dividends paid	配当金の支払額
Other	その他
Net cash generated from (used in) financing activities	**財務活動によるキャッシュ・フロー**
Net increase/(decrease) in cash and cash equivalents	**現金及び現金同等物の増減額**
Cash and cash equivalents at the beginning of the year	現金及び現金同等物の期首残高
Effects of exchange rate changes on the balance of cash and cash equivalents	現金及び現金同等物に係る為替変動による影響額
Cash and cash equivalents at the end of the year	**現金及び現金同等物の期末残高**

2. IFRS基準書別 会計用語

ここでは，実務的に使用頻度の高い基準書で使用されている用語（及び関連する用語）について解説しています。

IAS/IFRS	基準書
IAS 1	"Presentation of Financial Statements"（財務諸表の表示）
IAS 2	"Inventories"（棚卸資産）
IAS 7	"Statement of Cash Flows"（キャッシュ・フロー計算書）
IAS 8	"Accounting Policies, Changes in Accounting Estimates and Errors"（会計方針，会計上の見積りの変更及び誤謬）
IAS 10	"Events after the Reporting Period"（後発事象）
IAS 12	"Income Taxes"（法人所得税）
IAS 16	"Property, Plant and Equipment"（有形固定資産）
IAS 19	"Employee Benefits"（従業員給付）
IAS 20	"Accounting for Government Grants and Disclosure of Government Assistance"（政府補助金の会計処理及び政府援助の開示）
IAS 21	"The Effects of Changes in Foreign Exchange Rates"（外国為替レート変動の影響）
IAS 23	"Borrowing Costs"（借入コスト）
IAS 24	"Related Party Disclosures"（関連当事者についての開示）
IAS 27	"Separate Financial Statements"（個別財務諸表）
IAS 28	"Investments in Associates and Joint Ventures"（関連会社及び共同支配企業に対する投資）
IAS 32	"Financial Instruments: Presentation"（金融商品：表示）
IAS 33	"Earnings Per Share"（1株当たり利益）
IAS 34	"Interim Financial Reporting"（期中財務報告）
IAS 36	"Impairment of Assets"（資産の減損）
IAS 37	"Provisions, Contingent Liabilities and Contingent Assets"（引当金，偶発負債及び偶発資産）
IAS 38	"Intangible Assets"（無形資産）
IAS 40	"Investment Property"（投資不動産）
IFRS 1	"First-time Adoption of International Financial Reporting Standards"（国際財務報告基準の初度適用）
IFRS 2	"Share-based Payment"（株式に基づく報酬）
IFRS 3	"Business Combinations"（企業結合）
IFRS 5	"Non-current Assets Held for Sale and Discontinued Operations"（売却目的で保有する非流動資産及び非継続事業）
IFRS 7	"Financial Instruments: Disclosures"（金融商品：開示）
IFRS 8	"Operating Segments"（事業セグメント）
IFRS 9	"Financial Instruments"（金融商品）

IAS/IFRS	基準書
IFRS 10	"Consolidated Financial Statements"（連結財務諸表）
IFRS 11	"Joint Arrangements"（共同支配の取決め）
IFRS 12	"Disclosure of Interests in Other Entities"（他の企業への関与の開示）
IFRS 13	"Fair Value Measurement"（公正価値測定）
IFRS 15	"Revenue from Contracts with Customers"（顧客との契約から生じる収益）
IFRS 16	"Leases"（リース）

付録

共通

英　語	日本語
解　説	
accrual basis	発生主義
取引や事象を，現金受渡時点ではなく，経済的資源や請求権の発生時点で認識するもの	
asset	資産
過去の事象の結果として企業が支配し，かつ将来の経済的便益が当該企業に流入することが期待される資源	
capital	資本
持分参加者の投下資金であり，企業が維持すべき対象。持分	
comparability	比較可能性
財務諸表の質的特性の1つ	
current cost	現在原価
測定基礎の1つで，資産であれば，現時点で取得するとしたときに支払う金額	
disclosure	開示
財務諸表の本表や注記により情報を開示すること	
equity	持分
企業の資産から負債を控除した残余に対する請求権	
expense	費用
会計期間における資産の減少または負債の増加という形での経済的便益の減少で，持分参加者への分配以外のもの	
gain	利得
広義の収益（income）のうち，狭義の収益（revenue）以外のもので，主として企業の通常の事業過程以外から稼得したものを指すが，IFRS上は狭義の収益と特段区別はされていない	
going concern	継続企業
予見しうる将来にわたって，企業が事業活動を継続するという前提	
historical cost	取得原価
測定基礎の1つで，資産であれば，取得したときに支払った金額	
income	（広義の）収益
会計期間における資産の増加または負債の減少という形での経済的便益の増加で，持分参加者からの出資以外のもの	
liability	負債
過去の事象から発生した企業の現在の債務で，その決済により，経済的便益を有する資源が当該企業から流出することが予想されるもの	
loss	損失
広義の費用（expense）のうち，主として企業の通常の事業過程以外から発生したものを指すが，IFRS上はその他の費用と特段区別はされていない	
matching (of cost with revenue)	費用収益の対応
費用と収益を対応させて計上するという原則	

materiality	重要性
目的適合性の1要素で，質的または量的な影響の大きさのこと	
measurement	測定
財務諸表への計上を決定（認識）した後，その計上金額を決定するプロセス	
measurement base	測定の基礎
取得原価，現在原価，実現可能価額，現在価値の4つ	
present value	現在価値
測定基礎の1つで，資産であれば，将来キャッシュ・フロー（流入）の現在価値	
realisable value	実現可能価額
測定基礎の1つで，資産であれば，通常の事業過程で処分することにより得られる金額	
recognition	認識
財務諸表への計上を決定するプロセス	
relevance	目的適合性
財務諸表の質的特性の1つ	
revenue	（狭義の）収益
広義の収益（income）のうち，主として企業の通常の事業過程で稼得したもの	
substance over form	実質主義
形式よりも実質を優先するというIFRSの原則の1つ	

IAS 1 "Presentation of Financial Statements"（財務諸表の表示）

【基準書の内容】	
財務諸表の構成やその内容など，IFRS に準拠する財務諸表の表示についての全般的事項を規定している	
英　語	日本語
解　説	
accounting policy	会計方針
企業が財務諸表を作成・表示するにあたって適用する特定の原則，基準，慣行，ルール及び実務	
a complete set of financial statements	完全な1組の財務諸表
構成要素は，財政状態計算書，包括利益計算書，持分変動計算書，キャッシュ・フロー計算書，注記，（一定の場合には）比較対象期間のうち最も早い年度の期首時点の財政状態計算書	
classification	分類
財務諸表における科目の分類	
comparative information	比較情報
当期の情報と比較するための前期以前の情報（過年度財務諸表等）	
estimation	見積り（見積もること）
財務諸表の構成要素に不確実性がある場合において，財務諸表作成時に入手可能な情報に基づいて，その合理的な金額を算出すること	
impracticable	実務上不可能な
ある要求事項について，あらゆる合理的な努力を行ったとしても，それを適用することができないという状況	
notes (to financial statements)	注記
財務諸表の本体に追加する形で，財務諸表作成の基礎や採用している具体的な会計方針，またその他の情報（財務諸表に表示している項目の説明や個別の項目の分解など）等を開示するもの	
presentation	表示
財務諸表における表示	
statement of cash flows	キャッシュ・フロー計算書
1会計期間のキャッシュ・フローの内訳を示す計算書	
statement of changes in equity	持分変動計算書
1会計期間の資本の変動内訳を示す計算書	
statement of comprehensive income	包括利益計算書
1会計期間の企業の所有者（株主）以外との取引による資本の変動（単純にいうと経営成績）を示す計算書で，従来の損益計算書にその他の包括利益の要素を加えたもの	
statement of financial position	財政状態計算書
企業の期末時点の財政状態を表現したもので，従来の貸借対照表と同様	

IAS 2 "Inventories"（棚卸資産）

【基準書の内容】	
原価の決定及び正味実現可能価額への評価減を含むその後の費用認識に関する指針のほか，棚卸資産に原価を配分するために用いられる原価算定方式に関する指針も提供するなど，棚卸資産の全般的な会計処理を規定している	

英　語	日本語
解　説	
cost formula	原価算定方式
先入先出法や加重平均法など，棚卸資産の原価を売上原価や期末残高に配分する方法	
finished goods	製品
棚卸資産の1つで，製造が完了したもの	
first-in, first-out (FIFO)	先入先出法
原価算定方式の1つで，先に入庫したものから順に出庫されるという仮定に基づく方式	
inventory	棚卸資産
通常の事業過程において販売目的で保有されている製品や商品，製造過程にある仕掛品，製造過程で消費する原材料等	
last-in, first-out (LIFO)	後入先出法
原価算定方式の1つで，後に入庫したものから順に出庫されるという仮定に基づく方式。IFRSでは後入先出法の使用は認められていない	
(the) lower of cost and net realisable value	低価法
取得原価と正味実現可能価額のいずれか低いほうで財政状態計算書上の価額とする方法	
net realisable value (NRV)	正味実現可能価額
通常の事業過程における見積売価から，完成までに要する見積原価及び販売に要する見積費用を控除した額	
raw material	原材料
棚卸資産の1つで，まだ製造工程に投入されていないもの	
specific identification of cost	個別法
代替性のない棚卸資産の原価算定方式	
standard cost method	標準原価法
原価算定方式ではなく，原価の直接的な測定方法であり，IFRSでは実際原価に近似する場合のみ簡便法として使用が認められる	
weighted average cost formula	加重平均法
原価算定方式の1つで，期首の原価と期中に購入・製造したものの原価との加重平均により，個々の原価を算定する方式	
work in process	仕掛品
棚卸資産の1つで，製造の過程にあるもの	

IAS 7 "Statement of Cash Flows"（キャッシュ・フロー計算書）

【基準書の内容】

1会計期間のキャッシュ・フローの営業・投資・財務活動への分類等，企業のキャッシュ（現金及び現金同等物）の変動実績に関する開示方法を規定している

英　語	日本語
解　説	
cash	現金
手許現金及び要求払預金	
cash equivalent	現金同等物
短期の流動性の高い投資のうち，容易に一定金額に換金可能であり，かつ価値の変動について僅少なリスクしか負わないもの	
cash flow	キャッシュ・フロー
現金及び現金同等物の流入及び流出	
direct method	直接法
営業活動によるキャッシュ・フローについて，主要な区分ごとに収入総額と支出総額を分けて表示する方法	
financing activity	財務活動
拠出資本や借入金の規模や構成に変動をもたらす活動	
indirect method	間接法
営業活動によるキャッシュ・フローについて，収入総額と支出総額を分けず，純損益からスタートし，非資金項目等の種々の調整を行う形で表示する方法	
investing activity	投資活動
有形固定資産などの長期性資産への投資やその処分等の活動	
non-cash transaction	非資金取引
現金及び現金同等物の増減を伴わない取引（例えば，リース資産の取得）で，注記による開示が必要とされる	
operating activity	営業活動
企業の主たる収益稼得活動をいうが，投資活動や財務活動に含まれないその他の活動も含む	

IAS 8 "Accounting Policies, Changes in Accounting Estimates and Errors"
(会計方針,会計上の見積りの変更及び誤謬)

【基準書の内容】	
会計方針の選択及び適用,会計方針の変更,会計上の見積りの変更,並びに誤謬の訂正の会計処理及び開示を規定している	
英　語	日本語
解　説	
accounting estimate	会計上の見積り
財務諸表の構成要素に不確実性がある場合において,財務諸表作成時に入手可能な情報に基づいて,その合理的な金額を算出した結果	
accounting policy	会計方針
企業が財務諸表を作成表示するにあたって適用する特定の原則,基準,慣行,ルール及び実務	
change in accounting estimate	会計上の見積りの変更
新しい情報や展開をもとに,資産や負債を再度評価し,それにより現状の帳簿価額を修正すること等を指す。過年度の誤謬の訂正とは異なり,会計上の見積りの変更の影響は,それを行った期の純損益に含めて認識する必要がある	
change in accounting policy	会計方針の変更
会計方針の変更が許容されるのは,①新しい基準書等で要求される場合,②より信頼性及び目的適合性が高い情報が提供できるようになる場合に限られ,①の場合はその経過措置(もしあれば)に従い,②の場合は基本的に遡及適用する必要がある	
cumulative effect	累積的影響
会計方針の変更を遡及適用することによる当期残高への影響	
prior period error	過年度の誤謬
信頼性の高い情報の不使用または誤用により生じた,過去の財務諸表における脱漏または誤表示。遡及的に修正し,修正再表示する必要がある	
prospective application	将来に向かっての適用
会計方針の変更についていうと,変更時点から新しい会計方針を適用すること。遡及適用に対する用語	
retrospective application	遡及適用
新しい会計方針について,あたかも過去からその会計方針が適用されていたかのように適用すること	
retrospective restatement	遡及的修正再表示
あたかも過年度の誤謬がなかったかのように,財務諸表項目の金額及び表示を修正すること	
voluntary change in accounting policy	自発的な会計方針の変更
会計方針の変更のうち,新しいIFRSの基準書等で要求されるもの以外の変更	

IAS 10 "Events after the Reporting Period"（後発事象）

【基準書の内容】	
後発事象が発生した場合の財務諸表の修正や必要な開示について規定している	
英　語	日本語
解　説	
adjusting event after reporting period	修正を要する後発事象
後発事象のうち，報告期間の末日に存在した状況についての証拠を提供する事象で，財務諸表の金額等の修正が必要になるもの	
date when financial statements are authorised for issue	財務諸表の発行承認日
財務諸表の発行承認日以前に発生した事象が後発事象となる	
end of reporting period	報告期間の末日
いわゆる期末日を指し，この日以降に発生した事象が後発事象となる	
estimate of financial effect	財務的影響の見積り
重要な「修正を要しない後発事象」については，その財務的影響の見積りを開示する必要がある	
event after reporting period	後発事象
報告期間の末日と財務諸表の発行承認日との間に発生する事象	
nature of the event	（当該）事象の性質
重要な「修正を要しない後発事象」については，その性質を開示する必要がある	
non-adjusting event after reporting period	修正を要しない後発事象
後発事象のうち，報告期間の末日後に新たに発生した状況を示す事象で，日本基準でいう開示後発事象に相当するもの	

IAS 12 "Income Taxes"(法人所得税)

【基準書の内容】	
法人所得税(当期税金及び繰延税金)の会計処理や開示を規定している	
英　語	日本語
解　説	
accounting profit	会計上の利益
会計上の利益であり,税務上の利益(課税所得)とは区別される	
carryforward of unused tax credits	繰越税額控除
税額控除のうち翌期以降に使用されるもの。将来その使用対象となる課税所得(税額)が稼得される可能性が高い場合,繰延税金資産が認識される	
carryforward of unused tax losses	税務上の繰越欠損金
当期以前に発生した欠損金のうち翌期以降に繰り越されるもの。将来その使用対象となる課税所得が稼得される可能性が高い場合,繰延税金資産が認識される	
components of tax expense	税金費用の内訳
主要な(major)税金費用の内訳は開示対象となる	
current tax	当期税金
実際に納付すべき(または還付を受ける)税額で,繰延税金に対する用語	
current tax expense	当期税金費用(法人税,住民税及び事業税)
当期の税金計算の結果,実際に納付すべき税額。繰延税金費用に対する用語	
deductible temporary difference	将来減算一時差異
一時差異のうち,解消の際に課税所得を減額させるもので,繰延税金資産の計上対象となる(繰延税金資産が回収可能と判断された場合)	
deferred tax	繰延税金
繰延税金資産・負債の認識に伴い発生するもので,当期税金に対する用語	
deferred tax assets	繰延税金資産
繰延税金資産は,一定の例外を除き,①将来減算一時差異,②税務上の繰越欠損金,③繰越税額控除について,回収可能と判断された場合に認識される	
deferred tax expense	繰延税金費用(法人税等調整額)
当期の税効果計算の結果,税金費用として認識される額。当期税金費用に対する用語	
deferred tax liabilities	繰延税金負債
繰延税金負債は,一定の例外を除き,将来加算一時差異について認識される	
income tax	法人所得税
所得を課税標準として課される国内外のすべての税金。課税標準が所得ではない税金(例えば,日本の住民税均等割等)はIFRSにおける法人所得税には該当しない	
recoverability	回収可能性
繰延税金資産が認識される条件として,繰延税金資産が回収可能(recoverable)であることが必要である	
taxable profit	税務上の利益(課税所得)
税務上の利益(課税所得)であり,会計上の利益とは区別される	

taxable temporary difference	将来加算一時差異
一時差異のうち，解消の際に課税所得を増額させるもので，基本的に繰延税金負債の計上対象となる	
tax base	税務基準額
一時差異を計算する際に会計上の金額（carrying amount）と比較される金額	
tax expense	税金費用
当期税金費用と繰延税金費用の合計額	
tax planning	タックス・プランニング
将来の税務コストの削減や税務リスクの低減を達成するための計画をいい，繰延税金資産の回収可能性を判断するにあたって考慮される	
tax rate	税率
繰延税金資産及び負債は，報告期間の末日において制定されている（または実質的に制定されている）法定税率に基づき，それらが回収及び決済される時点に適用されると予想される税率に基づいて測定される	
temporary difference	一時差異
資産及び負債の会計上の金額と税務上の金額の差異であり，将来減算一時差異と将来加算一時差異に分類される	
uncertain tax position (UTP)	不確実な税務ポジション
端的には，税務当局と見解が相違する（つまり，税務上の処理の一部または全部を否認される）可能性のある項目。不確実な税務ポジションも考慮に入れて税金費用を見積もる必要がある	
undistributed profit	未配分利益
子会社等が親会社に配当せずに保有している利益。将来加算一時差異を構成するが，親会社がその解消時期をコントロールでき，予見しうる将来（foreseeable future）にそれが解消しない可能性が高い場合（例えば，配当させない方針の場合）には，繰延税金負債を認識しない	
valuation allowance	評価性引当額
繰延税金資産のうち回収不能と判断された部分	

IAS 16 "Property, Plant and Equipment"（有形固定資産）

【基準書の内容】	
有形固定資産について，その認識及び帳簿価額の算定，またそれに関連して認識すべき減価償却費及び減損損失など，有形固定資産全般の会計処理や開示を規定している	
英　語	日本語
解　説	
accumulated depreciation	減価償却累計額
過去の減価償却費の累計額	
accumulated impairment losses	減損損失累計額
過去の減損損失の累計額	
cost model	原価モデル
当初認識後の測定として，有形固定資産項目を取得原価から減価償却累計額及び減損損失累計額を控除した価額で計上する方法。再評価モデルに対する用語	
depreciable amount	償却可能額
資産の取得原価から残存価額を控除した額	
depreciation	減価償却（費）
資産の償却可能額をその耐用年数にわたって規則的に配分すること	
depreciation method	減価償却方法
減価償却方法は，その資産についての企業による将来の経済的便益の消費パターンを反映するものである必要がある	
diminishing balance method	定率法
減価償却方法の1つで，定率法によると，減価償却費が毎期逓減していく	
property, plant and equipment (PP&E)	有形固定資産
製品の製造や役務の提供に使用する目的等で企業が保有し，1会計期間を超えて使用されると予想される有形の資産	
residual value	残存価額
資産の耐用年数終了時点における処分可能価額（見積処分コスト控除後）の現時点での予測額	
revaluation model	再評価モデル
当初認識後の測定として，公正価値が信頼性をもって測定できる有形固定資産につき，再評価実施日の公正価値からその後の減価償却累計額及び減損損失累計額を控除した価額で計上する方法。原価モデルに対する用語	
straight-line method	定額法
減価償却方法の1つで，定額法によると，減価償却費が毎期一定になる	
unit of production method	生産高比例法
減価償却方法の1つで，毎期の生産高に基づいて減価償却費を決定する方法	
useful life	耐用年数
企業がその資産を使用すると予測される期間など	

IAS 19 "Employee Benefits"（従業員給付）

【基準書の内容】

従業員給付（従業員が提供した役務と交換に企業から得る対価）に関する会計処理や開示を規定しており，有給休暇を含む短期従業員給付，退職後給付，その他の長期従業員給付，解雇給付等をカバーしている

英　語	日本語
解　説	
actuarial assumption	数理計算上の仮定
確定給付債務等の金額を数理計算するにあたって用いられる仮定で，従業員の離職率や死亡率といった人口統計上の変数や将来の給与上昇等の財務上の変数を含む	
actuarial gains and losses	数理計算上の差異
数理計算上の仮定の変更や実績値との差異により生じる確定給付債務の現在価値の変動であり，発生時にその全額をその他の包括利益として認識する	
asset ceiling	資産上限額（アセット・シーリング）
制度からの返還（または将来の掛金の減額）の形で利用可能な経済的便益の現在価値であり，確定給付制度が積立超過である場合の資産計上の上限額を意味する	
compensated absence	有給休暇
未消化の有給休暇を繰り越せる累積型の制度がある場合には，従業員が役務を提供した期の期末で未消化有給休暇日数のうち一定の部分に費用及び負債を認識する必要がある	
current service cost	当期勤務費用
勤務費用のうち，当期の従業員の勤務による給付見積額の増加額（確定給付債務の現在価値の変動額）	
defined benefit cost	確定給付費用
確定給付制度について発生する費用	
defined benefit obligation	確定給付（制度）債務
確定給付制度における債務で，数理計算上の仮定に基づく現在価値計算により算定される	
defined benefit plan	確定給付制度
退職後給付制度のうち，確定拠出制度以外のもの。企業が従業員（退職者を含む）に対して，合意した給付を支給するという債務を負う	
defined contribution plan	確定拠出制度
退職後給付制度のうち，企業が一定の掛金を基金等に支払い，仮に基金に十分な資産がない場合でも，企業はそれ以上の債務を負わないもの	
discount rate	割引率
確定給付債務の現在価値を算定する際の割引計算に用いられる率で，期末時点の優良社債の市場利回りを基礎として決定される	
employee benefit	従業員給付
従業員が提供した勤務などと交換に，企業が従業員に与える対価。従業員給付には様々な形態があるが，本基準書では，短期従業員給付・退職後給付・その他の長期従業員給付・解雇給付の4つに分類して会計処理を規定している	
net defined benefit asset	確定給付資産の純額（退職給付に係る資産）
報告期間の末日において，制度資産が確定給付債務を上回っている部分。ただし，計上額にアセット・シーリング（資産上限額）と呼ばれる一定の制限がある	

net defined benefit liability	確定給付負債の純額（退職給付に係る負債）
報告期間の末日において，確定給付債務が制度資産を上回っている部分	
net interest on the net defined benefit liability [asset]	確定給付負債［資産］の純額に係る利息純額
確定給付費用の1つで，確定給付債務から制度資産を控除したネットの金額に（確定給付債務を求める際に用いた）割引率を乗じて計算される	
other long-term employee benefits	その他の長期従業員給付
従業員給付の一形態であり，短期従業員給付，退職後給付，解雇給付以外のすべて従業員給付。例えば，長期勤続休暇がこれに該当する。退職後給付とは異なり，すべての再測定結果を純損益で認識する（その他の包括利益では認識しない）	
past service cost	過去勤務費用
勤務費用のうち，制度改訂（確定給付制度の導入や変更）または縮小により発生する，過去の期間の従業員の勤務に対応する確定給付債務の現在価値の変動額。権利確定しているか否かに関わらず，制度改訂時に費用処理する	
plan assets	制度資産
退職後給付のために保有する資産	
post-employment benefit	退職後給付
従業員給付の一形態で，雇用関係の終了後に支払われるもの（解雇給付及び短期従業員給付を除く）	
post-employment benefit plan	退職後給付制度
企業が従業員に対して退職後給付を支給する公式または非公式の取決め。退職後給付制度は，確定拠出制度か確定給付制度のいずれかに分類される	
remeasurement	再測定
確定給付負債（資産）の再測定結果（例えば，数理計算上の差異）は発生時にその全額をその他の包括利益として認識し，事後的な純損益へのリサイクリングも行わない	
service cost	勤務費用
確定給付費用の1つで，当期勤務費用・過去勤務費用・確定給付制度の清算損益により構成される	
settlement of employee benefit obligations	従業員給付債務の清算
確定給付制度に係る給付について，すべての追加的な債務（法的債務または推定的債務）を解消する取引	
short-term employee benefit	短期従業員給付
従業員給付の一形態で，従業員が関連する役務を提供した期間の末日後12か月以内に決済されると予想されるもの（解雇給付を除く）。例えば，給料や年次有給休暇	
termination benefit	解雇給付
従業員給付の一形態で，企業が従業員を解雇する場合などに，雇用の終了と交換に支給されるもの。企業が給付の申し出を撤回することができなくなった時点と，関連するリストラ費用がIAS第37号に基づいて認識された時点のいずれか早い時点で認識し，その給付の性質に応じた測定を行う必要がある	

IAS 20 "Accounting for Government Grants and Disclosure of Government Assistance"（政府補助金の会計処理及び政府援助の開示）

【基準書の内容】	
政府補助金の会計処理と開示，及びその他の形態の政府援助に関する開示を規定している	
英　語	日本語
解　説	
deferred income	繰延収益
資産に関する補助金については，繰延収益として処理する方法がある	
forgivable loan	返済免除条件付融資
一定の条件を満たせば，返済が免除される融資	
government assistance	政府援助
一定の条件を満たす企業または企業群に対して，経済的便益を提供することを目的とする政府の活動	
government grant	政府補助金
企業が一定の条件を過去に満たしたこと，またはそれを将来満たすことの見返りとして，政府が企業へ資源を移転するという形の援助	
grants related to assets	資産に関する補助金
政府補助金のうち，補助を受ける企業が固定資産を取得することを主要な条件とするものであり，その基本的な会計処理としては，繰延収益として処理する方法と，補助金額を控除して資産の帳簿価額を算定する方法がある	
grants related to income	収益に関する補助金
政府補助金のうち，資産に関する補助金以外のものであり，その基本的な会計処理としては，「その他の収益」（other income）のような一般的科目で処理する方法と，関連する費用から控除する方法がある	
nature and extent of government grant	政府補助金の性質と範囲
政府補助金の性質と範囲は開示の対象となる	
non-monetary grants	非貨幣性の補助金
例えば，企業が使用するための土地の移転であり，非貨幣性の補助金は公正価値により測定される	
related expense	関連費用
収益に関する補助金については，関連費用から控除する形で表示する方法がある	
repayment of grant	補助金の返還
補助金の返還は基本的に会計上の見積りの変更に該当し，資産に関する補助金と収益に関する補助金のそれぞれについて会計処理が定められている	
unfulfilled condition	未履行の条件
認識した政府援助に関する未履行の条件は，その他の偶発事象とともに開示の対象となる	

IAS 21 "The Effects of Changes in Foreign Exchange Rates"（外国為替レート変動の影響）

【基準書の内容】	
企業の財務諸表に外貨建取引及び在外営業活動体の活動結果を反映するための方法と，財務諸表を表示通貨に換算するための方法を規定している	
英　語	日本語
解　説	
closing rate	決算日レート
決算日レートは外貨建貨幣性項目等の換算に使用される	
exchange difference	為替差額
ある通貨を他の通貨に換算することにより生じる差額で，純損益で認識される場合とその他の包括利益で認識される場合がある	
exchange rate	為替レート
外国為替の取引における外貨との交換比率	
exchange rate at the date of the transaction	取引日レート
取引日レートは，外貨建非貨幣性項目のうち取得原価で測定されているもの等の換算に使用される	
foreign currency	外国通貨
企業の機能通貨以外の通貨	
foreign currency transaction	外貨建取引
外国通貨による取引	
foreign operation	在外営業活動体
報告企業と異なる国または通貨に基盤を置いて活動している子会社，関連会社，共同支配企業，または支店	
functional currency	機能通貨
企業が営業活動を行う主たる経済環境における通貨。例えば，シンガポール子会社が主として米ドルにより取引を行っている場合，（シンガポールドルではなく）米ドルがその子会社の機能通貨となる可能性もある	
net investment in a foreign operation	在外営業活動体に対する純投資
在外営業活動体の純資産に占める報告企業の持分の額	
presentation currency	表示通貨
財務諸表を表示する通貨で，表示通貨が機能通貨と異なる場合には，表示通貨への換算が必要になる	
spot exchange rate	直物為替レート
為替を即時受渡する際の為替レートで，一般にいう為替レートは直物為替レートを指し，為替予約に係る予約レート（forward exchange rate）に対する用語	

IAS 23 "Borrowing Costs"（借入コスト）

【基準書の内容】	
適格資産の取得等に直接起因する借入コスト及びその他の借入コストの会計処理や開示を規定している	
英　語	日本語
解　説	
borrowing costs	借入コスト
企業の資金の借入に関連して発生する利息及びその他の費用	
borrowing costs eligible for capitalisation	資産化に適格な借入コスト
資産化に適格な借入コスト以外の借入コストは，費用として認識される	
capitalisation of borrowing costs	借入コストの資産化
借入コストを適格資産の取得原価の一部として処理すること	
capitalisation rate	資産化率
適格資産を取得するために特別に行った借入を除く，企業の当期中の借入金残高に対する借入コストの割合（加重平均）であり，適格資産の取得に係る支出にこの資産化率を乗じることで，資産化される借入コストの額が算定される	
(to) cease capitalisation	資産化を終了する
企業は，資産の使用または販売に向けた準備活動が実質的にすべて完了した時点で，借入コストの資産化を終了しなければならない	
commencement date (for capitalisation)	（資産化の）開始日
資産化を開始する日で，①資産に係る支出の発生，②借入コストの発生，③資産の使用または販売に向けた準備活動への着手，という条件を最初に充足した日	
expenditure on a qualifying asset	適格資産に係る支出
資産化される借入コストの額を算定する際，資産化率を乗じる対象	
qualifying asset	適格資産
企業の意図した使用または販売が可能となるまでに相当の期間を要する資産であり，建設期間中の有形固定資産や投資不動産，開発期間中の無形資産などが適格資産になりうる	
(to) suspend capitalisation	資産化を中断する
企業は，適格資産の開発を中断している期間中は，借入コストの資産化も中断する必要がある	

IAS 24 "Related Party Disclosures"(関連当事者についての開示)

【基準書の内容】	
企業の財務諸表は関連当事者の存在並びに関連当事者との取引及び未決済残高の影響を受けている可能性があり，その点に注意が払われるよう，関連当事者に関する開示を規定している	
英　語	日本語
解　説	
close members of the family of a person	個人の近親者
その個人に影響を与えるかまたは影響を受けると予測される親族	
control over (the) reporting entity	報告企業に対する支配
報告企業に対する支配を有している個人またはその近親者は関連当事者に該当する	
fellow subsidiary	兄弟会社
兄弟会社は，報告企業と同一のグループの一員として，関連当事者に該当する	
joint control over (the) reporting entity	報告企業に対する共同支配
報告企業に対する共同支配を有している個人またはその近親者は関連当事者に該当する	
member of key management personnel	経営幹部の一員
報告企業または報告企業の親会社の経営幹部の一員である個人またはその近親者は関連当事者に該当する	
outstanding balance	未決済残高
関連当事者との取引に係る未決済残高及びそれに関連する貸倒引当金の残高は開示対象となる	
related party	関連当事者
報告企業と一定の関連のある個人または企業	
related party transaction	関連当事者との取引
報告企業と関連当事者との間の資源，役務または債務の移転をいい，対価のやり取りの有無を問わない	
reporting entity	報告企業
財務諸表を作成する会社であり，報告企業と一定の関連がある個人または企業が関連当事者となる	
significant influence over (the) reporting entity	報告企業に対する重大な影響力
報告企業に対する重大な影響力を有している個人またはその近親者は関連当事者に該当する	
ultimate controlling party	最終的な支配当事者
報告企業の最終的な支配当事者が親会社と異なる場合には，最終的な支配当事者の名称等を開示する必要がある	

IAS 27 "Separate Financial Statements"(個別財務諸表)

【基準書の内容】
旧IAS第27号「連結及び個別財務諸表」のうち,連結財務諸表に関係する会計処理等はIFRS第10号「連結財務諸表」等に切り出されたため,現状では子会社,共同支配企業及び関連会社に対する投資の個別財務諸表上の会計処理について規定している

英 語	日本語
解 説	
investments in subsidiaries, jointly controlled entities, and associates	子会社,共同支配企業及び関連会社に対する投資
個別財務諸表において,子会社,共同支配企業及び関連会社に対する投資は,以下のいずれかの方法により会計処理される ● 取得原価による会計処理 ● IFRS第9号に従った会計処理 ● IAS第28号に従った会計処理(持分法)	
separate financial statements	個別財務諸表
企業が表示する財務諸表のうち,子会社,共同支配企業及び関連会社に対する投資の会計処理を上記のいずれの方法で行うかを(本基準書の要求事項を条件として)企業が選択できるもの	

IAS 28 "Investments in Associates and Joint Ventures"（関連会社及び共同支配企業に対する投資）

【基準書の内容】	
関連会社の定義や関連会社に対する投資についての会計処理のほか，共同支配企業に対する投資の会計処理も規定している	
英　語	日本語
解　説	
associate	関連会社
投資企業が重要な影響力を有している企業	
distribution received from an investee	被投資企業から受け取った分配
持分法では，被投資企業から受け取った分配は，投資の帳簿価額の減額として処理される	
equity method	持分法
関連会社や共同支配企業に対する投資につき，当初は取得原価で認識するが，その後の被投資企業の純資産に対する投資企業の持分の変動に応じて，投資額を修正する会計処理の方法	
investee	被投資企業
投資企業からの投資を受け入れている側の企業で，複数の投資企業が被投資企業を共同で支配している等の場合には共同支配企業に該当し，投資企業が被投資企業に重要な影響力を有している等の場合には関連会社に該当する	
investment in a joint venture	共同支配企業に対する投資
共同支配企業に対する投資は，原則として持分法により会計処理される	
investment in an associate	関連会社に対する投資
関連会社に対する投資は，原則として持分法により会計処理される	
investor	投資企業
被投資企業に投資している側の企業	
investor's proportionate interest in an investee	投資企業の被投資企業に対する比例持分
持分法では，投資企業は，被投資企業に対する比例持分の変動に応じて，投資額を修正する	
investor's share of the other comprehensive income of an investee	被投資企業のその他の包括利益のうち投資企業の持分額
持分法では，被投資企業のその他の包括利益のうち投資企業の持分額は，投資企業のその他の包括利益として認識される	
investor's share of the profit or loss of an investee	被投資企業の純損益のうち投資企業の持分額
持分法では，被投資企業の純損益のうち投資企業の持分額は，投資企業の純損益として認識される	
joint venture	共同支配企業
共同支配の取決め（joint arrangement）のうち，共同支配の当事者がその取決めに関する純資産に対する権利を有しているもの	
significant influence	重要な影響力
被投資企業の財務及び営業の方針の決定に関与する力（パワー）ではあるが，支配または共同支配には該当しないもの。議決権割合が20％以上の場合には，明らかな反証がない限りは，重要な影響力を有していると推定される	

IAS 32 "Financial Instruments: Presentation"（金融商品：表示）

【基準書の内容】	
主として金融商品の分類（金融資産・金融負債・資本性金融商品），関連損益の分類，及び金融資産・負債の相殺に関して規定しており，IFRS第9号「金融商品」における金融資産・負債の認識及び測定に関する原則や，IFRS第7号「金融商品：開示」における開示の原則を補足するものという位置づけになっている	
英　語	日本語
解　説	
compound financial instrument	複合金融商品
複数の金融商品が組み合わされている金融商品	
equity component	資本部分
金融商品が負債部分と資本部分の両方を含んでいる場合には，その構成部分ごとに金融負債と資本性金融商品として区分して会計処理する必要がある	
equity instrument	資本性金融商品
企業の資産から負債を控除した残余に対する持分を証する契約で，例えば株式が該当する	
financial asset	金融資産
金融資産とは，①現金，②他の企業が発行する資本性金融商品，③他の企業から金融資産を受け取る契約上の権利，または金融資産等を有利な条件で他の企業と交換する契約上の権利，④その企業の資本性金融商品で決済される契約のうち一定のもの，をいう	
financial instrument	金融商品
一方の企業にとっての金融資産と，他方の企業にとっての金融負債または資本性金融商品の双方を生じさせる契約	
financial liability	金融負債
金融負債とは，①他の企業に金融資産を支払う契約上の義務，または金融資産等を不利な条件で他の企業と交換する契約上の義務，②その企業の資本性金融商品で決済される契約のうち一定のもの，をいう	
liability component	負債部分
金融商品が負債部分と資本部分の両方を含んでいる場合には，その構成部分ごとに金融負債と資本性金融商品として区分して会計処理する必要がある	
offsetting of financial assets and liabilities	金融資産・負債の相殺
企業が，①法的に強制力のある相殺の権利と②それを実行する意図を有している場合には，金融資産と金融負債は相殺され，純額で財政状態計算書に表示される	
treasury share	自己株式
企業が自らの資本性金融商品を買い戻す場合の当該資本性金融商品。自己株式は資本から控除され，その購入，売却または発行等により，利得または損失は認識されない	

IAS 33 "Earnings Per Share"（1株当たり利益）

【基準書の内容】	
1株当たり利益の算定及び表示に関して規定している	

英　語	日本語
解　説	
anti-dilution	逆希薄化
文字通り希薄化の逆で，転換型金融商品の転換等を仮定した場合の1株当たり利益の増加	
basic earnings per share	基本的1株当たり利益
親会社の普通株主に帰属する損益を，当期中の発行済普通株式数の加重平均で除したもの	
contingent share agreement	条件付株式発行契約
一定の条件を満たす場合に株式を発行するという契約	
cumulative preference share	累積型優先株式
配当を受け取る優先権が累積する優先株式	
diluted earnings per share	希薄化後1株当たり利益
希薄化性潜在的普通株式による影響を調整した後の1株当たり利益	
dilution	希薄化
転換型金融商品の転換，オプションやワラントの行使，または特定の条件の充足による普通株式の発行等を仮定した場合の1株当たり利益の減少または1株当たり損失の増加	
dilutive potential ordinary share	希薄化性潜在的普通株式
普通株式への転換等により1株当たり利益が減少する場合または1株当たり損失が増加する場合の潜在的普通株式	
discontinued operation	非継続事業
非継続事業を報告する企業は，包括利益計算書または注記において，非継続事業に係る基本的1株当たり利益及び希薄化後1株当たり利益を開示する必要がある	
earnings per share (EPS)	1株当たり利益
端的には利益を発行済株式総数で除したもので，基本的1株当たり利益と希薄化後1株当たり利益がある	
non-cumulative preference share	非累積型優先株式
配当を受け取る優先権が累積せず，単年度で失効する優先株式	
options, warrants and their equivalents	オプション，ワラント及びその同等物
所有者に対して普通株式の購入の権利を付与する金融商品	
ordinary share	普通株式
他のすべての資本性金融商品に劣後する資本性金融商品	
potential ordinary share	潜在的普通株式
その所有者に普通株式を付与する可能性がある金融商品またはその他の契約	
preference dividend	優先配当
優先株式からの配当	
preference share	優先株式
その株主に優先権（通常は配当に関する優先権）が付与されている株式	

IAS 34 "Interim Financial Reporting"（期中財務報告）

【基準書の内容】

企業がIFRSに準拠した期中財務報告の公表を強制されたり，または自発的に公表したりする場合に適用される基準書。期中財務報告に関する最低限の開示内容を規定し，また期中報告期間に係る完全な財務諸表または要約財務諸表に適用される認識及び測定の原則も規定している。なお，どのような場合に期中財務報告を行う必要があるかについては規定しておらず，各国の規制に委ねられる。

英　語	日本語
解　説	
a complete set of financial statements	完全な1組の財務諸表
IAS第1号「財務諸表の表示」に規定する財務諸表で，構成要素は，財政状態計算書，包括利益計算書，持分変動計算書，キャッシュ・フロー計算書，注記等	
annual	年次の，年間の
期中報告期間を表すinterimに対する用語	
a set of condensed financial statements	1組の要約財務諸表
構成要素は，要約財政状態計算書，要約包括利益計算書，要約持分変動計算書，要約キャッシュ・フロー計算書，一定の説明的注記等	
cyclicality of operations	事業活動の循環性
事業活動の季節性及び循環性については，注記により説明する必要がある	
explanatory note	説明的注記
直近の年次財務報告期間の末日からの財政状態や経営成績の変化を理解する上で重要な事象や取引について説明するもの	
greater use of estimation methods	より多くの見積りの方法の使用
期中財務報告書作成にあたっては，例えば税金費用や年金費用等の処理に代表されるように，年次財務報告書に比べ，より多くの見積りの方法が用いられる	
heading and subtotal	見出し及び小計
期中財務報告書に含まれる要約財務諸表においては，少なくとも直近の年次財務諸表中に掲記された各見出し及び小計を含んでいる必要がある	
interim financial report	期中財務報告書
期中報告期間に係る完全な1組の財務諸表または1組の要約財務諸表のいずれかを含む財務報告書	
interim period	期中報告期間
1事業年度全体よりも短い財務報告の期間で，半期のみならず四半期も含む	
on a year-to-date basis	年初からの累計で
期中財務報告目的の測定は，年初からの累計を基準として行われる	
seasonality of operations	事業活動の季節性
事業活動の季節性及び循環性については，注記により説明する必要がある	

IAS 36 "Impairment of Assets"（資産の減損）

【基準書の内容】	
企業が資産に回収可能価額以上の帳簿価額を付さないよう，資産が減損した場合の減損損失の認識と減損した資産についての一定の開示を要求するとともに，企業が減損損失を戻入しなければならない状況も規定している	
英　語	日本語
解　説	
carrying amount	帳簿価額
資産が財務状態計算書に認識されている金額。資産または資金生成単位の回収可能価額が帳簿価額を下回る場合に減損損失が認識される	
cash-generating unit (CGU)	資金生成単位
他の資産または資産グループからのキャッシュ・インフローとは，ほぼ独立したキャッシュ・インフローを生成するものとして識別される資産グループの最小単位	
corporate assets	全社資産
検討対象の資金生成単位と他の資金生成単位の両方の将来キャッシュ・フローの獲得に寄与する資産	
estimate of future cash flows	将来キャッシュ・フローの見積り
使用価値を算定する際の将来キャッシュ・フローの見積りは，資産の現在の状態をもとに行い，コミットしていない将来のリストラクチャリング等を反映させることはできない	
fair value less costs of disposal	処分コスト控除後の公正価値
資産等の公正価値から処分に直接要する増分コストを控除した額	
impairment loss	減損損失
資産または資金生成単位の回収可能価額が帳簿価額を下回る場合には，帳簿価額を回収可能価額まで減額する必要があり，その減額分が減損損失となる	
impairment test [testing]	減損テスト
減損損失を認識する必要があるかどうかを判定するためのテスト	
indication of impairment	減損の兆候
減損の兆候がある場合には，資産の回収可能価額を見積もらなければならない。なお，減損の兆候に関しては，indication that an asset may be impaired のようないい方もする	
(to) recognise an impairment loss	減損損失を認識する
逆に「減損損失を戻入する」は，(to) reverse an impairment loss	
recoverable amount	回収可能価額
文字通り，資産等から回収可能な金額であり，処分コスト控除後の公正価値と使用価値のいずれか高い金額	
value in use	使用価値
資産等から生じると見込まれる将来キャッシュ・フローの現在価値	
weighted average cost of capital (WACC)	加重平均資本コスト
使用価値を算定する際の割引率（discount rate）は，対象となる資産に固有の割引率を用いるのが原則だが，それがない場合には企業の加重平均資本コストが用いられることがある	

IAS 37 "Provisions, Contingent Liabilities and Contingent Assets"（引当金，偶発負債及び偶発資産）

【基準書の内容】	
引当金，偶発負債及び偶発資産に関して，会計処理や注記による開示を規定している	
英　語	日本語
解　説	
constructive obligation	推定的債務
確立された過去の実務慣行等により，企業が外部の第三者に何らかの責務を受諾することを表明しており，その結果，企業がその責務を果たすであろうという期待が外部の第三者に生じている場合のその債務	
contingent asset	偶発資産
過去の事象から発生し得る（潜在的な）資産のうち，将来の不確実な事象の発生または不発生によってのみその存在が確認されるもの（例えば，還付される可能性のある税金）。偶発資産は財務諸表には認識してはならない。ただし，経済的便益の流入の可能性が高い場合には開示の必要があり，またそれがほぼ確実になった場合には財務諸表上で「資産」として認識される	
contingent liability	偶発負債
①過去の事象から発生し得る（潜在的な）債務のうち，将来の不確実な事象の発生または不発生によってのみ，その存在が確認される債務，または②過去の事象から発生した現在の債務であるが，債務決済のために経済的便益が流出する可能性が高くないか，また債務の金額が十分な信頼性をもって測定できないという理由で認識されていない債務。偶発負債は，引当金とは異なり財務諸表には認識されないが，経済的便益の流出可能性がほとんどない場合を除いて，注記による開示の必要がある	
legal obligation	法的債務
契約や法律に基づく債務	
most likely outcome	最も起こりそうな結果
引当金の測定方法の1つとして，最も起こりそうな結果（金額）で見積もる方法がある	
obligating event	偶発発生事象
（その決済以外に企業に現実的な選択肢がない）法的債務または推定的債務を生じさせる事象	
onerous contract	不利な契約
企業にとって不利な契約であり，正確には，契約上の義務の履行に不可避なコストが，契約から得られる経済的便益を上回る契約。不利な契約から生じる現在の債務は引当金の設定対象となる	
present obligation	現在の債務
引当金の設定対象となるもので，現在の債務には法的債務のほか推定的債務も含まれる	
probability-weighted expected value	発生確率で加重平均した期待値
引当金の測定方法の1つとして，発生可能性のあるすべての結果を，その発生確率で加重平均した期待値として見積もる方法がある	
probable	発生の可能性が高い
本基準書ではmore likely than not（発生の可能性が50％より高い）と同義	
provision	引当金
時期または金額が不確実な負債。①過去の事象から生じる現在の債務であって，②将来において経済的便益が流出する可能性が高く，③信頼性をもって測定できる，という3つの要件を満たす場合に認識される	

IAS 38 "Intangible Assets"（無形資産）

【基準書の内容】	
他の基準で別途取り扱われているものを除き，無形資産に関する全般的な会計処理や開示を規定している	
英　語	日本語
解　説	
accumulated amortisation	（無形資産の）償却累計額
過去の償却費の累計額	
accumulated impairment losses	減損損失累計額
過去の減損損失の累計額	
amortisation	（無形資産の）償却
無形資産の償却可能価額をその耐用年数にわたって規則的に配分することをいい，有形固定資産の depreciation に相当する	
development	開発
研究成果または他の知識を新製品等の計画や設計に適用することをいい，開発フェーズに係る支出については一定の場合には無形資産として認識される	
finite	（耐用年数が）有限の，確定できる
耐用年数を確定できる無形資産の償却可能価額は，その耐用年数にわたり規則的に配分される	
identifiable	識別可能な
無形資産が識別可能とは，その無形資産が①企業から分離可能（個別に売却等可能）な場合，または②契約やその他の法的な権利から生じている場合，をいう	
indefinite	（耐用年数が）確定できない
耐用年数が確定できない無形資産は償却されないが，減損テストを行う必要がある。ちなみに infinite（無限の）とは区別する必要がある	
in-process research and development project	仕掛中の研究開発プロジェクト
仕掛中の研究開発プロジェクトが企業結合により取得された場合で，それが無形資産の定義を満たす場合には，取得企業はそのプロジェクトを「のれん」とは区別して資産として認識する	
intangible asset	無形資産
物理的実体のない識別可能な非貨幣性資産	
internally generated intangible assets	自己創設の無形資産
自己創設の無形資産については，一般的な無形資産の認識要件に加えて，追加の認識要件がある。例えば，自己創設のブランドなどは無形資産としては認識されない	
research	研究
新規の科学的知識等を得る目的で実施される基礎的な調査。研究フェーズに係る支出は費用として認識されるため，研究から生じた無形資産は基本的に認識されない	
useful life	耐用年数
無形資産が企業によって利用可能と予想される期間など	

IAS 40 "Investment Property"(投資不動産)

【基準書の内容】	
投資不動産に関する会計処理や開示を規定している	
英　語	日本語
解　説	
cost model	原価モデル
当初認識の後，通常の減価償却累計額控除後（かつ減損損失累計額控除後）の原価で投資不動産を測定する方法。原価モデルを選択する場合，投資不動産の公正価値等を別途開示する必要がある	
disposal of investment property	投資不動産の処分
投資不動産の処分から生じる利得または損失は純損益として認識される	
fair value model	公正価値モデル
当初認識の後，投資不動産を公正価値で測定する方法。公正価値の変動は損益として認識される	
investment property	投資不動産
賃貸収益や価値増加の目的で保有する不動産（土地や建物の全部または一部）であり，自己使用目的の不動産（IAS第16号の対象）や販売目的の不動産（IAS第2号の対象）は除かれる	
owner-occupied property	自己使用不動産
財またはサービスの供給等，または管理の目的で保有している不動産であり，投資不動産に対する用語	
transfer to [from] investment property classification	投資不動産への［からの］振替
例えば，自己使用の終了に伴う投資目的への変更など，不動産の使用目的の変更がある場合には，投資不動産への振替が行われることもある（逆の場合も同様）	

IFRS 1 "First-time Adoption of International Financial Reporting Standards"（国際財務報告基準の初度適用）

【基準書の内容】	
IFRS以外の会計基準を採用していた企業が，初めてIFRSを採用する場合についての取扱いを規定している	
英　語	日本語
解　説	
comparative information	比較情報
IFRSの初度適用の際には，直近で開示するIFRSに準拠した財務諸表に加えて最低でも1年分の比較情報（comparative prior-year information）を開示することを要求している	
date of transition to IFRS	IFRS移行日
最初のIFRS財務諸表において，IFRSによる完全な比較情報を表示する最初の期間の期首。IFRS開始財政状態計算書の作成基準日	
deemed cost	みなし原価
IFRSの初度適用の際に，有形固定資産等の原価の代用として使用することが許容される金額で，その有形固定資産等の公正価値など	
exemption	免除規定
IFRSの初度適用にあたっては，従前の資産及び負債の認識，測定及び分類等の見直しが必要になるが，いくつかの項目については免除規定がある	
first IFRS financial statements	最初のIFRS財務諸表
明示的，かつ無限定にIFRSに準拠している旨を示して，IFRSを採用する最初の財務諸表	
first IFRS reporting period	最初のIFRS報告期間
比較情報を含む最初のIFRS財務諸表が対象とする期間のうち，直近の期間	
first-time adopter	初度適用企業
IFRSに基づく財務諸表を初めて作成する企業	
opening IFRS statement of financial position	IFRS開始財政状態計算書
IFRS移行日現在の財政状態計算書	
previous GAAP	従前のGAAP
IFRS採用の直前に採用していた会計基準	
reconciliation	調整（表）
IFRSの初度適用にあたっては，従前のGAAPによる純資産や包括利益（または当期純損益）等について，IFRSに基づく包括利益への調整表の開示が必要となる	
retrospective application of IFRS	IFRSの遡及適用
IFRSの初度適用にあたっては，基本的にはIFRSを遡及的に適用する必要があるが，企業結合等の一定の項目については免除規定がある	

IFRS 2 "Share-based Payment"（株式に基づく報酬）

【基準書の内容】	
企業が従業員またはその他の関係者と株式に基づく報酬取引を行っている場合の会計処理や開示を規定している	
英　語	日本語
解　説	
cash-settled share-based payment	現金決済型の株式に基づく報酬
株式に基づく報酬取引の一形態であり，企業が，自社の資本性金融商品の価格を基礎とする金額の「負債」（後に現金決済される）を負うことを対価として，財またはサービスを取得する取引。負担する負債の公正価値により，対価として受け取った財またはサービスも測定される	
equity-settled share-based payment	持分決済型の株式に基づく報酬
株式に基づく報酬取引の一形態であり，企業が，自社の資本性金融商品（株式やストック・オプション等）を対価として，財またはサービスを受け取る取引など。受け取った財やサービスの公正価値により，対応する資本の増加も測定される（信頼性をもって見積もれない場合を除く）	
exercise date	権利行使日
（ストック・）オプションを行使する日	
exercise price	権利行使価格
（ストック・）オプションを行使する際の価格	
grant date	付与日
企業と他の当事者（従業員等）が株式に基づく報酬契約に合意した日（当該株式に基づく報酬契約に基づき，権利が付与される日）	
measurement date	測定日
付与された資本性金融商品の公正価値を測定する日。従業員等との取引については，基本的に付与日が測定日となる	
performance condition	業績条件
権利確定条件のうち，勤務条件に加えて，一定の業績目標を達成することを求めるもの。株式市場条件（market-based performance condition）とそれ以外のもの（例えば，利益目標など）がある	
service condition	勤務条件
権利確定条件のうち，従業員などに所定の期間の勤務を完了することを求めるもの	
share-based payment transaction	株式に基づく報酬取引
財またはサービス（例えば，従業員の勤務）の対価として，企業の資本性金融商品やそれを基礎とする現金等を取引相手（例えば，従業員）に与える取引。株式に基づく報酬取引には，①持分決済型，②現金決済型，③持分決済と現金決済の選択ができるもの，がある	
share option	ストック・オプション
一定の期間，所定の価格で企業の株式を取得する権利を付与する契約	
vesting condition	権利確定条件
株式に基づく報酬契約において，資本性金融商品や現金等を受け取る権利を得るために充足すべき条件。権利確定条件には，①一定期間の勤務を条件とする勤務条件や②業績目標の達成を条件とする業績条件がある	
vesting period	権利確定期間
株式に基づく報酬契約に係る権利確定条件が（その間に）充足されるべき期間	

IFRS 3 "Business Combinations"（企業結合）

【基準書の内容】	
企業結合における全般的な会計処理や開示を規定している。具体的には，識別可能な取得資産及び引受負債の認識及び測定，「のれん」や割安購入益の認識及び測定，また関連する被取得企業の非支配持分の認識及び測定などに関する規定がある	
英　語	日本語
解　説	
acquiree	被取得企業
企業結合において，取得企業により支配を獲得された企業	
acquirer	取得企業
企業結合において，被取得企業の支配を獲得した企業	
acquisition date	取得日
取得企業が被取得企業に対する支配を獲得した日。多くの場合，契約上の企業結合実施日と一致する	
acquisition-date fair value	取得日の公正価値
取得法においては，取得資産及び引受負債の測定に取得日の公正価値が使用される	
acquisition method	取得法
企業結合の会計処理方法で，取得企業により取得される被取得企業の資産及び負債を，原則として取得日の公正価値で測定する方法	
acquisition-related cost	取得関連コスト
取得企業側で取得に関連して発生する種々の費用（外部アドバイザーなどへの報酬等）。資本証券の発行費用等の例外を除いて，基本的に発生時の費用とされる	
assets acquired	取得した資産
取得企業が取得する被取得企業の資産	
bargain purchase	割安購入（益）
計算された「のれん」がマイナスになる場合，つまり割安で購入できた場合をいい，日本基準でいう「負ののれん」に相当する。取得日における純損益として処理される	
business	事業
投資家等に対して，配当等の形でのリターンを直接的に提供する目的で実施及び管理される活動及び資産の統合された組合せ。インプット（例えば，原材料），プロセス（例えば，製造プロセス），及びアウトプット（例えば，製品）の3要素で構成される。取得対象が「事業」に該当しない場合には，企業結合に該当しないため，資産の取得として会計処理する	
business combination	企業結合
取得企業が被取得企業の事業（business）の支配を獲得する取引	
business combination achieved in stages	段階的に達成された企業結合
取得企業が被取得企業の支配を段階的に獲得する形態の企業結合	
closing date	クロージング日
契約に基づく最終的な取得企業及び被取得企業の義務が履行される日であり，具体的には取得企業側が対価を決済し，被取得企業側が資産及び負債を引き渡す日	

consideration transferred	対価
取得企業が企業結合の対価として引き渡す現金や株式等	
contingent consideration	条件付対価
企業結合後の特定の事象または取引の結果に依存して，企業結合日後に被取得企業の旧所有者に対して追加的に引き渡される取得対価。取得日の公正価値によって認識され，取得日後の公正価値の変動があった場合には一定の会計処理が要求される	
goodwill	のれん
企業結合において，取得企業が引き渡した対価の公正価値が，取得した資産の公正価値（から引き受けた負債の公正価値を控除したもの）を上回る場合のその差額をいい，個別には識別されない将来の経済的便益を意味する	
identifiable intangible asset	識別可能な無形資産
企業結合の結果取得される無形資産のうち，資産として認識できるもので，「のれん」とは区別される	
indemnification asset	補償資産
企業結合において，被取得企業側が取得企業に対して行う契約上の補償（例えば，資産や負債の偶発性に係る補償）について，取得企業側が資産として認識したもの	
liabilities assumed	引き受けた負債
取得企業が引き受ける被取得企業の負債	
non-controlling interest (NCI)	非支配持分
子会社に対する持分のうち，親会社に帰属しないもので，従来の少数株主持分（minority interest）。企業結合にあたって，非支配持分は購入のれん方式（partial goodwill method）または全部のれん方式（full goodwill method）により測定される	
reacquired right	再取得した権利
取得企業が企業結合前に被取得企業に使用を認めていた権利（例えば，技術ライセンス契約）を，企業結合の結果，取得企業が取得した場合のその権利	
reverse acquisition	逆取得
取得企業の決定において，法律上の被取得企業が会計上は取得企業とされるような企業結合	

IFRS 5 "Non-current Assets Held for Sale and Discontinued Operations"（売却目的で保有する非流動資産及び非継続事業）

【基準書の内容】	
売却目的で保有する非流動資産の会計処理，非継続事業の表示や開示を規定している	
英　語	日本語
解　説	
component of an entity	企業の構成単位
事業活動上及び財務報告目的で，企業の他の部分から明確に区分できる事業活動及びキャッシュ・フローをいい，非継続事業に分類されず使用目的で保有されているとすれば，単一の資金生成単位（CGU）または資金生成単位のグループとなるべき単位	
continuing operation	継続事業
非継続事業以外の事業	
continuing use	継続的な使用
帳簿価額は，売却取引による回収のほか，「継続的な使用」により回収される場合もある	
discontinued operation	非継続事業
すでに処分されたかまたは売却目的保有に分類されている企業の構成単位で，①独立の主要な事業分野等，②独立の主要な事業分野等を処分する計画の一部，③転売のために取得した子会社，のいずれかに該当するもの。非継続事業の経営成績は，包括利益計算書上で区分表示される	
disposal group	処分グループ
処分や売却等の方法により，単一の取引として処分される資産のグループ，及びそれに直接関連して移転される負債	
held for sale	売却目的保有の
非流動資産（または処分グループ）の帳簿価額が，継続的な使用よりも主として売却取引により回収される場合には，その非流動資産（または処分グループ）は売却目的保有に分類される。売却目的保有に分類された非流動資産（または処分グループ）は，帳簿価額か売却コスト控除後の公正価値のいずれか低い金額で測定され，減価償却は中止される	
non-current asset (that is) to be abandoned	廃棄予定の非流動資産
廃棄予定の非流動資産（または処分グループ）は売却目的保有には分類できない	
sale transaction	売却取引
帳簿価額が主として「売却取引」により回収される場合とは，①現況で即時に売却することが可能であり，かつ②その売却の可能性が非常に高い（highly probable）場合をいう	

IFRS 7 "Financial Instruments: Disclosures"(金融商品：開示)

【基準書の内容】	
企業の財政状態及び業績からみた金融商品の重要性，金融商品から生じる企業のリスクの性質及び程度，またそのリスク管理方法に関連する財務諸表上の開示を規定している	
英　語	日本語
解　説	
allowance account for credit losses	信用損失引当金（貸倒引当金）
金融資産の分類ごとの信用損失引当金（期首残高と期末残高の調整）は開示の対象となる	
credit risk	信用リスク
金融商品の取引に係る他方の当事者の債務不履行により損失を被るリスク	
currency risk	為替リスク
為替レートの変動により，金融商品の公正価値または将来キャッシュ・フローが変動するリスク	
exposure	エクスポージャー
リスクにさらされていること	
fair value	公正価値
測定日時点の市場参加者間の秩序ある取引において，資産の売却により受け取る，または負債の移転により支払うであろう価格。金融資産・負債の種類ごとの公正価値は開示の対象となる	
financial asset pledged as collateral	担保として差し入れた金融資産
担保として差し入れた金融資産は開示の対象となる	
interest rate risk	金利リスク
市場金利の変動により，金融商品の公正価値または将来キャッシュ・フローが変動するリスク	
liquidity risk	流動性リスク
企業の金融負債に関連する債務の履行が困難になるリスク	
market risk	市場リスク
市場価格の変動により，金融商品の公正価値またはキャッシュ・フローが変動するリスク	
other price risk	その他の価格リスク
金利リスクまたは為替リスク以外で，市場価格の変動により，金融商品の公正価値または将来キャッシュ・フローが変動するリスク	
qualitative disclosure	定性的開示
定量的開示に対する用語で，金融商品から生じるリスクの管理に関する経営者の目的，方針，及び手続きなどを説明するもの	
quantitative disclosure	定量的開示
定性的開示に対する用語で，金融商品から生じるリスクなどを数値として示すもの	
reclassification of financial instrument	金融商品の分類の変更
金融商品の分類の変更は開示の対象となる	
transfer of financial assets	金融資産の譲渡
金融資産の譲渡は，その全体の認識の中止の有無にかかわらず，開示の対象となる	

IFRS 8 "Operating Segments"（事業セグメント）

【基準書の内容】	
事業セグメントについての情報の開示のほか，製品及びサービス，地域別情報，また主要顧客に関連する情報の開示についても規定している	
英　語	日本語
解　説	
aggregation criteria	集約基準
報告セグメントを決定する際に考慮される基準で，いくつかの事業セグメントが類似の経済的特徴を有している場合等に，複数のセグメントを単一のセグメントとして集約すること	
chief operating decision maker (CODM)	最高経営意思決定者
事業セグメントの業績を評価し，資源を配分する機能を意味し，通常最高経営責任者（CEO）や最高執行責任者（COO）がこれに該当するが，経営会議等のグループがこれに該当することも考えられる	
entity-wide disclosure	全社情報の開示
企業が単一の報告セグメントしか有しない場合でも，製品及びサービスに関する情報など，一定の全社情報の開示は必要となる	
geographical information	地域別情報
地域別の収益及び非流動資産に係る情報は開示対象となる	
inter-segment	セグメント間の
inter-segment sales（セグメント間売上）のような使い方をする	
major customer	主要な顧客
主要な顧客との取引に係る情報は開示対象となる	
operating segment	事業セグメント
企業の構成単位であって，①その単位で事業活動を行って収益を稼得，費用を負担しており，②その単位で最高経営意思決定者が業績評価を行って資源の配分方法を決定しており，③その単位で区分された財務情報が入手可能なもの	
products and services	製品及びサービス
製品及びサービスは，全社情報の開示の一環として開示対象となる	
quantitative threshold	定量的な基準値
報告セグメントを決定する際に考慮される基準で，収益，純損益，資産等が全セグメント合計の10％以上など，一定の定量的な基準値を満たす事業セグメントを報告対象とするもの	
reportable segment	報告セグメント
報告の対象となる事業セグメント（または特定の条件に合致して集計された事業セグメントの合計数値）をいい，報告セグメントは量的基準や集約基準等に基づいて決定される	

IFRS 9 "Financial Instruments"（金融商品）

【基準書の内容】	
IFRS第9号「金融商品」の最終版（2014年公表）で，従来のIAS第39号「金融商品：認識及び測定」及びIFRS第9号の過去のすべてのフェーズのバージョンを置き換えたもの。「分類及び測定」・「減損」・「ヘッジ会計」について規定している	
英　語	日本語
解　説	
accounting mismatch	会計上のミスマッチ
資産または負債の測定や関連する利得または損失の認識を異なる基準に基づいて行うことにより生じる測定または認識の不整合。企業が公正価値オプションを適用することができるのは，会計上のミスマッチを除去または低減できる場合に限られる	
amortised cost	償却原価
当初認識額をもとに額面金額との差額を実効金利法に基づいて調整した結果で金融商品を測定する方法。事業モデルが「回収」で，キャッシュ・フローの特性によるテストを満たす場合，金融資産は償却原価で測定される（公正価値オプションを適用する場合を除く）。また，金融負債は，一定のものを除いては，基本的に実効金利法に基づく償却原価で測定される	
business model test	事業モデルによるテスト
それぞれの金融資産がどのような目的で保有・管理されているかを判定するもので，事業モデルには「回収」・「回収及び売却」・「その他」の3つがある。例えば，「回収」は，契約上のキャッシュ・フローを回収するために金融資産を保有することを意味する	
cash flow characteristics test	契約上のキャッシュ・フローの特性によるテスト
金融資産の契約条件によって発生するキャッシュ・フローが元本及び利息のみかどうかを判定するもの	
cash flow hedge	キャッシュ・フロー・ヘッジ
キャッシュ・フローの変動に対するエクスポージャーのうち，認識済の資産または負債に関連する特定のリスク（例えば，変動利付債券に係る将来の支払金利変動リスク），または実行可能性が非常に高い予定取引に起因し，かつ純損益に影響し得るものに対するヘッジ	
credit-impaired financial asset	信用減損のある金融資産
見積将来キャッシュ・フローに不利な影響を与える事象（例えば，債務者の重大な財政的困難）が発生している金融資産	
derecognition	認識の中止
過去に認識した金融資産または金融負債を財政状態計算書から取り除くこと	
effective interest method	実効金利法
金融資産または負債の当初認識額と額面金額の差額につき，実効利回りを考慮した複利計算で各期の配分額（金利収益または費用）を決定し，償却原価を計算する方法。日本基準でいう利息法に相当する	
expected credit loss (ECL)	予想信用損失
信用損失を債務不履行発生確率でウェイト付けした期待値	
fair value hedge	公正価値ヘッジ
認識済の資産または負債等の公正価値変動に対するエクスポージャーのうち，特定のリスクに起因し，かつ純損益に影響し得るものに対するヘッジ	

fair value option	公正価値オプション
本来は償却原価またはFVTOCIの負債性金融商品（例えば，債券）をFVTPLに指定できるという選択肢（一定の要件あり）	
fair value through other comprehensive income (FVTOCI / FVOCI)	その他の包括利益を通じて公正価値（で測定する区分）
金融資産の区分の1つで，公正価値で測定され，変動はその他の包括利益として計上されるもの。例えば，債券については，事業モデルが「回収及び売却」で，キャッシュ・フローの特性によるテストを満たす場合，公正価値オプションを適用しない限りはFVTOCIとなる	
fair value through profit or loss (FVTPL / FVPL)	純損益を通じて公正価値（で測定する区分）
金融資産（または負債）の区分の1つで，公正価値で測定され，変動は純損益として計上されるもの。例えば，株式については，トレーディング目的のものはFVTPL，それ以外のものもOCIオプションを適用しない限りはFVTPLとなる	
firm commitment	確定約定
将来の特定の日に所定の数量の資源を所定の価格で交換することを約する拘束力のある契約	
forecast transaction	予定取引
確定ではないが，予想される将来の取引	
hedge accounting	ヘッジ会計
ヘッジ対象とヘッジ手段から生じる損益を相殺し，ヘッジの効果を会計上表現する手法	
hedged item	ヘッジ対象
公正価値またはキャッシュ・フローの変動リスクがあり，ヘッジ手段によりヘッジされる対象	
hedge effectiveness	ヘッジの有効性
ヘッジ対象の公正価値またはキャッシュ・フローの変動がヘッジ手段によりどの程度相殺されているかという割合。指定期間を通じたヘッジの有効性の確保がヘッジ会計の要件とされている	
hedge of a net investment in a foreign operation	在外営業活動体に対する純投資のヘッジ
海外子会社への出資など，在外営業活動体に対する純投資に対するヘッジをいう	
hedging instrument	ヘッジ手段
ヘッジ対象の公正価値またはキャッシュ・フローの変動リスクをヘッジするものとして指定されたデリバティブ等の金融商品など	
hedging relationship	ヘッジ関係
ヘッジ関係には大きく分けて，①公正価値ヘッジ，②キャッシュ・フロー・ヘッジ，③在外営業活動体に対する純投資のヘッジの3種類がある	
held for trading	売買目的保有の
主として短期間に売却（または買戻し）を行う目的で取得（または発生した）金融資産（または金融負債）を指す	
loss allowance	損失評価引当金
金融資産，リース債権，契約資産などに係る予想信用損失に対する引当金	
other comprehensive income option (OCI option)	OCIオプション
本来はFVTPLの資本性金融商品（例えば，株式）をFVTOCIに指定できるという選択肢（一定の要件あり）	

IFRS 10 "Consolidated Financial Statements"（連結財務諸表）

【基準書の内容】	
従来のIAS第27号「連結及び個別財務諸表」のうち，連結財務諸表に関係する会計処理を取り扱う新基準書であり，「支配」の定義やどのような事業体を連結対象とすべきかを規定している	
英　語	日本語
解　説	
agent	代理人
支配の有無を判断するためには，意思決定者が本人または代理人のどちらに該当するかを判断する必要がある。代理人は被投資企業を支配することはできないため，基本的に投資先を連結することはない	
attributable to non-controlling interest	非支配持分に帰属する
純損益やその他の包括利益のうち非支配持分に帰属する部分	
attributable to owners of the parent	親会社の所有者に帰属する
純損益やその他の包括利益のうち親会社の所有者に帰属する部分	
change in (the) level of ownership interest in subsidiary	子会社に対する所有持分の変動
子会社に対する親会社の持分変動のうち，支配の喪失とならないものは，持分（資本）の内部で会計処理される	
consolidated financial statements	連結財務諸表
親会社及びその子会社の資産，負債，資本，収益，費用及びキャッシュ・フローを，単一の経済的実体のものとして表示する企業集団の財務諸表	
control	支配
投資企業（investor）が被投資企業（investee）への関与から生じる変動リターン（variable return）にさらされ，または変動リターンに対する権利を有しており，かつ，被投資企業に対する力（パワー）を通じてそれらのリターンに影響を及ぼすことができる場合には，被投資企業を支配していることになる	
group	企業集団
親会社及びその全ての子会社	
loss of control of subsidiary	子会社に対する支配の喪失
子会社に対する支配を喪失したときは，その子会社の資産，負債及び関連する持分（資本）の構成要素について認識の中止を行い，関連して発生する利得または損失は純損益で認識する	
non-controlling interest (NCI)	非支配持分
親会社の所有者の持分以外の持分で，従来の少数株主持分（minority interest）	
parent	親会社
他の企業（子会社）を支配している企業	
power	力（パワー）
被投資企業の関連する活動を左右する現在の能力	
protective rights	防御的な権利
権利を有する当事者の利益を保護するように設計された権利（例えば，一定の拒否権）で，当該権利が関係する企業に対する力（パワー）を与えないもの	

relevant activities	関連性のある活動
被投資企業のリターンに重要な影響を及ぼす被投資企業の活動	
reporting date	報告日
連結財務諸表の作成に用いる親会社及び子会社の財務諸表は同じ報告日である必要があり，それが異なる場合には，（実務上不可能な場合を除き）子会社は連結目的で仮決算を行う必要がある	
return	リターン
被投資企業への関与から生じるリターンには，利益のみならず，損失も含まれる。リターンの典型例は配当であり，その他被投資企業に対する投資の価値変動などもリターンの1つである	
silo	サイロ
被投資企業の一部を別個の事業体とみなしたもの。支配の有無を判断する対象（単位）としては，被投資企業全体だけではなく，被投資企業の一部（特定資産）に対する力（パワー）を有しているかも判断しなければならない	
subsidiary	子会社
他の企業（親会社）に支配されている企業	
uniform accounting policies	統一的な会計方針
企業集団は，類似の状況における同様の取引等の報告にあたって，統一的な会計方針を用いる必要がある	
voting rights	議決権
支配の検討にあたり，議決権に基づいて力（パワー）の有無を判定する場合，まずは投資者が投資先の議決権の過半数を有しているかどうかが重要になる	

IFRS 11 "Joint Arrangements"（共同支配の取決め）

【基準書の内容】	
従来のIAS第31号「ジョイント・ベンチャーに対する持分」を置き換える新基準書であり，共同支配の取決めの会計処理について規定している	
英　語	日本語
解　説	
equity method	持分法
共同支配企業に対する持分につき，当初は取得原価で認識するが，その後の共同支配企業の純資産に対する共同支配投資企業の持分の変動に応じて，投資額を修正する会計処理の方法	
joint arrangement	共同支配の取決め
複数の当事者が共同支配を有する取決め。共同支配の取決めは，共同支配企業または共同支配事業のいずれかに分類される	
joint control	共同支配
契約上合意された支配の共有。共同支配は，関連性のある活動の意思決定に際して，支配を共有する当事者の一致した合意（unanimous consent）を必要とする場合にのみ存在する	
joint operation	共同支配事業（ジョイント・オペレーション）
共同支配の取決めのうち，共同支配の当事者が，その取決めに関する「資産に対する権利及び負債に対する義務」を有しているもの。従来のIAS第31号における「共同支配の資産」（jointly controlled asset）及び「共同支配の営業活動」（jointly controlled operation）に相当する	
joint operator	共同支配事業者
共同支配事業（joint operation）に対して共同支配を有する当事者。共同支配事業の資産，負債，収益及び費用に対する自らの持分相当額を認識する	
joint venture	共同支配企業（ジョイント・ベンチャー）
共同支配の取決めのうち，共同支配の当事者が，その取決めに関する「純資産に対する権利」を有しているもの	
joint venturer	共同支配投資者
共同支配企業（joint venture）に対して共同支配を有する当事者。持分法により会計処理を行う	
separate vehicle	別個のビークル
別個に識別可能な財務構造（financial structure）であり，例えば，株式会社などがこれに該当する。共同支配の取決めが別個のビークルを通じて組成されていない場合は，その取決めは共同支配事業に該当する	

IFRS 12 "Disclosure of Interests in Other Entities"（他の企業への関与の開示）

【基準書の内容】	
従来のIAS第27号「連結及び個別財務諸表」の連結財務諸表に関係する開示規定，及び従来の第28号「関連会社に対する投資」やIAS第31号「ジョイント・ベンチャーに対する持分」の開示規定を切り出した新基準書であり，子会社，共同支配の取決め，関連会社及びストラクチャード・エンティティに対する企業の持分に関する開示を規定している	
英　語	日本語
解　説	
interest in another entity	他の企業への関与
本基準書では，企業を他の企業の業績からのリターンの変動性にさらすような関与（契約上及び非契約上）を意味する。投資企業は，以下のような他の企業への関与に関する情報を開示する必要がある ● 子会社（subsidiaries） ● 共同支配の取決め（joint arrangements） 　…共同支配企業（joint ventures）及び共同支配事業（joint operations） ● 関連会社（associates） ● 非連結の組成された企業（unconsolidated structured entities）	
structured entity	ストラクチャード・エンティティ（組成された企業）
その企業を支配している主体の決定にあたって，議決権または類似の権利が決定的な要因とならないように設計された企業（例えば，証券化の際のビークルなど）。ストラクチャード・エンティティについては，連結・非連結のものそれぞれについて一定の開示が求められる	

IFRS 13 "Fair Value Measurement"（公正価値測定）

【基準書の内容】	
IFRSにおける公正価値測定に関する単一のガイダンスであり，IFRSに基づいて公正価値測定を行う場合に，金融資産及び負債並びに非金融資産及び負債の公正価値をどのように測定すべきかを規定している	
英　語	日本語
解　説	
active market	活発な市場
継続的な価格付けの情報を提供するのに十分な頻度及び取引量をもって，資産または負債が取引される市場	
cost approach	コスト・アプローチ
公正価値測定に際して，資産の用役能力を再調達するために現在必要とされる金額（いわゆる現在再調達原価）を用いるアプローチ。例えば，現在再調達原価法がこれに該当する	
exit price	出口価格
資産を売却する際に受け取るであろう（または負債を移転する際に支払うであろう）価格であり，入口価格（entry price）に対する用語。公正価値は出口価格として定義されている	
fair value	公正価値
測定日時点の市場参加者（market participant）間の秩序ある取引（orderly transaction）において，資産の売却により受け取る，または負債の移転により支払うであろう価格	
fair value hierarchy	公正価値ヒエラルキー
公正価値を測定する際のインプットについて，観察可能性に応じて3つのレベルに区分し，優先順位付けしたもの	
income approach	インカム・アプローチ
公正価値測定に際して，将来発生するキャッシュ・フロー（または収益及び費用）を割り引くことで，現在価値を算出するアプローチ。例えば，DCF法がこれに該当する	
input	インプット
公正価値測定のための入力値。評価手法の適用にあたっては，適切なインプットを選択する必要があるが，関連性のある観察可能なインプット（observable inputs）の使用を最大限にし，観察不能なインプット（unobservable inputs）の使用を最小限にする必要がある	
level 1 inputs	レベル1のインプット
測定日において企業がアクセス可能な，同一の資産または負債に関する活発な市場における（調整なしの）相場価格	
level 2 inputs	レベル2のインプット
レベル1に含まれる相場価格以外の，直接または間接的に観察可能な，資産または負債に関するインプット（例えば，活発な市場における類似の資産の相場価格）	
level 3 inputs	レベル3のインプット
資産または負債に関する観察不能なインプット（例えば，企業自身のデータを用いた見積り）	
market approach	マーケット・アプローチ
公正価値測定に際して，同一または類似の資産または負債の市場から得られる価格及び関連する情報を利用するアプローチ。例えば，同一資産の取引所の公表価格を用いて評価する方法がこれに該当する	

most advantageous market	最も有利な市場
取引コスト及び輸送コストを考慮したうえで，資産の売却により受け取る金額が最大となる（または負債の移転により支払う金額が最小となる）市場	
principal market	主要な市場
資産または負債について，活動の量や水準（取引量や取引額）が最も大きい市場	
valuation technique	評価手法
公正価値の評価にあたって用いる技法。マーケット・アプローチ，インカム・アプローチ，及びコスト・アプローチがある	

IFRS 15 "Revenue from Contracts with Customers"（顧客との契約から生じる収益）

【基準書の内容】	

従来の収益認識に関する基準書や規定をすべて置き換える新基準書であり，収益を生じさせるすべての契約に適用される認識及び測定モデルを規定している。基本原則として，収益は，約束した財またはサービスの顧客への移転を表すように，またそれと交換に企業が権利を得ると見込む対価を反映した金額で認識する（具体的には，5つのステップから構成される収益認識モデルが定められている）。また，収益の区分ごとの開示など，開示に関する規定も含まれている

英　語	日本語
解　説	
adjusted market assessment approach	調整後市場評価アプローチ
独立販売価格の見積りに際して，財またはサービスを販売する市場を評価し，顧客が支払ってもよいと考える価格を見積もるという方法	
contract	契約
強制可能な権利及び義務を生じさせる当事者間の合意（文書による場合に限らず，口頭による場合や取引慣行による場合を含む）。財またはサービスと引換えに得る対価の回収可能性が高いなど，一定の要件を満たす場合には，「契約」を識別する（ステップ1）	
contract asset	契約資産
企業が顧客に移転した財またはサービスと交換に受け取る対価に対する企業の権利で，当該権利が時の経過以外の何か（例えば，企業の将来の履行）を条件としているもの。条件の観点で，債権とは区別される	
contract cost	契約コスト
契約獲得の増分コスト（incremental costs of obtaining a contract）及び契約履行コスト（costs incurred to fulfil a contract）については，回収が見込まれるなどの一定の場合には資産計上され，事後的に償却及び減損テストが行われる	
contract liability	契約負債
顧客に財またはサービスを移転する企業の義務のうち，企業が顧客から対価を受け取っている（またはその期限が到来している）もの	
expected cost plus a margin approach	予想コストにマージンを加算するアプローチ
独立販売価格の見積りに際して，履行義務を充足するためのコストを予想し，それに適切なマージンを加算するという方法	
five-step model (framework)	5ステップの収益認識モデル
本基準書では，「(1)顧客との契約の識別➡(2)契約における履行義務の識別➡(3)取引価格の算定➡(4)取引価格の履行義務への配分➡(5)履行義務の充足による収益の認識」という5つのステップから構成される収益認識モデルが採用されている	
performance obligation	履行義務
財またはサービスを移転するという顧客との契約上の約束。契約条件及び商慣行を評価し，約束した財またはサービス，あるいはそれらの組合せのうち，独立した履行義務として会計処理すべきものを識別する（ステップ2）	
receivable	債権
企業が顧客に移転した財またはサービスと交換に受け取る対価に対する企業の権利で，無条件のもの（時の経過のみが要求されている）。条件の観点で，契約資産は区別される	

residual approach	残余アプローチ
独立販売価格の見積りに際して，「取引価格の総額」から「他の財またはサービスの独立販売価格の合計」を控除するという方法。財またはサービスの独立販売価格の変動性が高い，または不確実な場合に限って使用が認められる	
revenue recognition	収益認識
企業は，履行義務を充足した時点で，または充足するに従って一定の期間にわたり，収益を認識する（ステップ5）	
significant financing component	重要な金融要素
対価の前払いや後払いなどの場合に契約に含まれる金利部分のうち重要なものであり，取引価格の算定にあたって分離する必要がある（ただし，1年以内の場合を除く）。当該金利部分は金融収益または費用として表示する	
stand-alone selling price	独立販売価格
企業が財またはサービスを独立して顧客に提供する場合の価格であり，独立販売価格の比率に基づき，取引価格をそれぞれの独立した履行義務に配分する（ステップ4）	
transaction price	取引価格
約束した財またはサービスの顧客への移転と引換えに，企業が権利を得ると見込んでいる対価の金額。変動対価や重要な金融要素も考慮し，取引価格を算定する（ステップ3）	
variable consideration	変動対価
文字どおり，対価のうち変動するもので，値引きやリベート，インセンティブなどが該当する。変動対価については，期待値または最も可能性の高い金額のいずれか適切な方法により見積もる必要がある（ただし，一定の制限あり）	

付　録

IFRS 16 "Leases"（リース）

【基準書の内容】	
従来のIAS 第17号「リース」を置き換える新基準書。借手は，単一のオンバランス・モデルに基づき，ほとんどのリースを貸借対照表に認識することが求められる。一方，貸手の会計処理は，基本的に従来から変更されていない	
英　語	日本語
解　説	
control	支配
本基準書では，借手が資産の使用を指図でき，かつ，それにより得られる経済的便益のほぼすべてを享受できることを意味する。特定された対象資産の使用を借手が「支配」しているかどうかにより，契約にリースが含まれているかどうかの判断を行う	
finance lease	ファイナンス・リース
原資産の所有に伴うリスクと経済価値が実質的にすべて移転するリース（貸手にとっての分類）。ファイナンス・リースの貸手は，リース開始日において，原資産の認識を中止し，代わりにリースに係る未収入金を認識する	
head lease	ヘッド・リース
サブリースに対する用語で，当初の貸手と借手との間のリース	
interest rate implicit in (the) lease	リース計算上の利子率
「リース料総額と無保証残存価値（unguaranteed residual value）の現在価値の合計」を「原資産の公正価値と貸手の初期直接コストの合計」と等しくするような（計算上の）利子率。割引率として使用される	
lease	リース
資産（原資産）を使用する権利を，対価との交換により，一定期間にわたって移転する契約（またはそのような契約の一部）	
lease component	リース構成要素
リース契約に含まれるリースとしての構成要素。非リース構成要素に対する用語	
lease liability	リース負債
リース料の支払義務。リースの借手は，リース開始日において（使用権資産とともに）リース負債を認識する（ただし，短期リースや少額資産のリースついては簡便法あり）。リース負債は，リース期間にわたり支払われるリース料総額の現在価値に基づいて測定される	
lease payments	リース料
リース期間にわたって原資産を使用する権利の対価として，借手から貸手に対して行われる支払い	
lease term	リース期間
リース開始日から起算した解約不能期間＋延長オプション期間（借手が延長オプションを行使することが合理的に確実な場合）＋解約オプション期間（借手が解約オプションを行使しないことが合理的に確実な場合）	
lessee	リースの借手
—	
lessee's incremental borrowing rate	借手の追加借入利率
リースの借手が追加的に借入を行う際に適用されるべき利率。リース計算上の利子率が使用できない場合に割引率として使用される	

lessor	リースの貸手
—	

non-lease component	非リース構成要素
リース契約に含まれる，リース以外の財またはサービス（例えば，維持管理）の取引に係る合意。リース構成要素に対する用語。借手は原則として非リース構成要素をリース構成要素と区別して会計処理する（ただし実務上の簡便法あり）	
operating lease	オペレーティング・リース
原資産の所有に伴うリスクと経済価値の実質的移転を伴わないリース（貸手にとっての分類）。オペレーティング・リースの貸手は，原資産を引き続き認識し，リース料総額をリース期間にわたって，定額法等により収益として認識する	
right-of-use asset	使用権資産
借手が原資産を（リース期間にわたり）使用する権利を表す資産。リースの借手は，リース開始日において（リース負債とともに）使用権資産を認識する。使用権資産は，リース負債の金額に一定の調整を加えた金額として測定される	
sale and leaseback transaction	セール・アンド・リースバック取引
所有物件をいったん売却し，その購入者から当該物件のリースを受ける取引。売手（借手）及び買手（貸手）は，収益認識の基準（IFRS第15号）に基づいて売却が生じたかどうかを判断し，売却と判断された場合には「売却取引＋リース取引」として会計処理するが，それ以外の場合は金融取引として会計処理する	
short-term lease	短期リース
リース開始日において，リース期間が12か月以内であるリース	
sub-lease	サブリース
貸手から借手にリースされた原資産を，借手がさらに（第三者に）リースすること	
underlying asset	原資産
リースの対象となる資産	

付　録

3. 国際税務の分野別　税務用語

ここでは，海外進出企業が関係する国際税務の分野で使用される用語について解説しています。

	分　野
（1）	移転価格税制（TP: Transfer Pricing Taxation）
（2）	外国子会社配当益金不算入制度（Foreign Dividend Exclusion）
（3）	外国税額控除制度（FTC: Foreign Tax Credits）
（4）	恒久的施設（PE: Permanent Establishment）
（5）	税務デュー・デリジェンス（TDD: Tax Due Diligence）
（6）	租税条約（Tax Treaties）
（7）	タックス・ヘイブン対策税制（CFC Rules）

なお，特に外国税額控除制度やタックス・ヘイブン対策税制などに関しては，日本独自の用語について海外とのコミュニケーションを行う場合，単語だけでなく，その単語の意味合いや制度内容の説明を付加することが望ましいと考えられます。

(1) 移転価格税制（TP: Transfer Pricing Taxation）

【概　要】
日本企業とその国外関連者との取引について，取引価格を独立企業間価格に引き直して課税所得を計算するものであり，国外関連者との取引を通じた恣意的な所得の移転を防止することを目的とした税制

英　語	日本語
解　説	
advance pricing arrangement (APA)	事前確認（制度）
独立企業間価格の算定方法の合理性等につき税務当局が事前に確認する制度をいい，企業が確認された内容に基づいて申告を行う限りにおいて，移転価格課税は行われない	
APA rollback	ロールバック（遡及適用）
事前確認（APA）の結果を，（将来年度のみならず）過年度にも適用すること	
arm's length price (ALP)	独立企業間価格
独立の第三者間で取引される際に成立するであろう価格水準	
best method rule	ベスト・メソッド・ルール
独立企業間価格の算定方法について，事案に応じた最適な手法を選択すべき，という原則。	
bilateral advance pricing arrangement (BAPA)	二国間 APA，バイラテラル APA
事前確認（APA）のうち，関係する2か国の税務当局から確認を受けるもの	
Commissioner's Directive on the Operation of Transfer Pricing	移転価格事務運営要領
日本の国税庁が発行している，移転価格税制の執行に関する指針	
comparable transaction	比較対象取引
独立企業間価格の算定の基礎となる比準取引	
comparable uncontrolled price method (CUP method)	独立価格比準法
独立企業間価格の算定方法の1つで，独立企業間の同種の取引で同様の状況下で行われた取引を比較対象とし，その価格を国外関連取引の価格と比較する方法	
competent authority (CA)	権限ある当局
租税条約により，相互協議（MAP）を行うべき者として定められている者	
contemporaneous documentation	同時文書（化）
移転価格の文書化を確定申告期限までに行うこと	
controlled transaction	国外関連取引
国外関連者との取引	
corresponding [correlative] adjustment	対応的調整
関連者の一方が移転価格課税（増額更正）された場合に，相互協議における合意に従い，他方の国外関連者に対して還付（減額更正）を行って二重課税を排除すること	
cost contribution arrangement (CCA) cost sharing arrangement (CSA)	費用分担契約
研究開発活動等の一定の活動に係る費用を，複数の企業が共同で負担することを取り決める契約	

cost-plus method (CPM)	原価基準法
独立企業間価格の算定方法の1つで，「国外関連取引に係る棚卸資産の売手（製造会社など）の製造原価等の額に通常の利潤の額を加算して計算した金額」をもって独立企業間価格とする方法	
Country-by-Country Report (CbC Report)	国別報告書（国別報告事項）
移転価格文書の1つで，多国籍企業グループが事業を行う国ごとの情報をサマリーしたもの。事業を行う国ごとの収入金額，税引前当期利益の額，納付税額などの情報を記載する	
documentation	文書化
文字どおり移転価格関連の文書を作成すること	
donation to foreign related party	国外関連者に対する寄附金
国外関連者に対する「資産や経済的利益の贈与または無償の供与」をいい，日本の税制上，国外関連者に対する寄附金は全額損金不算入となる	
foreign related party [person]	国外関連者
発行済株式総数の50％以上の株式を直接または間接に保有する関係にある外国法人（形式基準）。あるいは，50％以上の出資関係がない場合でも役員関係，取引依存関係，資金依存関係等で実質的な支配関係にある外国法人（実質基準）	
function and risk	機能とリスク
移転価格税制の基本的な考え方として，日本企業または国外関連者が有している機能や負担しているリスクに応じて，リターンが決まるべきという考え方がある	
intangible property	無形資産
無形資産は，「重要な価値を有し，所得の源泉となるもの」として，例えば，①技術革新を要因として形成される特許権，営業秘密等，②従業員等が経営，営業，生産，研究開発，販売促進等の企業活動における経験等を通じて形成したノウハウ等，③生産工程，交渉手順及び開発，販売，資金調達等に係る取引網等，を含む	
inter-quartile range	四分位レンジ
データ（例えば，比較対象取引の利益率など）を小さい順に並べたときの25％目から75％目の値のレンジ（範囲）	
intra-group service (IGS)	企業グループ内の役務提供
企業グループ内の役務提供をいい，多くの場合，日本企業が海外子会社等に対して行う経営・財務・業務・事務管理等の面でのサポートを指し，その対価は移転価格税制の対象となる	
local file	ローカルファイル（独立企業間価格を算定するために必要と認められる書類）
移転価格文書の1つで，国外関連取引の内容を記載し，その取引に係る独立企業間価格を算定するもの。日本においては，一定金額以上の国外関連取引について，ローカルファイルの同時文書化義務が定められている	
master file	マスターファイル（事業概況報告事項）
移転価格文書の1つで，多国籍企業グループの組織構造，事業の概要，財務状況等に関する情報を記載するもの。移転価格税制に係るグループのポリシーや全体像を示す文書という位置付け	
mutual agreement procedure (MAP)	相互協議
租税条約締結国の税務当局間で行われる協議。主として移転価格税制について，二重課税の排除のために行われる	

OECD Transfer Pricing Guidelines for Multinational Enterprises and Tax Administrations	OECD移転価格ガイドライン
OECDが，移転価格に関連する税務上の問題について，多国籍企業及び各国の税務当局のための解決の方策を示したもの．法的拘束力は有しないが，実務上は国際的なコンセンサスとして機能している	
pre-filing consultation	事前相談
事前確認を受けようとする法人が，事前確認の申出前に，事前確認を申し出ようとする独立企業間価格の算定方法等について国税局の担当課等と行う相談	
primary adjustment	第一次調整
第二次調整に対する用語で，当初の移転価格課税を指す	
profit level indicator (PLI)	利益水準指標
移転価格分析で用いられる，利益率などの利益水準の指標	
profit split method (PSM)	利益分割法
独立企業間価格の算定方法の1つで，対象となる国外関連取引について，日本企業と国外関連者の利益の合計額を計算し（切り出し計算），それを両者の寄与度を表す一定のアロケーション・ファクターで配分し，それをもとに独立企業間価格を算定する方法	
resale price method (RPM)	再販売価格基準法
独立企業間価格の算定方法の1つで，「国外関連取引に係る棚卸資産の買手（販売会社など）が独立第三者に対して当該棚卸資産を販売した対価の額から通常の利潤の額を控除して計算した金額」をもって独立企業間価格とする方法	
residual profit split method (RPSM)	残余利益分割法
独立企業間価格の算定方法の1つで，まず重要な無形資産を有しない非関連者間取引において通常得られる基本的利益の金額を日本企業及び国外関連者に配分し，配分後の残額である超過利益または残余利益を，それぞれが有する重要な無形資産の価値に応じて（例えば，重要な無形資産の開発のために支出した費用等の額に応じて）合理的に配分することにより，各関連者が稼得すべき利益を決定し，これをもとに独立企業間価格を算定する方法	
secondary adjustment	第二次調整
みなし配当やみなし出資といった第二次取引に対する源泉税や資本税の課税	
secondary transaction	第二次取引
国外関連取引に関して，一方の関連者が移転価格課税による増額更正を受けた場合，相互協議の結果，他方の関連者の所得を減額する対応的調整が行われることがある．この場合，当該他方の関連者から一方の関連者に見合いの金額の送金が行われない場合には，本来一方の関連者が保有すべき資産を，他方の関連者が保有していることになる．第二次取引は，これを一方の関連者から他方の関連者に対する資産の流出と考え，配当や出資とみなすものである	
secret comparable	シークレット・コンパラブル
課税当局が（調査対象会社の）同業者に対する質問検査を通じて収集した比較対象取引に関する情報．移転価格税制に基づく調査や更正処分にあたり，独立企業間価格を算定するために必要な帳簿書類等の提示・提出がなされない場合等に使用される	

transactional net margin method (TNMM)	取引単位営業利益法
独立企業間価格の算定方法の1つで，取引単位ごとに，検証の対象とする会社（通常は海外子会社）と類似の事業活動を行う会社の営業利益率とを比較することにより，独立企業間価格を算定する方法。主として当事者の一方に（例えば，単純な製造機能等の）基本的な機能しかなく，当該当事者が独自の機能を果たしていない場合に適した算定方法	
unrelated party [person]	非関連者
日本企業と特殊の関係にない者	

(2) 外国子会社配当益金不算入制度（Foreign Dividend Exclusion）

【概　要】	
外国子会社配当益金不算入制度とは，外国子会社からの配当を原則として95％益金不算入とするもの。本制度により，海外子会社で稼得した利益は，大きな追加の税負担なしに日本へ還流させることが可能となっている（ただし，配当源泉税は純粋な税務コストとなる）	
英　語	日本語
解　説	
creditable	税額控除の対象となる
外国子会社から受ける配当については，その配当源泉税に外国税額控除は適用できない	
deductible	損金の額に算入できる
外国子会社配当益金不算入制度の適用を受ける配当については，その配当源泉税を原則として損金の額に算入することはできない	
deductible dividend	損金算入配当
支払側で損金算入される配当。外国子会社において損金算入される配当については，外国子会社配当益金不算入制度の対象外（つまり，益金算入）となる	
foreign subsidiary	外国子会社
外国子会社配当益金不算入制度でいう外国子会社とは，日本企業がその発行済株式等の25％以上（ただし，租税条約による軽減あり）を配当等の支払義務が確定する日以前6か月以上引き続き保有している外国法人をいう	
foreign withholding tax on dividend	外国配当源泉税
外国子会社配当益金不算入制度の適用を受ける配当については，その配当源泉税に外国税額控除は適用できず，原則として損金の額に算入することもできない	
holding period	保有期間
海外子会社が外国子会社配当益金不算入制度でいう外国子会社に該当するためには，（配当等の支払義務が確定する日以前）6か月以上の保有期間が要求されている	
holding ratio	保有比率
海外子会社が外国子会社配当益金不算入制度でいう外国子会社に該当するためには，25％以上の保有比率が要求されている（ただし，この25％という保有比率は，租税条約により軽減されることがある）	
repatriation	利益還流，資金還流
外国子会社配当益金不算入制度の導入により，海外で稼得した利益は，大きな追加の税負担なしに日本へ還流させることが可能となっている	

(3) 外国税額控除制度（FTC: Foreign Tax Credits）

【概要】

外国税額控除とは，国際的な二重課税を排除するために，外国法人税を一定の条件のもと日本の法人税等から差し引く制度をいう。日本の法人税等は全世界所得について課税されるため，国外源泉所得が海外でも課税された場合には二重課税が生じる。そこで，外国税額控除により，海外で納付した税金を日本の法人税から差し引けることとしている

英　語	日本語
解　説	
claim for refund	還付請求
所得に対する法人税の額が発生せず，繰越控除余裕額がある場合には，外国税額控除による還付が発生することがある	
creditable foreign tax	控除対象外国法人税
外国法人税のうち，外国税額控除の対象となるもの。foreign tax eligible for a credit のような言い方も可能	
credit limit	控除限度額
外国税額控除の控除限度額は，概念的には，日本での納税額のうち国外源泉所得に対応する部分（つまり，二重課税が発生する部分）として計算される	
excess credit limit	控除余裕額
外国法人税の額が控除限度額を下回るときのその余裕額をいい，将来3年にわたり繰越可能	
excess foreign tax	控除限度超過額
外国法人税の額が控除限度額を上回るときのその超過額をいい，将来3年にわたり繰越可能	
foreign source income	国外源泉所得
居住地国（日本）以外の国で得た所得で，外国税額控除の控除限度額の計算に影響を与える	
foreign tax	外国法人税
日本の外国税額控除制度にいう外国法人税とは，日本の法人税に相当する税で，外国またはその地方公共団体により法人の所得を課税標準として課される税をいう	
local tax	地方税
地方税のうち，住民税（inhabitant tax）には法人税と同様に外国税額控除の制度があるが，事業税（enterprise tax）には外国税額控除の制度は存在しない	
tax sparing credit	みなし外国税額控除
一般に租税条約に規定され，端的には，実際には海外で支払っていない税金をあたかも支払ったかのように日本の税金から控除するもの。開発途上国等への投資促進を目的とする制度	
unused credit limit	繰越控除余裕額
外国法人税の額が控除限度額を下回るときのその余裕額につき，将来3年にわたり繰り越すもの	
unused foreign tax (credit)	繰越控除限度超過額
外国法人税の額が控除限度額を上回るときのその超過額につき，将来3年にわたり繰り越すもの	
withholding tax	源泉税
外国源泉税は，外国子会社配当に係るもの等を除き，外国税額控除の対象となるケースが多い	
worldwide income	全世界所得
国内源泉所得と国外源泉所得の合計で，外国税額控除の控除限度額の計算に影響を与える	

(4) 恒久的施設（PE: Permanent Establishment）

【概　要】
恒久的施設（PE：Permanent Establishment）とは，事業を行う一定の場所であって，企業がその場所を通じてその事業の全部または一部を行っている場所をいう。例えば，日本企業が海外で事業を行うために設けた（海外）支店などがこれに該当する。事業所得については，一般に「PEなければ課税なし」という原則がある

英　語	日本語
【解　説】	
agent	代理人
企業に代わって行動する者。ある国の代理人が企業の名において契約を締結する権限を有し，かつ，その権限を反復して行使する場合には，当該企業はその国にPEを有するものとされる（ただし，独立代理人に該当する場合を除く）	
attributable income principle	帰属主義
企業がある国にPEを有し，そのPEを通じて事業を行う場合，その国の税務当局は当該PEに帰属する所得に対してのみ課税できるという考え方。総合主義（entire income principle）に対する用語	
attributable to	〜に帰属する
帰属主義においては，PEに帰属する所得が課税対象となる	
Authorised OECD Approach (AOA)	OECD承認アプローチ
OECDモデル租税条約第7条（事業所得）におけるPE帰属所得の算定方法。端的には，PEの果たす機能及び事実関係に基づいて外部取引，資産，リスク及び資本をPEに帰属させるとともに，独立企業間価格の算定方法を適用して，PEと本店等との内部取引を認識する	
branch	支店
支店は，OECDモデル租税条約においてPEとして例示されている	
broker	仲立人
他人間の法律行為（契約など）の成立を媒介する者。一般に仲立人が独立代理人に該当する場合には，PEに該当しない	
building site	建築工事現場
建築工事現場については，一定期間（例えば1年）を超えるとPEに該当することが多い	
commissionaire	コミッショネア（問屋）
自己の名をもって他人のために物品の販売または買入れをすることを業とする者。OECDモデル租税条約では，general commission agentという呼び方をしている。一般にコミッショネアが独立代理人に該当する場合には，PEに該当しない	
construction or installation project	建設または据付プロジェクト
建設または据付プロジェクトについては，一定期間（例えば1年）を超えるとPEに該当することが多い	
dependent agent	従属代理人
法律的・経済的に本人（企業）に従属している代理人で，独立代理人に対する用語。基本的に当該企業のPEに該当する	
factory	工場
工場は，OECDモデル租税条約においてPEとして例示されている	
fixed place of business	事業を行う一定の場所
OECDモデル租税条約におけるPEは，「事業を行う一定の場所」であって，企業がその場所を通じてその事業の全部または一部を行っている場所とされている	

independent agent	独立代理人
本人（企業）から独立して業務を行う一定の代理人で，従属代理人に対する用語。基本的に当該企業のPEには該当しない。OECDモデル租税条約では，agent of an independent statusという呼び方をしている	
office	事務所
事務所は，OECDモデル租税条約においてPEとして例示されている	
place of management	事業の管理の場所
事業を管理している場所は，OECDモデル租税条約においてPEとして例示されている	
preparatory or auxiliary activity	準備的または補助的な活動
例えば，情報の提供など，企業の生産性に貢献するものではあるが，実際の利得の実現とは関係が薄い活動。準備的または補助的な性格の活動を行うことのみを目的として，事業を行う一定の場所を保有する場合，一般にその場所はPEには該当しない	
representative office	駐在員事務所
駐在員事務所が準備的または補助的な活動のみを行う場合，一般にPEには該当しない	
service PE	サービスPE
企業がある国に従業員等を派遣して役務提供（例えば，コンサルティング・サービス）を行う場合，その従業員等をその国における派遣元企業のPEとして取り扱うという考え方	

(5) 税務デュー・デリジェンス（TDD: Tax Due Diligence）

【概　要】
税務デュー・デリジェンスは，潜在的な租税債務を含む簿外負債の把握を行うための調査で，海外企業を買収する際の税務デュー・デリジェンスは通常現地の専門家が実施する

英　語	日本語
解　説	
acquirer	買手
買収対象会社を買収する会社	
asset purchase	資産買収
買収形態の1つで，海外に新会社を設立し（または既存の海外子会社を利用して），その海外子会社が買収対象会社の資産等を買収する方法。株式買収に対する用語	
carried-forward tax losses	繰越欠損金
過年度に発生した税務上の損失で，将来の課税所得と相殺できるもの	
change of control (CoC)	株主変更
買収による株主変更は，優遇税制の終了や繰越欠損金の失効等を通じて，買収対象会社の税務ポジションに影響を与える可能性がある。change of ownershipも同様の意味で使われる	
financial due diligence (FDD)	財務デュー・デリジェンス
買収対象会社の財務内容の調査であり，財務諸表の分析等により，資産の実在性や含み損益の実態，また租税債務を含む簿外負債の把握を行うもの	
forfeiture of carried-forward tax losses	繰越欠損金の切捨て
買収対象会社が繰越欠損金の残高を保有している場合，買収による株主の変更により，繰越欠損金が自動的に切捨てになるケースがある	
history of tax audits	税務調査履歴
買収対象会社が過去に受けた税務調査についての情報をいう。税務デュー・デリジェンスにおいては，調査終了年度について，指摘事項とその顛末を把握し，現状の税務リスクの判断の参考とする。ただし，より大きなリスクがあるのが調査未了年度で，通常租税債権の時効についても併せて確認する	
legal due diligence (LDD)	法務デュー・デリジェンス
買収対象会社の法的な観点からの調査であり，予定されている取引の障害となりうる法律上の問題点を検出するほか，買収価格のベースとなる企業評価や今後の事業計画に影響のある項目をピックアップするもの	
open tax years	税務調査未了年度
税務調査履歴に関係する用語で，税務調査未了年度は当然ながら税務調査終了年度よりも税務リスクが高い	
potential tax liability	潜在的租税債務
いまだ顕在化していないものの，買収対象会社に潜在的に存在する租税債務で，例えば買収後の税務調査により顕在化する可能性があるもの	
representation and warranty	表明・保証
買収契約書（株式譲渡契約書など）において，その取引に関連する各種の事実について各当事者がそれが真実であることを表明・保証するものをいい，その事実が真実でない場合には金銭による補償の請求などを可能とする補償条項が通常セットで規定される。税務デュー・デリジェンスの関係では，必要な申告や納税が適正に行われていることなどが表明・保証の対象となる	

share purchase	株式買収
買収形態の１つで，買収対象会社の株式を取得する方法。資産買収に対する用語	
share sale agreement (SSA) share purchase agreement (SPA)	株式譲渡契約書
税務デュー・デリジェンスの結果検出された事項は，買収の際の株式譲渡契約書の基礎となる。例えば，簿外の租税債務の存在は買収価格の調整項目となることが多く，また偶発債務（潜在的租税債務）についてはそれが実際に発生しないという売手側の表明・保証を契約書の条項として含める必要がある	
statute of limitations	時効
買収対象会社の税務リスクを判断するうえで，租税債権の時効は重要な情報となり，税務調査未了年度のうち，消滅時効にかかっていない年度が税務リスクの観点から特に重要とされる	
target	買収対象会社
文字通り，買収の対象となる会社	
tax exposure	税務エクスポージャー
税務リスクにさらされていることをいい，税務リスクとほぼ同義	
tax position	税務ポジション
過去の所得または欠損の発生状況や税金の納付状況，また繰越欠損金の残高等の買収対象会社の全般的な状況	
tax risk	税務リスク
端的には買収後に買収対象会社において買収前の期間に対応する追加の税金負担が発生する可能性。過去の税務申告書やその根拠資料，また担当者へのインタビューにより，税目ごとに税務リスクの高い項目を把握し，定量化できるものは定量化する必要がある	
vendor	売手
買収対象会社の現所有者	

(6) 租税条約 (Tax Treaties)

【概　要】	
租税条約とは，二重課税の排除や脱税の防止などを目的として，主権国家の間で締結される成文による合意をいう	
英　語	日本語
解　説	
anti-conduit provision	導管取引防止規定
導管取引に対して租税条約の適用を認めない（条約相手国の居住者を受益者として取り扱わない）とする規定。主に，配当・利子・使用料等の条項に盛り込まれている	
anti-treaty shopping provision	トリーティー・ショッピング防止規定
トリーティー・ショッピングに対応するために租税条約に定められる濫用防止規定	
application form for income tax convention	租税条約に関する届出書
租税条約による源泉税等の減免を受ける場合には，通常何らかの届出書等の提出が必要であり，日本ではこの租税条約に関する届出書がそれに該当する	
certificate of residence	居住者証明（書）
権限ある当局（税務当局）が法人や個人について自国の居住者であることを証明するもの。租税条約に基づく租税の減免等を受けるためには，（租税条約に関する届出書に加えて）居住者証明（書）が必要になる場合がある	
commentary	コメンタリー
OECDモデル租税条約には，コメンタリー（解説）があり，その解釈に利用される	
conduit	導管
第三国の居住者への所得の支払いにあたり，条約の特典を利用するため，条約相手国の居住者を経由させる場合のその条約相手国の居住者（中間会社）	
domestic tax law	国内法
海外における課税関係を考える際には，その国の国内法と（日本との）租税条約の内容をセットで検討する必要がある	
double taxation relief	二重課税防止規定
租税条約には，国際的な二重課税を防止するための規定が盛り込まれている	
exchange of information	情報交換
租税条約には，国際的な租税回避取引の防止のために，情報交換の規定が設けられている	
exchange of notes (E/N)	交換公文
国家間で書簡を往復させて権利義務を設定するもので，広義の条約に含まれる。議定書と同様，租税条約の解釈が記載されていることがある	
Japan - U.S. tax treaty	日米租税条約
日本とX国の租税条約は，通常Japan-X tax treatyのような言い方をするが，例えば日米租税条約の正式名称は，"CONVENTION BETWEEN THE GOVERNMENT OF JAPAN AND THE GOVERNMENT OF THE UNITED STATES OF AMERICA FOR THE AVOIDANCE OF DOUBLE TAXATION AND THE PREVENTION OF FISCAL EVASION WITH RESPECT TO TAXES ON INCOME"である	
limitation on benefits (LOB) provision	特典制限条項（LOB条項）
一定の条件を満たした者にしか租税条約の適用を認めないという形で，租税条約の特典を制限する条項	

mutual agreement procedure (MAP)	相互協議
租税条約締結国の税務当局間で行われる協議。主として移転価格税制について，二重課税の排除のために実施される	
OECD Model Tax Convention on Income and on Capital	OECDモデル租税条約
OECD（経済協力開発機構）が公表している租税条約のひな型。法的拘束力を有するものではないが，特に先進国の間での国際的なコンセンサスとして機能している	
preservation clause	プリザベーションの原則
国内法上の減免措置や納税者にとって有利な取扱いが租税条約の締結によって損なわれることはない，という原則。すなわち，基本的には，租税条約により租税が減免されることはあっても，租税条約が新たな課税関係を創出することはないということを意味する	
principal purposes test (PPT)	主要目的テスト
取引の主たる目的が租税条約の特典の享受である場合には，その取引に租税条約の適用を認めないとする考え方（租税条約上の規定）	
protocol	議定書
租税条約に付随して国会の承認を得るもので，議定書には租税条約の解釈が記載されていることがある	
reduction or exemption	減免
租税条約の規定により，源泉税などは減免の対象となることが多い。なお，(tax) reliefの一語で減免を指すこともできる	
saving clause	セービングの原則
自国の居住者に対する自国での課税関係は租税条約の影響を受けない，という原則	
source rule	ソース・ルール
所得の源泉地（国内源泉所得か国外源泉所得か）の決定基準。ソース・ルールが国内法と租税条約で異なっている場合，租税条約が優先される	
treaty shopping	トリーティー・ショッピング
本来であれば租税条約の特典を享受することのできない者が，租税条約の一方の締約国に中間会社を置くなどして，租税条約の特典を受けることをいい，「条約漁り」とも訳される	

(7) タックス・ヘイブン対策税制（CFC Rules）

【概　要】	
低税率国に所在する海外子会社を利用した租税回避行為を防止することを目的として，低税率国の海外子会社の所得を日本企業の所得と合算して，日本で課税する税制	
英　語	日本語
解　説	
administration and control test	管理支配基準
経済活動基準の1つで，外国関係会社がその本店所在地国において事業の管理，支配及び運営を自ら行っていることを確認する基準	
aggregation of income	合算課税
タックス・ヘイブン対策税制による合算課税には，会社単位の合算課税と受動的所得の合算課税があり，いずれも保有割合（請求権等勘案合算割合）を乗じることにより合算課税の対象となる金額が計算される	
black list company	ブラックリスト国所在会社
特定外国関係会社の1つで，外国関係会社のうち，「租税に関する情報の交換に関する国際的な取組への協力が著しく不十分な国または地域として財務大臣が指定する国または地域」に本店または主たる事務所を有するもの	
business purpose test	事業基準
経済活動基準の1つで，外国関係会社の主たる事業が，株式等または債券の保有，工業所有権等または著作権の提供，船舶または航空機の貸付などの事業ではないことを確認する基準（一定の例外あり）	
cash box	（事実上の）キャッシュ・ボックス
一般には軽課税国の利用を目的とし，豊富な資本を持ちながら，能動的な事業遂行やリスク管理に必要な機能をほとんど果たしていない事業体を指す用語。日本の税制上は特定外国関係会社の1つであり，外国関係会社のうち，総資産に対する受動的所得の割合や，総資産に占める金融資産等の割合に関する一定の基準に抵触するものがこれに該当する	
controlled foreign company (CFC)	被支配外国法人
一般にタックス・ヘイブン対策税制の適用対象となる法人を指し，日本の税制では「外国関係会社」がこれに該当する	
country of location test	所在地国基準
経済活動基準の1つで，外国関係会社が事業を主としてその本店所在地国において行っていることを確認する基準	
de facto control	実質支配
外国関係会社には，居住者または内国法人との間に実質支配関係がある外国法人も含まれる	
de minimis rule	デミニマス基準（少額所得除外基準）
受動的所得の金額が少額である場合（部分適用対象金額が2,000万円以下など）には，受動的所得の合算課税を適用しないという基準	
economic activity test	経済活動基準
従来の適用除外基準に相当するもので，端的には，外国関係会社がその国に所在することに経済合理性があるか否かを判定するための基準。特定外国関係会社以外の外国関係会社については，（租税負担割合が20％未満でも）経済活動基準を充足できれば会社単位の合算課税は行われない	

effective tax rate (for CFC purposes)	租税負担割合
租税負担割合は，各国の法定税率（statutory tax rate）ではなく，その外国関係会社固有のものであり，大まかには以下の算式で計算される $$租税負担割合＝\frac{所得に対して課される外国法人税}{現地法令上の課税所得＋（配当等以外の）非課税所得}$$	
foreign company	外国法人
内国法人以外の法人	
foreign related company	外国関係会社
外国法人のうち，日本資本（内国法人等）により50％超保有されている，または実質支配されている外国法人。この外国関係会社が日本の税制上のCFCに該当する	
paper company	ペーパー・カンパニー
特定外国関係会社の1つで，外国関係会社のうち，主たる事業を行うに必要と認められる固定施設を有しておらず，本店所在地国においてその事業の管理，支配及び運営を自ら行っていないもの	
passive income	受動的所得
従来の資産性所得に相当するもので，企業の能動的な活動を必要としない所得であり，持分比率25％未満の株式等に係る配当など一定のもの	
regional headquarters	地域統括会社
外国関係会社のうち，内国法人の100％子会社で，複数の被統括会社に対して統括業務を行っており，その他一定の要件を充足するもの。経済活動基準のうち，事業基準や非関連者基準に特例が定められている	
specified foreign related company	特定外国関係会社
外国関係会社のうち，①ペーパー・カンパニー，②事実上のキャッシュ・ボックス，③ブラックリスト国所在会社に該当するもの。基本的に会社単位の合算課税の対象となる（ただし，租税負担割合が30％以上の場合を除く）	
substance test	実体基準
経済活動基準の1つで，外国関係会社がその本店所在地国において主たる事業を行うために必要と認められる事務所等の固定施設を有していることを確認する基準	
unrelated party test	非関連者基準
経済活動基準の1つで，外国関係会社がその事業を主として関連者以外の者との間で行っていることを確認する基準（一定の例外あり）	

4. 知っていると便利！　e-mail 表現

　ここでは，例えば，海外子会社の担当者とメールでやり取りをする際に，知っておくと便利な表現をまとめています。
　まず，「(1) 標準的な構成」において，英文メールにおける標準的な構成と構成単位ごとのポイントを解説します。
　次に，「(2) 資料のやり取りに関する便利表現」において，具体的な場面を念頭に置いた便利な表現をピックアップしています。

(1)　標準的な構成
　以下は英文メールの大まかな構成の例です。

Dear Mr. Smith,
　①宛名
（スミス様）

My name is Taro Yamada, and I am an accounting manager at ABC Corporation.
　　　　　　　　　　　　　　　　　②自己紹介
（ABC Corporation の経理部マネジャーの山田太郎と申します。）

With regard to Z project, we are requesting that you provide us with the financial
　　　　　　　　　　　　　③本題（資料依頼）
（Zプロジェクトに関して，今週末までに XYZ Corporation の

statements of XYZ Corporation by the end of this week.
財務諸表の提出をお願い致します。）

Should you have any questions, please do not hesitate to contact us.
　　　　　　　　　　　　　　　④結び
（ご質問があれば，ご遠慮なくご連絡ください。）

Kind regards,

Taro Yamada
　⑤署名
（山田太郎）

付　録

構成単位ごとのポイントは以下のとおりです。

構成単位①　宛名
- Dear Mr. XX
- Dear Ms. XX

☞ポイント
- まず，Mr./Ms. からコミュニケーションを始めて，ファースト・ネームに切り替えるのが無難です。
- 例えば，日本語では「ジョー」という同じ響きでも，一般に Jo は女性，Joe は男性など，Mr. と Ms. を使い分ける際には注意を要します。相手が男性か女性かわからない場合は，性別を予測して Mr. や Ms. を付けるよりも，Dear Alex Smith のようにフルネームで書くのが安全です。
- ただし，企業の文化にもよりますが，海外子会社の担当者なら，最初から Dear Alex などファースト・ネームを使うことも可能で，この場合は性別を気にしなくてよいというメリットがあります。
- 各国の海外子会社の担当者にメールを一斉送信する場合には，Dear Colleagues や Dear All のようないい方もできます。

構成単位②　自己紹介
I am【役職】at/from【会社】
(私は【会社】の【役職】です。)

☞ポイント
- 初回のメールでは自己紹介が必要です。
- なお，単発のプロジェクトに関してメールを送る際には，以下のようにそのプロジェクトに関するメールであることを示すのが望ましいと考えられます。
  I am currently working on【プロジェクト名】.
  (私は現在【プロジェクト名】を担当しています。)

構成単位③　本題（ここでは，資料依頼）
We are requesting that you provide us with【資料名】by【期限】
(【期限】までに【資料名】の提出をお願いします。)

☞ポイント
- 資料の依頼にどの程度丁寧な表現を使うかは状況によります。
- 毎月依頼しているようなものなら，特に丁寧な表現は不要です。
- 逆に急な依頼で新しい資料を要求する場合などは We apologise (apologize) for the short notice, but …（急なお願いで申し訳ないのですが…）などの表現を加えつつ，丁寧な依頼文を使います。
- 上と同じ内容を，より丁寧にいうと，以下のようになります。
  We would like you to provide us with【資料名】by【期限】
  (【期限】までに【資料名】の提出をお願いしたいと考えております。)

- これをさらに丁寧にすると，以下のとおりです。
  We would appreciate it if you could provide us with【資料名】by【期限】
  (【期限】までに【資料名】をご提出頂けると幸甚に存じます。)
- なお，期限については，急ぎのときは「by【期限】」の代わりに，as soon as possible（できるだけ早く）を使います。
- 逆に，それほど急ぎではないときは，when you have a chance（ご都合のよろしいときに）を付けることもあります。

構成単位④　結び

Should you have any questions, please do not hesitate to contact us.
（ご質問があれば，遠慮なくご連絡ください。）

ポイント

- この部分はほぼ定型文ですが，いくつかバリエーションがあります。
- 例えば，「返事をもらいたい」ということをはっきりさせたい場合には，We look forward to hearing from you.（お返事をお待ちしています。）等の表現を使います。
- また，急ぎで連絡がほしいときは，We look forward to hearing from you soon.（早めにご返信ください）などの表現を付け加えます。
- さらに，長い付き合いになりそうな場合は，We look forward to working with you.（これから一緒に働けるのを楽しみにしています）などの表現を付け加えたりもします。

構成単位⑤　署名

Kind regards, / Best regards,
【自分の名前】

ポイント

- 海外子会社の担当者とのやり取りであれば，この程度の丁寧さで問題ないと思われます。
- もっと丁寧な表現を使うのであれば，Yours sincerely, で代替可能です。
- 逆に親しみを表現するのであれば，軽く Regards, としておけば十分です。

付　録

(2) 資料のやり取りに関する便利表現

　ここでは，海外の担当者と連絡をとる用件として多い資料のやり取りの際に使える便利な表現を簡単に列挙しています。「(1)標準的な構成」でいえば，「③本題」の部分に使える表現です。

A. 資料の依頼

「(1)標準的な構成　③本題」をご参照ください。

B. 資料の督促

- This is to remind you that【資料名】is now past due.
  （【資料名】の提出期限が過ぎているので，念のため連絡しました。）
- Despite the request, we have still not received【資料名】
  （以前お願いした【資料名】について，まだ受け取っておりません。…やや強い）
- In the light of the problem, we trust you will address the matter promptly.
  （この問題に鑑みれば，早急に対応して頂けるものと信じております。…かなり強い）

ポイント

- 国にもよりますが，海外では，日本ほど期限を守るという意識がない担当者も多いので，このような督促の表現は特に重要です。
- 督促は，最初から強い表現を使うよりも，徐々にトーンを変えていくほうが効果的です。
- また，資料の提出が遅れがちな担当者には，リマインダーとして，期日前に以下のようなメールを送っておくことも有効と考えられます。
  This is to remind you that the deadline for【資料名】is【日付】
  （【資料名】の提出期限は【日付】なので，念のためご連絡させて頂きます。）

C. 資料の受領

- We have received【資料名】
  （【資料名】を受領しました。）
- Thank you for【資料名】
  （【資料名】をお送り頂き，ありがとうございます。）

ポイント

- 資料を受け取った場合，まずは受領の確認メールを送るのが一般的です。

D. 資料の内容についての確認

- We have some follow-up questions about【資料名】
  （【資料名】について，いくつか追加の質問があります。）
- Would you clarify what you mean by【わからない単語】?
  （【わからない単語】はどういう意味か明確にして頂けないでしょうか。）
- Would you provide us with more details on【もう少し知りたい内容】?
  （【もう少し知りたい内容】について，詳細を教えて頂けないでしょうか。）
- Is our understanding correct that【確認したい内容（文の形）】?

（【確認したい内容】という我々の理解は正しいでしょうか。）
- Do you think 【報告事項】 has significant impact on our project?
（【報告事項】はプロジェクトに大きな影響を与えると思われますか。）

E. 資料に関する問題点の指摘

- There seems to be a discrepancy between A on page XX and B on page XX.
（XX ページの A と XX ページの B の間に不整合があるように見受けられます。）
- Would you let us know how we could reconcile these two figures?
（この 2 つの数値をどのように調整すればよいか（一致するか）教えてください。）

ポイント

■ 資料に誤りがあると思われる場合でも，それをズバリ指摘せず，It seems / It looks like / It appears のように，「そう見受けられる」的な表現を使うほうが相手に嫌な印象を与えないと思われます。

F. 海外子会社への情報の提供

- I am writing to inform you that 【情報提供（文の形）】
（【情報提供】をご報告させて頂きます。）
- This is to announce that 【情報提供（文の形）】
（【情報提供】をご報告させて頂きます。）
- Attached please find 【資料名】.
（添付の【資料名】をご参照ください。）

ポイント

■ 情報の詳細を説明するために，上記のようなフレーズを使って，そのメールが情報提供を目的としていることを明確にしておくと，コミュニケーションがスムーズです。

G. 拒否する

- We received your request.
（ご依頼は受領しました。）
- We are sorry to inform you, however, that we cannot accept your request.
（残念ながら，ご依頼をお受けすることはできません。）
- This is due to the fact that 【日本側の事情（文の形）】
（これは，【日本側の事情】のためです。）

ポイント

■ 期限延長など，海外の担当者の要求を断る場合には，きっちりと断りの表現を用いる必要がありますが，一方でそれが受け容れられない日本側の事情もしっかりと説明する必要があります。
■ もし，何か代替案を示せるのであれば，Alternatively, や As an alternative, （他の選択肢としては,）と文を始めて，代替案を伝えてあげることも可能です。

H. 感謝する

- We appreciate your assistance.
（ご協力に感謝致します。（ご協力よろしくお願い致します。））
- We appreciate your consideration.
（ご配慮に感謝致します。（ご配慮頂けると幸いです。））

ポイント

- Thank you for XX と We appreciate XX はほぼ同じように使えますが，後者のほうがフォーマルです。
- Thank you for XX, We appreciate XX とも事後的な「お礼」だけではなく，事前の「お願い」という意味でも使うことができます。
- We appreciate XX の代わりに We would appreciate XX とすると，事後的な「お礼」ではなく，事前の「お願い」であることが明確になります。
- なお，Thank you in advance.（よろしくお願いします。）などの表現は，相手がお願いに対応してくれることを前提としている点で，若干図々しい印象を与える可能性があります。

I. 謝罪する

- We apologise for the inconvenience.
（ご迷惑をおかけして申し訳ありません。）
- Please accept our apologies for the inconvenience.
（ご迷惑をおかけして申し訳ありません。）
- We appreciate your patience.
（お待たせして申し訳ありません。）
- We appreciate your understanding.
（ご理解に感謝致します。）

ポイント

- We apologise for XX の代わりに，We regret XX や We deeply regret XX の表現を用いることもできますが，apologise を使ったほうが，より謝罪の意図が明確になります。
- 海外とのコミュニケーションでは，日本人が通常謝罪する局面でも，相手に感謝の意を述べるほうが適切な場合が多いので，海外の担当者とのやりとりにおいて，上記のような謝罪のフレーズを使うことは限定的と考えられます。

著者紹介

佐和　周（さわ　あまね）

公認会計士，税理士
佐和公認会計士事務所　代表
関西学院大学非常勤講師

1999年	東京大学経済学部を卒業，同年朝日監査法人（現 有限責任 あずさ監査法人）に入所。日系グローバル企業や外資系企業の監査のほか，財務デュー・デリジェンス業務や企業価値評価業務等に従事。
2008年	英国ケンブリッジ大学経営大学院（Cambridge Judge Business School）首席修了（MBA）。
2009年	KPMG税理士法人に転籍。日系グローバル企業や外資系企業の税務申告のほか，国内・海外税務デュー・デリジェンス業務や国際税務に係るアドバイザリー業務等に従事。
2011年	佐和公認会計士事務所を開設。財務・会計・税務の面から，日本企業の海外進出をサポートしている。

主な著書

『海外進出・展開・撤退の会計・税務Q&A』，『海外進出企業の税務調査対策チェックリスト』，『M&Aにおける 財務・税務デュー・デリジェンスのチェックリスト』，『これだけは押さえておこう 国際税務のよくあるケース50』，『これだけは押さえておこう 海外取引の経理実務ケース50』，『海外進出企業の資金・為替管理Q&A: 調達から投資・回収・還元まで』，『29年度税制改正後のタックス・ヘイブン対策税制』（共著），『アジア進出・展開・撤退の税務』，『ケース別 税効果会計の実務Q&A』（以上，中央経済社）など。その他，旬刊『経理情報』，月刊『国際税務』，週刊『税務通信』など，雑誌への寄稿も多数。

英和・和英
海外取引で使える会計・税務用語辞典

2018年12月10日　第1版第1刷発行
2024年 9 月15日　第1版第3刷発行

著　者　佐　和　　　周
発行者　山　本　　　継
発行所　㈱中央経済社
発売元　㈱中央経済グループ
　　　　パブリッシング

〒101-0051　東京都千代田区神田神保町1-35
電話　03（3293）3371（編集代表）
　　　03（3293）3381（営業代表）
https://www.chuokeizai.co.jp
印刷・製本／昭和情報プロセス㈱

© 2018
Printed in Japan

＊頁の「欠落」や「順序違い」などがありましたらお取り替えいたしますので発売元までご送付ください。（送料小社負担）

ISBN978-4-502-28181-5　C3034

JCOPY〈出版者著作権管理機構委託出版物〉本書を無断で複写複製（コピー）することは，著作権法上の例外を除き，禁じられています。本書をコピーされる場合は事前に出版者著作権管理機構（JCOPY）の許諾を受けてください。
JCOPY〈https://www.jcopy.or.jp　eメール：info@jcopy.or.jp〉

●実務・受験に愛用されている読みやすく正確な内容のロングセラー！

定評ある税の法規・通達集シリーズ

所得税法規集
日本税理士会連合会
中央経済社 編

❶所得税法 ❷同施行令・同施行規則・同関係告示 ❸租税特別措置法(抄) ❹同施行令・同施行規則・同関係告示(抄) ❺震災特例法・同施行令・同施行規則(抄) ❻復興財源確保法(抄) ❼復興特別所得税に関する政令・同省令 ❽災害減免法・同施行令(抄) ❾国外送金等調書提出法・同施行令・同施行規則・同関係告示

所得税取扱通達集
日本税理士会連合会
中央経済社 編

❶所得税取扱通達(基本通達／個別通達) ❷租税特別措置法関係通達 ❸国外送金等調書提出法関係通達 ❹災害減免法関係通達 ❺震災特例法関係通達 ❻索引

法人税法規集
日本税理士会連合会
中央経済社 編

❶法人税法 ❷同施行令・同施行規則・法人税申告書一覧表 ❸減価償却耐用年数省令 ❹法人税法関係告示 ❺地方法人税法・同施行令・同施行規則 ❻租税特別措置法(抄) ❼同施行令・同施行規則・同関係告示 ❽震災特例法・同施行令・同施行規則(抄) ❾復興財源確保法(抄) ❿復興特別法人税に関する政令・同省令 ⓫租特透明化法・同施行令・同施行規則

法人税取扱通達集
日本税理士会連合会
中央経済社 編

❶法人税取扱通達(基本通達／個別通達) ❷租税特別措置法関係通達(法人税編) ❸連結納税基本通達 ❹租税特別措置法関係通達(連結納税編) ❺減価償却耐用年数省令 ❻機械装置の細目と個別年数 ❼耐用年数の適用等に関する取扱通達 ❽震災特例法関係通達 ❾復興特別法人税関係通達 ❿索引

相続税法規通達集
日本税理士会連合会
中央経済社 編

❶相続税法 ❷同施行令・同施行規則・同関係告示 ❸土地評価審議会令・同省令 ❹相続税法基本通達 ❺財産評価基本通達 ❻相続税法関係個別通達 ❼租税特別措置法(抄) ❽同施行令・同施行規則(抄)・同関係告示 ❾租税特別措置法(相続税法の特例)関係通達 ❿震災特例法・同施行令・同施行規則(抄)・同関係告示 ⓫震災特例法関係通達 ⓬災害減免法・同施行令(抄) ⓭国外送金等調書提出法・同施行令・同施行規則・同関係通達 ⓮民法(抄)

国税通則・徴収法規集
日本税理士会連合会
中央経済社 編

❶国税通則法 ❷同施行令・同施行規則・同関係告示 ❸同関係通達 ❹租税特別措置法・同施行令・同施行規則(抄) ❺国税徴収法 ❻同施行令・同施行規則 ❼滞調法・同施行令・同施行規則 ❽税理士法・同施行令・同施行規則・同関係告示 ❾電子帳簿保存法・同施行令・同施行規則・同関係告示・同関係通達 ❿行政手続オンライン化法・同国税関係法令に関する省令・同関係告示 ⓫行政手続法 ⓬行政不服審査法 ⓭行政事件訴訟法(抄) ⓮組織的犯罪処罰法(抄) ⓯没収保全と滞納処分との調整令 ⓰犯罪収益規則(抄) ⓱麻薬特例法

消費税法規通達集
日本税理士会連合会
中央経済社 編

❶消費税法 ❷同別表第三等に関する法令 ❸同施行令・同施行規則・同関係告示 ❹消費税法基本通達 ❺消費税申告書様式等 ❻消費税法等関係取扱通達等 ❼租税特別措置法(抄) ❽同施行令・同施行規則(抄)・同関係通達 ❾消費税転嫁対策法・同ガイドライン ❿震災特例法・同施行令(抄)・同関係告示 ⓫震災特例法関係通達 ⓬税制改革法等 ⓭地方税法(抄) ⓮同施行令・同施行規則(抄) ⓯所得税・法人税政令(抄) ⓰輸徴法令 ⓱関税法令(抄) ⓲国税定率法令(抄)

登録免許税・印紙税法規集
日本税理士会連合会
中央経済社 編

❶登録免許税法 ❷同施行令・同施行規則 ❸租税特別措置法・同施行令・同施行規則(抄) ❹震災特例法・同施行令・同施行規則(抄) ❺印紙税法 ❻同施行令・同施行規則 ❼印紙税法基本通達 ❽租税特別措置法・同施行令・同施行規則(抄) ❾印紙税額一覧表 ❿震災特例法・同施行令・同施行規則(抄) ⓫震災特例法関係通達等

中央経済社